VECTOR
MECHANICS FOR ENGINEERS: STATICS

Vector
Mechanics for Engineers

STATICS

FERDINAND P. BEER
Professor and Head, Department of Mechanics
Lehigh University

E. RUSSELL JOHNSTON, JR.
Professor, Department of Civil Engineering
University of Connecticut

1962

McGRAW-HILL BOOK COMPANY
New York, San Francisco, Toronto, London

PREFACE

The main objective of a first course in mechanics should be to develop in the engineering student the ability to analyze any problem in a simple and logical manner and to apply to its solution a few, well-understood basic principles. It is hoped that this text, designed for the first course in statics offered in the sophomore year, and the volume that follows, *Vector Mechanics for Engineers: Dynamics,* will help the instructor achieve this goal.†

Vector algebra is introduced early in the text and used in the presentation and the discussion of the fundamental principles of mechanics. Vector methods are also used to solve many problems, particularly three-dimensional problems where their application results in a simpler and more concise solution. The emphasis in this text, however, remains on the correct understanding of the principles of mechanics and on their application to the solution of engineering problems, and vector algebra is presented chiefly as a convenient tool.‡

One of the characteristics of the approach used in these volumes is that the mechanics of *particles* has been clearly separated from the mechanics of *rigid bodies.* This approach makes it possible to consider simple practical applications at an early stage and to postpone the introduction of more difficult concepts. In this volume, for example, the statics of particles is treated first (Chap. 2); after the rules of addition and subtraction of vectors have been introduced, the principle of equilibrium of a particle is immediately applied to practical situations involving only concurrent forces. The statics of rigid bodies is considered in Chaps. 3 and 4. In Chap. 3, the vector and

† Both texts are also available in a single volume, *Vector Mechanics for Engineers: Statics and Dynamics.*

‡ In a parallel text, *Mechanics for Engineers: Statics,* second edition, the use of vector algebra is limited to the addition and subtraction of vectors.

scalar products of two vectors are introduced and used to define the moment of a force about a point and about an axis. The presentation of these new concepts is followed by a thorough and rigorous discussion of equivalent systems of forces leading, in Chap. 4, to many practical applications involving the equilibrium of rigid bodies under general force systems. In the volume on dynamics, the same division is observed. The basic concepts of force, mass, and acceleration, of work and energy, and of impulse and momentum are introduced and first applied to problems involving only particles. Thus the student may familiarize himself with the three basic methods used in dynamics and learn their respective advantages before facing the difficulties associated with the motion of rigid bodies.

Since this text is designed for a first course in statics, new concepts have been presented in simple terms and every step explained in detail. On the other hand, by discussing the broader aspects of the problems considered, a definite maturity of approach has been achieved. For example, the concepts of partial constraints and of statical indeterminacy are introduced early in the text and used throughout.

A large number of optional sections have been included. These sections are indicated by asterisks and may thus easily be distinguished from those which form the core of the basic statics course. They may be omitted without prejudice to the understanding of the rest of the text. Among the topics covered in these additional sections are applications to hydrostatics, shear and bending-moment diagrams for beams, equilibrium of cables, products of inertia and Mohr's circle, and the method of virtual work. In addition, the method of the force polygon and string polygon for the analysis of coplanar forces has been covered in an Appendix. The sections on beams are especially useful when the course in statics is immediately followed by a course in mechanics of materials.

The fact that mechanics is essentially a *deductive* science based on a few fundamental principles has been stressed. Derivations have been presented in their logical sequence and with all the rigor warranted at this level. However, the learning process being largely *inductive*, simple applications have been considered first. Thus the statics of particles precedes the statics of rigid bodies, and problems involving internal forces are postponed until Chap. 6. Also, in Chap. 4, equilibrium problems involving only coplanar forces are considered first and solved by ordinary algebra, while problems involving three-dimensional forces and requiring the full use of vector algebra are discussed in the second part of the chapter.

Free-body diagrams are introduced early, and their importance is emphasized throughout the text.   They are used not
only to solve equilibrium problems but also to express the
equivalence of two systems of forces or, more generally, of two
systems of vectors.   This approach is particularly useful as a
preparation for the study of the dynamics of rigid bodies.   As
will be shown in the volume on dynamics, by placing the
emphasis on "free-body-diagram equations" rather than on the
standard algebraic equations of motion, a more intuitive and
more complete understanding of the fundamental principles of
dynamics may be achieved.

The material presented in the text and most of the problems
require no previous mathematical knowledge beyond algebra,
trigonometry, and elementary calculus, and all the elements of
vector algebra necessary to the understanding of the text have
been carefully presented in Chaps. 2 and 3.   In general, a
greater emphasis has been placed on the correct understanding
of the basic mathematical concepts involved than on the nimble
manipulation of mathematical formulas.   In this connection, it
should be mentioned that the determination of the centroids of
composite areas precedes the calculation of centroids by integration, thus making it possible to establish the concept of
moment of area firmly before introducing the use of integration.

Since students are often given no formal training in the use of
the slide rule, special notes have been included in Chap. 2,
stressing the proper use of the slide rule in the solution of problems involving proportions or trigonometric relations.

The text has been divided into units, each consisting of one or
several theory sections, one or several Sample Problems, and a
large number of problems to be assigned.   Each unit corresponds to a well-defined topic and generally may be covered
in one lesson.   In a number of cases, however, the instructor
will find it desirable to devote more than one lesson to a given
topic.   The Sample Problems have been set up in much the
same form that a student will use in solving the assigned problems.   They thus serve the double purpose of amplifying the
text and demonstrating the type of neat and orderly work that
the student should cultivate in his own solutions.   Most of the
problems to be assigned are of a practical nature and should
appeal to the engineering student.   They are primarily designed, however, to illustrate the material presented in the text
and to help the student understand the basic principles of mechanics.   The problems have been grouped according to the
portions of material they illustrate and have been arranged in
order of increasing difficulty.   Problems requiring special

attention have been indicated by asterisks.   Answers to all even-numbered problems are given at the end of the book.

The authors wish to acknowledge gratefully the many helpful comments and suggestions offered by the users of the first edition of *Mechanics for Engineers.*

FERDINAND P. BEER
E. RUSSELL JOHNSTON, JR.

CONTENTS

ix

LIST OF SYMBOLS

a Constant; radius; distance

$\mathbf{A}, \mathbf{B}, \mathbf{C}, \ldots$ Reactions at supports and connections

$A, B, C, \ldots$ Points

A Area

b Width; distance

c Constant

C Centroid

d Distance

e Base of natural logarithms

$\mathbf{F}$ Force; friction force

g Acceleration of gravity

G Center of gravity; constant of gravitation

h Height; sag of cable

$\mathbf{i}, \mathbf{j}, \mathbf{k}$ Unit vectors along coordinate axes

$I, I_x, \ldots$ Moment of inertia

$\bar{I}$ Centroidal moment of inertia

J Polar moment of inertia

k Spring constant

k_x, k_y, k_o Radius of gyration

$\bar{k}$ Centroidal radius of gyration

l Length

L Length; span

m Mass

$\mathbf{M}$ Couple; moment

$\mathbf{M}_o$ Moment about point O

$\mathbf{M}_o^R$ Moment resultant about point O

M Magnitude of couple or moment; mass of earth

M_{OL} Moment about axis OL

$\mathbf{N}$ Normal component of reaction

O Origin of coordinates

p Pressure

$\mathbf{P}$ Force; vector

$P_{xy}, \ldots$ Product of inertia

Q   Force; vector

r   Position vector

r Radius; distance; polar coordinate

R   Resultant force; resultant vector; reaction

R Radius of earth

s   Position vector

s Distance; length of arc; length of cable

S   Force; vector

t Thickness

T   Force

T Tension

u Rectangular coordinate

U Work

v Rectangular coordinate

V   Vector product; shearing force

V Volume; potential energy; shear

w Load per unit length

W, W Weight; load

x, y, z Rectangular coordinates; distances

$\bar{x}, \bar{y}, \bar{z}$ Rectangular coordinates of centroid or center of gravity

α, β, γ Angles

γ Specific weight

δ Elongation

$\delta \mathbf{r}$ Virtual displacement

δU Virtual work

λ Unit vector along a line

η Efficiency

θ Angular coordinate; angle; polar coordinate

μ Coefficient of friction

ρ Density

ϕ Angle of friction; angle

VECTOR
MECHANICS FOR ENGINEERS: STATICS

1. INTRODUCTION

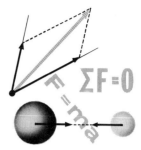

1.1. What Is Mechanics?   Mechanics may be defined as that science which describes and predicts the conditions of rest or motion of bodies under the action of forces.   It is divided into three parts: mechanics of *rigid bodies*, mechanics of *deformable bodies*, and mechanics of *fluids*.

The mechanics of rigid bodies is subdivided into *statics* and *dynamics*, the former dealing with bodies at rest, the latter with bodies in motion.   In this part of the study of mechanics, bodies are assumed to be perfectly rigid.   Actual structures and machines, however, are never absolutely rigid and deform under the loads to which they are subjected.   But these deformations are usually small and do not appreciably affect the conditions of equilibrium or motion of the structure under consideration.   They are important, though, as far as the resistance of the structure to failure is concerned and are studied in mechanics of materials, which is a part of the mechanics of deformable bodies.   The third division of mechanics, the mechanics of fluids, is subdivided into the study of *incompressible fluids* and of *compressible fluids*.   An important subdivision of the study of incompressible fluids is *hydraulics*, which deals with problems involving liquids.

Mechanics is a physical science, since it deals with the study of physical phenomena.   However, some associate mechanics with mathematics, while many consider it as an engineering subject.   Both these views are justified in part.   Mechanics is the foundation of most engineering sciences and is an indispensable prerequisite to their study.   However, it does not have the *empiricism* found in many engineering sciences; by its rigor and the emphasis it places on deductive reasoning it resembles mathematics.   But, again, it is not an *abstract* or even a *pure* science; mechanics is an *applied* science.   The purpose of mechanics is to explain and predict physical phenomena and thus to lay the foundations for engineering applications.

1.2. Fundamental Concepts and Principles. Although the study of mechanics goes back to the time of Aristotle (384–322 B.C.) and Archimedes (287–212 B.C.), one has to wait until Newton (1642–1727) to find a satisfactory formulation of its fundamental principles. These principles were later expressed in a modified form by D'Alembert, Lagrange, and Hamilton. Their validity remained unchallenged, however, until Einstein formulated his *theory of relativity* (1905). While its limitations have now been recognized, *newtonian mechanics* still remains the basis of today's engineering sciences.

The basic concepts used in mechanics are *space, time, mass,* and *force*. These concepts cannot be truly defined; they should be accepted on the basis of our intuition and experience and used as a mental frame of reference for our study of mechanics.

The concept of *space* is associated with the notion of the position of a point *P*. The position of *P* may be defined by three lengths measured from a certain reference point, or *origin*, in three given directions. These lengths are known as the *coordinates* of *P*.

To define an event, it is not sufficient to indicate its position in space. The *time* of the event should also be given.

The concept of *mass* is used to characterize and compare bodies on the basis of certain fundamental mechanical experiments. Two bodies of the same mass, for example, will be attracted by the earth in the same manner; they will also offer the same resistance to a change in translational motion.

A *force* represents the action of one body on another. It may be exerted by actual contact or at a distance, as in the case of gravitational forces and magnetic forces. A force is characterized by its *point of application*, its *magnitude*, and its *direction;* a force is represented by a *vector* (Sec. 2.2).

In newtonian mechanics, space, time, and mass are absolute concepts, independent of each other. (This is not true in *relativistic mechanics,* where the time of an event depends upon its position, and where the mass of a body varies with its velocity.) On the other hand, the concept of force is not independent of the other three. Indeed, one of the fundamental principles of newtonian mechanics listed below indicates that the resultant force acting on a body is related to the mass of the body and to the manner in which its velocity varies with time.

We shall study the conditions of rest or motion of particles and rigid bodies in terms of the four basic concepts we have introduced.   By *particle* we mean a very small amount of matter which may be assumed to occupy a single point in space. A *rigid body* is a combination of a large number of particles occupying fixed positions with respect to each other.   The study of the mechanics of particles is obviously a prerequisite to that of rigid bodies.   Besides, the results obtained for a particle may be used directly in a large number of problems dealing with the conditions of rest or motion of actual bodies.

The study of elementary mechanics rests on six fundamental principles based on experimental evidence:

The Parallelogram Law for the Addition of Forces.   This states that two forces acting on a particle may be replaced by a single force, called their *resultant,* obtained by drawing the diagonal of the parallelogram which has sides equal to the given forces (Sec. 2.1).

The Principle of Transmissibility.   This states that the conditions of equilibrium or of motion of a rigid body will remain unchanged if a force acting at a given point of the rigid body is replaced by a force of the same magnitude and same direction, but acting at a different point, provided that the two forces have the same line of action (Sec. 3.2).

Newton's Three Fundamental Laws.   Formulated by Sir Isaac Newton in the latter part of the seventeenth century, these laws may be stated as follows:

FIRST LAW.   If the resultant force acting on a particle is zero, the particle will remain at rest (if originally at rest) or will move with constant speed in a straight line (if originally in motion) (Sec. 2.9).

SECOND LAW.   If the resultant force acting on a particle is not zero, the particle will have an acceleration proportional to the magnitude of the resultant and in the direction of this resultant force.

As we shall see in Sec. 12.1, this law may be stated as

$$\mathbf{F} = m\mathbf{a} \tag{1.1}$$

where $\mathbf{F}$, m, and $\mathbf{a}$ represent, respectively, the resultant force acting on the particle, the mass of the particle, and the acceleration of the particle, expressed in a consistent system of units.

THIRD LAW.   The forces of action and reaction between bodies in contact have the same magnitude, same line of action, and opposite sense (Sec. 6.1).

Newton's Law of Gravitation.   This states that two particles of mass M and m are mutually attracted with equal and opposite forces $\mathbf{F}$ and $-\mathbf{F}$ of magnitude F given by the formula

$$F = G\frac{Mm}{r^2} \qquad (1.2)$$

where $r =$ distance between the two particles
$\quad\ G =$ a universal constant called the *constant of gravitation*

A particular case of great importance is that of the attraction of the earth on a particle located on its surface. The force $\mathbf{F}$ exerted by the earth on the particle is then defined as the *weight* $\mathbf{W}$ of the particle. Taking M equal to the mass of the earth, m equal to the mass of the particle, and r equal to the radius R of the earth, and introducing the constant

$$g = \frac{GM}{R^2} \qquad (1.3)$$

the magnitude W of the weight of a particle of mass m may be expressed as†

$$W = mg \qquad (1.4)$$

The value of R in formula (1.3) depends upon the elevation of the point considered; it also depends upon its latitude, since the earth is not truly spherical. The value of g therefore varies with the position of the point considered. As long as the point actually remains on the surface of the earth, it is sufficiently accurate in most engineering computations to assume that g equals 32.2 ft/sec².

  As noted earlier, the six fundamental principles listed above are based on experimental evidence; they cannot be derived mathematically. On these principles rests most of the intricate structure of newtonian mechanics. For more than two centuries a tremendous number of problems dealing with the conditions of rest and motion of rigid bodies, deformable bodies, and fluids have been solved by applying these fundamental principles. Many of the solutions obtained could be checked experimentally, thus providing a further verification of the principles from which they were derived. It is only recently that Newton's mechanics was found at fault, in the study of the motion of atoms and in the study of the motion of certain planets, where it must be supplemented by the theory of rela-

---

† A more accurate definition of the weight $\mathbf{W}$ should take into account the rotation of the earth.

tivity.   But on the human or engineering scale, where velocities are small compared with the velocity of light, Newton's
mechanics has yet to be disproved.

1.3. Units.   With the four basic concepts introduced in the
preceding section are associated the units of *length, time,
mass,* and *force.*   These four units are not independent.   As
we shall see in greater detail in Sec. 12.2, three of these units
may be defined arbitrarily, but the fourth one must be chosen
in accordance with formula (1.1).

The fundamental units chosen by engineers everywhere are
the units of length, time, and force.   The standard unit of
length used by American engineers is the *foot* (ft), subdivided
into 12 *inches* (in.); a multiple of the foot is the *mile,* equal to
5,280 ft.   The standard unit of time is the *second* (sec); a multiple of the second is the *hour* (hr), equal to 3,600 sec.   The
standard unit of force is the *pound* (lb), defined as the force
(weight) with which a certain mass of platinum is attracted by
the earth at the latitude of 45° and at sea level.   Multiples of
the pound frequently used are the *kilopound* (kip, or k), equal
to 1,000 lb, and the *ton,* equal to 2,000 lb.

All quantities other than length, time, and force should be
expressed in units obtained from the fundamental units ft, sec,
and lb.   For example, an area, obtained by multiplying a
length (ft) by a length (ft), should be expressed in ft².   A pressure, obtained by dividing a force (lb) by an area (ft²), should
be expressed in lb/ft².   The magnitude of a velocity, obtained
by dividing a length (ft) by a time (sec), should be expressed in
ft/sec.   An acceleration, obtained by dividing a velocity (ft/
sec) by a time (sec), should be expressed in ft/sec².   Since, according to formula (1.1), a mass may be obtained by dividing
the magnitude of a force (lb) by that of an acceleration (ft/
sec²), a mass should be expressed in lb-sec²/ft.

A useful check of our computations may be obtained if we
carry out the computations with the units as well as the numerical values.   For example, the magnitude of the moment
of a 10-lb force about a point 2 ft from its line of action may
be determined as follows (Sec. 3.5):

$$M = Fd = (10 \text{ lb})(2 \text{ ft}) = 20 \text{ lb-ft}$$

The unit lb-ft obtained by multiplying lb by ft is the correct
unit for the moment of a force; if another unit had been obtained, we would have known that some mistake had been
made.

Sometimes a quantity is expressed in units other than the

standard units.   For example, the magnitude of a velocity may be given as $v = 30$ mph (miles per hour).   To express this magnitude in ft/sec, we shall proceed as follows:

First we write
$$v = 30\,\frac{\text{miles}}{\text{hr}}$$

Since we want to get rid of the unit miles and introduce instead the unit feet, we should multiply the right-hand member of the equation by an expression containing miles in the denominator and feet in the numerator.   But, since we do not want to change the value of the right-hand member, the expression used should have a value equal to unity.   The quotient 5,280 ft/1 mile is such an expression.   Operating in a similar way to transform the unit hour into seconds, we write

$$v = \left(30\,\frac{\text{miles}}{\text{hr}} \right) \left(\frac{5{,}280\text{ ft}}{1\text{ mile}} \right) \left(\frac{1\text{ hr}}{3{,}600\text{ sec}} \right)$$

Carrying out the numerical computations and canceling out units which appear both in the numerator and the denominator, we obtain

$$v = 44\,\frac{\text{ft}}{\text{sec}} = 44\text{ ft/sec}$$

1.4. Method of Problem Solution.   The student should approach a problem in mechanics as he would approach an actual engineering situation.   By drawing on his own experience and on his intuition, he will find it easier to understand and formulate the problem.   Once the problem has been clearly stated, however, there is no place in its solution for the student's particular fancy.   *The solution must be based on the six fundamental principles stated above or on theorems derived from them.*   Every step taken must be justified on that basis.   Strict rules must be followed, which lead to the solution in an almost automatic fashion, leaving no room for the student's intuition or "feeling."   After an answer has been obtained, it should be checked.   Here again, the student may call upon his common sense and personal experience.   If not completely satisfied with the result obtained, he should carefully check his formulation of the problem, the validity of the methods used for its solution, and the accuracy of his computations.

The *statement* of a problem should be clear and precise.   It should contain the given data and indicate what information is required.   A neat drawing showing all quantities involved should be included.   Separate diagrams should be drawn for all bodies involved, indicating clearly the forces acting on each body. These diagrams are known as *free-body diagrams* and are described in detail in Secs. 2.10 and 4.2.

The *fundamental principles* of mechanics listed in Sec. 1.2 *will be used to write equations* expressing the conditions of rest or motion of the bodies considered. Each equation should be clearly related to one of the free-body diagrams. The student will then proceed to solve the problem, observing strictly the usual rules of algebra and recording neatly the various steps taken.

After the answer has been obtained, it should be *carefully checked*. Mistakes in reasoning may often be detected by checking the units, as indicated in Sec. 1.3. Errors in computation will usually be found by substituting the numerical values obtained into an equation which has not yet been used and verifying that the equation is satisfied. The importance of correct computations in engineering cannot be overemphasized.

1.5. Numerical Accuracy. The accuracy of the solution of a problem depends upon two items: (1) the accuracy of the given data; (2) the accuracy of the computations performed.

The solution cannot be more accurate than the less accurate of these two items. For example, if the loading of a bridge is known to be 75,000 lb with a possible error of 100 lb either way, the relative error which measures the degree of accuracy of the data is

$$\frac{100 \text{ lb}}{75,000 \text{ lb}} = 0.0013 = 0.13 \text{ per cent}$$

It would then be meaningless, in computing the reaction at one of the bridge supports, to record it as 14,322 lb. The accuracy of the solution cannot be greater than 0.13 per cent, no matter how accurate the computations are, and the possible error in the answer may be as large as $(0.13/100)(14,322 \text{ lb}) \approx 20 \text{ lb}$. The solution should be properly recorded as $14,320 \pm 20 \text{ lb}$.

In engineering problems, the data are seldom known with an accuracy greater than 0.2 per cent. It is therefore unnecessary to carry out computations with a greater accuracy. In almost all cases, the slide rule will provide the desired accuracy. On looking at the main scales of a 10-in. slide rule, it will be observed that the number 502 may be easily interpolated between the graduations corresponding, respectively, to 500 and 505. It might possibly be mistaken for 501 or 503, but no larger error in reading or in adjusting the rule will be made if a minimum of care is observed.   The error involved is thus at most 1 unit out of 500; the relative error is 0.2 per cent.   For other positions on the rule, the absolute error will be different (for example, 2 units out of 1,000); owing to the logarithmic nature of the scales, however, the relative error will remain 0.2 per cent.

It is sometimes said that the accuracy obtained on the slide rule is *three significant figures*.   This is correct as far as the central portion of the scale is concerned, where numbers such as 298, 299, 300, 301 may be easily read.   The third significant figure, however, becomes doubtful toward the right end of the scale, where it is difficult to tell 997 from 998.   On the other hand, one should be able, toward the left end of the scale, to estimate the fourth significant figure within a couple of units. The relative error between 996 and 998 is the same as between 1,002 and 1,004 (0.2 per cent in both cases).   We should therefore define the accuracy of a computation by the possible relative error involved, rather than by the number of significant figures obtained, and we shall attempt to obtain all answers with an accuracy of about 0.2 per cent.   A practical rule consists in using four figures to record readings taken on a 10-in. slide rule between 1 and 2 and three figures to record readings between 2 and 10.   Unless otherwise indicated, the data given in a problem should be assumed known with a comparable degree of accuracy.   A force of 40 lb, for example, should actually be read 40.0 lb, and a force of 15 lb should be read 15.00 lb.

2. STATICS OF PARTICLES

FORCES IN A PLANE

2.1. Force on a Particle. Resultant of Two Forces. A force represents the action of one body on another. It is characterized by its *point of application,* its *magnitude,* and its *direction.* In this chapter we shall study the effect of forces on particles. The use of the word "particles" does not imply that we shall restrict our study to that of small corpuscles. It means that the size and shape of the bodies under consideration will not affect the solution of the problems treated in this chapter and that all the forces acting on a given body will be assumed to have the same point of application. Each force will thus be completely defined by its magnitude and direction.

The magnitude of a force is characterized by a certain number of units; as was indicated in Sec. 1.3, the standard units used by American engineers to measure the magnitude of a force are the pound (lb) and its multiples, the kilopound (kip, or k), equal to 1,000 lb, and the ton, equal to 2,000 lb. The direction of a force is defined by the *line of action* and the *sense* of the force. The line of action is the infinite straight line along which the force acts; it is characterized by the angle it forms with some fixed axis (Fig. 2.1). The force itself is represented by a segment of that line; through the use of an appropriate scale, the length of this segment may be chosen to represent the magnitude of the force. Finally, the sense of the force should be indicated by an arrowhead. It is important, in defining a force, to indicate its sense. Two forces, such as those shown in Figs. 2.1*a* and 2.1*b*, having the same magnitude and the same line of action but different sense, will have directly opposite effects on a particle.

Experimental evidence shows that two forces **P** and **Q** acting on a particle *A* (Fig. 2.2*a*) may be replaced by a single force **R** which has the same effect on the particle (Fig. 2.2*c*). This

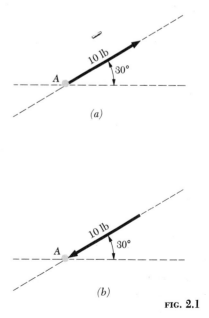

FIG. 2.1

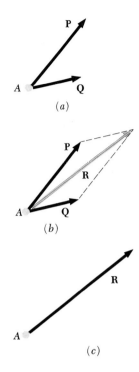

(a)

(b)

(c)

FIG. 2.2

force is called the *resultant* of the forces **P** and **Q** and may be obtained, as shown in Fig. 2.2*b*, by constructing a parallelogram, using **P** and **Q** as two sides of the parallelogram. *The diagonal that passes through A represents the resultant.* This is known as the *parallelogram law* for the addition of two forces. This law is based on experimental evidence; it cannot be proved or derived mathematically.

2.2. Vectors. It appears from the above that forces do not obey the rules of addition defined in ordinary arithmetic or algebra. For example, two forces acting at a right angle to each other, one of 4 lb and the other of 3 lb, add up to a force of 5 lb, *not* to a force of 7 lb. Forces are not the only expressions which follow the parallelogram law of addition. As we shall see later, *displacements, velocities, accelerations, momenta* are other examples of physical quantities possessing magnitude and direction and which are added according to the parallelogram law. All these quantities may be represented mathematically by *vectors,* while those physical quantities which do not have direction, such as *volume, mass,* or *energy,* are represented by ordinary numbers or *scalars.*

Vectors are defined as *mathematical expressions possessing magnitude and direction, which add according to the parallelogram law.*† Vectors are represented by arrows in the illustrations and will be distinguished from scalar quantities in this text through the use of boldface type (**P**). In longhand writing, a vector may be characterized by drawing a short arrow above the letter used to represent it ($\vec{P}$), or by underlining the letter (P̲). The last method is gaining wider acceptance since it can also be used on a typewriter. The magnitude of a vector defines the length of the arrow used to represent the vector.

† Some expressions have magnitude and direction, but do not add according to the parallelogram law. While these expressions may be represented by arrows, they *cannot* be considered as vectors.

A group of such expressions are the finite rotations of a rigid body. Place a closed book on a table in front of you, so that it lies in the usual fashion, with its front cover up and its binding to the left. Now rotate it through 180° about an axis parallel to the binding (Fig. 2.3*a*); this rotation may be represented by an arrow of length equal to 180 units and oriented as shown. Picking up the book as it lies in its new position, rotate it now through 180° about a horizontal

FIG. 2.3. Finite rotations of a rigid body

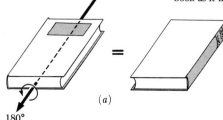

180°

(a)

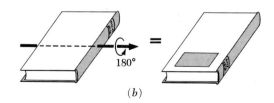

180°

(b)

In this text, italic type will be used to denote the magnitude of a vector. Thus, the magnitude of the vector **P** will be referred to as *P*.

A vector used to represent a force acting on a given particle has a well-defined point of application, namely, the particle itself. Such a vector is said to be a *fixed*, or *bound*, vector and cannot be moved without modifying the conditions of the problem. Other physical quantities, however, such as couples (see Chap. 3), are represented by vectors which may be freely moved in space; these vectors are called *free* vectors. Still other physical quantities, such as forces acting on a rigid body (see Chap. 3), are represented by vectors which may be moved, or slid, along their line of action; they are known as *sliding* vectors.

Two vectors which have the same magnitude and the same direction are said to be *equal*, whether or not they also have the same point of application (Fig. 2.4); equal vectors may be denoted by the same letter.

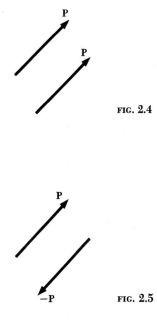

FIG. 2.4

The *negative vector* of a given vector **P** is defined as a vector having the same magnitude as **P** and a direction opposite to that of **P** (Fig. 2.5); the negative of the vector **P** is denoted by −**P**. The vectors **P** and −**P** are commonly referred to as *equal and opposite* vectors. Clearly, we have

$$\mathbf{P} + (-\mathbf{P}) = 0$$

FIG. 2.5

2.3. Addition of Vectors. We saw in the preceding section that, by definition, vectors add according to the parallelogram law. Thus the sum of two vectors **P** and **Q** is obtained by attaching the two vectors to the same point *A* and constructing a parallelogram, using **P** and **Q** as two sides of the parallelo-

---

axis perpendicular to the binding (Fig. 2.3*b*); this second rotation may be represented by an arrow 180 units long and oriented as shown. But the book could have been placed in this final position through a single 180-degree rotation about a vertical axis (Fig. 2.3*c*). We conclude that the sum of the two 180-degree rotations represented by arrows directed respectively along the *z* and *x* axes is a 180-degree rotation represented by an arrow directed along the *y* axis (Fig. 2.3*d*). Clearly, the finite rotations of a rigid body *do not* obey the parallelogram law of addition; therefore they *cannot* be represented by vectors.

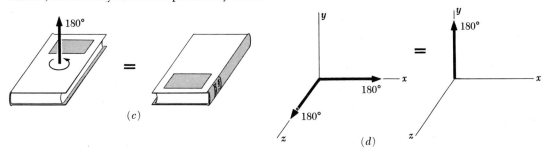

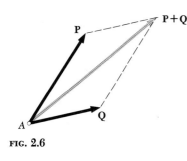

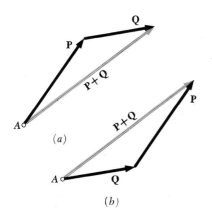

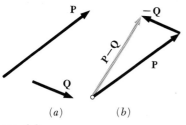

gram (Fig. 2.6).   The diagonal that passes through A represents the sum of the vectors **P** and **Q**, and this sum is denoted by **P** + **Q**.   The fact that the sign + is used to denote both vector and scalar addition should not cause any confusion if vector and scalar quantities are always carefully distinguished. Thus, we should note that the magnitude of the vector **P** + **Q** is *not*, in general, equal to the sum $P + Q$ of the magnitudes of the vectors **P** and **Q**.

Since the parallelogram constructed on the vectors **P** and **Q** does not depend upon the order in which **P** and **Q** are selected, we conclude that the addition of two vectors is *commutative*, and we write

$$\mathbf{P} + \mathbf{Q} = \mathbf{Q} + \mathbf{P} \tag{2.1}$$

From the parallelogram law, we can derive an alternate method for determining the sum of two vectors.   This method, known as the *triangle rule*, is derived as follows: Consider Fig. 2.6, where the sum of the vectors **P** and **Q** has been determined by the parallelogram law.   Since the side of the parallelogram opposite **Q** is equal to **Q** in magnitude and direction, we could draw only half of the parallelogram (Fig. 2.7a).   The sum of the two vectors may thus be found by *arranging P and Q in tip-to-tail fashion and then connecting the tail of P with the tip of Q*.   In Fig. 2.7b, the other half of the parallelogram is considered, and the same result is obtained.   This confirms the fact that vector addition is commutative.

The *subtraction* of a vector is defined as the addition of the corresponding negative vector.   Thus, the vector **P** − **Q** representing the difference between the vectors **P** and **Q** is obtained by adding to **P** the negative vector −**Q** (Fig. 2.8).   We write

$$\mathbf{P} - \mathbf{Q} = \mathbf{P} + (-\mathbf{Q}) \tag{2.2}$$

Here again we should observe that, while the same sign is used to denote both vector and scalar subtraction, confusion will be avoided if care is taken to distinguish between vector and scalar quantities.

We shall now consider the *sum of three or more vectors*. The sum of three vectors **P**, **Q**, and **S** will, *by definition*, be obtained by first adding the vectors **P** and **Q**, and then by adding the vector **S** to the vector **P** + **Q**.   We thus write

$$\mathbf{P} + \mathbf{Q} + \mathbf{S} = (\mathbf{P} + \mathbf{Q}) + \mathbf{S} \tag{2.3}$$

Similarly, the sum of four vectors will be obtained by adding the fourth vector to the sum of the first three.   It follows that the sum of any number of vectors may be obtained by applying repeatedly the parallelogram law to successive pairs of vectors until all the given vectors are replaced by a single vector.

If the given vectors are *coplanar,* i.e., if they are contained in the same plane, their sum may be easily obtained graphically.   In that case, the repeated application of the triangle rule will be preferred to the application of the parallelogram law.   In Fig. 2.9 the sum of three vectors **P**, **Q**, and **S** was obtained in that manner.   The triangle rule was first applied to obtain the sum **P** + **Q** of the vectors **P** and **Q**; it was applied again to obtain the sum of the vectors **P** + **Q** and **S**.   The determination of the vector **P** + **Q**, however, could have been omitted and the sum of the three vectors could have been obtained directly, as shown in Fig. 2.10, by *arranging the given vectors in tip-to-tail fashion and connecting the tail of the first vector with the tip of the last one.*   This is known as the *polygon rule* for the addition of vectors.

We observe that the result obtained would have been unchanged if, as shown in Fig. 2.11, the vectors **Q** and **S** had been replaced by their sum **Q** + **S**.   We may thus write

$$\blacktriangleright \qquad \mathbf{P} + \mathbf{Q} + \mathbf{S} = (\mathbf{P} + \mathbf{Q}) + \mathbf{S} = \mathbf{P} + (\mathbf{Q} + \mathbf{S}) \qquad (2.4)$$

which expresses the fact that vector addition is *associative.* Recalling that vector addition has also been shown, in the case of two vectors, to be commutative, we write

$$\mathbf{P} + \mathbf{Q} + \mathbf{S} = (\mathbf{P} + \mathbf{Q}) + \mathbf{S} = \mathbf{S} + (\mathbf{P} + \mathbf{Q})$$
$$= \mathbf{S} + (\mathbf{Q} + \mathbf{P}) = \mathbf{S} + \mathbf{Q} + \mathbf{P} \qquad (2.5)$$

This expression, as well as others which may be obtained in the same way, shows that the order in which several vectors are added together is immaterial (Fig. 2.12).

Product of a Scalar and a Vector.   Since it is convenient to denote the sum **P** + **P** by 2**P**, the sum **P** + **P** + **P** by 3**P**, and, in general, to represent the sum of *n* equal vectors **P** by the product *n***P**, we shall define the product *n***P** of a positive integer *n* and a vector **P** as a vector having the same direction as **P** and the magnitude *nP*.   Extending this definition to include all scalars, and recalling the definition of a negative vector given in Sec. 2.2, we define the product *k***P** of a scalar *k* and a vector **P** as a vector having the same direction as **P** (if *k* is positive), or a direction opposite to that of **P** (if *k* is negative), and a magnitude equal to the product of *P* and of the absolute value of *k* (Fig. 2.13).

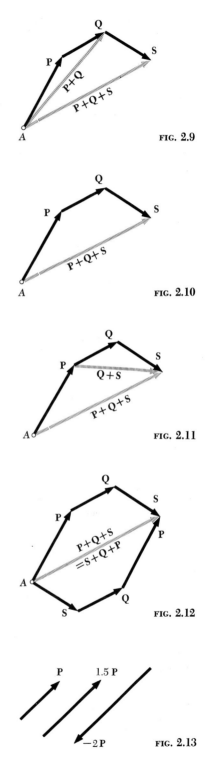

FIG. 2.9

FIG. 2.10

FIG. 2.11

FIG. 2.12

FIG. 2.13

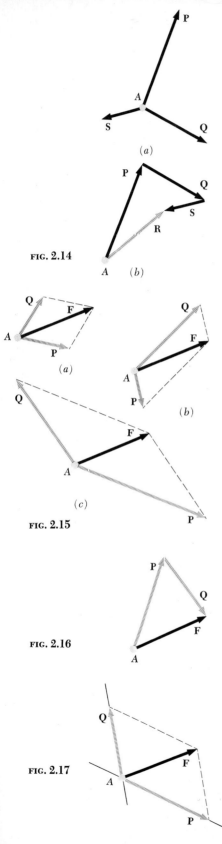

FIG. 2.14

FIG. 2.15

FIG. 2.16

FIG. 2.17

2.4. Resultant of Several Concurrent Forces. Consider a particle *A* acted upon by several coplanar forces, i.e., by several forces contained in the same plane (Fig. 2.14*a*). Since the forces considered here all pass through *A*, they are also said to be *concurrent*. The vectors representing the forces acting on *A* may be added by the polygon rule (Fig. 2.14*b*). Since the use of the polygon rule is equivalent to the repeated application of the parallelogram law, the vector **R** thus obtained represents the resultant of the given concurrent forces, i.e., the single force which has the same effect on the particle *A* as the given forces. As indicated above, the order in which the vectors **P**, **Q**, and **S** representing the given forces are added together is immaterial.

2.5 Resolution of a Force into Components. We have seen that two or more forces acting on a particle may be replaced by a single force which has the same effect on the particle. Conversely, a single force **F** acting on a particle may be replaced by two or more forces which, together, have the same effect on the particle. These forces are called the *components* of the original force **F**, and the process of substituting them for **F** is called *resolving the force* **F** *into components*.

Clearly, for each force **F** there exist an infinite number of possible sets of components. Sets of *two components* **P** *and* **Q** are the most important as far as practical applications are concerned. But, even then, the number of ways in which a given force **F** may be resolved into two components is unlimited (Fig. 2.15). Two cases are of particular interest:

1. *One of the Two Components*, **P**, *Is Known*. The second component, **Q**, is obtained by applying the triangle rule and joining the tip of **P** to the tip of **F** (Fig. 2.16); the magnitude and direction of **Q** are determined graphically or by trigonometry. Once **Q** has been determined, both components **P** and **Q** should be applied at *A*.

2. *The Line of Action of Each Component Is Known*. The magnitude and sense of the components are obtained by applying the parallelogram law and drawing lines, through the tip of **F**, parallel to the given lines of action (Fig. 2.17). This process leads to two well-defined components, **P** and **Q**, which may be determined graphically or by applying the law of sines.

Many other cases may be encountered; for example, the direction of one component may be known while the magnitude of the other component is to be as small as possible (see Sample Prob. 2.2). In all cases the appropriate triangle or parallelogram is drawn, which satisfies the given conditions.

SAMPLE PROBLEM 2.1

The two forces **P** and **Q** act on a bolt A.   Determine their resultant.

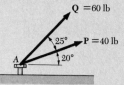

Graphical Solution.   A parallelogram with sides equal to **P** and **Q** is drawn to scale.   The magnitude and direction of the resultant are measured and found to be

$$R = 98 \text{ lb} \qquad \alpha = 35° \qquad\qquad R = 98 \text{ lb} \measuredangle\, 35° \quad \blacktriangleleft$$

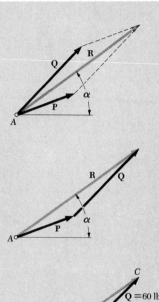

The triangle rule may also be used.   Forces **P** and **Q** are drawn in tip-to-tail fashion.   Again the magnitude and direction of the resultant are measured.

$$R = 98 \text{ lb} \qquad \alpha = 35° \qquad\qquad R = 98 \text{ lb} \measuredangle\, 35° \quad \blacktriangleleft$$

Trigonometric Solution.   The triangle rule is again used; two sides and the included angle are known.   We apply the law of cosines.

$$R^2 = P^2 + Q^2 - 2\,P\,Q\,\cos B$$
$$R^2 = (40 \text{ lb})^2 + (60 \text{ lb})^2 - 2(40 \text{ lb})(60 \text{ lb}) \cos 155°$$
$$R = 97.7 \text{ lb}$$

Now, applying the law of sines, we write

$$\frac{\sin A}{Q} = \frac{\sin B}{R}$$
$$\frac{\sin A}{60 \text{ lb}} = \frac{\sin 155°}{97.7 \text{ lb}}$$

Noting that $\sin 155° = \sin 25°$, and setting the slide rule as shown, we read

$$A = 15.0° \qquad \alpha = 20° + A = 35.0°$$
$$R = 97.7 \text{ lb} \measuredangle\, 35° \quad \blacktriangleleft$$

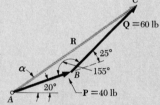

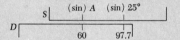

Alternate Trigonometric Solution.   We construct the right triangle BCD and compute

$$CD = (60 \text{ lb}) \sin 25° = 25.4 \text{ lb}$$
$$BD = (60 \text{ lb}) \cos 25° = 54.4 \text{ lb}$$

Then, using triangle ACD, we obtain

$$\tan A = \frac{25.4 \text{ lb}}{94.4 \text{ lb}} \qquad A = 15.0°$$
$$R \sin A = 25.4 \qquad R = 97.7 \text{ lb}$$

Again,

$$\alpha = 20° + A = 35.0° \qquad\qquad R = 97.7 \text{ lb} \measuredangle\, 35° \quad \blacktriangleleft$$

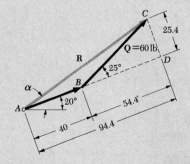

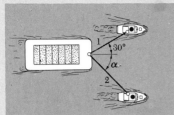

SAMPLE PROBLEM 2.2

A barge is pulled by two tugboats. If the resultant of the forces exerted by the tugboats is a 5,000-lb force directed along the axis of the barge, find (a) the tension in each of the ropes, knowing that $\alpha = 45°$, (b) the value of α such that the tension in rope 2 is minimum.

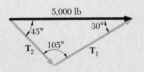

a. **Tension for $\alpha = 45°$.** *Graphical Solution.* The parallelogram law is used; the diagonal (resultant) is known to be equal to 5,000 lb and to be directed to the right. The sides are drawn parallel to the ropes. If the drawing is done to scale, we measure

$$T_1 = 3{,}700 \text{ lb} \qquad T_2 = 2{,}600 \text{ lb} \blacktriangleleft$$

Trigonometric Solution. The triangle rule may be used. We note that the triangle shown represents half of the parallelogram shown above. Using the law of sines, we write

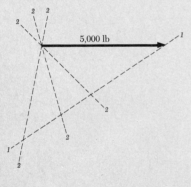

$$\frac{T_1}{\sin 45°} = \frac{T_2}{\sin 30°} = \frac{5{,}000 \text{ lb}}{\sin 105°}$$

or, since $\sin 105° = \sin 75°$,

$$\frac{T_1}{\sin 45°} = \frac{T_2}{\sin 30°} = \frac{5{,}000 \text{ lb}}{\sin 75°}$$

The values of T_1 and T_2 may be obtained in one setting of the slide rule.

$$T_1 = 3{,}660 \text{ lb} \qquad T_2 = 2{,}590 \text{ lb} \blacktriangleleft$$

b. **Value of α for Minimum T_2.** To determine the value of α such that the tension in rope 2 is minimum, the triangle rule is again used. In the sketch shown, line *1-1* is the known direction of $\mathbf{T}_1$. Several possible directions of $\mathbf{T}_2$ are shown by the lines *2-2*. We note that the minimum value of T_2 occurs when $\mathbf{T}_1$ and $\mathbf{T}_2$ are perpendicular. The minimum value of T_2 is

$$T_2 = (5{,}000 \text{ lb}) \sin 30° = 2{,}500 \text{ lb}$$

Corresponding values of T_1 and α are

$$T_1 = (5{,}000 \text{ lb}) \cos 30° = 4{,}330 \text{ lb}$$
$$\alpha = 90° - 30° \qquad\qquad \alpha = 60° \blacktriangleleft$$

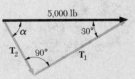

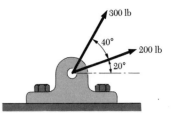

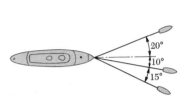

FIG. P 2.1

PROBLEMS†

2.1 and 2.2. Determine graphically the magnitude and direction of the resultant of the two forces shown, using in each problem (*a*) the parallelogram law, (*b*) the triangle rule.

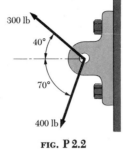

FIG. P 2.2

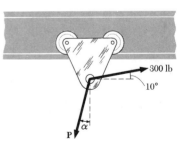

FIG. P 2.3

2.3. A disabled ocean liner is being towed by three tugboats as shown. The tension in each cable is 5,000 lb.   (*a*) Determine graphically the resultant force acting on the bow of the liner.   (*b*) If the tugboats cannot operate safely when the angle between any two of the cables is less than 10°, where should the tugboats be located in order to produce the largest resultant force parallel to the axis of the liner?   What is the magnitude of this resultant?

2.4. Two structural members *B* and *C* are riveted to the bracket *A*. Knowing that the tension in member *B* is 2,500 lb and that the tension in *C* is 2,000 lb, determine graphically the magnitude and direction of the resultant force acting on the bracket.

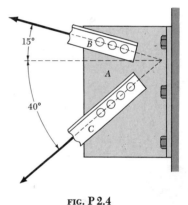

FIG. P 2.4

2.5. Solve Prob. 2.4 by trigonometry.

2.6. In raising the lid of a box, the two forces shown are applied at edge *A*.   Determine by trigonometry the resultant of the two applied forces.

2.7. Determine by trigonometry the magnitude and direction of the force **P** so that the resultant of **P** and the 300-lb force is a vertical force of 900 lb directed downward.

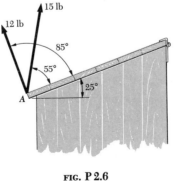

FIG. P 2.6

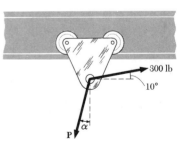

FIG. P 2.7

† Answers to all even-numbered problems are given at the end of the book.

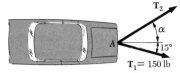

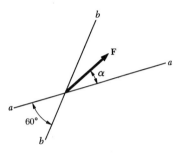

FIG. P 2.10 AND P 2.11

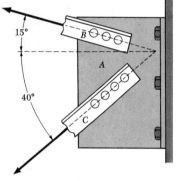

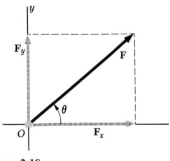

FIG. P 2.12

FIG. 2.18

2.8. A disabled automobile is being pulled by means of two ropes. Knowing that the tension in rope *1* is 150 lb, determine the magnitude and direction of the tension in rope *2* so that the resultant is a 200-lb force parallel to the axis of the automobile. Check the answer graphically.

2.9. If the angle α is equal to $30°$, determine the tension T_2 so that the resultant force exerted at A is parallel to the axis of the automobile.

2.10. The force **F** of magnitude 800 lb is to be resolved into two components along the lines *a-a* and *b-b*. Determine by trigonometry the angle α, knowing that the component of **F** along the line *a-a* is to be 500 lb.

2.11. The force **F** of magnitude 800 lb is to be resolved into two components along the lines *a-a* and *b-b*. Determine by trigonometry the angle α, knowing that the component of **F** along the line *b-b* is to be 600 lb.

2.12. The tension in member B is 1,500 lb. If the resultant of the forces exerted by members B and C is to be horizontal, determine the tension in member C.

2.13. If the resultant of the two forces T_1 and T_2 is parallel to the axis of the automobile, find the value of α for which the tension T_2 is minimum. What is the corresponding value of T_2?

2.6. Rectangular Components of a Force.   Unit Vectors.† In many problems it will be found desirable to resolve a force into two components which are perpendicular to each other. In Fig. 2.18, the force **F** has been resolved into a component $\mathbf{F}_x$ along the *x* axis and a component $\mathbf{F}_y$ along the *y* axis. The parallelogram drawn to obtain the two components is a *rectangle*, and $\mathbf{F}_x$ and $\mathbf{F}_y$ are called *rectangular components*.

The *x* and *y* axes are usually chosen horizontal and vertical, respectively, as in Fig. 2.18; they may, however, be chosen in any two perpendicular directions, as shown in Fig. 2.19. In determining the rectangular components of a force, the student should think of the construction lines shown in Figs. 2.18 and 2.19 as being *parallel* to the *x* and *y* axes, rather than *per-*

---

† The properties established in Secs. 2.6 and 2.7 may be readily extended to the rectangular components of any vector quantity.

pendicular to these axes. This practice will help avoid mistakes in determining *oblique* components as in Sec. 2.5.

We shall, at this point, introduce two vectors of magnitude 1, directed respectively along the positive x and y axes. These vectors are called *unit vectors* and are denoted by **i** and **j**, respectively (Fig. 2.20). Recalling the definition of the product of a scalar and a vector given in Sec. 2.3, we note that the rectangular components $\mathbf{F}_x$ and $\mathbf{F}_y$ of a force **F** may be obtained by multiplying respectively the unit vectors **i** and **j** by appropriate scalars (Fig. 2.21). We write

$$\mathbf{F}_x = F_x\mathbf{i} \qquad \mathbf{F}_y = F_y\mathbf{j} \tag{2.6}$$

and

$$\mathbf{F} = F_x\mathbf{i} + F_y\mathbf{j} \tag{2.7}$$

While the scalars F_x and F_y may be positive or negative, depending upon the sense of $\mathbf{F}_x$ and of $\mathbf{F}_y$, their absolute values are respectively equal to the magnitudes of the component forces $\mathbf{F}_x$ and $\mathbf{F}_y$. The scalars F_x and F_y are called the *scalar components* of the force **F**, while the actual component forces $\mathbf{F}_x$ and $\mathbf{F}_y$ should be referred to as the *vector components* of **F**. However, when there exists no possibility of confusion, the vector as well as the scalar components of **F** may be referred to simply as the *components* of **F**. We note that the scalar component F_x is positive when the vector component $\mathbf{F}_x$ has the same sense as the unit vector **i** (i.e., the same sense as the positive x axis) and negative when $\mathbf{F}_x$ has the opposite sense. A similar conclusion may be drawn regarding the sign of the scalar component F_y.

Denoting by F the magnitude of the force **F** and by θ the angle between **F** and the x axis, measured counterclockwise from the positive x axis (Fig. 2.21), we may express the scalar components of **F** as follows:

$$F_x = F \cos \theta \qquad F_y = F \sin \theta \tag{2.8}$$

We note that the relations obtained hold for any value of the angle θ from $0°$ to $360°$, and that they define the signs as well as the absolute values of the scalar components F_x and F_y.

Example 1. An 800-lb force is exerted on a bolt A as shown in Fig. 2.22a. Determine the horizontal and vertical components of the force.

In order to obtain the correct sign for the scalar components F_x and F_y, the value $\theta = 180° - 35° = 145°$ should be substituted for θ in the relations (2.8). However, it will be found more practical to deter-

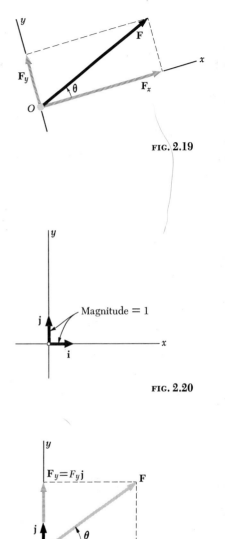

FIG. 2.19

FIG. 2.20

FIG. 2.21

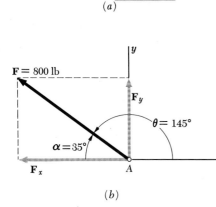

F= 800 lb

35°

A

(a)

F= 800 lb

$\mathbf{F}_y$

$\theta = 145°$

$\alpha = 35°$

$\mathbf{F}_x$

A

x

(b)

FIG. 2.22

mine by inspection the signs of F_x and of F_y (Fig. 2.22b) and to use the trigonometric functions of the angle $\alpha = 35°$, which may be read directly on the slide rule. We write therefore

$$F_x = -F \cos \alpha = -(800 \text{ lb}) \cos 35° = -655 \text{ lb}$$
$$F_y = +F \sin \alpha = +(800 \text{ lb}) \sin 35° = +459 \text{ lb}$$

The vector components of $\mathbf{F}$ are thus

$$\mathbf{F}_x = -(655 \text{ lb})\mathbf{i} \qquad \mathbf{F}_y = +(459 \text{ lb})\mathbf{j}$$

and we may write $\mathbf{F}$ in the form

$$\mathbf{F} = -(655 \text{ lb})\mathbf{i} + (459 \text{ lb})\mathbf{j}$$

Example 2. A man pulls with a force of 75 lb on a rope attached to a building, as shown in Fig. 2.23a. What are the horizontal and vertical components of the force exerted by the rope at point A?

It is seen from Fig. 2.23b that

$$F_x = +(75 \text{ lb}) \cos \alpha \qquad F_y = -(75 \text{ lb}) \sin \alpha$$

Observing that $AB = 25$ ft, we find from Fig. 2.23a

$$\cos \alpha = \frac{20 \text{ ft}}{AB} = \frac{20 \text{ ft}}{25 \text{ ft}} = \frac{4}{5} \qquad \sin \alpha = \frac{15 \text{ ft}}{AB} = \frac{15 \text{ ft}}{25 \text{ ft}} = \frac{3}{5}$$

We thus obtain

$$F_x = +(75 \text{ lb}) \frac{4}{5} = +60 \text{ lb} \qquad F_y = -(75 \text{ lb}) \frac{3}{5} = -45 \text{ lb}$$

and write

$$\mathbf{F} = (60 \text{ lb})\mathbf{i} - (45 \text{ lb})\mathbf{j}$$

When a force $\mathbf{F}$ is defined by its rectangular components F_x and F_y (see Fig. 2.21), the angle θ defining its direction can be obtained by writing

$$\tan \theta = \frac{F_y}{F_x} \tag{2.9}$$

The magnitude F of the force may be obtained by applying the Pythagorean theorem and writing

$$F = \sqrt{F_x^2 + F_y^2} \tag{2.10}$$

However, once θ has been found, it is usually easier to determine the magnitude of the force by the process of solving one of the formulas (2.8) for F.

Example 3. A force $\mathbf{F} = (700 \text{ lb})\mathbf{i} + (1,500 \text{ lb})\mathbf{j}$ is applied to a bolt A. Determine the magnitude of the force and the angle θ it forms with the horizontal.

First, we draw a diagram showing the two rectangular components of the force and the angle θ (Fig. 2.24a). Rather than θ, however, we

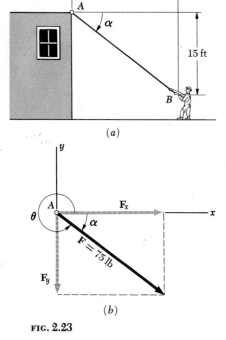

A

20 ft

α

15 ft

B

(a)

y

A

$\mathbf{F}_x$

x

θ

α

$F = 75$ lb

$\mathbf{F}_y$

(b)

FIG. 2.23

shall determine its complement β (Fig. 2.24*b*) because β being smaller than 45°, its tangent is more easily found on the slide rule.

We write

$$F_y \tan \beta = F_x$$
$$(1,500 \text{ lb}) \tan \beta = 700 \text{ lb} \qquad (2.11)$$

and obtain
$$\beta = 25.0°$$

We then write
$$F \sin \beta = F_x$$
$$F \sin 25.0° = 700 \text{ lb} \qquad (2.12)$$

and obtain
$$F = 1,656 \text{ lb}$$

The magnitude of the force is thus 1,656 lb, and the angle θ it forms with the x axis is $\theta = 90.0° - 25.0° = 65.0°$.

Use of the Slide Rule. On most slide rules, β and F may be conveniently determined in the following way (Fig. 2.25):

FIRST STEP. Move the slide until one of the extremities of the trigonometric scale (in the present case the left one) coincides with the *larger* of the two components (1,500 lb) read on the D scale.

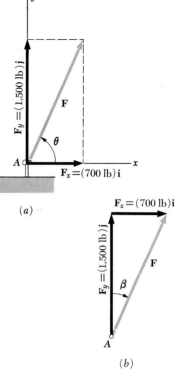

(a)

(b)

FIG. **2.24**

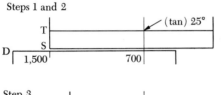

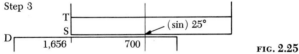

FIG. **2.25**

SECOND STEP. Move the indicator until the hairline coincides with the *smaller* of the two components (700 lb). Angle β may then be read *on the* T *scale* under the hairline since the rule is set to perform the product defined by Eq. (2.11).

THIRD STEP. Without touching the indicator, move the slide until angle β (25.0°) is read *on the* S *scale* under the hairline. The value of F (1,656 lb) may then be read on the D scale opposite one of the extremities of the trigonometric scale since the rule is set to perform the product defined by Eq. (2.12).

Remark. If the smaller of the two components is less than one-tenth of the larger one, the ST scale should be used in the second step, instead of the T scale, and the angle found will be less than 5.7°. The third step may then be omitted since, within the accuracy of the slide rule, the magnitude F of the force may be assumed equal to the larger of the two components (see Sample Prob. 2.3).

2.7. Addition of Forces by Summing x and y Components.

It was seen in Sec. 2.1 that forces should be added according

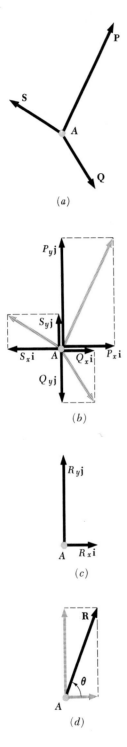

(a)

(b)

(c)

(d)

FIG. 2.26

to the parallelogram law. From this law, two other methods, more readily applicable to the *graphical* solution of problems, were derived in Secs. 2.3 and 2.4: the triangle rule for the addition of two forces and the polygon rule for the addition of three or more forces. It was also seen that the force triangle used to define the resultant of two forces could be used to obtain a *trigonometric* solution.

When three or more forces are to be added, no practical trigonometric solution may be obtained from the force polygon which defines the resultant of the forces. In this case, an *analytic* solution of the problem may be obtained by resolving each force into two rectangular components. Consider, for instance, three forces $\mathbf{P}$, $\mathbf{Q}$, and $\mathbf{S}$ acting on a particle A (Fig. 2.26a). Their resultant $\mathbf{R}$ is defined by the relation

$$\mathbf{R} = \mathbf{P} + \mathbf{Q} + \mathbf{S}$$

Resolving each force into its rectangular components, we write

$$R_x\mathbf{i} + R_y\mathbf{j} = P_x\mathbf{i} + P_y\mathbf{j} + Q_x\mathbf{i} + Q_y\mathbf{j} + S_x\mathbf{i} + S_y\mathbf{j}$$
$$= (P_x + Q_x + S_x)\mathbf{i} + (P_y + Q_y + S_y)\mathbf{j}$$

from which it follows that

$$R_x = P_x + Q_x + S_x \qquad R_y = P_y + Q_y + S_y$$

or, for short,

$$R_x = \Sigma F_x \qquad R_y = \Sigma F_y \qquad (2.13)$$

We thus conclude that *the scalar components R_x and R_y of the resultant $\mathbf{R}$ of several forces acting on a particle are obtained by adding algebraically the corresponding scalar components of the given forces.*†

In practice, the determination of the resultant $\mathbf{R}$ is carried out in three steps as illustrated in Fig. 2.26. First, the given forces shown in Fig. 2.26a are resolved into their x and y components (Fig. 2.26b). Adding these components, we obtain the x and y components of $\mathbf{R}$ (Fig. 2.26c). Finally, the resultant $\mathbf{R} = R_x\mathbf{i} + R_y\mathbf{j}$ is determined by applying the parallelogram law (Fig. 2.26d). The procedure just described will be carried out most efficiently if the computations are arranged in a table. While it is the only practical analytic method for adding three or more forces, it is also often preferred to the trigonometric solution in the case of the addition of two forces.

† Clearly, this result also applies to the addition of other vector quantities, such as velocities, accelerations, or momenta.

SAMPLE PROBLEM 2.3

Four forces act on bolt A as shown. Determine the resultant of the forces on the bolt.

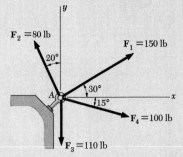

Solution. The x and y components of each force are determined by trigonometry as shown and are entered in the table below. According to the convention adopted in Sec. 2.6, the scalar number representing a force component is positive if the force component has the same sense as the corresponding coordinate axis. Thus, x components acting to the right and y components acting upward are represented by positive numbers.

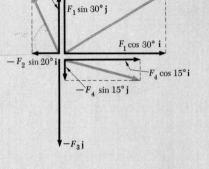

Force	Magnitude, lb	x component, lb	y component, lb
F_1	150	+129.9	+75.0
F_2	80	−27.4	+75.2
F_3	110	0	−110.0
F_4	100	+96.6	−25.9
		$R_x = +199.1$	$R_y = +14.3$

Thus, the resultant **R** of the four forces is

$$\mathbf{R} = R_x\mathbf{i} + R_y\mathbf{j} \qquad \mathbf{R} = (199.1\text{ lb})\mathbf{i} + (14.3\text{ lb})\mathbf{j} \blacktriangleleft$$

The magnitude and direction of the resultant may now be determined. In the triangle shown,

$$R_x \tan \alpha = R_y \qquad (199.1\text{ lb}) \tan \alpha = 14.3\text{ lb}$$

The smaller component (14.3 lb) being less than one-tenth of the larger component (199.1 lb), we use the ST scale and read $\alpha = 4.1°$. Since within the accuracy of the slide rule the sine and tangent of this angle are equal, the magnitude of **R** may be assumed equal to that of the larger component,

$$\mathbf{R} = 199.1\text{ lb} \measuredangle 4.1° \blacktriangleleft$$

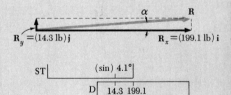

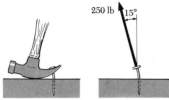

250 lb 15°

FIG. P 2.14

PROBLEMS

2.14. In removing a nail, a force of 250 lb is applied by a hammer in the direction shown.   What are the horizontal and vertical components of this force?

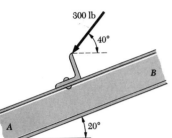

300 lb
40°
B
A
20°

FIG. P 2.15

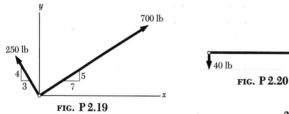

P
30°
20°

FIG. P 2.16

2.15. Determine the components of the 300-lb force in directions parallel and perpendicular to the beam *AB*.

2.16. The force **P** must have a 60-lb component acting up the incline.   Determine the magnitude of **P** and of its component perpendicular to the incline.

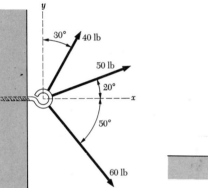

y
30°   40 lb
50 lb
20°
x
50°
60 lb

FIG. P 2.17

B
24 ft
A
10 ft

FIG. P 2.18

2.17. Determine the *x* and *y* components of each of the forces shown.

2.18. The tension in the telephone-pole guy wire is 390 lb.   Determine the horizontal and vertical components of the force acting on the anchor at *A*.

2.19. Determine the *x* and *y* components of each of the forces shown.

2.20 and 2.21. The *x* and *y* components of a force **F** are as shown.   Determine the magnitude and direction of the force **F**.

y
700 lb
250 lb
4
3   5
7
x

FIG. P 2.19

500 lb
40 lb

FIG. P 2.20

2.22. Determine the resultant of the four forces shown.

2.23. Using *x* and *y* components, solve part *a* of Prob. 2.3.

2.24. Using *x* and *y* components, solve Prob. 2.4.

2.25. Determine the resultant of the three forces of Prob. 2.17.

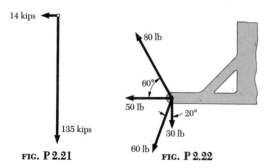

14 kips
135 kips

FIG. P 2.21

80 lb
60°
50 lb
20°
30 lb
60 lb

FIG. P 2.22

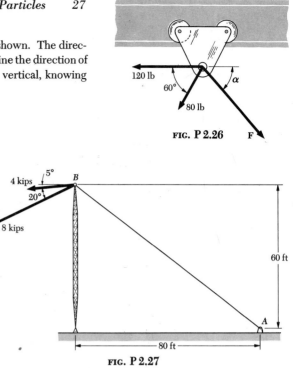

2.26. A hoist trolley is subjected to the three forces shown. The direction of the force **F** may be varied. If possible, determine the direction of the force **F** so that the resultant of the three forces is vertical, knowing that the magnitude of **F** is (*a*) 240 lb, (*b*) 140 lb.

2.27. Two cables which have known tensions are attached at point *B*. A third cable *AB* is used as a guy wire and is also attached at *B*. Determine the required tension in *AB* so that the resultant of the forces exerted by the three cables will be vertical.

FIG. P 2.26

2.28. The resultant of the three forces shown must be a 100-lb force directed to the right along line *a-a*. Determine the required magnitude and direction of the force **F**.

2.29. Show that the forces $\mathbf{P} = P_x\mathbf{i} + P_y\mathbf{j}$ and $\mathbf{Q} = Q_x\mathbf{i} + Q_y\mathbf{j}$ are perpendicular to each other if and only if $P_xQ_x + P_yQ_y = 0$.

FIG. P 2.27

2.8. Equilibrium of a Particle.

In the preceding sections, we discussed the methods for determining the resultant of several forces acting on a particle. Although this has not occurred in any of the problems considered so far, it is quite possible for the resultant to be zero. In such a case, the net effect of the given forces is zero, and the particle is said to be in equilibrium. We thus have the following definition: *When the resultant of all the forces acting on a particle is zero, the particle is in equilibrium.*

A particle which is acted upon by two forces will be in equilibrium if the two forces have the same magnitude, same line of action, and opposite sense. The resultant of the two forces is then zero. Such a case is shown in Fig. 2.27.

Another case of equilibrium of a particle is represented in Fig. 2.28*a*, where four forces are shown acting on *A*. In Fig. 2.28*b*, the resultant of the given forces is determined by the polygon rule. Starting from point *O* with $\mathbf{F}_1$ and arranging the forces in tip-to-tail fashion, we find that the tip of $\mathbf{F}_4$ coincides with the starting point *O*. Thus the resultant **R** of the given system of forces is zero, and the particle is in equilibrium.

The closed polygon drawn in Fig. 2.28*b* provides a *graphical* expression of the equilibrium of *A*. To express *algebraically*

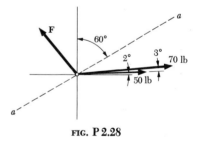

FIG. P 2.28

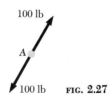

FIG. 2.27

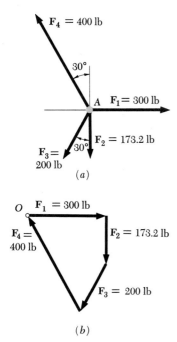

FIG. 2.28

the conditions for the equilibrium of a particle, we write

▶ $$\mathbf{R} = \Sigma\mathbf{F} = 0 \tag{2.14}$$

Resolving each force $\mathbf{F}$ into rectangular components, we have

$$\Sigma(F_x\mathbf{i} + F_y\mathbf{j}) = 0 \quad \text{or} \quad (\Sigma F_x)\mathbf{i} + (\Sigma F_y)\mathbf{j} = 0$$

We conclude that the necessary and sufficient conditions for the equilibrium of a particle are

▶ $$\Sigma F_x = 0 \qquad \Sigma F_y = 0 \tag{2.15}$$

Returning to the particle shown in Fig. 2.28a we check that the equilibrium conditions are satisfied.

$$\Sigma F_x = 300\ \text{lb} - (200\ \text{lb})\sin 30° - (400\ \text{lb})\sin 30°$$
$$= 300\ \text{lb} - 100\ \text{lb} - 200\ \text{lb} = 0$$
$$\Sigma F_y = -173.2\ \text{lb} - (200\ \text{lb})\cos 30° + (400\ \text{lb})\cos 30°$$
$$= -173.2\ \text{lb} - 173.2\ \text{lb} + 346.4\ \text{lb} = 0$$

2.9. Newton's First Law of Motion. In the latter part of the seventeenth century, Sir Isaac Newton formulated three fundamental laws upon which the science of mechanics is based. The first of these laws can be stated as follows:

If the resultant force acting on a particle is zero, the particle will remain at rest (if originally at rest) or will move with constant speed in a straight line (if originally in motion).

From this law and from the definition of equilibrium given in Sec. 2.8, it is seen that a particle in equilibrium either is at rest or is moving in a straight line with constant speed. In the following section, various problems concerning the equilibrium of a particle will be considered.

2.10. Problems Involving the Equilibrium of a Particle. Free-body Diagram. In practice, a problem in engineering mechanics is derived from an actual physical situation. A sketch showing the physical conditions of the problem is known as a *space diagram.*

The methods of analysis discussed in the preceding sections apply to a system of forces acting on a particle. A large number of problems involving actual structures, however, may be reduced to problems concerning the equilibrium of a particle. This is done by choosing a significant particle and drawing a separate diagram showing this particle and all the forces acting on it. Such a diagram is called a *free-body diagram.*

As an example, consider the crate, weighing 140 lb, shown in the space diagram of Fig. 2.29a. This crate was lying between two buildings, and it is now being lifted onto a truck, which will remove it. The crate is supported by a vertical cable, which is joined at *A* to two ropes which pass over pulleys attached to the buildings at *B* and *C*. It is desired to determine the tension in each of the ropes *AB* and *AC*.

In order to solve this problem, a free-body diagram must be drawn, showing a particle in equilibrium. Since we are interested in the rope tensions, the free-body diagram should include at least one of these tensions and, if possible, both tensions. Point *A* is seen to be a good free body for this problem. The free-body diagram of point *A* is shown in Fig. 2.29*b*. It represents point *A* and the three forces acting on *A*, namely, the 140-lb force exerted by the crate and the two forces $\mathbf{T}_{AB}$ and $\mathbf{T}_{AC}$ representing respectively the tension in rope *AB* and the tension in rope *AC*. These two forces are shown acting away from point *A*. No other detail is included in the free-body diagram.

Since point *A* is in equilibrium, the three forces acting on it must form a closed triangle when drawn in tip-to-tail fashion. This *force triangle* has been drawn in Fig. 2.29*c*. The values T_{AB} and T_{AC} of the tension in the ropes may be found graphically if the triangle is drawn to scale, or they may be found by trigonometry. If the latter method of solution is chosen, we use the law of sines and write

$$\frac{T_{AB}}{\sin 60^\circ} = \frac{T_{AC}}{\sin 40^\circ} = \frac{140\text{ lb}}{\sin 80^\circ}$$

$$T_{AB} = 123.2\text{ lb} \qquad T_{AC} = 91.4\text{ lb}$$

When a particle is in *equilibrium under three forces*, the problem may always be solved by drawing a force triangle. When a particle is in *equilibrium under more than three forces*, the problem may be solved graphically by drawing a force polygon. If an analytic solution is desired, the *equations of equilibrium* given in Sec. 2.8 should be solved:

$$\Sigma F_x = 0 \qquad \Sigma F_y = 0 \qquad (2.15)$$

These equations may be solved for no more than *two unknowns;* similarly, the force triangle used in the case of equilibrium under three forces may be solved for two unknowns.

The more common types of problems are those where the two unknowns represent (1) the two components (or the magnitude and direction) of a single force, (2) the magnitude of two forces each of known direction. Problems involving the determination of the maximum or minimum value of the magnitude of a force are also encountered (see Probs. 2.34 and 2.37).

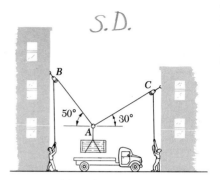

S.D.

(*a*) Space diagram

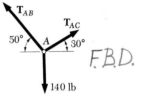

F.B.D.

(*b*) Free-body diagram

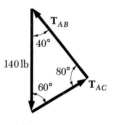

(*c*) Force triangle

FIG. **2.29**

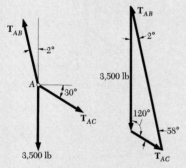

SAMPLE PROBLEM 2.4

In a ship-unloading operation, a 3,500-lb automobile is supported by a cable. A rope is tied to the cable at A and pulled in order to center the automobile over its intended position. The angle between the cable and the vertical is 2°, while the angle between the rope and the horizontal is 30°. What is the tension in the rope?

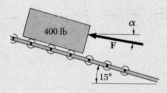

Solution. Point A is chosen as a free body, and the complete free-body diagram is drawn. T_{AB} is the tension in the cable AB, and T_{AC} is the tension in the rope. Drawing the force triangle and using the law of sines, we write

$$\frac{T_{AB}}{\sin 120°} = \frac{T_{AC}}{\sin 2°} = \frac{3,500 \text{ lb}}{\sin 58°}$$

$$T_{AB} = 3,570 \text{ lb} \qquad T_{AC} = 144 \text{ lb} \qquad \blacktriangleleft$$

SAMPLE PROBLEM 2.5

Determine the magnitude and direction of the smallest force **F** which will maintain the package shown in equilibrium. Note that the force exerted by the rollers on the package is perpendicular to the incline.

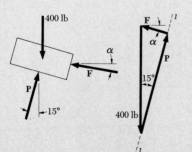

Solution. We choose the package as a free body and assume that it may be treated as a particle. Since three forces act on the free body, we draw a force triangle to express that it is in equilibrium. Line *1-1* represents the known direction of **P**. In order to obtain the minimum value of the force **F**, we choose the direction of **F** perpendicular to that of **P**. From the geometry of the triangle obtained, we find

$$F = (400 \text{ lb}) \sin 15° = 103.6 \text{ lb} \qquad \alpha = 15°$$

$$F = 103.6 \text{ lb} \ \diagdown 15° \qquad \blacktriangleleft$$

SAMPLE PROBLEM 2.6

A small boat is moored by means of three ropes tied to posts on the banks of a stream. The stream flow exerts a force on the boat which acts directly downstream. The tensions in ropes A and B are measured and found to be $A = 120$ lb and $B = 80$ lb. Determine the magnitude of the force exerted by the flow and the tension in rope C.

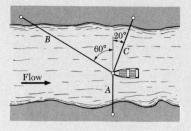

Solution. The boat is taken as a free body. It is acted upon by four forces directed as shown. Each force is resolved into its x and y components.

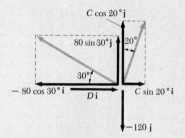

$$\mathbf{A} = -(120\text{ lb})\mathbf{j}$$
$$\mathbf{B} = -(80\text{ lb})\cos 30°\mathbf{i} + (80\text{ lb})\sin 30°\mathbf{j}$$
$$= -(69.3\text{ lb})\mathbf{i} + (40\text{ lb})\mathbf{j}$$
$$\mathbf{C} = C\sin 20°\mathbf{i} + C\cos 20°\mathbf{j}$$
$$= 0.342\,C\mathbf{i} + 0.940\,C\mathbf{j}$$
$$\mathbf{D} = D\mathbf{i}$$

Since the boat is in equilibrium, the resultant of the forces must be zero. Thus

$$\mathbf{R} = \mathbf{A} + \mathbf{B} + \mathbf{C} + \mathbf{D} = 0$$

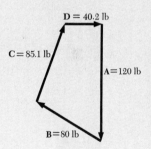

Substituting for $\mathbf{A}$, $\mathbf{B}$, $\mathbf{C}$, and $\mathbf{D}$ the expressions obtained above, and factoring the unit vectors $\mathbf{i}$ and $\mathbf{j}$, we have

$$(-69.3\text{ lb} + 0.342\,C + D)\mathbf{i} + (-120\text{ lb} + 40\text{ lb} + 0.940\,C)\mathbf{j} = 0$$

This equation will be satisfied if, and only if, the coefficients of $\mathbf{i}$ and $\mathbf{j}$ are equal to zero. We thus obtain the following two equilibrium equations, which express, respectively, that the sum of the x components and the sum of the y components of the given forces must be zero.

$(\Sigma F_x = 0\!:)\qquad -69.3\text{ lb} + 0.342C + D = 0$

$(\Sigma F_y = 0\!:)\qquad -120\text{ lb} + 40\text{ lb} + 0.940C = 0$

Solving these equations, we find

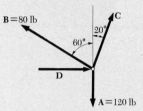

$$C = +85.1\text{ lb}\qquad D = +40.2\text{ lb}\quad \blacktriangleleft$$

In drawing the free-body diagram, we assumed a sense for each unknown force. A positive sign in the answer indicates that the assumed sense is correct. The complete force polygon may be drawn to check the results.

31

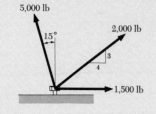

5,000 lb

2,000 lb

15°

3

4

1,500 lb

SAMPLE PROBLEM 2.7

A bolt is used to anchor three guy wires as shown. The tension in each wire is given. Determine the magnitude and direction of the force exerted by the foundation on the bolt.

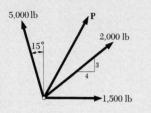

5,000 lb   **P**

2,000 lb

15°

3

4

1,500 lb

Solution. A free-body diagram of the bolt is drawn; the force exerted by the foundation is **P**. No attempt is made to guess the direction or sense of **P** (although in this case it is easily seen that **P** has a downward component). We assume that **P** is directed to the right and upward and write

$$\mathbf{P} = P_x\mathbf{i} + P_y\mathbf{j}$$

Since the bolt is in equilibrium, the resultant must be zero; therefore,

$$\Sigma F_x = 0 \qquad \Sigma F_y = 0$$

Positive sense is to the right for the x components and upward for the y components. The components of the 2,000-lb force are computed directly from the given slope of the force.

$\Sigma F_x = 0:$ $-(5,000 \text{ lb}) \sin 15° + (2,000 \text{ lb})\frac{4}{5} + 1,500 \text{ lb} + P_x = 0$

$-1,294 \text{ lb} + 1,600 \text{ lb} + 1,500 \text{ lb} + P_x = 0$
$+1,806 \text{ lb} + P_x = 0 \qquad P_x = -1,806 \text{ lb}$

$\Sigma F_y = 0:$ $+(5,000 \text{ lb}) \cos 15° + (2,000 \text{ lb})\frac{3}{5} + P_y = 0$

$+4,830 \text{ lb} + 1,200 \text{ lb} + P_y = 0$
$+6,030 \text{ lb} + P_y = 0 \qquad P_y = -6,030 \text{ lb}$

Thus the force **P** is

$$\mathbf{P} = P_x\mathbf{i} + P_y\mathbf{j}$$
$$\mathbf{P} = -(1,806 \text{ lb})\mathbf{i} - (6,030 \text{ lb})\mathbf{j}$$

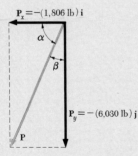

$\mathbf{P}_x = -(1,806 \text{ lb})\,\mathbf{i}$

α

β

$\mathbf{P}_y = -(6,030 \text{ lb})\,\mathbf{j}$

P

The magnitude and direction of **P** are now determined.

$$P_y \tan \beta = P_x$$

$$(6,030 \text{ lb}) \tan \beta = 1,806 \text{ lb}$$

$$\beta = 16.7° \qquad \alpha = 90° - 16.7° = 73.3°$$

$$P \sin \beta = P_x$$

$$P \sin 16.7° = 1,806 \text{ lb}$$

$$\mathbf{P} = 6,300 \text{ lb} \ \angle\!\!\!/ \ 73.3° \quad \blacktriangleleft$$

PROBLEMS

2.30 through 2.32. Two cables are tied together at C and loaded as shown. Determine the tension in AC and BC.

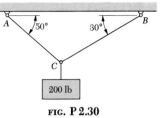

FIG. P 2.30

2.33. If the length of cable BC is increased to 10 ft in Prob. 2.32, determine the new tension in AC and BC.

FIG. P 2.31

FIG. P 2.32

2.34. A 600-lb block is supported by the two cables AC and BC. (a) For what value of α is the tension in cable AC minimum? (b) What are the corresponding values of the tension in cables AC and BC?

2.35. A 600-lb block is supported by the two cables AC and BC. Determine (a) the value of α for which the larger of the cable tensions is as small as possible, (b) the corresponding values of the tension in cables AC and BC.

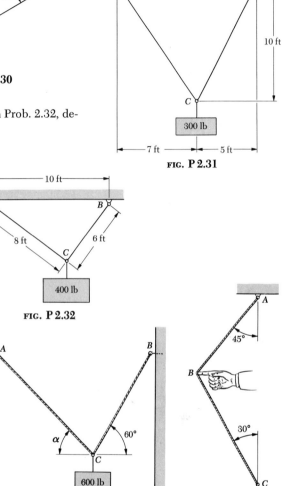

FIG. P 2.34 AND P 2.35

FIG. P 2.36

2.36. A man stretches an elastic cord AC by applying his finger at B. Determine the magnitude and direction of the force exerted by the man, knowing that the tension in both parts of the cord is 5 lb.

2.37. Two ropes are tied together at C. If the maximum permissible tension in each rope is 750 lb, what is the maximum force F that may be applied? In what direction must this maximum force act?

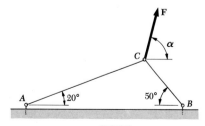

FIG. P 2.37

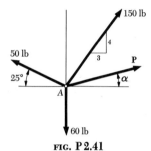

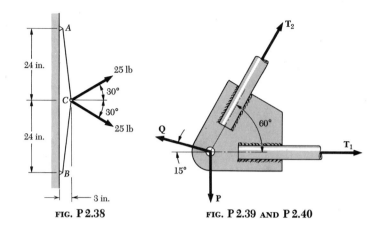

FIG. P 2.38

FIG. P 2.39 AND P 2.40

2.38. Two strings are tied together at C and loaded as shown. Determine the tension in AC and BC.

2.39. Two forces **P** and **Q** of magnitude $P = 1,000$ lb and $Q = 1,200$ lb are applied to the aircraft connection shown. Knowing that the connection is in equilibrium, determine the tensions T_1 and T_2.

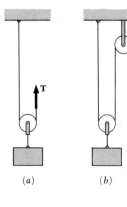

FIG. P 2.41

2.40. Two forces **P** and **Q** are applied to the aircraft connection shown. At a certain instant, when the connection is in equilibrium, it is found that $T_1 = 560$ lb and $T_2 = 120$ lb. Determine the corresponding values of P and Q.

2.41. A particle A is in equilibrium under the action of the four forces shown. Determine the magnitude and direction of **P**.

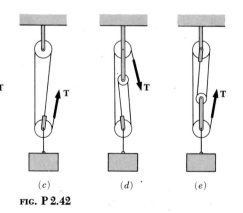

(a)   (b)   (c)   (d)   (e)

FIG. P 2.42

2.42. A 600-lb crate is supported by several rope-and-pulley arrangements as shown. Determine for each arrangement the tension in the rope. (The tension in the rope is the same on each side of a simple pulley. This can be proved by the methods of Chap. 4.)

2.43. Solve parts b and d of Prob. 2.42 assuming that the free end of the rope is attached to the crate.

2.44. A 1,500-lb crate is lifted by a crane cable *CD*. A cable sling *ACB* is 5 ft long and can be attached to the crate in each of the two ways shown. Determine the tension in the cable sling in each case.

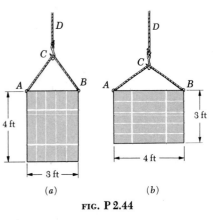

(*a*) (*b*)

FIG. P 2.44

2.45. A portable bin and its contents weigh 750 lb. Determine the shortest chain sling *ACB* which may be used to lift the loaded bin if the tension in the chain sling is not to exceed 900 lb.

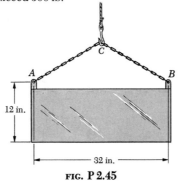

FIG. P 2.45

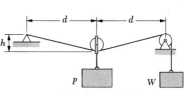

FIG. P 2.46 AND P 2.47

°2.46. If in the diagram shown $W = 80$ lb, $P = 10$ lb, and $d = 20$ in., determine the value of h consistent with equilibrium.

°2.47. Express the weight W required to maintain equilibrium in terms of P, d, and h.

°2.48. A 500-lb crate is to be supported by the rope-and-pulley arrangement shown. Determine the required magnitude and direction of the force **T**.

°2.49. For any given value of α in Prob. 2.37, there is a maximum force **F** which may be applied without exceeding the permissible tension in either of the ropes. Considering only cases in which both ropes remain taut, determine the magnitude of the maximum force **F** as a function of the angle α.

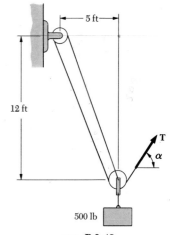

FIG. P 2.48

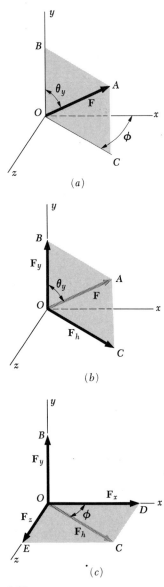

(a)

(b)

(c)

FIG. **2.30**

FORCES IN SPACE

2.11. Rectangular Components of a Force in Space. The problems considered in the first part of this chapter involved only two dimensions; they could be formulated and solved in a single plane. In this section and in the remaining sections of the chapter, we shall discuss problems involving the three dimensions of space.

Consider a force **F** acting at the origin O of the system of rectangular coordinates x, y, z. To define the direction of **F**, we may draw the vertical plane $OBAC$ containing **F** and shown in Fig. 2.30*a*. This plane passes through the vertical y axis; its orientation is defined by the angle ϕ it forms with the xy plane, while the direction of **F** within the plane is defined by the angle θ_y that **F** forms with the y axis. The force **F** may be resolved into a vertical component **F**$_y$ and a horizontal component **F**$_h$; this operation, shown in Fig. 2.30*b*, is carried out inside plane $OBAC$ according to the rules developed in the first part of the chapter. The corresponding scalar components are

$$F_y = F \cos \theta_y \qquad\qquad F_h = F \sin \theta_y \qquad (2.16)$$

But **F**$_h$ may be resolved into two rectangular components **F**$_x$ and **F**$_z$ along the x and z axes, respectively. This operation, shown in Fig. 2.30*c*, is carried out inside the xz plane. We obtain the following expressions for the corresponding scalar components:

$$\begin{aligned} F_x &= F_h \cos \phi = F \sin \theta_y \cos \phi \\ F_z &= F_h \sin \phi = F \sin \theta_y \sin \phi \end{aligned} \qquad (2.17)$$

The given force **F** has thus been resolved into three rectangular vector components **F**$_x$, **F**$_y$, **F**$_z$, directed along the three axes of coordinates.

Applying the Pythagorean theorem to the triangles OAB and OCD of Fig. 2.30, we write

$$\begin{aligned} F^2 &= (OA)^2 = (OB)^2 + (BA)^2 = F_y^2 + F_h^2 \\ F_h^2 &= (OC)^2 = (OD)^2 + (DC)^2 = F_x^2 + F_z^2 \end{aligned}$$

Eliminating F_h^2 from these two equations and solving for F, we obtain the following relation between the magnitude of **F** and its rectangular scalar components:

$$F = \sqrt{F_x^2 + F_y^2 + F_z^2} \qquad (2.18)$$

The relationship existing between the force **F** and its three components **F**$_x$, **F**$_y$, **F**$_z$ is more easily visualized if a "box" having F_x, F_y, F_z for edges is drawn as shown in Fig. 2.31. The force **F** is then represented by the diagonal *OA* of this box. Fig. 2.31*b* shows the right triangle *OAB* used to derive the first of the formulas (2.16): $F_y = F \cos \theta_y$. In Fig. 2.31*a* and *c*, two other right triangles have also been drawn: *OAD* and *OAE*. These triangles are seen to occupy in the box positions comparable with that of triangle *OAB*. Denoting by θ_x and θ_z, respectively, the angles that **F** forms with the *x* and *z* axes, we may derive two formulas similar to $F_y = F \cos \theta_y$. We thus write

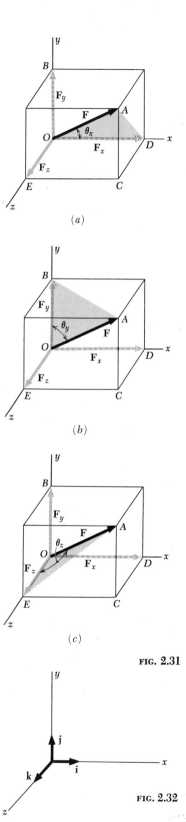

▶ $$F_x = F \cos \theta_x \qquad F_y = F \cos \theta_y \qquad F_z = F \cos \theta_z \qquad (2.19)$$

The three angles θ_x, θ_y, θ_z define the direction of the force **F**; they are more commonly used for this purpose than the angles θ_y and ϕ introduced at the beginning of this section. The cosines of θ_x, θ_y, θ_z are known as the direction cosines of the force **F**.

Introducing the unit vectors **i**, **j**, and **k**, directed respectively along the *x*, *y*, and *z* axes (Fig. 2.32), we may express **F** in the form

▶ $$\mathbf{F} = F_x \mathbf{i} + F_y \mathbf{j} + F_z \mathbf{k} \qquad (2.20)$$

where the scalar components F_x, F_y, F_z are defined by the relations (2.19).

Example 1. A 100-lb force forms angles of 60, 45, and 120°, respectively, with the *x*, *y*, and *z* axes. Find the components F_x, F_y, and F_z of the force.

Substituting $F = 100$ lb, $\theta_x = 60°$, $\theta_y = 45°$, $\theta_z = 120°$ into formulas (2.19), we write

$$F_x = (100 \text{ lb}) \cos 60° = +50.0 \text{ lb}$$
$$F_y = (100 \text{ lb}) \cos 45° = +70.7 \text{ lb}$$
$$F_z = (100 \text{ lb}) \cos 120° = -50.0 \text{ lb}$$

Carrying into Eq. (2.20) the values obtained for the scalar components of **F**, we have

$$\mathbf{F} = (50.0 \text{ lb})\mathbf{i} + (70.7 \text{ lb})\mathbf{j} - (50.0 \text{ lb})\mathbf{k}$$

As in the case of two-dimensional problems, the plus sign indicates that the component has the same sense as the corresponding axis, and the minus sign that it has the opposite sense.

The angle a force **F** forms with an axis should be measured from the positive side of the axis and will always be comprised between 0 and 180°. An angle θ_x smaller than 90° (acute) indicates that **F** (assumed attached at *O*) is on the same side of

(*a*)

(*b*)

(*c*)

FIG. 2.31

FIG. 2.32

the yz plane as the positive x axis; $\cos \theta_x$ and F_x will then be positive. An angle θ_x larger than 90° (obtuse) would indicate that $\mathbf{F}$ is on the other side of the yz plane; $\cos \theta_x$ and F_x would then be negative. In Example 1 the angles θ_x and θ_y are acute, while θ_z is obtuse: consequently, F_x and F_y are positive, while F_z is negative.

Substituting into (2.20) the expressions obtained for F_x, F_y, F_z in (2.19), we write

$$\mathbf{F} = F\,(\cos \theta_x \mathbf{i} + \cos \theta_y \mathbf{j} + \cos \theta_z \mathbf{k}) \qquad (2.21)$$

which shows that the force $\mathbf{F}$ may be expressed as the product of the scalar F and of the vector

$$\boldsymbol{\lambda} = \cos \theta_x \mathbf{i} + \cos \theta_y \mathbf{j} + \cos \theta_z \mathbf{k} \qquad (2.22)$$

Clearly, the vector $\boldsymbol{\lambda}$ is a vector of magnitude equal to 1 and of the same direction as $\mathbf{F}$ (Fig. 2.33). We shall refer to $\boldsymbol{\lambda}$

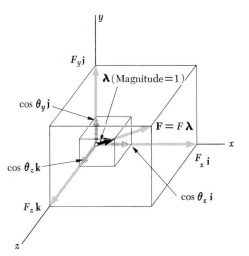

FIG. 2.33

as the *unit vector* along the line of action of $\mathbf{F}$. It follows from (2.22) that the components of the unit vector $\boldsymbol{\lambda}$ are respectively equal to the direction cosines of the line of action of $\mathbf{F}$:

$$\lambda_x = \cos \theta_x \qquad \lambda_y = \cos \theta_y \qquad \lambda_z = \cos \theta_z \qquad (2.23)$$

We should observe that the values of the three angles θ_x, θ_y, θ_z are not independent. Expressing that the sum of the squares of the components of $\boldsymbol{\lambda}$ is equal to the square of its magnitude, we write

$$\lambda_x^2 + \lambda_y^2 + \lambda_z^2 = 1$$

or, substituting for λ_x, λ_y, λ_z from (2.23),

▶ $$\cos^2 \theta_x + \cos^2 \theta_y + \cos^2 \theta_z = 1 \qquad (2.24)$$

In Example 1, for instance, once the values $\theta_x = 60°$ and $\theta_y = 45°$ have been selected, the value of θ_z *must* be equal to $60°$ or $120°$ in order to satisfy identity (2.24).

When the components F_x, F_y, F_z of a force F are given, the magnitude F of the force is obtained from (2.18). The relations (2.19) may then be solved for the direction cosines, and the angles θ_x, θ_y, θ_z characterizing the direction of F may be found. However, these relations may also be written in the form

▶ $$\frac{\cos \theta_x}{F_x} = \frac{\cos \theta_y}{F_y} = \frac{\cos \theta_z}{F_z} = \frac{1}{F} \qquad (2.25)$$

which is better adapted to the use of the slide rule. Note that the relations obtained express that the components and the magnitudes of the unit vector λ and of the force F (i.e., the sides and the diagonals of the two "boxes" shown in Fig. 2.33) must be respectively proportional.

Example 2. A force F has the components $F_x = 20$ lb, $F_y = -30$ lb, $F_z = 60$ lb. Determine its magnitude F and the angles θ_x, θ_y, θ_z it forms with the axes of coordinates.

From formula (2.18) we obtain

$$F = \sqrt{F_x^2 + F_y^2 + F_z^2} = \sqrt{(20 \text{ lb})^2 + (-30 \text{ lb})^2 + (60 \text{ lb})^2}$$
$$= \sqrt{4{,}900 \text{ lb}} = 70 \text{ lb}$$

Substituting the values of the components and of the magnitude of F into (2.25), we obtain

$$\frac{\cos \theta_x}{20 \text{ lb}} = \frac{\cos \theta_y}{-30 \text{ lb}} = \frac{\cos \theta_z}{60 \text{ lb}} = \frac{1}{70 \text{ lb}}$$

$$\theta_x = 73.4° \qquad \theta_y = 115.4° \qquad \theta_z = 31.0°$$

Note that, F_y being negative, the value of θ_y must be larger than $90°$; thus θ_y is equal not to $64.6°$ but to its supplement, $115.4°$.

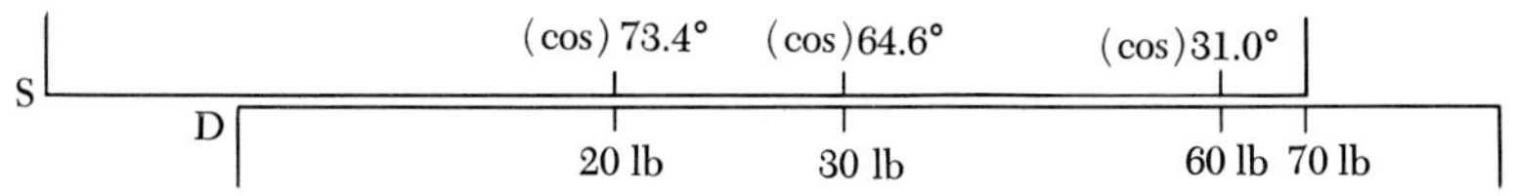

FIG. 2.34

Use of the Slide Rule. The angles θ_x, θ_y, θ_z defined by formula (2.25) are found on the slide rule by bringing one of the extremities of the S scale to coincide with F on the D scale. The values of θ_x, θ_y, θ_z are then read directly on the S scale (using angles corresponding to cosines) above F_x, F_y, F_z, respectively.   The sketch of Fig. 2.34 shows the rule set to read the values corresponding to Example 2.

2.12. Force Defined by Its Magnitude and Two Points on Its Line of Action.   In many applications, the direction of a force $\mathbf{F}$ is defined by the coordinates of two points, $M(x_1, y_1, z_1)$ and $N(x_2, y_2, z_2)$, located on its line of action (Fig. 2.35).   Con-

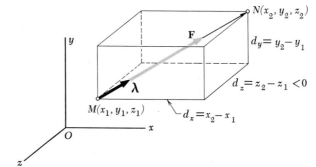

FIG. 2.35

sider the vector $\overrightarrow{MN}$ joining M and N and of the same sense as $\mathbf{F}$; we shall denote its scalar components by d_x, d_y, d_z, respectively, and its magnitude (i.e., the distance from M to N) by d. Since the vector $\overrightarrow{MN}$ has the same direction as $\mathbf{F}$ and, thus, the same direction as the unit vector $\boldsymbol{\lambda}$, we may express it as the product of d and $\boldsymbol{\lambda}$ and write

$$\overrightarrow{MN} = d_x\mathbf{i} + d_y\mathbf{j} + d_z\mathbf{k} = \boldsymbol{\lambda}\, d \qquad (2.26)$$

Recalling that $\mathbf{F}$ is equal to the product of F and $\boldsymbol{\lambda}$, we also have

$$\mathbf{F} = F_x\mathbf{i} + F_y\mathbf{j} + F_z\mathbf{k} = \boldsymbol{\lambda}\, F \qquad (2.27)$$

Observing that the coefficients of the unit vectors $\mathbf{i}$, $\mathbf{j}$, $\mathbf{k}$, and $\boldsymbol{\lambda}$ in Eqs. (2.26) and (2.27) must be proportional, we write

$$\frac{F_x}{d_x} = \frac{F_y}{d_y} = \frac{F_z}{d_z} = \frac{F}{d} \qquad (2.28)$$

The relations (2.28) considerably simplify the determination of the components of a force $\mathbf{F}$ of given magnitude F when the line of action of $\mathbf{F}$ is defined by two points M and N. Subtracting the coordinates of M from those of N, we first determine the components of the vector $\overrightarrow{MN}$ and the distance d

from M to N.

$$d_x = x_2 - x_1 \qquad d_y = y_2 - y_1 \qquad d_z = z_2 - z_1$$

$$d = \sqrt{d_x^2 + d_y^2 + d_z^2} \tag{2.29}$$

Substituting for F and for d_x, d_y, d_z, and d into the relations (2.28), we obtain the components F_x, F_y, F_z of the force. This computation, which is easily performed on the slide rule, has been carried out in Sample Prob. 2.8. Since the vector $\overrightarrow{MN}$ was chosen to have the same sense as $\mathbf{F}$, the components F_x, F_y, and F_z will have, respectively, the same signs as d_x, d_y, and d_z.

Comparing Eqs. (2.22) and (2.26), we may also write the proportions

▶
$$\frac{\cos \theta_x}{d_x} = \frac{\cos \theta_y}{d_y} = \frac{\cos \theta_z}{d_z} = \frac{1}{d} \tag{2.30}$$

These relations may be used to obtain the angles θ_x, θ_y, θ_z that $\mathbf{F}$ forms with the coordinate axes, directly from the components d_x, d_y, d_z, and the distance d.

2.13. Addition of Concurrent Forces in Space. We shall determine the resultant $\mathbf{R}$ of two or more forces in space by summing their rectangular components. Graphical or trigonometric methods are generally not practical in the case of forces in space.

The method followed here is similar to that used in Sec. 2.7 with coplanar forces. Setting

$$\mathbf{R} = \Sigma \mathbf{F}$$

we resolve each force into its rectangular components and write

$$R_x \mathbf{i} + R_y \mathbf{j} + R_z \mathbf{k} = \Sigma (F_x \mathbf{i} + F_y \mathbf{j} + F_z \mathbf{k})$$

$$= (\Sigma F_x) \mathbf{i} + (\Sigma F_y) \mathbf{j} + (\Sigma F_z) \mathbf{k}$$

from which it follows that

▶
$$R_x = \Sigma F_x \qquad R_y = \Sigma F_y \qquad R_z = \Sigma F_z \tag{2.31}$$

The magnitude of the resultant $\mathbf{R}$ and the angles θ_x, θ_y, θ_z it forms with the axes of coordinates are obtained by the method of Sec. 2.11. We write

▶
$$R = \sqrt{R_x^2 + R_y^2 + R_z^2} \tag{2.32}$$

▶
$$\frac{\cos \theta_x}{R_x} = \frac{\cos \theta_y}{R_y} = \frac{\cos \theta_z}{R_z} = \frac{1}{R} \tag{2.33}$$

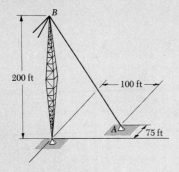

SAMPLE PROBLEM 2.8

A tower guy wire is anchored by means of a bolt at A. The tension in the wire is 2,500 lb. Determine (*a*) the components F_x, F_y, F_z of the force acting on the bolt, (*b*) the angles θ_x, θ_y, θ_z defining the direction of the force.

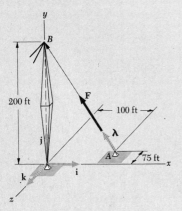

a. **Components of the Force.** The line of action of the force acting on the bolt passes through A and B; and the force is directed from A to B. The components of the vector AB, which has the same direction as the force, are

$$d_x = -100 \text{ ft} \qquad d_y = +200 \text{ ft} \qquad d_z = +75 \text{ ft}$$

The total distance from A to B is

$$d = \sqrt{d_x^2 + d_y^2 + d_z^2} = 236 \text{ ft}$$

Introducing the unit vectors **i**, **j**, **k** along the axes of coordinates, and the unit vector $\boldsymbol{\lambda}$ along AB, we write

$$\overrightarrow{AB} = -(100 \text{ ft})\mathbf{i} + (200 \text{ ft})\mathbf{j} + (75 \text{ ft})\mathbf{k} = (236 \text{ ft})\,\boldsymbol{\lambda} \qquad (1)$$

$$\mathbf{F} = F_x\mathbf{i} + F_y\mathbf{j} + F_z\mathbf{k} = (2,500 \text{ lb})\boldsymbol{\lambda} \qquad (2)$$

Expressing that the coefficients of the unit vectors in (1) and (2) are proportional, we write

$$\frac{F_x}{-100 \text{ ft}} = \frac{F_y}{+200 \text{ ft}} = \frac{F_z}{+75 \text{ ft}} = \frac{2,500 \text{ lb}}{236 \text{ ft}}$$

and obtain

$$F_x = -1,060 \text{ lb} \qquad F_y = +2,120 \text{ lb} \qquad F_z = +794 \text{ lb} \qquad \blacktriangleleft$$

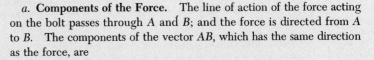

b. **Direction of Force.** Recalling that the components of the unit vector $\boldsymbol{\lambda}$ are respectively equal to the direction cosines of **F**, we write

$$\cos \theta_x\mathbf{i} + \cos \theta_y\mathbf{j} + \cos \theta_z\mathbf{k} = \boldsymbol{\lambda} \qquad (3)$$

$$\mathbf{F} = -(1,060 \text{ lb})\mathbf{i} + (2,120 \text{ lb})\mathbf{j} + (794 \text{ lb})\mathbf{k} = (2,500 \text{ lb})\,\boldsymbol{\lambda} \qquad (4)$$

Expressing that the coefficients of the unit vectors in (3) and (4) are proportional, we have

$$\frac{\cos \theta_x}{-1,060 \text{ lb}} = \frac{\cos \theta_y}{+2,120 \text{ lb}} = \frac{\cos \theta_z}{+794 \text{ lb}} = \frac{1}{2,500 \text{ lb}}$$

$$\theta_x = 180° - 64.9° = 115.1° \qquad \theta_y = 32.0° \qquad \theta_z = 71.5° \qquad \blacktriangleleft$$

This result may also be obtained by using proportions involving the components of the vector AB instead of the components of **F**.

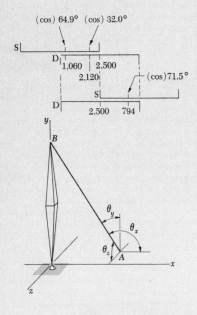

42

SAMPLE PROBLEM 2.9

In order to move a wrecked truck, two cables are attached to the truck at A and pulled by winches B and C as shown. Determine the resultant of the forces exerted on the truck by the two cables, knowing that the tension is 2,000 lb in cable AB and 1,500 lb in cable AC.

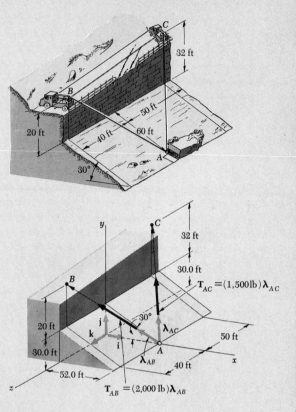

Solution. The force exerted by each cable on the truck will be resolved into x, y, and z components. We first determine the components and magnitudes of the vectors AB and AC, measuring them from the truck toward each winch.

Cable AB (A to B):
$$d_x = -52 \text{ ft} \qquad d_y = +50 \text{ ft}$$
$$d_z = +40 \text{ ft} \qquad d = 82.5 \text{ ft}$$

Cable AC (A to C):
$$d_x = -52 \text{ ft} \qquad d_y = +62 \text{ ft}$$
$$d_z = -50 \text{ ft} \qquad d = 95.1 \text{ ft}$$

Denoting by $\mathbf{i}$, $\mathbf{j}$, $\mathbf{k}$ the unit vectors along the coordinate axes, and by $\boldsymbol{\lambda}_{AB}$ the unit vector along AB, we write

$$\overrightarrow{AB} = -(52 \text{ ft})\mathbf{i} + (50 \text{ ft})\mathbf{j} + (40 \text{ ft})\mathbf{k} = (82.5 \text{ ft})\boldsymbol{\lambda}_{AB}$$
$$\mathbf{T}_{AB} = \qquad F_x\mathbf{i} + \qquad F_y\mathbf{j} + \qquad F_z\mathbf{k} = (2{,}000 \text{ lb})\boldsymbol{\lambda}_{AB}$$

and find the components of $\mathbf{T}_{AB}$ by proportions. We have

$$\mathbf{T}_{AB} = -(1{,}260 \text{ lb})\mathbf{i} + (1{,}212 \text{ lb})\mathbf{j} + (970 \text{ lb})\mathbf{k}$$

Denoting by $\boldsymbol{\lambda}_{AC}$ the unit vector along AC, we write in a similar way

$$\overrightarrow{AC} = -(52 \text{ ft})\mathbf{i} + (62 \text{ ft})\mathbf{j} - (50 \text{ ft})\mathbf{k} = (95.1 \text{ ft})\boldsymbol{\lambda}_{AC}$$
$$\mathbf{T}_{AC} = \qquad F_x\mathbf{i} + \qquad F_y\mathbf{j} + \qquad F_z\mathbf{k} = (1{,}500 \text{ lb})\boldsymbol{\lambda}_{AC}$$

and, by proportions,

$$\mathbf{T}_{AC} = -(820 \text{ lb})\mathbf{i} + (978 \text{ lb})\mathbf{j} - (788 \text{ lb})\mathbf{k}$$

The resultant $\mathbf{R}$ of the forces exerted by the two cables is

$$\mathbf{R} = \mathbf{T}_{AB} + \mathbf{T}_{AC} = -(2{,}080 \text{ lb})\mathbf{i} + (2{,}190 \text{ lb})\mathbf{j} + (182 \text{ lb})\mathbf{k}$$

The magnitude R of the resultant is

$$R = \sqrt{(-2{,}080)^2 + (2{,}190)^2 + (182)^2} = 3{,}030 \text{ lb} \qquad \blacktriangleleft$$

Recalling that the direction cosines of the resultant represent the components of the unit vector $\boldsymbol{\lambda}_R$ directed along $\mathbf{R}$, we write

$$\cos\theta_x\mathbf{i} + \quad \cos\theta_y\mathbf{j} + \quad \cos\theta_z\mathbf{k} = \boldsymbol{\lambda}_R$$
$$\mathbf{R} = -(2{,}080 \text{ lb})\mathbf{i} + (2{,}190 \text{ lb})\mathbf{j} + (182 \text{ lb})\mathbf{k} = (3{,}030 \text{ lb})\boldsymbol{\lambda}_R$$

and, by proportions,

$$\frac{\cos\theta_x}{-2{,}080 \text{ lb}} = \frac{\cos\theta_y}{+2{,}190 \text{ lb}} = \frac{\cos\theta_z}{+182 \text{ lb}} = \frac{1}{3{,}030 \text{ lb}}$$

$$\theta_x = 180° - 46.6° = 133.4° \qquad \theta_y = 43.7° \qquad \theta_z = 86.6° \qquad \blacktriangleleft$$

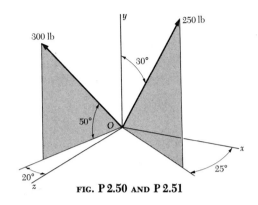

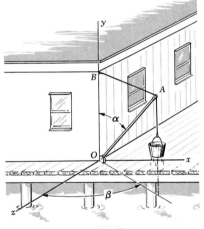

FIG. P 2.50 AND P 2.51

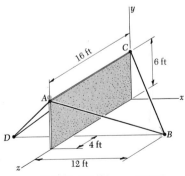

FIG. P 2.52

PROBLEMS

2.50. Determine (*a*) the *x*, *y*, and *z* components of the 250-lb force, (*b*) the angles θ_x, θ_y, and θ_z that the force forms with the coordinate axes.

2.51. Determine (*a*) the *x*, *y*, and *z* components of the 300-lb force, (*b*) the angles θ_x, θ_y, and θ_z that the force forms with the coordinate axes.

2.52. A force of 500 lb, directed along the axis of the boom from *A* to *O*, is exerted on the support at *O*. Knowing that $\alpha = 35°$ and $\beta = 65°$, determine (*a*) the *x*, *y*, and *z* components of the force exerted at *O*, (*b*) the angles θ_x, θ_y, and θ_z for the force exerted at *O*.

2.53. A gun is aimed so that it will fire at a point *A* which is 30° east of north and is 15 ft above the gun in elevation. The horizontal distance from the gun to point *A* is 50 ft. If at a given instant the recoil force of the gun is 80 lb, determine (*a*) the *x*, *y*, and *z* components of the recoil force, (*b*) the values of θ_x, θ_y, and θ_z. (Assume the *x* axis is toward the east, the *y* axis is up, and the *z* axis is south.)

2.54. A 400-lb force acts at the origin in a direction defined by the angles $\theta_y = 80.0°$ and $\theta_z = 46.0°$. It is also known that the *x* component of the force is positive. Determine the value of θ_x and the components of the force.

2.55. A force acts at the origin in a direction defined by the angles $\theta_x = 125.0°$ and $\theta_z = 65.0°$. It is known that the *y* component of the force is +3.20 lb. Determine the magnitude of the force and the value of θ_y.

2.56. A precast-concrete wall section is temporarily held by the cables shown. If the tension in cable *AB* is 700 lb, determine the components of the force exerted on the wall section at *A*.

2.57. Knowing that the tension in cable *BC* is 900 lb, determine the components of the force exerted on the wall section at *C*.

2.58. Determine the magnitude and direction of the force $\mathbf{F} = 150\mathbf{i} - 75\mathbf{j} + 200\mathbf{k}$ (lb).

2.59. Determine the magnitude and direction of the force $\mathbf{F} = -150\mathbf{i} - 350\mathbf{j} + 200\mathbf{k}$ (lb).

FIG. P 2.56, P 2.57, AND P 2.62

2.60. Determine the angles θ_x, θ_y, and θ_z which define the direction of the force exerted on point A in Prob. 2.56.

2.61. Determine the angles θ_x, θ_y, and θ_z which define the direction of the force exerted on point C in Prob. 2.57.

2.62. The tension in cable AB is 700 lb and the tension in cable BC is 900 lb. Determine the components of the resultant of the forces exerted by the cables on point B.

2.63. Several guy wires are attached to the top of the tower at A. The tension in AB is 5,200 lb and the tension in AC is 3,500 lb. Determine the resultant of the two forces exerted by these two cables on point A.

2.64. Knowing that the tension in AC is 7,000 lb, determine the required values of the tension in AB and AD so that the resultant of the three forces applied at A is vertical.

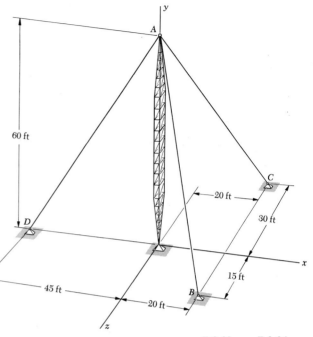

FIG. P 2.63 AND P 2.64

2.65. Determine the two possible values of θ_y for a force $\mathbf{F}$, (*a*) if the force forms equal angles with the positive x, y, and z axes, (*b*) if the force forms equal angles with the positive y and z axes and an angle of 45° with the positive x axis.

2.14. Equilibrium of a Particle in Space.

According to the definition given in Sec. 2.8, a particle A is in equilibrium if the resultant of all the forces acting on A is zero. The components R_x, R_y, R_z of the resultant are given by the relations (2.31); expressing that the components of the resultant are zero, we write

$$\Sigma F_x = 0 \qquad \Sigma F_y = 0 \qquad \Sigma F_z = 0 \qquad (2.34)$$

Equations (2.34) represent the necessary and sufficient conditions for the equilibrium of a particle in space. They may be used to solve problems dealing with the equilibrium of a particle and involving no more than three unknowns.

To solve such problems, we first should draw a free-body diagram showing the particle in equilibrium and *all* the forces acting on it. We may then write the equations of equilibrium (2.34) and solve them for three unknowns. In the more common types of problems, these unknowns will represent (1) the three components of a single force or (2) the magnitude of three forces each of known direction.

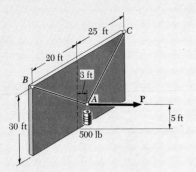

SAMPLE PROBLEM 2.10

A 500-lb weight is hung by means of two cables AB and AC, which are attached to the top of a vertical wall. A horizontal force $\mathbf{P}$ perpendicular to the wall holds the weight in the position shown. Determine the magnitude of $\mathbf{P}$ and the tension in each cable.

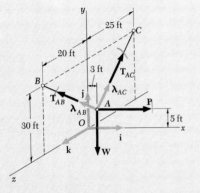

Solution. Point A is chosen as a free body; this point is subjected to four forces, three of which are of unknown magnitude.

Introducing the unit vectors $\mathbf{i}, \mathbf{j}, \mathbf{k}$, we resolve each force into rectangular components.

$$\mathbf{P} = P\mathbf{i} \qquad \mathbf{W} = -500\mathbf{j} \qquad (1)$$

In the case of $\mathbf{T}_{AB}$ and $\mathbf{T}_{AC}$, it is necessary first to determine the components and magnitudes of the vectors $\overrightarrow{AB}$ and $\overrightarrow{AC}$. Denoting by $\boldsymbol{\lambda}_{AB}$ the unit vector along AB, we write

$$\overrightarrow{AB} = -(3\text{ ft})\mathbf{i} + (25\text{ ft})\mathbf{j} + (20\text{ ft})\mathbf{k} \qquad AB = 32.2\text{ ft}$$

$$\boldsymbol{\lambda}_{AB} = \frac{\overrightarrow{AB}}{32.2\text{ ft}} = -0.0932\mathbf{i} + 0.776\mathbf{j} + 0.621\mathbf{k}$$

$$\mathbf{T}_{AB} = T_{AB}\boldsymbol{\lambda}_{AB} = -0.0932T_{AB}\mathbf{i} + 0.776T_{AB}\mathbf{j} + 0.621T_{AB}\mathbf{k} \qquad (2)$$

Denoting by $\boldsymbol{\lambda}_{AC}$ the unit vector along AC, we write in a similar way

$$\overrightarrow{AC} = -(3\text{ ft})\mathbf{i} + (25\text{ ft})\mathbf{j} - (25\text{ ft})\mathbf{k} \qquad AC = 35.5\text{ ft}$$

$$\boldsymbol{\lambda}_{AC} = \frac{\overrightarrow{AC}}{35.5\text{ ft}} = -0.0845\mathbf{i} + 0.704\mathbf{j} - 0.704\mathbf{k}$$

$$\mathbf{T}_{AC} = T_{AC}\boldsymbol{\lambda}_{AC} = -0.0845T_{AC}\mathbf{i} + 0.704T_{AC}\mathbf{j} - 0.704T_{AC}\mathbf{k} \qquad (3)$$

Since point A is in equilibrium, we must have

$$\Sigma\mathbf{F} = 0: \qquad \mathbf{T}_{AB} + \mathbf{T}_{AC} + \mathbf{P} + \mathbf{W} = 0$$

or, substituting from (1), (2), (3) for the various forces and factoring $\mathbf{i}, \mathbf{j}, \mathbf{k}$,

$$(-0.0932T_{AB} - 0.0845T_{AC} + P)\mathbf{i}$$
$$+ (0.776T_{AB} + 0.704T_{AC} - 500)\mathbf{j} + (0.621T_{AB} - 0.704T_{AC})\mathbf{k} = 0$$

Setting the coefficients of $\mathbf{i}, \mathbf{j}, \mathbf{k}$ equal to zero, we write three scalar equations, which express that the sums of the x, y, and z components of the forces are respectively equal to zero.

$$(\Sigma F_x = 0:) \qquad -0.0932T_{AB} - 0.0845T_{AC} + P = 0$$
$$(\Sigma F_y = 0:) \qquad +0.776T_{AB} + 0.704T_{AC} - 500 = 0$$
$$(\Sigma F_z = 0:) \qquad +0.621T_{AB} - 0.704T_{AC} = 0$$

Solving these equations, we obtain

$$P = 60\text{ lb} \qquad T_{AB} = 358\text{ lb} \qquad T_{AC} = 316\text{ lb} \quad \blacktriangleleft$$

PROBLEMS

2.66. A load W is supported by three cables as shown. Determine the value of W, knowing that the tension in cable BD is 200 lb.

2.67. A load W is supported by three cables as shown. Determine the value of W, knowing that the tension in cable CD is 450 lb.

2.68. A load W of magnitude 262 lb is supported by three cables as shown. Determine the tension in each cable.

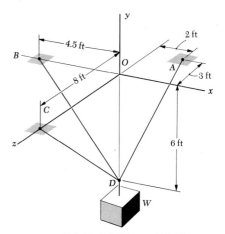

FIG. P 2.66, P 2.67, AND P 2.68

2.69. Three cables are joined at D where an upward force of 6,000 lb is applied. Determine the tension in each cable.

2.70. A 50-lb load is supported by three ropes which are attached to a ceiling as shown. Determine the tension in each rope.

2.71. A pole AB is used to support a 180-lb weight which hangs very close to the intersection of two smooth walls. It is known that the force exerted on point B by the pole must be directed along the pole and that the force exerted on point B by a wall must be perpendicular to the wall. Determine the force exerted on B by the pole and by each wall, when $a = 6$ ft, $b = 2$ ft, and $h = 3$ ft.

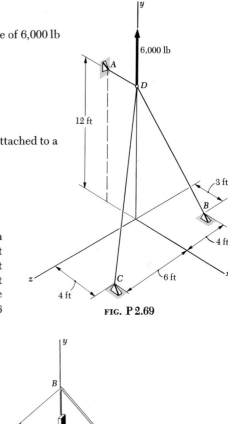

FIG. P 2.69

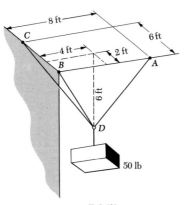

FIG. P 2.70

FIG. P 2.71

47

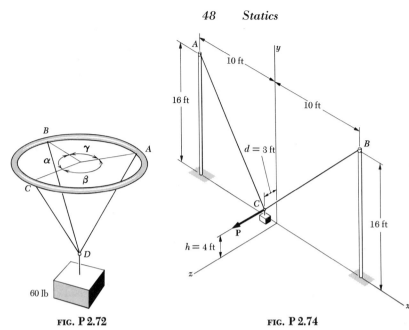

FIG. P 2.72

FIG. P 2.74

2.72. A 60-lb weight is hung by three strings which are attached to a ring and are tied together at D. The diameter of the ring is 24 in., and the length of each string is 20 in. If $\alpha = \beta = \gamma$, determine the tension in each string.

2.73. If, in Prob. 2.72, $\alpha = 80°$, $\beta = 130°$, and $\gamma = 150°$, determine the tension in each string.

2.74. A 500-lb weight is hung by means of two cables AC and BC, which are attached to the top of vertical posts. A horizontal force $\mathbf{P}$, perpendicular to the plane containing the posts, holds the weight in the position shown. Determine the magnitude of $\mathbf{P}$ and the tension in each cable.

2.75. A 20-lb instrument is hung inside a box by means of three strings. If the instrument hangs directly in the center of the box and the strings are tied together at a point D, 3 in. below the top of the box, determine the tension in each string.

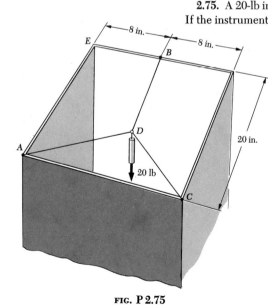

FIG. P 2.75

2.76. Solve Prob. 2.75 assuming that string BD is removed and replaced by a string between D and E.

2.77. Solve Prob. 2.75 assuming that point D is located only ½ in. below the top of the box. (Explain why this arrangement results in higher tensions.)

2.78. A pole *AB* of length 10 ft is used to support a 180-lb weight as shown in Prob. 2.71. If the force exerted on point *B* by the pole must not exceed 300 lb, determine (*a*) the smallest value of *h* that may be used, (*b*) the area of the floor in which point *A* must be located.

°**2.79.** In Prob. 2.74 the weight is held in equilibrium by a force **P** of magnitude 200 lb. Determine the value of *d* and of *h* for this equilibrium position.

REVIEW PROBLEMS

2.80. A chain loop of length 5 ft is placed around a 1- by 1-ft piece of lumber as shown. Knowing that the weight lifted by the crane hook is 800 lb, determine the tension in the chain in each case.

2.81. Knowing that the magnitude of the force **P** is 500 lb, determine the resultant of the three forces applied at *A*.

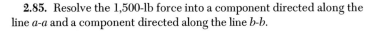

(*a*)   (*b*)

FIG. P 2.80

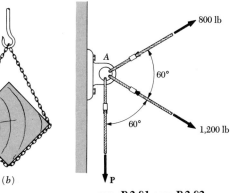

FIG. P 2.81 AND P 2.82

2.82. Determine the magnitude of the force **P** for which the resultant of the three forces applied at *A* is 2,000 lb.

2.83. Three cables are connected at *D*, which lies 4 ft below the *x* axis, and support the load *W* = 600 lb. Determine the tension in each cable.

2.84. Determine the angles θ_x, θ_y, and θ_z for the force exerted (*a*) at *A* by cable *AD*, (*b*) at *B* by cable *BD*, (*c*) at *C* by cable *CD*.

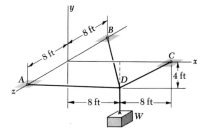

FIG. P 2.83 AND P 2.84

2.85. Resolve the 1,500-lb force into a component directed along the line *a-a* and a component directed along the line *b-b*.

2.86. Resolve the 1,500-lb force into a component directed along the line *a-a* and a component directed along the line *c-c*.

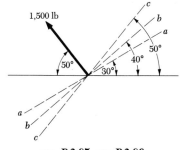

FIG. P 2.85 AND P 2.86

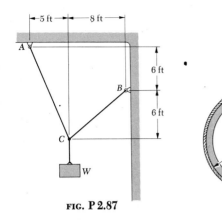

FIG. P 2.87

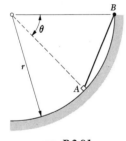

FIG. P 2.88

2.87. Two cables are tied together at C and loaded as shown.   Knowing that the maximum permissible tension in AC and in BC is 650 lb, determine the largest weight W which can be safely supported.

2.88. A small pulley is attached to the end of a rope which is looped around a pipe of radius r and weight W.   Determine (a) the angle θ, (b) the tension in the rope if $r = 10$ in. and $W = 100$ lb.

FIG. P 2.89 AND P 2.90

2.89. Two forces, $\mathbf{P}$ and $\mathbf{P'}$, of the same magnitude P, and a 200-lb force are applied at A.   Determine the required magnitude P and angle α if the resultant of the three forces is to be a vertical upward force of 250 lb.

2.90. Knowing that $\alpha = 60°$, determine the required common magnitude P of the two forces $\mathbf{P}$ and $\mathbf{P'}$ if the resultant of the three forces acting at A is to be vertical.   What is the corresponding magnitude of the resultant?

2.91. A particle A of weight W is supported by a string on a circular cylindrical surface as shown.   Assuming that the force $\mathbf{N}$ exerted on A by the surface is normal to the surface, show that $N = W \tan \theta/2$. What is the corresponding tension in the string?

FIG. P 2.91

3. RIGID BODIES. EQUIVALENT SYSTEMS OF FORCES

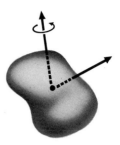

3.1. Rigid Bodies. External and Internal Forces. In the preceding chapter it was assumed that each of the bodies considered could be treated as a single particle. Such a view, however, is not always possible, and a body, in general, should be treated as a combination of a large number of particles. The size of the body will have to be taken into consideration, as well as the fact that forces will act on different particles and thus will have different points of application.

Most of the bodies considered in elementary mechanics are assumed to be *rigid*, a *rigid body* being defined as one which does not deform. Actual structures and machines, however, are never absolutely rigid and deform under the loads to which they are subjected. But these deformations are usually small and do not appreciably affect the conditions of equilibrium or motion of the structure under consideration. They are important, though, as far as the resistance of the structure to failure is concerned, and are considered in the study of mechanics of materials.

Forces acting on rigid bodies may be separated into two groups: (1) *external forces;* (2) *internal forces.*

1. The *external forces* represent the action of other bodies on the rigid body under consideration. They are entirely responsible for the external behavior of the rigid body. They will either cause it to move or assure that it remains at rest. We shall be concerned only with external forces in this chapter and in Chaps. 4 and 5.

2. The *internal forces* are the forces which hold together the particles forming the rigid body. If the rigid body is structurally composed of several parts, the forces holding the component parts together are also defined as internal forces. Internal forces will be considered in Chaps. 6 and 7.

FIG. 3.1

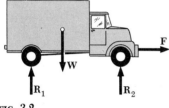

FIG. 3.2

As an example of external forces, we shall consider the forces acting on a disabled truck that men are pulling forward by means of a rope attached to the front bumper (Fig. 3.1). The external forces acting on the truck are shown in a *free-body diagram* (Fig. 3.2). Let us first consider the *weight* of the truck. Although it embodies the effect of the earth's pull on each of the particles forming the truck, the weight may be represented by the single force **W**. The *point of application* of this force, i.e., the point at which the force acts, is defined as the *center of gravity* of the truck. It will be seen in Chap. 5 how centers of gravity may be determined. The weight **W** tends to make the truck move vertically downward. In fact, it would actually cause the truck to move downward, i.e., to fall, if it were not for the presence of the ground. The ground opposes the downward motion of the truck by means of the reactions $\mathbf{R}_1$ and $\mathbf{R}_2$. These forces are exerted *by* the ground *on* the truck and must therefore be included among the external forces acting on the truck.

The men pulling on the rope exert the force **F**. The point of application of **F** is on the front bumper. The force **F** tends to make the truck move forward in a straight line and does actually make it move, since no external force opposes this motion. (Rolling resistance has been neglected here for simplicity.) This forward motion of the truck, during which all straight lines remain parallel to themselves (the floor of the truck remains horizontal, and its walls remain vertical), is known as a *translation.* Other forces might cause the truck to move differently. For example, the force exerted by a jack placed under the front axle would cause the truck to pivot about its rear axle. Such a motion is a *rotation.* It may be concluded, therefore, that each of the *external forces* acting on a *rigid body* is capable, if unopposed, of imparting to the rigid body a motion of translation or rotation, or both.

3.2. Principle of Transmissibility. Equivalent Forces. The *principle of transmissibility* states that the conditions of equilibrium or of motion of a rigid body will remain unchanged if a force **F** acting at a given point of the rigid body is replaced by a force **F′** of the same magnitude and same direction, but acting at a different point, *provided that the two forces have the same line of action* (Fig. 3.3). The two forces **F** and **F′** have the same effect on the rigid body and are said to be *equivalent.* This principle, which states in fact that the action of a force may be *transmitted* along its line of action, is based on experimental evidence.   It *cannot* be derived from the properties established so far in this text and must therefore be accepted as an experimental law.

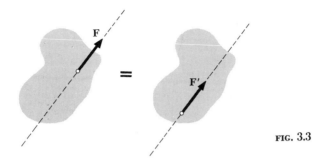

FIG. 3.3

It was indicated in Chap. 2 that the forces acting on a particle are vectors.   These vectors had a well-defined point of application, namely, the particle itself, and were therefore fixed, or bound, vectors.   In the case of forces acting on a rigid body, however, the point of application of the force does not matter, as long as the line of action remains unchanged.   Thus forces acting on a rigid body are *sliding vectors,* i.e., vectors which may be allowed to slide along their line of action.

Returning to the example of the truck, we first observe that the line of action of the force **F** is a horizontal line passing through both the front and the rear bumpers of the truck (Fig. 3.4).   Using the principle of transmissibility, we may therefore

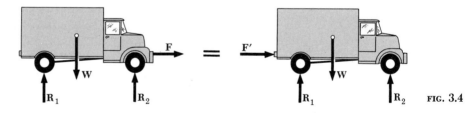

FIG. 3.4

replace **F** by an *equivalent force* **F'** acting on the rear bumper. In other words, the conditions of motion are unaffected, and all the other external forces acting on the truck (**W**, **R**₁, **R**₂) remain unchanged if the men push on the rear bumper instead of pulling on the front bumper.

The principle of transmissibility and the concept of equivalent forces have limitations, however.   Consider, for example, a short bar AB acted upon by equal and opposite axial forces $\mathbf{P}_1$ and $\mathbf{P}_2$, as shown in Fig. 3.5a.   According to the principle of transmissibility, the force $\mathbf{P}_2$ may be replaced by a force $\mathbf{P}'_2$ having the same magnitude, same direction, and same line of action, but acting at A instead of B (Fig. 3.5b).   The forces $\mathbf{P}_1$ and $\mathbf{P}'_2$ acting on the same particle may be added according to the rules of Chap. 2, and, being equal and opposite, their sum is found equal to zero.   The original system of forces shown in Fig. 3.5a is thus equivalent to no force at all (Fig. 3.5c) from the point of view of the external behavior of the bar.

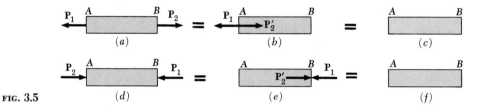

FIG. 3.5

Consider now the two equal and opposite forces $\mathbf{P}_1$ and $\mathbf{P}_2$ acting on the bar AB as shown in Fig. 3.5d.   The force $\mathbf{P}_2$ may be replaced by a force $\mathbf{P}'_2$ having the same magnitude, same direction, and same line of action, but acting at B instead of A (Fig. 3.5e).   The forces $\mathbf{P}_1$ and $\mathbf{P}'_2$ may then be added, and their sum is found again to be zero (Fig. 3.5f).   From the point of view of the mechanics of rigid bodies, the systems shown in Fig. 3.5a and d are thus equivalent.   But the *internal forces* and *deformations* produced by the two systems are clearly different. The bar of Fig. 3.5a is in *tension* and, if not absolutely rigid, will increase in length slightly; the bar of Fig. 3.5d is in *compression* and, if not absolutely rigid, will decrease in length slightly. Thus, while the principle of transmissibility may be used freely to determine the conditions of motion or equilibrium of rigid bodies and to compute the external forces acting on these bodies, it should be avoided, or at least used with care, in determining internal forces and deformations.

3.3. Vector Product of Two Vectors.   In order to gain a better understanding of the effect of a force on a rigid body, we shall introduce a new concept, the concept of *moment of a force about a point*.   This concept will be more clearly understood, and we shall be able to apply it more effectively, if we first add to the mathematical tools at our disposal by defining the *vector product* of two vectors.

The vector product of two vectors **P** and **Q** is defined as the vector **V** which satisfies the following conditions:

1. The line of action of **V** is perpendicular to the plane containing **P** and **Q** (Fig. 3.6).

2. The magnitude of **V** is the product of the magnitudes of **P** and **Q** and of the sine of the angle θ formed by **P** and **Q** (the measure of which will always be 180° or less); we thus have

$$V = PQ \sin \theta \tag{3.1}$$

3. The sense of **V** is such that a man located at the tip of **V** will observe as counterclockwise the rotation through θ which brings the vector **P** in line with the vector **Q**; note that if **P** and **Q** do not have a common point of application, they should first be redrawn from the same point.   The three vectors **P**, **Q**, and **V**—taken in that order—are said to form a *right-handed triad.*†

As stated above, the vector **V** satisfying these three conditions (which define it uniquely) is referred to as the vector product of **P** and **Q**; it is represented by the mathematical expression

$$V = P \times Q \tag{3.2}$$

Because of the notation used, the vector product of two vectors **P** and **Q** is also referred to as the *cross product* of **P** and **Q**.

It follows from Eq. (3.1) that, when two vectors **P** and **Q** have either the same direction or opposite directions, their vector product is zero.   In the general case when the angle θ formed by the two vectors is neither 0° nor 180°, Eq. (3.1) may be given a simple geometric interpretation: the magnitude V of the vector product of **P** and **Q** measures the area of the parallelogram which has **P** and **Q** for sides (Fig. 3.7).   The vector product **P** $\times$ **Q** will therefore remain unchanged if we replace **Q** by a vector **Q′** coplanar with **P** and **Q** and such that the line joining the tips of **Q** and **Q′** is parallel to **P**.   We write

$$V = P \times Q = P \times Q' \tag{3.3}$$

From the third condition used to define the vector product **V** of **P** and **Q**, namely, the condition stating that **P**, **Q**, and **V** must form a right-handed triad, it follows that vector products *are not*

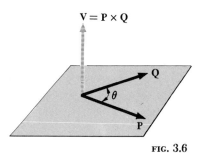

$V = P \times Q$

FIG. 3.6

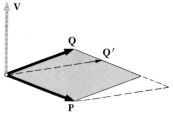

FIG. 3.7

---

† We should note that the x, y, and z axes used in Chap. 2 form a right-handed system of axes and that the unit vectors **i**, **j**, **k** defined in Sec. 2.11 form a right-handed triad.

commutative, i.e., $\mathbf{Q} \times \mathbf{P}$ is not equal to $\mathbf{P} \times \mathbf{Q}$. Indeed, we may easily check that $\mathbf{Q} \times \mathbf{P}$ is represented by the vector $-\mathbf{V}$ equal and opposite to $\mathbf{V}$. We thus write

$$\mathbf{Q} \times \mathbf{P} = -(\mathbf{P} \times \mathbf{Q}) \tag{3.4}$$

Example. Let us compute the vector product $\mathbf{V} = \mathbf{P} \times \mathbf{Q}$ of the vector $\mathbf{P}$ of magnitude 6 lying in the zx plane at an angle of 30° with the x axis, and of the vector $\mathbf{Q}$ of magnitude 4 lying along the x axis (Fig. 3.8).

It follows immediately from the definition of the vector product that the vector $\mathbf{V}$ must lie along the y axis, have the magnitude

$$V = PQ \sin \theta = (6)(4) \sin 30° = 12$$

and be directed upward.

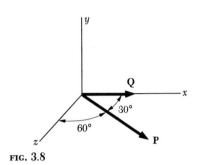

FIG. 3.8

We saw that the commutative property does not apply to vector products. We may wonder whether the *distributive* property holds, i.e., whether the relation

$$\mathbf{P} \times (\mathbf{Q}_1 + \mathbf{Q}_2) = \mathbf{P} \times \mathbf{Q}_1 + \mathbf{P} \times \mathbf{Q}_2 \tag{3.5}$$

is valid. The answer is *yes*. Many readers are probably willing to accept without formal proof an answer which they intuitively feel is correct. However, since the entire structure of vector algebra and of statics depends upon the relation (3.5), we shall take time out actually to derive it.

We may, without any loss of generality, assume that $\mathbf{P}$ is directed along the y axis (Fig. 3.9a). Denoting by $\mathbf{Q}$ the sum of $\mathbf{Q}_1$ and $\mathbf{Q}_2$, we drop perpendiculars from the tips of $\mathbf{Q}$, $\mathbf{Q}_1$, and $\mathbf{Q}_2$ onto the zx plane, defining in this way the vectors $\mathbf{Q}'$, $\mathbf{Q}'_1$, and $\mathbf{Q}'_2$. These vectors will be referred to, respectively, as the *projections* of $\mathbf{Q}$, $\mathbf{Q}_1$, and $\mathbf{Q}_2$ on the zx plane. Recalling the property expressed by Eq. (3.3), we note that the left-hand member of Eq. (3.5) may be replaced by $\mathbf{P} \times \mathbf{Q}'$ and that, similarly, the vector products $\mathbf{P} \times \mathbf{Q}_1$ and $\mathbf{P} \times \mathbf{Q}_2$ may, respectively, be replaced by $\mathbf{P} \times \mathbf{Q}'_1$ and $\mathbf{P} \times \mathbf{Q}'_2$. Thus, the relation to be proved may be written in the form

$$\mathbf{P} \times \mathbf{Q}' = \mathbf{P} \times \mathbf{Q}'_1 + \mathbf{P} \times \mathbf{Q}'_2 \tag{3.5'}$$

We now observe that $\mathbf{P} \times \mathbf{Q}'$ may be obtained from $\mathbf{Q}'$ by multiplying this vector by the scalar P and rotating it counterclockwise through 90° in the zx plane (Fig. 3.9b); the other two vector products in (3.5') may be obtained in the same manner from $\mathbf{Q}'_1$ and $\mathbf{Q}'_2$, respectively. Now, since the projection of a parallelogram onto an arbitrary plane is a parallelogram, the projection $\mathbf{Q}'$ of the sum $\mathbf{Q}$ of $\mathbf{Q}_1$ and $\mathbf{Q}_2$ must be the sum of the projections $\mathbf{Q}'_1$ and $\mathbf{Q}'_2$ of $\mathbf{Q}_1$ and $\mathbf{Q}_2$ on the same plane (Fig. 3.9a).   This relation between the vectors $\mathbf{Q}'$, $\mathbf{Q}'_1$, and $\mathbf{Q}'_2$ will

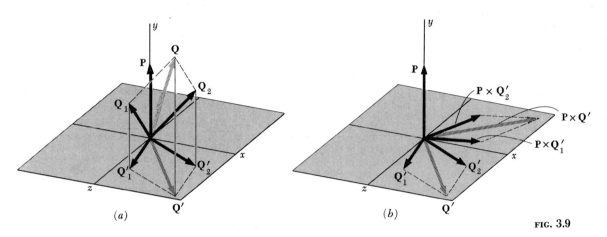

FIG. 3.9

still hold after the three vectors have been multiplied by the scalar P and rotated through 90° (Fig. 3.9b).   Thus the relation (3.5') has been proved and we can now be sure that the distributive property holds for vector products.

The third property, the associative property, does not apply to vector products; we have in general

$$(\mathbf{P} \times \mathbf{Q}) \times \mathbf{S} \neq \mathbf{P} \times (\mathbf{Q} \times \mathbf{S}) \qquad (3.6)$$

3.4.   Vector Products Expressed in Terms of Rectangular Components.   We shall now determine the vector product of any two of the unit vectors, $\mathbf{i}, \mathbf{j}, \mathbf{k}$, defined in Chap. 2.   Consider first the product $\mathbf{i} \times \mathbf{j}$ (Fig. 3.10a).   Since both vectors have a magnitude equal to one and since they are at a right angle to each other, their vector product will also be a unit vector. This unit vector must be $\mathbf{k}$, since the vectors $\mathbf{i}, \mathbf{j}, \mathbf{k}$ are mutually perpendicular and form a right-handed triad.   On the other hand, the product $\mathbf{j} \times \mathbf{i}$ will be equal to $-\mathbf{k}$ since the 90-degree rotation which brings $\mathbf{j}$ into $\mathbf{i}$ is observed as counterclockwise by a man located at the tip of $-\mathbf{k}$ (Fig. 3.10b).   Finally, it should be observed that the vector product of a unit vector by itself, such as $\mathbf{i} \times \mathbf{i}$, is equal to zero, since both vectors have the same direction.   The vector products of the various possible pairs of unit vectors are

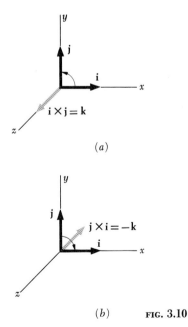

FIG. 3.10

$$i \times i = 0 \qquad j \times i = -k \qquad k \times i = j$$
$$i \times j = k \qquad j \times j = 0 \qquad k \times j = -i \quad (3.7)$$
$$i \times k = -j \qquad j \times k = i \qquad k \times k = 0$$

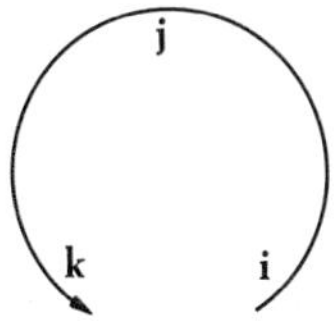

FIG. 3.11

By arranging the three letters representing the unit vectors in a circle (Fig. 3.11), we may simplify the determination of the sign of the vector product of two unit vectors: The product of two unit vectors will be positive if they follow each other in counterclockwise order, and negative otherwise.

We may now easily express the vector product $\mathbf{V}$ of two given vectors $\mathbf{P}$ and $\mathbf{Q}$ in terms of the rectangular components of these vectors. Resolving $\mathbf{P}$ and $\mathbf{Q}$ into components, we first write

$$\mathbf{V} = \mathbf{P} \times \mathbf{Q} = (P_x\mathbf{i} + P_y\mathbf{j} + P_z\mathbf{k}) \times (Q_x\mathbf{i} + Q_y\mathbf{j} + Q_z\mathbf{k})$$

Making use of the distributive property, we express $\mathbf{V}$ as the sum of vector products such as $P_x\mathbf{i} \times Q_y\mathbf{j}$. Observing that each of the expressions obtained is equal to the vector product of two unit vectors, such as $\mathbf{i} \times \mathbf{j}$, multiplied by the product of two scalars, such as P_xQ_y, and recalling the identities (3.7), we obtain, after factoring $\mathbf{i}$, $\mathbf{j}$, and $\mathbf{k}$,

$$\mathbf{V} = (P_yQ_z - P_zQ_y)\mathbf{i} + (P_zQ_x - P_xQ_z)\mathbf{j} + (P_xQ_y - P_yQ_x)\mathbf{k}$$
$$(3.8)$$

The rectangular components of the vector product $\mathbf{V}$ are thus found to be

$$V_x = P_yQ_z - P_zQ_y$$
$$V_y = P_zQ_x - P_xQ_z \qquad (3.9)$$
$$V_z = P_xQ_y - P_yQ_x$$

Returning to Eq. (3.8), we observe that its right-hand member represents the expansion of a determinant. The vector product $\mathbf{V}$ may thus be expressed in the following form, more easily memorized:[†]

$$\mathbf{V} = \begin{vmatrix} \mathbf{i} & \mathbf{j} & \mathbf{k} \\ P_x & P_y & P_z \\ Q_x & Q_y & Q_z \end{vmatrix} \qquad (3.10)$$

[†] Any determinant consisting of 3 rows and 3 columns may be evaluated by repeating the first and second columns and forming products along each diagonal line. The sum of the products obtained along the dashed lines is then subtracted from the sum of the products obtained along the solid lines.

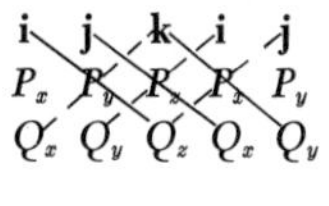

$$\begin{matrix} \mathbf{i} & \mathbf{j} & \mathbf{k} & \mathbf{i} & \mathbf{j} \\ P_x & P_y & P_z & P_x & P_y \\ Q_x & Q_y & Q_z & Q_x & Q_y \end{matrix}$$

3.5.   Moment of a Force about a Point.   Let us now consider a force **F** acting on a rigid body (Fig. 3.12).   As we know, the force **F** is represented by a vector which defines its magnitude and direction.   However, the effect of the force on the rigid body depends also upon its point of application A.   The position of A may be conveniently defined by the vector **r** which joins the fixed reference point O with A; this vector is known as the *position vector* of A.†   The position vector **r** and the force **F** define the plane shown in Fig. 3.12.

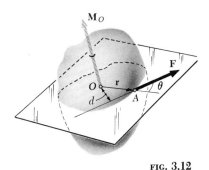

FIG. 3.12

We shall define the *moment of* **F** *about* O as the vector product of **r** and **F**:

$$\mathbf{M}_o = \mathbf{r} \times \mathbf{F} \tag{3.11}$$

According to the definition of the vector product given in Sec. 3.3, the moment $\mathbf{M}_o$ must be perpendicular to the plane containing O and **F**; thus, *the line of action of* $\mathbf{M}_o$ *represents the axis about which the body tends to rotate* when attached at O and subjected to the force **F**.

The sense of $\mathbf{M}_o$ is defined by the sense of the rotation which would bring the vector **r** in line with the vector **F**; but this rotation is the rotation that **F** tends to impart to the body.   Thus *the sense of the moment* $\mathbf{M}_o$ *characterizes the sense of the rotation that* **F** *tends to impart to the rigid body;* this rotation will be observed as *counterclockwise* by an observer located at the tip of $\mathbf{M}_o$.   Another way of stating the relationship existing between the sense of $\mathbf{M}_o$ and the sense of rotation of the rigid body is furnished by the *right-hand rule:* Close your right hand and hold it so that your fingers are curled in the sense of the rotation that **F** tends to impart to the rigid body; your thumb will indicate the sense of the moment $\mathbf{M}_o$.

Finally, denoting by θ the angle between the lines of action of the position vector **r** and the force **F**, we find that the magnitude of the moment of **F** about O is

$$M_o = rF \sin \theta = Fd \tag{3.12}$$

where d represents the perpendicular distance from O to the line of action of **F**.   A force being expressed in pounds and a

---

† We may easily verify that position vectors obey the law of vector addition and, thus, are truly vectors.   Consider, for example, the position vectors **r** and **r′** of A with respect to two reference points O and $O′$, and the position vector **s** of O with respect to $O′$ (Fig. 3.37a, Sec. 3.14).   We check that the position vector $\mathbf{r′} = \overrightarrow{O′A}$ may be obtained from the position vectors $\mathbf{s} = \overrightarrow{O′O}$ and $\mathbf{r} = \overrightarrow{OA}$ by applying the triangle rule for the addition of vectors.

distance in feet or inches, the moment of a force will be expressed in lb-ft or lb-in. Since the tendency of a force $\mathbf{F}$ to make a rigid body rotate about an axis perpendicular to the force depends upon the distance of $\mathbf{F}$ from that axis, as well as upon the magnitude of $\mathbf{F}$, we note that *the magnitude of* $\mathbf{M}_o$ *measures the tendency of the force* $\mathbf{F}$ *to impart to the rigid body a rotational motion* when the body is attached at O.

We may observe that the moment $\mathbf{M}_o$ of a force about a point, while it depends upon the magnitude, the line of action, and the sense of the force, does *not* depend upon the actual position of the point of application of the force along its line of action. Conversely, the moment $\mathbf{M}_o$ of a force $\mathbf{F}$ does not characterize the position of the point of application of $\mathbf{F}$.

However, as we shall see presently, the moment $\mathbf{M}_o$ of a force $\mathbf{F}$ of given magnitude and direction *completely defines the line of action of* $\mathbf{F}$. Indeed, the line of action of $\mathbf{F}$ must lie in a plane through O perpendicular to the moment $\mathbf{M}_o$; its distance d from O must be equal to the quotient M_o/F of the magnitudes of $\mathbf{M}_o$ and $\mathbf{F}$; and the sense of $\mathbf{M}_o$ determines whether the line of action of $\mathbf{F}$ is to be drawn on one side or the other of the point O.

We recall from Sec. 3.2 that the principle of transmissibility states that two forces $\mathbf{F}$ and $\mathbf{F}'$ are equivalent (i.e., have the same effect on a rigid body) if they have the same magnitude, same direction, and same line of action. This principle may now be restated as follows: *Two forces* $\mathbf{F}$ *and* $\mathbf{F}'$ *are equivalent if, and only if, they are equal* (i.e., have the same magnitude and same direction) *and have equal moments about a given point* O. The necessary and sufficient condition for two forces $\mathbf{F}$ and $\mathbf{F}'$ to be equivalent is thus

$$\mathbf{F} = \mathbf{F}' \qquad \text{and} \qquad \mathbf{M}_o = \mathbf{M}_o' \qquad (3.13)$$

We should observe that it follows from this statement that if the relations (3.13) hold for a given point O, they will hold for any other point.

Problems Involving Only Two Dimensions. Many applications deal with two-dimensional structures, i.e., structures which have length and breadth, but only negligible depth, and which are subjected to forces contained in the plane of the structure. Two-dimensional structures and the forces acting on them may be readily represented on a sheet of paper or on a blackboard. Their analysis is therefore considerably simpler than that of three-dimensional structures and forces.

Consider, for example, a rigid slab acted upon by a force $\mathbf{F}$

(Fig. 3.13). The moment of **F** about a point O chosen in the plane of the figure is represented by a vector $\mathbf{M}_O$ perpendicular to that plane and of magnitude Fd. In the case of Fig. 3.13*a* the vector $\mathbf{M}_O$ points *out* of the paper, while in the case of Fig. 3.13*b* it points *into* the paper. As we look at the figure, we observe the action of **F** in the first case as counterclockwise, and in the second case as clockwise. Therefore, it is natural to refer to the sense of the moment of **F** about O in Fig. 3.13*a* as counterclockwise $\mathanswer$, and in Fig. 3.13*b* as clockwise $\mathanswer$.

Since the moment of a force **F** acting in the plane of the figure must be perpendicular to that plane, we need only specify the *magnitude* and the *sense* of the moment of **F** about O. This may be done by assigning to the magnitude M_O of the moment a positive or negative sign, according to whether the vector $\mathbf{M}_O$ points out of or into the paper.

3.6. Varignon's Theorem. The distributive property of vector products may be used to determine the moment of the resultant of several *concurrent forces*. If several forces $\mathbf{F}_1$, $\mathbf{F}_2$, . . . are applied at the same point A (Fig. 3.14), and if we denote by **r** the position vector of A, it follows immediately from formula (3.5) that

$$\blacktriangleright \quad \mathbf{r} \times (\mathbf{F}_1 + \mathbf{F}_2 + \ldots) = \mathbf{r} \times \mathbf{F}_1 + \mathbf{r} \times \mathbf{F}_2 + \ldots \quad (3.14)$$

In words, *the moment about a given point O of the resultant of several concurrent forces is equal to the sum of the moments of the various forces about the same point O.* This property was originally established by the French mathematician Varignon (1654–1722), long before the introduction of vector algebra, and is known as *Varignon's Theorem.*

The relation (3.14) makes it possible to replace the direct determination of the moment of a force **F** by the determination of the moments of two or more component forces. As we shall see in the next section, **F** will generally be resolved into components parallel to the coordinate axes. However, it may be found more expeditious in some instances to resolve **F** into components which are not parallel to the coordinate axes (see Sample Prob. 3.3).

3.7. Rectangular Components of the Moment of a Force. In general, the determination of the moment of a force in space will be considerably simplified if the force and the position vector of its point of application are resolved into rectangular x, y, and z components. Consider, for example, the moment $\mathbf{M}_O$ about O of a force **F** of components F_x, F_y, and F_z, applied at a point A of coordinates x, y, and z (Fig. 3.15). Observing that

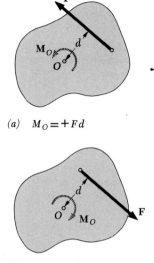

(*a*) $M_O = +Fd$

(*b*) $M_O = -Fd$

FIG. 3.13

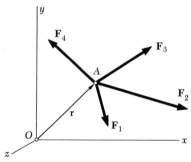

FIG. 3.14

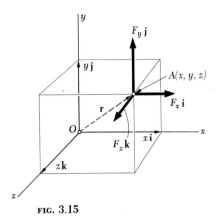

FIG. 3.15

the components of the position vector **r** are respectively equal to the coordinates x, y, and z of the point A, we write

$$\mathbf{r} = x\mathbf{i} + y\mathbf{j} + z\mathbf{k} \qquad (3.15)$$
$$\mathbf{F} = F_x\mathbf{i} + F_y\mathbf{j} + F_z\mathbf{k} \qquad (3.16)$$

Substituting for **r** and **F** from (3.15) and (3.16) into

$$\mathbf{M}_O = \mathbf{r} \times \mathbf{F} \qquad (3.11)$$

and recalling the results obtained in Sec. 3.4, we write the moment $\mathbf{M}_O$ of **F** about O in the form

$$\mathbf{M}_O = M_x\mathbf{i} + M_y\mathbf{j} + M_z\mathbf{k} \qquad (3.17)$$

where the components M_x, M_y, and M_z are defined by the relations

$$M_x = yF_z - zF_y$$
$$M_y = zF_x - xF_z \qquad (3.18)$$
$$M_z = xF_y - yF_x$$

As we shall see in Sec. 3.10, the scalar components M_x, M_y, and M_z of the moment $\mathbf{M}_O$ measure the tendency of the force **F** to impart to a rigid body a motion of rotation about the x, y, and z axes, respectively. Substituting from (3.18) into (3.17), we may also write $\mathbf{M}_O$ in the form of the determinant

$$\mathbf{M}_O = \begin{vmatrix} \mathbf{i} & \mathbf{j} & \mathbf{k} \\ x & y & z \\ F_x & F_y & F_z \end{vmatrix} \qquad (3.19)$$

In the case of *problems involving only two dimensions*, the force **F** may be assumed to lie in the xy plane (Fig. 3.16). Carrying $z = 0$ and $F_z = 0$ into the relations (3.19), we obtain

$$\mathbf{M}_O = (xF_y - yF_x)\mathbf{k}$$

We check that the moment of **F** about O is perpendicular to the plane of the figure and that it is completely defined by the scalar

$$M_O = M_z = xF_y - yF_x \qquad (3.20)$$

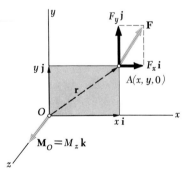

FIG. 3.16

As noted earlier, a positive value for M_O indicates that the vector $\mathbf{M}_O$ points out of the paper (the force **F** tends to rotate the body counterclockwise about O), and a negative value that the vector $\mathbf{M}_O$ points into the paper (the force **F** tends to rotate the body clockwise about O).

SAMPLE PROBLEM 3.1

A 100-lb vertical force is applied to the end of a lever which is attached to a shaft at O. Determine (a) the moment of the 100-lb force about O; (b) the magnitude of the horizontal force applied at A which creates the same moment about O; (c) the smallest force applied at A which creates the same moment about O; (d) how far from the shaft a 240-lb vertical force must act to create the same moment about O; (e) whether any one of the forces obtained in parts b, c, and d is equivalent to the original force.

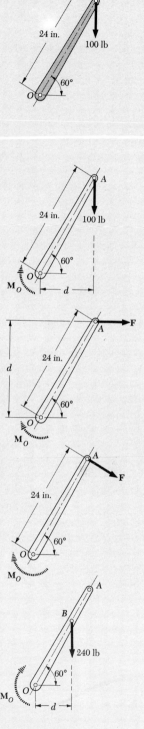

a. **Moment about O.** The perpendicular distance from O to the line of action of the 100-lb force is

$$d = (24 \text{ in.}) \cos 60° = 12 \text{ in.}$$

The magnitude of the moment about O of the 100-lb force is

$$M_O = Fd = (100 \text{ lb})(12 \text{ in.}) = 1{,}200 \text{ lb-in.}$$

Since the force tends to rotate the lever clockwise about O, the moment will be represented by a vector $\mathbf{M}_O$ perpendicular to the plane of the figure and pointing *into* the paper. We express this fact by writing

$$\mathbf{M}_O = 1{,}200 \text{ lb-in.} \ \ \text{◄}$$

b. **Horizontal Force.** In this case, we have

$$d = (24 \text{ in.}) \sin 60° = 20.8 \text{ in.}$$

Since the moment about O must be 1,200 lb-in., we write

$$M_O = Fd \qquad 1{,}200 \text{ lb-in.} = F(20.8 \text{ in.})$$
$$F = 57.8 \text{ lb} \qquad\qquad \mathbf{F} = 57.8 \text{ lb} \rightarrow \ \text{◄}$$

c. **Smallest Force.** Since $M_O = Fd$, the smallest value of $\mathbf{F}$ occurs when d is maximum. We choose the force perpendicular to OA and find $d = 24$ in.; thus

$$M_O = Fd \qquad 1{,}200 \text{ lb-in.} = F(24 \text{ in.})$$
$$F = 50 \text{ lb} \qquad\qquad \mathbf{F} = 50 \text{ lb} \ \text{↖} \ 30° \ \text{◄}$$

d. **240-lb Vertical Force.** In this case $M_O = Fd$ yields

$$1{,}200 \text{ lb-in.} = (240 \text{ lb})d \qquad d = 5 \text{ in.}$$

but $\qquad\qquad OB \cos 60° = d \qquad\qquad OB = 10 \text{ in.} \ \text{◄}$

e. None of the forces considered in parts b, c, and d is equivalent to the original 100-lb force. Although they have the same moment about O, they have different x and y components. In other words, although each force tends to rotate the shaft in the same manner, each causes the lever to pull on the shaft in a different way.

63

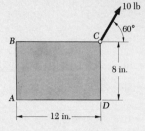

SAMPLE PROBLEM 3.2

A 10-lb force acts on the corner of a 12- by 8-in. plate as shown. Determine the moment $\mathbf{M}_A$ of the force about A.

Solution. The moment $\mathbf{M}_A$ is obtained by forming the vector product

$$\mathbf{M}_A = \mathbf{r} \times \mathbf{F}$$

Resolving the position vector $\mathbf{r}$ and the force $\mathbf{F}$ into rectangular components, we write

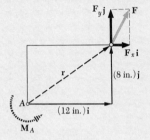

$$\mathbf{r} = \ xi + \ yj = (12 \text{ in.})\mathbf{i} + (8 \text{ in.})\mathbf{j}$$
$$\mathbf{F} = F_x\mathbf{i} + F_y\mathbf{j} = (10 \text{ lb}) \cos 60°\mathbf{i} + (10 \text{ lb}) \sin 60°\mathbf{j}$$
$$= (5 \text{ lb})\mathbf{i} + (8.66 \text{ lb})\mathbf{j}$$

Recalling the relations (3.7) for the cross products of unit vectors, we obtain

$$\mathbf{M}_A = \mathbf{r} \times \mathbf{F} = [(12 \text{ in.})\mathbf{i} + (8 \text{ in.})\mathbf{j}] \times [(5 \text{ lb})\mathbf{i} + (8.66 \text{ lb})\mathbf{j}]$$
$$= (104 \text{ lb-in.})\mathbf{k} - (40 \text{ lb-in.})\mathbf{k} = +(64 \text{ lb-in.})\mathbf{k}$$

The moment $\mathbf{M}_A$ is a vector perpendicular to the plane of the figure and pointing *out* of the paper.

$$\mathbf{M}_A = +(64 \text{ lb-in.})\mathbf{k} \qquad \mathbf{M}_A = 64 \text{ lb-in.} \ \rangle \ \blacktriangleleft$$

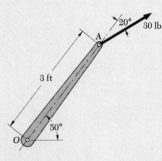

SAMPLE PROBLEM 3.3

A 30-lb force acts on the end of the 3-ft lever as shown. Determine the moment of the force about O.

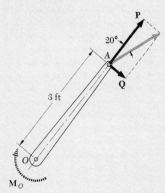

Solution. The force is replaced by two components, one component $\mathbf{P}$ in the direction of OA and one component $\mathbf{Q}$ perpendicular to OA. Since O is on the line of action of $\mathbf{P}$, the moment of $\mathbf{P}$ about O is zero and the moment of the 30-lb force reduces to the moment of $\mathbf{Q}$, which is clockwise and, thus, represented by a negative scalar.

$$Q = (30 \text{ lb}) \sin 20° = 10.26 \text{ lb}$$
$$M_O = -Q(3 \text{ ft}) = -(10.26 \text{ lb})(3 \text{ ft}) = -30.8 \text{ lb-ft} \ \blacktriangleleft$$

Since the value obtained for the scalar M_O is negative, the moment $\mathbf{M}_O$ points *into* the paper. We write

$$\mathbf{M}_O = 30.8 \text{ lb-ft} \ \rangle \ \blacktriangleleft$$

64

SAMPLE PROBLEM 3.4

A 6-ft pole AB is held by three guy wires as shown. Determine the moment about O of the force exerted by wire BE on point B. The tension in wire BE is known to be 210 lb.

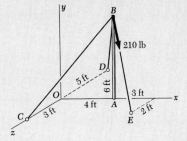

Solution. The moment $\mathbf{M}_O$ about O of the force exerted by wire BE on point B is obtained by forming the vector product

$$\mathbf{M}_O = \mathbf{r} \times \mathbf{F} \tag{1}$$

where $\mathbf{r}$ is the position vector of point B,

$$\mathbf{r} = (4 \text{ ft})\mathbf{i} + (6 \text{ ft})\mathbf{j} \tag{2}$$

and where $\mathbf{F}$ is the 210-lb force exerted by wire BE.

To determine the rectangular components of $\mathbf{F}$, we first compute the components and the magnitude of the vector $\overrightarrow{BE}$ which has the same direction as $\mathbf{F}$.

$$d_x = +3 \text{ ft} \qquad d_y = -6 \text{ ft} \qquad d_z = +2 \text{ ft} \qquad d = 7 \text{ ft}$$

Expressing that the components and the magnitudes of the force $\mathbf{F}$ and of the vector $\overrightarrow{BE}$ are proportional, we write

$$\frac{F_x}{+3 \text{ ft}} = \frac{F_y}{-6 \text{ ft}} = \frac{F_z}{+2 \text{ ft}} = \frac{210 \text{ lb}}{7 \text{ ft}}$$

$$F_x = +90 \text{ lb} \qquad F_y = -180 \text{ lb} \qquad F_z = +60 \text{ lb}$$

$$\mathbf{F} = F_x\mathbf{i} + F_y\mathbf{j} + F_z\mathbf{k} = (90 \text{ lb})\mathbf{i} - (180 \text{ lb})\mathbf{j} + (60 \text{ lb})\mathbf{k} \tag{3}$$

Substituting for $\mathbf{r}$ and $\mathbf{F}$ from (2) and (3) into (1), and recalling the relations (3.7), we obtain

$$\mathbf{M}_O = \mathbf{r} \times \mathbf{F} = (4\mathbf{i} + 6\mathbf{j}) \times (90\mathbf{i} - 180\mathbf{j} + 60\mathbf{k})$$
$$= (4)(-180)\mathbf{k} + (4)(60)(-\mathbf{j}) + (6)(90)(-\mathbf{k}) + (6)(60)\mathbf{i}$$
$$\mathbf{M}_O = 360\mathbf{i} - 240\mathbf{j} - 1{,}260\mathbf{k} \qquad \text{lb-ft} \quad \blacktriangleleft$$

Alternate Solution. As indicated in Sec. 3.7, the moment $\mathbf{M}_O$ may be expressed in the form of a determinant. Substituting for x, y, z the coordinates of point B and for F_x, F_y, F_z the values obtained above for the components of the 210-lb force, we have

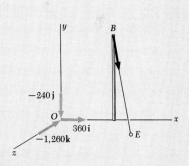

$$\mathbf{M}_O = \begin{vmatrix} \mathbf{i} & \mathbf{j} & \mathbf{k} \\ x & y & z \\ F_x & F_y & F_z \end{vmatrix} = \begin{vmatrix} \mathbf{i} & \mathbf{j} & \mathbf{k} \\ 4 & 6 & 0 \\ 90 & -180 & 60 \end{vmatrix}$$

$$\mathbf{M}_O = 360\mathbf{i} - 240\mathbf{j} - 1{,}260\mathbf{k} \qquad \text{lb-ft} \quad \blacktriangleleft$$

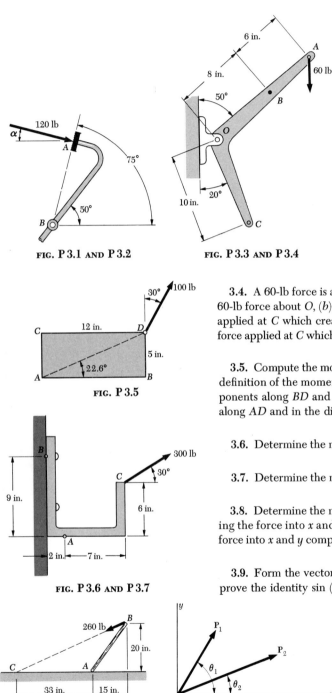

FIG. P 3.1 AND P 3.2

FIG. P 3.3 AND P 3.4

FIG. P 3.5

FIG. P 3.6 AND P 3.7

FIG. P 3.8

FIG. P 3.9

PROBLEMS

3.1. A 120-lb force is applied to the brake pedal at A. Knowing that the distance AB is 8 in., determine the moment of the force about B when α is $30°$.

3.2. Knowing that the distance AB is 8 in., determine the maximum moment about B which can be caused by the 120-lb force. In what direction should the force act?

3.3. A 60-lb force is applied at A as shown. Determine (*a*) the moment of the. 60-lb force about O, (*b*) the smallest force applied at B which creates the same moment about O.

3.4. A 60-lb force is applied at A. Determine (*a*) the moment of the 60-lb force about O, (*b*) the magnitude and sense of the horizontal force applied at C which creates the same moment about O, (*c*) the smallest force applied at C which creates the same moment about O.

3.5. Compute the moment of the 100-lb force about A (*a*) by using the definition of the moment of a force, (*b*) by resolving the force into components along BD and CD, (*c*) by resolving the force into components along AD and in the direction perpendicular to AD.

3.6. Determine the moment of the 300-lb force about A.

3.7. Determine the moment of the 300-lb force about B.

3.8. Determine the moment of the 260-lb force about A (*a*) by resolving the force into x and y components acting at B, (*b*) by resolving the force into x and y components acting at C.

3.9. Form the vector product $\mathbf{P}_1 \times \mathbf{P}_2$ and use the result obtained to prove the identity $\sin(\theta_1 - \theta_2) = \sin\theta_1 \cos\theta_2 - \cos\theta_1 \sin\theta_2$.

3.10. A force $\mathbf{F} = F_x\mathbf{i} + F_y\mathbf{j}$ acts at a point A of coordinates x_1 and y_1. Derive an expression for the moment of $\mathbf{F}$ about a second point B of coordinates x_2 and y_2.

3.11. The line of action of a force **P** passes through the two points $A(x_1, y_1)$ and $B(x_2, y_2)$. If the force is directed from A to B, determine the moment of the force about the origin.

3.12. A force $\mathbf{F} = F_x\mathbf{i} + F_y\mathbf{j}$ acts at a point of coordinates x and y. Derive an expression for the perpendicular distance d from the line of action of **F** to the origin O of the system of coordinates.

3.13. Determine the moment about the origin O of the force $\mathbf{F} = -2\mathbf{i} - 3\mathbf{j} + 5\mathbf{k}$ which acts at a point A. Assume that the position vector of A is $(a)\,\mathbf{r} = \mathbf{i} + \mathbf{j} + \mathbf{k}$, $(b)\,\mathbf{r} = 4\mathbf{i} + 6\mathbf{j} - 10\mathbf{k}$, $(c)\,\mathbf{r} = 4\mathbf{i} + 3\mathbf{j} - 5\mathbf{k}$.

3.14. Determine the moment about the origin O of the force $\mathbf{F} = 4\mathbf{i} + 10\mathbf{j} + 6\mathbf{k}$ which acts at a point A. Assume that the position vector of A is $(a)\,\mathbf{r} = 2\mathbf{i} - 3\mathbf{j} + 4\mathbf{k}$, $(b)\,\mathbf{r} = 2\mathbf{i} + 6\mathbf{j} + 3\mathbf{k}$, $(c)\,\mathbf{r} = 2\mathbf{i} + 5\mathbf{j} + 6\mathbf{k}$.

3.15. A precast-concrete wall section is temporarily held by cables as shown. Knowing that the tension in cable AB is 700 lb, determine the moment about the origin of coordinates O of the force exerted on the wall section at A.

3.16. Knowing that the tension in cable BC is 900 lb, determine the moment about the origin of coordinates O of the force exerted on the wall section at C.

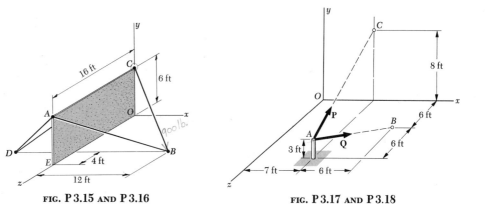

FIG. P 3.15 AND P 3.16   FIG. P 3.17 AND P 3.18

3.17. A force **P** of magnitude 260 lb is applied at point A as shown. Determine the rectangular components of the moment of **P** about the origin of coordinates O.

3.18. A force **Q** of magnitude 300 lb is applied at a point A as shown. Determine the rectangular components of the moment of **Q** about the origin of coordinates O.

3.19. A force **P** acts along the diagonal of a face of a rectangular box as shown. Determine the moment of **P** about the origin *O*.

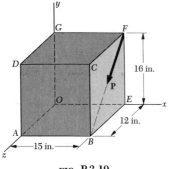

FIG. P 3.19

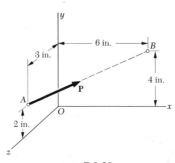

FIG. P 3.20

3.20. The line of action of the force **P** of magnitude 700 lb passes through the two points *A* and *B* as shown. Compute the moment of **P** about *O* using the position vector (*a*) of point *A*, (*b*) of point *B*.

3.21. In Prob. 3.19, determine the perpendicular distance from the line of action of **P** to the origin *O*.

3.22. In Prob. 3.20, determine the perpendicular distance from the line of action of **P** to the origin *O*.

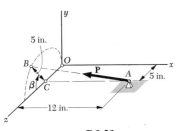

FIG. P 3.23

3.23. The line of action of the force **P** passes through points *A* and *B*. Knowing that the magnitude of **P** is 260 lb, determine the rectangular components of the moment of **P** about the origin *O* (*a*) in terms of β, (*b*) when $\beta = 60°$, (*c*) when $\beta = 120°$.

3.24. A single force **F** acts at a point *A* of coordinates $x = y = z = a$. Show that $M_x + M_y + M_z = 0$; i.e., show that the *algebraic* sum of the rectangular components of the moment of **F** about *O* is zero.

3.8. Scalar Product of Two Vectors. We shall now expand our knowledge of vector algebra and introduce the *scalar product* of two vectors.

The scalar product of two vectors **P** and **Q** is defined as the product of the magnitudes of **P** and **Q** and of the cosine of the angle θ formed by **P** and **Q** (Fig. 3.17). The scalar product of **P** and **Q** is denoted by **P** · **Q**. We write therefore

$$\mathbf{P} \cdot \mathbf{Q} = PQ \cos \theta \tag{3.21}$$

Note that the expression just defined is not a vector, but a *scalar,* which explains the name *scalar product;* because of the notation used, **P** · **Q** is also referred to as the *dot product* of the vectors **P** and **Q**.

FIG. 3.17

It follows from its very definition that the scalar product of two vectors is *commutative,* i.e., that

$$\mathbf{P} \cdot \mathbf{Q} = \mathbf{Q} \cdot \mathbf{P} \tag{3.22}$$

To prove that the scalar product is also *distributive,* we must prove the relation

$$\mathbf{P} \cdot (\mathbf{Q}_1 + \mathbf{Q}_2) = \mathbf{P} \cdot \mathbf{Q}_1 + \mathbf{P} \cdot \mathbf{Q}_2 \tag{3.23}$$

We may, without any loss of generality, assume that $\mathbf{P}$ is directed along the y axis (Fig. 3.18). Denoting by $\mathbf{Q}$ the sum of $\mathbf{Q}_1$ and $\mathbf{Q}_2$, and by θ_y the angle $\mathbf{Q}$ forms with the y axis, we express the left-hand member of (3.23) as follows:

$$\mathbf{P} \cdot (\mathbf{Q}_1 + \mathbf{Q}_2) = \mathbf{P} \cdot \mathbf{Q} = PQ \cos \theta_y = PQ_y \tag{3.24}$$

where Q_y is the y component of $\mathbf{Q}$. We may, in a similar way, express the right-hand member of (3.23) as

$$\mathbf{P} \cdot \mathbf{Q}_1 + \mathbf{P} \cdot \mathbf{Q}_2 = P(Q_1)_y + P(Q_2)_y \tag{3.25}$$

Since $\mathbf{Q}$ is the sum of $\mathbf{Q}_1$ and $\mathbf{Q}_2$, its y component must be equal to the sum of the y components of $\mathbf{Q}_1$ and $\mathbf{Q}_2$. Thus, the expressions obtained in (3.24) and (3.25) are equal and the relation (3.23) has been proved.

As far as the third property—the associative property—is concerned, we note that this property cannot apply to scalar products. Indeed, $(\mathbf{P} \cdot \mathbf{Q}) \cdot \mathbf{S}$ has no meaning, since $\mathbf{P} \cdot \mathbf{Q}$ is not a vector, but a scalar.

We shall now express the scalar product of two vectors $\mathbf{P}$ and $\mathbf{Q}$ in terms of their rectangular components. Resolving $\mathbf{P}$ and $\mathbf{Q}$ into components, we first write

$$\mathbf{P} \cdot \mathbf{Q} = (P_x \mathbf{i} + P_y \mathbf{j} + P_z \mathbf{k}) \cdot (Q_x \mathbf{i} + Q_y \mathbf{j} + Q_z \mathbf{k})$$

Making use of the distributive property, we express $\mathbf{P} \cdot \mathbf{Q}$ as the sum of scalar products such as $P_x \mathbf{i} \cdot Q_x \mathbf{i}$ and $P_x \mathbf{i} \cdot Q_y \mathbf{j}$. But we may easily check from the definition of the scalar product that the scalar products of the unit vectors are either zero or one.

$$\begin{array}{lll} \mathbf{i} \cdot \mathbf{i} = 1 & \mathbf{j} \cdot \mathbf{j} = 1 & \mathbf{k} \cdot \mathbf{k} = 1 \\ \mathbf{i} \cdot \mathbf{j} = 0 & \mathbf{j} \cdot \mathbf{k} = 0 & \mathbf{k} \cdot \mathbf{i} = 0 \end{array} \tag{3.26}$$

Thus, the expression obtained for $\mathbf{P} \cdot \mathbf{Q}$ reduces to

$$\mathbf{P} \cdot \mathbf{Q} = P_x Q_x + P_y Q_y + P_z Q_z \tag{3.27}$$

In the particular case when $\mathbf{P}$ and $\mathbf{Q}$ are equal, we check that

$$\mathbf{P} \cdot \mathbf{P} = P_x^2 + P_y^2 + P_z^2 = P^2 \tag{3.28}$$

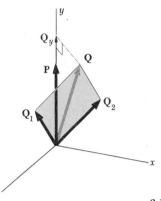

FIG. 3.18

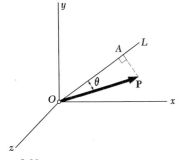

FIG. 3.19

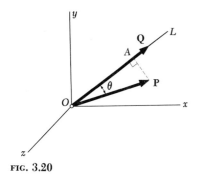

FIG. 3.20

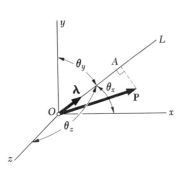

FIG. 3.21

Applications.   1. *Angle formed by two given vectors.*   Let two vectors be given in terms of their components.

$$\mathbf{P} = P_x\mathbf{i} + P_y\mathbf{j} + P_z\mathbf{k}$$
$$\mathbf{Q} = Q_x\mathbf{i} + Q_y\mathbf{j} + Q_z\mathbf{k}$$

To determine the angle formed by the two vectors we shall equate the expressions obtained in (3.21) and (3.27) for their scalar product:

$$PQ \cos \theta = P_xQ_x + P_yQ_y + P_zQ_z$$

Solving for $\cos \theta$, we write

$$\cos \theta = \frac{P_xQ_x + P_yQ_y + P_zQ_z}{PQ} \tag{3.29}$$

2. *Projection of a Vector on a Given Axis.*   Consider a vector $\mathbf{P}$ forming an angle θ with an axis, or directed line, OL (Fig. 3.19).   The *projection of* $\mathbf{P}$ *on the axis* OL is defined as the scalar

$$P_{OL} = P \cos \theta \tag{3.30}$$

We note that the projection P_{OL} is equal in absolute value to the length of the segment OA; it will be positive if OA has the same sense as the axis OL, i.e., if θ is acute, and negative otherwise.   If $\mathbf{P}$ and OL are at a right angle, the projection of $\mathbf{P}$ on OL is zero.

Consider now a vector $\mathbf{Q}$ directed along OL and of the same sense as OL (Fig. 3.20).   The scalar product of $\mathbf{P}$ and $\mathbf{Q}$ may be expressed as

$$\mathbf{P} \cdot \mathbf{Q} = PQ \cos \theta = P_{OL}Q \tag{3.31}$$

from which it follows that

$$P_{OL} = \frac{\mathbf{P} \cdot \mathbf{Q}}{Q} = \frac{P_xQ_x + P_yQ_y + P_zQ_z}{Q} \tag{3.32}$$

In the particular case when the vector selected along OL is the unit vector $\boldsymbol{\lambda}$ (Fig. 3.21), we write

$$P_{OL} = \mathbf{P} \cdot \boldsymbol{\lambda} \tag{3.33}$$

Resolving $\mathbf{P}$ and $\boldsymbol{\lambda}$ into rectangular components, and recalling from Sec. 2.11 that the components of $\boldsymbol{\lambda}$ along the coordinate axes are respectively equal to the direction cosines of OL, we express the projection of $\mathbf{P}$ on OL as

$$P_{OL} = P_x \cos \theta_x + P_y \cos \theta_y + P_z \cos \theta_z \tag{3.34}$$

where θ_x, θ_y, and θ_z denote the angles that the axis OL forms with the coordinate axes.

3.9. Mixed Triple Product of Three Vectors. We define the *mixed triple product* of the three vectors **S**, **P**, and **Q** as the scalar expression

$$\mathbf{S} \cdot (\mathbf{P} \times \mathbf{Q}) \qquad (3.35)$$

obtained by forming the scalar product of **S** with the vector product of **P** and **Q**.†

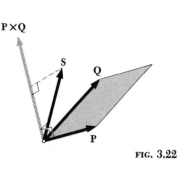

A simple geometrical interpretation may be given for the mixed triple product of **S**, **P**, and **Q** (Fig. 3.22). We first recall from Sec. 3.3 that the vector **P** × **Q** is perpendicular to the plane containing **P** and **Q**, and that its magnitude is equal to the area of the parallelogram constructed on **P** and **Q**. On the other hand, Eq. (3.31) indicates that the scalar product of **S** and **P** × **Q** may be obtained by multiplying the magnitude of **P** × **Q** (i.e., the area of the parallelogram built on **P** and **Q**) by the projection of **S** on the vector **P** × **Q** (i.e., by the projection of **S** on the normal to the plane containing the parallelogram). The mixed triple product is thus equal, in absolute value, to the volume of the parallelepiped having the vectors **S**, **P**, and **Q** for sides (Fig. 3.23). We may check that the sign of the mixed triple product will be positive if **S**, **P**, and **Q** form a right-handed triad, and negative if they form a left-handed triad [i.e., **S** · (**P** × **Q**) will be negative if the rotation which brings **P** into line with **Q** is observed as clockwise from the tip of **S**]. The mixed triple product will be zero if **S**, **P**, and **Q** are coplanar.

FIG. 3.22

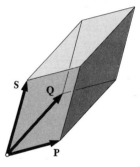

FIG. 3.23

Since the parallelepiped defined in the preceding paragraph is independent of the order in which the three vectors are taken, the six mixed triple products which may be formed with **S**, **P**, and **Q** will all have the same absolute value, although not the same sign. We check that

$$\mathbf{S} \cdot (\mathbf{P} \times \mathbf{Q}) = \mathbf{P} \cdot (\mathbf{Q} \times \mathbf{S}) = \mathbf{Q} \cdot (\mathbf{S} \times \mathbf{P})$$
$$= -\mathbf{S} \cdot (\mathbf{Q} \times \mathbf{P}) = -\mathbf{P} \cdot (\mathbf{S} \times \mathbf{Q}) = -\mathbf{Q} \cdot (\mathbf{P} \times \mathbf{S}) \qquad (3.36)$$

Arranging in a circle and in counterclockwise order the letters representing the three vectors (Fig. 3.24), we note that the sign of the mixed triple product is conserved if the vectors are permuted in such a way that they are still read in counterclockwise order. Such a permutation is said to be a *circular permutation*. It also follows from (3.36) that the mixed triple product of **S**, **P**, and **Q** may be defined equally well as **S** · (**P** × **Q**) or (**S** × **P**) · **Q**.

FIG. 3.24

---

† Another kind of triple product will be introduced later (Chap. 15): the *vector triple product* **S** × (**P** × **Q**).

We shall now express the mixed triple product of the vectors **S**, **P**, and **Q** in terms of the rectangular components of these vectors. Denoting **P** × **Q** by **V**, and using formula (3.27) to express the scalar product of **S** and **V**, we write

$$\mathbf{S} \cdot (\mathbf{P} \times \mathbf{Q}) = \mathbf{S} \cdot \mathbf{V} = S_x V_x + S_y V_y + S_z V_z$$

Substituting from the relations (3.9) for the components of **V**, we obtain

$$\mathbf{S} \cdot (\mathbf{P} \times \mathbf{Q}) = S_x(P_y Q_z - P_z Q_y) + S_y(P_z Q_x - P_x Q_z) \\ + S_z(P_x Q_y - P_y Q_x) \quad (3.37)$$

This expression may be written in a more compact form if we observe that it represents the expansion of a determinant:

$$\mathbf{S} \cdot (\mathbf{P} \times \mathbf{Q}) = \begin{vmatrix} S_x & S_y & S_z \\ P_x & P_y & P_z \\ Q_x & Q_y & Q_z \end{vmatrix} \quad (3.38)$$

By applying the rules governing the permutation of rows in a determinant, we could easily verify the relations (3.36) which were derived earlier from geometrical considerations.

3.10. Moment of a Force about a Given Axis. Now that we have further increased our knowledge of vector algebra, we shall introduce a new concept, the concept of *moment of a force about an axis.* Consider again a force **F** acting on a rigid body and the moment **M**$_O$ of that force about O (Fig. 3.25). Let OL be an axis through O; *we define the moment M_{OL} of **F** about OL as the projection OC of the moment **M**$_O$ on the axis OL.* Denoting by **λ** the unit vector along OL, and recalling the expressions (3.33) and (3.11) obtained earlier for the projection of a vector on a given axis and for the moment **M**$_O$ of a force **F**, we write

$$M_{OL} = \boldsymbol{\lambda} \cdot \mathbf{M}_O = \boldsymbol{\lambda} \cdot (\mathbf{r} \times \mathbf{F}) \quad (3.39)$$

which shows that the moment M_{OL} of **F** about the axis OL is the scalar obtained by forming the mixed triple product of **λ**, **r**, and **F**. Expressing M_{OL} in the form of a determinant, we write

$$M_{OL} = \begin{vmatrix} \lambda_x & \lambda_y & \lambda_z \\ x & y & z \\ F_x & F_y & F_z \end{vmatrix} \quad (3.40)$$

where $\lambda_x, \lambda_y, \lambda_z$ = direction cosines of axis OL
x, y, z = coordinates of point of application of **F**
F_x, F_y, F_z = components of force **F**

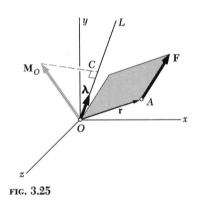

FIG. 3.25

The physical significance of the moment M_{OL} of a force $\mathbf{F}$ about a fixed axis OL becomes more apparent if we resolve $\mathbf{F}$ into two rectangular components $\mathbf{F}_1$ and $\mathbf{F}_2$, with $\mathbf{F}_1$ parallel to OL and $\mathbf{F}_2$ lying in a plane P perpendicular to OL (Fig. 3.26). Resolving $\mathbf{r}$ similarly into two components $\mathbf{r}_1$ and $\mathbf{r}_2$, and substituting for $\mathbf{F}$ and $\mathbf{r}$ into (3.39), we write

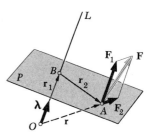

FIG. 3.26

$$M_{OL} = \boldsymbol{\lambda} \cdot [(\mathbf{r}_1 + \mathbf{r}_2) \times (\mathbf{F}_1 + \mathbf{F}_2)]$$
$$= \boldsymbol{\lambda} \cdot (\mathbf{r}_1 \times \mathbf{F}_1) + \boldsymbol{\lambda} \cdot (\mathbf{r}_1 \times \mathbf{F}_2) + \boldsymbol{\lambda} \cdot (\mathbf{r}_2 \times \mathbf{F}_1) + \boldsymbol{\lambda} \cdot (\mathbf{r}_2 \times \mathbf{F}_2)$$

Noting that all mixed triple products, except the last one, involve coplanar vectors and, therefore, are equal to zero, we have†

$$M_{OL} = \boldsymbol{\lambda} \cdot (\mathbf{r}_2 \times \mathbf{F}_2) \tag{3.41}$$

The vector product $\mathbf{r}_2 \times \mathbf{F}_2$ is perpendicular to the plane P and represents the moment of the component $\mathbf{F}_2$ of $\mathbf{F}$ about the point B where OL intersects P.   Therefore, the scalar M_{OL}, which will be positive if $\mathbf{r}_2 \times \mathbf{F}_2$ and OL have the same sense, and negative otherwise, measures the tendency of $\mathbf{F}_2$ to make the rigid body rotate about the fixed axis OL.   Since the other component $\mathbf{F}_1$ of $\mathbf{F}$ does not tend to make the body rotate about OL, we conclude that *the moment M_{OL} of $\mathbf{F}$ about OL measures the tendency of the force $\mathbf{F}$ to impart to the rigid body a motion of rotation about the fixed axis OL.*

It follows from the definition of the moment of a force about an axis that the moment of $\mathbf{F}$ about a coordinate axis is equal to the component of $\mathbf{M}_O$ along that axis.   Substituting successively each of the unit vectors $\mathbf{i}$, $\mathbf{j}$, and $\mathbf{k}$ for $\boldsymbol{\lambda}$ in (3.39), we check that the expressions thus obtained for the *moments of $\mathbf{F}$ about the coordinate axes* are respectively equal to the expressions obtained in Sec. 3.7 for the components of the moment $\mathbf{M}_O$ of $\mathbf{F}$ about O.

$$\begin{aligned} M_x &= yF_z - zF_y \\ M_y &= zF_x - xF_z \\ M_z &= xF_y - yF_x \end{aligned} \tag{3.18}$$

We observe that, just as the components F_x, F_y, and F_z of a force $\mathbf{F}$ acting on a rigid body measure, respectively, the tendency of $\mathbf{F}$ to move the rigid body in the x, y, and z directions, the moments M_x, M_y, and M_z of $\mathbf{F}$ about the coordinate axes measure the tendency of $\mathbf{F}$ to impart to the rigid body a motion of rotation about the x, y, and z axes, respectively.

† Note that, since the expression (3.41) obtained for M_{OL} does not contain the vector $\mathbf{r}_1$, it is clear that the value of M_{OL} is independent of the choice of the point O used in the original definition of the moment M_{OL}.

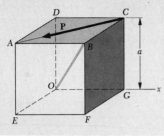

SAMPLE PROBLEM 3.5

A cube of side a is acted upon by a force $\mathbf{P}$ as shown. Determine the moment of $\mathbf{P}$ (a) about O, (b) about the x axis, (c) about the diagonal OB of the cube. (d) Using the result of part c, determine the perpendicular distance from OB to AC.

a. **Moment about O.** Choosing x, y, and z axes as shown, we resolve the force $\mathbf{P}$ and the position vector $\mathbf{r}$ of its point of application into rectangular components.

$$\mathbf{r} = a\mathbf{i} + a\mathbf{j} = a(\mathbf{i} + \mathbf{j})$$
$$\mathbf{P} = -(P/\sqrt{2})\mathbf{i} + (P/\sqrt{2})\mathbf{k} = (P/\sqrt{2})(-\mathbf{i} + \mathbf{k})$$

The moment of $\mathbf{P}$ about O is

$$\mathbf{M}_O = \mathbf{r} \times \mathbf{P} = a(\mathbf{i} + \mathbf{j}) \times (P/\sqrt{2})(-\mathbf{i} + \mathbf{k})$$
$$\mathbf{M}_O = (aP/\sqrt{2})(\mathbf{i} - \mathbf{j} + \mathbf{k}) \quad \blacktriangleleft$$

b. **Moment about x axis.** Projecting $\mathbf{M}_O$ on the x axis, we write

$$M_x = \mathbf{i} \cdot \mathbf{M}_O = \mathbf{i} \cdot (aP/\sqrt{2})(\mathbf{i} - \mathbf{j} + \mathbf{k})$$
$$M_x = aP/\sqrt{2} \quad \blacktriangleleft$$

We verify that M_x is also the x component of the moment $\mathbf{M}_O$.

c. **Moment about Diagonal OB.** The moment of $\mathbf{P}$ about OB is obtained by projecting $\mathbf{M}_O$ on OB. Denoting by $\boldsymbol{\lambda}$ the unit vector along OB, we note that

$$\boldsymbol{\lambda} = \frac{\overrightarrow{OB}}{OB} = \frac{a\mathbf{i} + a\mathbf{j} + a\mathbf{k}}{a\sqrt{3}} = (1/\sqrt{3})(\mathbf{i} + \mathbf{j} + \mathbf{k})$$

and write

$$M_{OB} = \boldsymbol{\lambda} \cdot \mathbf{M}_O = (1/\sqrt{3})(\mathbf{i} + \mathbf{j} + \mathbf{k}) \cdot (aP/\sqrt{2})(\mathbf{i} - \mathbf{j} + \mathbf{k})$$
$$M_{OB} = (aP/\sqrt{6})(1 - 1 + 1) \qquad M_{OB} = aP/\sqrt{6} \quad \blacktriangleleft$$

Alternate Method. The moment of $\mathbf{P}$ about OB may also be expressed in the form of a determinant:

$$M_{OB} = \begin{vmatrix} \lambda_x & \lambda_y & \lambda_z \\ x & y & z \\ F_x & F_y & F_z \end{vmatrix} = \begin{vmatrix} 1/\sqrt{3} & 1/\sqrt{3} & 1/\sqrt{3} \\ a & a & 0 \\ -P/\sqrt{2} & 0 & P/\sqrt{2} \end{vmatrix} = aP/\sqrt{6}$$

d. **Perpendicular Distance from OB to AC.** We first observe that $\mathbf{P}$ is perpendicular to the diagonal OB. This may be checked by forming the scalar product of $\mathbf{P}$ and $\boldsymbol{\lambda}$ and verifying that it reduces to zero:

$$\mathbf{P} \cdot \boldsymbol{\lambda} = (P/\sqrt{2})(-\mathbf{i} + \mathbf{k}) \cdot (1/\sqrt{3})(\mathbf{i} + \mathbf{j} + \mathbf{k}) = (P/\sqrt{6})(-1 + 0 + 1) = 0$$

The moment M_{OB} may then be expressed as the product of P and the perpendicular distance d from OB to AC. Using the value of M_{OB} found in part c, we write

$$aP/\sqrt{6} = Pd \qquad d = a/\sqrt{6} \quad \blacktriangleleft$$

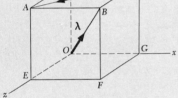

74

PROBLEMS

3.25. Given the vectors $\mathbf{P} = 2\mathbf{i} + \mathbf{j} + 2\mathbf{k}$, $\mathbf{Q} = 3\mathbf{i} + 4\mathbf{j} - 5\mathbf{k}$, and $\mathbf{S} = -4\mathbf{i} + \mathbf{j} - 2\mathbf{k}$, compute the scalar products $\mathbf{P} \cdot \mathbf{Q}$, $\mathbf{P} \cdot \mathbf{S}$, and $\mathbf{Q} \cdot \mathbf{S}$.

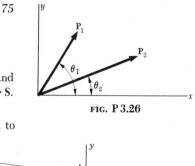

FIG. P 3.26

3.26. Form the scalar product $\mathbf{P}_1 \cdot \mathbf{P}_2$ and use the result obtained to prove the identity $\cos(\theta_1 - \theta_2) = \cos\theta_1 \cos\theta_2 + \sin\theta_1 \sin\theta_2$.

3.27. Several cables are attached to the top of the tower at A.   Determine the angle formed by cables AB and AC.

3.28. Determine the angle formed by cables AD and AB.

3.29. A force $\mathbf{P}$ of magnitude 420 lb is directed along the line AB from point A to point B.   Determine the projection of $\mathbf{P}$ on the line AC.

3.30. A force $\mathbf{Q}$ of magnitude 420 lb is directed along line AC from point A to point C.   Determine the projection of $\mathbf{Q}$ on line AB.

3.31. Knowing that the tension in cable AB is 210 lb, determine (*a*) the angle formed by AB and AC, (*b*) the projection on AC of the force exerted by cable AB at point A.

3.32. Knowing that the tension in cable AB is 210 lb, determine (*a*) the angle between cable AB and a line joining points B and C, (*b*) the projection on that line of the force exerted by cable AB at point B.

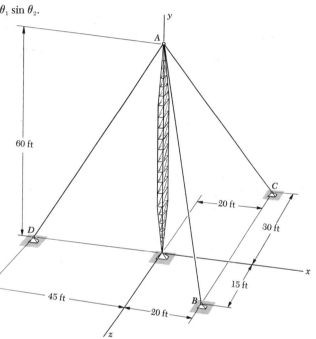

FIG. P 3.27 AND P 3.28

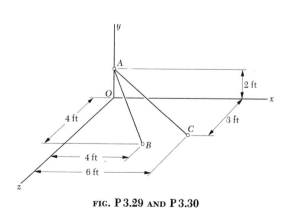

FIG. P 3.29 AND P 3.30

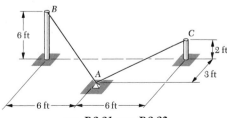

FIG. P 3.31 AND P 3.32

3.33. Given the vectors $\mathbf{P} = \mathbf{i} + \mathbf{j} + \mathbf{k}$, $\mathbf{Q} = \mathbf{i} + \mathbf{j}$, and $\mathbf{S} = \mathbf{i}$, compute $\mathbf{P} \cdot (\mathbf{Q} \times \mathbf{S})$, $(\mathbf{P} \times \mathbf{Q}) \cdot \mathbf{S}$, and $(\mathbf{S} \times \mathbf{Q}) \cdot \mathbf{P}$.

3.34. Given the vectors $\mathbf{P} = \mathbf{i} + 2\mathbf{j} + 3\mathbf{k}$, $\mathbf{Q} = 2\mathbf{i} - \mathbf{j} - 5\mathbf{k}$, and $\mathbf{S} = S_x\mathbf{i} + 3\mathbf{j} + \mathbf{k}$, determine the value of S_x for which the three vectors are coplanar.

3.35. A crane is oriented so that the end of the 50-ft boom AO lies in the yz plane. At the instant shown the tension in cable AB is 1,000 lb. Determine the moment about each of the coordinate axes of the force exerted on A by the cable AB.

3.36. The 50-ft crane boom AO lies in the yz plane. Determine the maximum permissible tension in the cable AB if the absolute value of the moments about the coordinate axes of the force exerted on A must be as follows: $M_x \leqslant 40{,}000$ lb-ft, $M_y \leqslant 8{,}000$ lb-ft, $M_z \leqslant 9{,}000$ lb-ft.

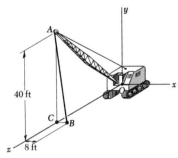

FIG. P 3.35 AND P 3.36

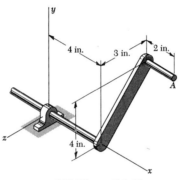

FIG. P 3.37 AND P 3.38

3.37. A single force $\mathbf{F}$ of unknown magnitude and direction acts at point A of the crank shown. Determine the moment M_x of $\mathbf{F}$ about the x axis, knowing that $M_y = +90$ lb-in. and $M_z = -220$ lb-in.

3.38. The primary purpose of the crank shown is, of course, to produce a moment about the x axis. Show that a single force acting at A and having a moment M_x different from zero about the x axis must also have a moment different from zero about at least one of the other coordinate axes.

3.39. A force $\mathbf{P}$ of magnitude 50 lb acts along the diagonal of a face of a rectangular box as shown. Determine the moment of $\mathbf{P}$ about (a) a line joining corners G and C, (b) a line joining corners O and C.

3.40. A force $\mathbf{P}$ of magnitude 50 lb acts along the diagonal of a face of a rectangular box as shown. Determine the moment of $\mathbf{P}$ about (a) a line joining corners A and C, (b) a line joining corners D and E.

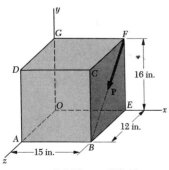

FIG. P 3.39 AND P 3.40

3.41. An irregular pyramid is acted upon by a force **P** of magnitude 75 lb as shown. Determine the moment of **P** about (*a*) edge *AD*, (*b*) edge *AB*, (*c*) edge *AC*.

3.42. Solve Prob. 3.41 assuming that the force **P** is replaced by the force **Q** = 50**i** + 25**j** + 50**k** acting at point *D*.

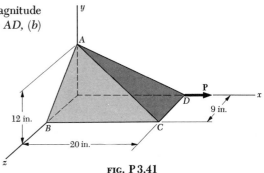

FIG. P 3.41

3.43. A 5- by 12-ft rectangular plate has one edge located along the *x* axis as shown. A force **P** of magnitude 1,400 lb is applied to the plate at *C*. Determine the moment of **P** about (*a*) edge *OA*, (*b*) the diagonal *OB*.

3.44. A 5- by 12-ft rectangular plate has one edge located along the *x* axis as shown. A force **P** of magnitude 1,400 lb is applied to the plate at *C*. Determine the moment of **P** about (*a*) the *y* axis, (*b*) the diagonal *DA*.

3.45. A regular tetrahedron has six edges each of length *a*. A single force **P** is directed along one edge. Determine the moment of **P** about each of the other five edges.

3.46. Two forces **F**₁ and **F**₂ in space have the same magnitude *F*. Prove that the moment of **F**₁ about the line of action of **F**₂ is equal to the moment of **F**₂ about the line of action of **F**₁.

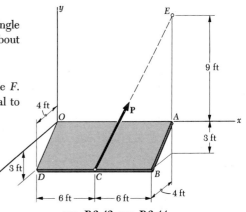

FIG. P 3.43 AND P 3.44

°3.47. In Prob. 3.39, use the result obtained in part *b* to determine the perpendicular distance between the lines *OC* and *BF*.

°3.48. In Prob. 3.40, use the result obtained in part *b* to determine the perpendicular distance between the lines *DE* and *BF*.

3.11. Moment of a Couple. *Two forces* **F** *and* −**F**, *having the same magnitude, parallel lines of action, and opposite sense are said to form a couple* (Fig. 3.27).   Clearly, the sum of the components of the two forces in any direction is zero. The sum of the moments of the two forces about a given point, however, is not zero.   While the two forces will not translate the body on which they act, they will tend to make it rotate.
    Denoting by **r**_A and **r**_B, respectively, the position vectors of

FIG. 3.27

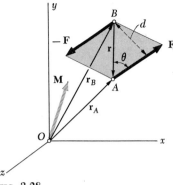

FIG. 3.28

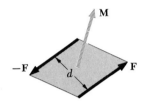

FIG. 3.29

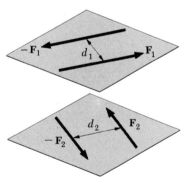

FIG. 3.30

the points of application of **F** and $-$**F** (Fig. 3.28), we find that the sum of the moments of the two forces about O is

$$\mathbf{r}_A \times \mathbf{F} + \mathbf{r}_B \times (-\mathbf{F}) = (\mathbf{r}_A - \mathbf{r}_B) \times \mathbf{F}$$

Setting $\mathbf{r}_A - \mathbf{r}_B = \mathbf{r}$, where **r** is the vector joining the points of application of the two forces, we conclude that the sum of the moments of **F** and $-$**F** about O is represented by the vector

$$\mathbf{M} = \mathbf{r} \times \mathbf{F} \tag{3.42}$$

The vector **M** is called the *moment of the couple;* it is a vector perpendicular to the plane containing the two forces and its magnitude is

$$M = rF \sin \theta = Fd \tag{3.43}$$

where d is the perpendicular distance between the lines of action of **F** and $-$**F**.   The sense of **M** is defined by the right-hand rule.

Since the vector **r** in (3.42) is independent of the choice of the origin O of the coordinate axes, we note that the same result would have been obtained if the moments of **F** and $-$**F** had been computed about a different point O'.   Thus, the moment **M** of a couple is a *free vector* (Sec. 2.2) which may be applied at any point (Fig. 3.29).

From the definition of the moment of a couple, it also follows that two couples, one consisting of the forces $\mathbf{F}_1$ and $-\mathbf{F}_1$, the other of the forces $\mathbf{F}_2$ and $-\mathbf{F}_2$ (Fig. 3.30), will have equal moments if

$$F_1 d_1 = F_2 d_2 \tag{3.44}$$

and if the two couples lie in parallel planes (or in the same plane) and have the same sense.

3.12. Equivalent Couples.   Consider the three couples shown in Fig. 3.31, which are made to act successively on the same rectangular box.   As seen in the preceding section, the only motion a couple may impart to a rigid body is a rotation. Since each of the three couples shown has the same moment **M** (same direction and same magnitude $M = 120$ lb-in.), we may expect the three couples to have the same effect on the box.

As reasonable as this conclusion may appear, we should not accept it hastily.   While intuitive feeling is of great help in the study of mechanics, it should not be accepted as a substitute for logical reasoning.   Before stating that two systems (or groups) of forces have the same effect on a rigid body, we should prove that fact on the basis of the experimental evidence introduced so far. This evidence consists of the parallelogram law for the addition of two forces (Sec. 2.1) and of the principle of transmissibility (Sec. 3.2). Therefore, we shall state that *two systems of forces are equivalent* (i.e., they have the same effect on a rigid body) *if we can transform one of them into the other by means of one or several of the following operations:* (1) replacing two forces acting on the same particle by their resultant; (2) resolving a force into two components; (3) canceling two equal and opposite forces acting on the same particle; (4) attaching to the same particle two equal and opposite forces; (5) moving a force along its line of action. Each of these operations is easily justified on the basis of the parallelogram law or the principle of transmissibility.

Let us now prove that *two couples having the same moment* **M** *are equivalent*. First, we shall consider two couples contained in the same plane, and we shall assume that this plane coincides with the plane of the figure (Fig. 3.32). The first couple consists of the forces $\mathbf{F}_1$ and $-\mathbf{F}_1$, of magnitude F_1 and at a distance d_1 from each other (Fig. 3.32a), and the second couple of the forces $\mathbf{F}_2$ and $-\mathbf{F}_2$, of magnitude F_2 and at a distance d_2 from each other (Fig. 3.32d). Since the two couples have the same moment **M** perpendicular to the plane of the figure, they must have the same sense (assumed here counterclockwise) and the relation

$$F_1 d_1 = F_2 d_2 \qquad (3.44)$$

must be satisfied. To prove that they are equivalent, we shall show that the first couple may be transformed into the second by means of the operations listed above.

Denoting by *A, B, C, D* the points of intersection of the lines of action of the two couples, we first slide the forces $\mathbf{F}_1$ and $-\mathbf{F}_1$ until they are attached, respectively, at *A* and *B*, as shown in Fig. 3.32b. The force $\mathbf{F}_1$ is then resolved into a component **P** along line *AB* and a component **Q** along *AC* (Fig. 3.32c); similarly, the force $-\mathbf{F}_1$ is resolved into $-\mathbf{P}$ along *AB* and $-\mathbf{Q}$ along *BD*. The forces **P** and $-\mathbf{P}$ have the same magnitude, same line of action, and opposite sense; they may be moved along their common line of action until they are applied at the

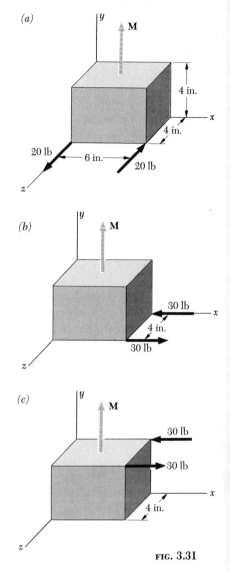

(a)

(b)

(c)

FIG. 3.31

FIG. 3.32

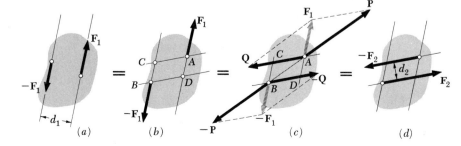

(a)　(b)　(c)　(d)

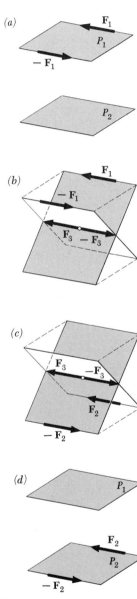

(a)

(b)

(c)

(d)

FIG. 3.33

same point and then canceled. Thus the couple formed by $\mathbf{F}_1$ and $-\mathbf{F}_1$ reduces to a couple consisting of $\mathbf{Q}$ and $-\mathbf{Q}$.

We shall now show that the forces $\mathbf{Q}$ and $-\mathbf{Q}$ are respectively equal to the forces $-\mathbf{F}_2$ and $\mathbf{F}_2$. The moment of the couple formed by $\mathbf{Q}$ and $-\mathbf{Q}$ may be obtained by computing the moment of $\mathbf{Q}$ about B; similarly, the moment of the couple formed by $\mathbf{F}_1$ and $-\mathbf{F}_1$ is the moment of $\mathbf{F}_1$ about B. But, by Varignon's theorem, the moment of $\mathbf{F}_1$ is equal to the sum of the moments of its components $\mathbf{P}$ and $\mathbf{Q}$. Since the moment of $\mathbf{P}$ about B is zero, the moment of the couple formed by $\mathbf{Q}$ and $-\mathbf{Q}$ must be equal to the moment of the couple formed by $\mathbf{F}_1$ and $-\mathbf{F}_1$. Recalling (3.44), we write

$$Qd_2 = F_1d_1 = F_2d_2 \qquad \text{and} \qquad Q = F_2$$

Thus the forces $\mathbf{Q}$ and $-\mathbf{Q}$ are respectively equal to the forces $-\mathbf{F}_2$ and $\mathbf{F}_2$, and the couple of Fig. 3.32a is equivalent to the couple of Fig. 3.32d.

Next we shall consider two couples contained in parallel planes P_1 and P_2 and prove that they are equivalent if they have the same moment. In view of the foregoing we may assume that the couples consist of forces of the same magnitude F acting along parallel lines (Fig. 3.33a and d). We propose to show that the couple contained in plane P_1 may be transformed into the couple contained in plane P_2 by means of the standard operations listed above.

Let us consider the two planes defined respectively by the lines of action of $\mathbf{F}_1$ and $-\mathbf{F}_2$, and of $-\mathbf{F}_1$ and $\mathbf{F}_2$ (Fig. 3.33b). At a point on their line of intersection we attach two forces $\mathbf{F}_3$ and $-\mathbf{F}_3$, respectively equal to $\mathbf{F}_1$ and $-\mathbf{F}_1$. The couple formed by $\mathbf{F}_1$ and $-\mathbf{F}_3$ may be replaced by a couple consisting of $\mathbf{F}_3$ and $-\mathbf{F}_2$ (Fig. 3.33c), since both couples have clearly the same moment and are contained in the same plane. Similarly, the couple formed by $-\mathbf{F}_1$ and $\mathbf{F}_3$ may be replaced by a couple consisting of $-\mathbf{F}_3$ and $\mathbf{F}_2$. Canceling the two equal and opposite forces $\mathbf{F}_3$ and $-\mathbf{F}_3$, we obtain the desired couple in plane P_2 (Fig. 3.33d). Thus, we conclude that two couples having the same moment $\mathbf{M}$ are equivalent, whether they are contained in the same plane or in parallel planes.

The property we have just established is very important for the correct understanding of the mechanics of rigid bodies. It indicates that, when a couple acts on a rigid body, it does not matter where the two forces forming the couple act, or what magnitude and direction they have. The only thing which counts is the *moment* of the couple (magnitude and direction).

Couples with the same moment will have the same effect on the rigid body.

3.13. Couples May Be Represented by Vectors. Since couples which have the same moment are equivalent, there is no need to draw the actual forces forming a given couple in order to define its effect on a rigid body (Fig. 3.34*a*). It is suf-

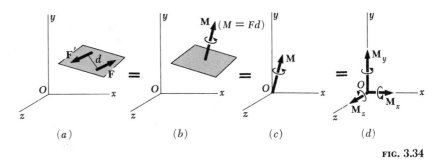

$$(a) \qquad (b) \qquad (c) \qquad (d)$$

FIG. 3.34

ficient to draw a vector equal in magnitude and direction to the moment **M** of the couple (Fig. 3.34*b*); this vector is called a *couple vector*. Note that a solid arrow is used to distinguish the couple vector, *which represents the couple itself,* from the vector representing the *moment* of the couple, and that the symbol ↄ is added to avoid any confusion with vectors representing forces. A couple vector, like the moment of a couple, is a free vector. Its point of application, therefore, may be chosen at the origin of the system of coordinates, if so desired (Fig. 3.34*c*). Furthermore, the couple vector **M** may be resolved into component vectors $\mathbf{M}_x$, $\mathbf{M}_y$, and $\mathbf{M}_z$, directed along the axes of coordinates (Fig. 3.34*d*) and representing couples acting, respectively, in the *yz, zx,* and *xy* planes.

The representation of a couple by means of a vector is convenient. This representation, however, should be *justified,* i.e., we should show that the arrows used to represent couples possess the characteristics of vectors (see Sec. 2.2); more specifically, we should prove that they obey the parallelogram law of addition.

Consider two intersecting planes P_1 and P_2 and two couples acting respectively in P_1 and P_2. We may, without any loss of generality, assume that the couple in P_1 consists of two forces $\mathbf{F}_1$ and $-\mathbf{F}_1$ perpendicular to the line of intersection of the two planes and acting respectively at A and B (Fig. 3.35*a*). Similarly, we assume that the couple in P_2 consists of two forces $\mathbf{F}_2$ and $-\mathbf{F}_2$ perpendicular to AB and acting respectively at A and B. It is clear that the resultant **R** of $\mathbf{F}_1$ and $\mathbf{F}_2$ and the resultant

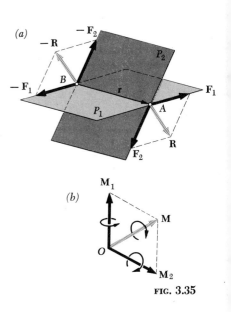

FIG. 3.35

$-\mathbf{R}$ of $-\mathbf{F}_1$ and $-\mathbf{F}_2$ form a couple.   Denoting by $\mathbf{r}$ the vector joining B to A, and recalling the definition of the moment of a couple (Sec. 3.11), we express the moment $\mathbf{M}$ of the resulting couple as follows:

$$\mathbf{M} = \mathbf{r} \times \mathbf{R} = \mathbf{r} \times (\mathbf{F}_1 + \mathbf{F}_2)$$

and, by Varignon's theorem,

$$\mathbf{M} = \mathbf{r} \times \mathbf{F}_1 + \mathbf{r} \times \mathbf{F}_2$$

But the first term in the expression obtained represents the moment $\mathbf{M}_1$ of the couple in P_1, and the second term the moment $\mathbf{M}_2$ of the couple in P_2.   We have

$$\mathbf{M} = \mathbf{M}_1 + \mathbf{M}_2 \tag{3.45}$$

and we conclude that the sum of two couples of moments $\mathbf{M}_1$ and $\mathbf{M}_2$ is a couple of moment $\mathbf{M}$ equal to the vector sum of $\mathbf{M}_1$ and $\mathbf{M}_2$.   Clearly, the same relation holds between the corresponding couple vectors; thus, couple vectors obey the parallelogram law of addition (Fig. 3.35b).

Summarizing the results obtained in this section, we conclude that *a couple may be truly represented by a vector*.   This vector, called a couple vector, is equal to the moment of the couple; it is a *free vector* and may be applied at any point.   Couple vectors may be added or resolved according to the parallelogram law.

3.14. Resolution of a Given Force into a Force at O and a Couple.   Consider a force $\mathbf{F}$ acting on a rigid body at a point A defined by the position vector $\mathbf{r}$ (Fig. 3.36a).   Suppose that for some reason we would rather have the force act at point O. We know that we can move $\mathbf{F}$ along its line of action (principle of transmissibility); but we cannot move it to a point O away from the original line of action without modifying the action of $\mathbf{F}$ on the rigid body.

We may, however, attach two forces at point O, one equal to $\mathbf{F}$ and the other equal to $-\mathbf{F}$, without modifying the action of the original force on the rigid body (Fig. 3.36b).   As a result of this transformation, a force $\mathbf{F}$ is now applied at O; the other two

FIG. 3.36

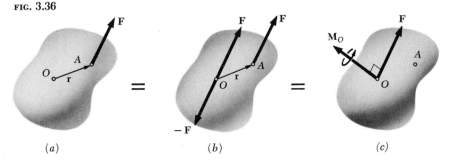

(a)   (b)   (c)

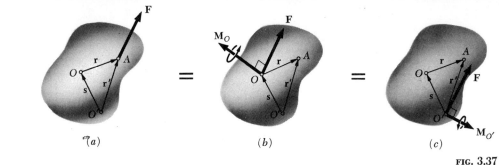

FIG. 3.37

forces form a couple of moment $\mathbf{M}_o = \mathbf{r} \times \mathbf{F}$. Thus, *any force F acting on a rigid body may be moved to an arbitrary point O, provided that a couple is added, of moment equal to the moment of F about O.* The couple tends to impart to the rigid body the same motion of rotation about O that the force $\mathbf{F}$ tended to produce before it was transferred to O. The couple is represented by a couple vector $\mathbf{M}_o$ perpendicular to the plane containing $\mathbf{r}$ and $\mathbf{F}$. Since $\mathbf{M}_o$ is a free vector, it may be applied anywhere; for convenience, however, the couple vector is usually attached at O, together with $\mathbf{F}$, and the combination obtained is referred to as a *force-couple system* (Fig. 3.36c).

If the force $\mathbf{F}$ had been moved from A to a different point O' (Fig. 3.37a and c), the moment $\mathbf{M}_{o'} = \mathbf{r}' \times \mathbf{F}$ of $\mathbf{F}$ about O' should have been computed, and a new force-couple system, consisting of $\mathbf{F}$ and of the couple vector $\mathbf{M}_{o'}$, would have been attached at O'. The relation existing between the moments of $\mathbf{F}$ about O and O' is obtained by writing

$$\mathbf{M}_{o'} = \mathbf{r}' \times \mathbf{F} = (\mathbf{r} + \mathbf{s}) \times \mathbf{F} = \mathbf{r} \times \mathbf{F} + \mathbf{s} \times \mathbf{F}$$
$$\mathbf{M}_{o'} = \mathbf{M}_o + \mathbf{s} \times \mathbf{F} \qquad (3.46)$$

where s is the vector joining O' to O. Thus, the moment $\mathbf{M}_{o'}$ of $\mathbf{F}$ about O' is obtained by adding to the moment $\mathbf{M}_o$ of $\mathbf{F}$ about O the vector product $\mathbf{s} \times \mathbf{F}$ representing the moment about O' of the force $\mathbf{F}$ applied at O.

This result could also have been established by observing that, in order to transfer to O' the force-couple system attached at O (Fig. 3.37b and c), the couple vector $\mathbf{M}_o$ may be freely moved to O'; to move the force $\mathbf{F}$ from O to O', however, it is necessary to add to $\mathbf{F}$ a couple vector $\mathbf{s} \times \mathbf{F}$ representing the moment about O' of the force $\mathbf{F}$ applied at O. Thus, the couple vector $\mathbf{M}_{o'}$ must be the sum of $\mathbf{M}_o$ and $\mathbf{s} \times \mathbf{F}$.

As noted above, the force-couple system obtained by transferring a force $\mathbf{F}$ from a point A to a point O consists of $\mathbf{F}$ and of a couple vector $\mathbf{M}_o = \mathbf{r} \times \mathbf{F}$ perpendicular to $\mathbf{F}$. Conversely, any force-couple system consisting of a force $\mathbf{F}$ and of a couple vector $\mathbf{M}_o$ which are *mutually perpendicular* may be replaced by a single equivalent force. This is done by moving the force $\mathbf{F}$ in the plane perpendicular to $\mathbf{M}_o$ until its moment about O becomes equal to the couple vector $\mathbf{M}_o$ to be eliminated.

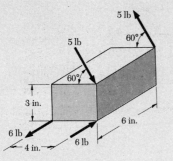

SAMPLE PROBLEM 3.6

Two couples act on a rectangular box as shown. Replace these two couples by a single equivalent couple.

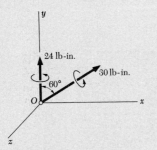

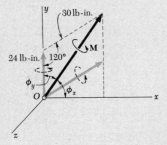

Solution. Each of the given couples is represented by a couple vector which is perpendicular to the plane of the couple and of a magnitude equal to the moment of the couple.   The sense of each vector is obtained by applying the right-hand rule, and for convenience both couple vectors are attached at the origin.

The single couple equivalent to the two given couples will be represented by the resultant of the two couple vectors.   The magnitude of the resultant couple vector **M** is obtained from the law of cosines.

$$M^2 = (24)^2 + (30)^2 - (2)(24)(30) \cos 120°$$

$$M = 46.9 \text{ lb-in.}$$

The angle ϕ_y that the resultant couple vector forms with the vertical is obtained from the law of sines.

$$\frac{\sin \phi_y}{30 \text{ lb-in.}} = \frac{\sin 120°}{46.9 \text{ lb-in.}} \qquad \phi_y = 33.6°$$

The angle that the couple vector forms with the x axis is

$$\phi_x = 90° - 33.6° = 56.4°$$

and the angle it forms with the z axis is $\phi_z = 90°$.   Thus the resultant couple vector **M** is defined by

$$M = 46.9 \text{ lb-in.} \qquad \phi_x = 56.4° \qquad \phi_y = 33.6° \qquad \phi_z = 90° \quad \blacktriangleleft$$

The single couple equivalent to the two original couples is a couple of moment $M = 46.9$ lb-in., acting in a plane parallel to the z axis and forming an angle of 33.6° with the horizontal plane.   This couple may be formed in many ways, for example, by the two 7.82-lb forces shown.

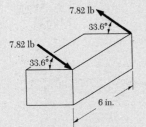

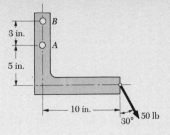

SAMPLE PROBLEM 3.7

A 50-lb force is applied to a corner plate as shown. Determine (a) an equivalent force-couple system at A, (b) an equivalent system consisting of a 150-lb force at B and another force at A.

a. **Force-couple System at A.** We resolve the 50-lb force into x and y components.

$$\mathbf{F} = F_x\mathbf{i} + F_y\mathbf{j} = (50 \text{ lb}) \sin 30°\mathbf{i} - (50 \text{ lb}) \cos 30°\mathbf{j}$$
$$\mathbf{F} = (25.0 \text{ lb})\mathbf{i} - (43.3 \text{ lb})\mathbf{j} \quad \blacktriangleleft$$

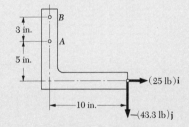

The force $\mathbf{F}$ may be moved to A if a couple is added, of moment $\mathbf{M}_A$ equal to the moment about A of the force $\mathbf{F}$ in its original position. We write

$$\mathbf{M}_A = \mathbf{r} \times \mathbf{F} = [(10 \text{ in.})\mathbf{i} - (5 \text{ in.})\mathbf{j}] \times [(25.0 \text{ lb})\mathbf{i} - (43.3 \text{ lb})\mathbf{j}]$$
$$= (-433 \text{ lb-in.} + 125 \text{ lb-in.})\mathbf{k}$$
$$\mathbf{M}_A = -(308 \text{ lb-in.})\mathbf{k} \quad \blacktriangleleft$$

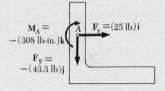

b. **Forces at A and B.** We shall assume that the couple $\mathbf{M}_A$ found in part *a* consists of two 150-lb forces $\mathbf{P}$ and $-\mathbf{P}$ acting respectively at B and A. The moment of $\mathbf{P}$ about A must be equal to the moment $\mathbf{M}_A$ of the couple. Denoting by θ the angle that $\mathbf{P}$ forms with the horizontal, we have

$$\mathbf{P} = (150 \text{ lb}) \cos \theta \, \mathbf{i} + (150 \text{ lb}) \sin \theta \, \mathbf{j}$$
$$\mathbf{M}_A = (3 \text{ in.})\mathbf{j} \times \mathbf{P} = -(450 \text{ lb-in.}) \cos \theta \, \mathbf{k}$$

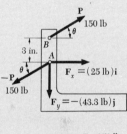

Substituting for $\mathbf{M}_A$ the expression found in part *a* for the moment of the couple, we write

$$-(308 \text{ lb-in.})\mathbf{k} = -(450 \text{ lb-in.}) \cos \theta \, \mathbf{k}$$

$$\cos \theta = \frac{308 \text{ lb-in.}}{450 \text{ lb-in.}} = 0.684 \qquad \theta = \pm 46.8°$$

Having found the direction of the forces $\mathbf{P}$ and $-\mathbf{P}$, we complete the solution by determining the resultant $\mathbf{Q}$ of the forces $\mathbf{F}$ and $-\mathbf{P}$ acting at A.

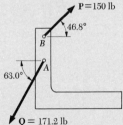

$$\mathbf{Q} = \mathbf{F} - \mathbf{P} = (25.0\mathbf{i} - 43.3\mathbf{j}) - (150 \cos \theta \, \mathbf{i} + 150 \sin \theta \, \mathbf{j})$$
$$\mathbf{Q} = (25.0 - 150 \cos \theta)\mathbf{i} - (43.3 + 150 \sin \theta)\mathbf{j}$$

Since we have found two possible values for θ, there will be two pairs of forces $\mathbf{P}$ and $\mathbf{Q}$ forming a system equivalent to the original 50-lb force:

$$\mathbf{P} = 150 \text{ lb } \measuredangle 46.8° \text{ at } B \qquad \mathbf{Q} = 171.2 \text{ lb } \measuredangle 63.0° \text{ at } A \quad \blacktriangleleft$$

or

$$\mathbf{P} = 150 \text{ lb } \measuredangle 46.8° \text{ at } B \qquad \mathbf{Q} = 101.8 \text{ lb } \measuredangle 40.3° \text{ at } A \quad \blacktriangleleft$$

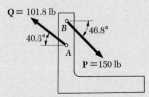

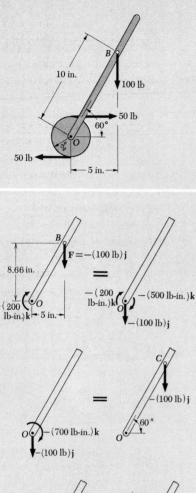

SAMPLE PROBLEM 3.8

Replace the couple and force shown by an equivalent single force applied to the lever. Determine the distance from the shaft to the point of application of this equivalent force.

Solution. First the given force and couple are replaced by an equivalent force-couple system at O. We move the force $\mathbf{F} = -(100\ \text{lb})\mathbf{j}$ to O and at the same time add a couple of moment $\mathbf{M}_o$ equal to the moment about O of the force in its original position.

$$\mathbf{M}_o = \overrightarrow{OB} \times \mathbf{F} = (5\mathbf{i} + 8.66\mathbf{j}) \times (-100\mathbf{j}) = -(500\ \text{lb-in.})\mathbf{k}$$

This couple is added to the couple of moment $-(200\ \text{lb-in.})\mathbf{k}$ formed by the two 50-lb forces, and a couple of moment $-(700\ \text{lb-in.})\mathbf{k}$ is obtained. This last couple may be eliminated by applying $\mathbf{F}$ at a point C chosen in such a way that

$$-(700\ \text{lb-in.})\mathbf{k} = \overrightarrow{OC} \times \mathbf{F}$$
$$= [(OC)\cos 60°\mathbf{i} + (OC)\sin 60°\mathbf{j}] \times (-100\ \text{lb})\mathbf{j}$$
$$= -(OC)\cos 60°\ (100\ \text{lb})\mathbf{k}$$

We conclude that

$$(OC)\cos 60° = 7\ \text{in.} \qquad OC = 14\ \text{in.} \quad \blacktriangleleft$$

Alternate Solution. Since the effect of a couple does not depend on its location, the couple of moment $-(200\ \text{lb-in.})\mathbf{k}$ may be moved to B; we thus obtain a force-couple system at B. The couple may now be eliminated by applying $\mathbf{F}$ at a point C chosen in such a way that

$$-(200\ \text{lb-in.})\mathbf{k} = \overrightarrow{BC} \times \mathbf{F}$$
$$= -(BC)\cos 60°\ (100\ \text{lb})\mathbf{k}$$

We conclude that

$$(BC)\cos 60° = 2\ \text{in.} \qquad BC = 4\ \text{in.}$$
$$OC = OB + BC = 10\ \text{in.} + 4\ \text{in.} \qquad OC = 14\ \text{in.} \quad \blacktriangleleft$$

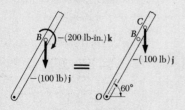

PROBLEMS

3.49. The two couples shown are applied to a 6- by 8-in. plate. Knowing that $P_1 = P_2 = 30$ lb and $Q_1 = Q_2 = 40$ lb, prove that their sum is zero (*a*) by adding their moments, (*b*) by combining $\mathbf{P}_1$ and $\mathbf{Q}_1$ into their resultant $\mathbf{R}_1$, combining $\mathbf{P}_2$ and $\mathbf{Q}_2$ into their resultant $\mathbf{R}_2$, and then showing that $\mathbf{R}_1$ and $\mathbf{R}_2$ are equal and opposite and have the same line of action.

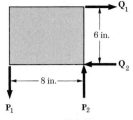

FIG. P 3.49

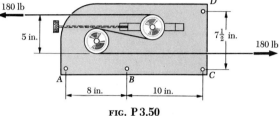

FIG. P 3.50

3.50. A couple formed by two 180-lb forces is applied to the pulley assembly shown. Determine an equivalent couple which is formed by (*a*) vertical forces acting at *A* and *C*, (*b*) the smallest possible forces acting at *B* and *D*, (*c*) the smallest possible forces which can be attached to the assembly.

3.51. Four 1-in.-diameter pegs are attached to a board as shown. Two strings are passed around the pegs and pulled with forces of magnitude $P = 16$ lb and $Q = 40$ lb. Determine the resultant couple acting on the board.

3.52. Four pegs are attached to a board as shown. Two strings are passed around the pegs and pulled with forces of magnitude $P = 16$ lb and $Q = 40$ lb. Determine the required diameter of the pegs if the resultant couple applied to the board is to be 300 lb-in. clockwise.

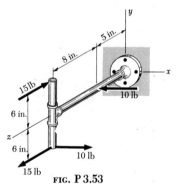

FIG. P 3.51 AND P 3.52

3.53. Determine the components of a single couple equivalent to the two couples shown. Check the result obtained by adding the moments of the individual forces about the coordinate axes.

3.54. The axles and drive shaft of an automobile are acted upon by the three couples shown. Replace these three couples by a single equivalent couple.

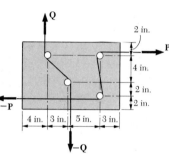

FIG. P 3.53

3.55. Three shafts are connected to a gear box as shown. Shaft *A* is horizontal and shafts *B* and *C* lie in the vertical *yz* plane. Determine the components of the resultant couple exerted on the gear box.

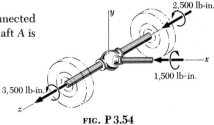

FIG. P 3.54

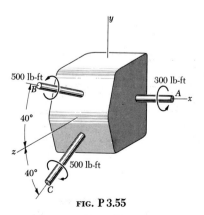

FIG. P 3.55

3.56. The couple vectors $\mathbf{M}_1$ and $\mathbf{M}_2$ represent couples which are contained in the planes ABC and ACD, respectively. Assuming that $M_1 = M_2 = M$, determine a single couple equivalent to the two given couples.

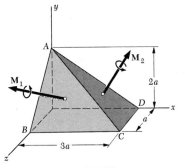

FIG. P 3.56

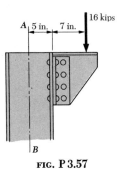

FIG. P 3.57

3.57. A crane column supports a 16-kip load as shown. Reduce the load to an axial force along AB and a couple.

3.58. A 65-lb force is applied to a bent plate as shown. Determine an equivalent force-couple system (*a*) at A, (*b*) at B.

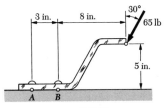

FIG. P 3.58

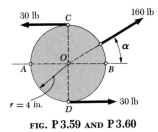

FIG. P 3.59 AND P 3.60

3.59. Knowing that $\alpha = 30°$, replace the force and couple shown by a single force applied at a point located (*a*) on line AB, (*b*) on line CD. In each case determine the distance from the center O to the point of application of the force.

3.60. The force and couple shown are to be replaced by an equivalent single force. Determine the required value of α so that the line of action of the single equivalent force will pass through point B.

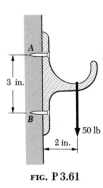

FIG. P 3.61

3.61. A hook is held by screws at A and B. (*a*) Replace the 50-lb load shown by an equivalent force-couple system at B. (*b*) Find two horizontal forces at A and B which form a couple equivalent to the couple found in part *a*.

3.62. A force **P** is applied to a beam *AB* at a point *C* as shown. Find the vertical forces $\mathbf{F}_A$ and $\mathbf{F}_B$, applied, respectively, at *A* and *B*, which form a system equivalent to **P**.

3.63. The 60-lb force is applied in a direction perpendicular to the handle at *A* ($\beta = 0$). When the rod is in the vertical position ($\alpha = 0$), replace the 60-lb force by (*a*) an equivalent force-couple system at *B*, (*b*) an equivalent system formed by two parallel forces at *B* and *C*.

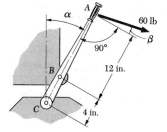

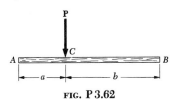

FIG. P 3.62

FIG. P 3.63 AND P 3.64

°3.64. Replace the 60-lb force by an equivalent system formed by two parallel forces at *B* and *C*. Show (*a*) that these forces are parallel to the 60-lb force, (*b*) that the magnitude of these forces is independent of both α and β.

3.65. A 25-kip load is applied eccentrically on a column. Determine the components of the force and couple at *G* which are equivalent to the 25-kip load.

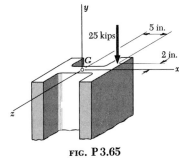

FIG. P 3.65

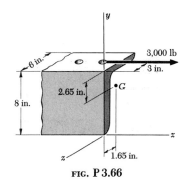

FIG. P 3.66

3.66. A 3,000-lb force is applied on the outside face of the short leg of a rolled angle section. Determine the components of the force and couple at *G* which are equivalent to the 3,000-lb load.

3.67. In Prob. 3.35, determine the magnitude and direction of the force and couple at *O* equivalent to the 1,000-lb force exerted on point *A* by the cable *AB*.

3.68. A precast-concrete wall section is temporarily held by cables as shown. The tension in cable *AB* is 700 lb. Replace the force exerted on the wall section at *A* by a force-couple system located (*a*) at the origin of coordinates *O*, (*b*) at point *E*.

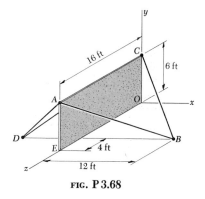

FIG. P 3.68

3.69. Five separate force-couple systems act at the corners of a rectangular box as shown. Find two force-couple systems which are equivalent.

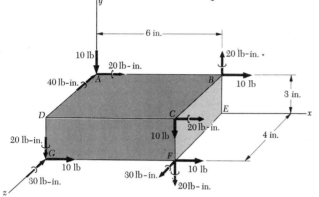

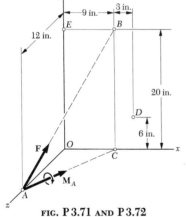

FIG. P 3.69

3.70. Determine which of the force-couple systems given in Prob. 3.69 is equivalent to a force-couple system located at the origin O and consisting of $F = -10j$ and $M_o = 60i - 60k$.

3.71. The force-couple system at A consists of the force $\mathbf{F}$ of magnitude 25 lb and the couple $\mathbf{M}_A$ of moment 250 lb-in. Replace this force-couple system by an equivalent force-couple system at D.

3.72. The force-couple system at A consists of the force $\mathbf{F}$ of magnitude 25 lb and the couple $\mathbf{M}_A$ of moment 250 lb-in. Replace this force-couple system by an equivalent force-couple system at E.

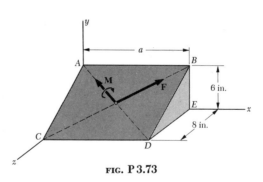

FIG. P 3.71 AND P 3.72

FIG. P 3.73

3.73. Determine the dimension a for which the force-couple system shown may be replaced by a single equivalent force. If $F = 200$ lb and $M = 1,000$ lb-in., determine the point where the line of action of the single equivalent force intersects the yz plane.

3.15. Reduction of a System of Forces to One Force and One Couple.

Consider a system of forces $\mathbf{F}_1$, $\mathbf{F}_2$, $\mathbf{F}_3$, etc., acting on a rigid body at the points A_1, A_2, A_3, etc., defined by the position vectors $\mathbf{r}_1$, $\mathbf{r}_2$, $\mathbf{r}_3$, etc. (Fig. 3.38a).   As seen in the preceding sec-

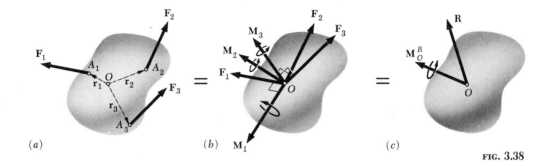

(a)   (b)   (c)

FIG. 3.38

tion, $\mathbf{F}_1$ may be moved from A_1 to a given point O if a couple of moment $\mathbf{M}_1$ equal to the moment $\mathbf{r}_1 \times \mathbf{F}_1$ of $\mathbf{F}_1$ about O is added to the original system of forces.   Repeating this procedure with $\mathbf{F}_2$, $\mathbf{F}_3$, etc., we obtain the system shown in Fig. 3.38b, consisting of forces acting at O and of couples.   Since the forces are now concurrent, they may be added vectorially and replaced by their resultant $\mathbf{R}$.   Similarly, the couple vectors $\mathbf{M}_1$, $\mathbf{M}_2$, $\mathbf{M}_3$, etc., may be added vectorially and replaced by a single couple vector $\mathbf{M}_O^R$.   Any system of forces, however complex, may thus be reduced to an *equivalent force-couple system acting at a given point O* (Fig. 3.38c).   We should note that, while each of the couple vectors $\mathbf{M}_1$, $\mathbf{M}_2$, $\mathbf{M}_3$, etc., in Fig. 3.38b is perpendicular to the corresponding force, the resultant force $\mathbf{R}$ and the resultant couple vector $\mathbf{M}_O^R$ in Fig. 3.38c will not, in general, be perpendicular to each other.

The equivalent force-couple system is defined by the equations

$$\mathbf{R} = \Sigma\mathbf{F} \qquad \mathbf{M}_O^R = \Sigma\mathbf{M}_O = \Sigma(\mathbf{r} \times \mathbf{F}) \qquad (3.47)$$

which express that the force $\mathbf{R}$ is obtained by adding all the forces of the system, while the moment $\mathbf{M}_O^R$ of the couple, called *moment resultant* of the system, is obtained by adding the moments about O of all the forces of the system.

Once a given system of forces has been reduced to a force and a couple at a point O, it may easily be reduced to a force and a couple at another point O'.   While the resultant force $\mathbf{R}$ will remain unchanged, the new couple vector $\mathbf{M}_{O'}^R$ will be equal to the sum of the couple vector $\mathbf{M}_O^R$ and of the moment about O'

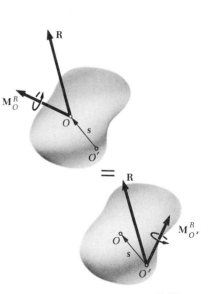

FIG. 3.39

of the force $\mathbf{R}$ attached at O (Fig. 3.39).   We have

$$\mathbf{M}_{O'}^R = \mathbf{M}_O^R + \mathbf{s} \times \mathbf{R} \qquad (3.48)$$

In practice, the reduction of a given system of forces to a single force $\mathbf{R}$ at O and a couple $\mathbf{M}_O^R$ will be carried out in terms of components.   Resolving each position vector $\mathbf{r}$ and each force $\mathbf{F}$ of the system into rectangular components, we write

$$\mathbf{r} = x\mathbf{i} + y\mathbf{j} + z\mathbf{k} \qquad (3.49)$$
$$\mathbf{F} = F_x\mathbf{i} + F_y\mathbf{j} + F_z\mathbf{k} \qquad (3.50)$$

Substituting for $\mathbf{r}$ and $\mathbf{F}$ into (3.47) and factoring the unit vectors $\mathbf{i}$, $\mathbf{j}$, $\mathbf{k}$, we obtain $\mathbf{R}$ and $\mathbf{M}_O^R$ in the form

$$\mathbf{R} = R_x\mathbf{i} + R_y\mathbf{j} + R_z\mathbf{k} \qquad \mathbf{M}_O^R = M_x^R\mathbf{i} + M_y^R\mathbf{j} + M_z^R\mathbf{k} \quad (3.51)$$

The components R_x, R_y, R_z represent, respectively, the sums of the x, y, and z components of the given forces and measure the tendency of the system to impart to the rigid body a motion of translation in the x, y, or z direction.   Similarly, the components M_x^R, M_y^R, M_z^R represent, respectively, the sums of the moments of the given forces about the x, y, and z axes and measure the tendency of the system to impart to the rigid body a motion of rotation about the x, y, or z axis.

If the magnitude and direction of the force $\mathbf{R}$ are desired, they may be obtained from the components R_x, R_y, R_z by means of the relations (2.18) and (2.25) of Sec. 2.11; similar computations will yield the magnitude and direction of the couple vector $\mathbf{M}_O^R$.

3.16.   Equivalent Systems of Forces.   We have seen in the preceding section that any system of forces acting on a rigid body may be reduced to a force-couple system at a given point O.   This equivalent force-couple system characterizes completely the effect of the given system on the rigid body. *Two systems of forces are equivalent, therefore, if they may be reduced to the same force-couple system at a given point O.* Recalling that the force-couple system at O is defined by the relations (3.47), we state: *Two systems of forces $\mathbf{F}_1$, $\mathbf{F}_2$, $\mathbf{F}_3$, etc., and $\mathbf{F}_1'$, $\mathbf{F}_2'$, $\mathbf{F}_3'$, etc., are equivalent if, and only if, the sums of the forces and the sums of the moments about a given point O of the forces of the two systems are, respectively, equal.* Expressed mathematically, the necessary and sufficient conditions for the two systems of forces to be equivalent are

$$\Sigma\mathbf{F} = \Sigma\mathbf{F}' \qquad \text{and} \qquad \Sigma\mathbf{M}_O = \Sigma\mathbf{M}_O' \qquad (3.52)$$

Note that, to prove that two systems of forces are equivalent, the second of the relations (3.52) needs to be established with respect to *only one point O.* It will hold, however, with respect to *any point* if the two systems are equivalent.

Resolving the forces and moments in (3.52) into their rectangular components, we may express the necessary and sufficient conditions for the equivalence of two systems of forces as follows:

$$\Sigma F_x = \Sigma F'_x \qquad \Sigma F_y = \Sigma F'_y \qquad \Sigma F_z = \Sigma F'_z$$
$$\Sigma M_x = \Sigma M'_x \qquad \Sigma M_y = \Sigma M'_y \qquad \Sigma M_z = \Sigma M'_z \tag{3.53}$$

These equations have a simple physical significance. They express that two systems of forces are equivalent if they tend to impart to a given rigid body (1) the same translation in the x, y, and z directions, respectively, and (2) the same rotation about the x, y, and z axes, respectively.

3.17. Further Reduction of a System of Forces. We saw in Sec. 3.15 that any given system of forces may be reduced to an equivalent force-couple system at O, consisting of a force $\mathbf{R}$ equal to the sum of the forces of the system, and of a couple vector $\mathbf{M}_O^R$ equal to the moment resultant of the system.

When $\mathbf{R} = 0$, the force-couple system reduces to the couple vector $\mathbf{M}_O^R$. The given system of forces may then be reduced to a single couple, called the *resultant couple* of the system.

We shall now investigate the conditions under which a given system of forces may be reduced to a single force. It follows from Sec. 3.14 that the force-couple system at O may be replaced by a single force $\mathbf{R}$ acting along a new line of action if $\mathbf{R}$ and $\mathbf{M}_O^R$ are mutually perpendicular. The systems of forces which may be reduced to a single force, or *resultant*, are therefore the systems for which the force $\mathbf{R}$ and the couple vector $\mathbf{M}_O^R$ are mutually perpendicular. While this condition *is generally not satisfied* by systems of forces in space, it *will be satisfied* by systems consisting (1) of concurrent forces, (2) of coplanar forces, or (3) of parallel forces. We shall discuss these cases separately.

1. *Concurrent forces* are applied at the same point and may therefore be added directly into their resultant $\mathbf{R}$. Thus, they always reduce to a single force. Concurrent forces have been discussed in detail in Chap. 2.

2. *Coplanar forces* act in the same plane, which we shall assume here to be the plane of the figure (Fig. 3.40a). The sum $\mathbf{R}$ of the forces of the system will also lie in the plane of the figure, while the moment of each force about O, and thus the moment resultant $\mathbf{M}_O^R$, will be perpendicular to that plane. The force-couple system at O consists therefore of a force $\mathbf{R}$

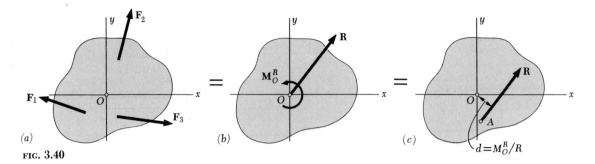

(a)

(b)

(c)

$d = M_O^R / R$

FIG. 3.40

and a couple vector $\mathbf{M}_O^R$ which are mutually perpendicular (Fig. 3.40b).† They may be reduced to a single force $\mathbf{R}$ by moving $\mathbf{R}$ in the plane of the figure until its moment about O becomes equal to $\mathbf{M}_O^R$. The distance from O to the line of action of $\mathbf{R}$ is $d = M_O^R / R$ (Fig. 3.40c).

As noted in Sec. 3.15, the reduction of a system of forces is considerably simplified if the forces are resolved into rectangular components. The force-couple system at O is then characterized by the components

$$R_x = \Sigma F_x \qquad R_y = \Sigma F_y \qquad M_z^R = M_O^R = \Sigma M_O \quad (3.54)$$

To reduce the system to a single force $\mathbf{R}$ we shall express that the moment of $\mathbf{R}$ about O must be equal to $\mathbf{M}_O^R$. Denoting by x and y the coordinates of the point of application A of the resultant, and recalling formula (3.20), we write

$$xR_y - yR_x = M_O^R$$

which represents the equation of the line of action of $\mathbf{R}$. We may also determine directly the x and y intercepts of the line of action of the resultant by noting that M_O^R must be equal to the moment about O of the y component of $\mathbf{R}$ when $\mathbf{R}$ is attached at B (Fig. 3.41a), and to the moment of its x component when $\mathbf{R}$ is attached at C (Fig. 3.41b).

† Since the couple vector $\mathbf{M}_O^R$ is perpendicular to the plane of the figure, it has been represented by the symbol ↻. A counterclockwise couple ↺ corresponds to a vector pointing out of the paper, and a clockwise couple ↻ to a vector pointing into the paper.

FIG. 3.41

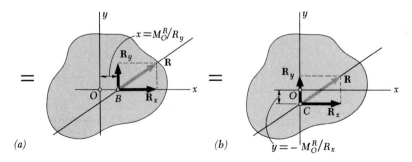

(a)

(b)

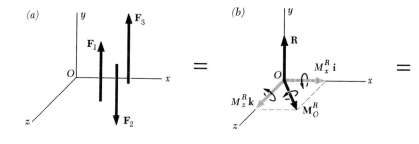
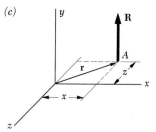

FIG. 3.42

3. *Parallel forces* have parallel lines of action and may or
may not have the same sense. Assuming here that the forces
are parallel to the y axis (Fig. 3.42a), we note that their sum $\mathbf{R}$
will also be parallel to the y axis. On the other hand, since the
moment of a given force must be perpendicular to that force,
the moment about O of each force of the system, and thus the
moment resultant $\mathbf{M}_O^R$, will lie in the zx plane. The force-couple
system at O consists therefore of a force $\mathbf{R}$ and a couple vector
$\mathbf{M}_O^R$ which are mutually perpendicular (Fig. 3.42b). They may
be reduced to a single force $\mathbf{R}$ (Fig. 3.42c) or, if $\mathbf{R} = 0$, to a
single couple of moment $\mathbf{M}_O^R$.

In practice, the force-couple system at O will be characterized by the components

$$R_y = \Sigma F_y \qquad M_x^R = \Sigma M_x \qquad M_z^R = \Sigma M_z \qquad (3.55)$$

The reduction of the system to a single force may be carried
out by moving $\mathbf{R}$ to a new point of application $A(x, 0, z)$
chosen so that the moment of $\mathbf{R}$ about O is equal to $\mathbf{M}_O^R$. We
write

$$\mathbf{r} \times \mathbf{R} = \mathbf{M}_O^R$$

$$(x\mathbf{i} + z\mathbf{k}) \times R_y\mathbf{j} = M_x^R\mathbf{i} + M_z^R\mathbf{k}$$

Computing the vector products and equating the coefficients of
the corresponding unit vectors in both members of the equation,
we obtain two scalar equations which define the coordinates of A:

$$-zR_y = M_x^R \qquad\qquad xR_y = M_z^R$$

These equations express that the moments of $\mathbf{R}$ about the x and
z axes must, respectively, be equal to M_x^R and M_z^R.

In the general case of a system of forces in space, the force-
couple system at O consists of a force $\mathbf{R}$ and a couple vector
$\mathbf{M}_O^R$ which are not perpendicular, and neither of which is zero
(Fig. 3.43a). Thus, the system of forces *cannot* be reduced
to a single force or a single couple. The couple vector, however, may be replaced by two other couple vectors obtained by
resolving $\mathbf{M}_O^R$ into a component $\mathbf{M}_1$ along $\mathbf{R}$ and a component
$\mathbf{M}_2$ in a plane perpendicular to $\mathbf{R}$ (Fig. 3.43b). The couple

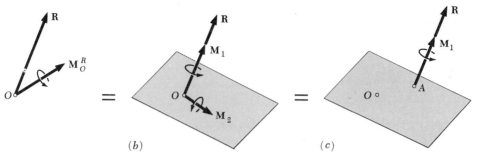

(a)　　　　　　　　　(b)　　　　　　　　　　　(c)

FIG. 3.43

vector M_2 and the force R may then be replaced by a single force R acting along a new line of action.   The original system of forces thus reduces to R and to the couple vector M_1 (Fig. 3.43c), i.e., to R and a couple acting in the plane perpendicular to R.   This particular force-couple combination is called a *wrench*.   The force R and the couple vector M_1 tend, at the same time, to translate the rigid body on which they act in the direction of R and to rotate it about the line of action of R.   The line of action of R is known as the *axis of the wrench*, and the ratio M_1/R is called the *pitch* of the wrench.

Recalling the expression (3.32) obtained for the projection of a vector on the line of action of another vector, we note that the projection of M_O^R on the line of action of R is

$$M_1 = \frac{R \cdot M_O^R}{R} \tag{3.56}$$

We thus have †

$$\text{Pitch of wrench} = \frac{M_1}{R} = \frac{R \cdot M_O^R}{R^2} \tag{3.57}$$

An important particular case of the reduction of a system of forces to a force-couple system occurs when both the force R and the couple vector M_O^R are equal to zero.   The system of forces is said to be *equivalent to zero*.   Such a system has no effect on the rigid body on which it acts, and the rigid body is said to be in *equilibrium*.   This case will be considered in detail in the next chapter.

† The expressions obtained for the projection of the couple vector on the line of action of R and for the pitch of the wrench are independent of the choice of point O.   Using the relation (3.48), we check that if a different point O' had been used, the numerator in (3.56) and (3.57) would be

$$R \cdot M_{O'}^R = R \cdot (M_O^R + s \times R) = R \cdot M_O^R + R \cdot (s \times R)$$

Since the mixed triple product $R \cdot (s \times R)$ is identically equal to zero, we have

$$R \cdot M_{O'}^R = R \cdot M_O^R \tag{3.58}$$

and conclude that the scalar product $R \cdot M_O^R$ is independent of the choice of point O.

SAMPLE PROBLEM 3.9

A 12-ft beam is subjected to the forces shown. Reduce the given system of forces to (a) an equivalent force-couple system at A, (b) an equivalent force-couple system at B, (c) a single force or resultant.

Note. Since the reactions at the supports are not included in the given system of forces, the given system will not maintain the beam in equilibrium.

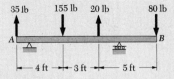

a. **Force-couple System at A.** The force-couple system at A equivalent to the given system of forces consists of a force **R** and a couple $\mathbf{M}_A^R$ defined as follows:

$$\mathbf{R} = \Sigma\mathbf{F}$$
$$= (35\text{ lb})\mathbf{j} - (155\text{ lb})\mathbf{j} + (20\text{ lb})\mathbf{j} - (80\text{ lb})\mathbf{j} = -(180\text{ lb})\mathbf{j}$$
$$\mathbf{M}_A^R = \Sigma(\mathbf{r} \times \mathbf{F})$$
$$= (4\mathbf{i}) \times (-155\mathbf{j}) + (7\mathbf{i}) \times (20\mathbf{j}) + (12\mathbf{i}) \times (-80\mathbf{j}) = -(1{,}440\text{ lb-ft})\mathbf{k}$$

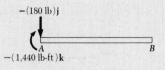

The equivalent force-couple system at A is thus

$$\mathbf{R} = 180\text{ lb} \downarrow \qquad M_A^R = 1{,}440\text{ lb-ft} \; \rangle \quad \blacktriangleleft$$

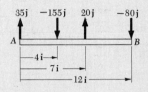

b. **Force-couple System at B.** We shall find a force-couple system at B equivalent to the force-couple system at A determined in part *a*. The force **R** is unchanged, but a new couple $\mathbf{M}_B^R$ must be determined, the moment of which is equal to the moment about B of the force-couple system determined in part *a*. Thus, we have

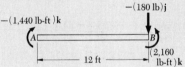

$$\mathbf{M}_B^R = \mathbf{M}_A^R + \overrightarrow{BA} \times \mathbf{R}$$
$$= -(1{,}440\text{ lb-ft})\mathbf{k} + (-12\text{ ft})\mathbf{i} \times (-180\text{ lb})\mathbf{j}$$
$$= -(1{,}440\text{ lb-ft})\mathbf{k} + (2{,}160\text{ lb-ft})\mathbf{k} = +(720\text{ lb-ft})\mathbf{k}$$

The equivalent force-couple system at B is thus

$$\mathbf{R} = 180\text{ lb} \downarrow \qquad M_B^R = 720\text{ lb-ft} \; \rangle \quad \blacktriangleleft$$

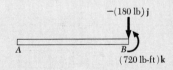

c. **Single Force or Resultant.** The resultant of the given system of forces is equal to **R** and its point of application must be such that the moment of **R** about A is equal to $\mathbf{M}_A^R$. We write

$$\mathbf{r} \times \mathbf{R} = \mathbf{M}_A^R$$
$$x\mathbf{i} \times (-180\text{ lb})\mathbf{j} = -(1{,}440\text{ lb-ft})\mathbf{k}$$
$$-x(180\text{ lb})\mathbf{k} = -(1{,}440\text{ lb-ft})\mathbf{k}$$

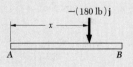

and conclude that $x = 8$ ft. Thus, the single force equivalent to the given system is defined as

$$\mathbf{R} = 180\text{ lb} \downarrow \qquad x = 8\text{ ft} \quad \blacktriangleleft$$

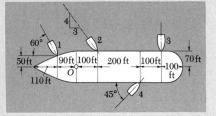

SAMPLE PROBLEM 3.10

Four tugboats are used to bring an ocean liner to its pier. Each tugboat exerts a 5,000-lb force in the direction shown. Determine (a) the equivalent force-couple system at the foremast O, (b) the point on the hull where a single, more powerful tugboat should push to produce the same effect as the original four tugboats.

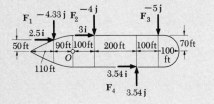

a. **Force-couple System at O.** Each of the given forces is resolved into components in the diagram shown (kip units are used). The force-couple system at O equivalent to the given system of forces consists of a force $\mathbf{R}$ and a couple $\mathbf{M}_O^R$ defined as follows:

$$\mathbf{R} = \Sigma\mathbf{F}$$
$$= (2.50\mathbf{i} - 4.33\mathbf{j}) + (3.00\mathbf{i} - 4.00\mathbf{j}) + (-5.00\mathbf{j}) + (3.54\mathbf{i} + 3.54\mathbf{j})$$
$$= 9.04\mathbf{i} - 9.79\mathbf{j}$$
$$\mathbf{M}_O^R = \Sigma(\mathbf{r} \times \mathbf{F})$$
$$= (-90\mathbf{i} + 50\mathbf{j}) \times (2.50\mathbf{i} - 4.33\mathbf{j})$$
$$+ (100\mathbf{i} + 70\mathbf{j}) \times (3.00\mathbf{i} - 4.00\mathbf{j})$$
$$+ (400\mathbf{i} + 70\mathbf{j}) \times (-5.00\mathbf{j})$$
$$+ (300\mathbf{i} - 70\mathbf{j}) \times (3.54\mathbf{i} + 3.54\mathbf{j})$$
$$= (390 - 125 - 400 - 210 - 2,000 + 1,062 + 248)\mathbf{k}$$
$$= -1,035\mathbf{k}$$

The equivalent force-couple system at O is thus

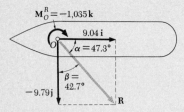

$$\mathbf{R} = (9.04 \text{ kips})\mathbf{i} - (9.79 \text{ kips})\mathbf{j} \qquad \mathbf{M}_O^R = -(1,035 \text{ kip-ft})\mathbf{k}$$
or $\quad \mathbf{R} = 13.33 \text{ kips} \; \measuredangle \; 47.3° \qquad \mathbf{M}_O^R = 1,035 \text{ kip-ft} \; \rangle$ ◄

Remark. Since all the forces are contained in the plane of the figure, we could have expected the sum of their moments to be perpendicular to that plane. Note that the moment of each force component could have been obtained directly from the diagram by forming the product of its magnitude and its perpendicular distance to O, and assigning to this product a positive or a negative sign, depending upon the sense of the moment.

b. **Single Tugboat.** The force exerted by a single tugboat must be equal to $\mathbf{R}$ and its point of application A must be such that the moment of $\mathbf{R}$ about O is equal to $\mathbf{M}_O^R$. Observing that the position vector of A is

$$\mathbf{r} = x\mathbf{i} + 70\mathbf{j}$$

we write

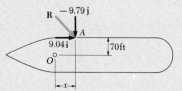

$$\mathbf{r} \times \mathbf{R} = \mathbf{M}_O^R$$
$$(x\mathbf{i} + 70\mathbf{j}) \times (9.04\mathbf{i} - 9.79\mathbf{j}) = -1,035\mathbf{k}$$
$$-x(9.79)\mathbf{k} - 633\mathbf{k} = -1,035\mathbf{k}$$

$$x = 41.1 \text{ ft} \quad ◄$$

SAMPLE PROBLEM 3.11

Three cables are attached to a bracket as shown. Replace the forces exerted by the cables by an equivalent force-couple system at A.

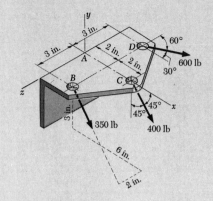

Solution. We first determine the position vectors of the points of application B, C, D and resolve the given forces into rectangular components.

$$r_B = 2i + 3k \qquad F_B = 300i - 150j + 100k$$
$$r_C = 4i \qquad F_C = 283i - 283j$$
$$r_D = 2i - 3k \qquad F_D = 520i \qquad - 300k$$

The force-couple system at A equivalent to the given forces consists of a force R and a couple M_A^R defined as follows:

$$R = \Sigma F \qquad M_A^R = \Sigma(r \times F)$$

The force R is readily obtained by adding respectively the x, y, and z components of the given forces.

$$R = \Sigma F = (1{,}103\ \text{lb})i - (433\ \text{lb})j - (200\ \text{lb})k \quad \blacktriangleleft$$

The computation of M_A^R will be facilitated if we express each of the moments $r \times F$ in the form of a determinant (Sec. 3.7).

$$r_B \times F_B = \begin{vmatrix} i & j & k \\ 2 & 0 & 3 \\ 300 & -150 & 100 \end{vmatrix} = 450i + 700j - 300k$$

$$r_C \times F_C = \begin{vmatrix} i & j & k \\ 4 & 0 & 0 \\ 283 & -283 & 0 \end{vmatrix} = -1{,}132k$$

$$r_D \times F_D = \begin{vmatrix} i & j & k \\ 2 & 0 & -3 \\ 520 & 0 & -300 \end{vmatrix} = -960j$$

Adding the expressions obtained, we have

$$M_A^R = \Sigma(r \times F) = (450\ \text{lb-in.})i - (260\ \text{lb-in.})j - (1{,}432\ \text{lb-in.})k \quad \blacktriangleleft$$

The components of the force R and of the couple M_A^R along the coordinate axes are shown in the adjoining sketch.

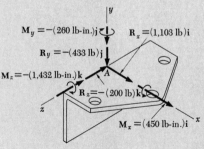

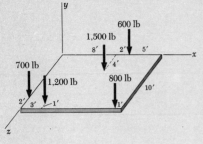

A 10- by 15-ft slab supports five columns which exert on the slab the forces indicated.   Determine the magnitude and point of application of the single force equivalent to the given forces.

Solution.   We shall first reduce the given system of forces to a force-couple system at the origin O of the coordinates.   This force-couple system consists of a force $\mathbf{R}$ and a couple $\mathbf{M}_O^R$ defined as follows:

$$\mathbf{R} = \Sigma\mathbf{F} \qquad \mathbf{M}_O^R = \Sigma(\mathbf{r} \times \mathbf{F})$$

The position vectors of the points of application of the various forces are determined and the computations are arranged in tabular form.

$\mathbf{r}$, ft	$\mathbf{F}$, lb	$\mathbf{r} \times \mathbf{F}$, lb-ft
$10\mathbf{i}$	$-\ 600\mathbf{j}$	$-\ 6{,}000\mathbf{k}$
$8\mathbf{k}$	$-\ 700\mathbf{j}$	$5{,}600\mathbf{i}$
$14\mathbf{i} + 10\mathbf{k}$	$-\ 800\mathbf{j}$	$8{,}000\mathbf{i} - 11{,}200\mathbf{k}$
$3\mathbf{i} + 9\mathbf{k}$	$-1{,}200\mathbf{j}$	$10{,}800\mathbf{i} - 3{,}600\mathbf{k}$
$8\mathbf{i} + 4\mathbf{k}$	$-1{,}500\mathbf{j}$	$6{,}000\mathbf{i} - 12{,}000\mathbf{k}$
	$\mathbf{R} = -4{,}800\mathbf{j}$	$\mathbf{M}_O^R = 30{,}400\mathbf{i} - 32{,}800\mathbf{k}$

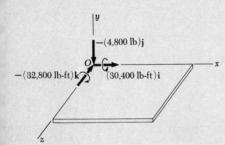

Since the force $\mathbf{R}$ and the couple vector $\mathbf{M}_O^R$ are mutually perpendicular, the force-couple system obtained may be reduced further to a single force $\mathbf{R}$.   The new point of application of $\mathbf{R}$ will be selected in the plane of the slab and in such a way that the moment of $\mathbf{R}$ about O will be equal to $\mathbf{M}_O^R$.   Denoting by $\mathbf{r}$ the position vector of the desired point of application, and by x and z its coordinates, we write

$$\mathbf{r} \times \mathbf{R} = \mathbf{M}_O^R$$
$$(x\mathbf{i} + z\mathbf{k}) \times (-4{,}800\mathbf{j}) = 30{,}400\mathbf{i} - 32{,}800\mathbf{k}$$
$$-4{,}800x\mathbf{k} + 4{,}800z\mathbf{i} = 30{,}400\mathbf{i} - 32{,}800\mathbf{k}$$

from which it follows that

$$-4{,}800x = -32{,}800 \qquad 4{,}800z = 30{,}400$$
$$x = 6.83 \text{ ft} \qquad z = 6.33 \text{ ft}$$

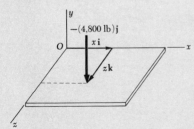

We conclude that the resultant of the given system of forces is

$$\mathbf{R} = 4{,}800 \text{ lb} \downarrow \quad \text{at} \quad x = 6.83 \text{ ft}, z = 6.33 \text{ ft} \quad \blacktriangleleft$$

PROBLEMS

3.74. A 12-ft beam is loaded in the various ways represented in the figure.   Find two loadings which are equivalent.

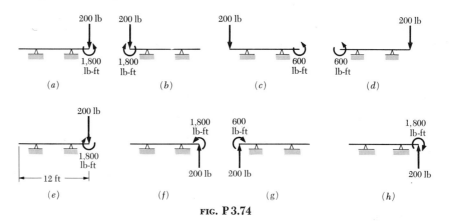

FIG. P 3.74

3.75. A 12-ft beam is loaded as shown.   Determine the loading of Prob. 3.74 which is equivalent to this loading.

3.76. For the truss and loading shown, determine the resultant of the loads and the distance from point *A* to its line of action.

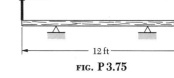

FIG. P 3.75

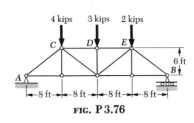

FIG. P 3.76

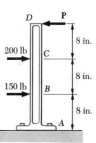

FIG. P 3.77

3.77. Three horizontal forces are applied as shown to a machine arm.   Determine the resultant of the loads and the point where its line of action intersects *AD* if the magnitude of **P** is (*a*) *P* = 50 lb, (*b*) *P* = 500 lb, (*c*) *P* = 350 lb.

3.78. Replace the three forces acting on the gear by an equivalent force-couple system at *O*.

3.79. Replace the two belt tensions by an equivalent force-couple system at *A*.

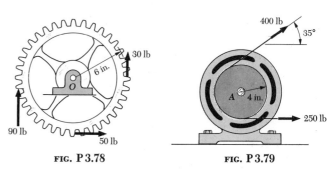

FIG. P 3.78   FIG. P 3.79

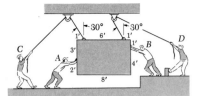

FIG. P 3.80

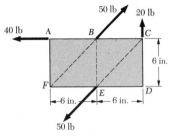

FIG. P 3.81

3.80. In order to move a 173-lb crate, two men push on it while two other men pull on it by means of ropes. The force exerted by man *A* is 150 lb, and that exerted by man *B* is 50 lb; both forces are horizontal. Man *C* pulls with a force equal to 80 lb and man *D* with a force equal to 120 lb. Both cables form an angle of 30° with the vertical. Determine the resultant of all forces acting on the crate.

3.81. A 6- by 12-in. plate is subjected to four loads. Find the resultant of the four loads and the two points at which the line of action of the resultant intersects the edge of the plate.

3.82. An angle bracket is subjected to the system of forces shown. Find the resultant of the system and the point of intersection of its line of action with (*a*) line *AB*, (*b*) line *BC*.

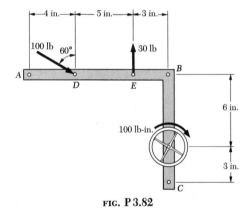

FIG. P 3.82

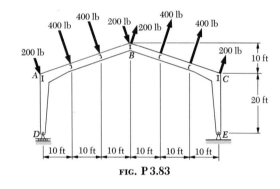

FIG. P 3.83

3.83. The roof of a building frame is subjected to the wind loading shown. Determine (*a*) the equivalent force-couple system at *D*, (*b*) the resultant of the loading and its line of action.

3.84. Two cables exert forces of 18 kips each on a truss of weight $W = 40$ kips. Find the resultant force acting on the truss and the point of intersection of its line of action with the line *AB*.

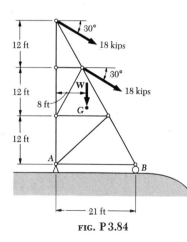

FIG. P 3.84

3.85. A force **P** and a couple **M** of moment 200 lb-in. are applied at *A* to a plate cut in the shape of a regular hexagon of side $a = 5$ in. Determine the force **P** for which the resultant of the system is directed along (*a*) side *BC*, (*b*) side *CD*, (*c*) side *DE*.

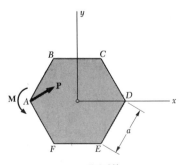

FIG. P 3.85

3.86. In Prob. 3.85, determine the force **P** for which the resultant of the system is directed along a line joining (*a*) points *F* and *C*, (*b*) points *E* and *B*.

3.87. A force **P** of given magnitude *P* is applied to the edge of a circular plate of radius *a* as shown.   (*a*) Replace **P** by a force-couple system at point *D*.   (*b*) Determine the value of *θ* for which the moment of the equivalent force-couple system at *D* is maximum.

3.88. A force **P** of given magnitude *P* is applied to the edge of a circular plate of radius *a* as shown.   (*a*) Replace **P** by an equivalent force-couple system at the point *E* obtained by drawing the perpendicular from *B* to the *x* axis.   (*b*) Determine the value of *θ* for which the moment of the equivalent force-couple system at *E* is maximum.

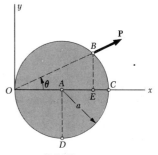

FIG. P 3.87 AND P 3.88

°3.89. Two forces, each of magnitude *P*, are applied to the edge of a circular disk as shown.   Knowing that the line of action of the resultant of the two forces is tangent to the edge of the disk, determine the required value of *β*.

3.90. Two forces, both parallel to the *yz* plane, are applied to the pipe as shown.   Determine the components of the force and couple at *A* equivalent to the two forces.

3.91. Two forces, both parallel to the *yz* plane, are applied to the pipe as shown.   Determine the components of the force and couple at *B* equivalent to the two forces.

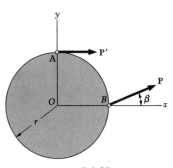

FIG. P 3.89

3.92. What is the smallest additional force **P** that can be applied at point *E* in order to transform the system of forces into a system equivalent to a single force applied at the origin of coordinates?

3.93. In drilling a hole in a wall, a man applies a vertical 30-lb force at *B* on the brace and bit, while pushing at *C* with a 10-lb force.   The brace lies in the horizontal *xz* plane.   (*a*) Determine the other components of the total force which should be exerted at *C* if the bit is not to be bent about the *y* and *z* axes (i.e., if the system of forces applied on the brace is to have zero moment about both the *y* and *z* axes).   (*b*) Reduce the 30-lb force and the total force at *C* to an equivalent force and couple at *A*.

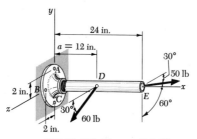

FIG. P 3.90, P 3.91, AND P 3.92

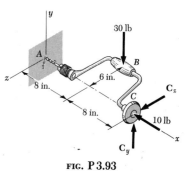

FIG. P 3.93

3.94. A concrete foundation mat of 16-ft radius supports four equally spaced columns, each of which is located 14 ft from the center of the mat. Determine the magnitude and the point of application of the resultant of the four loads.

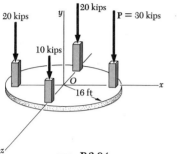

FIG. P 3.94

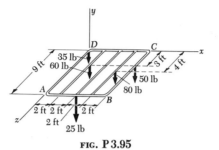

FIG. P 3.95

3.95. Five loads are suspended from the rack shown. Determine the magnitude and line of action of the resultant of the five loads.

3.96. A marine crane is mounted on a 100- by 50-ft barge; the crane supports an 80-kip load, and a 100-kip load is stored on the deck at E. Determine the magnitude and point of application of the smallest additional load which should be placed on the deck if the resultant of the three loads is to pass through the center of the barge.

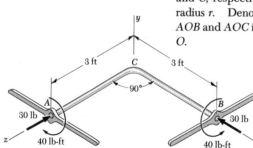

FIG. P 3.96

3.97. Three vertical loads P_1, P_2, and P_3 are applied at points A, B, and C, respectively, on the perimeter of a horizontal circular plate of radius r. Denoting the center of the plate by O, determine the angles AOB and AOC if the resultant of the three loads is to pass through point O.

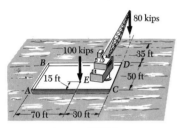

3.98. Two men are threading the ends of a bent pipe simultaneously. Each of the men applies a 40-lb-ft couple and a force of 30 lb directed along the axis of the section he is threading. The thread at A is to be right-handed, and that at B is to be left-handed. (*a*) Replace the given system of forces by a force at C and a couple. (*b*) Show that the given system may be reduced to a single force and determine the line of action of the force.

FIG. P 3.98

°3.99. Three forces act on a cube of side a as shown. Determine the magnitude of $\mathbf{F}_3$, knowing that $F_1 = F_2 = P$ and that the system may be reduced to a single force $\mathbf{R}$. Also determine the magnitude of $\mathbf{R}$ and its line of action.

3.100. Three forces act on a cube of side a as shown. Determine the magnitude and axis of the wrench equivalent to the three forces, if $F_1 = F_2 = F_3 = P$.

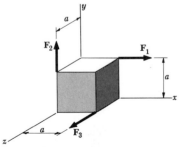

FIG. P 3.99 AND P 3.100

3.101. Solve Prob. 3.100 if $F_1 = F_2 = P$ and $F_3 = 0$.

3.102. A rectangular block is acted upon by the five forces shown, which are directed along the edges. Reduce the system of forces to (*a*) a force-couple system at the origin, (*b*) a wrench (specify the axis and pitch of the wrench).

3.103. Solve Prob. 3.102 if the 10-lb forces are replaced by 20-lb forces.

3.104. Two forces of magnitude *P* act along the diagonals of the faces of a cube of side *a* as shown. Replace the two forces by a system consisting of (*a*) a single force at *O* and a couple, (*b*) a wrench (specify the axis and pitch of the wrench).

°3.105. In Prob. 3.94 determine the range of permissible values of the load **P** if the resultant of the four loads must be located so that (*a*) it is not more than 4 ft from the *yz* plane, (*b*) it is not more than 4 ft from the center of the mat.

°3.106. In Prob. 3.90 consider the dimension *a* as a variable and determine the force and couple at the origin of coordinates which are equivalent to the two forces shown. For what value of *a* is the moment of the couple minimum?

3.107. (*a*) Reduce the wrench shown to a system consisting of two forces perpendicular to the *y* axis and applied respectively at *A* and *B*. (*b*) Solve part *a* assuming $R = 60$ lb, $M = 400$ lb-in., $a = 5$ in., and $b = 10$ in.

3.108. Knowing that $R = 70$ lb and $M = 140$ lb-in., replace the given wrench by a system of two forces chosen in such a way that one force acts at point *B* and the other force lies in the *xz* plane.

3.109. Show that, in general, a wrench may be replaced by two forces chosen in such a way that one force passes through a given point while the other force lies in a given plane.

°3.110. Show that a wrench may be replaced by two perpendicular forces, one of which is applied at a given point.

°3.111. Show that a wrench may be replaced by two forces, one of which has a prescribed line of action.

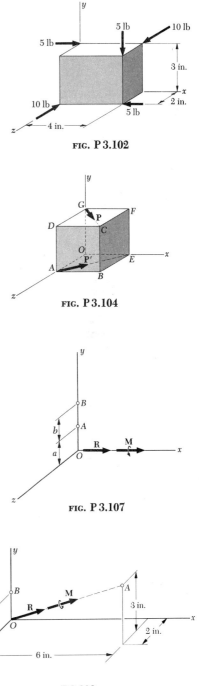

FIG. P3.102

FIG. P3.104

FIG. P3.107

FIG. P3.108

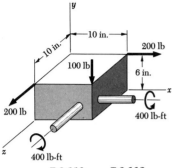

FIG. P3.112 AND P3.113

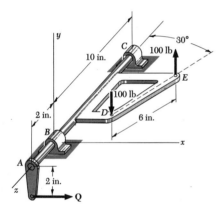

FIG. P3.116

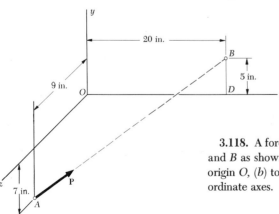

FIG. P3.118

REVIEW PROBLEMS

3.112. Replace the forces and couples shown by an equivalent force-couple system at the origin of coordinates.

3.113. Determine the magnitude of the single force equivalent to the system shown and find the point where its line of action intersects each of the coordinate planes.

3.114. Find the resultant of the system shown and the point of intersection of its line of action with (*a*) line *AB*, (*b*) line *BD*, (*c*) line *DE*.

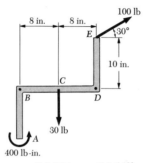

FIG. P3.114 AND P3.115

3.115. Determine the magnitude and sense of the single vertical force **P** which must be applied at *D* if the line of action of the resultant of the entire system is to pass through point *B*.

3.116. A 600-lb-in. couple formed by two 100-lb forces and a force **Q** of magnitude 150 lb are applied to the assembly shown. Replace this system of forces (*a*) by an equivalent force-couple system at *B*, (*b*) by an equivalent wrench (specify the pitch and axis of the wrench).

3.117. The corners of a square plate of side *a* are lettered *A*, *B*, *C*, and *D* clockwise as viewed from above. The plate supports loads *W*, 2*W*, 3*W*, and 4*W* at the corners *A*, *B*, *C*, and *D*, respectively. Determine where the line of action of the resultant of the four loads intersects the plate.

3.118. A force **P** of magnitude 500 lb acts along a line joining points *A* and *B* as shown. Determine the moment of **P** with respect (*a*) to the origin *O*, (*b*) to a line forming equal angles with each of the positive coordinate axes.

3.119. Three forces act on a plate as shown. Determine (*a*) an equivalent force-couple system at *C*, (*b*) the points where the line of action of the resultant intersects the edge of the plate.

3.120. Determine the force **Q** which must be applied at *C* if the line of action of the entire system is to pass through both points *B* and *D*.

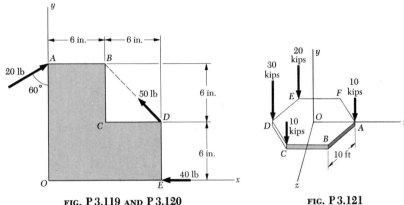

FIG. P 3.119 AND P 3.120   FIG. P 3.121

3.121. A concrete foundation mat, in the shape of a regular hexagon of side 10 ft, supports four column loads as shown. Determine where the line of action of the resultant of the four loads intersects the mat.

3.122. In Prob. 3.121 determine the magnitude of the downward loads which must be applied at *B* and *F* if the resultant of all six loads is to pass through the center of the mat.

3.123. Two wrenches, each with its axis perpendicular to the *y* axis, are applied to a gear box as shown. Determine (*a*) an equivalent force-couple system at the origin *O*, (*b*) a single equivalent wrench (specify the axis and pitch of the wrench).

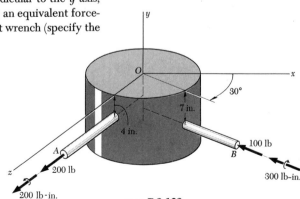

FIG. P 3.123

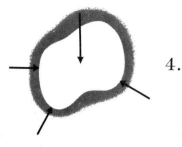

4. EQUILIBRIUM OF RIGID BODIES

4.1. Rigid Body in Equilibrium. *A rigid body is said to be in equilibrium when the external forces acting on it form a system of forces equivalent to zero,* i.e., when the external forces may be reduced to no force and no couple. Setting $\mathbf{R}$ and $\mathbf{M}_O^R$ equal to zero in the relations (3.47), we obtain the following necessary and sufficient conditions for the equilibrium of a rigid body:

$$\Sigma\mathbf{F} = 0 \qquad \Sigma\mathbf{M}_O = \Sigma(\mathbf{r} \times \mathbf{F}) = 0 \qquad (4.1)$$

Resolving each force and each moment into its rectangular components, we find that the necessary and sufficient conditions for the equilibrium of a rigid body may also be expressed by the six scalar equations

$$\Sigma F_x = 0 \qquad \Sigma F_y = 0 \qquad \Sigma F_z = 0 \qquad (4.2)$$
$$\Sigma M_x = 0 \qquad \Sigma M_y = 0 \qquad \Sigma M_z = 0 \qquad (4.3)$$

Equations (4.2) express the fact that the components of the external forces in the x, y, and z directions are balanced; Eqs. (4.3) express the fact that the moments of the external forces about the x, y, and z axes are balanced. The system of the external forces, therefore, will impart no motion of translation or rotation to the rigid body considered.

4.2. Free-body Diagram. In solving a problem concerning the equilibrium of a rigid body, it is essential to consider *all* the forces acting on the body; it is equally important to exclude any force which is not directly applied on the body. Omitting a force or adding an extraneous one would destroy the conditions of equilibrium. Therefore, the first step in the solution of the problem should consist in drawing a *free-body diagram* of the rigid body under consideration. Free-body diagrams have already been used on many occasions in Chap. 2. However, in view of their importance to the solution of equilibrium problems, we shall summarize here the various steps which must be followed in drawing a free-body diagram.

First, a clear decision is made regarding the choice of the free body to be used. This body is then detached from the ground and separated from any other body. The contour of the body thus isolated is sketched.

All external forces are then indicated. These forces represent the action exerted *on* the free body *by* the ground and the bodies which have been detached; they should be applied at the various points where the free body was supported by the ground or connected to the other bodies. The *weight* of the free body should also be included among the external forces, since it represents the attraction exerted by the earth on the various particles forming the free body. As will be seen in Chap. 5, the weight should be applied at the center of gravity of the body. When the free body is made of several parts, the forces the various parts exert on each other should *not* be included among the external forces. These forces are internal forces as far as the free body is concerned.

The magnitude and direction of the *known external forces* should be clearly marked on the free-body diagram. Care should be taken to indicate the sense of the force exerted *on* the free body, not that of the force exerted *by* the free body. Known external forces generally include the *weight* of the free body and *forces applied* for a given purpose.

Unknown external forces usually consist of the *reactions*—also called sometimes *constraining forces*—through which the ground and other bodies oppose a possible motion of the free body and thus constrain it to remain in the same position. Reactions are exerted at the points where the free body is *supported* or *connected* to other bodies. They will be discussed in detail in Secs. 4.3 and 4.8.

The free-body diagram should also include dimensions, since these may be needed in the computation of moments of forces. Any other detail, however, should be omitted.

EQUILIBRIUM IN TWO DIMENSIONS

4.3. Reactions at Supports and Connections for a Two-dimensional Structure. In the first part of this chapter we shall consider the equilibrium of a two-dimensional structure, i.e., we shall assume that the structure considered and the forces applied to it are contained in the plane of the figure. Clearly, the reactions needed to maintain the structure in the same position will also be contained in the plane of the figure.

The reactions exerted on a two-dimensional structure may be

divided into three groups, corresponding to three types of *supports*, or *connections:*

1. *Reactions Equivalent to a Force with Known Line of Action.*   Supports and connections causing reactions of this group include *rollers, rockers, smooth surfaces, short links and cables, collars on smooth rods,* and *pins in smooth slots.*   Each of these supports and connections can prevent motion in one direction only.   They are shown in Fig. 4.1, together with the reaction they produce.   Reactions of this group involve *one unknown,* namely, the magnitude of the reaction; this magnitude should be denoted by an appropriate letter.   The line of action of the reaction is known and should be indicated clearly in the free-body diagram.   The sense of the reaction must be as shown in Fig. 4.1 in the case of a smooth surface (away from the surface) or of a cable (tension in the direction of the cable).   The reaction may be directed either way in the case of double-track rollers, links, collars on rods, and pins in slots.   Single-track rollers and rockers are generally assumed to be reversible, and thus the corresponding reactions may also be directed either way.

2. *Reactions Equivalent to a Force of Unknown Direction.* Supports and connections causing reactions of this group include *smooth pins in fitted holes, hinges,* and *rough surfaces.* They can prevent translation of the free body in all directions, but they cannot prevent the body from rotating about the connection.   Reactions of this group involve *two unknowns* and are usually represented by their x and y components.   In the case of a rough surface, the component normal to the surface must be directed away from the surface.

3. *Reactions Equivalent to a Force and a Couple.*   These reactions are caused by *fixed supports* which oppose any motion of the free body and thus constrain it completely.   Fixed supports actually produce forces over the entire surface of contact; these forces, however, form a system which may be reduced to a force and a couple.   Reactions of this group involve *three unknowns,* namely, the two components of the force and the moment of the couple.

When the sense of an unknown force or couple is not clearly apparent, no attempt should be made at determining it.   Instead, the sense of the force or couple should be arbitrarily assumed; the sign of the answer obtained will indicate whether the assumption is correct or not.

4.4. Equilibrium of a Rigid Body in Two Dimensions.   The conditions stated in Sec. 4.1 for the equilibrium of a rigid body become considerably simpler in the case of a two-dimensional

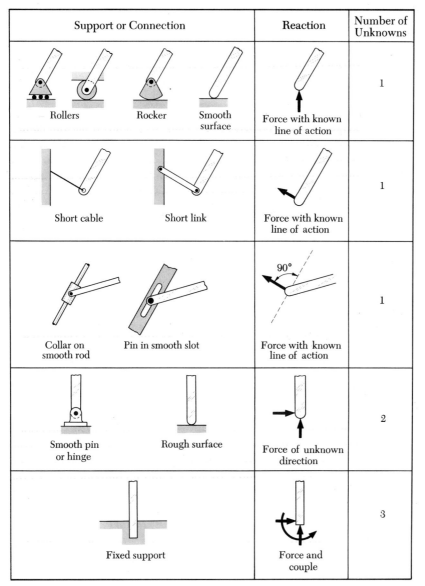

Support or Connection	Reaction	Number of Unknowns
Rollers Rocker Smooth surface	Force with known line of action	1
Short cable Short link	Force with known line of action	1
Collar on smooth rod Pin in smooth slot	Force with known line of action	1
Smooth pin or hinge Rough surface	Force of unknown direction	2
Fixed support	Force and couple	3

FIG. 4.1. Reactions at supports and connections

structure. Choosing the x and y axes in the plane of the structure, we have

$$F_z = 0 \qquad M_x = M_y = 0 \qquad M_z = M_0$$

for each of the forces applied to the structure. Thus, the six equations of equilibrium derived in Sec. 4.1 reduce to

$$\Sigma F_x = 0 \qquad \Sigma F_y = 0 \qquad \Sigma M_0 = 0 \qquad (4.4)$$

and to three trivial identities $0 = 0$. Since the third of the equations (4.4) must be satisfied regardless of the choice of the origin O, we may write the equations of equilibrium for a two-dimensional structure in the more general form

$$\Sigma F_x = 0 \qquad \Sigma F_y = 0 \qquad \Sigma M_A = 0 \qquad (4.5)$$

where A is any point in the plane of the structure.   <u>The three equations obtained may be solved for no more than *three unknowns.*</u>

We saw in the preceding sections that unknown forces usually consist of reactions, and that the number of unknowns corresponding to a given reaction depends upon the type of support or connection causing that reaction.   Referring to Sec. 4.3, we check that the equilibrium equations (4.5) may be used to determine the reactions of two rollers and one cable, or of one fixed support, or of one roller and one smooth pin in a fitted hole, etc.

Consider, for instance, the truss shown in Fig. 4.2*a*, which is subjected to the given forces **P**, **Q**, and **S**.   The truss is held in place by a smooth pin at A and a roller at B.   The pin prevents point A from moving by exerting on the truss a force which may be resolved into the components $\mathbf{A}_x$ and $\mathbf{A}_y$; the roller keeps the truss from rotating about A by exerting the vertical force **B**.   The free-body diagram of the truss is shown in Fig. 4.2*b*; it includes the reactions $\mathbf{A}_x$, $\mathbf{A}_y$, and **B** as well as the applied forces **P**, **Q**, **S**, and the weight **W** of the truss. Expressing that the sum of the moments about A of all the forces shown in Fig. 4.2*b* is zero, we write the equation $\Sigma M_A = 0$, which may be solved for the magnitude B since it does not contain A_x or A_y.   Expressing, then, that the sum of the x components and the sum of the y components of the forces are zero, we write the equations $\Sigma F_x = 0$ and $\Sigma F_y = 0$, which may be solved for the components A_x and A_y, respectively.

Additional equations could be obtained by expressing that the sum of the moments of the external forces about points other than A is zero.   We could write, for instance, $\Sigma M_B = 0$.   Such a statement, however, does not contain any new information, since it has already been established that the system of the forces shown in Fig. 4.2*b* is equivalent to zero. The additional equation *is not independent* and cannot be used to determine a fourth unknown.   It will be useful, however, for checking the solution obtained from the original three equations of equilibrium.

While the three equations of equilibrium cannot be *augmented* by additional equations, any of them may be *replaced* by another equation.   Thus, an alternate system of equations of equilibrium is

$$\Sigma F_x = 0 \qquad \Sigma M_A = 0 \qquad \Sigma M_B = 0 \qquad (4.6)$$

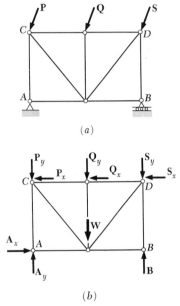

(a)

(b)

FIG. 4.2

where the line AB is chosen in a direction different from the y direction (Fig. 4.2b). These equations are sufficient conditions for the equilibrium of the truss. The first two equations indicate that the external forces must reduce to a single vertical force at A. Since the third equation requires that the moment of this force be zero about a point B which is not on its line of action, the force must be zero and the rigid body is in equilibrium.

A third possible set of equations of equilibrium is

$$\Sigma M_A = 0 \qquad \Sigma M_B = 0 \qquad \Sigma M_C = 0 \qquad (4.7)$$

where the points A, B, and C are not in a straight line (Fig. 4.2b). The first equation requires that the external forces reduce to a single force at A; the second equation requires that this force pass through B; the third, that it pass through C. Since the points A, B, C are not in a straight line, the force must be zero and the rigid body is in equilibrium.

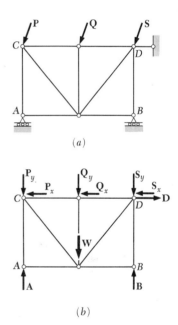

(a)

(b)

The equation $\Sigma M_A = 0$, which expresses that the sum of the moments of the forces about pin A is zero, possesses a more definite physical meaning than either of the other two equations (4.7). These two equations express a similar idea of balance, but with respect to points about which the rigid body is not actually hinged. They are, however, as useful as the first equation, and our choice of equilibrium equations should not be unduly influenced by the physical meaning of these equations. Indeed, it will be desirable in practice to choose equations of equilibrium containing only one unknown, since this eliminates the necessity of solving simultaneous equations. Equations containing only one unknown may be obtained by summing moments about the point of intersection of the lines of action of two unknown forces or, if these forces are parallel, by summing components in a direction perpendicular to their common direction. In the case of the truss of Fig. 4.3, for example, which is held by rollers at A and B and a short link at D, the reactions at A and B may be eliminated by summing x components. The reactions at A and D will be eliminated by summing moments about C and the reactions at B and D by summing moments about D. The equations obtained are

$$\Sigma F_x = 0 \qquad \Sigma M_C = 0 \qquad \Sigma M_D = 0$$

Each of these equations contains only one unknown.

4.5. Statically Indeterminate Reactions. Partial Constraints. In each of the two examples considered in the preceding section (Figs. 4.2 and 4.3), the reactions to be de-

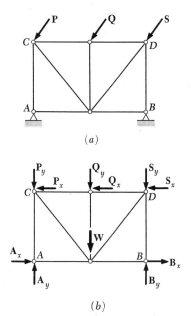

(a)

(b)

**FIG. 4.4. Statically indeter-
minate reactions**

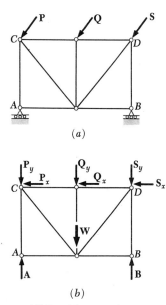

(a)

(b)

FIG. 4.5. Partial constraints

termined involved *three unknowns;* these unknowns were obtained by solving the three equations of equilibrium.   Besides,
the types of supports used were such that the rigid body could
not possibly move under the given loads or under any other
loading conditions.   In such cases, the reactions are said to
be *statically determinate* and the rigid body is said to be *completely constrained.*

Consider now the truss shown in Fig. 4.4a, which is held
by smooth pins at A and B.   We note from the free-body diagram of Fig. 4.4b that the reactions involve *four unknowns.*
Since, as was pointed out in Sec. 4.4, only three independent
equilibrium equations are available, there are *more unknowns
than equations* and all the unknowns cannot be determined.
While the equations $\Sigma M_A = 0$ and $\Sigma M_B = 0$ yield the vertical components B_y and A_y, respectively, the equation $\Sigma F_x =
0$ gives only the sum $A_x + B_x$ of the horizontal components
of the reactions at A and B.   The components A_x and B_x are
said to be *statically indeterminate.*   They could be determined by considering the deformations produced in the truss
by the given loading, but this method is beyond the scope of
statics and belongs to the study of mechanics of materials.

The supports used to hold the truss shown in Fig. 4.5a consist of rollers at A and B.   The corresponding reactions, shown
in Fig. 4.5b, involve *two unknowns.*   Since three equations
of equilibrium must still be satisfied, there are *fewer unknowns
than equations* and one of the equilibrium equations will not be
satisfied.   While the equations $\Sigma M_A = 0$ and $\Sigma M_B = 0$ can
be satisfied by a proper choice of reactions at A and B, the
equation $\Sigma F_x = 0$ will not be satisfied unless the sum of the
horizontal components of the applied forces happens to be
zero.   The physical significance of this result is clear: Equilibrium cannot be maintained under general loading conditions;
while any vertical motion is prevented, the truss is free to
move horizontally.   The truss is said to be only *partially constrained.*†

It appears from the above that, if a rigid body is to be completely constrained and if the reactions at its supports are to
be statically determinate, *there must be as many unknowns
as there are equations of equilibrium.*   We should note, however, that while *necessary* this condition is *not sufficient.*

---

† Partially constrained bodies are often referred to as *unstable.*   However,
in order to avoid any confusion between this type of instability, due to insuffi-
cient constraints, and the type of instability considered in Chap. 10, which relates to the behavior of a rigid body when its equilibrium is disturbed, we shall
restrict the use of the words *stable* and *unstable* to the latter case.

Consider, for example, the truss shown in Fig. 4.6a, which is held by rollers at A, B, and E.   While there are three unknown reactions, **A**, **B**, and **E** (Fig. 4.6b), we find that the equation $\Sigma F_x = 0$ will not be satisfied unless the sum of the horizontal components of the applied forces happens to be zero.   There is a sufficient number of constraints, but these constraints are not properly arranged; we say that the truss is *improperly constrained*.   Since only two equilibrium equations are left for determining the three unknowns, the reactions will be statically indeterminate.   Thus, improper constraints also produce statical indeterminacy.

Another example of improper constraints—and of the accompanying statical indeterminacy—is provided by the truss shown in Fig. 4.7.   This truss is held by a smooth pin at A and by rollers at B and C, which altogether involve four unknowns.   Choosing the equilibrium equations $\Sigma M_A = 0$, $\Sigma F_x = 0$, and $\Sigma F_y = 0$, we find that the first equation cannot be satisfied under general loading conditions, while the other two yield only the sums $A_x + B$ and $A_y + C$.   The examples of Figs. 4.6 and 4.7 lead us to conclude that *a rigid body is improperly constrained whenever the supports,* even though they may provide a sufficient number of reactions, *are arranged in such a way that the reactions must be either concurrent or parallel.*†

Supports involving statically indeterminate reactions should be used with care in the *design* of structures, and only with a full knowledge of the problems they may cause.   On the other hand, the *analysis* of structures possessing statically indeterminate reactions often may be partially carried out by the methods of statics.   In the case of the truss of Fig. 4.4, for example, the vertical components of the reactions at A and B were obtained from the equilibrium equations.

For obvious reasons, supports producing partial or improper constraints should be avoided in the design of stationary structures.   However, a partially or improperly constrained structure will not necessarily collapse; under particular loading conditions, equilibrium may be maintained.   For example, the trusses of Figs. 4.5 and 4.6 will be in equilibrium if the applied forces **P**, **Q**, and **S** are vertical.   Besides, structures which are designed to move *should* be only partially constrained.   A railroad car, for instance, would be of little use if it were completely constrained by having its brakes applied permanently.

† Because this situation arises from an inadequate arrangement or *geometry* of the supports, it is often referred to as *geometric instability.*

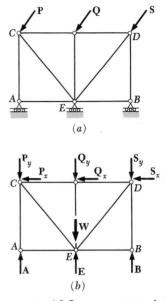

FIG. 4.6. Improper constraints

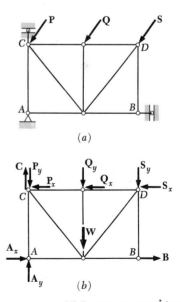

FIG. 4.7. Improper constraints

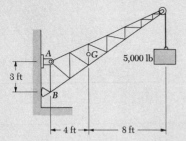

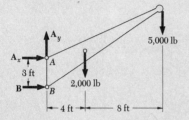

SAMPLE PROBLEM 4.1

A fixed crane weighs 2,000 lb and is used to lift a load of 5,000 lb. It is held in place by a smooth pin at A and a rocker at B. The center of gravity is located at G. Determine the components of the reactions at A and B.

Solution. A free-body diagram of the crane is drawn. Since the reaction at a smooth pin is a force of unknown direction, the reaction at A is represented by its components A_x and A_y. Since the reaction at a rocker is perpendicular to the rocker surface, the reaction at B will be horizontal. We assume that A_x, A_y, and B act in the directions shown on the free-body diagram.

Determination of **B.** We express that the sum of the moments of all external forces about point A is zero. The equation obtained will contain neither A_x nor A_y since the moments of A_x and A_y about A are zero. Multiplying the magnitude of each force by its perpendicular distance from B, and recalling that counterclockwise is positive, we write

$$+\rotatebox{0}{$\curvearrowleft$}\ \Sigma M_A = 0: \qquad +B(3\text{ ft}) - (2,000\text{ lb})(4\text{ ft}) - (5,000\text{ lb})(12\text{ ft}) = 0$$

$$B = +22,700\text{ lb} \qquad\qquad \mathbf{B} = 22,700\text{ lb} \rightarrow \qquad \blacktriangleleft$$

Since the result is positive, the reaction is directed as assumed.

Determination of $\mathbf{A}_x$. The magnitude A_x is determined by expressing that the sum of the horizontal components of all external forces is zero. We write

$$\xrightarrow{+}\ \Sigma F_x = 0: \qquad A_x + B = 0 \qquad A_x + 22,700\text{ lb} = 0$$

$$A_x = -22,700\text{ lb} \qquad\qquad \mathbf{A}_x = 22,700\text{ lb} \leftarrow \qquad \blacktriangleleft$$

Determination of $\mathbf{A}_y$. The sum of the vertical components must also equal zero.

$$+\uparrow \Sigma F_y = 0: \qquad A_y - 2,000\text{ lb} - 5,000\text{ lb} = 0$$

$$A_y = +7,000\text{ lb} \qquad\qquad \mathbf{A}_y = 7,000\text{ lb} \uparrow \qquad \blacktriangleleft$$

Adding vectorially the components $\mathbf{A}_x$ and $\mathbf{A}_y$, we find that the reaction at A is 23,700 lb $\measuredangle$ 17.2°.

Check. The values obtained for the reactions may be checked by recalling that the sum of the moments of all external forces about any point must be zero. For example, considering point B, we write

$$+\rotatebox{0}{$\curvearrowleft$}\ \Sigma M_B = -(2,000\text{ lb})(4\text{ ft}) - (5,000\text{ lb})(12\text{ ft}) + (22,700\text{ lb})(3\text{ ft}) = 0$$

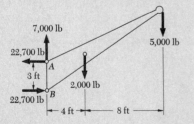

116

SAMPLE PROBLEM 4.2

Three loads are applied to a truss as shown. The truss is supported by a roller at A and by a smooth pin at B. Determine the reactions at A and B.

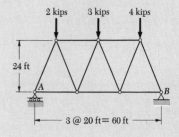

Solution. A free-body diagram of the truss is drawn. The reaction at A is vertical and is denoted by **A**. The reaction at B is represented by components $\mathbf{B}_x$ and $\mathbf{B}_y$. Each component is assumed to act in the direction shown.

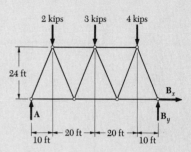

Equilibrium Equations. We write the following three equilibrium equations and solve for the reactions indicated:

$$\xrightarrow{+} \Sigma F_x = 0: \qquad B_x = 0 \qquad\qquad\qquad\qquad B_x = 0 \blacktriangleleft$$

$$+\,\rotatebox{0}{$\circlearrowleft$}\ \Sigma M_A = 0:$$

$$-(2\text{ kips})(10\text{ ft}) - (3\text{ kips})(30\text{ ft}) - (4\text{ kips})(50\text{ ft}) + B_y(60\text{ ft}) = 0$$
$$B_y = +5.17\text{ kips} \qquad\qquad B_y = 5.17\text{ kips}\uparrow \blacktriangleleft$$

$$+\,\rotatebox{0}{$\circlearrowleft$}\ \Sigma M_B = 0:$$

$$A(60\text{ ft}) - (2\text{ kips})(50\text{ ft}) - (3\text{ kips})(30\text{ ft}) - (4\text{ kips})(10\text{ ft}) = 0$$
$$A = +3.83\text{ kips} \qquad\qquad A = 3.83\text{ kips}\uparrow \blacktriangleleft$$

Check. The results are checked by adding the vertical components of all the external forces.

$$+\uparrow\Sigma F_y = +5.17\text{ kips} + 3.83\text{ kips} - 2\text{ kips} - 3\text{ kips} - 4\text{ kips} = 0$$

Remark. In this problem the reactions at both A and B are vertical; however, these reactions are vertical for different reasons. At A, the truss is supported by a roller; hence the reaction cannot have any horizontal component. At B, the horizontal component of the reaction is zero because it must satisfy the equilibrium equation $\Sigma F_x = 0$ and none of the other forces acting on the truss has a horizontal component.

We could have noticed at first glance that the reaction at B was vertical and dispensed with the horizontal component $\mathbf{B}_x$. This, however, is a bad practice. In following it, we would run the risk of forgetting the component $\mathbf{B}_x$ when the loading conditions require such a component (i.e., when a horizontal load is included). Also, the component $\mathbf{B}_x$ was found to be zero by using and solving an equilibrium equation, $\Sigma F_x = 0$. By setting $\mathbf{B}_x$ equal to zero immediately, we might not realize that we actually make use of this equation and thus might lose track of the number of equations available for solving the problem.

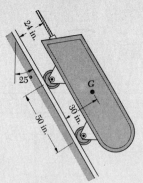

SAMPLE PROBLEM 4.3

A loading car is at rest on a track forming an angle of 25° with the vertical. The gross weight of the car and its load is 5,500 lb, and it is applied at a point 30 in. from the track, halfway between the two axles. The car is held by a cable attached 24 in. from the track. Determine the tension in the cable and the reaction at each pair of wheels.

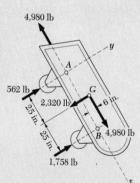

Solution. A free-body diagram of the car is drawn. The reaction at each wheel is perpendicular to the track, and the tension force **T** is parallel to the track. For convenience, we choose the x axis parallel to the track and the y axis perpendicular to the track. The 5,500-lb weight is then resolved into x and y components.

$$W_x = +(5,500 \text{ lb}) \cos 25° = +4,980 \text{ lb}$$

$$W_y = -(5,500 \text{ lb}) \sin 25° = -2,320 \text{ lb}$$

Equilibrium Equations. We take moments about A to eliminate **T** and $\mathbf{R}_1$ from the computation.

$$+{\Large\rangle}\ \Sigma M_A = 0:$$

$$-(2,320 \text{ lb})(25 \text{ in.}) - (4,980 \text{ lb})(6 \text{ in.}) + R_2(50 \text{ in.}) = 0$$

$$R_2 = +1,758 \text{ lb} \qquad \mathbf{R}_2 = 1,758 \text{ lb} \nearrow \quad \blacktriangleleft$$

Now, taking moments about B to eliminate **T** and $\mathbf{R}_2$ from the computation, we write

$$+{\Large\rangle}\ \Sigma M_B = 0: \qquad (2,320 \text{ lb})(25 \text{ in.}) - (4,980 \text{ lb})(6 \text{ in.}) - R_1(50 \text{ in.}) = 0$$

$$R_1 = +562 \text{ lb} \qquad \mathbf{R}_1 = 562 \text{ lb} \nearrow \quad \blacktriangleleft$$

The value of T is found by writing

$$\searrow\ +\Sigma F_x = 0: \qquad +4,980 \text{ lb} - T = 0$$

$$T = +4,980 \text{ lb} \qquad \mathbf{T} = 4,980 \text{ lb} \nwarrow \quad \blacktriangleleft$$

The computed values of the reactions are shown in the adjacent sketch.

Check. The computations are verified by writing

$$\nearrow\ +\Sigma F_y = +562 \text{ lb} + 1,758 \text{ lb} - 2,320 \text{ lb} = 0$$

A check could also have been obtained by computing moments about any point except A or B.

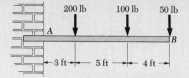

SAMPLE PROBLEM 4.4

A cantilever beam is loaded as shown. The beam is fixed at the left end and free at the right end. Determine the reaction at the fixed end.

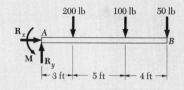

Solution. The portion of the beam which is embedded in the wall is subjected to a large number of forces. These forces, however, are equivalent to a force of components R_x and R_y and a couple **M**.

Equilibrium Equations

$\xrightarrow{+} \Sigma F_x = 0:$ $R_x = 0$ $R_x = 0$ ◄

$+\uparrow \Sigma F_y = 0:$ $R_y - 200\,\text{lb} - 100\,\text{lb} - 50\,\text{lb} = 0$
                   $R_y = +350\,\text{lb}$ $R_y = 350\,\text{lb} \uparrow$ ◄

$+\,\rotatebox[origin=c]{180}{$\circlearrowleft$}\, \Sigma M_A = 0:$

$-(200\,\text{lb})(3\,\text{ft}) - (100\,\text{lb})(8\,\text{ft}) - (50\,\text{lb})(12\,\text{ft}) + M = 0$
         $M = +2{,}000\,\text{lb-ft}$ $\mathbf{M = 2{,}000\,\text{lb-ft}}$ ◄

The reaction at the fixed end consists of a vertical upward force of 350 lb and of a 2,000-lb-ft counterclockwise couple.

Check. The results may be checked by computing moments about any point. Choosing point B, we write

$+\,\rotatebox[origin=c]{180}{$\circlearrowleft$}\, \Sigma M_B = 2{,}000\,\text{lb-ft} - (350\,\text{lb})(12\,\text{ft}) + (200\,\text{lb})(9\,\text{ft}) + (100\,\text{lb})(4\,\text{ft}) = 0$

SAMPLE PROBLEM 4.5

A 400-lb weight is attached to the lever AO as shown. The constant of the spring BC is $k = 250$ lb/in., and the spring is unstretched when $\theta = 0$. Determine the position or positions of equilibrium.

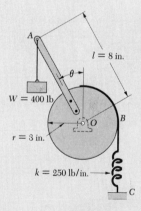

Solution. *Force Exerted by Spring.* Denoting by s the deflection of the spring from its undeformed position, and noting that $s = r\theta$, we write

$$F = ks = kr\theta$$

Equilibrium Equation. Summing the moments of **W** and **F** about O, we write

$+\,\rotatebox[origin=c]{180}{$\circlearrowleft$}\, \Sigma M_O = 0:.$ $Wl \sin\theta - r(kr\theta) = 0$ $\sin\theta = \dfrac{kr^2}{Wl}\theta$

Substituting the given data, we obtain

$$\sin\theta = \frac{(250\,\text{lb/in.})(3\,\text{in.})^2}{(400\,\text{lb})(8\,\text{in.})}\theta \qquad \sin\theta = 0.7030\,\theta$$

Solving by trial and error, we find

$$\theta = 0 \qquad \theta = 80.4° \quad ◄$$

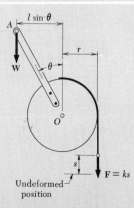

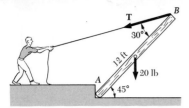

FIG. P4.1

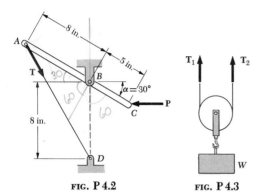

FIG. P4.2

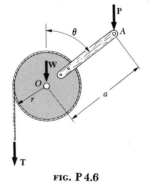

FIG. P4.3

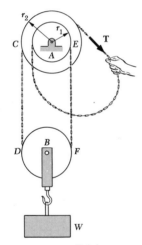

FIG. P4.4

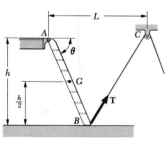

FIG. P4.5

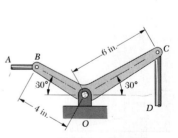

FIG. P4.6

FIG. P4.7 AND P4.8

PROBLEMS

4.1. A man raises a 12-ft joist weighing 20 lb by pulling on a rope. Find the tension T in the rope and the reaction at A.

4.2. A 13-in. lever is hinged at B and attached to a control cable at A. Knowing that the magnitude of the force **P** is 400 lb, find the tension in the cable and the reaction at B.

4.3. A load W is supported by the pulley as shown. Prove that, if the pulley is in equilibrium, the tensions T_1 and T_2 are both equal to $W/2$.

4.4. The chain hoist shown may be used to raise a weight W by pulling on the free end of the chain with a smaller force **T**. (*a*) Derive an expression for the magnitude of **T** in terms of W, r_1, and r_2. (*b*) If $W = 3$ tons, $r_1 = 7$ in., and $r_2 = 7.5$ in., determine the magnitude of the required force **T**.

4.5. The ladder AB, of length L and weight W, can be raised by the cable BC. Determine the tension T required to raise end B just off the floor (*a*) in terms of W and θ, (*b*) if $h = 8$ ft, $L = 10$ ft, and $W = 35$ lb.

4.6. A vertical force **P** is applied to the handle of a winch of weight **W**. Determine the tension in the hoisting cable (*a*) in terms of P, W, r, a, and θ, (*b*) if $P = 40$ lb, $W = 20$ lb, $r = 4$ in., $a = 12$ in., and $\theta = 75°$.

4.7. Two links AB and CD are connected by a bell crank as shown. The tension in link AB is 100 lb. Determine the tension in CD and the reaction at O.

4.8. Find the maximum force which may be safely exerted by link AB on the bell crank if the maximum allowable value for the reaction at O is 500 lb.

4.9. Determine the reactions at A and B for the truss and loading shown.   Note that the roller rests on a 30° incline.

4.10. Determine the reactions at A and B for the truss of Prob. 4.9, if the horizontal 4-kip load is directed to the left.

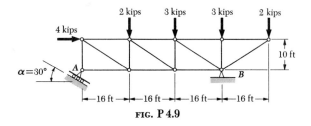

FIG. P 4.9

4.11. Determine the reactions at A and B for the truss of Prob. 4.9, if the horizontal 4-kip load is removed.

4.12. Determine the reaction at A and B for the truss and loading of Prob. 4.9, if the roller at A rests on a horizontal plane.

4.13. A movable bracket is held at rest by a cable attached at C and by frictionless rollers at A and B.   For the loading shown, determine the tension in the cable and the reactions at A and B.

FIG. P 4.13

4.14. A light bar AD is suspended from a cable BE and supports an 800-lb load at point C.   The extremities A and D of the bar are in contact with smooth, vertical walls.   (*a*) If $d = 8$ in., determine the tension in cable BE and the reactions at A and D.   (*b*) Find the maximum distance d which may be safely used if the maximum allowable value for the reaction at A is 500 lb.

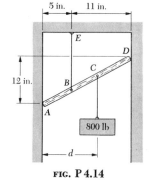

FIG. P 4.14

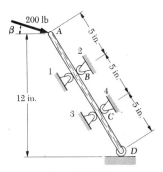

FIG. P 4.15

4.15. A light rod, supported by rollers at B, C, and D, is subjected to a 200-lb force applied at A.   If $\beta = 0$, determine (*a*) the reactions at B, C, and D, (*b*) the rollers which may safely be removed for this loading.

4.16. Solve Prob. 4.15 when the 200-lb force is directed vertically downward, i.e., when $\beta = 90°$.

4.17. A man holds a 3-ft wooden bar at both ends while another man tightens screws into the bar with a screw driver, applying a couple of magnitude 10 lb-ft.   Find the smallest forces that the first man may apply to hold the bar in place while a screw is being tightened (*a*) in the middle of the bar, (*b*) 1 ft from the end of the bar.

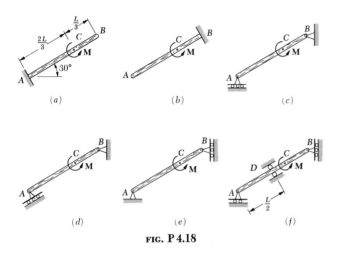

(a)   (b)   (c)

(d)   (e)   (f)

FIG. P 4.18

4.18. A couple **M** is applied to a bar of length L which may be supported in six different ways as shown. In each case determine the reactions at the supports.

4.19. Determine the reactions at the points of support of the pulley assembly of Prob. 3.50, assuming in turn the following types of connections: (a) a pin in a fitted hole at A and a pin in a horizontal slot at C, (b) a pin in a fitted hole at A and a pin in a vertical slot at D, (c) a tightly clinched rivet at A.

4.20. Determine the reactions at the points of support of the pulley assembly of Prob. 3.50, assuming in turn the following types of connections: (a) a pin in a horizontal slot at B and a pin in a fitted hole at D, (b) a pin in a vertical slot at B and a pin in a fitted hole at D, (c) a tightly clinched rivet at B.

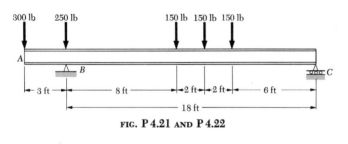

FIG. P 4.21 AND P 4.22

4.21. Determine the reactions at B and C for the beam and loading shown.

4.22. Assuming that the maximum allowable value of the reaction at B is 2,000 lb and that the reaction at C must be directed upward, determine the largest additional downward force **P** which may safely be applied at point A.

4.23. The crane supports a 500-lb load. Find the reactions for each of the three types of supports shown.

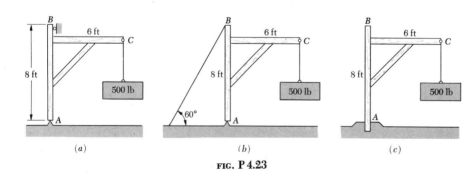

(a)   (b)   (c)

FIG. P 4.23

4.24. A slender, uniform bar is 24 in. long and weighs 15 lb. Determine the reactions for each of the four types of supports shown.

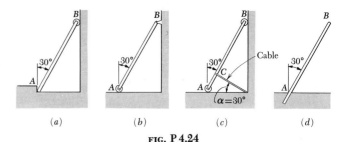

(a)　　　(b)　　　(c)　　　(d)

FIG. P 4.24

4.25. Determine the reactions at the points of support of the angle bracket of Prob. 3.82, assuming in turn the following types of connections: (*a*) a pin in a fitted hole at *A* and a pin in a horizontal slot at *B*, (*b*) a pin in a horizontal slot at *A* and a pin in a fitted hole at *B*, (*c*) a firmly clinched rivet at *B*.

4.26. Determine the reactions at the points of support of the angle bracket of Prob. 3.82, assuming in turn the following types of connections: (*a*) a pin in a fitted hole at *A* and a pin in a vertical slot at *C*, (*b*) a pin in a horizontal slot at *A* and a pin in a fitted hole at *C*, (*c*) a firmly clinched rivet at *C*.

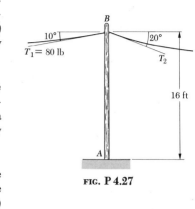

FIG. P 4.27

4.27. A 16-ft telephone pole weighing 300 lb is used to support the ends of two wires. The tension in the wire to the left is 80 lb and, at the point of support, the wire forms an angle of 10° with the horizontal. (*a*) If the tension T_2 is zero, determine the reaction at the base *A*. (*b*) Determine the largest and smallest allowable tension T_2, if the magnitude of the couple at *A* may not exceed 600 lb-ft.

4.28. A workbench seat *ABC* is held in the position shown by a vertical bar *DE* and supports a 175-lb man. (*a*) Determine the reaction at *A*. (*b*) If the inside diameter of the collar is slightly larger than the bar, the collar will bear only at points *G* and *H*. Determine the magnitude of the horizontal forces developed at *G* and *H*.

FIG. P 4.28

4.29. In the pivoted motor mount, or Rockwood drive, the weight of the motor is used to maintain tension in the drive belt. When the motor is at rest, the tensions T_1 and T_2 may be assumed equal. The weight of the motor is 175 lb, and the diameter of the drive pulley is 6 in. Assuming that the weight of the platform *AB* is negligible, determine the tension in the belt and the reaction at *C* when the motor is at rest.

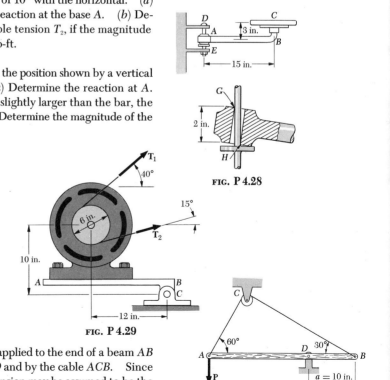

FIG. P 4.29

4.30. A force **P** of magnitude 40 lb is applied to the end of a beam *AB* which is supported by a smooth pin at *D* and by the cable *ACB*. Since the cable passes over a pulley at *C*, the tension may be assumed to be the same in the portions *AC* and *BC* of the cable. Determine the tension in the cable and the reaction at *D*.

FIG. P 4.30

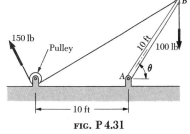

FIG. P 4.31

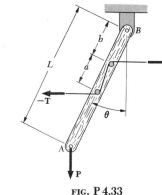

FIG. P 4.33

*4.31. Find the angle θ for which the boom AB is in equilibrium. Neglect the weight of the boom.

*4.32. Solve Prob. 4.31 assuming that the 100-lb force applied at B is directed horizontally to the right.

*4.33. The control rod AB is acted upon by the vertical force $\mathbf{P}$ and by two forces of magnitude T exerted by the cable which passes over frictionless pulleys of negligible diameter. Assuming that the free ends of the cable remain horizontal, determine the value of θ corresponding to equilibrium.

*4.34. For the control rod of Prob. 4.33 the following values are given: $L = 20$ in., $a = 8$ in., $b = 5$ in., $T = 150$ lb, and $P = 100$ lb. If possible, determine the value of θ corresponding to equilibrium (a) neglecting the diameter of the pulleys, (b) assuming that the diameter of each pulley is 1 in., (c) neglecting the diameter of the pulleys and assuming that the force $\mathbf{P}$ is directed horizontally to the right.

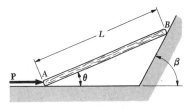

FIG. P 4.35

*4.35. A uniform, slender rod of length L and weight W is held in the position shown by the horizontal force $\mathbf{P}$. Knowing that both the floor at A and the surface at B are smooth, determine the angle θ corresponding to equilibrium (a) in terms of P, W, L, and β, (b) if $P = 10$ lb, $W = 20$ lb, $L = 30$ in., and $\beta = 60°$.

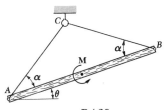

FIG. P 4.36

*4.36. A uniform rod of length L and weight W is suspended by two cords of equal length. If a couple $\mathbf{M}$ is applied to the rod, find the angle θ formed by the axis of the rod and the horizontal. Also, prove that if both cords are to remain taut, the magnitude of $\mathbf{M}$ must be less than $\frac{1}{2} WL \sin \alpha$.

*4.37. Two wheels A and B, of weight W and $2W$, respectively, are connected by a rod of negligible weight and are free to roll on $45°$ inclines. Determine the angle θ that the rod forms with the incline AC when the system is in equilibrium.

*4.38. In the problems listed below, the rigid bodies considered were completely constrained and the reactions were statically determinate. For each of these rigid bodies it is possible to create an improper set of constraints by changing either a dimension of the body or the direction of a reaction. In each problem determine the value of α or of a which results in improper constraints. (a) Prob. 4.2, (b) Prob. 4.9, (c) Prob. 4.24c, (d) Prob. 4.30.

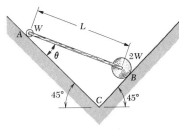

FIG. P 4.37

124

4.39. Twelve identical rectangular plates, 2 by 3 ft, weighing 100 lb each, are held in a vertical plane as shown. All connections consist of smooth pins, rollers, or short links. In each case, determine whether (*a*) the plate is completely, partially, or improperly constrained, (*b*) the reactions are statically determinate or indeterminate, (*c*) the equilibrium of the plate is maintained in the position shown. Also, wherever possible, compute the reactions.

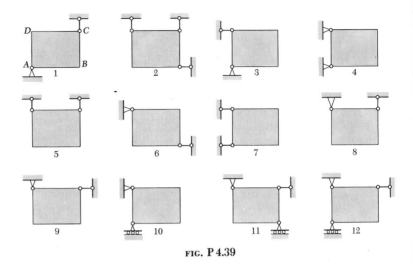

FIG. P 4.39

4.40. A small truss is supported in eight different ways as shown. All connections consist of smooth pins, rollers, or short links. For each structure, answer the questions listed in Prob. 4.39, and, wherever possible, compute the reactions, assuming that the magnitude of the force **P** is 10 kips.

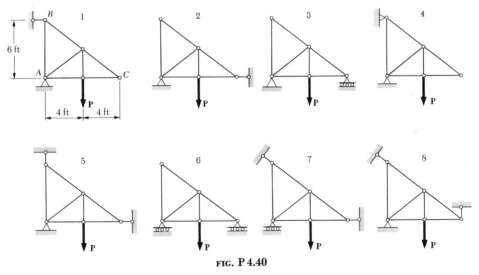

FIG. P 4.40

4.6. Equilibrium of a Two-force Body. A particular case of equilibrium which is of considerable interest is that of a rigid body subjected to two forces. Such a body is commonly called a *two-force body*. We shall show that, *if a two-force body is in equilibrium, the two forces must have the same magnitude, same line of action, and opposite sense.*

125

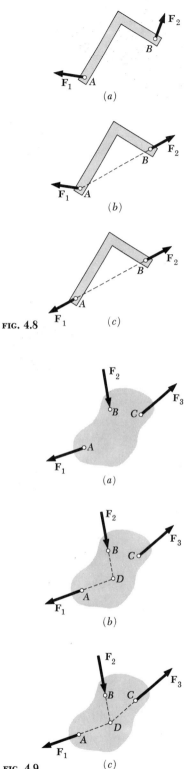

FIG. 4.8

FIG. 4.9

Consider a corner plate subjected to two forces $\mathbf{F}_1$ and $\mathbf{F}_2$ acting at A and B, respectively (Fig. 4.8a). If the plate is to be in equilibrium, the sum of the moments of $\mathbf{F}_1$ and $\mathbf{F}_2$ about any axis must be zero. First, we sum moments about A: since the moment of $\mathbf{F}_1$ is obviously zero, the moment of $\mathbf{F}_2$ must also be zero and the line of action of $\mathbf{F}_2$ must pass through A (Fig. 4.8b). Summing moments about B, we prove similarly that the line of action of $\mathbf{F}_1$ must pass through B (Fig. 4.8c). Both forces have the same line of action (line AB). From the equation $\Sigma F_x = 0$ or $\Sigma F_y = 0$, it is seen that they must have also the same magnitude but opposite sense.

If several forces act at two points A and B, the forces acting at A may be replaced by their resultant $\mathbf{F}_1$ and those acting at B by their resultant $\mathbf{F}_2$. Thus a two-force body may be more generally defined as *a rigid body subjected to forces acting at only two points.* The resultants $\mathbf{F}_1$ and $\mathbf{F}_2$ then must have the same line of action, same magnitude, and opposite sense.

Although problems dealing with the equilibrium of two-force bodies may be solved by the general methods studied in the preceding sections, it is sometimes desirable to make use of the property we have just established to simplify certain problems so that simple trigonometric or geometric relations can be used.

4.7. Equilibrium of a Three-force Body. Another case of equilibrium that is of great interest is that of a *three-force body,* i.e., a rigid body subjected to three forces or, more generally, *a rigid body subjected to forces acting at only three points.* Consider a rigid body subjected to a system of forces which may be reduced to three forces $\mathbf{F}_1$, $\mathbf{F}_2$, and $\mathbf{F}_3$ acting at A, B, and C, respectively (Fig. 4.9a). We shall show that, if the body is in equilibrium, *the lines of action of the three forces must be either concurrent or parallel.*

Since the rigid body is in equilibrium, the sum of the moments of $\mathbf{F}_1$, $\mathbf{F}_2$, and $\mathbf{F}_3$ about any axis must be zero. Assuming that the lines of action of $\mathbf{F}_1$ and $\mathbf{F}_2$ intersect, and denoting their point of intersection by D, we sum moments about D (Fig. 4.9b); since the moments of $\mathbf{F}_1$ and $\mathbf{F}_2$ about D are zero, the moment of $\mathbf{F}_3$ about D must also be zero and the line of action of $\mathbf{F}_3$ must pass through D (Fig. 4.9c). The three lines of action are concurrent. The only exception occurs when none of the lines intersect; the lines of action must then be parallel.

Although problems concerning three-force bodies may be solved by the general methods of Secs. 4.3 to 4.5, the property just established may be used to solve them either graphically or from simple trigonometric or geometric relations.

SAMPLE PROBLEM 4.6

A 500-lb cylindrical tank, 8 ft in diameter, is to be raised over a 2-ft obstruction. A cable is wrapped around the tank and pulled horizontally as shown. The corner of the obstruction at A is rough. Find the required tension in the cable and the reaction at A.

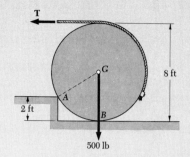

Solution. When the tank is just about to be raised, there is no force acting at B. Since the corner at A is rough, the reaction $\mathbf{R}$ is of unknown magnitude and direction. The only other forces acting on the tank are its 500-lb weight and the force $\mathbf{T}$ exerted by the cable. The tank is thus a three-force body, and the three forces must be concurrent. The reaction $\mathbf{R}$, therefore, will pass through the point of intersection C of the lines of action of the 500-lb weight and the tension force $\mathbf{T}$.

We compute

$$\cos\phi = \frac{GH}{AG} = \frac{2\text{ ft}}{4\text{ ft}} = 0.500 \qquad \phi = 60°$$

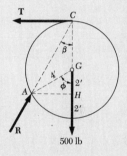

Since β is the corresponding inscribed angle, we find

$$\beta = \frac{\phi}{2} = 30°$$

A force triangle is drawn as shown, and we compute

$$T = (500\text{ lb})\tan 30° \qquad\qquad T = 288\text{ lb} \blacktriangleleft$$

$$R = \frac{500\text{ lb}}{\cos 30°} = 577\text{ lb} \qquad \mathbf{R} = 577\text{ lb} \measuredangle 60° \blacktriangleleft$$

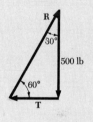

Remark. It should be noted that $\mathbf{R}$ is not normal to the surface of the tank. Therefore, the surfaces of the obstruction and of the tank must be rough if the tank is to be raised in the described manner. This point is discussed fully in Chap. 8.

PROBLEMS

4.41. Using the method of Sec. 4.7, solve Prob. 4.1.

4.42. Using the method of Sec. 4.7, solve Prob. 4.2.

4.43. Using the method of Sec. 4.7, solve Prob. 4.7.

4.44. Using the method of Sec. 4.7, solve Prob. 4.8.

4.45. Using the method of Sec. 4.7, solve Prob. 4.23a and b.

4.46. Using the method of Sec. 4.7, solve Prob. 4.24a and b.

4.47. In Prob. 4.15, determine (a) the value of β for which the reaction at C is zero, (b) the corresponding reactions at B and D.

4.48. In Prob. 4.15, determine (a) the value of β for which the reaction at B is zero, (b) the corresponding reactions at C and D.

4.49. A uniform plate girder weighs 6,000 lb. It is held by two crane cables as shown; the cable attached at B forms an angle of 30° with the vertical. If the girder is to be held in a horizontal position, determine the direction of the cable attached at A and the tension in each cable.

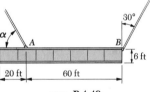

FIG. P 4.49

4.50. A weight W is to be supported by the bell crank shown. Determine the horizontal force **P** which must be applied at A and the magnitude and direction of the reaction at B.

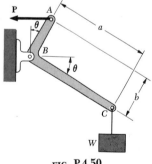

FIG. P 4.50

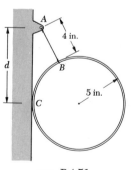

FIG. P 4.51

4.51. A thin ring, of radius 5 in., weighs 3 lb and is held against a smooth wall by a 4-in. string AB. Determine the angle the string forms with the wall and the tension in the string. Also find the distance d and the reaction at C.

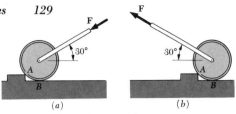

FIG. P 4.52

4.52. A 600-lb roller, 2 ft in diameter, is used on a lawn. Determine the force **F** required to make it roll over a 3-in. obstruction (*a*) if the roller is pushed as shown, (*b*) if the roller is pulled as shown.

°4.53. A slender rod of length 2*r* and weight *W* is attached to a collar at *B* and rests on a smooth circular cylinder of radius *r*. Knowing that the collar may slide freely along a vertical guide, determine the value of θ corresponding to equilibrium.

°4.54. A slender rod *AB* of length *L* and weight *W* is held by a cable *BC* and by a pin at *A* which may slide in a smooth vertical slot. Determine the values of α and θ for which the rod is in equilibrium.

°4.55. A 4-ft rod, of uniform cross section, is held in equilibrium as shown, with one end against a smooth, vertical wall and the other end attached to a cord. Find the length of the cord.

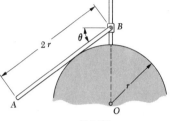

FIG. P 4.53

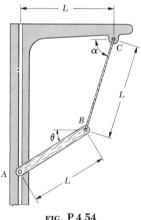

FIG. P 4.54

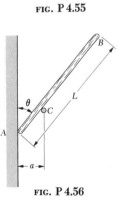

FIG. P 4.55

°4.56. A slender rod of length *L* and weight *W* is lodged between a smooth wall and a smooth peg. Determine the angle θ between the rod and the wall corresponding to equilibrium.

FIG. P 4.56

EQUILIBRIUM IN THREE DIMENSIONS

4.8. Reactions at Supports and Connections for a Three-dimensional Structure.   The reactions on a three-dimensional structure range from the single force of known direction exerted by a smooth surface to the force-couple system exerted by a fixed support.   Consequently, the number of unknowns associated with the reaction at a support or connection may vary from one to six in problems involving the equilibrium of a three-dimensional structure.   Various types of supports and connections are shown in Fig. 4.10 with the corresponding reactions.   A simple way of determining the type of reaction corresponding to a given support or connection and the number of unknowns involved is to find which of the six fundamental motions (translation in x, y, and z directions, rotation about the x, y, and z axes) are allowed and which motions are prevented.

Ball supports, smooth surfaces, and cables, for example, prevent translation in one direction only and thus exert a single force of known line of action; they each involve one unknown, namely, the magnitude of the reaction.   Rollers on rough surfaces and wheels on rails prevent translation in two directions; the corresponding reactions consist of two unknown force components.   Rough surfaces in direct contact and ball-and-socket supports prevent translation in three directions; these supports involve three unknown force components.

Some supports and connections may prevent rotation as well as translation; the corresponding reactions include, then, couples as well as forces.   The reaction at a fixed support, for example, which prevents any motion (rotation as well as translation), consists of three unknown forces and three unknown couples.   A universal joint, which is designed to allow rotation about two axes, will exert a reaction consisting of three unknown force components and one unknown couple.

Other supports and connections are primarily intended to prevent translation; their design, however, is such that they also prevent some rotations.   The corresponding reactions consist essentially of force components but may also include couples. One group of supports of this type includes hinges and bearings designed to support radial loads only (for example, journal bearings, roller bearings).   The corresponding reactions consist of two force components but may also include two couples.   Another group includes pin-and-bracket supports, hinges, and bearings designed to support an axial thrust as well as a radial load (for example, ball bearings).   The corresponding reactions

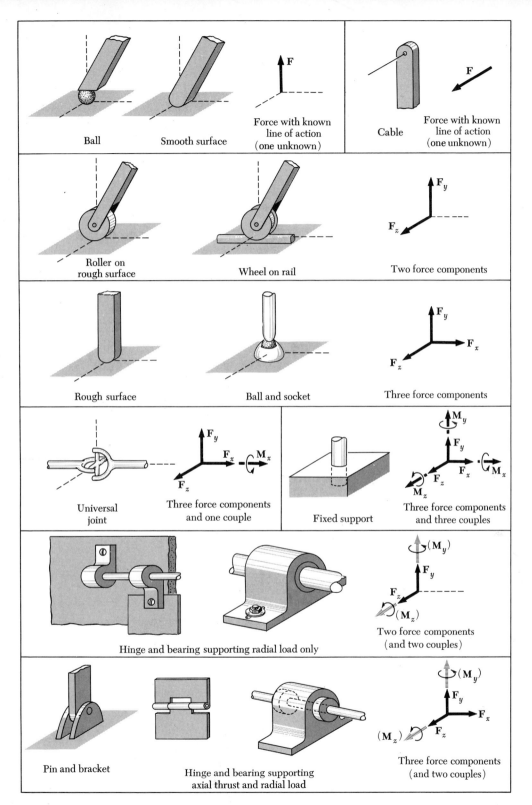

Ball

Smooth surface

Force with known
line of action
(one unknown)

Cable

Force with known
line of action
(one unknown)

Roller on
rough surface

Wheel on rail

Two force components

Rough surface

Ball and socket

Three force components

Universal
joint

Three force components
and one couple

Fixed support

Three force components
and three couples

Hinge and bearing supporting radial load only

Two force components
(and two couples)

Pin and bracket

Hinge and bearing supporting
axial thrust and radial load

Three force components
(and two couples)

FIG. 4.10. Reactions at supports and connections

consist of three force components but may include two couples. However, these supports will not exert any appreciable couples under normal conditions of use. Therefore, only force components should be included in their analysis, unless it is found that couples are necessary to maintain the equilibrium of the rigid body, or unless the support is known to have been specifically designed to exert a couple.

4.9. Equilibrium of a Rigid Body in Three Dimensions. We saw in Sec. 4.1 that six scalar equations are required to express the conditions for the equilibrium of a rigid body in the general three-dimensional case.

$$\Sigma F_x = 0 \qquad \Sigma F_y = 0 \qquad \Sigma F_z = 0 \qquad (4.2)$$
$$\Sigma M_x = 0 \qquad \Sigma M_y = 0 \qquad \Sigma M_z = 0 \qquad (4.3)$$

These equations may be solved for no more than *six unknowns,* which generally will represent reactions at supports or connections.

In most problems the scalar equations (4.2) and (4.3) will be more conveniently obtained if we first express in vector form the conditions for the equilibrium of the rigid body considered. We write

$$\Sigma \mathbf{F} = 0 \qquad \Sigma \mathbf{M}_0 = \Sigma(\mathbf{r} \times \mathbf{F}) = 0 \qquad (4.1)$$

and express the forces **F** and position vectors **r** in terms of scalar components and unit vectors. Next we compute all vector products, either directly, or by means of determinants (see Sec. 3.7). Equating to zero the coefficients of the unit vectors in each of the two relations (4.1), we obtain the desired scalar equations.

If the reactions involve more than six unknowns, there are more unknowns than equations and some of the reactions are *statically indeterminate* (see Sample Prob. 4.9). If the reactions involve less than six unknowns, there are more equations than unknowns and some of the equations of equilibrium cannot be satisfied under general loading conditions; the rigid body is only *partially constrained.* Under the particular loading conditions corresponding to a given problem, however, the extra equations often reduce to trivial identities such as $0 = 0$ and may be disregarded; although only partially constrained, the rigid body remains in equilibrium (see Sample Probs. 4.7 and 4.8). Even with six or more unknowns, it is possible that some equations of equilibrium will not be satisfied. This may occur when the supports are such that the reactions are forces which must either be parallel or intersect the same line; the rigid body is then *improperly constrained.*

SAMPLE PROBLEM 4.7

A ladder used to reach high shelves in a storeroom is supported by two flanged wheels A and B mounted on a rail and by an unflanged wheel C resting against a rail fixed to the wall. A man stands on the ladder and leans to the right. The line of action of the 240-lb combined weight of the man and ladder intersects the floor at point D. Determine the components of the reactions at A, B, and C.

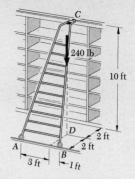

Solution. A free-body diagram of the ladder is drawn; there are five unknown reaction components, two at each flanged wheel and one at the unflanged wheel. The ladder is therefore only partially constrained; it is free to roll along the rails. It is, however, in equilibrium under the given vertical load since the equation $\Sigma F_x = 0$ is satisfied.

Since the ladder is in equilibrium, the forces acting on it must form a system equivalent to zero. We write therefore

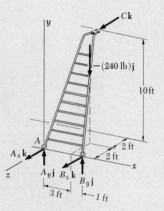

$\Sigma \mathbf{F} = 0$:

$$A_y\mathbf{j} + A_z\mathbf{k} + B_y\mathbf{j} + B_z\mathbf{k} - (240\text{ lb})\mathbf{j} + C\mathbf{k} = 0$$
$$(A_y + B_y - 240\text{ lb})\mathbf{j} + (A_z + B_z + C)\mathbf{k} = 0 \qquad (1)$$

$\Sigma \mathbf{M}_A = \Sigma(\mathbf{r} \times \mathbf{F}) = 0$:
$$4\mathbf{i} \times (B_y\mathbf{j} + B_z\mathbf{k}) + (3\mathbf{i} - 2\mathbf{k}) \times (-240\mathbf{j}) + (2\mathbf{i} + 10\mathbf{j} - 4\mathbf{k}) \times C\mathbf{k} = 0$$

Computing the vector products, we have†

$$4B_y\mathbf{k} - 4B_z\mathbf{j} - 720\mathbf{k} - 480\mathbf{i} - 2C\mathbf{j} + 10C\mathbf{i} = 0$$
$$(10C - 480)\mathbf{i} - (4B_z + 2C)\mathbf{j} + (4B_y - 720)\mathbf{k} = 0 \qquad (2)$$

Setting the coefficients of $\mathbf{i}$, $\mathbf{j}$, $\mathbf{k}$ equal to zero in Eq. (2), we obtain the following three scalar equations, which express that the sum of the moments about each coordinate axis must be zero:

$$10C - 480 = 0 \qquad C = +48\text{ lb} \qquad \blacktriangleleft$$
$$4B_z + 2C = 0 \qquad B_z = -24\text{ lb} \qquad \blacktriangleleft$$
$$4B_y - 720 = 0 \qquad B_y = +180\text{ lb} \qquad \blacktriangleleft$$

Setting the coefficients of $\mathbf{j}$ and $\mathbf{k}$ equal to zero in Eq. (1), we obtain two scalar equations expressing that the sums of the components in the y and z directions are equal to zero. Substituting for B_y, B_z, and C the values obtained above, we write

$$A_y + B_y - 240 = 0 \qquad A_y + 180 - 240 = 0 \qquad A_y = +60\text{ lb} \qquad \blacktriangleleft$$
$$A_z + B_z + C = 0 \qquad A_z - 24 + 48 = 0 \qquad A_z = -24\text{ lb} \qquad \blacktriangleleft$$

†*Remark.* The moments in this Sample Problem and in Sample Probs. 4.8 and 4.9 could also be expressed in the form of determinants (see Sample Prob. 3.11, page 99).

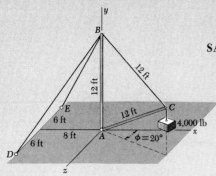

SAMPLE PROBLEM 4.8

The derrick shown supports a 4,000-lb load. It is held by a ball and socket at A and by two cables attached at points D and E. In the position shown, the derrick stands in a vertical plane forming an angle $\phi = 20°$ with the xy plane. Determine the tension in each cable and the components of the reaction at A.

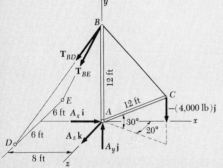

Solution. A free-body diagram of the derrick is drawn. Since the directions of the forces exerted at B by the cables are known, these forces involve one unknown each, namely, the magnitudes T_{BD} and T_{BE}. The reaction at A is a force of unknown direction and is represented by three unknown components. Since there are only five unknowns, the derrick is partially constrained. It may rotate freely about the y axis; it is, however, in equilibrium under the given loading since the equation $\Sigma M_y = 0$ is satisfied.

The components of the forces $\mathbf{T}_{BD}$ and $\mathbf{T}_{BE}$ may be obtained by proportions from the components of the vectors $\overrightarrow{BD}$ and $\overrightarrow{BE}$. We write

$$\overrightarrow{BD} = -(8 \text{ ft})\mathbf{i} - (12 \text{ ft})\mathbf{j} + (6 \text{ ft})\mathbf{k} \qquad BD = 15.62 \text{ ft}$$
$$\overrightarrow{BE} = -(8 \text{ ft})\mathbf{i} - (12 \text{ ft})\mathbf{j} - (6 \text{ ft})\mathbf{k} \qquad BE = 15.62 \text{ ft}$$
$$\mathbf{T}_{BD} = T_{BD} \, (\overrightarrow{BD}/BD) = T_{BD} \, (-0.512\mathbf{i} - 0.768\mathbf{j} + 0.384\mathbf{k})$$
$$\mathbf{T}_{BE} = T_{BE} \, (\overrightarrow{BE}/BE) = T_{BE} \, (-0.512\mathbf{i} - 0.768\mathbf{j} - 0.384\mathbf{k})$$

We also resolve the position vector of point C into rectangular components

$$\overrightarrow{AC} = (12 \text{ ft}) \, (\cos 30° \cos 20°\mathbf{i} + \sin 30°\mathbf{j} + \cos 30° \sin 20°\mathbf{k})$$

$$\overrightarrow{AC} = (9.77 \text{ ft})\mathbf{i} + (6 \text{ ft})\mathbf{j} + (3.55 \text{ ft})\mathbf{k}$$

Since the derrick is in equilibrium, the forces acting on it must form a system equivalent to zero. We write therefore

$$\Sigma \mathbf{F} = 0: \quad A_x\mathbf{i} + A_y\mathbf{j} + A_z\mathbf{k} + \mathbf{T}_{BD} + \mathbf{T}_{BE} - (4{,}000 \text{ lb})\mathbf{j} = 0$$
$$(A_x - 0.512T_{BD} - 0.512T_{BE})\mathbf{i}$$
$$+ (A_y - 0.768T_{BD} - 0.768T_{BE} - 4{,}000 \text{ lb})\mathbf{j}$$
$$+ (A_z + 0.384T_{BD} - 0.384T_{BE})\mathbf{k} = 0 \qquad (1)$$
$$\Sigma \mathbf{M}_A = \Sigma(\mathbf{r} \times \mathbf{F}) = 0:$$
$$12\mathbf{j} \times T_{BD} \, (-0.512\mathbf{i} - 0.768\mathbf{j} + 0.384\mathbf{k})$$
$$+ 12\mathbf{j} \times T_{BE} \, (-0.512\mathbf{i} - 0.768\mathbf{j} - 0.384\mathbf{k})$$
$$+ (9.77\mathbf{i} + 6\mathbf{j} + 3.55\mathbf{k}) \times (-4{,}000\mathbf{j}) = 0$$
$$(4.61T_{BD} - 4.61T_{BE} + 14{,}200)\mathbf{i}$$
$$+ (6.14T_{BD} + 6.14T_{BE} - 39{,}080)\mathbf{k} = 0 \qquad (2)$$

Setting the coefficients of $\mathbf{i}$ and $\mathbf{k}$ equal to zero in Eq. (2), we obtain two scalar equations which may be solved for T_{BD} and T_{BE}:

$$T_{BD} = 1{,}640 \text{ lb} \qquad T_{BE} = 4{,}720 \text{ lb} \quad \blacktriangleleft$$

Setting the coefficients of $\mathbf{i}$, $\mathbf{j}$, $\mathbf{k}$ equal to zero in Eq. (1), we obtain three more scalar equations which yield

$$A_x = +3{,}260 \text{ lb} \qquad A_y = +8{,}880 \text{ lb} \qquad A_z = +1{,}183 \text{ lb} \quad \blacktriangleleft$$

SAMPLE PROBLEM 4.9

A 500-lb marquee, 8 by 10 ft, is held in a horizontal position by two horizontal hinges at A and B and by a cable CD attached to a point D located 5 ft directly above B. Determine the tension in the cable and the components of the reactions at the hinges.

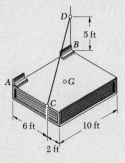

Solution. A free-body diagram of the marquee is drawn. The reactions involve seven unknowns, namely, the force $\mathbf{T}$ exerted by the cable and three unknown components at each hinge. Since we cannot write more than six independent equations, the problem is indeterminate and cannot be solved completely by the methods of statics.

The components of the force $\mathbf{T}$ may be obtained by proportions from the components of the vector $\overrightarrow{CD}$. We write

$$\overrightarrow{CD} = -(6\text{ ft})\mathbf{i} + (5\text{ ft})\mathbf{j} - (10\text{ ft})\mathbf{k} \qquad CD = 12.69\text{ ft}$$
$$\mathbf{T} = T(\overrightarrow{CD}/CD) = -0.473T\mathbf{i} + 0.394T\mathbf{j} - 0.788T\mathbf{k}$$

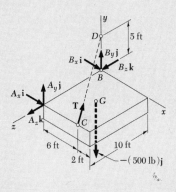

Since the marquee is in equilibrium, the forces acting on it must form a system equivalent to zero. We write therefore

$$\Sigma\mathbf{F} = 0: \quad A_x\mathbf{i} + A_y\mathbf{j} + A_z\mathbf{k} + B_x\mathbf{i} + B_y\mathbf{j} + B_z\mathbf{k} + \mathbf{T} - (500\text{ lb})\mathbf{j} = 0$$
$$(A_x + B_x - 0.473T)\mathbf{i}$$
$$+ (A_y + B_y + 0.394T - 500\text{ lb})\mathbf{j}$$
$$+ (A_z + B_z - 0.788T)\mathbf{k} = 0 \qquad (1)$$

$$\Sigma\mathbf{M}_B = \Sigma(\mathbf{r} \times \mathbf{F}) = 0:$$
$$10\mathbf{k} \times (A_x\mathbf{i} + A_y\mathbf{j} + A_z\mathbf{k})$$
$$+ (6\mathbf{i} + 10\mathbf{k}) \times (-0.473T\mathbf{i} + 0.394T\mathbf{j} - 0.788T\mathbf{k})$$
$$+ (4\mathbf{i} + 5\mathbf{k}) \times (-500\mathbf{j}) = 0$$
$$(-10A_y - 3.94T + 2,500)\mathbf{i} + 10A_x\mathbf{j} + (2.36T - 2,000)\mathbf{k} = 0 \quad (2)$$

Setting the coefficients of the unit vectors equal to zero in Eq. (2), we write three scalar equations which yield

$$T = 846\text{ lb} \qquad A_x = 0 \qquad A_y = -83.3\text{ lb} \quad \blacktriangleleft$$

Setting the coefficients of the unit vectors equal to zero in Eq. (1), we obtain three more scalar equations. After substituting the values of T, A_x, and A_y into these equations, we obtain

$$B_x = +400\text{ lb} \qquad B_y = +250\text{ lb} \qquad A_z + B_z = +667\text{ lb} \quad \blacktriangleleft$$

The z components of the reactions at the hinges cannot be determined separately; only their sum is known. Other equations of equilibrium may be written; such equations, however, are not independent of the six equations used above, and they cannot be used to determine A_z and B_z. If the hinge at B were modified so that it could not exert any axial thrust, we would then obtain $B_z = 0$ and $A_z = +667$ lb.

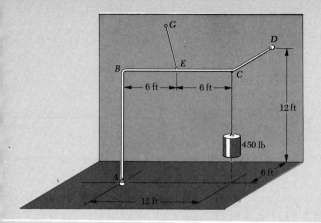

SAMPLE PROBLEM 4.10

A 450-lb load hangs from the corner C of a rigid piece of pipe $ABCD$ which has been bent as shown. The pipe is supported by the ball-and-socket joints A and D fastened, respectively, to the floor and to a vertical wall, and by a cable attached at the mid-point E of the portion BC of the pipe and at a point G on the wall. Determine (a) where G should be located if the tension in the cable is to be minimum, (b) the corresponding minimum value of the tension.

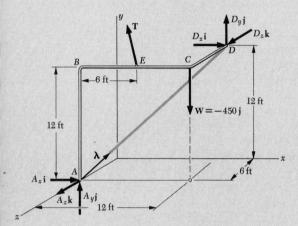

Solution. The free-body diagram of the pipe includes the load $\mathbf{W} = -450\mathbf{j}$, the reactions at A and D, and the force $\mathbf{T}$ exerted by the cable. To eliminate the reactions at A and D from the computations, we express that the sum of the moments of the forces about AD is zero. Denoting by $\boldsymbol{\lambda}$ the unit vector along AD, we write

$$\Sigma M_{AD} = 0: \qquad \boldsymbol{\lambda} \cdot (\overrightarrow{AE} \times \mathbf{T}) + \boldsymbol{\lambda} \cdot (\overrightarrow{AC} \times \mathbf{W}) = 0 \quad (1)$$

The second term in Eq. (1) may be computed as follows:

$$\overrightarrow{AC} \times \mathbf{W} = (12\mathbf{i} + 12\mathbf{j}) \times (-450\mathbf{j}) = -5{,}400\mathbf{k}$$

$$\boldsymbol{\lambda} = \frac{\overrightarrow{AD}}{AD} = \frac{12\mathbf{i} + 12\mathbf{j} - 6\mathbf{k}}{18} = \tfrac{2}{3}\mathbf{i} + \tfrac{2}{3}\mathbf{j} - \tfrac{1}{3}\mathbf{k}$$

$$\boldsymbol{\lambda} \cdot (\overrightarrow{AC} \times \mathbf{W}) = (\tfrac{2}{3}\mathbf{i} + \tfrac{2}{3}\mathbf{j} - \tfrac{1}{3}\mathbf{k}) \cdot (-5{,}400\mathbf{k}) = +1{,}800$$

Substituting the value obtained into Eq. (1), we write

$$\boldsymbol{\lambda} \cdot (\overrightarrow{AE} \times \mathbf{T}) = -1{,}800 \text{ lb-ft} \qquad (2)$$

Minimum Value of Tension. Recalling the commutative property for mixed triple products, we rewrite Eq. (2) in the form

$$\mathbf{T} \cdot (\boldsymbol{\lambda} \times \overrightarrow{AE}) = -1{,}800 \text{ lb-ft} \qquad (3)$$

which shows that the projection of $\mathbf{T}$ on the vector $\boldsymbol{\lambda} \times \overrightarrow{AE}$ is a constant. It follows that $\mathbf{T}$ is minimum when parallel to the vector

$$\boldsymbol{\lambda} \times \overrightarrow{AE} = (\tfrac{2}{3}\mathbf{i} + \tfrac{2}{3}\mathbf{j} - \tfrac{1}{3}\mathbf{k}) \times (6\mathbf{i} + 12\mathbf{j}) = 4\mathbf{i} - 2\mathbf{j} + 4\mathbf{k}$$

Using proportions, we write

$$\mathbf{T}_{\min} = T(\tfrac{2}{3}\mathbf{i} - \tfrac{1}{3}\mathbf{j} + \tfrac{2}{3}\mathbf{k}) \qquad (4)$$

Substituting for $\mathbf{T}$ and $\boldsymbol{\lambda} \times \overrightarrow{AE}$ in Eq. (3), we find $T = -300$. Carrying this value into (4), we obtain

$$\mathbf{T}_{\min} = -200\mathbf{i} + 100\mathbf{j} - 200\mathbf{k} \qquad T_{\min} = 300 \text{ lb} \quad \blacktriangleleft$$

Location of G. Denoting by $x, y, 0$ the coordinates of point G where the cable is attached to the wall, and observing that the vector $\overrightarrow{EG}$ has the same direction as the force $\mathbf{T}_{\min}$, we write

$$\frac{x-6}{-200} = \frac{y-12}{+100} = \frac{0-6}{-200} \qquad x = 0 \qquad y = 15 \text{ ft} \quad \blacktriangleleft$$

PROBLEMS

4.57. The 10-ft flagpole *OB* forms an angle of 60° with the vertical; it is held by a ball and socket at *O* and by two braces. Knowing that the distance *OA* is 3 ft, determine the components of the reaction at *O* and the tension in each brace caused by the 100-lb load.

4.58. A surveying instrument weighing 15 lb is mounted on a tripod. The legs of the tripod are equally spaced and form an angle of 20° with the vertical. Find the reaction of the ground on each leg, neglecting the weight of the tripod and assuming (*a*) that the tripod is rigid and the ground is smooth, (*b*) that the screws connecting the legs to the instrument mount are loose and that the ground is sufficiently rough to keep the legs from sliding.

4.59. A 7-ft boom supports an 1,800-lb load as shown. The boom is held by a ball and socket at *A* and by the two cables *BC* and *BD*. Neglecting the weight of the boom, determine the tension in each cable and the reaction at *A*.

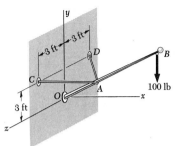

FIG. P 4.57

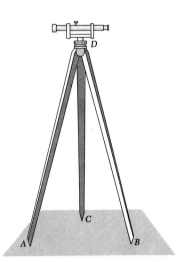

FIG. P 4.58

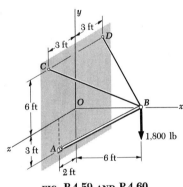

FIG. P 4.59 AND P 4.60

4.60. A 7-ft boom is held by a ball and socket at *A* and by two cables. In addition to the vertical 1,800-lb load shown, a force of magnitude *P* is also applied at *B* in the direction of the positive *x* axis. Determine (*a*) the required magnitude *P* if the tension is to be the same in both cables, (*b*) the corresponding reaction at *A*.

4.61. A 4- by 6-ft plate weighing 900 lb is lifted by three cables which are joined at point *D* directly above the center of the plate. Determine the tension in each cable.

4.62. Solve Prob. 4.61 assuming that cable *BD* is replaced by a cable connecting points *D* and *E*.

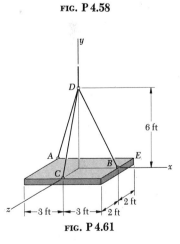

FIG. P 4.61

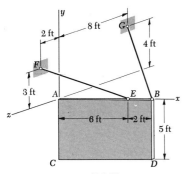

FIG. P 4.63

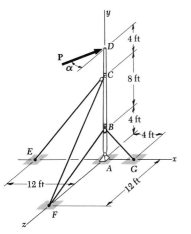

FIG. P 4.64

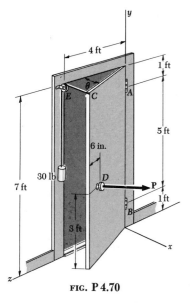

FIG. P 4.70

4.63. A 5- by 8-ft sign of uniform density weighs 270 lb and is supported by a ball and socket at A and by two cables.   Determine the tension in each cable and the reaction at A.

4.64. A 16-ft boom is held by a ball and socket at A and by two cables ECF and FBG which pass around frictionless pulleys at C and B.   A horizontal load P of magnitude 900 lb is applied at the top of the boom at D. If P is parallel to the z axis ($\alpha = 0$), determine the reaction at A and the tension in each cable.

°4.65. In Prob. 4.64, determine the limiting values of the horizontal angle α if both the cables are to remain taut.

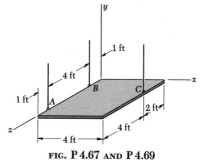

FIG. P 4.67 AND P 4.69

4.66. In Sample Prob. 4.8, determine the horizontal angle ϕ for which the tension in BE is maximum (*a*) if neither cable may become slack, (*b*) if cables BE and BD are replaced by rods which can withstand either a tension or a compression force.

4.67. The rectangular plate shown weighs 60 lb and is supported by three wires.   Determine the tension in each wire.

4.68. A load W is placed on the plate of Prob. 4.67.   Knowing that the weight of the plate is 60 lb, determine the magnitude of the load W and the point where the load should be placed if the tension is to be 50 lb in each of the three wires.

4.69. Determine the magnitude and location of the smallest load which must be placed on the 60-lb plate if the tensions in the three wires are to be equal.

4.70. A 40-lb door is made self-closing by attaching to it a 30-lb weight by means of a cable CE.   The door is held open by a force P applied at the knob D, in a direction perpendicular to the door.   Determine the magnitude of P and the components of the reactions at A and B when $\theta = 90°$.   It is assumed that the hinge at A does not exert any axial thrust.

4.71. The door of a bank vault weighs 12,000 lb and is supported by two hinges as shown. Determine the components of the reaction at each hinge.

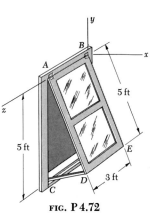

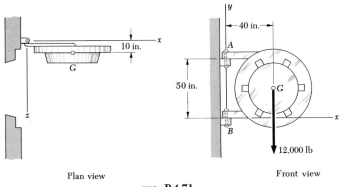

Plan view   Front view

FIG. P 4.71

4.72. A 3- by 5-ft storm window weighs 15 lb and is held by hinges at *A* and *B*. In the position shown, it is held away from the side of the house by a 2-ft stick *CD*. Assuming that the hinge at *A* does not exert any axial thrust, determine the magnitude of the force exerted by the stick and the components of the reactions at *A* and *B*.

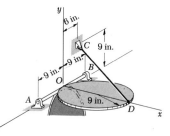

FIG. P 4.72

4.73. Solve Prob. 4.72 assuming that the hinge at *A* is removed.

4.74. A uniform pipe cover of radius 9 in. and weight 60 lb is held in a horizontal position by the cable *CD*. Assuming that the bearing at *B* does not exert any axial thrust, determine the tension in the cable and the components of the reactions at *A* and *B*.

FIG. P 4.74

4.75. Solve Prob. 4.74 assuming that the bearings at *A* and *B* are removed and are replaced by a single hinge at *O*.

4.76. A generator is mounted on a platform which is held by bolts at *A*, *B*, and *C*. The generator and platform, as a unit, weigh 60 lb and have a combined center of gravity located at $x = 10$ in. and $z = 8$ in. If a 500-lb-in. couple is applied to the horizontal shaft, determine the vertical component of the reactions at *A*, *B*, and *C*.

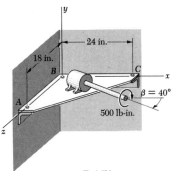

FIG. P 4.76

4.77. In Prob. 4.76 determine the smallest allowable value of the horizontal angle β, if the bolts are removed and the platform simply rests on its supports.

4.78. A uniform circular plate of radius *r* and weight *W* is supported by three vertical wires, each of length *h*, equally spaced around the edge. Determine the horizontal angle θ through which the plate rotates when a couple $\mathbf{M}_0$ is applied in the plane of the plate. Assume that θ is small.

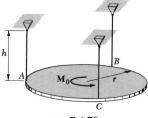

FIG. P 4.78

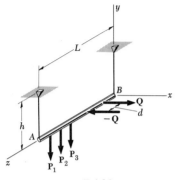

FIG. P 4.81

4.79. In Prob. 4.78, show that the angle θ is independent of the location of the points where the vertical wires are attached to the edge of the plate, provided that A, B, and C do not lie on the same side of a diameter. Assume that θ is small.

°4.80. In Prob. 4.78, determine the magnitude of the couple $\mathbf{M}_0$ required to rotate the plate through an angle θ.   Do *not* assume that θ is small.

°4.81. A bar AB, of negligible weight, is suspended from two wires and supports several vertical loads $\mathbf{P}_1$, $\mathbf{P}_2$, and $\mathbf{P}_3$.   Determine the angle θ through which the bar rotates when two horizontal forces forming a couple of magnitude $M_0 = Qd$ are applied to the bar.   Also show that the axis of rotation coincides with the axis of the wrench which is equivalent to the total loading.   Assume that θ is small.

4.82. The uniform rod AB weighs 24 lb; it is supported by a ball and socket at B and the cord CD which is attached to the mid-point of the rod C.   Knowing that the rod leans against a smooth vertical wall at A, determine the tension in the cord and the reactions at A and B.

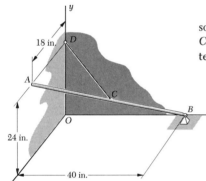

FIG. P 4.82

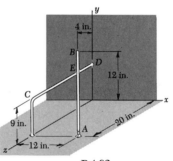

FIG. P 4.83

4.83. The rod AB is uniform and weighs 25 lb.   It is supported by a ball and socket at A and leans against both the rod CD and the vertical wall.   Assuming the wall and the rods to be smooth, determine (*a*) the components of the force which rod CD exerts on AB, (*b*) the components of the reactions at A and B.   (*Hint.* The force exerted by CD on AB must be perpendicular to both rods.)

4.84. Two rods are welded together to form a T-shaped lever which leans against a smooth vertical wall at D and is supported by bearings at A and B.   A vertical force $\mathbf{P}$ of magnitude 120 lb is applied at the mid-point of rod DC. Determine the reaction at D.

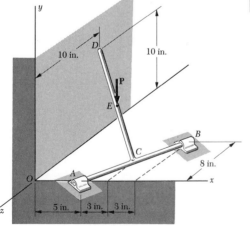

FIG. P 4.84

4.85. Solve Prob. 4.84 assuming that the vertical force P is replaced by a force **Q** of magnitude 300 lb acting at E and directed along a line joining point E and the origin O.

4.86. A bent plate is held by two ball-and-socket joints and a cord AB. Determine the tension in the cord if a 100-lb force is applied at D as shown.

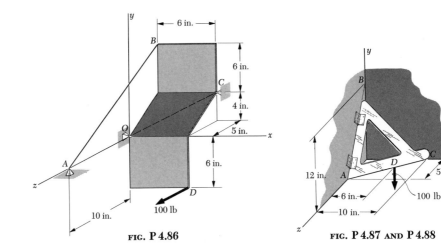

FIG. P 4.86

FIG. P 4.87 AND P 4.88

4.87. The bracket shown is held by hinges located along line AB and bears against a smooth vertical wall at C. Neglecting the weight of the bracket, determine the reaction at C when a 100-lb load is applied as shown.

4.88. Determine the magnitude and direction of the smallest force **P** which should be applied at C to keep the bracket from bearing against the wall.

4.89. In Prob. 4.86 the cord AB is removed and replaced by a force **P** applied at B. Determine the magnitude and direction of the smallest force **P** required to hold the plate.

REVIEW PROBLEMS

4.90. The frame shown is held by a pin at A and by a cable BDC which passes over a frictionless pulley at D. Determine the reaction at A and the tension in the cable when $\alpha = 45°$ and $P = 200$ lb.

4.91. The frame shown is held by a pin at A and by a cable BDC which passes over a frictionless pulley at D. If $P = 200$ lb, determine (*a*) the value of α for which the tension in the cable is maximum, (*b*) the corresponding reaction at A and tension in the cable.

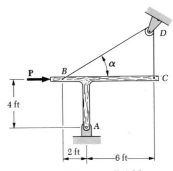

FIG. P 4.90 AND P 4.91

4.92. A 600-lb-in. couple formed by 100-lb forces acting at D and E is applied to the assembly shown.   Knowing that a line joining D and E forms an angle of 30° with the yz plane, determine the force **Q** required for equilibrium and the components of the reactions at B and C. It is assumed that the bearing at C does not exert any axial thrust.

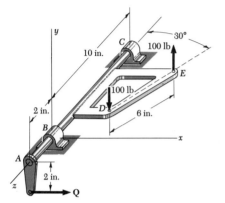

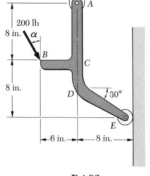

FIG. P 4.92

FIG. P 4.93

4.93. (*a*) Determine the reactions at A and E, if $\alpha = 0$.   (*b*) Determine the values of α for which the magnitude of the reaction at E is 120 lb.

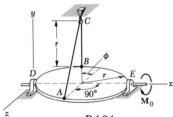

FIG. P 4.94

4.94. The circular plate of radius r is supported by bearings at D and E and by the cable ACB which passes over a frictionless pulley at C.   The pulley is located at a distance r directly above point B.   A couple $\mathbf{M}_0$ is applied to the plate as shown.   (*a*) Express the tension in the cable in terms of M_0, r, and ϕ.   (*b*) Determine the tension in the cable and the reactions at D and E when $\phi = 0$.   (*c*) Determine the range of values of ϕ for which the bearings and cable can maintain the plate in equilibrium. Bearing E does not exert any axial thrust.

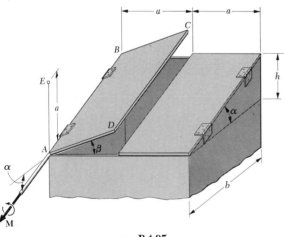

FIG. P 4.95

4.95. A shaft is attached to the left half of the lid of a box so that it is collinear with the axis of the hinges located along edge AB.   Denoting by W the weight of $ABCD$, determine the couple **M** which must be applied to the shaft in order to hold the left half of the lid in the position shown.

4.96. Three identical rectangular plates, weighing 40 lb each, are held by a pin at A and by a cable as shown.   In each case determine (*a*) the value of θ for which the tension in the cable is minimum, (*b*) the minimum cable tension and the corresponding reaction at A, (*c*) the value of θ for which the plate is improperly constrained.

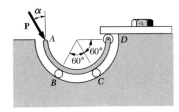

FIG. **P 4.96**

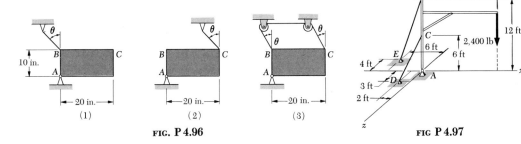

FIG **P 4.97**

4.97. Determine the tension in cables BE and CD.

4.98. Knowing that $\alpha = 0$, determine the reactions at B, C, and D for the semicircular rod shown.

4.99. Determine the range of values of α for which the semicircular rod can be maintained in equilibrium by the small wheel at D and the rollers at B and C.

FIG. **P 4.98** AND **P 4.99**

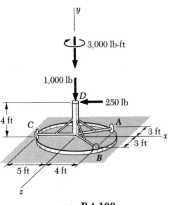

FIG. **P 4.100**

4.100. An experimental radar antenna is to be mounted on the base shown which may roll on a 5-ft-radius track.   Each wheel has a single flange on the inner side of the track.   Wheels A and B are free to rotate, but a brake is applied to wheel C to keep it from moving.   Determine the components of the reactions at A, B, and C for the loading shown.

4.101. In Prob. 4.84, assuming that the bearing at B does not exert any axial thrust, determine the reactions at A, B, and D.

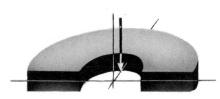

5. DISTRIBUTED FORCES:
CENTROIDS AND CENTERS OF GRAVITY

AREAS AND LINES

5.1. Center of Gravity of a Two-dimensional Body. We have assumed so far that the attraction exerted by the earth on a rigid body could be represented by a single force **W**. This force, called the weight of the body, was to be applied at the *center of gravity* of the body (Sec. 3.1). Actually, the earth exerts a force on each of the particles forming the body. The action of the earth on a rigid body should thus be represented by a large number of small forces distributed over the entire body. We shall see in this chapter, however, that all these small forces may be replaced by a single equivalent force **W**. We shall also learn to determine the center of gravity, i.e., the point of application of the resultant **W**, for various shapes of bodies.

Let us first consider a flat horizontal plate (Fig. 5.1). We may divide the plate into n small elements. The coordinates of the first element are denoted by x_1 and y_1, those of the second element by x_2 and y_2, etc. The forces exerted by the earth on the elements of plate will be denoted, respectively, by $\Delta\mathbf{W}_1$, $\Delta\mathbf{W}_2, \ldots, \Delta\mathbf{W}_n$. These forces or weights are directed toward

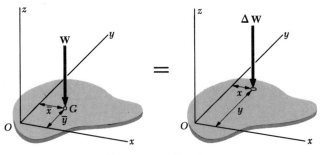

$$\Sigma M_y : \bar{x} W = \Sigma\, x\, \Delta W$$
$$\Sigma M_x : \bar{y} W = \Sigma\, y\, \Delta W$$

FIG. 5.1. Center of gravity of a plate

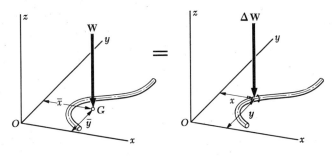

$$\Sigma M_y: \quad \bar{x}W = \Sigma x \ \Delta W$$
$$\Sigma M_x: \quad \bar{y}W = \Sigma y \ \Delta W$$

FIG. 5.2. Center of gravity of a wire

the center of the earth; however, for all practical purposes they may be assumed parallel. Their resultant is therefore a single force in the same direction. The magnitude W of this force is obtained by adding the magnitudes of the elementary weights,

$$\Sigma F_z: \qquad W = \Delta W_1 + \Delta W_2 + \cdots + \Delta W_n \qquad (5.1)$$

To obtain the coordinates $\bar{x}$ and $\bar{y}$ of the point G where the resultant $\mathbf{W}$ should be applied, we write that the moments of $\mathbf{W}$ about the y and x axes are equal to the sum of the corresponding moments of the elementary weights,

$$\begin{aligned} \Sigma M_y: & \quad \bar{x}W = x_1\Delta W_1 + x_2\Delta W_2 + \cdots + x_n\Delta W_n \\ \Sigma M_x: & \quad \bar{y}W = y_1\Delta W_1 + y_2\Delta W_2 + \cdots + y_n\Delta W_n \end{aligned} \qquad (5.2)$$

If we now increase the number of elements into which the plate is divided and simultaneously decrease the size of each element, we obtain at the limit the following expressions:

$$\blacktriangleright \qquad W = \int dW \qquad \bar{x}W = \int x \, dW \qquad \bar{y}W = \int y \, dW \qquad (5.3)$$

These equations define the weight $\mathbf{W}$ and the coordinates $\bar{x}$ and $\bar{y}$ of the center of gravity G of a flat plate. The same equations may be derived for a wire lying in the xy plane (Fig. 5.2). We shall observe, in the latter case, that the center of gravity G will generally not be located on the wire.

5.2. Centroids of Areas and Lines. In the case of a homogeneous plate of uniform thickness, the magnitude ΔW of the weight of an element of plate may be expressed as

$$\Delta W = \gamma t \ \Delta A$$

where $\gamma =$ specific weight (weight per unit volume) of material
  $t =$ thickness of plate
  $\Delta A =$ area of element

If γ is expressed in lb/ft³, t in feet, and ΔA in square feet, we check that ΔW is expressed in pounds. Similarly, we may ex-

145

press the magnitude W of the weight of the entire plate in the form

$$W = \gamma t A$$

where A is the total area of the plate.

Substituting for ΔW and W in the moment equations (5.2) and dividing throughout by γt, we write

$$\Sigma M_y: \quad \bar{x}A = x_1\,\Delta A_1 + x_2\,\Delta A_2 + \cdots + x_n\,\Delta A_n$$
$$\Sigma M_x: \quad \bar{y}A = y_1\,\Delta A_1 + y_2\,\Delta A_2 + \cdots + y_n\,\Delta A_n \tag{5.4}$$

If we increase the number of elements into which the area A is divided and simultaneously decrease the size of each element, we obtain at the limit

$$\blacktriangleright \qquad \bar{x}A = \int x\,dA \qquad \bar{y}A = \int y\,dA \tag{5.5}$$

These equations define the coordinates $\bar{x}$ and $\bar{y}$ of the center of gravity of a homogeneous plate. The point of coordinates $\bar{x}$ and $\bar{y}$ is also known as the *centroid C of the area A of the* plate (Fig. 5.3). If the plate is not homogeneous, the equations cannot be used to determine the center of gravity of the plate; they still define, however, the centroid of the area.

The integral $\int x\,dA$ is known as the *first moment of the area A with respect to the y axis.* Similarly, the integral $\int y\,dA$ defines the *first moment of A with respect to the x axis.* It is seen from Eqs. (5.5) that, if the centroid of an area is located on a coordinate axis, the first moment of the area with respect to that axis is zero.

In the case of a homogeneous wire of uniform cross section, the magnitude ΔW of the weight of an element of wire may be expressed as

$$\Delta W = \gamma a\,\Delta L$$

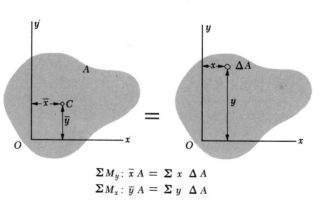

$$\Sigma M_y: \ \bar{x}\,A = \Sigma\,x\ \Delta A$$
$$\Sigma M_x: \ \bar{y}\,A = \Sigma\,y\ \Delta A$$

FIG. 5.3. Centroid of an area

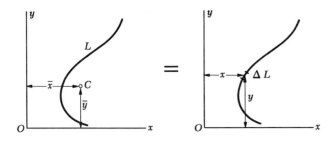

$$\Sigma M_y : \bar{x} L = \Sigma x \; \Delta L$$
$$\Sigma M_x : \bar{y} L = \Sigma y \; \Delta L$$

FIG. 5.4. Centroid of a line

where γ = specific weight of material

a = cross-sectional area of wire

ΔL = length of element

The center of gravity of the wire then coincides with the *centroid C of the line L* defining the shape of the wire (Fig. 5.4). The coordinates $\bar{x}$ and $\bar{y}$ of the centroid of the line L are obtained from the equations

$$\bar{x}L = \int x \, dL \qquad \bar{y}L = \int y \, dL \qquad (5.6)$$

An area A is said to be *symmetrical about an axis BB'* if to every point P of the area corresponds a point P' of the same area such that the line PP' is perpendicular to BB' and is divided into two equal parts by that axis (Fig. 5.5). A line L is said to be symmetrical about BB' if it satisfies similar conditions. When an area A or a line L possesses an axis of symmetry BB', the centroid of the area or line must be located on that axis. If the axis of symmetry is chosen as the y axis, the coordinate $\bar{x}$ of the centroid is found to be zero, since to every product $x \, dA$ or $x \, dL$ appearing in the first integral in Eqs. (5.5) or (5.6) will correspond a product of equal magnitude but of opposite sign. It follows that, if an area or line possesses two axes of symmetry, the centroid of the area or line is located at the intersection of the two axes of symmetry (Fig. 5.6). This property enables us to determine immediately the centroid of areas such as circles, ellipses, squares, rectangles, equilateral triangles, or any other symmetrical figures, as well as the centroid of lines in the shape of the circumference of a circle, the perimeter of a square, etc.

An area is said to be *symmetrical about a center O* if to every point P of the area corresponds a point P' of the same area such that the line PP' is divided into two equal parts by O (Fig. 5.7). A line L is said to be symmetrical about O if it satisfies similar conditions. A reasoning similar to that used above would show that, when an area A or line L possesses a center of symmetry O, the point O must be the centroid of the area or line. It

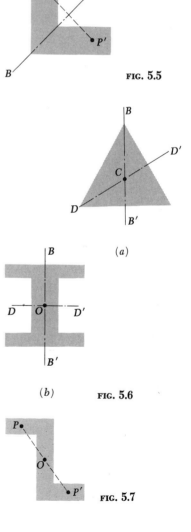

FIG. 5.5

(a)

(b) **FIG. 5.6**

FIG. 5.7

147

Shape		$\bar{x}$	$\bar{y}$	Area
Triangular area	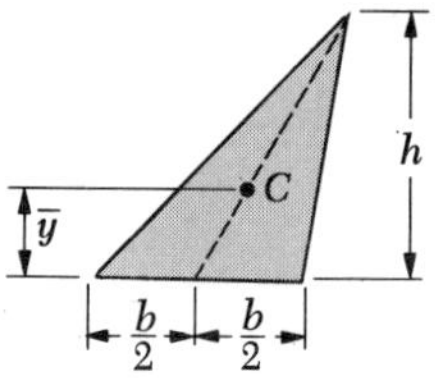		$\dfrac{h}{3}$	$\dfrac{bh}{2}$
Quarter-circular area	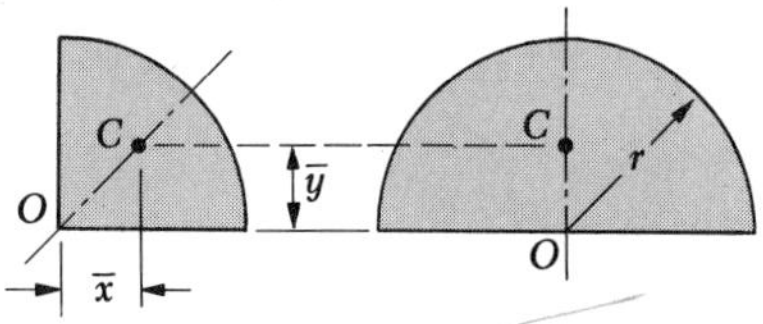	$\dfrac{4r}{3\pi}$	$\dfrac{4r}{3\pi}$	$\dfrac{\pi r^2}{4}$
Semicircular area		0	$\dfrac{4r}{3\pi}$	$\dfrac{\pi r^2}{2}$
Quarter-elliptical area	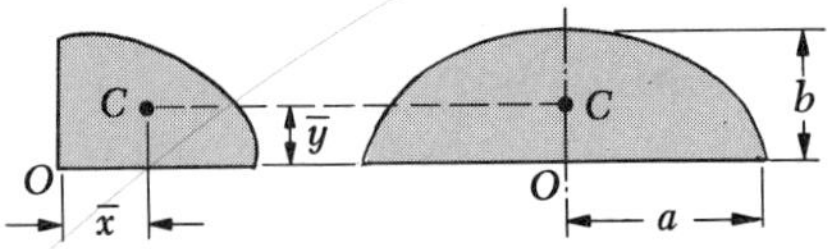	$\dfrac{4a}{3\pi}$	$\dfrac{4b}{3\pi}$	$\dfrac{\pi ab}{4}$
Semielliptical area		0	$\dfrac{4b}{3\pi}$	$\dfrac{\pi ab}{2}$
Semiparabolic area	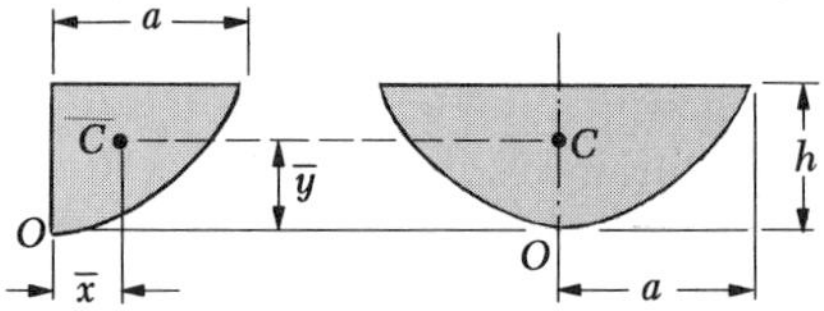	$\dfrac{3a}{8}$	$\dfrac{3h}{5}$	$\dfrac{2ah}{3}$
Parabolic area		0	$\dfrac{3h}{5}$	$\dfrac{4ah}{3}$
Parabolic spandrel	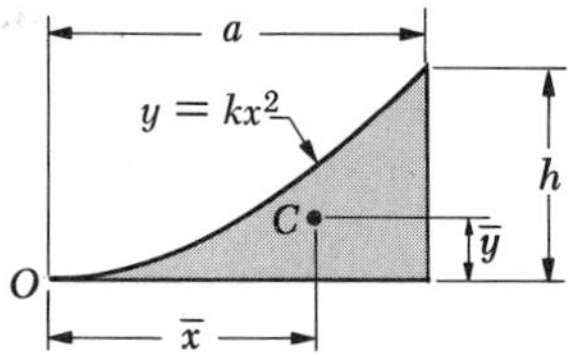	$\dfrac{3a}{4}$	$\dfrac{3h}{10}$	$\dfrac{ah}{3}$
General spandrel	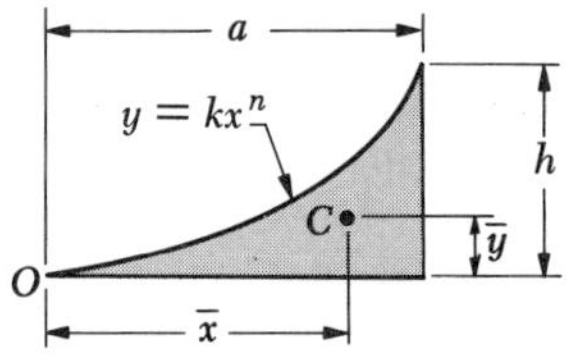	$\dfrac{n+1}{n+2}a$	$\dfrac{n+1}{4n+2}h$	$\dfrac{ah}{n+1}$
Circular sector	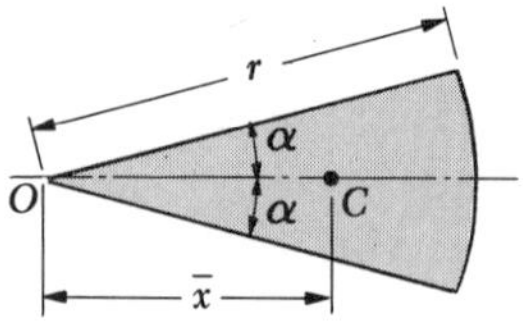	$\dfrac{2r\sin\alpha}{3\alpha}$	0	αr^2

FIG. 5.8A. Centroids of common shapes of areas

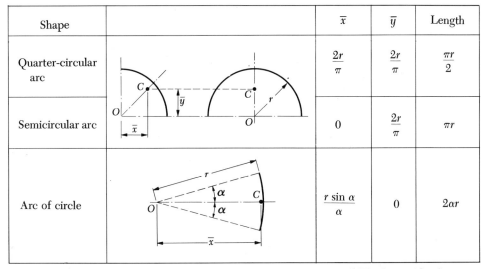

Shape		$\bar{x}$	$\bar{y}$	Length
Quarter-circular arc		$\dfrac{2r}{\pi}$	$\dfrac{2r}{\pi}$	$\dfrac{\pi r}{2}$
Semicircular arc		0	$\dfrac{2r}{\pi}$	πr
Arc of circle		$\dfrac{r \sin \alpha}{\alpha}$	0	$2\alpha r$

FIG. 5.8B. Centroids of common shapes of lines

should be noted that a figure possessing a center of symmetry does not necessarily possess an axis of symmetry (Fig. 5.7), while a figure possessing two axes of symmetry does not necessarily possess a center of symmetry (Fig. 5.6a). However, if a figure possesses two axes of symmetry at a right angle to each other, the point of intersection of these axes will be a center of symmetry (Fig. 5.6b).

Centroids of unsymmetrical areas and lines and of areas and lines possessing only one axis of symmetry will be determined by the methods of Secs. 5.4 and 5.5. Centroids of common shapes of areas and lines are shown in Fig. 5.8A and B. The formulas defining these centroids will be derived in the Sample Problems and Problems following Secs. 5.4 and 5.5.

5.3. Composite Plates and Wires. In many instances, a flat plate may be divided into rectangles, triangles, or other common shapes shown in Fig. 5.8A. The abscissa $\overline{X}$ of its center of gravity G may be determined from the abscissas $\overline{x}_1$, $\overline{x}_2$, ...

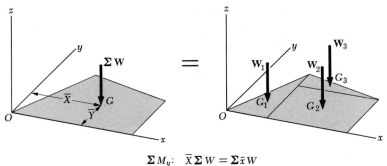

ΣM_y: $\quad \overline{X} \Sigma W = \Sigma \overline{x} W$
ΣM_x: $\quad \overline{Y} \Sigma W = \Sigma \overline{y} W$

FIG. 5.9. Center of gravity of a composite plate

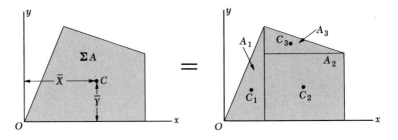

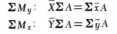

FIG. 5.10. Centroid of a composite area

$$\Sigma M_y: \quad \overline{X}\Sigma A = \Sigma \overline{x}A$$
$$\Sigma M_x: \quad \overline{Y}\Sigma A = \Sigma \overline{y}A$$

of the centers of gravity of the various parts by expressing that the moment of the weight of the whole plate about the y axis is equal to the sum of the moments of the weights of the various parts about the same axis (Fig. 5.9). The ordinate $\overline{Y}$ of the center of gravity of the plate is found in a similar way by equating moments about the x axis.

▶ $\quad \Sigma M_y: \quad \overline{X}(W_1 + W_2 + \cdots + W_n)$
$$= \overline{x}_1 W_1 + \overline{x}_2 W_2 + \cdots + \overline{x}_n W_n$$
▶ $\quad \Sigma M_x: \quad \overline{Y}(W_1 + W_2 + \cdots + W_n) \qquad (5.7)$
$$= \overline{y}_1 W_1 + \overline{y}_2 W_2 + \cdots + \overline{y}_n W_n$$

If the plate is homogeneous and of uniform thickness, the center of gravity coincides with the centroid C of its area. The abscissa $\overline{X}$ of the centroid of the area may then be determined by expressing that the first moment of the composite area with respect to the y axis is equal to the sum of the first moments of the elementary areas with respect to the same axis (Fig. 5.10). The ordinate $\overline{Y}$ of the centroid is found in a similar way by equating first moments of areas with respect to the x axis.

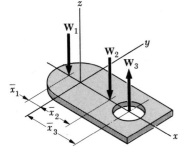

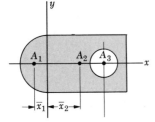

▶ $\quad \Sigma M_y: \quad \overline{X}(A_1 + A_2 + \cdots + A_n)$
$$= \overline{x}_1 A_1 + \overline{x}_2 A_2 + \cdots + \overline{x}_n A_n$$
▶ $\quad \Sigma M_x: \quad \overline{Y}(A_1 + A_2 + \cdots + A_n) \qquad (5.8)$
$$= \overline{y}_1 A_1 + \overline{y}_2 A_2 + \cdots + \overline{y}_n A_n$$

Care should be taken to record the moment of each area with the appropriate sign. First moments of areas, just like moments of forces, may be positive or negative. For example, an area whose centroid is located to the left of the y axis will have a negative first moment with respect to that axis. Also, the area of a hole should be recorded with a negative sign (Fig. 5.11).

Similarly, it is possible in many cases to determine the center of gravity of a composite wire or the centroid of a composite line by dividing the wire or line into simpler elements (Sample Prob. 5.3).

	$\overline{x}$	A	$\overline{x}A$
A_1 Semicircle	−	+	−
A_2 Full rectangle	+	+	+
A_3 Circular hole	+	−	−

FIG. 5.11

150

SAMPLE PROBLEM 5.1

Determine the center of gravity of the thin homogeneous plate shown.

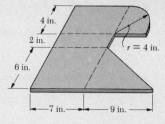

Solution. Since the plate is homogeneous, we may locate the center of gravity by determining the centroid of the area of the plate. The area is divided into its component parts: a rectangle, a triangle, and a quarter circle. Coordinate axes are chosen with the origin at the lower left corner of the plate. The centroid of each component part is indicated in the figure, and $\bar{x}$ and $\bar{y}$ are computed for each component. The moments of the component areas with respect to the coordinate axes are determined in the following table:

Component	A	$\bar{x}$	$\bar{y}$	$\bar{x}A$	$\bar{y}A$
Rectangle......	84	3.5	6.0	294	504
Triangle.......	27	10.0	2.0	270	54
Quarter circle...	12.56	8.7	9.7	109.2	121.8
	$\Sigma A =$ 123.6	....	...	$\Sigma \bar{x}A =$ 673.2	$\Sigma \bar{y}A =$ 679.8

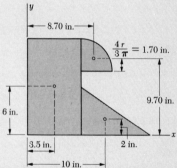

Substituting the values obtained from the table into the equations defining the centroid of a composite area, we obtain

$$\bar{X}\Sigma A = \Sigma \bar{x}A: \qquad \bar{X}(123.6) = 673.2 \qquad\qquad \bar{X} = 5.45 \text{ in.} \blacktriangleleft$$

$$\bar{Y}\Sigma A = \Sigma \bar{y}A: \qquad \bar{Y}(123.6) = 679.8 \qquad\qquad \bar{Y} = 5.50 \text{ in.} \blacktriangleleft$$

The above values of $\bar{X}$ and $\bar{Y}$ define the centroid of the area and also the center of gravity of the plate. The center of gravity, of course, is actually located halfway between the upper and lower faces of the plate.

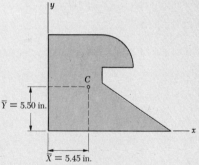

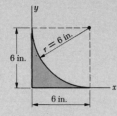

SAMPLE PROBLEM 5.2

Determine the centroid of the area shown.

Solution. Since the area is symmetrical with respect to a line drawn at 45° through the origin, the centroid must be located on this line; therefore, $\overline{X} = \overline{Y}$. The given area may be obtained by subtracting a quarter circle from a square. The centroid of the quarter circle is obtained from Fig. 5.8A and the following table is constructed:

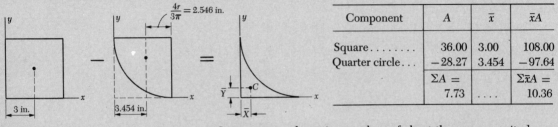

Component	A	$\overline{x}$	$\overline{x}A$
Square........	36.00	3.00	108.00
Quarter circle...	−28.27	3.454	−97.64
	$\Sigma A =$ 7.73	....	$\Sigma \overline{x}A =$ 10.36

Since we are subtracting numbers of about the same magnitude, accuracy greater than standard is required in the table in order to obtain standard accuracy (0.2 per cent) in the result.

$$\overline{X}\Sigma A = \Sigma \overline{x}A: \qquad \overline{X}(7.73) = 10.36 \qquad \overline{X} = \overline{Y} = 1.34 \text{ in.} \blacktriangleleft$$

SAMPLE PROBLEM 5.3

The figure shown is made of a thin homogeneous wire. Determine the dimension b such that the center of gravity will be located at point G.

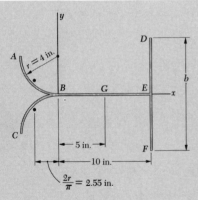

Solution. Since the figure is formed of homogeneous wire, its center of gravity may be located by determining the centroid of the corresponding line. The origin is arbitrarily placed at point B, and the line is divided into three segments ABC, BGE, and DEF.

Segment	L	$\overline{x}$	$\overline{x}L$
ABC	12.56	−2.55	−32.0
BGE	10.00	5.00	50.0
DEF	b	10.00	$10b$
	$\Sigma L =$ 22.56 + b	......	$\Sigma \overline{x}L =$ 18 + 10b

Since the value of $\overline{X}$ is known to be 5 in., the value of b is determined as follows:

$$\overline{X}\Sigma L = \Sigma \overline{x}L: \qquad 5(22.56 + b) = 18 + 10b \qquad b = 18.96 \text{ in.} \blacktriangleleft$$

PROBLEMS

5.1 through 5.12. Locate the centroid of the plane area shown.

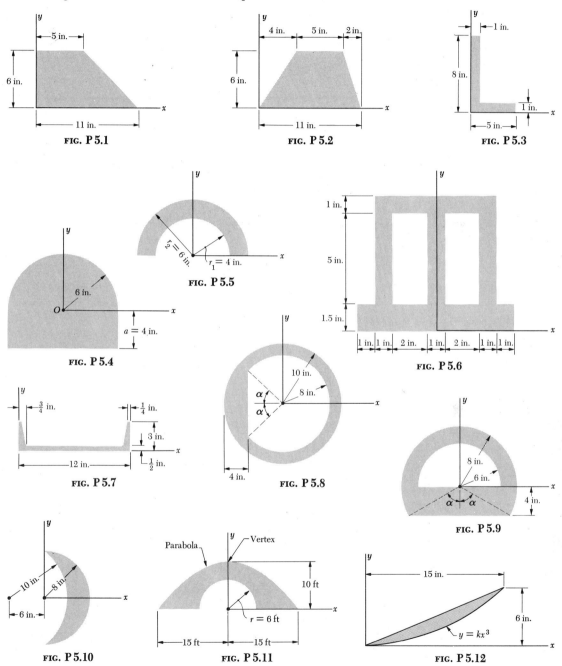

FIG. P 5.1

FIG. P 5.2

FIG. P 5.3

FIG. P 5.4

FIG. P 5.5

FIG. P 5.6

FIG. P 5.7

FIG. P 5.8

FIG. P 5.9

FIG. P 5.10

FIG. P 5.11

FIG. P 5.12

5.13. Locate the centroid of the shaded area in terms of a, b, and h.

5.14. Determine the abscissa of the centroid of the circular segment in terms of r and α.

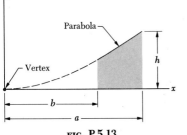

FIG. P 5.13

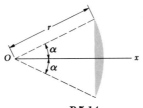

FIG. P 5.14

5.15 through 5.18. A thin homogeneous wire is bent to form the *perimeter* of the figure indicated.   Locate the center of gravity of the wire figure thus formed.

    5.15. Fig. P 5.1.
    5.16. Fig. P 5.4.
    5.17. Fig. P 5.10.
    5.18. Fig. P 5.14.

5.19. For the plane area of Prob. 5.4, determine the value of the dimension a for which the centroid of the area is located at the origin O.

5.20. For the semiannular area of Prob. 5.5, determine the ratio r_1 to r_2 for which the centroid of the area is located at the point of intersection of the inner circle and the y axis.

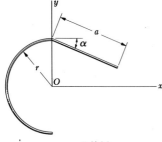

FIG. P 5.21

5.21. The figure shown is formed of a thin homogeneous wire.   Determine the length a of the straight portion and the angle α for which the center of gravity of the entire figure is located at the origin O.

°5.22. Locate the centroid C in Prob. 5.5 in terms of r_1 and r_2 and show that, as r_1 approaches r_2, the location of C approaches that for a semicircular arc of radius $\frac{1}{2}(r_1 + r_2)$.

5.23. A semicircular rod of weight W and radius r is attached to a pin at A.   If the surface at B is smooth, determine the reactions at A and B.

5.24. A semicircular rod of weight W is hinged at A; a weight W_1 is attached to the rod at point B.   Derive an expression for the magnitude of θ in terms of W and W_1.

°5.25. A semicircular rod of weight W is hinged at A; a weight W_1 is attached to the rod at a point D.   Denoting by α the angle formed by the radii AO and OD, derive an expression for the angle θ in terms of W, W_1, and α.

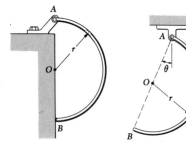

FIG. P 5.23   FIG. P 5.24 AND P 5.25

°**5.26.** If in Prob. 5.25 the weight W_1 is equal in magnitude to the weight of the rod W, determine where W_1 should be attached to the rod so that the angle θ will be maximum. Also determine the corresponding maximum value of θ.

°**5.27.** A curved slot is cut in a uniform disk of radius r. The disk is mounted on a frictionless shaft at O and is in equilibrium in the position shown. After a weight W_1 has been attached to the rim of the disk at A, the disk takes a new position of equilibrium in which line BOC is vertical. At what point on the rim should a second weight W_2 be attached, and how large should W_2 be, if the center of gravity of the disk and the two weights is to be located at O?

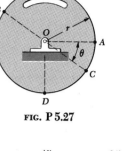

FIG. P 5.27

5.28. The plan view of a cam of uniform thickness is shown. Locate by approximate means the center of gravity of the cam.

5.29. A plate of uniform thickness is cut as shown. Locate by approximate means the center of gravity of the plate.

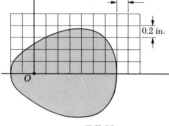

FIG. P 5.28

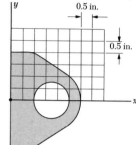

FIG. P 5.29

5.30. Divide the parabolic spandrel shown into five vertical sections and determine by approximate means the x coordinate of its centroid; approximate the spandrel by rectangles of the form $bcc'b'$. What is the percentage error in the answer obtained? (See Fig. 5.8A for exact answer.)

5.31. Solve Prob. 5.30 using rectangles of the form $bdd'b'$.

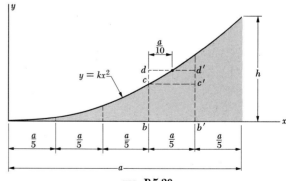

FIG. P 5.30

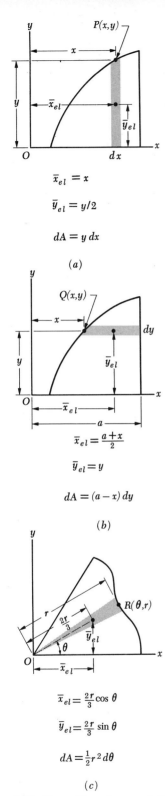

$$\bar{x}_{el} = x$$

$$\bar{y}_{el} = y/2$$

$$dA = y\,dx$$

(a)

$$\bar{x}_{el} = \frac{a+x}{2}$$

$$\bar{y}_{el} = y$$

$$dA = (a - x)\,dy$$

(b)

$$\bar{x}_{el} = \frac{2r}{3}\cos\theta$$

$$\bar{y}_{el} = \frac{2r}{3}\sin\theta$$

$$dA = \tfrac{1}{2}r^2\,d\theta$$

(c)

FIG. 5.12. Centroids and areas of differential elements

5.4. Determination of Centroids by Integration.   The centroid of an area bounded by analytical curves (i.e., curves defined by algebraic equations) is usually determined by computing the integrals in Eqs. (5.5) of Sec. 5.2.

$$\bar{x}A = \int x\,dA \qquad \bar{y}A = \int y\,dA \qquad (5.5)$$

If the element of area dA is chosen equal to a small square of sides dx and dy, the determination of each of these integrals requires a *double integration* in x and y.   A double integration is also necessary if polar coordinates are used and if dA is chosen equal to a small square of sides dr and $r\,d\theta$.

In most cases, however, it is possible to determine the coordinates of the centroid of an area by performing a single integration.   This is achieved by choosing for dA a thin rectangle or strip, or a thin sector or pie-shaped element (Fig. 5.12).   The coordinates of the centroid of the area under consideration are then obtained by expressing that the first moment of the entire area with respect to each of the coordinate axes is equal to the sum (or integral) of the corresponding moments of the elements of area.   Denoting by $\bar{x}_{el}$ and $\bar{y}_{el}$ the coordinates of the centroid of the element dA, we write

$$\Sigma M_y: \qquad \bar{x}A = \int \bar{x}_{el}\,dA$$
$$\Sigma M_x: \qquad \bar{y}A = \int \bar{y}_{el}\,dA \qquad (5.9)$$

If the area itself is not already known, it may also be computed from these elements.

The coordinates $\bar{x}_{el}$ and $\bar{y}_{el}$ of the centroid of the element of area should be expressed in terms of the coordinates of a point located on the curve bounding the area under consideration.   Also, the element of area dA should be expressed in terms of the coordinates of the point and their differentials. This has been done in Fig. 5.12 for three common types of elements; the pie-shaped element of part c should be used when the equation of the curve bounding the area is given in polar coordinates.   The appropriate expressions should be substituted in formulas (5.9), and the equation of the curve should be used to express one of the coordinates in terms of the other. The integration is thus reduced to a single integration which may be performed according to the usual rules of calculus.

The centroid of a line defined by an algebraic equation may be determined by computing the integrals in Eqs. (5.6) of Sec. 5.2.

$$\bar{x}L = \int x\,dL \qquad \bar{y}L = \int y\,dL \qquad (5.6)$$

The element dL should be replaced by one of the following expressions, depending upon the type of equation used to define the line (these expressions may be derived by using the Pythagorean theorem).

$$dL = \sqrt{1 + (dy/dx)^2}\, dx$$
$$dL = \sqrt{1 + (dx/dy)^2}\, dy$$
$$dL = \sqrt{r^2 + (dr/d\theta)^2}\, d\theta$$

The equation of the line is then used to express one of the coordinates in terms of the other, and the integration may be performed by the methods of calculus.

5.5. Theorems of Pappus-Guldinus. These theorems, which were first formulated by the Greek geometer Pappus during the third century A.D. and later restated by the Swiss mathematician Guldinus, or Guldin (1577–1643), deal with surfaces and bodies of revolution.

A *surface of revolution* is a surface which may be generated by rotating a plane curve about a fixed axis. For example (Fig. 5.13), the surface of a sphere may be obtained by rotating a

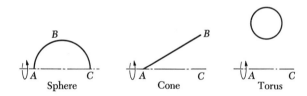

FIG. 5.13. Generating a surface of revolution

semicircular arc ABC about the diameter AC; the surface of a cone by rotating a straight line AB about an axis AC; the surface of a torus or ring by rotating the circumference of a circle about a nonintersecting axis. A *body of revolution* is a body which may be generated by rotating a plane area about a fixed axis. A solid sphere may be obtained by rotating a semicircular area, a cone by rotating a triangular area, and a solid torus by rotating a full circular area (Fig. 5.14).

THEOREM I. *The area of a surface of revolution is equal to the length of the generating curve times the distance traveled by the centroid of the curve while the surface is being generated.*

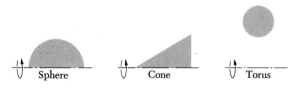
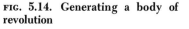

FIG. 5.14. Generating a body of revolution

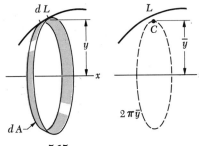

FIG. 5.15

Proof. Consider an element dL of the line L (Fig. 5.15) which is revolved about the x axis. The area dA generated by the element dL is equal to $2\pi y\, dL$. Thus, the entire area generated by L is $A = \int 2\pi y\, dL$. But we saw in Sec. 5.2 that the integral $\int y\, dL$ is equal to $\bar{y}L$. We have therefore

$$A = 2\pi\bar{y}L \tag{5.10}$$

where $2\pi\bar{y}$ is the distance traveled by the centroid of L. It should be noted that the generating curve should not cross the axis about which it is rotated; if it did, the two sections on either side of the axis would generate areas of opposite signs and the theorem would not apply.

THEOREM II. *The volume of a body of revolution is equal to the generating area times the distance traveled by the centroid of the area while the body is being generated.*

Proof. Consider an element dA of the area A which is revolved about the x axis (Fig. 5.16). The volume dV generated by the element dA is equal to $2\pi y\, dA$. Thus, the entire volume generated by A is $V = \int 2\pi y\, dA$. But since the integral $\int y\, dA$ is equal to $\bar{y}A$ (Sec. 5.2), we have

$$V = 2\pi\bar{y}A \tag{5.11}$$

where $2\pi\bar{y}$ is the distance traveled by the centroid of A. Again, it should be noted that the theorem does not apply if the axis of rotation intersects the generating area.

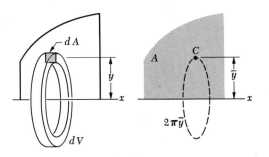

FIG. 5.16

The theorems of Pappus-Guldinus offer a simple way for computing the area of surfaces of revolution and the volume of bodies of revolution. They may also be used conversely to determine the centroid of a plane curve when the area of the surface generated by the curve is known or to determine the centroid of a plane area when the volume of the body generated by the area is known (see Sample Prob. 5.8).

SAMPLE PROBLEM 5.4

Determine by direct integration the centroid of a parabolic spandrel.

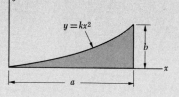

Solution. The value of k is determined by substituting $x = a$ and $y = b$ in the given equation. We have $b = ka^2$ and $k = b/a^2$. The equation of the curve is thus

$$y = \frac{b}{a^2} x^2 \quad \text{or} \quad x = \frac{a}{b^{1/2}} y^{1/2}$$

Vertical Differential Element. We choose the differential element shown and find the total area of the figure.

$$A = \int dA = \int y \, dx = \int_0^a \frac{b}{a^2} x^2 \, dx = \left[\frac{b}{a^2} \frac{x^3}{3} \right]_0^a = \frac{ab}{3}$$

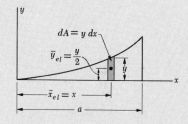

The moment of the differential element with respect to the y axis is $\bar{x}_{el} \, dA$; hence, the moment of the entire area with respect to this axis is

$$\int \bar{x}_{el} \, dA = \int xy \, dx = \int_0^a x \left(\frac{b}{a^2} x^2 \right) dx = \left[\frac{b}{a^2} \frac{x^4}{4} \right]_0^a = \frac{a^2 b}{4}$$

Thus, $\quad\quad \bar{x} A = \int \bar{x}_{el} \, dA \quad\quad \bar{x} \frac{ab}{3} = \frac{a^2 b}{4} \quad\quad \bar{x} = \tfrac{3}{4} a \quad \blacktriangleleft$

Likewise, the moment of the differential element with respect to the x axis is $\bar{y}_{el} \, dA$, and the moment of the entire area is

$$\int \bar{y}_{el} \, dA = \int \frac{y}{2} y \, dx = \int_0^a \frac{1}{2} \left(\frac{b}{a^2} x^2 \right)^2 dx = \left[\frac{b^2}{2a^4} \frac{x^5}{5} \right]_0^a = \frac{ab^2}{10}$$

Thus, $\quad\quad \bar{y} A = \int \bar{y}_{el} \, dA \quad\quad \bar{y} \frac{ab}{3} = \frac{ab^2}{10} \quad\quad \bar{y} = \tfrac{3}{10} b \quad \blacktriangleleft$

Horizontal Differential Element. The same result may be obtained by considering a horizontal element. The moments of the area are

$$\int \bar{x}_{el} \, dA = \int \frac{a + x}{2} (a - x) \, dy = \int_0^b \frac{a^2 - x^2}{2} \, dy$$

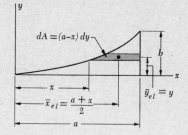

$$= \frac{1}{2} \int_0^b \left(a^2 - \frac{a^2}{b} y \right) dy = \frac{a^2 b}{4}$$

$$\int \bar{y}_{el} \, dA = \int y(a - x) \, dy = \int y \left(a - \frac{a}{b^{1/2}} y^{1/2} \right) dy$$

$$= \int_0^b \left(ay - \frac{a}{b^{1/2}} y^{3/2} \right) dy = \frac{ab^2}{10}$$

These moments are again substituted in the equations defining the centroid of the area to obtain $\bar{x}$ and $\bar{y}$.

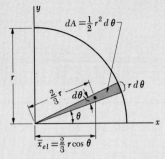

SAMPLE PROBLEM 5.5

Determine the centroid of a quarter circle by direct integration.

Solution. A differential element is chosen as shown, and the area of the quarter circle is determined.

$$A = \int dA = \int_0^{\pi/2} \tfrac{1}{2} r^2 \, d\theta = \tfrac{1}{4} \pi r^2$$

The moment of the area with respect to the y axis is

$$\int_0^{\pi/2} \bar{x}_{el} \, dA = \int_0^{\pi/2} (\tfrac{2}{3} r \cos \theta)(\tfrac{1}{2} r^2 \, d\theta) = \tfrac{1}{3} r^3 \int_0^{\pi/2} \cos \theta \, d\theta = \tfrac{1}{3} r^3$$

Thus,

$$\bar{x} A = \int \bar{x}_{el} \, dA \qquad \bar{x}(\tfrac{1}{4} \pi r^2) = \tfrac{1}{3} r^3 \qquad \bar{x} = \frac{4r}{3\pi}$$

Since the area is symmetrical with respect to a 45° line drawn through the origin, we have

$$\bar{x} = \bar{y} = \frac{4r}{3\pi} \quad \blacktriangleleft$$

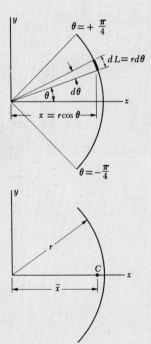

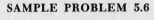

SAMPLE PROBLEM 5.6

Determine the centroid of the 90° circular arc shown.

Solution. The arc is symmetrical with respect to the x axis, and we note that $\bar{y} = 0$. Since the arc subtends an angle of $90° = \tfrac{1}{2}\pi$ radians, the length of arc is $L = \tfrac{1}{2}\pi r$. A differential element of arc is chosen as shown, and the moment of the entire arc with respect to the y axis is determined.

$$\int x \, dL = \int_{-\pi/4}^{\pi/4} (r \cos \theta)(r \, d\theta)$$

$$= r^2 \int_{-\pi/4}^{\pi/4} \cos \theta \, d\theta = \sqrt{2} \, r^2$$

Thus,

$$\bar{x} L = \int x \, dL \qquad \bar{x}(\tfrac{1}{2}\pi r) = \sqrt{2} \, r^2$$

$$\bar{x} = \frac{2\sqrt{2}}{\pi} r \quad \blacktriangleleft$$

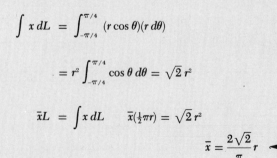

SAMPLE PROBLEM 5.7

The outside diameter of a steel flywheel is 8 ft, and the cross section of the rim is as shown. Determine the weight of the rim. Specific weight of steel = 490 lb/ft³.

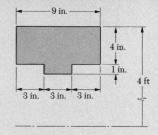

Solution. The volume of the rim may be found by applying Theorem II of Pappus-Guldinus, which states that the volume equals the product of the given cross-sectional area and of the distance traveled by its centroid in one complete revolution. However, the volume may be more easily obtained by considering the cross section as the sum of a 9- by 4-in. rectangle and a 3- by 1-in. rectangle. The volume of the rim is then equal to the sum of the volumes generated by rotating the rectangles about the x axis.

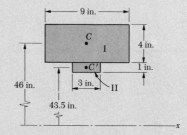

Com-ponent	Area	$\bar{y}$	Distance traveled by C	Volume
I	36 in.²	46.0 in.	$2\pi(46.0) = 289$ in.	$(36 \text{ in.}^2)(289 \text{ in.}) = 10{,}400 \text{ in.}^3$
II	3 in.²	43.5 in.	$2\pi(43.5) = 273$ in.	$(3 \text{ in.}^2)(273 \text{ in.}) = 819 \text{ in.}^3$
				Volume of rim $= 11{,}220$ in.³

Since the specific weight of steel is 490 lb/ft³, the weight of the rim is

$$W = \gamma V = \frac{490 \text{ lb/ft}^3}{1{,}728 \text{ in.}^3/\text{ft}^3} (11{,}220 \text{ in.}^3) \qquad W = 3{,}180 \text{ lb} \blacktriangleleft$$

SAMPLE PROBLEM 5.8

Using the theorems of Pappus-Guldinus, determine (a) the centroid of a semicircular area, (b) the centroid of a semicircular arc. We recall that the volume of a sphere is $\frac{4}{3}\pi r^3$ and that its surface area is $4\pi r^2$.

Solution. The volume of a sphere is equal to the product of the area of a semicircle and of the distance traveled by the centroid of the semicircle in one revolution about the x axis.

$$V = 2\pi \bar{y} A \qquad \tfrac{4}{3}\pi r^3 = 2\pi \bar{y}(\tfrac{1}{2}\pi r^2) \qquad \bar{y} = \frac{4r}{3\pi} \blacktriangleleft$$

Likewise, the area of a sphere is equal to the product of the length of the generating semicircle and of the distance traveled by its centroid in one revolution.

$$A = 2\pi \bar{y} L \qquad 4\pi r^2 = 2\pi \bar{y}(\pi r) \qquad \bar{y} = \frac{2r}{\pi} \blacktriangleleft$$

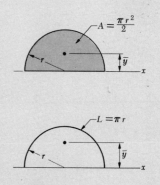

PROBLEMS

5.32 through 5.35. Determine by direct integration the centroid of the area shown.

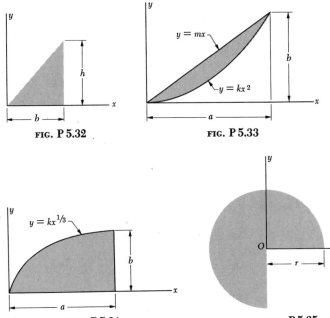

FIG. **P 5.32**   FIG. **P 5.33**

FIG. **P 5.34**   FIG. **P 5.35**

5.36 through 5.41. Derive by direct integration the expressions for $\bar{x}$ and $\bar{y}$ given in Fig. 5.8 for:

   5.36. A semicircular area.
   5.37. A quarter-elliptical area.
   5.38. A circular sector.
   5.39. A semiparabolic area.
   5.40. A general spandrel ($y = kx^n$).
   5.41. An arc of circle.

5.42. Determine by direct integration the centroid of the area bounded by the curves $y = x^2$ and $x = y^2$.

5.43. Determine by direct integration the centroid of the area located in the first quadrant and bounded by the curves $y = x^n$ and $x = y^n$, for $n > 1$.

°**5.44.** Determine by direct integration the centroid of the area shown.

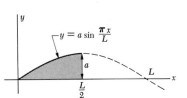

FIG. **P 5.44**

°**5.45.** Determine by direct integration the centroid of the area shown when $b = c$.

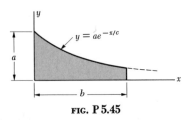

FIG. **P 5.45**

°5.46. Determine the location of the centroid of the area of Prob. 5.45 when b approaches infinity.

°5.47. Determine the centroid of the area shown.

°5.48. Determine the centroid of the area of Prob. 5.47 in terms of a.

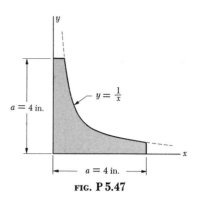

$a = 4$ in.

$y = \dfrac{1}{x}$

$a = 4$ in.

FIG. P 5.47

5.49. Determine the volume and total surface area of a right circular cone of height h and base radius r.

5.50. Determine the volume of the solid obtained by rotating the trapezoid of Prob. 5.1 about (a) the x axis, (b) the y axis.

5.51. Determine the volume of the solid obtained by rotating the semiparabolic area shown about (a) the y axis, (b) the x axis.

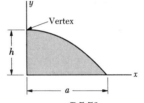

Vertex

h

a

FIG. P 5.51

5.52. Determine the surface area and the volume of the torus shown.

5.53. The inside diameter of a spherical tank is 6 ft.   What volume of liquid is required to fill the tank to a depth of 1.5 ft?

5.54. In Prob. 5.53, determine the area of the inside surface which is below the level of the liquid.

5.55. Determine the latitude of the parallel which divides the area of the northern hemisphere into two equal parts.

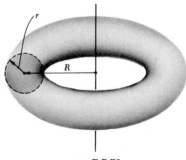

r

R

FIG. P 5.52

5.56. The excavation shown has been dug in a soil with a constant angle of repose $\phi = \tan^{-1}(\frac{3}{4})$.   The excavation is to be enlarged until the base radius is $r = 22$ ft and the width of the straight portion is $2r = 44$ ft. Assuming that the angle of repose of the soil will remain constant, determine the volume of soil which must be removed in the portion of the excavation to the left of the vertical plane *ABDE*.

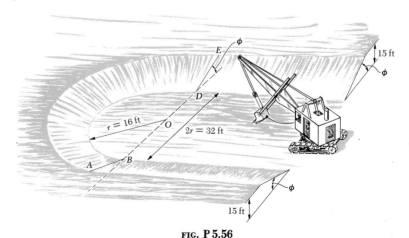

E

ϕ

15 ft

ϕ

D

$r = 16$ ft

O

$2r = 32$ ft

A

B

ϕ

15 ft

FIG. P 5.56

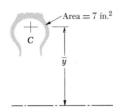

Area = 7 in.²

FIG. P 5.57

5.57. An automobile tire weighs 22 lb and has a cross-sectional area of 7 in.². The specific weight of the rubber used is 80 lb/ft³; determine the location of the centroid of the cross-sectional area.

5.58. A section of ring is cut into the two portions shown; the cross section of each portion is a semicircle. Determine the volume and the surface area, including the vertical cut, of portion *1*.

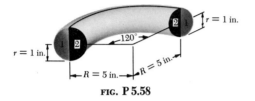

$r = 1$ in.

$r = 1$ in.

120°

$R = 5$ in.

$R = 5$ in.

FIG. P 5.58

5.59. Solve Prob. 5.58 for portion *2* of the ring.

5.60. In Prob. 5.58 determine the ratio of *r* to *R* for which the volume of portion *1* is twice the volume of portion *2*.

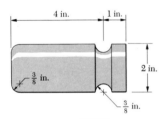

4 in.   1 in.

$\frac{3}{8}$ in.

2 in.

$\frac{3}{8}$ in.

FIG. P 5.61

FIG. P 5.63

t t

r b t

5.61. A brass plug is made from a 2-in.-diameter cylinder by machining it as shown. Determine the volume of the material removed in forming the semicircular groove.

5.62. In Prob. 5.61 determine the volume of the material removed in machining the quarter-circular rounding on the left end of the plug.

5.63. A hole of radius *r* is drilled in a flat plate of thickness *t*. In order to reinforce the plate, a metal "crack stopper" is welded around the hole as shown. Assuming that the cross section of the crack stopper is parabolic, determine the ratio *b/r* for which the total volume of metal used is the same as that of a plate without a hole.

5.64. Solve Prob. 5.63 assuming that the cross section of the crack stopper is triangular.

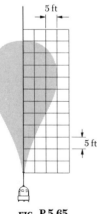

5 ft

5 ft

FIG. P 5.65

5.65. An experimental high-altitude balloon at a given time has the shape shown. Determine by approximate means (*a*) the volume of gas inside the balloon, (*b*) the surface area of the balloon.

*5.6. Distributed Loads on Beams. The concept of centroid of an area may be used to solve other problems, besides those dealing with the weight of flat plates. Consider, for example, a beam supporting a *distributed load;* this load may consist of the weight of materials supported directly or indirectly by the beam, or it may be caused by wind or hydrostatic pressure. The distributed load may be represented by plotting the load w supported per unit length (Fig. 5.17). The magnitude of the force exerted on an element of beam of length dx is thus $dW = w\,dx$, and the total load supported by the beam is

$$W = \int_0^L w\,dx$$

But the product $w\,dx$ is equal to the element of area dA shown in Fig. 5.17a, and W is thus equal to the total area A under the load curve,

$$W = \int dA = A$$

We shall now determine where a *single concentrated load* **W**, of the same magnitude W as the total distributed load, should be applied on the beam if it is to produce the same reactions at the supports (Fig. 5.17b). This concentrated load **W**, which represents the resultant of the given distributed loading, should be equivalent to this loading as far as the free-body diagram of the entire beam is concerned. The point of application P of the equivalent concentrated load **W** will therefore be obtained by expressing that the moment of **W** about point O is equal to the sum of the moments of the elementary loads d**W** about O:

$$(OP)W = \int x\,dW$$

or, since $dW = w\,dx = dA$ and $W = A$,

$$(OP)A = \int_0^L x\,dA \qquad\qquad (5.12)$$

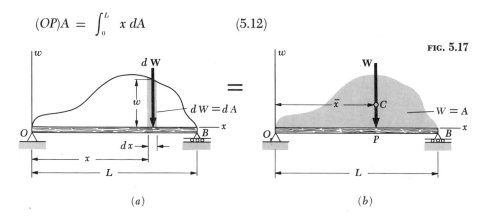

FIG. 5.17

(a)   (b)

Since the integral represents the first moment with respect to the w axis of the area under the load curve, it may be replaced by the product $\bar{x}A$. We have therefore $OP = \bar{x}$, where $\bar{x}$ is the distance from the w axis to the centroid C of the area A (this is *not* the centroid of the beam).

A distributed load on a beam may thus be replaced by a concentrated load; the magnitude of this single load is equal to the area under the load curve, and its line of action passes through the centroid of that area. It should be noted, however, that the concentrated load is equivalent to the given loading only as far as external forces are concerned. It may be used to determine reactions but should not be used to compute internal forces and deflections.

°5.7. Forces on Submerged Surfaces. Another example of the use of first moments and centroids of areas is obtained by considering the forces exerted on a *rectangular surface* submerged in a liquid. Consider the rectangular plate shown in Fig. 5.18; it has a length L, and its width, perpendicular to the plane of the figure, is assumed equal to unity. Since the gage pressure in a liquid is $p = \gamma h$, where γ is the specific weight of the liquid and h the vertical distance from the free surface, the pressure on the plate varies linearly with the distance x.

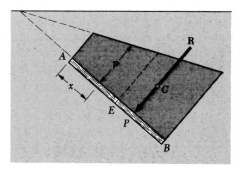

FIG. 5.18

The width of the plate being taken equal to unity, the pressure p is equal to the load w per unit length used in Sec. 5.6. The results obtained in that section may thus be used here, and we find that the magnitude of the resultant **R** of the forces exerted on one face of the plate is equal to the area under the pressure curve; we also find that the line of action of **R** passes through the centroid C of that area.

Noting that the area under the pressure curve is equal to $p_E L$, where p_E is the pressure at the center E of the plate and

L the length (or area) of the plate, we find that the magnitude R of the resultant may be obtained by multiplying the area of the plate by the pressure at the center E of the plate.   The resultant $\mathbf{R}$, however, *should not* be applied at E; as indicated above, its line of action passes through the centroid C of the area under the pressure curve.   The point of application P of the resultant $\mathbf{R}$ is known as the *center of pressure.*

We shall consider next the forces exerted by a liquid on a curved surface of constant width (Fig. 5.19*a*).   Since the de-

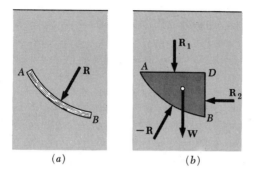

(*a*)   (*b*)   **FIG. 5.19**

termination of the resultant $\mathbf{R}$ of these forces by direct integration would not be easy, we shall consider the free body obtained by detaching the volume of liquid ABD bounded by the curved surface AB and by the two plane surfaces AD and DB shown in Fig. 5.19*b*.   The forces acting on the free body ABD consist of the weight $\mathbf{W}$ of the volume of liquid detached, the resultant $\mathbf{R}_1$ of the forces exerted on AD, the resultant $\mathbf{R}_2$ of the forces exerted on BD, and the resultant of the forces exerted *by the curved surface on the liquid.*   This last resultant is equal and opposite to, and has the same line of action as, the resultant $\mathbf{R}$ of the forces exerted *by the liquid on the curved surface;* we shall, therefore, denote it by $-\mathbf{R}$.   The forces $\mathbf{W}$, $\mathbf{R}_1$, and $\mathbf{R}_2$ may be determined by standard methods; after their values have been found, the force $-\mathbf{R}$ will be obtained by solving the equations of equilibrium for the free body of Fig. 5.19*b*.   The resultant $\mathbf{R}$ of the hydrostatic forces exerted on the curved surface will then be obtained by reversing the sense of $-\mathbf{R}$.

The methods outlined in this section may be used to determine the resultant of the hydrostatic forces exerted on the surface of dams or on rectangular gates and vanes.   Resultants of forces on submerged surfaces of variable width should be determined by the methods of Chap. 9.

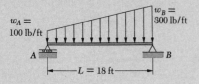

SAMPLE PROBLEM 5.9

A beam supports a distributed load as shown. (*a*) Determine the equivalent concentrated load. (*b*) Determine the reactions at the supports.

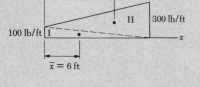

a. **Equivalent Concentrated Load.** The magnitude of the resultant of the load is equal to the area under the load curve, and the line of action of the resultant passes through the centroid of the same area. We divide the area under the load curve into two triangles and construct the following table:

Component	A	$\bar{x}$	$\bar{x}A$
Triangle I	900	6	5,400
Triangle II	2,700	12	32,400
	$\Sigma A = 3,600$	. . .	$\Sigma\bar{x}A = 37,800$

Thus,

$$\bar{X}\Sigma A = \Sigma\bar{x}A \qquad \bar{X}(3,600) = 37,800 \qquad \bar{X} = 10.5 \text{ ft}$$

The equivalent concentrated load is

$$W = 3,600 \text{ lb} \downarrow \blacktriangleleft$$

and its line of action is located at a distance

$$\bar{X} = 10.5 \text{ ft to the right of } A \blacktriangleleft$$

b. **Reactions.** The reaction at A is vertical and is denoted by $\mathbf{A}$; the reaction at B is represented by its components $\mathbf{B}_x$ and $\mathbf{B}_y$. The given load may be considered as the sum of two triangular loads as shown. The resultant of each triangular load is equal to the area of the triangle and acts at its centroid. We write the following equilibrium equations for the free body shown:

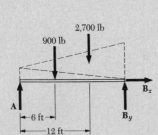

$$\xrightarrow{+} \Sigma F_x = 0: \qquad\qquad\qquad\qquad\qquad B_x = 0 \blacktriangleleft$$

$$+\circlearrowright \Sigma M_A = 0: \quad -(900 \text{ lb})(6 \text{ ft}) - (2,700 \text{ lb})(12 \text{ ft}) + B_y(18 \text{ ft}) = 0$$
$$B_y = 2,100 \text{ lb} \uparrow \blacktriangleleft$$

$$+\circlearrowright \Sigma M_B = 0: \quad +(900 \text{ lb})(12 \text{ ft}) + (2,700 \text{ lb})(6 \text{ ft}) - A(18 \text{ ft}) = 0$$
$$A = 1,500 \text{ lb} \uparrow \blacktriangleleft$$

Alternate Solution. The given distributed load may be replaced by its resultant, which was found in part *a*. The reactions may be determined by writing the equilibrium equations $\Sigma F_x = 0$, $\Sigma M_A = 0$, and $\Sigma M_B = 0$. We again obtain

$$B_x = 0 \qquad B_y = 2,100 \text{ lb} \uparrow \qquad A = 1,500 \text{ lb} \uparrow \blacktriangleleft$$

168

SAMPLE PROBLEM 5.10

The cross section of a concrete dam is as shown.   Consider a section of the dam 1 ft thick, and determine (a) the resultant of the reaction forces exerted by the ground on the base of the dam AB, (b) the resultant of the pressure forces exerted by the water on the face BC of the dam. Specific weight of concrete = 150 lb/ft³; of water = 62.4 lb/ft³.

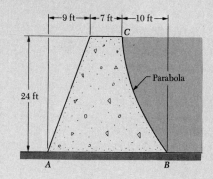

a. **Ground Reaction.**   As a free body we choose a section $ABDEA$, 1 ft thick, of the dam and water as shown.   The reaction forces exerted by the ground on the base AB are represented by an equivalent force-couple system at A.   Other forces acting on the free body are the weight of the dam, represented by the weights of its components $\mathbf{W}_1$, $\mathbf{W}_2$, and $\mathbf{W}_3$, the weight of the water $\mathbf{W}_4$, and the resultant $\mathbf{P}$ of the pressure forces exerted on section BD by the water to the right of section BD.   We have

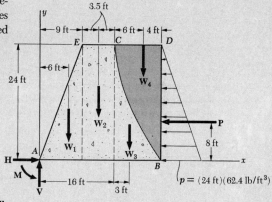

$$W_1 = \tfrac{1}{2}(9 \text{ ft})(24 \text{ ft})(1 \text{ ft})(150 \text{ lb/ft}^3) = 16,200 \text{ lb}$$
$$W_2 = (7 \text{ ft})(24 \text{ ft})(1 \text{ ft})(150 \text{ lb/ft}^3) = 25,200 \text{ lb}$$
$$W_3 = \tfrac{1}{3}(10 \text{ ft})(24 \text{ ft})(1 \text{ ft})(150 \text{ lb/ft}^3) = 12,000 \text{ lb}$$
$$W_4 = \tfrac{2}{3}(10 \text{ ft})(24 \text{ ft})(1 \text{ ft})(62.4 \text{ lb/ft}^3) = 9,980 \text{ lb}$$
$$P = \tfrac{1}{2}(24 \text{ ft})(1 \text{ ft})(24 \text{ ft})(62.4 \text{ lb/ft}^3) = 17,970 \text{ lb}$$

Equilibrium Equations

$$\Sigma F_x = 0: \qquad H - 17,970 \text{ lb} = 0 \qquad\qquad \mathbf{H} = 17,970 \text{ lb} \rightarrow \blacktriangleleft$$

$$\Sigma F_y = 0: \qquad V - 16,200 \text{ lb} - 25,200 \text{ lb} - 12,000 \text{ lb} - 9,980 \text{ lb} = 0$$
$$\mathbf{V} = 63,400 \text{ lb} \uparrow \blacktriangleleft$$

$$+\!\!\!\downarrow \Sigma M_A = 0: \qquad - (16,200 \text{ lb})(6 \text{ ft}) - (25,200 \text{ lb})(12.5 \text{ ft})$$
$$- (12,000 \text{ lb})(19 \text{ ft}) - (9,980 \text{ lb})(22 \text{ ft}) + (17,970 \text{ lb})(8 \text{ ft}) + M = 0$$
$$\mathbf{M} = 716,000 \text{ lb-ft} \, \downarrow \blacktriangleleft$$

We may replace the force-couple system obtained by a single force acting at a distance d to the right of A, where

$$d = \frac{716,000 \text{ lb-ft}}{63,400 \text{ lb}} = 11.30 \text{ ft} \quad \blacktriangleleft$$

b. **Resultant R of Water Forces.**   The parabolic section of water BCD is chosen as a free body.   The forces involved are the resultant $-\mathbf{R}$ of the forces exerted by the dam on the water, the weight $\mathbf{W}_4$, and the force $\mathbf{P}$. Since these forces must be concurrent, $-\mathbf{R}$ passes through the point of intersection F of $\mathbf{W}_4$ and $\mathbf{P}$.   A force triangle is drawn from which the magnitude and direction of $-\mathbf{R}$ are determined.   The resultant $\mathbf{R}$ of the forces exerted by the water on the face BC is equal and opposite:

$$R = 20,500 \text{ lb} \, \nearrow \, 29.0° \quad \blacktriangleleft$$

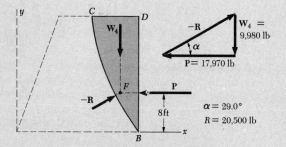

PROBLEMS

5.66 and 5.67. Determine the magnitude and location of the resultant of the distributed load shown.   Also calculate the reactions at *A* and *B*.

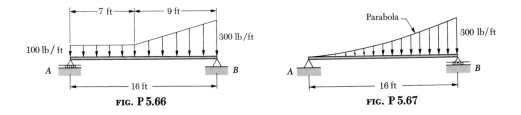

FIG. P 5.66   FIG. P 5.67

5.68 through 5.71. Determine the reactions at the beam supports for the given loading condition.

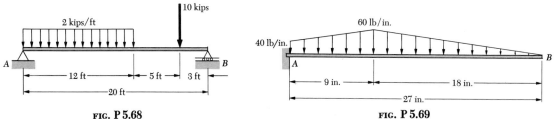

FIG. P 5.68   FIG. P 5.69

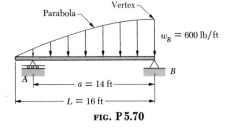

FIG. P 5.70

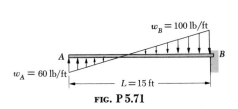

FIG. P 5.71

5.72. In Prob. 5.71 determine the ratio of w_A to w_B for which the reaction at *B* is equal to (*a*) a force and no couple, (*b*) a couple and no force. In each case express the reaction in terms of w_B and *L*.

5.73. Determine the ratio of w_A to w_B for which the reaction at *A* is equal to (*a*) a couple and no force, (*b*) a force and no couple.   In each case express the reaction in terms of w_A and *L*.

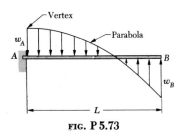

FIG. P 5.73

5.74. Solve Sample Prob. 5.9 in terms of the letter quantities w_A, w_B, and *L*.

5.75. A beam supports a uniformly distributed load w_1 and rests on soil which exerts a uniformly varying upward load as shown. Determine w_2 and w_3, corresponding to equilibrium. Knowing that at any point the soil can exert only an upward loading on the beam, state for what range of values of a/L the results obtained are valid.

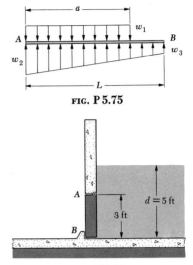

FIG. P 5.75

In the following problems, use $\gamma = 62.4 \text{ lb/ft}^3$ for the specific weight of fresh water.

5.76. A 3- by 3-ft gate is placed in a wall below water level as shown. (*a*) Determine the magnitude and location of the resultant of the forces exerted by the water on the gate. (*b*) If the gate is hinged at A, determine the force exerted by the sill on the gate at B.

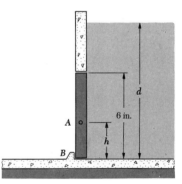

FIG. P 5.76

5.77. In Prob. 5.76 determine the depth of water d for which the force exerted by the sill on the gate at B is 1,500 lb.

5.78. An automatic valve consists of a square plate, 6 by 6 in., which is pivoted about a horizontal axis through A located at a distance $h = 2.5$ in. above the lower edge. Determine the depth of water d for which the valve will open.

5.79. If the valve shown is to open when the depth of water is $d = 12$ in., determine the distance h from the bottom of the valve to the pivot A.

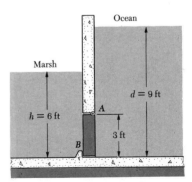

FIG. P 5.78 and P 5.79

5.80. A fresh-water marsh is drained to the ocean through an automatic tide gate which is 4 ft wide and 3 ft high. The gate is held by hinges located along its top edge at A and bears on a sill at B. At a given time, the water level in the marsh is $h = 6$ ft and in the ocean $d = 9$ ft. Determine the force exerted by the sill on the gate at B and the hinge reaction at A. (Specific weight of salt water $= 64 \text{ lb/ft}^3$.)

5.81. The automatic tide gate described in Prob. 5.80 is used to drain a fresh-water marsh into the ocean. If the water level in the marsh is $h = 6$ ft, determine the ocean level d for which the gate will open.

FIG. P 5.80

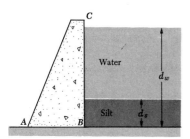

FIG. P 5.82

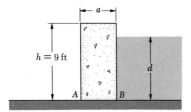

FIG. P 5.84

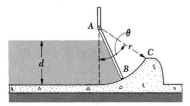

FIG. P 5.85, P 5.87, AND P 5.88

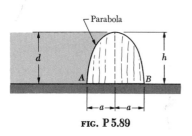

FIG. P 5.89

5.82. At the time of construction no silt was present behind the dam shown. At a later time silt has accumulated to a depth $d_s = 9$ ft. Knowing that $d_w = 24$ ft and assuming that the silt is equivalent to a liquid of specific weight $\gamma_s = 110$ lb/ft³, determine the magnitude and location of the resultant force exerted on the face BC. Consider a section of dam 1 ft thick.

5.83. For the dam of Prob. 5.82 determine the ratio of d_s to d_w for which (*a*) the resultant is 15 per cent larger than when $d_s = 0$, (*b*) the moment of the resultant about A is 15 per cent larger than when $d_s = 0$.

5.84. A uniform rectangular gate of weight W, height r, and length b is hinged at A. Denoting the specific weight of the fluid by γ, determine the required angle θ if the gate is to permit flow when $d = r$.

In the following problems, assume the specific weight of concrete to be $\gamma_c = 150$ lb/ft³.

5.85. Determine the minimum allowable value of the width a of the rectangular concrete dam if the dam is not to overturn about point A when $d = h = 9$ ft.

5.86. Solve Prob. 5.85 assuming that leakage occurs under the dam, causing an upward pressure on the bottom face AB which varies linearly from zero at A to the full hydrostatic pressure at B.

5.87. Concrete is a material which is weak in tension. In order to eliminate tension, the line of action of the resultant of the hydrostatic forces and of the weight of the dam must pass through the middle third of the base. Determine the minimum width a for which no tension will occur in the rectangular concrete dam shown when $d = h = 9$ ft.

5.88. Knowing that the width of the rectangular concrete dam is $a = 3$ ft and that its height is $h = 9$ ft, determine the maximum allowable value of the depth d of water if the dam is not to overturn about A.

5.89. A block of wood (specific weight $\gamma_1 = 40$ lb/ft³) is placed in a small channel to stop the flow of water. Assuming that $d = h$ and that no water leaks between the block and the floor of the channel, determine the maximum value of the ratio h/a for which the block will not overturn about point B.

5.90. Solve Prob. 5.89 assuming that leakage occurs under the block, causing an upward pressure on the base which varies linearly from zero at B to the full hydrostatic pressure at A.

5.91. A cylindrical drum, 10 ft long, is used as a temporary dam. Determine the resultant (magnitude and line of action) of the water pressure acting on the drum if $h = 2$ ft.

5.92. Solve Prob. 5.91 when $h = 4$ ft.

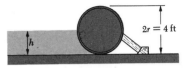

2r = 4 ft

FIG. P 5.91

VOLUMES

5.8. Center of Gravity of a Three-dimensional Body. Centroid of a Volume. The *center of gravity G* of a three-dimensional body is obtained by dividing the body into small elements and expressing that the weight **W** of the body attached at G is equivalent to the system of distributed forces $\Delta\mathbf{W}$ representing the weights of the small elements. Choosing the y axis vertical with positive sense upward (Fig. 5.20), and denoting by $\bar{\mathbf{r}}$ the position vector of G, we write that **W** is equal to the sum of the elementary weights $\Delta\mathbf{W}$ and that its moment about O is equal to the sum of the moments about O of the elementary weights:

$$\Sigma\mathbf{F}: \qquad\qquad -W\mathbf{j} = \Sigma(-\Delta W\mathbf{j}) \qquad\qquad (5.13)$$
$$\Sigma\mathbf{M}_O: \qquad \bar{\mathbf{r}} \times (-W\mathbf{j}) = \Sigma[\mathbf{r} \times (-\Delta W\mathbf{j})]$$

Rewriting the last equation in the form

$$\bar{\mathbf{r}}W \times (-\mathbf{j}) = (\Sigma\mathbf{r}\Delta W) \times (-\mathbf{j}) \qquad\qquad (5.14)$$

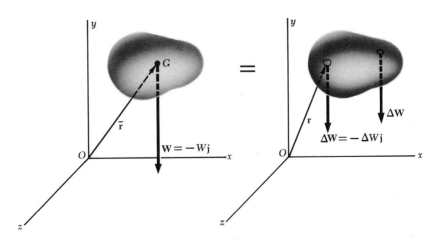

$W = -W\mathbf{j}$

$\Delta W = -\Delta W\mathbf{j}$

FIG. 5.20

we observe that the weight $\mathbf{W}$ of the body will be equivalent to the system of the elementary weights $\Delta\mathbf{W}$ if the following conditions are satisfied:

$$W = \Sigma\Delta W \qquad \bar{\mathbf{r}}W = \Sigma\mathbf{r}\Delta W$$

Increasing the number of elements and simultaneously decreasing the size of each element, we obtain at the limit

$$W = \int dW \qquad \bar{\mathbf{r}}W = \int \mathbf{r}\,dW \qquad (5.15)$$

We note that the relations obtained are independent of the orientation of the body.   For example, if the body and the axes of coordinates were rotated so that the z axis pointed upward, the unit vector $-\mathbf{j}$ would be replaced by $-\mathbf{k}$ in Eqs. (5.13) and (5.14), but the relations (5.15) would remain unchanged. Resolving the vectors $\bar{\mathbf{r}}$ and $\mathbf{r}$ into rectangular components, we verify that the second of the relations (5.15) is equivalent to the three scalar equations

▶ $\quad \bar{x}W = \int x\,dW \qquad \bar{y}W = \int y\,dW \qquad \bar{z}W = \int z\,dW \quad (5.16)$

If the body is made of a homogeneous material of specific weight γ, the magnitude dW of the weight of an infinitesimal element may be expressed in terms of the volume dV of the element, and the magnitude W of the total weight in terms of the total volume V.   We write

$$dW = \gamma\,dV \qquad W = \gamma V$$

Substituting for dW and W in the second of the relations (5.15), we write

$$\bar{\mathbf{r}}V = \int \mathbf{r}\,dV \qquad (5.17)$$

or, in scalar form,

▶ $\qquad \bar{x}V = \int x\,dV \qquad \bar{y}V = \int y\,dV \qquad \bar{z}V = \int z\,dV \quad (5.18)$

The point of coordinates $\bar{x}$, $\bar{y}$, $\bar{z}$ is also known as the *centroid C of the volume V* of the body.   If the body is not homogeneous, Eqs. (5.18) cannot be used to determine the center of gravity of the body; they still define, however, the centroid of the volume.

The integral $\int x\,dV$ is known as the *first moment of the volume with respect to the yz plane*.   Similarly, the integrals $\int y\,dV$ and $\int z\,dV$ define the first moments of the volume with respect to the zx plane and the xy plane, respectively.   It is seen from Eqs. (5.18) that, if the centroid of a volume is located in a coordinate plane, the first moment of the volume with respect to that plane is zero.

A volume is said to be symmetrical with respect to a given plane if to every point P of the volume corresponds a point P' of the same volume, such that the line PP' is perpendicular to the given plane and divided into two equal parts by that plane. The plane is said to be a *plane of symmetry* for the given volume.   When a volume V possesses a plane of symmetry, the centroid of the volume must be located in that plane.   When a volume possesses two planes of symmetry, the centroid of the volume must be located on the line of intersection of the two planes.   Finally, when a volume possesses three planes of symmetry which intersect in a well-defined point (i.e., not along a common line), the point of intersection of the three planes must coincide with the centroid of the volume.   This property enables us to determine immediately the centroid of the volume of spheres, ellipsoids, cubes, rectangular parallelepipeds, etc.

Centroids of unsymmetrical volumes or of volumes possessing only one or two planes of symmetry should be determined by integration (Sec. 5.10).   Centroids of common shapes of volumes are shown in Fig. 5.21.   It should be observed that the centroid of a volume of revolution in general *does not coincide* with the centroid of its cross section.   Thus, the centroid of a hemisphere is different from that of a semicircular area, and the centroid of a cone is different from that of a triangle.

5.9. Composite Bodies.   If a body can be divided into several of the common shapes shown in Fig. 5.21, its center of gravity G may be determined by expressing that the moment about O of its total weight is equal to the sum of the moments about O of the weights of the various component parts.   Proceeding as in Sec. 5.8, we obtain the following equations defining the coordinates $\overline{X}, \overline{Y}, \overline{Z}$ of the center of gravity G:

$$\overline{X}\Sigma W = \Sigma \overline{x}W \quad \overline{Y}\Sigma W = \Sigma \overline{y}W \quad \overline{Z}\Sigma W = \Sigma \overline{z}W \quad (5.19)$$

If the body is made of a homogeneous material, its center of gravity coincides with the centroid of its volume and the following equations may be used:

$$\overline{X}\Sigma V = \Sigma \overline{x}V \quad \overline{Y}\Sigma V = \Sigma \overline{y}V \quad \overline{Z}\Sigma V = \Sigma \overline{z}V \quad (5.20)$$

5.10. Determination of Centroids of Volumes by Integration.   The centroid of a volume bounded by analytical surfaces may be determined by computing the integrals given in Sec. 5.8.

$$\overline{x}V = \int x\,dV \quad \overline{y}V = \int y\,dV \quad \overline{z}V = \int z\,dV \quad (5.21)$$

Shape		$\bar{x}$	Volume
Hemisphere	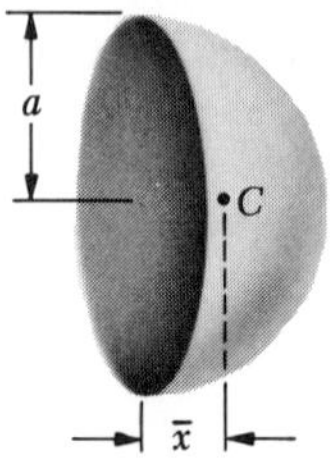	$\dfrac{3a}{8}$	$\dfrac{2}{3}\pi a^3$
Semiellipsoid of revolution	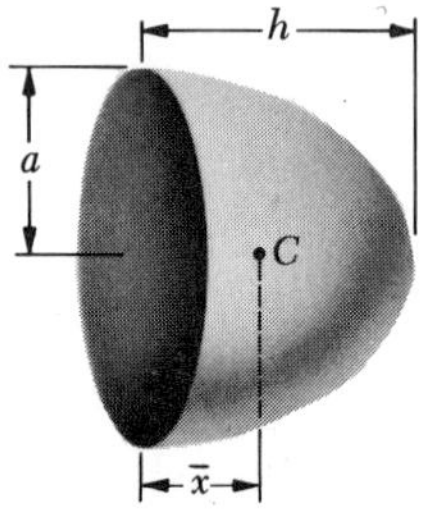	$\dfrac{3h}{8}$	$\dfrac{2}{3}\pi a^2 h$
Paraboloid of revolution	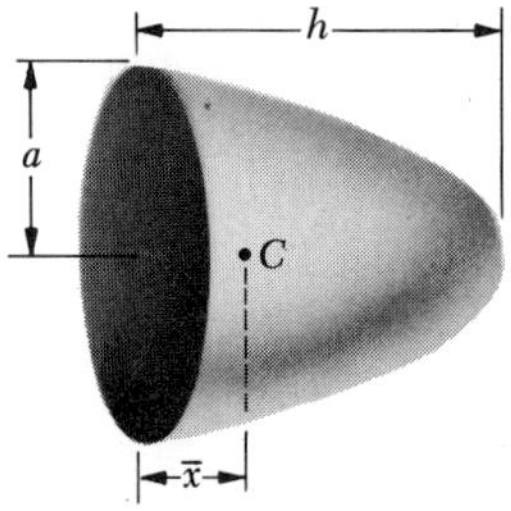	$\dfrac{h}{3}$	$\dfrac{1}{2}\pi a^2 h$
Cone	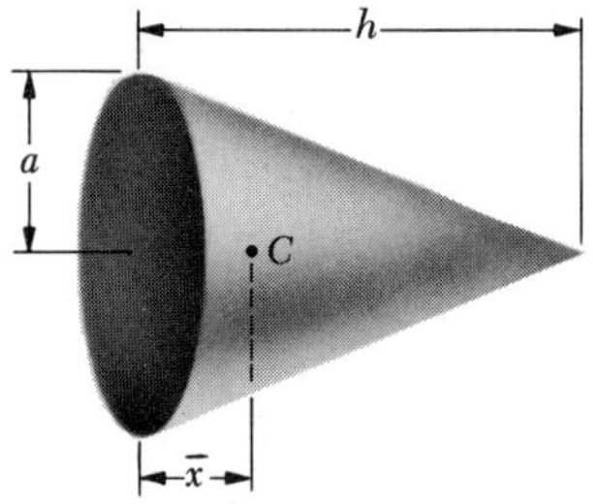	$\dfrac{h}{4}$	$\dfrac{1}{3}\pi a^2 h$
Pyramid	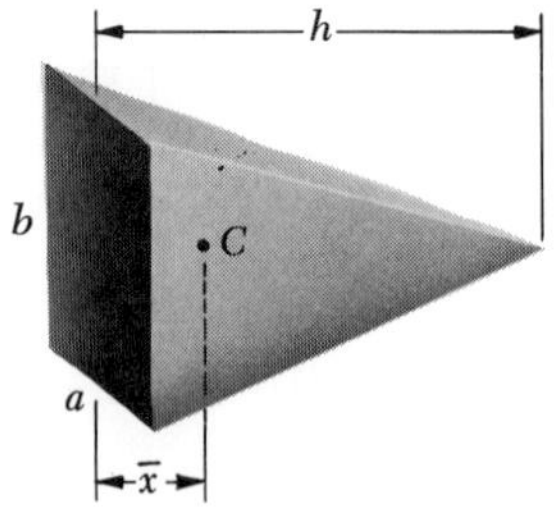	$\dfrac{h}{4}$	$\dfrac{1}{3}abh$

FIG. 5.21. Centroids of common shapes of volumes

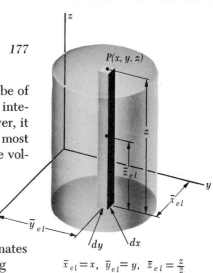

If the element of volume dV is chosen equal to a small cube of sides dx, dy, and dz, the determination of each of these integrals requires a *triple integration* in x, y, and z. However, it is possible to determine the coordinates of the centroid of most volumes by *double integration* if dV is chosen equal to the volume of a thin filament as shown in Fig. 5.22. The coordinates of the centroid of the volume are then obtained by writing

$$\bar{x}V = \int \bar{x}_{el}\, dV \qquad \bar{y}V = \int \bar{y}_{el}\, dV \qquad \bar{z}V = \int \bar{z}_{el}\, dV \qquad (5.22)$$

$$\bar{x}_{el} = x, \quad \bar{y}_{el} = y, \quad \bar{z}_{el} = \frac{z}{2}$$

$$dV = z\, dx\ dy$$

FIG. 5.22. Determination of the centroid of a volume by double integration

and substituting for the volume dV and the coordinates $\bar{x}_{el}$, $\bar{y}_{el}$, $\bar{z}_{el}$ the expressions given in Fig. 5.22. Using the equation of the surface to express z in terms of x and y, the integration is reduced to a double integration in x and y.

If the volume under consideration possesses *two planes of symmetry*, its centroid must be located on their line of intersection. Choosing the x axis along this line, we have

$$\bar{y} = \bar{z} = 0$$

and the only coordinate to determine is $\bar{x}$. This will be done most conveniently by dividing the given volume into thin slabs parallel to the yz plane. In the particular case of a body of revolution, these slabs are circular; their volume dV is given in Fig. 5.23. Substituting for $\bar{x}_{el}$ and dV into the equation

$$\bar{x}V = \int \bar{x}_{el}\, dV \qquad (5.23)$$

and expressing the radius r of the slab in terms of x, we may determine $\bar{x}$ by a single integration.

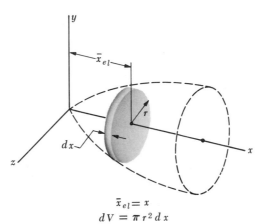

$$\bar{x}_{el} = x$$

$$dV = \pi r^2\, dx$$

FIG. 5.23. Determination of the centroid of a body of revolution

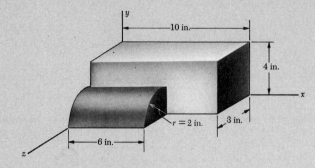

Determine the center of gravity of the homogeneous body shown.

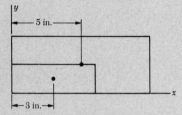

Solution. Since the body is homogeneous, its center of gravity coincides with its centroid. The body is made of a rectangular parallelepiped and a quarter cylinder, whose centroids are shown. The total volume and the moment of the volume with respect to each coordinate plane are determined from the table.

Component	V	$\bar{x}$	$\bar{y}$	$\bar{z}$	$\bar{x}V$	$\bar{y}V$	$\bar{z}V$
Parallelepiped..	120.0	5	2	1.5	600	240	180
Quarter cylinder	18.85	3	0.85	3.85	56.5	16.0	72.6
	$\Sigma V =$ 138.8	.	....	....	$\Sigma \bar{x}V =$ 656.5	$\Sigma \bar{y}V =$ 256.0	$\Sigma \bar{z}V =$ 252.6

Thus,

$$\bar{X}\Sigma V = \Sigma \bar{x}V: \qquad \bar{X}\,(138.8) = 656.5 \qquad\qquad \bar{X} = 4.73 \text{ in.} \quad \blacktriangleleft$$

$$\bar{Y}\Sigma V = \Sigma \bar{y}V: \qquad \bar{Y}\,(138.8) = 256.0 \qquad\qquad \bar{Y} = 1.84 \text{ in.} \quad \blacktriangleleft$$

$$\bar{Z}\Sigma V = \Sigma \bar{z}V: \qquad \bar{Z}\,(138.8) = 252.6 \qquad\qquad \bar{Z} = 1.82 \text{ in.} \quad \blacktriangleleft$$

SAMPLE PROBLEM 5.12

Determine the center of gravity of the homogeneous body of revolution shown.

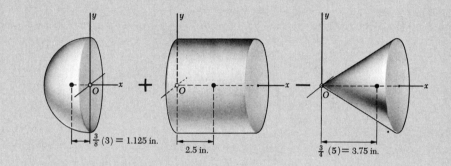

Solution. Because of symmetry, the center of gravity lies on the x axis. The body is seen to consist of a hemisphere, plus a cylinder, minus a cone, as shown.

$\frac{3}{8}(3) = 1.125$ in. 2.5 in. $\frac{3}{4}(5) = 3.75$ in.

Component	Volume	$\bar{x}$	$\bar{x}V$
Hemisphere....	$\frac{1}{2}\frac{4\pi}{3}(3)^3 = 56.5$	-1.125	-63.6
Cylinder	$\pi(3)^2(5) = 141.4$	$+2.50$	$+353.5$
Cone	$-\frac{\pi}{3}(3)^2(5) = -47.1$	$+3.75$	-176.6
	$\Sigma V = 150.8$	......	$\Sigma\bar{x}V = +113.3$

$\bar{X}\Sigma V = \Sigma\bar{x}V:$ $\bar{X}(150.8) = 113.3$ $\bar{X} = 0.75$ in. ◀

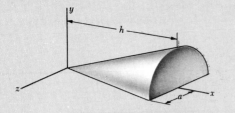

SAMPLE PROBLEM 5.13

Determine the location of the centroid of the half right circular cone shown.

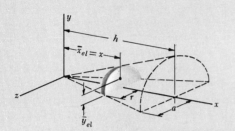

Solution. Since the xy plane is a plane of symmetry, the centroid lies in this plane and $\bar{z} = 0$. A slab of thickness dx is chosen as a differential element. The volume of this element is

$$dV = \tfrac{1}{2}\pi r^2 \, dx$$

The coordinates $\bar{x}_{el}$ and $\bar{y}_{el}$ of the centroid of the element are obtained from Fig. 5.8 (semicircular area).

$$\bar{x}_{el} = x \qquad \bar{y}_{el} = \frac{4r}{3\pi}$$

We observe that r is proportional to x and write

$$\frac{r}{x} = \frac{a}{h} \qquad r = \frac{a}{h}x$$

The volume of the body is

$$V = \int dV = \int_0^h \tfrac{1}{2}\pi r^2 \, dx = \int_0^h \tfrac{1}{2}\pi \left(\frac{a}{h}x\right)^2 dx = \frac{\pi a^2 h}{6}$$

The moment of the differential element with respect to the yz plane is $\bar{x}_{el} \, dV$; and the total moment of the body with respect to this plane is

$$\int \bar{x}_{el} \, dV = \int_0^h x(\tfrac{1}{2}\pi r^2) \, dx = \int_0^h x(\tfrac{1}{2}\pi)\left(\frac{a}{h}x\right)^2 dx = \frac{\pi a^2 h^2}{8}$$

Thus, $\qquad \bar{x}V = \int \bar{x}_{el} \, dV \qquad \bar{x}\frac{\pi a^2 h}{6} = \frac{\pi a^2 h^2}{8} \qquad \bar{x} = \tfrac{3}{4}h$ ◄

Likewise, the moment of the differential element with respect to the xz plane is $\bar{y}_{el} \, dV$; and the total moment is

$$\int \bar{y}_{el} \, dV = \int_0^h \frac{4r}{3\pi}(\tfrac{1}{2}\pi r^2) \, dx = \frac{2}{3}\int_0^h \left(\frac{a}{h}x\right)^3 dx = \frac{a^3 h}{6}$$

Thus, $\qquad \bar{y}V = \int \bar{y}_{el} \, dV \qquad \bar{y}\frac{\pi a^2 h}{6} = \frac{a^3 h}{6} \qquad \bar{y} = \frac{a}{\pi}$ ◄

PROBLEMS

5.93. A hemisphere and a cone are attached as shown. Determine the ratio h/a for which the centroid of the composite body is located in the plane between the hemisphere and the cone.

5.94. A paraboloid of revolution and a cylinder of the same radius a and height h are attached as shown. Determine the location of the centroid of the composite body.

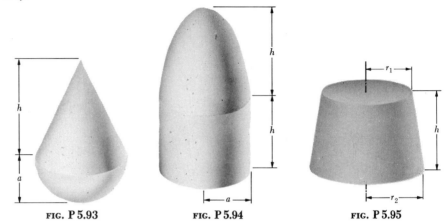

FIG. P 5.93   **FIG. P 5.94**   **FIG. P 5.95**

5.95. Locate the centroid of the frustum of a right circular cone when $r_1 = 8$ in., $r_2 = 10$ in., and $h = 6$ in.

5.96. A $\frac{3}{4}$-in.-diameter hole is drilled through the entire length of a taper as shown. Locate the center of gravity of the taper.

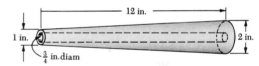

FIG. P 5.96

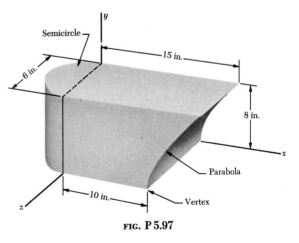

5.97. Locate the center of gravity of the block shown.

FIG. P 5.97

5.98 and 5.99. Locate the center of gravity of the link shown.

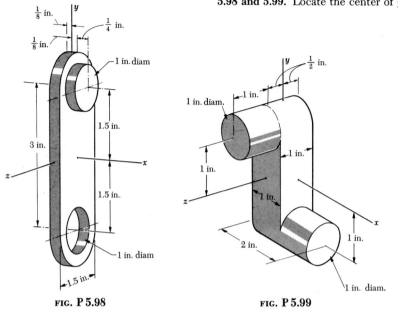

FIG. P 5.98

FIG. P 5.99

5.100. The brass sleeve is to be mounted on the pin of a machine part made of aluminum. Locate the center of gravity of the assembly. (Specific weights: brass = 530 lb/ft³; aluminum = 170 lb/ft³.)

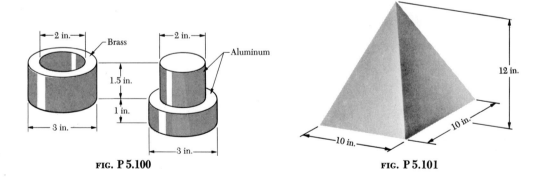

FIG. P 5.100

FIG. P 5.101

5.101. A regular pyramid 12 in. high, with a square base of side 10 in., is made of wood. Its four triangular faces are covered with steel sheets $\frac{1}{32}$ in. thick. Locate the center of gravity of the composite body. (Specific weights: steel = 490 lb/ft³; wood = 30 lb/ft³.)

5.102 and 5.103. Locate the center of gravity of the sheet-metal form shown.

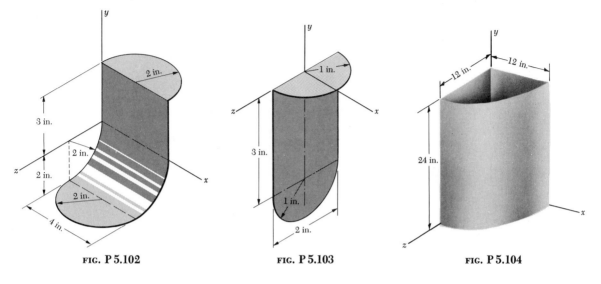

FIG. P 5.102   FIG. P 5.103   FIG. P 5.104

5.104. A wastebasket, designed to fit in the corner of a room, is 24 in. high and has a base in the shape of a quarter circle of radius 12 in. Locate the center of gravity of the wastebasket, knowing that it is made of sheet metal of uniform thickness.

5.105. Locate the centroid of the frustum of the right circular cone of Prob. 5.95, expressing the result in terms of r_1, r_2, and h.

5.106. Locate the center of gravity of a thin hemispherical shell of radius r and thickness t. (*Hint.* Consider the shell as formed by removing a hemisphere of radius r from a hemisphere of radius $r + t$; then neglect the terms containing t^2 and t^3, and keep those terms containing t.)

5.107. Derive by direct integration the expression given for $\bar{x}$ in Fig. 5.21 for a semiellipsoid of revolution.

5.108. Derive by direct integration the expression given for $\bar{x}$ in Fig. 5.21 for a paraboloid of revolution.

5.109 and 5.110. Locate the centroid of the volume obtained by rotating the area shown about the x axis.

5.111. Locate the centroid of the semiparaboloid of revolution shown.

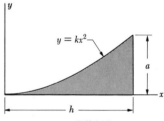

FIG. P 5.109

FIG. P 5.110

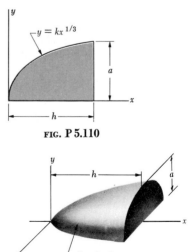

FIG. P 5.111

5.112. Locate the centroid of the volume shown, which was obtained by rotating the area of Fig. P 5.109 through 180° about the x axis.

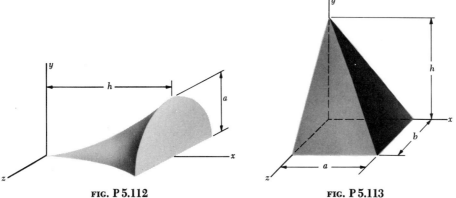

FIG. P 5.112

FIG. P 5.113

5.113. Locate the centroid of the volume of the irregular pyramid shown.

°5.114. Locate the centroid of the volume obtained by rotating the area of Prob. 5.47 about the y axis.

°5.115. A spherical tank is 12 ft in diameter and is filled with water to a depth of 9 ft. Determine by direct integration the center of gravity of the water in the tank.

°5.116. A hemispherical shell of radius a is partially filled with water. Using the result obtained in Prob. 5.106, determine for what depth of water the center of gravity of the water will coincide with the center of gravity of the shell.

FIG. P 5.117

°5.117. A right circular cone is made by welding a circular disk of sheet metal of radius a to a conical shell of the same gage and of generatrix l. For what ratio l/a will the center of gravity of this hollow cone coincide with the center of gravity of a solid cone of the same dimensions? (*Hint.* Consider the conical shell as the limiting case of the lateral surface of a regular pyramid when the number of faces of the pyramid approaches infinity.)

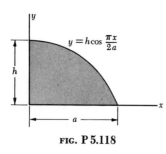

FIG. P 5.118

°5.118. Locate the centroid of the volume generated by revolving the portion shown of the cosine curve about the y axis. (*Hint.* Use as an element of volume a thin cylindrical shell of radius r and thickness dr.)

°5.119. Determine by direct integration the location of the centroid of the volume between the xz plane and the portion shown of the surface $y = h \sin (\pi x/a) \sin (\pi z/b)$.

°5.120. A circular cylinder of radius a is cut by an oblique plane as shown. Determine by direct integration the location of the centroid.

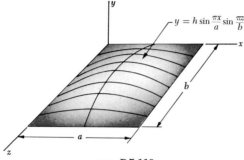

$$y = h \sin \frac{\pi x}{a} \sin \frac{\pi z}{b}$$

FIG. P 5.119

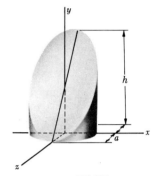

FIG. P 5.120

REVIEW PROBLEMS

5.121. Locate the centroid of the plane area shown.

5.122. Determine the volume of the solid generated by rotating the area shown about the y axis.

5.123. Determine the total surface area of the solid generated by rotating the area shown about the y axis.

5.124. Determine the reactions at A and B.

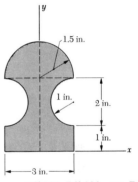

FIG. P 5.121, P 5.122, AND P 5.123

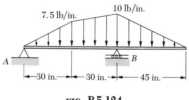

FIG. P 5.124

5.125. Locate the center of gravity of the sheet-metal form shown when $a = 1$ ft.

5.126. Determine the distance a so that the center of gravity of the sheet-metal form is located 1 ft from the y axis.

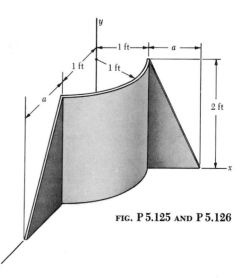

FIG. P 5.125 AND P 5.126

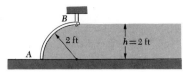

FIG. P 5.127

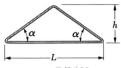

FIG. P 5.129

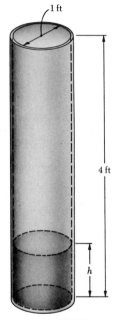

FIG. P 5.130

5.127. The gate shown is supported by hinges located along its top edge at B and rests on the floor of a channel at A. Knowing that the gate is 4 ft wide, determine the magnitude and direction of the resultant of the hydrostatic forces exerted on the gate when $h = 2$ ft.

5.128. Knowing that the gate of Prob. 5.127 is 4 ft wide and is made of sheet metal of uniform gage, determine the required weight of the gate if it is to prevent water from flowing when $h = 2$ ft.

5.129. A homogeneous wire is bent to form an isosceles triangle. Determine the angle α for which the center of gravity of the wire coincides with the centroid of the area enclosed by the wire.

5.130. Concrete is poured into a steel pipe of length 4 ft, inside diameter 1 ft, and weight 200 lb. To what depth should concrete be poured if the combined center of gravity of the pipe and concrete is to be as low as possible? (Specific weight of concrete = 150 lb/ft³.)

5.131. The production-line balancing of an automobile speedometer cup is done as follows. The unbalanced cup is placed on a frictionless shaft at O and is allowed to come to rest. A hole is then punched at A; the cup rotates through an angle θ and again comes to rest. The balancing is completed by punching additional holes at B and C. Knowing that the three holes are equal in size and are at the same distance from the shaft O, determine the required angle α in terms of the angle θ.

5.132. A simple beam AB of length L supports a distributed load $w = w_0(au^2 + bu^3)$ where $u = x/L$, with x measured from the left end A of the beam. Determine the ratio of b/a for which the reactions are equal in magnitude and direction.

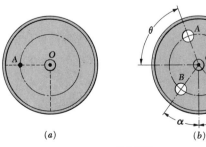

(a)   *(b)*

FIG. P 5.131

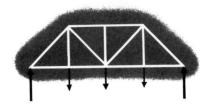

6. ANALYSIS OF STRUCTURES

6.1. Internal Forces. Newton's Third Law. The problems considered in the preceding chapters concerned the equilibrium of a single rigid body, and all forces involved were external to the rigid body. We shall now consider problems dealing with the equilibrium of structures made of several connected parts. These problems call not only for the determination of the external forces acting on the structure but also for the determination of the forces which hold together the various parts of the structure. From the point of view of the structure as a whole, these forces are *internal forces*.

Consider, for example, the crane shown in Fig. 6.1*a*, which carries a load *W*. The crane consists of three beams *AD*, *CF*, and *BE* connected by smooth pins; it is supported by a smooth pin at *A* and by a cable *DG*. The free-body diagram of the crane has been drawn in Fig. 6.1*b*. The external forces are shown in the diagram and include the weight **W**, the two components $\mathbf{A}_x$ and $\mathbf{A}_y$ of the reaction at *A*, and the force **T** exerted by the cable at *D*. The internal forces holding the various parts of the crane together do not appear in the diagram. If, however, the crane is dismembered and if a free-body diagram is drawn for each of its component parts, the forces holding the three beams together must also be represented, since these forces are external forces from the point of view of each component part (Fig. 6.1*c*).

It will be noted that the force exerted at *B* by member *BE* on member *AD* has been represented as equal and opposite to the force exerted at the same point by member *AD* on member *BE*; similarly, the force exerted at *E* by *BE* on *CF* is shown equal and opposite to the force exerted by *CF* on *BE*; and the components of the force exerted at *C* by *CF* on *AD* are shown equal and opposite to the components of the force exerted by *AD* on *CF*. This is in conformity with Newton's third law,

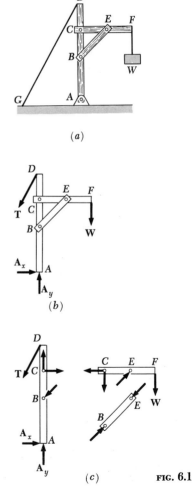

(*a*)

(*b*)

(*c*)　　　**FIG. 6.1**

which states that *the forces of action and reaction between bodies in contact have the same magnitude, same line of action, and opposite sense.*   As pointed out in Chap. 1, this law is one of the six fundamental principles of elementary mechanics and is based on experimental evidence.   Its application is essential to the solution of problems involving connected bodies.

TRUSSES

6.2. Definition of a Truss.   The truss is one of the major types of engineering structures.   It provides both a practical and an economical solution to many engineering situations, especially in the design of bridges and buildings.   A truss consists of straight members connected at joints; a typical truss is shown in Fig. 6.2a.   Truss members are connected at their extremities only; thus no member is continuous through a joint. In Fig. 6.2a, for example, there is no member AB; there are instead two distinct members AD and DB.   Actual structures are made of several trusses joined together to form a space framework.   Each truss is designed to carry those loads which act in its plane and thus may be treated as a two-dimensional structure.

In general, the members of a truss are slender and can support little lateral load; all loads, therefore, must be applied to the various joints, and not to the members themselves.   When a concentrated load is to be applied between two joints, or when a distributed load is to be supported by the truss, as in the case of a bridge truss, a floor system must be provided which, through the use of stringers and floor beams, transmits the load to the joints (Fig. 6.3).

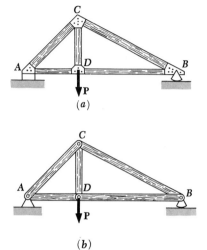

(a)

(b)

FIG. 6.2

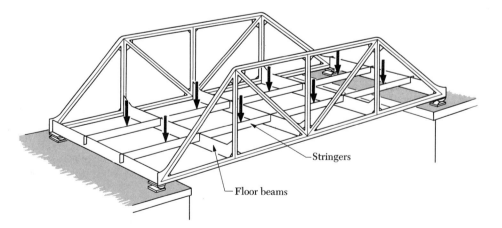

Stringers

Floor beams

FIG. 6.3

The weights of the members of the truss are also assumed to be applied to the joints, half of the weight of each member being applied to each of the two joints the member connects. Although the members are actually joined together by means of riveted and welded connections, it is customary to assume that the members are pinned together; therefore, the forces acting at each end of a member reduce to a single force and no couple. Thus, the only forces assumed to be applied to a truss member are a single force at each end of the member. Each member may then be treated as a two-force member, and the entire truss may be considered as a group of pins and two-force members (Fig. 6.2*b*). An individual member may be acted upon as shown in either of the two sketches of Fig. 6.4. In the first sketch, the forces tend to pull the member apart, and the member is in tension, while, in the second sketch, the forces tend to compress the member, and the member is in compression. Several typical trusses are shown in Fig. 6.5.

(*a*)   (*b*)

FIG. 6.4

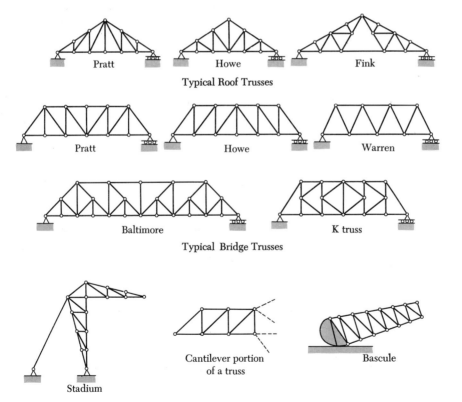

Pratt   Howe   Fink

Typical Roof Trusses

Pratt   Howe   Warren

Baltimore   K truss

Typical Bridge Trusses

Stadium

Cantilever portion
of a truss

Bascule

Other Types of Trusses

FIG. 6.5. Typical trusses

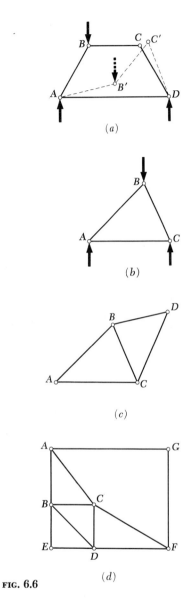

(a)

(b)

(c)

(d)

FIG. 6.6

6.3. Simple Trusses.   Consider the truss of Fig. 6.6a, which is made of four members connected by pins at A, B, C, and D.   If a load is applied at B, the truss will greatly deform and lose completely its original shape.   On the other hand, the truss of Fig. 6.6b, which is made of three members connected by pins at A, B, and C, will deform only slightly under a load applied at B.   The only possible deformation for this truss is one involving small changes in the length of its members.   The truss of Fig. 6.6b is said to be a *rigid truss*, the term rigid being used here to indicate that the truss *will not collapse*.

As shown in Fig. 6.6c, a larger rigid truss may be obtained by adding two members BD and CD to the basic triangular truss of Fig. 6.6b.   This procedure may be repeated as many times as desired, and the resulting truss will be rigid if, each time we add two new members, we attach them to separate existing joints and connect them at a new joint.†   A truss which may be constructed in this manner is called a *simple truss*.

It should be noted that a simple truss is not necessarily made only of triangles.   The truss of Fig. 6.6d, for example, is a simple truss which was constructed from triangle ABC by adding successively the joints D, E, F, and G.   On the other hand, rigid trusses are not always simple trusses, even when they appear to be made of triangles.   The Fink and Baltimore trusses shown in Fig. 6.5, for instance, are not simple trusses, since they cannot be constructed from a single triangle in the manner described above.   All the other trusses shown in Fig. 6.5 are simple trusses, as may be easily checked.   (For the K truss, start with one of the central triangles.)

Returning to the basic triangular truss of Fig. 6.6b, we note that this truss has three members and three joints.   The truss of Fig. 6.6c has two more members and one more joint, i.e., altogether five members and four joints.   Observing that every time two new members are added, the number of joints is increased by one, we find that in a simple truss the total number of members is $m = 2n - 3$, where n is the total number of joints.

6.4. Analysis of Trusses by the Method of Joints.   We saw in Sec. 6.2 that a truss may be considered as a group of pins and two-force members.   The truss of Fig. 6.2, whose free-body diagram is shown in Fig. 6.7a, may thus be dismembered, and a free-body diagram can be drawn for each pin and each

† The three joints must not be in a straight line.

member (Fig. 6.7*b*). Each member is acted upon by two forces, one at each end; these forces have the same magnitude, same line of action, and opposite sense (Sec. 4.6). Besides, Newton's third law indicates that the forces of action and reaction between a member and a pin are equal and opposite. Therefore, the forces exerted by a member on the two pins it connects must be directed along that member and be equal and opposite. The common magnitude of the forces exerted by a member on the two pins it connects is commonly referred to as the *force in the member* considered, even though this quantity is actually a scalar. Since the lines of action of all the internal forces in a truss are known, the analysis of a truss reduces to the computation of the forces in its various members and to the determination of whether each of its members is in tension or in compression.

Since the entire truss is in equilibrium, each pin must be in equilibrium. The fact that a pin is in equilibrium may be expressed by drawing its free-body diagram and writing two equilibrium equations (Sec. 2.8). If the truss contains n pins, there will be therefore $2n$ equations available, which may be solved for $2n$ unknowns. In the case of a simple truss, we have $m = 2n - 3$, that is, $2n = m + 3$, and the number of unknowns which may be determined from the free-body diagrams of the pins is thus $m + 3$. This means that the forces in all the members, as well as the two components of the reaction $\mathbf{R}_1$, and the reaction $\mathbf{R}_2$ may be found by considering the free-body diagrams of the pins.

The fact that the entire truss is a rigid body in equilibrium may be used to write three more equations involving the forces shown in the free-body diagram of Fig. 6.7*a*. Since they do not contain any new information, these equations are not independent from the equations associated with the free-body diagrams of the pins. Nevertheless, they may be used to determine immediately the components of the reactions at the supports. The arrangement of pins and members in a simple

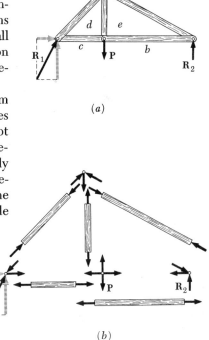

(*a*)

(*b*)

FIG. 6.7

truss is such that it will then always be possible to find a joint involving only two unknown forces.   These forces may be determined by the methods of Sec. 2.10 and their values transferred to the adjacent joints and treated as known quantities at these joints.   This procedure may be repeated until all unknown forces have been determined.

In order to expedite the analysis of trusses, it is desirable to establish a uniform method for denoting the various joints, members, loads, and forces.   This is done by using the following notation, known as *Bow's notation*.   A lower-case letter is assigned to every region between loads and reactions, moving clockwise around the truss, and to every area inside the truss (Fig. 6.7a).   Each joint, member, load, and force may then be denoted as follows:

1. *Joints*.   A joint is specified by naming *in clockwise order* the letters corresponding to all the areas adjacent to the joint.   For example, the joint at the left support (Fig. 6.7a) is joint *adc*, or joint *dca*, or joint *cad*.   For convenience, however, joints will be denoted sometimes by a number.

2. *Members*.   A member is specified by naming the letters of the two adjacent areas.   For example, the vertical member above the load **P** is member *de* or member *ed*.

3. *Loads*.   A load is specified by reading *in clockwise order* the letters of the two areas adjacent to the load.   The name of the load is then recorded with capital letters surmounted by an arrow.   For example, at joint *debc*, the load **P** is denoted by $\overrightarrow{BC}$.

4. *Forces Exerted by Members on Pins*.   As noted above, the forces exerted by a member on the two pins it connects must be directed along the member and be equal and opposite.   In considering the action of the member on one of the two pins, we denote the force it exerts by reading the letters of the two areas adjacent to the member *in clockwise order* with respect to the joint.   For example, the force exerted by member *ad* on pin *adc* is $\overrightarrow{AD}$, while the force exerted by the same member on pin *aed* is $\overrightarrow{DA}$.   The common magnitude of these forces commonly referred to as the force in member *ad*, may be denoted by either *AD* or *DA*.

We shall now proceed to analyze the truss of Fig. 6.7 by considering successively the equilibrium of each pin, starting with a joint at which only two forces are unknown.   In the truss considered, all pins are subjected to at least three unknown forces.   Therefore, the reactions at the supports must first be determined by considering the entire truss as a free body and using the equations of equilibrium of a rigid body.   We find in this way that $\mathbf{R}_1$ is vertical and determine the magnitudes of $\mathbf{R}_1$ and $\mathbf{R}_2$.

The number of unknown forces at joint *adc* is thus reduced to two; and these forces may be determined by considering the equilibrium of pin *adc*. The magnitude and sense of $\overrightarrow{AD}$ and $\overrightarrow{DC}$ are obtained from the corresponding force triangle (Fig. 6.8).

We may now proceed to joint *debc*, where only two forces, $\overrightarrow{DE}$ and $\overrightarrow{EB}$, are still unknown. $\overrightarrow{BC}$ is the given load $\mathbf{P}$ and hence is known; *CD* is the force exerted on the pin by the mem-

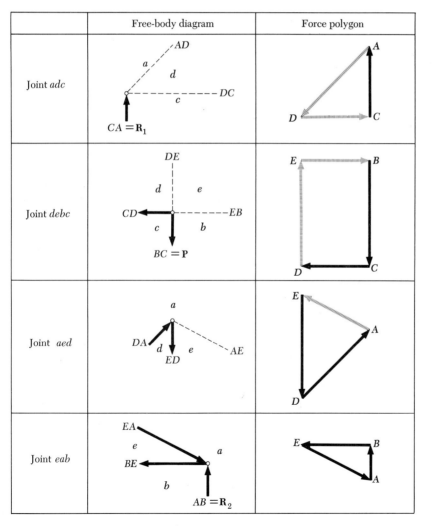

	Free-body diagram	Force polygon
Joint *adc*		
Joint *debc*		
Joint *aed*		
Joint *eab*		

FIG. 6.8

ber *cd* and, as indicated above, is equal and opposite to the force $\overrightarrow{DC}$ exerted by the same member on pin *adc*.

Next, joint *aed* is considered; its free-body diagram is shown in Fig. 6.8. It is noted that both $\overrightarrow{ED}$ and $\overrightarrow{DA}$ are known from the analysis of the preceding joints and that only $\overrightarrow{AE}$ is unknown. Since the equilibrium of each pin provides sufficient information to determine two unknowns, a check of our analysis is obtained at this joint. The force triangle is drawn, and the magnitude and sense of $\overrightarrow{AE}$ are determined. The check is obtained by verifying that the force $\overrightarrow{AE}$ and the member *ae* are parallel.

At joint *eab*, all the forces are known. Since the corresponding pin is in equilibrium, the force triangle must close and an additional check of the analysis is obtained.

From the free-body diagrams shown in Fig. 6.8, it is seen that some forces act away from a given joint and others toward it. If the force acts away from the joint, the corresponding member pulls on the pin and the member is in tension; if the force acts toward the joint, the corresponding member pushes on the pin and the member is in compression. For example, at joint *adc*, it is seen from the free-body diagram and the force triangle that force $\overrightarrow{AD}$ acts toward the joint; hence, member *ad* pushes on the pin and is in compression. If we consider joint *aed*, it is seen that $\overrightarrow{DA}$ also acts toward the joint; hence, member *ad* is again found to push and thus to be in compression.

*6.5. Joints under Special Loading Conditions. Consider the joint shown in Fig. 6.9*a*, which connects four members lying in two intersecting straight lines. The free-body diagram of Fig. 6.9*b* shows that the pin is subjected to two pairs of directly opposite forces. The corresponding force polygon, therefore, must be a parallelogram (Fig. 6.9*c*), and *the forces in opposite members must be equal.*

Consider next the joint shown in Fig. 6.10*a*, which connects three members and supports a load **P**. Two of the members lie in the same line, and the load **P** acts along the third member. The free-body diagram of the pin and the corresponding force polygon again will be as shown in Fig. 6.9*b* and *c*. Thus, *the forces in the two opposite members must be equal, and the force in the other member must equal P.* A particular case of special interest is shown in Fig. 6.10*b*. Since, in this case, no external load is applied to the joint, we have $P = 0$ and the force in member *cd* is zero. Member *cd* is said to be a *zero-force member.*

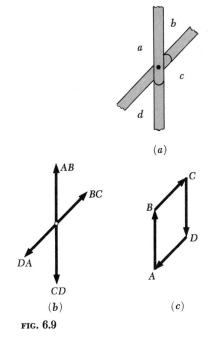

FIG. 6.9

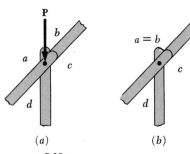

FIG. 6.10

Consider now a joint connecting two members only. From Sec. 2.8, we know that a particle which is acted upon by two forces will be in equilibrium if the two forces have the same magnitude, same line of action, and opposite sense. In the case of the joint of Fig. 6.11*a*, which connects two members lying in the same line, the equilibrium of the pin requires therefore that *the forces in the two members be equal.* In the case of the joint of Fig. 6.11*b*, equilibrium is impossible unless the forces in both members are zero. Members connected as shown in Fig. 6.11*b*, therefore, must be *zero-force members.*

Spotting the joints which are under the special loading conditions listed above will expedite the analysis of a truss. Consider, for example, a Howe truss loaded as shown in Fig. 6.12. All the members represented by dashed lines will be recognized as zero-force members. Joint *3* connects three members, two of which lie in the same line, and is not subjected to any external load; member *hi* is thus a zero-force member. Applying the same reasoning to joint *11*, we find that member *pq* is also a zero-force member. But joint *10* is now in the same situation as joints *3* and *11*, and member *po* must be a zero-force member. The examination of joints *3*, *10*, and *11* also shows that the forces in members *fh* and *if* are equal, that the forces in members *od* and *dq* are equal, and that the forces in members *ep* and *qe* are equal. Furthermore, now turning our attention to joint *9*, where the 4-kip load and member *no* are collinear, we note that the force in member *no* is 4 kips (tension) and that the forces in members *fn* and *pe* are equal. Hence, the forces in members *ep*, *eq*, and *fn* are equal.

Students, however, should be warned against misusing the rules established in this section. For example, it would be wrong to assume that the force in member *kj* is 5 kips or that

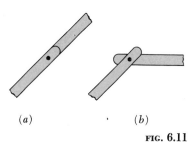

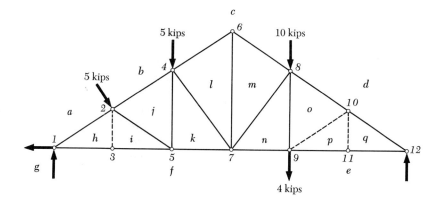

FIG. 6.12

the forces in members *bj* and *ha* are equal. The conditions discussed above do not apply to joints *2* and *4*. The forces in these members and in all remaining members should be found by carrying out the analysis of joints *1, 2, 4, 5, 6, 7, 8,* and *12* in the usual manner. Until they have become thoroughly familiar with the conditions of application of the rules established in this section, students would be well advised to draw the free-body diagrams of all pins and to write the corresponding equilibrium equations (or draw the corresponding force polygons), whether or not the joints considered fall into the categories listed above.

A final remark concerning zero-force members: These members are not useless. While they do not carry any load under the particular loading conditions shown, the zero-force members of Fig. 6.12 will probably carry loads if the loading conditions are changed. Besides, even in the case considered, these members are needed to support the weight of the truss and to maintain the truss in the desired shape.

*6.6. Space Trusses. When several straight members are joined together at their extremities to form a three-dimensional configuration, the structure obtained is called a *space truss.*

We recall from Sec. 6.3 that the most elementary two-dimensional rigid truss consisted of three members joined at their extremities to form the sides of a triangle; by adding two members at a time to this basic configuration, and connecting them at a new joint, it was possible to obtain a larger rigid structure which was defined as a simple truss. Similarly, the most elementary rigid space truss consists of six members joined at their extremities to form the edges of a tetrahedron *ABCD* (Fig. 6.13*a*). By adding three members at a time to this basic configuration, such as *AE, BE,* and *CE,* attaching them at separate existing joints, and connecting them at a new joint, we can obtain a larger rigid structure which is defined as a *simple space truss* (Fig. 6.13*b*).†
Observing that the basic tetrahedron has six members and four joints, and that, every time three members are added, the number of joints is increased by one, we conclude that in a simple space truss the total number of members is $m = 3n - 6$, where n is the total number of joints.

If a space truss is to be completely constrained and if the reactions at its supports are to be statically determinate, the supports should consist of a combination of balls, rollers, and balls and sockets providing six unknown reactions (see Sec. 4.9).

† The four joints must not lie in a plane.

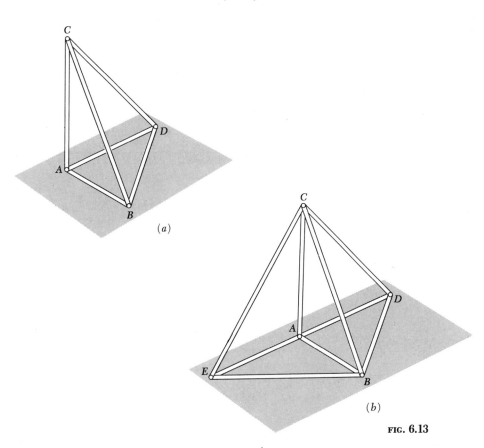

(a)

(b)

FIG. 6.13

These unknown reactions may be readily determined by solving the six equations expressing that the three-dimensional truss is in equilibrium.

Although the members of a space truss are actually joined together by means of riveted or welded connections, it is assumed that each joint consists of a ball-and-socket connection. Thus, no couple will be applied to the members of the truss and each member may be treated as a two-force member. The conditions of equilibrium for each joint will be expressed by the three equations $\Sigma F_x = 0$, $\Sigma F_y = 0$, and $\Sigma F_z = 0$. In the case of a simple space truss containing n joints, writing the conditions of equilibrium for each joint will thus yield $3n$ equations. Since $m = 3n - 6$, these equations suffice to determine all unknown forces (forces in m members and six reactions at the supports). However, to avoid solving many simultaneous equations, care should be taken to select joints in such an order that no selected joint will involve more than three unknown forces.

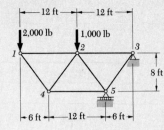

SAMPLE PROBLEM 6.1

Using the method of joints, determine the force in each member of the truss shown.

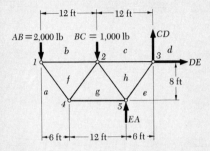

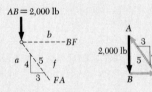

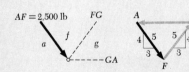

Solution. A free-body diagram of the entire truss is drawn; external forces acting on this free body consist of the applied loads and the reactions. The truss is then lettered, using Bow's notation. The applied loads are thus $\overrightarrow{AB}$ and $\overrightarrow{BC}$; the reactions are $\overrightarrow{CD}$, $\overrightarrow{DE}$, and $\overrightarrow{EA}$.

Equilibrium of Entire Truss

$+\,\rangle\ \Sigma M_3 = 0:\quad (2{,}000\text{ lb})(24\text{ ft}) + (1{,}000\text{ lb})(12\text{ ft}) - (EA)(6\text{ ft}) = 0$
$$EA = +10{,}000\text{ lb} \qquad EA = 10{,}000\text{ lb}\uparrow$$

$\stackrel{+}{\rightarrow}\Sigma F_x = 0: \qquad\qquad\qquad\qquad\qquad\qquad\qquad \overrightarrow{DE} = 0$

$+\uparrow\Sigma F_y = 0:\quad -2{,}000\text{ lb} - 1{,}000\text{ lb} + 10{,}000\text{ lb} + CD = 0$
$$CD = -7{,}000\text{ lb} \qquad \overrightarrow{CD} = 7{,}000\text{ lb}\downarrow$$

Joint 1. This joint is subjected to only two unknown forces, namely, the forces exerted by members bf and fa. A force triangle is used to determine $\overrightarrow{BF}$ and $\overrightarrow{FA}$. We note that member bf pulls on the joint and thus is in tension and that member fa pushes on the joint and thus is in compression. The magnitudes of the two forces are obtained from the proportion

$$\frac{2{,}000\text{ lb}}{4} = \frac{BF}{3} = \frac{FA}{5}$$

$$BF = 1{,}500\text{ lb } T \quad \blacktriangleleft$$
$$FA = 2{,}500\text{ lb } C \quad \blacktriangleleft$$

Joint 4. Since the force exerted by member af has been determined, only two unknown forces are now involved at this joint. Again, a force triangle is used to determine the unknown forces in members fg and ga.

$$FG = AF \qquad\qquad FG = 2{,}500\text{ lb } T \quad \blacktriangleleft$$
$$GA = (2)(\tfrac{3}{5}\,AF) \qquad GA = 3{,}000\text{ lb } C \quad \blacktriangleleft$$

Joint 2. Since more than three forces act at this joint, we determine the two unknown forces $\overrightarrow{CH}$ and $\overrightarrow{HG}$ by solving the equilibrium equations $\Sigma F_x = 0$ and $\Sigma F_y = 0$. We arbitrarily assume that both unknown forces act away from the joint, i.e., that the members are in tension. The positive value obtained for CH indicates that our assumption was correct; member ch is in tension. The negative value of HG indicates that our assumption was wrong; member hg is in compression.

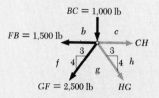

$$+\uparrow \Sigma F_y = 0: \qquad -1{,}000 - (\tfrac{4}{5})(2{,}500) - \tfrac{4}{5}HG = 0$$
$$HG = -3{,}750\ \text{lb} \qquad HG = 3{,}750\ \text{lb}\ C \ \blacktriangleleft$$

$$\xrightarrow{+}\ \Sigma F_x = 0: \qquad CH - 1{,}500 - (\tfrac{3}{5})(2{,}500) - (\tfrac{3}{5})(3{,}750) = 0$$
$$CH = +5{,}250\ \text{lb} \qquad CH = 5{,}250\ \text{lb}\ T \ \blacktriangleleft$$

Joint 5. The unknown force $\overrightarrow{HE}$ is assumed to act away from the joint. Summing x components, we write

$$\xrightarrow{+}\ \Sigma F_x = 0: \qquad \tfrac{3}{5}HE + 3{,}000 + (\tfrac{3}{5})(3{,}750) = 0$$
$$HE = -8{,}750\ \text{lb} \qquad HE = 8{,}750\ \text{lb}\ C \ \blacktriangleleft$$

Summing y components, we obtain a check of our computations:

$$+\uparrow \Sigma F_y = 10{,}000 - (\tfrac{4}{5})(3{,}750) - (\tfrac{4}{5})(8{,}750)$$
$$= 10{,}000 - 3{,}000 - 7{,}000 = 0 \qquad \text{(checks)}$$

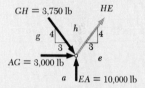

Joint 3. Using the computed values of $\overrightarrow{HC}$ and $\overrightarrow{EH}$, we may determine the reactions $\overrightarrow{CD}$ and $\overrightarrow{DE}$ by considering the equilibrium of this joint. Since these reactions have already been determined from the equilibrium of the entire truss, we will obtain two checks of our computations. We may also merely use the computed values of all forces acting on the joint (forces in members and reactions) and check that the joint is in equilibrium.

$$\xrightarrow{+}\ \Sigma F_x = -5{,}250 + (\tfrac{3}{5})(8{,}750) = -5{,}250 + 5{,}250 = 0 \qquad \text{(checks)}$$

$$+\uparrow \Sigma F_y = -7{,}000 + (\tfrac{4}{5})(8{,}750) = -7{,}000 + 7{,}000 = 0 \qquad \text{(checks)}$$

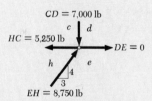

PROBLEMS

6.1 through 6.12. Using the method of joints, determine the force in each member of the truss shown.   State whether each member is in tension or compression.

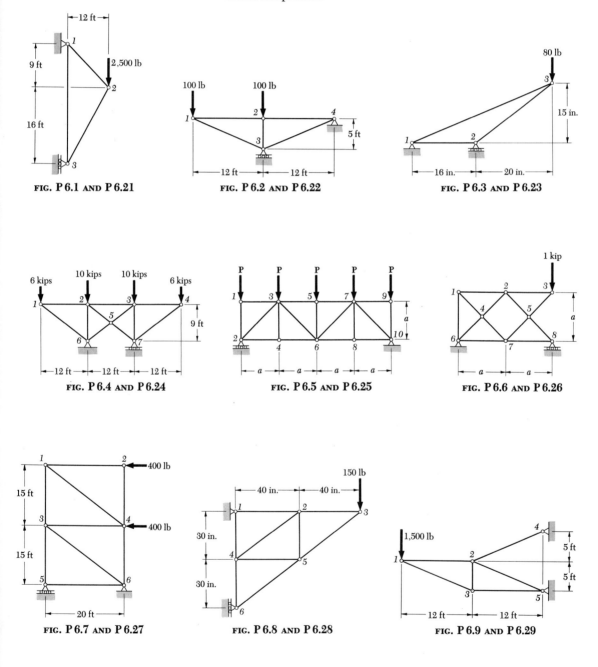

FIG. P 6.1 AND P 6.21

FIG. P 6.2 AND P 6.22

FIG. P 6.3 AND P 6.23

FIG. P 6.4 AND P 6.24

FIG. P 6.5 AND P 6.25

FIG. P 6.6 AND P 6.26

FIG. P 6.7 AND P 6.27

FIG. P 6.8 AND P 6.28

FIG. P 6.9 AND P 6.29

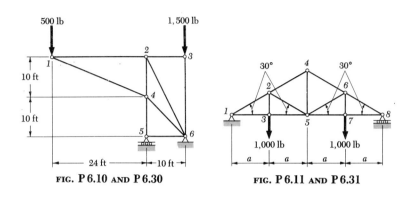

FIG. P6.10 AND P6.30

FIG. P6.11 AND P6.31

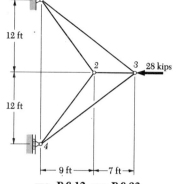

FIG. P6.12 AND P6.32

6.13 through 6.15. Determine the zero-force members in the truss shown for the given loading.

6.16. Indicate whether the trusses given in Probs. 6.4, 6.6, 6.10, 6.14, and 6.15 are simple trusses.

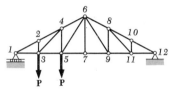

FIG. P6.13

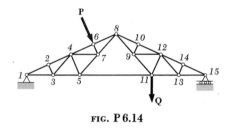

FIG. P6.14

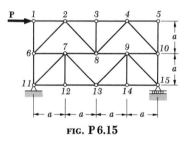

FIG. P6.15

°6.17. Twelve members, each of length L, are connected to form a regular octahedron. Determine the force in each member if two vertical loads are applied as shown.

°6.18. Six bars, each of length L, are connected to form a regular tetra-hedron which rests on a smooth hori-zontal surface. Determine the force in each of the six members when a ver-tical force **P** is applied at A.

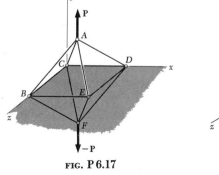

FIG. P6.17

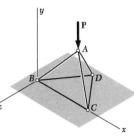

FIG. P6.18

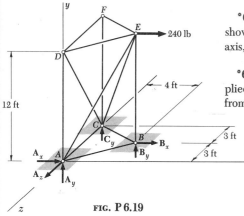

12 ft

FIG. P 6.19

*6.19. The three-dimensional truss is supported by the six reactions shown. If a 240-lb load is applied at E in a direction parallel to the x axis, determine (a) the reactions, (b) the force in each member.

*6.20. Solve Prob. 6.19 assuming that the horizontal 240-lb load is applied at E in a direction parallel to member FE and is directed away from the truss.

6.7. Graphical Analysis of Trusses: Maxwell's Diagram. The method of joints may be used as the basis for a graphical analysis of trusses. We shall develop this graphical analysis by considering the truss already discussed in Sec. 6.4. This truss is shown again in Fig. 6.14a, and a force polygon has been drawn to scale for each joint in Fig. 6.14b; the force in each member may now be measured from one of these force polygons. The number of lines which have to be drawn can be greatly reduced, however, if the various force polygons are superimposed. The resulting diagram is shown in Fig. 6.14c and is known as the *Maxwell diagram* of the truss.

FIG. 6.14

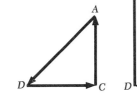

(a)

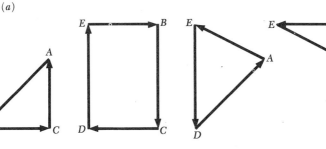

(b)

In order to draw the Maxwell diagram directly, we shall proceed as follows:

1. A lower-case letter is assigned to every region outside the truss, moving clockwise around the truss, and also to every area inside the truss (Fig. 6.14a).

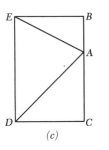

(c)

2. The reactions **R**$_1$ and **R**$_2$ are determined.   This is done either by drawing the string polygon or by solving the equations of equilibrium for the entire truss.

3. Selecting the external forces in clockwise order around the truss, we draw to scale the force polygon for the entire truss (line *ABCA* in Fig. 6.15*a*).   If a joint may be found which is acted upon by only two forces, the last two steps may be omitted or at least postponed.

4. A force polygon is then drawn for each joint by treating successively joints acted upon by only two unknown forces. All lines previously drawn may be used; thus, it is necessary to draw only two additional lines to complete each new force polygon.   For example, starting at joint *adc*, we draw a line parallel to *ad* through point *A* and a line parallel to *dc* through point *C*; this determines point *D* and thus completes the force triangle *ADC*, which corresponds to joint *adc* (Fig. 6.15*a*).   Considering next joint *debc*, we draw a line parallel to *de* through *D* and a line parallel to *eb* through *B*; we obtain point *E* and thus complete the force polygon *DEBC*, which corresponds to joint *debc* (Fig. 6.15*b*).   Next, we consider joint *aed* and draw a line parallel to *ae* through point *A* (Fig. 6.15*c*); we check that this line passes through the point *E* previously obtained.   This completes the force triangle *AED* corresponding to joint *aed* and also completes the Maxwell diagram.   At joint *eab*, all the forces are now known; we simply check that they form a closed triangle *EAB* (Fig. 6.15*d*).

5. The magnitude of the force in each member may now be measured on the Maxwell diagram.   Thus, the magnitude of the force in member *ad* is *AD*.   To determine whether a member is in tension or in compression, we shall determine whether it pulls or pushes on either of the two joints it connects.   For example, consider member *ad*, which connects joints *adc* and *aed*.   (*a*) We select one of these two joints, say, *adc*.   (*b*) We read the names of the areas adjacent to the member in clockwise order around the joint in Fig. 6.14*a*; we read *ad*.   (*c*) The direction of the force exerted on the joint is found by reading the corresponding letters of the Maxwell diagram in the same order (Fig. 6.14*c*).   Since force $\overrightarrow{AD}$ is directed down and to the left, member *ad* pushes on the joint and must be in compression. The same result may be found by considering joint *aed*.   The member is now read *da* and the corresponding force $\overrightarrow{DA}$. Since force $\overrightarrow{DA}$ is directed up and to the right, member *da* pushes on joint *aed* and is again found to be in compression.

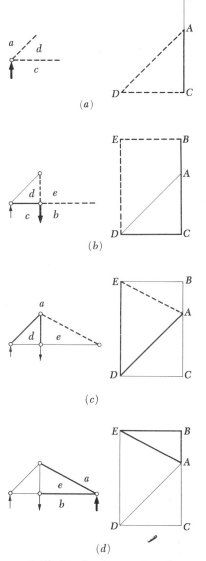

FIG. 6.15. Step-by-step construction of Maxwell's diagram

SAMPLE PROBLEM 6.2

By drawing Maxwell's diagram determine the force in each member of the truss considered in Sample Prob. 6.1.

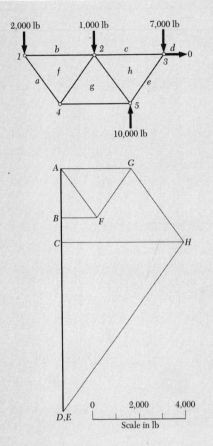

Solution. 1. The truss is drawn to scale; both the applied loads and the reactions are indicated. Using Bow's notation, a lower-case letter is assigned to each region outside the truss and to each individual area inside the truss.

2. By considering the entire truss as a free body, we compute the reactions (see Sample Prob. 6.1).

3. Selecting the external forces in clockwise order around the truss, we draw to scale the force polygon for the entire truss in tip-to-tail fashion; points A, B, C, D, and E are thus located on the Maxwell diagram.

4. Considering joint 1, where only two unknown forces exist, we now locate point F by drawing lines BF and AF, which are parallel to members bf and fa, respectively. We next consider joint 4, where there are now only two unknown forces and hence only one unknown point in the corresponding triangle of the Maxwell diagram. Lines FG and AG are drawn parallel to fg and ga, respectively; point G is located at the intersection of these lines. We next consider joint 2 and locate point H at the intersection of lines CH and GH which are drawn parallel to ch and hg, respectively. All the points of the Maxwell diagram have now been located. Since HE represents the force in member he, we may draw a line through point H parallel to member he; this line should pass through point E, which is already located. This provides a check on the accuracy of the drawing of the Maxwell diagram.

5. The magnitude and sense of the force in each member are determined from the Maxwell diagram; the magnitude is measured directly, and the sense is found as indicated in Sec. 6.7. The results are given in the table.

Member	Force
bf	1,500 lb T
fa	2,500 lb C
fg	2,500 lb T
ga	3,000 lb C
hg	3,750 lb C
ch	5,250 lb T
he	8,750 lb C

PROBLEMS

6.21 through 6.32. By drawing Maxwell's diagram, determine the force in each member of the truss shown.   Indicate whether the member is in tension or compression.   (The trusses appear on pages 200 and 201.)

6.33 through 6.37. By drawing Maxwell's diagram, determine the force in each member of the truss shown.   Indicate whether the member is in tension or compression.

6.38. Solve Prob. 6.37 assuming that the truss supports vertical 10-kip loads at joints *2, 4,* and *6.*

6.39. Solve Prob. 6.36 assuming that the 1,000-lb load supported at joint *1* is horizontal and directed to the left.

6.8. Analysis of Trusses by the Method of Sections.   The

method of joints and Maxwell's diagram are most effective when the forces in all the members of a truss are to be determined. If, however, the force in only one member or the forces in a very few members are desired, a third method, the method of sections, will prove more efficient.

Assume, for example, that we want to determine the force in member *BD* of the truss shown in Fig. 6.16*a*.   To do this, we must determine the force with which member *BD* acts on either joint *B* or joint *D*.   If we were to use the method of joints, we would choose either joint *B* or joint *D* as a free body. However, we may also choose as a free body a larger portion of the truss, composed of several joints and members, provided that the desired force is one of the external forces acting on that portion.   If, in addition, the portion of the truss is chosen so that there is a total of only three unknown forces acting upon it, the desired force may be obtained by solving the equations of equilibrium for this portion of the truss.   In practice, the portion of the truss to be utilized is obtained by *passing a section* through three members of the truss, one of which is the desired member, i.e., by drawing a line which divides the truss into two completely separate parts but does not intersect more than three members.   Either of the two portions of the truss obtained after the intersected members have been removed may then be used as a free body.†

In Fig. 6.16*a*, the section *nn* has been passed through members *BD, BE,* and *CE,* and the portion *ABC* of the truss is

---

† In the analysis of certain trusses, sections are passed which intersect more than three members; the forces in one, or possibly two, of the intersected members may be obtained if equilibrium equations can be found, each of which involves only one unknown (see Probs. 6.52 and 6.53).

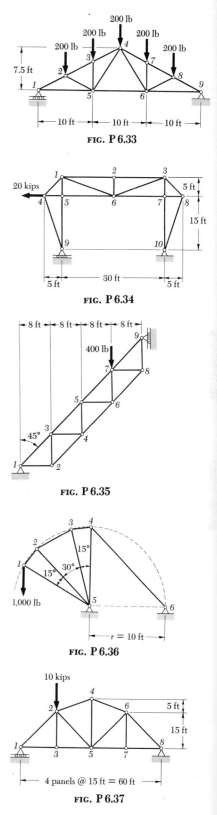

FIG. P 6.33

FIG. P 6.34

FIG. P 6.35

FIG. P 6.36

FIG. P 6.37

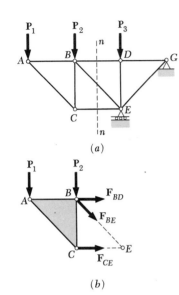

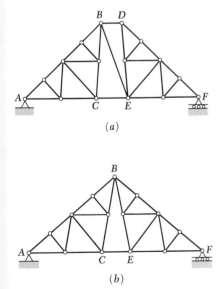

FIG. 6.16

FIG. 6.17

chosen as the free body (Fig. 6.16*b*).   The forces acting on the free body are the loads P_1 and P_2 at points A and B and the three unknown forces F_{BD}, F_{BE}, and F_{CE}.   Since it is not known whether the members removed were in tension or compression, the three forces have been arbitrarily drawn away from the free body as if the members were in tension.

The fact that the rigid body ABC is in equilibrium can be expressed by writing three equations which may be solved for the three unknown forces.   If only the force F_{BD} is desired, we need write only one equation, provided that the equation does not contain the other unknowns.   Thus the equation $\Sigma M_E = 0$ yields the value of the magnitude F_{BD} of the force F_{BD}.   A positive sign in the answer will indicate that our original assumption regarding the sense of F_{BD} was correct and that member BD is in tension; a negative sign will indicate that our assumption was incorrect and that BD is in compression.

On the other hand, if only the force F_{CE} is desired, an equation which does not involve F_{BD} or F_{BE} should be written; the appropriate equation is $\Sigma M_B = 0$.   Again a positive sign for the magnitude F_{CE} of the desired force indicates a correct assumption, hence tension; and a negative sign indicates an incorrect assumption, hence compression.

If only the force F_{BE} is desired, the appropriate equation is $\Sigma F_y = 0$.   Whether the member is in tension or compression is again determined from the sign of the answer.

When the force in only one member is determined, no independent check of the computation is available.   However, when all the unknown forces acting on the free body are determined, the computations can be checked by writing an additional equation.   For instance, if F_{BD}, F_{BE}, and F_{CE} are determined as indicated above, the computation can be checked by verifying that $\Sigma F_x = 0$.

*6.9. **Trusses Made of Several Simple Trusses.**   Consider two simple trusses ABC and DEF.   If they are connected by three bars BD, BE, and CE as shown in Fig. 6.17*a*, they will form together a rigid truss $ABDF$.   The trusses ABC and DEF can also be combined into a single rigid truss by joining joints B and D into a single joint B and by connecting joints C and E by a bar CE (Fig. 6.17*b*).   The truss thus obtained is known as a Fink truss.   It should be noted that the trusses of Fig. 6.17*a* and *b* are *not* simple trusses; they cannot be constructed from a triangular truss by adding successive pairs of members as prescribed in Sec. 6.3.   They are rigid trusses, however, as we may check by comparing the systems of connections used to hold the simple trusses ABC and DEF together (three bars in Fig.

6.17*a*, one smooth pin and one bar in Fig. 6.17*b*) with the systems of supports discussed in Secs. 4.4 and 4.5. Trusses made of several simple trusses rigidly connected are known as *compound trusses.*

It may be checked that in a compound truss the number of members *m* and the number of joints *n* are still related by the formula $m = 2n - 3$. If a compound truss is supported by a smooth pin and a roller (involving three unknown reactions), the total number of unknowns is $m + 3$ and this number is therefore equal to the number $2n$ of equations obtained by expressing that the *n* pins are in equilibrium. Compound trusses supported by a smooth pin and a roller, or by an equivalent system of supports, are *statically determinate, rigid,* and *completely constrained.* This means that all unknown reactions and forces in members can be determined by the methods of statics and that, all equilibrium equations being satisfied, the truss will neither collapse nor move. The forces in the members, however, cannot all be determined by the method of joints, except by solving a large number of simultaneous equations. In the case of the compound truss of Fig. 6.17*a*, for example, it will be found more expeditious to pass a section through members *BD*, *BE*, and *CE* to determine their forces.

Suppose, now, that the simple trusses *ABC* and *DEF* are connected by *four* bars *BD*, *BE*, *CD*, and *CE* (Fig. 6.18). The number of members *m* is now larger than $2n - 3$; the truss obtained is *overrigid,* and one of the four members *BD*, *BE*, *CD*, or *CE* is said to be *redundant.* If the truss is supported by a smooth pin at *A* and a roller at *F*, the total number of unknowns is $m + 3$. This number is now larger than the number $2n$ of available independent equations; the truss is *statically indeterminate.*

Finally, we shall assume that the two simple trusses *ABC* and *DEF* are joined by a smooth pin as shown in Fig. 6.19*a*. The number of members *m* is smaller than $2n - 3$. If the truss is supported by a smooth pin at *A* and a roller at *F*, the total number of unknowns is $m + 3$. This number is now smaller than the number $2n$ of equilibrium equations which should be satisfied; the truss is *nonrigid* and will collapse under its own weight. However, if two smooth pins are used to support it, the truss becomes *rigid* and will not collapse (Fig. 6.19*b*). We note that the total number of unknowns is now $m + 4$ and is thus equal to the number of equations. While necessary, this condition, however, is not sufficient for the equilibrium of a structure which ceases to be rigid when detached from its supports (see Sec. 6.12).

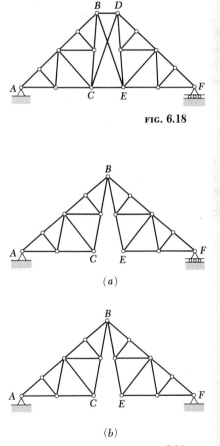

FIG. 6.18

(*a*)

(*b*)

FIG. 6.19

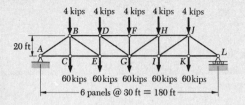

Determine the forces in members DE and HJ of the truss shown.

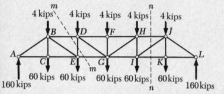

Solution. Considering the entire truss as a free body, we determine the reactions at A and L.

$$\mathbf{A} = 160 \text{ kips } \uparrow$$

$$\mathbf{L} = 160 \text{ kips } \uparrow$$

Force in Member HJ. Section nn is passed through the truss so that it intersects member HJ and only two additional members. After the intersected members have been removed, we choose the right-hand portion of the truss as a free body. Three unknown forces are involved; to eliminate the two forces passing through point I, we write

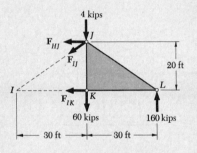

$$+ \circlearrowleft \Sigma M_I = 0:$$
$$(160 \text{ kips})(60 \text{ ft}) - (60 \text{ kips})(30 \text{ ft}) - (4 \text{ kips})(30 \text{ ft}) + F_{HJ}(20 \text{ ft}) = 0$$
$$F_{HJ} = -384 \text{ kips}$$

The sense of $\mathbf{F}_{HJ}$ was chosen assuming member HJ to be in tension; the negative sign obtained indicates that the member is in compression.

$$F_{HJ} = 384 \text{ kips } C \blacktriangleleft$$

Force in Member DE. Section mm is passed through the truss so that it intersects member DE and only two additional members. After the intersected members have been removed, the left-hand portion of the truss is chosen as a free body. Three unknown forces are again involved; since the equation $\Sigma F_y = 0$ involves only F_{DE} as an unknown, we write

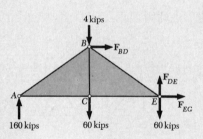

$$+ \uparrow \Sigma F_y = 0:$$
$$+160 \text{ kips} - 60 \text{ kips} - 4 \text{ kips} - 60 \text{ kips} + F_{DE} = 0$$
$$F_{DE} = -36 \text{ kips} \qquad\qquad F_{DE} = 36 \text{ kips } C \blacktriangleleft$$

SAMPLE PROBLEM 6.4

Determine the forces in members *FH*, *GH*, and *GI* of the roof truss shown.

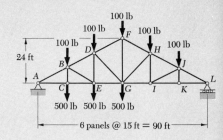

Solution. Section *nn* is passed through the truss as shown. The right-hand portion of the truss will be taken as a free body. Since the reaction at *L* acts on this free body, the value of **L** must be calculated separately, using the entire truss as a free body; the equation $\Sigma M_A = 0$ yields **L** = 750 lb ↑.

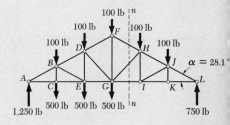

Force in Member *GI*. Using the portion *HLI* of the truss as a free body, the value of F_{GI} is obtained by writing

$+\circlearrowleft\ \Sigma M_H = 0$:

$$(750\text{ lb})(30\text{ ft}) - (100\text{ lb})(15\text{ ft}) - F_{GI}(16\text{ ft}) = 0$$
$$F_{GI} = +1{,}313\text{ lb} \qquad F_{GI} = 1{,}313\text{ lb } T \ \blacktriangleleft$$

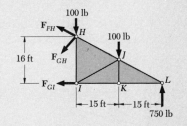

Force in Member *FH*. The value of F_{FH} is obtained from the equation $\Sigma M_G = 0$. We move $\mathbf{F}_{FH}$ along its line of action until it acts at point *F*, where it is resolved into its *x* and *y* components. The moment of $\mathbf{F}_{FH}$ with respect to point *G* is now equal to $(F_{FH} \cos \alpha)(24 \text{ ft})$.

$+\circlearrowleft\ \Sigma M_G = 0$:

$$(750\text{ lb})(45\text{ ft}) - (100\text{ lb})(30\text{ ft}) - (100\text{ lb})(15\text{ ft})$$
$$+ (F_{FH} \cos \alpha)(24\text{ ft}) = 0$$
$$F_{FH} = -1{,}382\text{ lb} \qquad F_{FH} = 1{,}382\text{ lb } C \ \blacktriangleleft$$

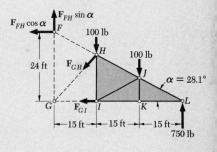

Force in Member *GH*. The value of F_{GH} is determined by first resolving the force $\mathbf{F}_{GH}$ into *x* and *y* components at point *G* and then solving the equation $\Sigma M_L = 0$.

$+\circlearrowleft\ \Sigma M_L = 0$:

$$(100\text{ lb})(30\text{ ft}) + (100\text{ lb})(15\text{ ft}) + (F_{GH} \cos \beta)(45\text{ ft}) = 0$$
$$F_{GH} = -137.2\text{ lb} \qquad F_{GH} = 137.2\text{ lb } C \ \blacktriangleleft$$

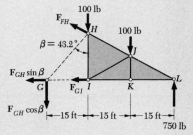

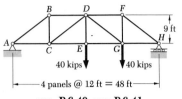

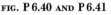

FIG. P 6.40 AND P 6.41

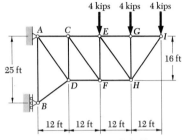

FIG. P 6.42 AND P 6.43

PROBLEMS

6.40. Determine the force in members *DF* and *DG* of the Howe truss shown.

6.41. Determine the force in members *FG* and *EG* of the Howe truss shown.

6.42. Determine the force in members *EF* and *CE* of the truss shown.

6.43. Determine the force in members *EH* and *FH* of the truss shown.

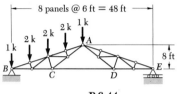

FIG. P 6.44

6.44. Determine the force in member *CD* of the Fink roof truss shown.

6.45. Determine the force in members *FH*, *GH*, and *GI* of the stadium truss shown.

6.46. Determine the force in members *DF*, *DE*, and *CE* of the stadium truss shown.

6.47. For the truss and loading of Sample Prob. 6.4, determine the force in members *BD*, *DE*, and *EG*.

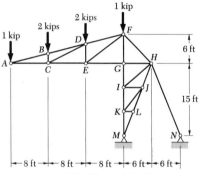

FIG. P 6.45 AND P 6.46

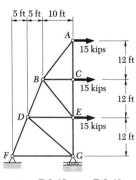

FIG. P 6.48 AND P 6.49

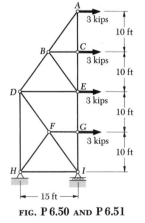

FIG. P 6.50 AND P 6.51

6.48. Determine the force in members *BD*, *BE*, and *CE* of the truss shown.

6.49. Determine the force in members *BD*, *DE*, and *EG* of the truss shown.

6.50. Determine the force in members *BE* and *DE* of the truss shown.

6.51. Determine the force in members *FH* and *DH* of the truss shown.

6.52. Determine the force in member *EH* of the K truss shown.   (*Hint.*   Use section *aa*.)

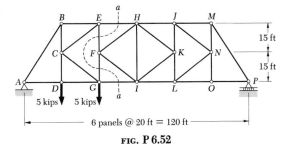

FIG. P 6.52

6.53. Determine the force in members *FK* and *JO* of the truss shown. (*Hint.*   Use section *aa*.)

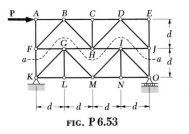

FIG. P 6.53

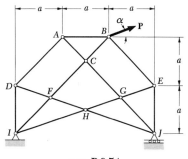

FIG. P 6.54

6.54. Determine the force in members *AB* and *EJ* of the truss shown, if $\alpha = 0°$.   (*Hint.*   Use portion *IBE* of the truss as a free body and apply to joints *C, F, G,* and *H* the results obtained in Sec. 6.5.)

6.55.   Solve Prob. 6.54 assuming that $\alpha = 90°$.

6.56. Solve Prob. 6.54 assuming that **P** $= 0$ and that a load **Q** is applied at joint *J* and is directed horizontally to the right.

6.57. The diagonal members in the center panel of the truss shown are very slender and can act only in tension; such members are known as *counters.*   Determine the force in members *CE* and *DF* and in the counter which is acting under the given loading.

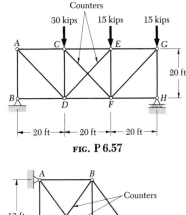

FIG. P 6.57

6.58. Solve Prob. 6.57 assuming that the 30-kip load has been removed.

6.59. Determine the force in member *CD* and in the counters which are acting under the given loading.   (See Prob. 6.57 for the definition of a counter.)

6.60. Solve Prob. 6.59 assuming that the 6-kip load has been removed.

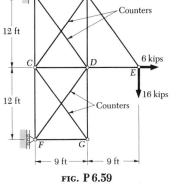

FIG. P 6.59

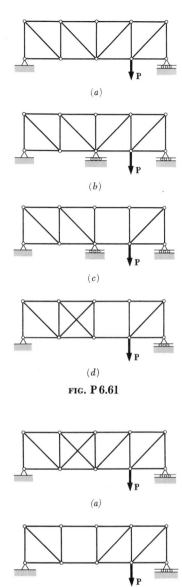

(a)

(b)

(c)

(d)

FIG. P 6.61

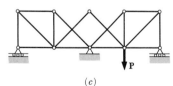

(a)

(b)

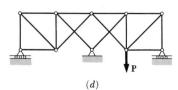

(c)

(d)

FIG. P 6.62

6.61 through 6.64. Classify each of the given structures as completely, partially, or improperly constrained; if completely constrained, further classify as determinate or indeterminate. (All members can act both in tension and in compression.)

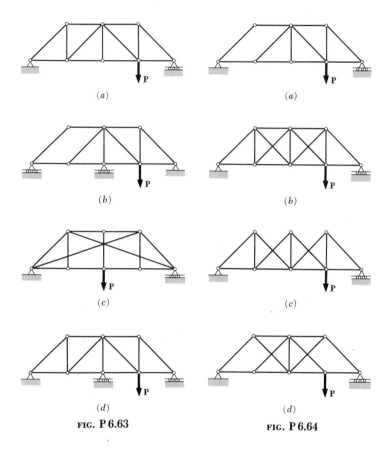

(a)   *(a)*

(b)   *(b)*

(c)   *(c)*

(d)   *(d)*

FIG. P 6.63   FIG. P 6.64

FRAMES AND MACHINES

6.10. Structures Containing Multiforce Members. Under Trusses, we have considered structures consisting entirely of pins and of straight two-force members. The forces acting on the two-force members were known to be directed along the members themselves. We shall now consider structures in which at least one of the members is a *multiforce* member, i.e., a member acted upon by three or more forces. These forces will generally not be directed along the members on which they act; their direction is unknown, and they should be represented therefore by two unknown components.

Frames and machines are structures containing multiforce members. *Frames* are designed to support loads and are usually stationary, fully constrained structures. *Machines* are designed to transmit and modify forces; they may or may not be stationary and will always contain moving parts.

6.11. Analysis of a Frame. As a first example of analysis of a frame, we shall consider again the crane described in Sec. 6.1, which carries a given load W (Fig. 6.20a). The free-body diagram of the entire frame is shown in Fig. 6.20b. This diagram may be used to determine the external forces acting on the frame. Summing moments about A, we first determine the force $\mathbf{T}$ exerted by the cable; summing x and y components, we then determine the components $\mathbf{A}_x$ and $\mathbf{A}_y$ of the reaction at the pin A.

In order to determine the internal forces holding the various parts of a frame together, we must dismember the frame and draw a free-body diagram for each of its component parts (Fig. 6.20c). First, the two-force members should be considered. In this frame, member BE is the only two-force member. The forces acting at each end of this member must have the same magnitude, same line of action, and opposite sense (Sec. 4.6). They are therefore directed along BE and will be denoted respectively by $\mathbf{F}_{BE}$ and $-\mathbf{F}_{BE}$. Their sense will be arbitrarily assumed as shown in Fig. 6.20c, and the correctness of this assumption will be checked later by the sign obtained for the common magnitude F_{BE} of the two forces.

Next, we consider the multiforce members, i.e., the members which are acted upon by three or more forces. According to Newton's third law, the force exerted at B by member BE on member AD must be equal and opposite to the force $\mathbf{F}_{BE}$ exerted by AD on BE. Similarly, the force exerted at E by member BE on member CF must be equal and opposite to the force $-\mathbf{F}_{BE}$ exerted by CF on BE. The forces that the two-force member BE exerts on AD and CF are therefore respectively equal to $-\mathbf{F}_{BE}$ and $\mathbf{F}_{BE}$; they have the same magnitude F_{BE} and opposite sense, and should be directed as shown in Fig. 6.20c.

At C two multiforce members are connected. Since neither the direction nor the magnitude of the forces acting at C is known, these forces will be represented by their x and y components. The components $\mathbf{C}_x$ and $\mathbf{C}_y$ of the force acting on member AD will be arbitrarily directed to the right and upward. Since, according to Newton's third law, the forces exerted by member CF on AD and by member AD on CF are equal and opposite, the components of the force acting on

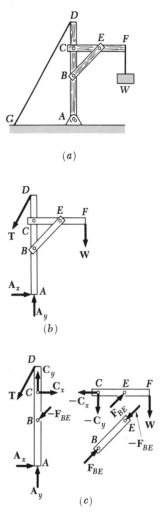

FIG. 6.20

member *CF must* be directed to the left and downward; they will be denoted, respectively, by $-\mathbf{C}_x$ and $-\mathbf{C}_y$. Whether the force $\mathbf{C}_x$ is actually directed to the right and the force $-\mathbf{C}_x$ is actually directed to the left will be determined later from the sign of their common magnitude C_x, a plus sign indicating that the assumption made was correct, and a minus sign that it was wrong. The free-body diagrams of the multiforce members are completed by showing the external forces acting at A, D, and F.†

The internal forces may now be determined by considering the free-body diagram of either of the two multiforce members. Choosing the free-body diagram of *CF*, for example, we write the equations $\Sigma M_C = 0$, $\Sigma M_E = 0$, and $\Sigma F_x = 0$, which yield the values of the magnitudes F_{BE}, C_y, and C_x, respectively. These values may be checked by verifying that member *AD* is also in equilibrium.

It should be noted that the free-body diagrams of the pins were not shown in Fig. 6.20*c*. This was because the pins were assumed to form an integral part of one of the two members they connected. This assumption can always be used to simplify the analysis of frames and machines. When a pin connects three or more members, however, or when a pin connects a support and two or more members, a clear decision must be made in choosing the member to which the pin will be assumed to belong. (If multiforce members are involved, the pin should be attached to one of these members.) The forces exerted on the pin by the other members or by the support should then be clearly identified. This is illustrated in Sample Prob. 6.7.

6.12. Frames Which Cease to Be Rigid When Detached from Their Supports. The crane analyzed in Sec. 6.11 was so constructed that it could keep the same shape without the help of its supports; it was therefore considered as a rigid body. Many frames, however, will collapse if detached from their supports; such frames cannot be considered as rigid bodies. Consider, for example, the frame shown in Fig. 6.21*a*, which consists of two members *AC* and *CB* carrying loads **P** and **Q** at their mid-points; the members are supported by pins at *A* and *B* and are connected by a pin at *C*. If detached from its sup-

---

† The use of a minus sign to distinguish the force exerted by one member on another from the equal and opposite force exerted by the second member on the first is not strictly necessary, since the two forces belong to different free-body diagrams and thus cannot easily be confused. In the Sample Problems, we shall represent by the same symbol equal and opposite forces which are applied to different free bodies.

ports, this frame will not maintain its shape; it should therefore be considered as made of *two distinct rigid parts AC* and
CB.

The equations $\Sigma F_x = 0$, $\Sigma F_y = 0$, $\Sigma M = 0$ (about any
given point) express the conditions for the *equilibrium of a
rigid body* (Chap. 4); we should use them, therefore, in connection with the free-body diagrams of rigid bodies, namely,
the free-body diagrams of members *AC* and *CB* (Fig. 6.21*b*).
Since these members are multiforce members, and since pins
are used at the supports and at the connection, the reactions
at *A* and *B* and the forces at *C* will each be represented by
two components.   In accordance with Newton's third law,
the components of the force exerted by *CB* on *AC* and the components of the force exerted by *AC* on *CB* will be represented

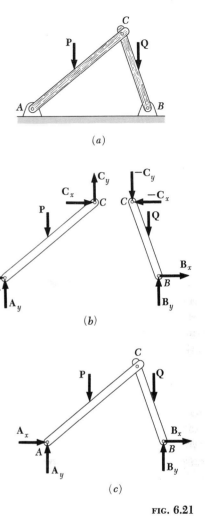

(*a*)

(*b*)

(*c*)

FIG. 6.21

by vectors of the same magnitude and opposite sense; thus, if the
first pair of components is denoted by $\mathbf{C}_x$ and $\mathbf{C}_y$, the second
pair will be denoted by $-\mathbf{C}_x$ and $-\mathbf{C}_y$.   We note that four
unknown force components act on free body *AC*, while only
three independent equations may be used to express that the
body is in equilibrium; similarly, four unknowns, but only three
equations, are associated with *CB*.   However, only six different
unknowns are involved in the analysis of the two members, and
altogether six equations are available to express that the members are in equilibrium.   Writing $\Sigma M_A = 0$ for free body *AC*
and $\Sigma M_B = 0$ for *CB*, we obtain two simultaneous equations
which may be solved for the common magnitude C_x of the components $\mathbf{C}_x$ and $-\mathbf{C}_x$, and for the common magnitude C_y of the
components $\mathbf{C}_y$ and $-\mathbf{C}_y$.   Writing, then, $\Sigma F_x = 0$ and
$\Sigma F_y = 0$ for each of the two free bodies, we obtain successively
the magnitudes A_x, A_y, B_x, and B_y.

We shall observe, now, that, since the equations of equilib-
rium $\Sigma F_x = 0$, $\Sigma F_y = 0$, $\Sigma M = 0$ (about any given point) are satisfied by the forces acting on free body *AC*, and since they are
also satisfied by the forces acting on free body *CB*, they must
be satisfied when the forces acting on the two free bodies are
considered simultaneously.   Since the internal forces at *C* cancel each other, we find that the equations of equilibrium must
be satisfied by the external forces shown on the free-body diagram of the frame *ACB* itself (Fig. 6.21*c*), although the frame is

not a rigid body. These equations may be used to determine some of the components of the reactions at A and B. We shall note, however, that *the reactions cannot be completely determined from the free-body diagram of the whole frame.* It is thus necessary to dismember the frame and to consider the free-body diagrams of its component parts (Fig. 6.21b), even when we are interested only in finding external reactions. This may be explained by the fact that the equilibrium equations obtained for free body ACB are *necessary conditions* for the equilibrium of a nonrigid structure, *but not sufficient conditions.*

The method of solution outlined in the second paragraph of this section involved simultaneous equations. We shall now discuss a more expeditious method, which utilizes the free body ACB as well as the free bodies AC and CB. Writing $\Sigma M_A = 0$ and $\Sigma M_B = 0$ for free body ACB, we obtain B_y and A_y. Writing $\Sigma M_C = 0$, $\Sigma F_x = 0$, and $\Sigma F_y = 0$ for free body AC, we obtain successively A_x, C_x, and C_y. Finally, writing $\Sigma F_x = 0$ for ACB, we obtain B_x.

We noted above that the analysis of the frame of Fig. 6.21 involves six unknown force components and six independent equilibrium equations (the equilibrium equations for the whole frame were obtained from the original six equations and, therefore, are not independent). Moreover, we checked that all unknowns could be actually determined and that all equations could be satisfied. The frame considered is *statically determinate and rigid.*† In general, to determine whether a structure is statically determinate and rigid, we should draw a free-body diagram for each of its component parts and count the reactions and internal forces involved. We should also determine the number of independent equilibrium equations (excluding equations expressing the equilibrium of the whole structure or of groups of component parts already analyzed). If there are more unknowns than equations, the structure is *statically indeterminate.* If there are fewer unknowns than equations, the structure is *nonrigid.* If there are as many unknowns as equations, *and if all unknowns may be determined and all equations satisfied* under general loading conditions, the structure is *statically determinate and rigid;* if, however, due to an *improper arrangement* of members and supports, all unknowns cannot be determined and all equations cannot be satisfied, the structure is *statically indeterminate and nonrigid.*

† The word "rigid" is used here to indicate that the frame will maintain its shape as long as it remains attached to its supports.

SAMPLE PROBLEM 6.5

In the small frame shown, members *EBF* and *ABCD* are connected by a pin at *B* and by the cable *EC*. A 75-lb load is supported by a second cable which passes over a pulley at *F* and is attached to the vertical member at *G*. Determine the tension in cable *EC* and the components of the pin reaction at *B*.

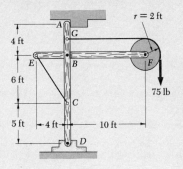

Entire Frame. The external reactions on the frame involve three unknowns; these reactions are determined by taking the entire frame as a free body.

$+\uparrow \Sigma F_y = 0$: $D_y - 75\,\text{lb} = 0$

$$D_y = +75\,\text{lb} \qquad \mathbf{D}_y = 75\,\text{lb} \uparrow$$

$+ \,\rangle\, \Sigma M_D = 0$: $-(75\,\text{lb})(12\,\text{ft}) + A(15\,\text{ft}) = 0$

$$A = +60\,\text{lb} \qquad \mathbf{A} = 60\,\text{lb} \leftarrow$$

$\xrightarrow{+}\, \Sigma F_x = 0$: $-60\,\text{lb} + D_x = 0$

$$D_x = +60\,\text{lb} \qquad \mathbf{D}_x = 60\,\text{lb} \rightarrow$$

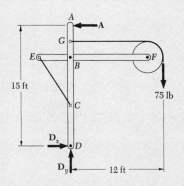

Since the values obtained are positive, the forces are directed as assumed in the diagram, i.e., $\mathbf{D}_x$ to the right, $\mathbf{D}_y$ up, and $\mathbf{A}$ to the left.

Members. The frame is dismembered; since only two members are connected at *B*, the components of the unknown forces acting on *EBF* and *ABCD* at *B* are, respectively, equal and opposite. The forces exerted at *E* and *C* by the cable *EC* are equal and opposite, and their direction is known. From the free-body diagram of the pulley, it is seen that the force exerted at *F* by the pulley on member *EBF* may be resolved into two 75-lb components as shown. The cable also exerts a 75-lb force on *ABCD* at point *G*.

Member *EBF*. Using the free body *EBF*, we write

$+ \,\rangle\, \Sigma M_E = 0$: $B_y(4\,\text{ft}) - (75\,\text{lb})(14\,\text{ft}) = 0$ $B_y = +263\,\text{lb}$ ◀

$+ \,\rangle\, \Sigma M_B = 0$: $(T\cos\alpha)(4\,\text{ft}) - (75\,\text{lb})(10\,\text{ft}) = 0$

$$T = +225\,\text{lb} \quad ◀$$

$\xrightarrow{+}\, \Sigma F_x = 0$: $+T\sin\alpha - B_x - 75\,\text{lb} = 0$ $B_x = +50.0\,\text{lb}$ ◀

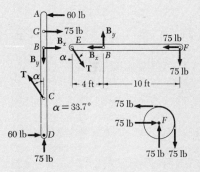

Since the values obtained are positive, the forces are directed as shown on the diagram: the forces $\mathbf{B}_x$ and $\mathbf{B}_y$ acting on member *ABCD* are directed, respectively, to the right and down, while the forces $\mathbf{B}_x$ and $\mathbf{B}_y$ acting on member *EBF* are directed, respectively, to the left and up.

Member *ABCD* (Check). The computations are checked by considering the free body *ABCD*. For example,

$\xrightarrow{+}\, \Sigma F_x = -60\,\text{lb} + 75\,\text{lb} + B_x - T\sin\alpha + 60\,\text{lb}$

$$= -60\,\text{lb} + 75\,\text{lb} + 50\,\text{lb} - (225\,\text{lb})\sin 33.7° + 60\,\text{lb} = 0$$

$$\text{(checks)}$$

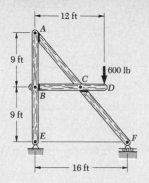

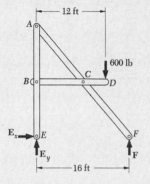

SAMPLE PROBLEM 6.6

Determine the components of the forces acting on each member of the frame shown.

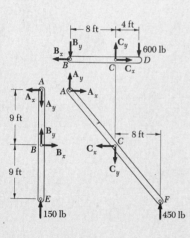

Entire Frame. Since the external reactions involve only three unknowns, we compute the reactions by considering the free-body diagram of the entire frame.

$+\circlearrowright \ \Sigma M_E = 0$: $-(600 \text{ lb})(12 \text{ ft}) + F(16 \text{ ft}) = 0$

$$F = +450 \text{ lb} \qquad\qquad \mathbf{F} = 450 \text{ lb} \uparrow \ \blacktriangleleft$$

$+\uparrow \Sigma F_y = 0$: $-600 \text{ lb} + 450 \text{ lb} + E_y = 0$

$$E_y = +150 \text{ lb} \qquad\qquad \mathbf{E}_y = 150 \text{ lb} \uparrow \ \blacktriangleleft$$

$\xrightarrow{+} \Sigma F_x = 0$: $\mathbf{E}_x = 0 \ \blacktriangleleft$

The frame is now dismembered; since only two members are connected at each joint, equal and opposite components are shown on each member at each joint.

Member *BCD*

$+\circlearrowright \ \Sigma M_B = 0$: $-(600 \text{ lb})(12 \text{ ft}) + C_y(8 \text{ ft}) = 0$ $C_y = +900 \text{ lb} \ \blacktriangleleft$

$+\circlearrowright \ \Sigma M_C = 0$: $-(600 \text{ lb})(4 \text{ ft}) + B_y(8 \text{ ft}) = 0$ $B_y = +300 \text{ lb} \ \blacktriangleleft$

$\xrightarrow{+} \Sigma F_x = 0$: $-B_x + C_x = 0$

We note that neither B_x nor C_x can be obtained by considering only member *BCD*. The positive values obtained for B_y and C_y indicate that the force components $\mathbf{B}_y$ and $\mathbf{C}_y$ are directed as assumed.

Member *ABE*

$+\circlearrowright \ \Sigma M_A = 0$: $B_x(9 \text{ ft}) = 0$ $B_x = 0 \ \blacktriangleleft$

$\xrightarrow{+} \Sigma F_x = 0$: $+B_x - A_x = 0$ $A_x = 0 \ \blacktriangleleft$

$+\uparrow \Sigma F_y = 0$: $-A_y + B_y + 150 \text{ lb} = 0$

                   $-A_y + 300 \text{ lb} + 150 \text{ lb} = 0$

$$A_y = +450 \text{ lb} \ \blacktriangleleft$$

Member *BCD*. Returning now to member *BCD*, we write

$\xrightarrow{+} \Sigma F_x = 0$: $-B_x + C_x = 0$ $0 + C_x = 0$ $C_x = 0 \ \blacktriangleleft$

Member *ACF* (Check). All unknown components have now been found; to check the results, verify that member *ACF* is in equilibrium.

$+\circlearrowright \ \Sigma M_C = (450 \text{ lb})(8 \text{ ft}) - A_y(8 \text{ ft}) - A_x(9 \text{ ft})$

         $= (450 \text{ lb})(8 \text{ ft}) - (450 \text{ lb})(8 \text{ ft}) - 0 = 0$ (checks)

SAMPLE PROBLEM 6.7

Determine the forces acting on each member of the frame shown.

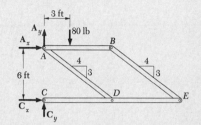

Entire Frame. The entire frame is chosen as a free body; although the reactions involve four unknowns, $\mathbf{A}_x$ and $\mathbf{C}_x$ may be determined by writing

$$+\!\!\curvearrowright \Sigma M_A = 0: \qquad -(80\text{ lb})(3\text{ ft}) + C_x(6\text{ ft}) = 0$$
$$C_x = +40\text{ lb} \qquad\qquad \mathbf{C}_x = 40\text{ lb} \rightarrow \quad \blacktriangleleft$$

$$\overset{+}{\rightarrow} \Sigma F_x = 0: \qquad A_x + C_x = 0$$
$$A_x = -40\text{ lb} \qquad\qquad \mathbf{A}_x = 40\text{ lb} \leftarrow \quad \blacktriangleleft$$

The equations of equilibrium of the entire frame are not sufficient to determine $\mathbf{A}_y$ and $\mathbf{C}_y$. The equilibrium of the various members must now be considered in order to proceed with the solution. In dismembering the frame, we have assumed that the pin at A is attached to member AB, and we have noted that both AD and BE are two-force members. The free-body diagrams of the various members are now considered separately.

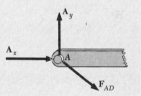

Member AB

$$+\!\!\curvearrowright \Sigma M_A = 0: \qquad -(80\text{ lb})(3\text{ ft}) + \tfrac{3}{5}F_{BE}(8\text{ ft}) = 0$$
$$F_{BE} = +50\text{ lb} \quad \blacktriangleleft$$

Member CDE. Since the force $\mathbf{F}_{BE}$ has been determined, we may compute $\mathbf{F}_{AD}$ by writing

$$+\!\!\curvearrowright \Sigma M_C = 0: \qquad \tfrac{3}{5}F_{AD}(8\text{ ft}) - \tfrac{3}{5}F_{BE}(16\text{ ft}) = 0$$
$$F_{AD} = +100\text{ lb} \quad \blacktriangleleft$$

Using $F_{AD} = +100$ lb, we now determine $\mathbf{C}_y$ by writing

$$+\!\uparrow \Sigma F_y = 0: \qquad C_y + \tfrac{3}{5}F_{AD} - \tfrac{3}{5}F_{BE} = 0$$
$$C_y = -30\text{ lb} \qquad\qquad \mathbf{C}_y = 30\text{ lb} \downarrow \quad \blacktriangleleft$$

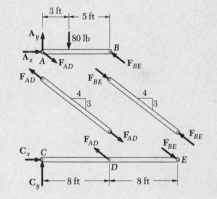

Entire Frame. Since $\mathbf{C}_y$ has been determined, we may return to the free-body diagram of the entire frame and write

$$+\!\uparrow \Sigma F_y = 0: \qquad C_y + A_y - 80\text{ lb} = 0$$
$$- 30\text{ lb} + A_y - 80\text{ lb} = 0$$
$$A_y = +110\text{ lb} \qquad\qquad \mathbf{A}_y = 110\text{ lb} \uparrow \quad \blacktriangleleft$$

Member AB (Check). We may check our computations by verifying that the equation $\Sigma F_y = 0$ is satisfied by the forces acting on member AB.

$$+\!\uparrow \Sigma F_y = A_y - \tfrac{3}{5}F_{AD} + \tfrac{3}{5}F_{BE} - 80\text{ lb}$$
$$= 110\text{ lb} - 60\text{ lb} + 30\text{ lb} - 80\text{ lb} = 0 \qquad \text{(checks)}$$

219

PROBLEMS

6.65. Determine the tension in member *BD* and the reaction at *C*.

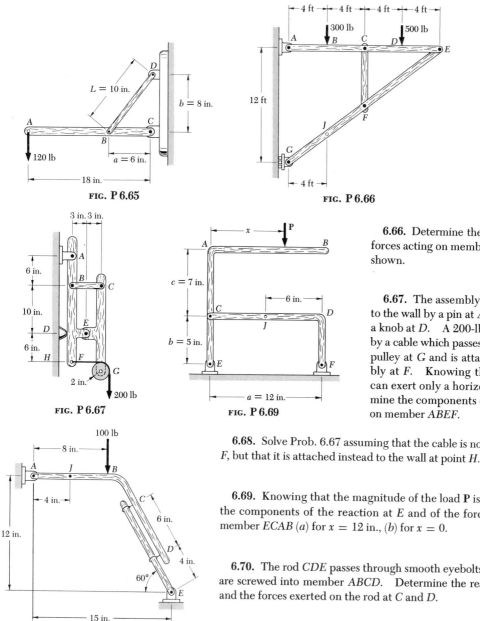

FIG. P 6.65

FIG. P 6.66

FIG. P 6.67

FIG. P 6.69

FIG. P 6.70

6.66. Determine the components of all forces acting on member *AE* of the frame shown.

6.67. The assembly shown is attached to the wall by a pin at *A* and bears against a knob at *D*.   A 200-lb load is supported by a cable which passes over a 2-in.-radius pulley at *G* and is attached to the assembly at *F*.   Knowing that the knob at *D* can exert only a horizontal force, determine the components of all forces acting on member *ABEF*.

6.68. Solve Prob. 6.67 assuming that the cable is not attached at point *F*, but that it is attached instead to the wall at point *H*.

6.69. Knowing that the magnitude of the load **P** is 180 lb, determine the components of the reaction at *E* and of the force exerted at *C* on member *ECAB* (*a*) for *x* = 12 in., (*b*) for *x* = 0.

6.70. The rod *CDE* passes through smooth eyebolts at *C* and *D* which are screwed into member *ABCD*.   Determine the reactions at *A* and *E* and the forces exerted on the rod at *C* and *D*.

6.71. Solve Prob. 6.69 in terms of *P*, *a*, *b*, and *c* for any value of *x*.

6.72. Determine the forces exerted on member *AB* if the frame is loaded by a clockwise couple of moment 120 lb-in. applied (*a*) at point *D*, (*b*) at point *E*.   (*c*) Determine the forces exerted on member *AB* if the frame is loaded by vertical forces applied at *D* and *E* which are equivalent to a 120-lb-in. clockwise couple.

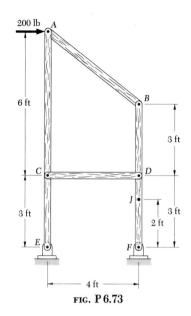

FIG. P 6.73

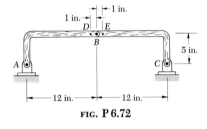

FIG. P 6.72

6.73. Determine the components of all forces acting on the two vertical members of the frame shown.

6.74. Determine the reactions at *E* and *F* and the force exerted on pin *C* for the frame shown.

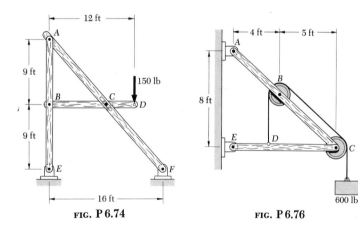

FIG. P 6.74

FIG. P 6.76

6.75. Determine the reactions at *E* and *F* and the force exerted on pin *C* for the frame of Prob. 6.74, assuming now that pin *C* is attached to member *ACF* and may slide in a horizontal slot in member *BD*.

6.76. Knowing that each pulley has a radius of 1 ft, determine the components of the reactions at *A* and *E*.

6.77. Determine the reactions at the supports for the beam shown.

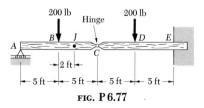

FIG. P 6.77

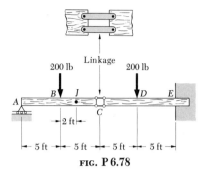

FIG. P 6.78

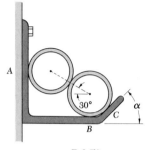

FIG. P 6.79

6.78. Determine the reactions at the supports for the beam shown.

6.79. Two equal lengths of steel tubing, of weight $2W$ each, are placed on two racks so that each rack supports half the weight of the tubing. Neglecting friction at all surfaces, determine the reactions exerted by the rack shown at A, B, and C when $\alpha = 45°$.

6.80. Determine the smallest value of the angle α for which equilibrium is possible in Prob. 6.79.

6.81. The axis of the three-hinged arch ABC is a parabola with its vertex at B. If $a = 25$ ft, determine the components of the reactions at A and C, and the components of the force exerted at B on segment AB.

6.82. Derive expressions for the components of the reaction at A in terms of the distance a. (*Hint.* Two expressions will be necessary for each component, one for $a < 30$ ft, the other for $a > 30$ ft.)

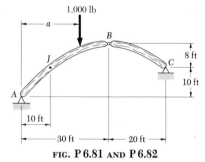

FIG. P 6.81 AND P 6.82

6.83. The tractor and scraper units shown are connected by a vertical pin located 2 ft behind the tractor wheels. The distance from C to D is 30 in. The center of gravity of the 16,000-lb tractor unit is located at G_t. The scraper unit and load together weigh 84,000 lb and have a combined center of gravity located at G_s. Knowing that the machine is at rest, with its brakes released, determine (*a*) the reactions at each of the four wheels, (*b*) the forces exerted on the tractor unit at C and D.

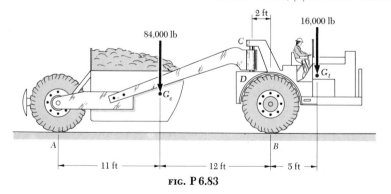

FIG. P 6.83

6.84. A trailer weighing 2,750 lb is attached to a 3,200-lb automobile by a ball-and-socket trailer hitch at *D*. Determine (*a*) the reactions at each of the six wheels when the automobile and trailer are at rest, (*b*) the additional load on each of the automobile wheels due to the trailer.

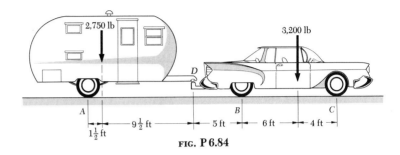

FIG. P 6.84

6.85. In order to obtain a better weight distribution over the four wheels of the automobile of Prob. 6.84, a compensating hitch of the type shown is used to attach the trailer to the automobile.   This hitch consists of two bar springs (only one is shown in the figure) which fit into bearings inside a support rigidly attached to the automobile.   The springs are also connected by chains to the trailer frame, and specially designed hooks make it possible to place both chains under a tension *T*.   Solve Prob. 6.84 assuming that such a compensating hitch is used and that the tension *T* in each chain is 440 lb.

6.86. In order to obtain a better weight distribution over the wheels of the automobile of Prob. 6.84, a compensating hitch of the type described in Prob. 6.85 is used to attach the trailer to the automobile.   (*a*) Determine the tension *T* required in each of the two chains if the additional load due to the trailer is to be evenly distributed over the four wheels of the automobile.   (*b*) What are the corresponding reactions at each of the six wheels of the trailer-automobile combination?

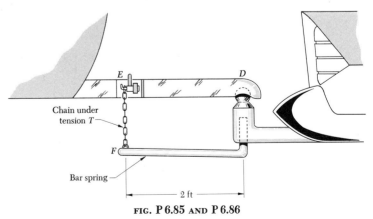

FIG. P 6.85 AND P 6.86

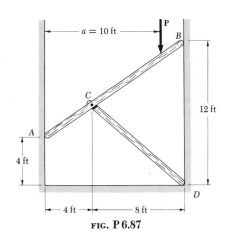

FIG. P 6.87

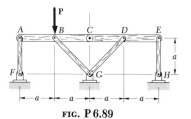

FIG. P 6.89

6.87. A load **P** of magnitude 100 lb is supported by two members AB and CD connected by a pin at C and placed between two smooth walls as shown. Determine the components of all forces exerted on member AB.

6.88. In Prob. 6.87, determine the range of values of the distance a for which the load **P** can be supported.

6.89. Determine the force in each of the links AF, BG, GD, and EH of the frame shown.

6.90. Solve Prob. 6.89, assuming that the force **P** is replaced by a clockwise couple of moment $\mathbf{M}_0$ applied to member ABC at B.

6.91. (*a*) Show that, when a frame supports a pulley at A, an equivalent loading of the frame and of each of its component parts may be obtained by removing the pulley and applying at A two forces equal and parallel to the forces of tension in the cable. (*b*) Further show that, if one end of the cable is attached to the frame at a point B, a force of magnitude equal to the tension should also be applied at B.

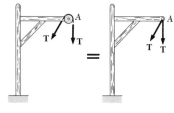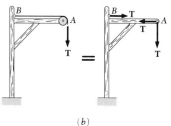

(*a*)   (*b*)

FIG. P 6.91

6.92 through 6.94. Determine the reactions at the supports for each of the trusses shown. Indicate whether the truss is rigid. The height of each truss is 12 ft; the length of each panel is 12 ft; and the magnitude of **P** is 4 kips.

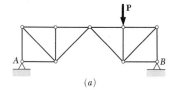
(*a*)

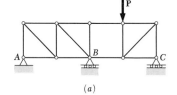
(*a*)

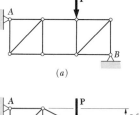
(*a*)

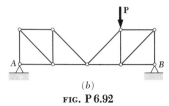
(*b*)

FIG. P 6.92

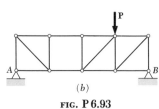
(*b*)

FIG. P 6.93

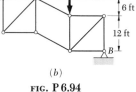
(*b*)

FIG. P 6.94

6.95. Determine the components of all forces acting on member *CDEF*.

6.96. Solve Prob. 6.95 assuming that the 200-lb force is attached at *B* instead of *A* and is directed horizontally to the right.

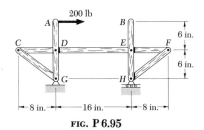

FIG. P 6.95

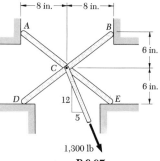

FIG. P 6.97

°6.97. Knowing that the surfaces at *A*, *B*, *D*, and *E* are smooth, determine (*a*) the reactions, (*b*) the components of the force exerted on member *ACE* at point *C*.

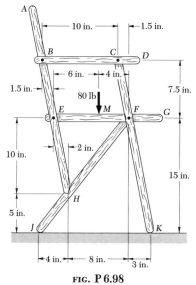

FIG. P 6.98

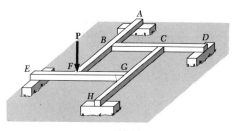

FIG. P 6.99

°6.98. In the folding chair shown, members *ABEH* and *CFK* are parallel. Determine the components of all forces acting on member *ABEH* when a 160-lb man sits in the chair. It may be assumed that the floor is perfectly smooth and that half the man's weight is carried by each side of the chair and is applied at point *M*.

°6.99. Four beams, each of length 2*a*, are nailed together at their midpoints to form the support system shown. Assuming that only vertical forces are exerted at the connections, determine the vertical reactions at *A*, *D*, *E*, and *H*.

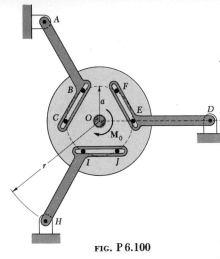

FIG. P 6.100

°6.100. Three arms are connected to a disk by six pins which are attached to the disk. The pins are equally spaced and are located at a distance a from the center of the disk. Each pin may slide freely in straight slots which are machined in the arms. If a couple of moment $\mathbf{M}_0$ is applied to the disk as shown, determine the reaction at D and the forces exerted on arm DEF at points E and F.

°6.101. Solve Prob. 6.100 assuming that the couple is removed and that a downward load $\mathbf{P}$ is applied at the center of the disk.

°6.102. In Prob. 6.65, knowing that the length BD must be 10 in., determine (a) another value of b for which the tension in BD has the same value as when $b = 8$ in., (b) the value of b for which the tension in BD is as small as possible.

6.13. Machines. Machines are structures designed to transmit and modify forces. Whether they are simple tools or include complicated mechanisms, their main purpose is to transform *input forces* into *output forces*. Consider, for example, a pair of cutting pliers used to cut a wire (Fig. 6.22a). If we apply two equal and opposite forces $\mathbf{P}$ and $-\mathbf{P}$ on their handles, they will exert two equal and opposite forces $\mathbf{Q}$ and $-\mathbf{Q}$ on the wire (Fig. 6.22b).

To determine the magnitude Q of the output forces when the magnitude P of the input forces is known (or, conversely, to determine P when Q is known), we draw a free-body diagram of the pliers *alone*, showing the input forces $\mathbf{P}$ and $-\mathbf{P}$ and the *reactions* $-\mathbf{Q}$ and $\mathbf{Q}$ that the wire exerts on the pliers (Fig. 6.22c). However, since a pair of pliers form a nonrigid structure, we must use one of the component parts as a free body in order to determine the unknown forces. Considering Fig. 6.22d, for example, and taking moments about A, we obtain the relation $Pa = Qb$, which defines the magnitude Q in terms of P or P in terms of Q. The same free-body diagram may be used to determine the components of the internal force at A; we find $A_x = 0$ and $A_y = P + Q$.

In the case of more complicated machines, it generally will be necessary to use several free-body diagrams and, possibly, to solve simultaneous equations involving various internal forces. The free bodies should be chosen to include the input forces and the reactions to the output forces, and the total number of unknown force components involved should not exceed the number of available independent equations. While it is advisable to check whether the problem is determinate before attempting to solve it, there is no point in discussing the rigidity of a machine. A machine includes moving parts and thus must be nonrigid.

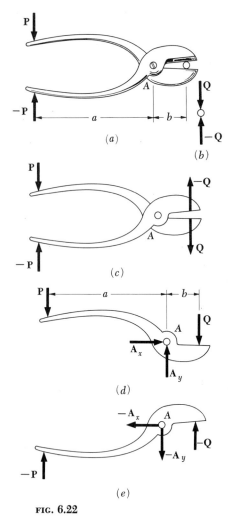

FIG. 6.22

SAMPLE PROBLEM 6.8

Determine the couple **M** which must be applied to the crank *CD* to hold the mechanism in equilibrium. The block at *D* is pinned to the crank *CD* and is free to slide in a slot cut in member *AB*.

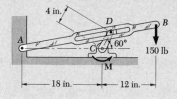

Solution. For the given position of the crank, we compute the following:

$$a = (4 \text{ in.}) \sin 60° = 3.46 \text{ in.}$$

$$b = (4 \text{ in.}) \cos 60° = 2.00 \text{ in.}$$

$$\tan \alpha = \frac{3.46}{20} \qquad \alpha = 9.8°$$

$$\sin \alpha = \frac{3.46}{c} \qquad c = 20.3 \text{ in.}$$

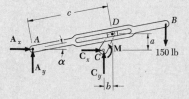

The mechanism is now dismembered; since the block at *D* slides freely along the slot, the internal force at *D* must be perpendicular to member *AB*.

Member *AB*

$$+ \text{\Large\rotatebox[origin=c]{-20}{$\downarrow$}} \; \Sigma M_A = 0: \qquad D(20.3 \text{ in.}) - (150 \text{ lb})(30 \text{ in.}) = 0$$
$$D = +222 \text{ lb}$$

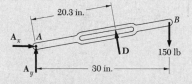

Member *CD*. The internal force **D** is resolved into its x and y components.

$$D_x = (222 \text{ lb}) \sin 9.8° = +37.8 \text{ lb}$$

$$D_y = -(222 \text{ lb}) \cos 9.8° = -218 \text{ lb}$$

We then write

$$+ \text{\Large\rotatebox[origin=c]{-20}{$\downarrow$}} \; \Sigma M_C = 0: \qquad M - (218 \text{ lb})(2 \text{ in.}) - (37.8 \text{ lb})(3.46 \text{ in.}) = 0$$
$$M = +567 \text{ lb-in.} \qquad \mathbf{M = 567 \text{ lb-in.}} \; \blacktriangleleft$$

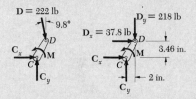

From the free-body diagram of the crank we may also obtain $C_x = -37.8 \text{ lb}$ and $C_y = +218 \text{ lb}$.

Entire Mechanism (Check). Considering the entire mechanism as a free body, we check that $\Sigma M_A = 0$.

$$+ \text{\Large\rotatebox[origin=c]{-20}{$\downarrow$}} \; \Sigma M_A = M - (150 \text{ lb})(30 \text{ in.}) + C_y(18 \text{ in.})$$
$$= 567 - 4{,}500 + (218)(18) = -9$$

Although ΣM_A is equal to -9 instead of zero, it is small compared with the quantities involved (4,500) and provides a satisfactory check.

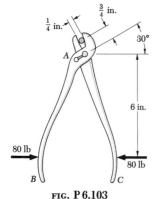

80 lb

B   C

FIG. P 6.103

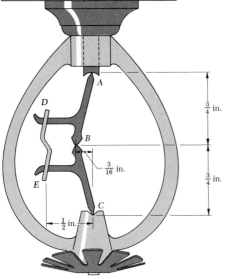

FIG. P 6.104

PROBLEMS

6.103. Two 80-lb forces are applied to the handles of the pliers as shown. Determine (*a*) the magnitude of the forces exerted on the rod, (*b*) the force exerted by the pin at *A* on portion *AB* of the pliers.

6.104. Water pressure in the supply system exerts a downward force of 25 lb on the vertical plug at *A*. Determine the tension in the fusible link *DE* and the force exerted on member *BCE* at *B*.

6.105. A cylinder weighs 500 lb and is lifted by a pair of tongs as shown. Determine the forces exerted at *D* and *C* on the tong *BCD*.

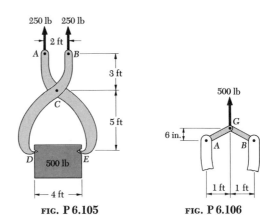

FIG. P 6.105   FIG. P 6.106

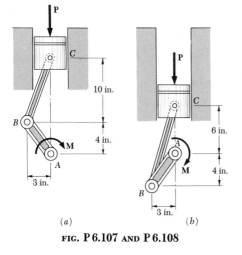

(*a*)   (*b*)

FIG. P 6.107 AND P 6.108

6.106. If the toggle shown is added to the tongs of Prob. 6.105 and the load is lifted by applying a single force at *G*, determine the forces exerted at *D* and *C* on the tong *BCD*.

6.107. A couple **M** of moment 210 lb-ft is applied to the crank of the engine system shown. For each of the two positions shown, determine the force **P** required to hold the system in equilibrium.

6.108. A force **P** of magnitude 500 lb is applied to the piston of the engine system shown. For each of the two positions shown, determine the couple **M** required to hold the system in equilibrium.

6.109. Two machine parts are connected by a pin at E which is attached to member CD and slides freely in a slot cut in member AB. If a couple $\mathbf{M}_D$ is applied to member CD, determine (a) the couple $\mathbf{M}_B$ required for equilibrium, (b) the reactions at B and D.

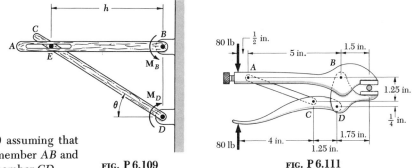

6.110. Solve Prob. 6.109 assuming that the pin at E is attached to member AB and slides freely in a slot cut in member CD.

FIG. P 6.109   FIG. P 6.111

6.111. Determine the magnitude of the gripping forces produced when two 80-lb forces are applied as shown.

6.112. In using the boltcutter shown, a man applies two 125-lb forces to the handles.   Determine the magnitude of the forces exerted by the cutter on the bolt.

6.113. In the pliers shown, the clamping jaws remain parallel as objects of various sizes are held.   If gripping forces of magnitude $Q = 450$ lb are desired, determine the magnitude P of the forces which must be applied.   Assume that pins B and E slide freely in the slots cut in the jaws.

6.114. In Prob. 6.113, show that the magnitude P of the required forces is independent of the position of the object gripped by the jaws. (*Hint.*   Determine P in terms of the distance a.)

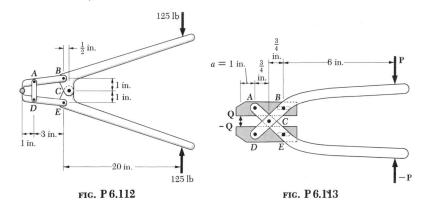

FIG. P 6.112   FIG. P 6.113

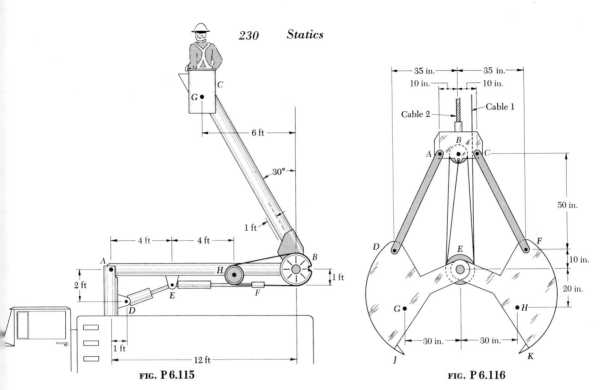

FIG. P 6.115

FIG. P 6.116

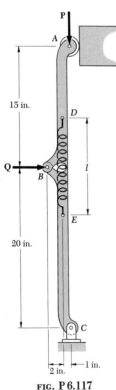

FIG. P 6.117

6.115. The truck shown is used to facilitate work on overhead wires by raising a pair of buckets to the required elevation. Two tubular members *AB* and *BC*, each of length 12 ft, form the main supporting mechanism; the position of *AB* is controlled by means of the hydraulic cylinder *DE*. Two 2-ft-diameter sheaves, one on each side, are rigidly attached to member *BC* at *B*. Cables are fastened to the sheaves, pass over pulleys at *H*, and are fastened to a common movable block at *F*. The position of block *F* is controlled by a second hydraulic cylinder *EF*. Knowing that the workmen, buckets, and equipment attached to the buckets together weigh 700 lb and have a combined center of gravity at *G*, determine the force which must be exerted by each hydraulic cylinder to maintain the position shown. Neglect the weight of the mechanism.

6.116. The total weight of the 1-yd clamshell bucket shown is 4,500 lb. The centers of gravity of sections *DEJ* and *EFK*, which weigh 2,000 lb each, are located at *G* and *H*, respectively. The double-sheave pulley *E* and a counterweight located at *E* together weigh 400 lb. Determine the tension in cable *1* and cable *2* for the position shown. (Neglect the effect of the horizontal distance between the cables.)

6.117. Since the brace shown must remain in position even when the magnitude of **P** is very small, a single safety spring is attached at *D* and *E*. The spring *DE* has a constant of 50 lb/in. and an unstretched length of 7 in. Knowing that *l* = 10 in. and that the magnitude of **P** is 800 lb, determine the force **Q** required to release the brace.

6.118. Members ACE and DCB are each of length 20 in. and are connected by a pin at their mid-points C.   A load **P** of magnitude 320 lb is applied to member DF.   If $h = 12$ in. and $a = 25$ in., determine (*a*) all forces acting on member DCB, (*b*) the tension in the spring AD, (*c*) the unstretched length of the spring knowing that the spring constant is 80 lb/in.

6.119. Show that the tension in the spring AD and the distance h are the same for any position of the load **P** on member DF.   (*Hint.*   Choose a as a parameter and determine the tension in AD in terms of a.)

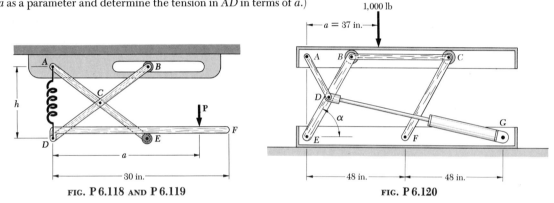

FIG. P 6.118 AND P 6.119

6.120. The top surface of the hydraulic-lift table shown is maintained at a given elevation by two identical linkage-and-hydraulic-cylinder systems; only one of the systems is shown.   Members EDB and CF are each of length 42 in.; member AD is 21 in. long and is pinned to the mid-point D of member EDB.   If a 2,000-lb load is placed on the table top so that half its weight is supported by the system shown, determine the force in members AD and BC and the force exerted by the hydraulic cylinder on point D.   Assume $\alpha = 60°$.

°6.121. In Prob. 6.120 show that the force exerted by the hydraulic cylinder is the same for any position of the load on the table top.   Assume $\alpha = 60°$.

6.122. The two gears are rigidly attached to shafts which are held by frictionless bearings at C, D, G, and H.   A couple of moment 480 lb-ft (counterclockwise when viewed from the positive x axis) is applied to shaft CDE at E.   Assuming that the bearings cannot exert any axial thrust, determine (*a*) the couple which must be applied at F to maintain equilibrium, (*b*) the reaction at B.

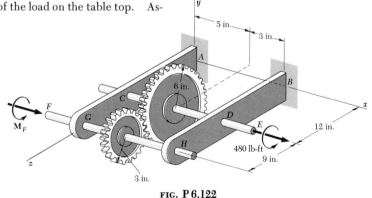

FIG. P 6.122

6.123. For the bevel-gear system shown, determine the required value of α if the ratio of M_B to M_A is to be 3.

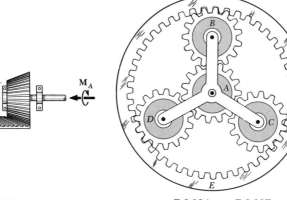

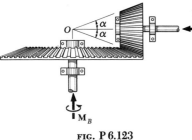

FIG. P 6.123

FIG. P 6.124 AND P 6.125

6.124. In the planetary-gear system shown, the radius of the central gear A is a, the radius of each planetary gear is b, and the radius of the outer gear E is $(a + 2b)$. In a particular gear system where $a = b = 2\frac{1}{4}$ in., a clockwise couple $\mathbf{M}_A$ is applied to gear A. If the system is to be in equilibrium, determine (a) the couple $\mathbf{M}_s$ which must be applied to the spider BCD, (b) the couple $\mathbf{M}_E$ which must be applied to the outer gear E.

6.125. In the planetary-gear system shown, the radius of the central gear A is a, the radius of each of the planetary gears is b, and the radius of the outer gear E is $(a + 2b)$. A clockwise couple of magnitude M_A is applied to the central gear A and a counterclockwise couple of magnitude $5M_A$ is applied to the spider BCD. If the system is to be in equilibrium, determine (a) the required ratio b/a, (b) the couple $\mathbf{M}_E$ which must be applied to the outer gear E.

*6.126. Two shafts AC and CF, which lie in the vertical xy plane, are connected by a universal joint at C. The bearings at B and D do not exert any axial force. A couple of moment 500 lb-ft (clockwise when viewed from the positive x axis) is applied to shaft CF at F. At a time when the arm of the crosspiece attached to shaft CF is horizontal, determine (a) the moment of the couple which must be applied to shaft AC at A to maintain equilibrium, (b) the reactions at B, D, and E. (*Hint.* The sum of the couples exerted on the crosspiece must be zero.)

*6.127. Solve Prob. 6.126 assuming that the arm of the crosspiece attached to shaft CF is vertical.

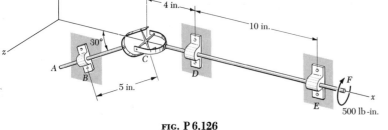

FIG. P 6.126

*6.128. The weight in ounces of letters placed on the postal scale shown is indicated on the moving dial by the stationary pointer *P*.   The scale is shown in its unloaded position.   It is known that the dial, the arm *AB*, and a counterweight together weigh 10 oz and have a combined center of gravity at *G*.   The distance *AG* is $1\frac{1}{4}$ in., and the length of the arm *AB* and of the link *CD* is 1.00 in.   At what angle θ should the 2-oz number be painted on the dial?   (*Hint.*   The weights of the tray, of *BC*, and of *CD* are unknown, but their effect must be considered.)

*6.129. A letter of unknown weight is placed on the postal scale of Prob. 6.128.   Knowing that the dial rotates counterclockwise through 45° before coming to rest, determine the weight of the letter.   (See hint of Prob. 6.128.)

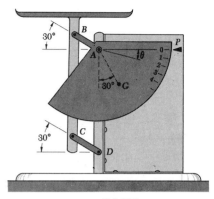

FIG. P 6.128

REVIEW PROBLEMS

6.130. Determine the reaction at *G* and all forces acting on member *BDFH*.

6.131. Each of the four bars shown is of length *L*.   Express the magnitude of the force **Q** required for equilibrium in terms of *P*, *a*, and *L*.

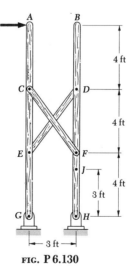

FIG. P 6.130

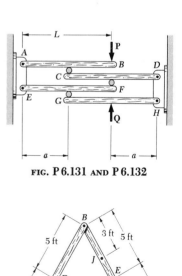

FIG. P 6.131 AND P 6.132

6.132. Each of the four bars shown is of length *L*.   Knowing that the magnitude of the force **P** is 100 lb and that *a* = 10 in. and *L* = 20 in., determine the magnitude of the force **Q** required for equilibrium.

6.133. A pipe weighs 20 lb-ft and is supported every 30 ft by a small frame; a typical frame is shown.   (*a*) Determine the components of the reactions and the components of the force exerted at *B* on member *AB*. (*b*) Determine the value of α for which the reactions are vertical.

FIG. P 6.133

6.134. The boom *CDE* is maintained in a horizontal position by a cable which passes over small pulleys at *A* and *F*.   For the loading shown, determine the force in members *AB, AC,* and *GH*.

6.135. Solve Prob. 6.134 assuming that the end *E* of the boom, where the 2-kip load is applied, has been raised 6 ft.

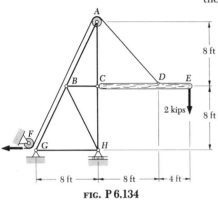

FIG. P 6.134

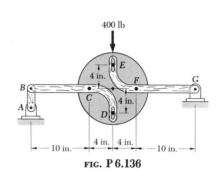

FIG. P 6.136

6.136. Two arms *BCD* and *EFG* are connected to a 10-in.-diameter disk by four pins which are attached to the disk.   Assuming that the pins at *D* and *E* may slide in the vertical slots, determine the components of all forces exerted on the disk when a 400-lb load is applied to the disk as shown.

6.137. Solve Prob. 6.136 assuming that the 400-lb load is applied to the top edge of member *EFG*.

6.138. An automobile front-wheel assembly supports 750 lb.   Determine the force exerted by the spring and the components of the forces exerted on the frame at points *A* and *D*.

FIG. P 6.138

6.139. An 800-lb weight may be supported by a small frame in each of the four ways shown.   The diameter of the pulley is 1 ft.   For each case, determine the force components and the couple representing the reaction at *A* and also the force exerted at *D* on the vertical member.

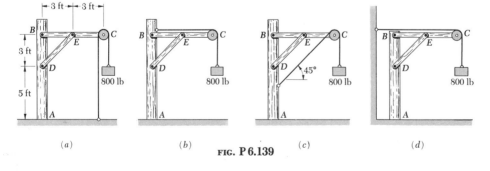

(*a*)   (*b*)   (*c*)   (*d*)

FIG. P 6.139

6.140. Knowing that the forces **P** and −**P** are equal and opposite and have a magnitude of 2 kips, determine the force in each member of the truss shown.

6.141. Determine the magnitude of the equal and opposite forces **P** and −**P** for which the forces in members 2-3 and 7-8 have the same absolute value.

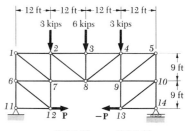

FIG. P 6.140 AND P 6.141

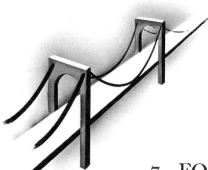

7. FORCES IN BEAMS AND CABLES

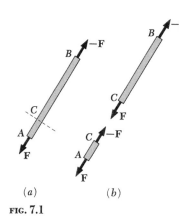

(a)   (b)

FIG. 7.1

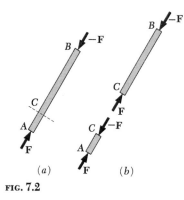

(a)   (b)

FIG. 7.2

7.1. Introduction. Internal Forces in Members. In preceding chapters, two basic problems involving structures were considered, (1) the determination of the external forces acting on a structure (Chap. 4) and (2) the determination of the forces which hold together the various members forming a structure (Chap. 6). We shall now consider the problem of determining the internal forces which hold together the various parts of a given member.

We shall first consider a *straight two-force member AB* (Fig. 7.1a). From Sec. 4.6, we know that the forces $\mathbf{F}$ and $-\mathbf{F}$ acting at A and B respectively must be directed along AB in opposite sense and have the same magnitude F. Let us cut, now, the member at C. To maintain the equilibrium of the free bodies AC and CB thus obtained, we must apply to AC a force $-\mathbf{F}$ equal and opposite to $\mathbf{F}$, and to CB a force $\mathbf{F}$ equal and opposite to $-\mathbf{F}$ (Fig. 7.1b). These new forces are directed along AB in opposite sense and have the same magnitude F. Since the two parts AC and CB were in equilibrium before the member was cut, *internal forces* equivalent to these new forces must have existed in the member itself. We see that, in the case of a straight two-force member, the internal forces acting on each part of the member are equivalent to an axial force. The magnitude F of this force does not depend upon the location of the section C and is referred to as the *force in member AB*. In the case considered, the member is in tension and will elongate under the action of the internal forces. In the case represented in Fig. 7.2, the member is in compression and will decrease in length under the action of the internal forces.

Next we shall consider a *multiforce member*. Take, for instance, member AD of the crane analyzed in Sec. 6.11. This crane is shown again in Fig. 7.3a, and the free-body diagram of member AD is drawn in Fig. 7.3b. We now cut member AD

at *J* and draw a free-body diagram for each of the portions *JD* and *AJ* of the member (Fig. 7.3c and d). Considering the free body *JD*, we find that its equilibrium will be maintained if we apply at *J* a force **F** to balance the vertical component of **T**, a force **V** to balance the horizontal component of **T**, and a couple **M** to balance the moment of **T** about *J*. Again we conclude that internal forces must have existed at *J* before member *AD* was cut. The internal forces acting on the portion *JD* of member *AD* are equivalent to the force-couple system shown in Fig. 7.3c. According to Newton's third law, the internal forces acting on *AJ* must be equivalent to an equal and opposite force-couple system, as shown in Fig. 7.3d. It clearly appears that the action of the internal forces in member *AD* *is not limited to producing tension or compression* as in the case of straight two-force members; the internal forces *also produce shear and bending*. The force **F** is again in this case called an *axial force;* the force **V** is called a *shearing force;* and the moment **M** of the couple is known as the *bending moment* at *J*. We note that, when determining internal forces in a member, we should clearly indicate on which portion of the member the forces are supposed to act. The deformation which will occur in member *AD* is sketched in Fig. 7.3e. The actual analysis of such a deformation is part of the study of mechanics of materials.

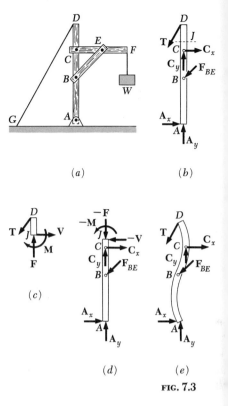

FIG. 7.3

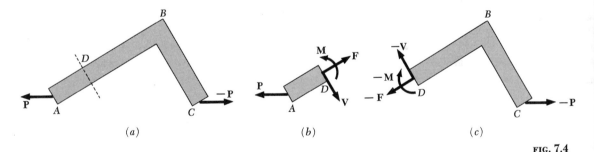

FIG. 7.4

It should be noted that, in a *two-force member which is not straight,* the internal forces are also equivalent to a force-couple system. This is shown in Fig. 7.4, where the two-force member *ABC* has been cut at *D*.

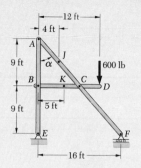

SAMPLE PROBLEM 7.1

In the frame shown, determine the internal forces (a) in member *ACF* at point *J* and (b) in member *BCD* at point *K*. This frame has been previously considered in Sample Prob. 6.6.

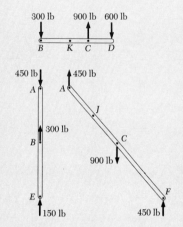

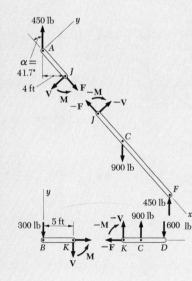

Solution. The reactions and the forces acting on each member of the frame are determined; this has been previously done in Sample Prob. 6.6, and the results are repeated here.

a. Internal Forces at J. Member *ACF* is cut at point *J*, and the two parts shown are obtained. The internal forces at *J* are represented by an equivalent force-couple system and may be determined by considering the equilibrium of either part. Considering the *free body AJ*, we write

$+\,\rotatebox{0}{)}\,\Sigma M_J = 0:$ $-(450\text{ lb})(4\text{ ft}) + M = 0$
$$M = +1{,}800\text{ lb-ft} \qquad \mathbf{M = 1{,}800\text{ lb-ft}} \; \rotatebox{0}{)} \quad \blacktriangleleft$$

$+\,\searrow\,\Sigma F_x = 0:$ $F - (450\text{ lb})\cos 41.7° = 0$
$$F = +336\text{ lb} \qquad\qquad \mathbf{F = 336\text{ lb}} \; \searrow \quad \blacktriangleleft$$

$+\,\nearrow\,\Sigma F_y = 0:$ $-V + (450\text{ lb})\sin 41.7° = 0$
$$V = +299\text{ lb} \qquad\qquad \mathbf{V = 299\text{ lb}} \; \swarrow \quad \blacktriangleleft$$

The internal forces at *J* are therefore equivalent to a couple **M**, an axial force **F**, and a shearing force **V**. The internal force-couple system acting on part *JCF* is equal and opposite.

b. Internal Forces at K. We cut member *BCD* at *K* and obtain the two parts shown. Considering the *free body BK*, we write

$+\,\rotatebox{0}{)}\,\Sigma M_K = 0:$ $(300\text{ lb})(5\text{ ft}) + M = 0$
$$M = -1{,}500\text{ lb-ft} \qquad \mathbf{M = 1{,}500\text{ lb-ft}} \; \rotatebox{0}{(} \quad \blacktriangleleft$$

$\xrightarrow{+}\,\Sigma F_x = 0:$ $F = 0$ $\mathbf{F = 0} \quad \blacktriangleleft$

$+\,\uparrow\,\Sigma F_y = 0:$ $-300\text{ lb} - V = 0$
$$V = -300\text{ lb} \qquad\qquad \mathbf{V = 300\text{ lb}} \; \uparrow \quad \blacktriangleleft$$

238

PROBLEMS

7.1 through 7.7. Determine the internal forces (axial force, shearing force, and bending moment) at point *J* of the structure indicated:

    7.1. Frame and loading of Prob. 6.69.
    7.2. Frame and loading of Prob. 6.66.
    7.3. Frame and loading of Prob. 6.73.
    7.4. Frame and loading of Prob. 6.70.
    7.5. Beam and loading of Prob. 6.77.
    7.6. Beam and loading of Prob. 6.78.
    7.7. Arch and loading of Prob. 6.81.

7.8 and 7.9. A steel channel forms one side of a flight of stairs. If one channel weighs w lb/ft, determine the internal forces at the center of one channel due to its own weight, (*a*) in terms of w, L, and θ, (*b*) if $w = 20$ lb/ft, $l = 12$ ft, and $h = 9$ ft.

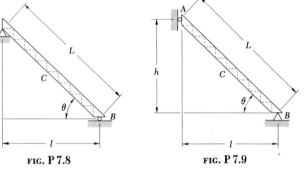

FIG. P 7.8   **FIG. P 7.9**

7.10. Determine the internal forces at points *J* and *K* of the adjustable hanger shown.

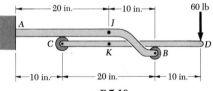

FIG. P 7.10

7.11 and 7.12. A half section of pipe, 1 ft long, rests on a smooth horizontal surface as shown. If the half section of pipe weighs 30 lb and has a diameter of 20 in., determine the bending moment at point *J* when $\theta = 90°$.

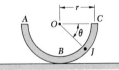

FIG. P 7.11 AND P 7.13

°**7.13 and 7.14.** A half section of pipe, 1 ft long and of weight W, rests on a smooth horizontal surface. Determine the internal forces at a point *J* in terms of W, r, and θ.

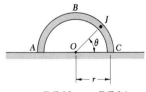

°**7.15.** In Prob. 7.13 determine the magnitude and location of the maximum internal axial force.

FIG. P 7.12 AND P 7.14

BEAMS

°7.2. Various Types of Loading and Support. A structural member designed to support loads applied at various points along the member is known as a *beam*. In most cases, the loads are perpendicular to the axis of the beam and will cause only shear and bending in the beam. When the loads are not at a right angle to the beam, they will also produce axial forces in the beam. Axial forces, however, may usually be neglected in the design of beams, since the ability of a beam to resist shear and especially bending is more critical than its ability to resist axial forces.

Beams are usually long, straight prismatic bars. Designing a beam consists essentially in selecting the cross section which will provide the most effective resistance to the shear and bending produced by the applied loads. The design of the beam, therefore, includes two distinct parts. In the first part, the shearing forces and bending moments produced by the loads are determined. The second part is concerned with the selection of the cross section best suited to resist the shearing forces and bending moments determined in the first part. This portion of the chapter, Beams, deals with the first part of the problem of beam design, namely, the determination of the shearing forces and bending moments in beams subjected to various loading conditions and supported in various ways. The second part of the problem belongs to the study of mechanics of materials.

A beam may be subjected to *concentrated loads* (Fig. 7.5a), to *distributed loads* (Fig. 7.5b), or to a combination of both. When the load w per unit length has a constant value over part of the beam (as between A and B in Fig. 7.5b), the load is said to be *uniformly distributed* over that part of the beam. The determination of the reactions at the supports may be considerably simplified if distributed loads are replaced by equivalent concentrated loads, as explained in Sec. 5.6. This substitution, however, should not be performed, or at least should be performed with care, when internal forces are being computed (see Sample Prob. 7.3).

Beams are classified according to the way in which they are supported. Several types of beams frequently used are shown in Fig. 7.6. The distance L between supports is called the *span*. It should be noted that the reactions will be determinate if the supports involve only three unknowns. The reactions will be statically indeterminate if more unknowns are involved; the methods of statics are not sufficient then to determine the reactions, and the properties of the beam with regard to its re-

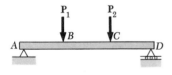

(*a*) Concentrated loads

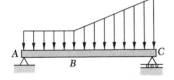

(*b*) Distributed loads

FIG. 7.5. Types of loadings

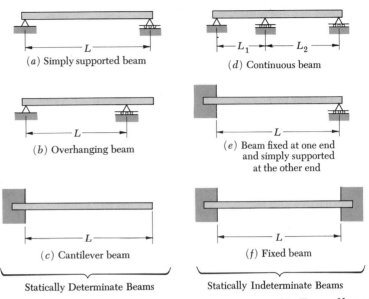

(a) Simply supported beam

(d) Continuous beam

(b) Overhanging beam

(e) Beam fixed at one end
and simply supported
at the other end

(c) Cantilever beam

(f) Fixed beam

Statically Determinate Beams

Statically Indeterminate Beams

FIG. 7.6. Types of beams

sistance to bending must be taken into consideration. Beams supported by two rollers are not shown here; such beams are only partially constrained and will move under certain loading conditions.

Sometimes two or more beams are connected by hinges to form a single continuous structure. Two examples of beams hinged at a point H are shown in Fig. 7.7. It will be noted that the reactions at the supports involve four unknowns and cannot be determined from the free-body diagram of the two-beam system. They can be determined, however, by considering the free-body diagram of each beam separately; six unknowns are involved (including two force components at the hinge), and six equations are available.

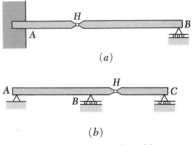

FIG. 7.7. Combined beams

*7.3. Shear and Bending Moment in a Beam. Consider a beam AB subjected to various concentrated and distributed loads (Fig. 7.8a). We propose to determine the shearing force and bending moment at any point of the beam. In the example considered here, the beam is simply supported, but the method used could be applied to any type of statically determinate beam.

First we determine the reactions at A and B by choosing the entire beam as a free body (Fig. 7.8b); writing $\Sigma M_A = 0$ and $\Sigma M_B = 0$, we obtain, respectively, $\mathbf{R}_B$ and $\mathbf{R}_A$.

To determine the internal forces at C, we cut the beam at C and draw the free-body diagrams of the portions AC and CB of the beam (Fig. 7.8c). Using the free-body diagram of AC, we may determine the shearing force $\mathbf{V}$ at C by equating to zero

241

the sum of the vertical components of all forces acting on AC. Similarly, the bending moment **M** at C may be found by equating to zero the sum of the moments about C of all forces and couples acting on AC.   We could have used just as well, however, the free-body diagram of CB † and determined the shearing force **V′** and the bending moment **M′** by equating to zero the sum of the vertical components and the sum of the moments about C of all forces and couples acting on AC.   While this possible choice of alternate free bodies may facilitate the computation of the numerical values of the shearing force and

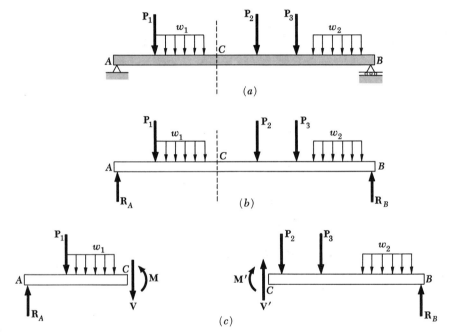

(a)

(b)

(c)

FIG. 7.8

bending moment, it makes it necessary to indicate on which portion of the beam the internal forces considered are acting. If the shearing force and bending moment, however, are to be computed at every point of the beam and efficiently recorded, we should not have to specify every time which portion of the beam is used as a free body.   We shall adopt, therefore, the following convention:

To determine the shearing force in a beam, *we shall always*

---

† The force and couple representing the internal forces acting on CB will now be denoted by **V′** and **M′**, rather than by $-$**V** and $-$**M** as done earlier, in order to avoid confusion when applying the sign convention which we are about to introduce.

assume that the internal forces **V** and **V′** are directed as shown in Fig. 7.8c.   A positive value obtained for their common magnitude V will indicate that this assumption was correct and that the shearing forces are actually directed as shown.   A negative value obtained for V will indicate that the assumption was wrong and that the shearing forces are directed in the opposite way.   Thus, only the magnitude V, together with a plus or minus sign, needs to be recorded to define completely the shearing forces at a given point of the beam.   The scalar V is commonly referred to as the *shear* at the given point of the beam.

Similarly, *we shall always assume* that the internal couples **M** and **M′** are directed as shown in Fig. 7.8c.   A positive value obtained for their magnitude M, commonly referred to as the bending moment, will indicate that this assumption was correct, and a negative value that it was wrong.   Summarizing the sign convention we have presented, we state:

The shear V and the bending moment M at a given point of a beam are said to be positive when the internal forces and couples acting on each portion of the beam are directed as shown in Fig. 7.9a.

This convention may be more easily remembered if we note that:

1. *The shear at C is positive when the* external *forces (loads and reactions) acting on the beam tend to shear off the beam at C as indicated in Fig. 7.9b.*

2. *The bending moment at C is positive when the* external *forces acting on the beam tend to bend the beam at C as indicated in Fig. 7.9c.*

It may also help to note that the situation described in Fig. 7.9, and corresponding to positive values of the shear and of the bending moment, is precisely the situation which occurs in the left half of a simply supported beam carrying a single concentrated load at its mid-point.   This particular example is fully discussed in the following section.

°7.4. Shear and Bending-moment Diagrams.   Now that shear and bending moment have been clearly defined in sense as well as in magnitude, we may easily record their values at any point of a beam by plotting these values against the distance x measured from one end of the beam.   The graphs obtained in this way are called, respectively, the *shear diagram* and the *bending-moment diagram.*   As an example, consider a simply supported beam AB of span L subjected to a single concentrated load **P** applied at its mid-point D (Fig. 7.10a).

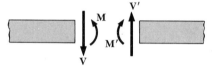

(*a*) Internal forces at section
(positive shear and positive bending moment)

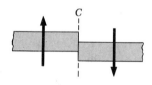

(*b*) Effect of external forces
(positive shear)

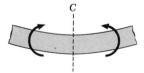

(*c*) Effect of external forces
(positive bending moment)

FIG. 7.9

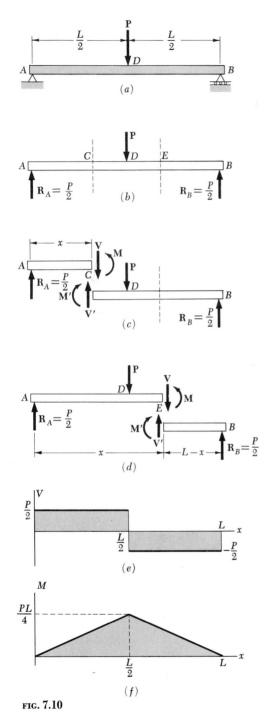

FIG. 7.10

We first determine the reactions at the supports from the free-body diagram of the entire beam (Fig. 7.10*b*); we find that the magnitude of each reaction is equal to $P/2$.

Next we cut the beam at a point C between A and D and draw the free-body diagrams of AC and CB (Fig. 7.10*c*). *Assuming that shear and bending moment are positive*, we direct the internal forces **V** and **V'** and the internal couples **M** and **M'** as indicated in Fig. 7.9*a*. Considering the free body AC and writing that the sum of the vertical components and the sum of the moments about C of the forces acting on the free body are zero, we find $V = +P/2$ and $M = +Px/2$. Both the shear and the bending moment are therefore positive; this may be checked by observing that the reaction at A tends to shear off and to bend the beam at C as indicated in Fig. 7.9*b* and *c*. We may plot V and M between A and D (Fig. 7.10*e* and *f*); the shear has a constant value $V = P/2$, while the bending moment increases linearly from $M = 0$ at $x = 0$ to $M = PL/4$ at $x = L/2$.

Cutting, now, the beam at a point E between D and B and considering the free body EB (Fig. 7.10*d*), we write that the sum of the vertical components and the sum of the moments about E of the forces acting on the free body are zero. We obtain $V = -P/2$ and $M = P(L - x)/2$. The shear is therefore negative and the bending moment positive; this may be checked by observing that the reaction at B bends the beam at E as indicated in Fig. 7.9*c* but tends to shear it off in a manner opposite to that shown in Fig. 7.9*b*. We can complete, now, the shear and bending-moment diagrams of Fig. 7.10*e* and *f*; the shear has a constant value $V = -P/2$ between D and B, while the bending moment decreases linearly from $M = PL/4$ at $x = L/2$ to $M = 0$ at $x = L$.

We shall note that, when a beam is subjected only to concentrated loads, the shear is of constant value between loads and the bending moment varies linearly between loads. On the other hand, when a beam is subjected to distributed loads, the shear and bending moment vary quite differently (see Sample Prob. 7.3).

SAMPLE PROBLEM 7.2

Draw the shear and bending-moment diagram for the beam and loading shown.

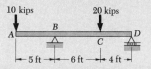

Solution. The reactions are determined by considering the entire beam as a free body; they are

$$\mathbf{R}_B = 23 \text{ kips} \uparrow \qquad \mathbf{R}_D = 7 \text{ kips} \uparrow$$

We first determine the internal forces just to the right of the 10-kip load at A. Considering the stub of beam to the left of section 1 as a free body and assuming V and M to be positive (according to the standard convention), we write

$$+\uparrow \Sigma F_y = 0: \qquad -10 \text{ kips} - V_1 = 0 \qquad V_1 = -10 \text{ kips}$$
$$+\circlearrowright \Sigma M_1 = 0: \qquad (10 \text{ kips})(0 \text{ ft}) + M_1 = 0 \qquad M_1 = 0$$

We next consider as a free body the portion of beam to the left of section 2 and write

$$+\uparrow \Sigma F_y = 0: \qquad -10 \text{ kips} - V_2 = 0 \qquad V_2 = -10 \text{ kips}$$
$$+\circlearrowright \Sigma M_2 = 0: \qquad (10 \text{ kips})(5 \text{ ft}) + M_2 = 0 \qquad M_2 = -50 \text{ kip-ft}$$

The shear and bending moment at sections 3, 4, 5, and 6 are determined in a similar way from the free-body diagrams shown. We obtain

$$V_3 = +13 \text{ kips} \qquad M_3 = -50 \text{ kip-ft}$$
$$V_4 = +13 \text{ kips} \qquad M_4 = +28 \text{ kip-ft}$$
$$V_5 = -7 \text{ kips} \qquad M_5 = +28 \text{ kip-ft}$$
$$V_6 = -7 \text{ kips} \qquad M_6 = 0$$

For several of the latter sections, the results may be more easily obtained by considering as a free body the portion of the beam to the right of the section. For example, considering the portion of the beam to the right of section 4, we write

$$+\uparrow \Sigma F_y = 0: \qquad V_4 - 20 \text{ kips} + 7 \text{ kips} = 0 \qquad V_4 = +13 \text{ kips}$$
$$+\circlearrowright \Sigma M_4 = 0: \qquad -M_4 + (7 \text{ kips})(4 \text{ ft}) = 0 \qquad M_4 = +28 \text{ kip-ft}$$

We may now plot the six points shown on the shear and bending-moment diagrams. As indicated in Sec. 7.4, the shear is of constant value between concentrated loads, and the bending moment varies linearly; we obtain therefore the shear and bending-moment diagrams shown.

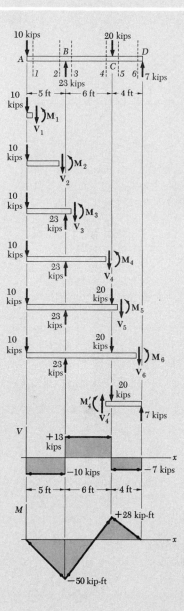

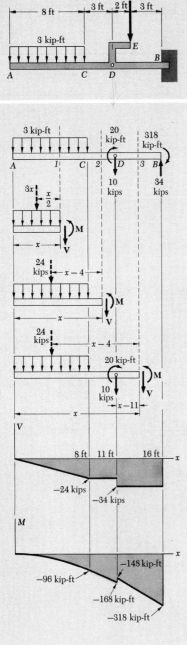

Draw the shear and bending-moment diagrams for the cantilever beam AB. The distributed load of 3 kips/ft extends over 8 ft of the beam and the 10-kip load is applied at E.

Solution. The 10-kip load is replaced by an equivalent force-couple system acting on the beam at point D. The reaction at B is determined by considering the entire beam as a free body.

From A to C. We determine the internal forces at a distance x from point A by considering the portion of beam to the left of section 1. That part of the distributed load acting on the free body is replaced by its resultant, and we write

$$+\uparrow \Sigma F_y = 0: \qquad -3x - V = 0 \qquad V = -3x \text{ kips}$$

$$+\rotatebox{90}{$\circlearrowleft$}\ \Sigma M_1 = 0: \qquad 3x(\tfrac{1}{2}x) + M = 0 \qquad M = -1.5x^2 \text{ kip-ft}$$

Since the free-body diagram shown may be used for all values of x smaller than 8 ft, the expressions obtained for V and M are valid in the region $0 < x < 8$ ft.

From C to D. Considering the portion of beam to the left of section 2 and again replacing the distributed load by its resultant, we obtain

$$+\uparrow \Sigma F_y = 0: \qquad -24 - V = 0 \qquad V = -24 \text{ kips}$$

$$+\rotatebox{90}{$\circlearrowleft$}\ \Sigma M_2 = 0: \qquad 24(x - 4) + M = 0 \qquad M = 96 - 24x \qquad \text{kip-ft}$$

These expressions are valid in the region 8 ft $< x <$ 11 ft.

From D to B. Using the portion of beam to the left of section 3, we obtain for the region 11 ft $< x <$ 16 ft

$$V = -34 \text{ kips} \qquad M = 226 - 34x \qquad \text{kip-ft}$$

The shear and bending-moment diagrams for the entire beam may now be plotted. We note that the couple of moment 20 kip-ft applied at point D introduces a discontinuity into the bending-moment diagram.

Forces in Beams and Cables 247

PROBLEMS

7.16 through 7.21. Draw the shear and bending-moment diagrams for the beam and loading shown.

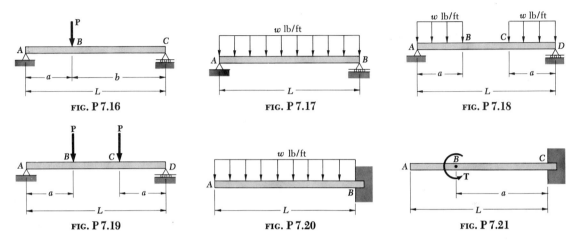

FIG. P 7.16   **FIG. P 7.17**   **FIG. P 7.18**

FIG. P 7.19   **FIG. P 7.20**   **FIG. P 7.21**

7.22 and 7.23. Draw the shear and bending-moment diagrams for the beam *AB*.

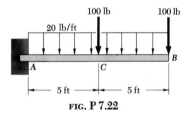

FIG. P 7.22   **FIG. P 7.23**

7.24. Draw the shear and bending-moment diagrams for the beam *AB* if *a* = 6 ft.

7.25. Draw the shear and bending-moment diagrams for the beam *AB* if the magnitude of the upward force **P** is 8 kips.

°7.26. Determine the distance *a* for which the maximum absolute value of the bending moment in the beam is as small as possible.

°7.27. Determine the magnitude of the upward force **P** for which the maximum absolute value of the bending moment in the beam is as small as possible.

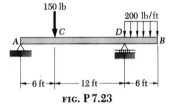

FIG. P 7.24 AND P 7.26

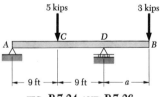

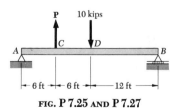

FIG. P 7.25 AND P 7.27

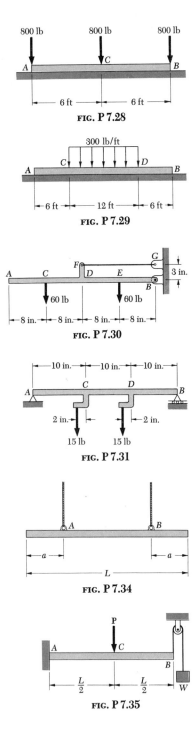

800 lb   800 lb   800 lb

A ‖ C ‖ B

|← 6 ft →|← 6 ft →|

FIG. P 7.28

300 lb/ft

C ↓↓↓↓↓↓↓ D

A ‖ B

|←6 ft→|← 12 ft →|←6 ft→|

FIG. P 7.29

A   C   F‖D   E   G

60 lb   60 lb   3 in. B

|←8 in.→|←8 in.→|←8 in.→|←8 in.→|

FIG. P 7.30

|← 10 in. →|← 10 in. →|← 10 in. →|

A   C   D   B

2 in.   2 in.

15 lb   15 lb

FIG. P 7.31

A   B

|← a →| |← a →|

|← L →|

FIG. P 7.34

P

A   C

B

|← L/2 →|← L/2 →| W

FIG. P 7.35

7.28 and 7.29. Assuming the upward reaction of the ground to be uniformly distributed, draw the shear and bending-moment diagrams for the beam AB.

7.30 and 7.31. Draw the shear and bending-moment diagrams for the beam AB.

7.32. Draw the shear and bending-moment diagrams for the beam and loading of Prob. 6.77.

7.33. Draw the shear and bending-moment diagrams for the beam and loading of Prob. 6.78.

°7.34. A uniform beam (w lb/ft) is to be picked up by crane cables attached at A and B. Determine the distance a from the ends of the beam to the points where the cables should be attached if the maximum absolute value of the bending moment in the beam is to be as small as possible. (*Hint.* Draw the bending-moment diagram in terms of a, L, and w, and then equate the maximum positive and negative bending moments obtained.)

°7.35. In order to reduce the bending moment in the cantilever beam AB, a cable and counterweight are permanently attached at end B. Determine the magnitude of the counterweight for which the maximum absolute value of the bending moment in the beam is as small as possible. (*a*) Consider only the case when the force **P** is actually applied at C. (*b*) Consider the more general case when the force **P** may either be applied at C or removed.

°7.5. Relations between Load, Shear, and Bending Moment. When a beam carries more than two or three concentrated loads, or when it carries distributed loads, the method outlined in Sec. 7.4 for plotting shear and bending moment may prove quite cumbersome. The construction of the shear diagram and, especially, of the bending-moment diagram will be greatly facilitated if certain relations existing between load, shear, and bending moment are taken into consideration.

Let us consider a simply supported beam AB carrying a distributed load w per unit length (Fig. 7.11a), and let C and C' be two points of the beam at a distance Δx from each other. The shear and bending moment at C will be denoted by V and M, respectively, and will be assumed positive; the shear and bending moment at C' will be denoted by $V + \Delta V$ and $M + \Delta M$.

We now shall detach the portion of beam CC' and draw its free-body diagram (Fig. 7.11b). The forces exerted on the free body include a load of magnitude $w\,\Delta x$ and internal forces and couples at C and C'. Since shear and bending moment have been assumed positive, the forces and couples will be directed as shown in the figure.

Relations between Load and Shear. Writing that the sum of the vertical components of the forces acting on the free body CC' is zero, we obtain

$$V - (V + \Delta V) - w\,\Delta x = 0$$
$$\Delta V = -w\,\Delta x$$

Dividing both members of the equation by Δx and then letting Δx approach zero, we obtain

$$\frac{dV}{dx} = -w \tag{7.1}$$

Formula (7.1) indicates that, for a beam loaded as shown in Fig. 7.11a, the slope dV/dx of the shear curve is negative; the numerical value of the slope at any point is equal to the load per unit length at that point.

Integrating (7.1) between points C and D, we obtain

$$V_D - V_C = -\int_{x_C}^{x_D} w\,dx \tag{7.2}$$

$$V_D - V_C = -(\text{area under load curve} \\ \text{between } C \text{ and } D) \tag{7.2'}$$

Note that this result could also have been obtained by considering the equilibrium of the portion of beam CD, since the area under the load curve represents the total load applied between C and D.

It should be observed that formula (7.1) *is not valid* at a point where a concentrated load is applied; the shear curve is discontinuous at such a point, as seen in Sec. 7.4. Similarly, formulas (7.2) and (7.2′) cease to be valid when concentrated loads are applied between C and D, since they do not take into account the sudden change in shear caused by a concentrated load. Formulas (7.2) and (7.2′), therefore, should be applied only between successive concentrated loads.

Relations between Shear and Bending Moment. Returning to the free-body diagram of Fig. 7.11b, and writing now that

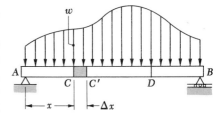

(a)

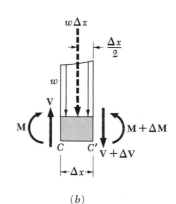

(b)

FIG. 7.11

the sum of the moments about C' is zero, we obtain

$$(M + \Delta M) - M - V\,\Delta x + w\,\Delta x \frac{\Delta x}{2} = 0$$

$$\Delta M = V\,\Delta x - \tfrac{1}{2}w(\Delta x)^2$$

Dividing both members of the equation by Δx and then letting Δx approach zero, we obtain

$$\frac{dM}{dx} = V \tag{7.3}$$

Formula (7.3) indicates that the slope dM/dx of the bending-moment curve is equal to the value of the shear. This is true at any point where the shear has a well-defined value, i.e., at any point where no concentrated load is applied. Formula (7.3) also shows that the shear is zero at points where the bending moment is maximum. This property facilitates the determination of the points where the beam is likely to fail under bending.

Integrating (7.3) between points C and D, we obtain

$$M_D - M_C = \int_{x_C}^{x_D} V\,dx \tag{7.4}$$

$$M_D - M_C = \text{area under shear curve}$$
$$\text{between } C \text{ and } D \tag{7.4'}$$

Note that the area under the shear curve should be considered positive where the shear is positive and negative where the shear is negative. Formulas (7.4) and (7.4') are valid even when concentrated loads are applied between C and D, as long as the shear curve has been correctly drawn. The formulas cease to be valid, however, if a *couple* is applied at a point between C and D, since they do not take into account the sudden change in bending moment caused by a couple (see Sample Prob. 7.7).

Example. Let us consider a simply supported beam AB of span L carrying a uniformly distributed load w (Fig. 7.12a). From the free-body diagram of the entire beam we determine the magnitude of the reactions at the supports: $R_A = R_B = wL/2$ (Fig. 7.12b). Next, we draw the shear diagram. Close to the end A of the beam, the shear is equal to R_A, that is, to $wL/2$, as we may check by considering as a free body a very small portion of the beam. Using formula (7.2), we may then determine the shear V at any distance x from A; we write

$$V - V_A = -\int_0^x w\,dx = -wx$$

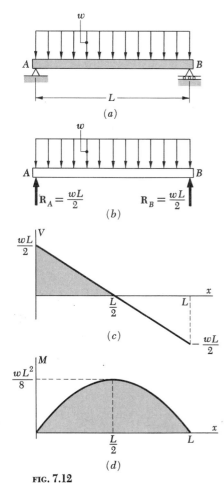

FIG. 7.12

$$V = V_A - wx = \frac{wL}{2} - wx = w\left(\frac{L}{2} - x\right)$$

The shear curve is thus an oblique straight line which crosses the x axis at $x = L/2$ (Fig. 7.12c). Considering, now, the bending moment, we first observe that $M_A = 0$. The value M of the bending moment at any distance x from A may then be obtained from formula (7.4); we have

$$M - M_A = \int_0^x V \, dx$$

$$M = \int_0^x w\left(\frac{L}{2} - x\right) dx = \frac{w}{2}(Lx - x^2)$$

The bending-moment curve is a parabola. The maximum value of the bending moment occurs when $x = L/2$, since V (and thus dM/dx) is zero for that value of x. Substituting $x = L/2$ in the last equation, we obtain $M_{max} = wL^2/8$.

In most engineering applications, the value of the bending moment needs to be known only at a few specific points. Once the shear diagram has been drawn, and after M has been determined at one of the ends of the beam, the value of the bending moment may then be obtained at any given point by computing the area under the shear curve and using formula (7.4'). For instance, since $M_A = 0$ for the beam of Fig. 7.12a, the maximum value of the bending moment for that beam may be obtained simply by measuring the area of the shaded triangle in the shear diagram of Fig. 7.12c. We have

$$M_{max} = \frac{1}{2}\frac{L}{2}\frac{wL}{2} = \frac{wL^2}{8}$$

We note that, in this example, the load curve is a horizontal straight line, the shear curve an oblique straight line, and the bending-moment curve a parabola. If the load curve had been an oblique straight line (first degree), the shear curve would have been a parabola (second degree) and the bending-moment curve a cubic (third degree). The shear and bending-moment curves will always be, respectively, one and two degrees higher than the load curve. With this in mind, we should be able to sketch the shear and bending-moment diagrams without actually determining the functions $V(x)$ and $M(x)$, once a few values of the shear and bending moment have been computed. The sketches obtained will be more accurate if we make use of the fact that, at any point where the curves are continuous, the slope of the shear curve is equal to $-w$ and the slope of the bending-moment curve is equal to V.

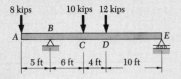

8 kips   10 kips 12 kips

SAMPLE PROBLEM 7.4

Draw the shear and bending-moment diagrams for the beam and loading shown.

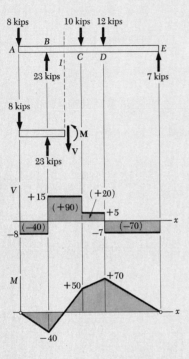

Solution. Considering the entire beam as a free body, we obtain the reactions

$$\mathbf{R}_B = 23 \text{ kips} \uparrow \qquad \mathbf{R}_E = 7 \text{ kips} \uparrow$$

We also note that at both A and E the bending moment is zero; thus two points (indicated by dots) are obtained on the bending-moment diagram.

Shear Diagram. Since $dV/dx = -w$, we find that between loads the slope of the shear diagram is zero (i.e., the shear is constant). The shear at any point is determined by dividing the beam into two parts and considering either part as a free body. For example, using the portion of beam to the left of section 1, we obtain

$$+\uparrow \Sigma F_y = 0: \qquad -8 + 23 - V = 0 \qquad V = +15 \text{ kips}$$

Bending-moment Diagram. We recall that the area under the shear curve between two points is equal to the change in bending moment between the same two points. For convenience, the area of each portion of the shear diagram is computed and is indicated on the diagram. Since the bending moment at the free end M_A is known to be zero, we write

$$M_B - M_A = -40 \qquad M_B = -40 \text{ kip-ft}$$

$$M_C - M_B = +90 \qquad M_C = +50 \text{ kip-ft}$$

$$M_D - M_C = +20 \qquad M_D = +70 \text{ kip-ft}$$

$$M_E - M_D = -70 \qquad M_E = 0$$

Since M_E is known to be zero, a check of the computations is obtained.

The shear being constant between successive loads, the slope dM/dx is constant and the bending-moment diagram is obtained by connecting the known points with straight lines. From the V and M diagrams we note that $V_{\max} = 15$ kips, and $M_{\max} = 70$ kip-ft.

SAMPLE PROBLEM 7.5

Draw the shear and bending-moment diagrams for the beam and loading shown.

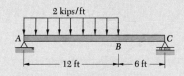

Solution. Considering the entire beam as a free body, we obtain the reactions

$$R_A = 16 \text{ kips} \uparrow \qquad R_C = 8 \text{ kips} \uparrow$$

Shear Diagram. The shear just to the right of A is $V_A = +16$ kips. Since the change in shear between two points is equal to *minus* the area under the load curve between the same two points, we obtain V_B by writing

$$V_B - V_A = -(2)(12) = -24$$

$$V_B = -24 + V_A = -24 + 16 = -8 \text{ kips}$$

The slope $dV/dx = -w$ being constant between A and B, the shear diagram between these two points is represented by a straight line. Between B and C, the area under the load curve is zero; therefore,

$$V_C - V_B = 0 \qquad V_C = V_B = -8 \text{ kips}$$

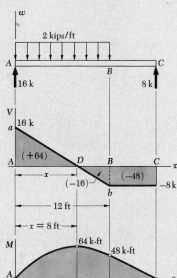

and the shear is constant between B and C.

Bending-moment Diagram. We note that the bending moment at each end of the beam is zero. In order to determine the maximum bending moment, we locate the section D of the beam where $V = 0$. Considering the portion of the shear diagram between A and B, we note that the triangles DAa and DBb are similar; thus,

$$\frac{x}{16 \text{ kips}} = \frac{12 - x}{8 \text{ kips}} \qquad x = 8 \text{ ft}$$

The maximum bending moment occurs at point D, where we have $dM/dx = V = 0$. The areas of the various portions of the shear diagram are computed and are given (in parentheses) on the diagram. Since the area of the shear diagram between two points is equal to the change in bending moment between the same two points, we write

$$M_D - M_A = +64 \text{ kip-ft} \qquad M_D = +64 \text{ kip-ft}$$

$$M_B - M_D = -16 \text{ kip-ft} \qquad M_B = +48 \text{ kip-ft}$$

$$M_C - M_B = -48 \text{ kip-ft} \qquad M_C = 0$$

The bending-moment diagram consists of an arc of parabola followed by a segment of straight line; the slope of the parabola at A is equal to the value of V at that point.

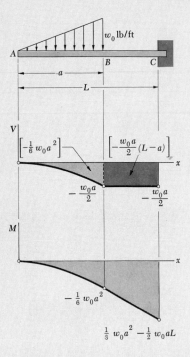

SAMPLE PROBLEM 7.6

Sketch the shear and bending-moment diagrams for the cantilever beam shown.

Solution. *Shear Diagram.* At the free end of the beam, we find $V_A = 0$. Between A and B, the area under the load curve is $\frac{1}{2}w_0 a$; we find V_B by writing

$$V_B - V_A = -\tfrac{1}{2}w_0 a \qquad V_B = -\tfrac{1}{2}w_0 a$$

Between B and C, the beam is not loaded; thus $V_C = V_B$. At A, we have $w = 0$, and therefore $dV/dx = 0$; between A and B, the loading increases linearly, and the shear diagram is parabolic. Between B and C, $w = 0$, and the shear diagram is a horizontal line.

Bending-moment Diagram. The bending moment at the free end of the beam is zero. We compute the area under the shear curve and write

$$M_B - M_A = -\tfrac{1}{6}w_0 a^2 \qquad M_B = -\tfrac{1}{6}w_0 a^2$$

$$M_C - M_B = -\tfrac{1}{2}w_0 a(L - a)$$

$$M_C = \tfrac{1}{3}w_0 a^2 - \tfrac{1}{2}w_0 aL$$

The sketch of the bending-moment diagram is completed by recalling that $dM/dx = V$. We find that between A and B the diagram is represented by a cubic curve and between B and C by a straight line.

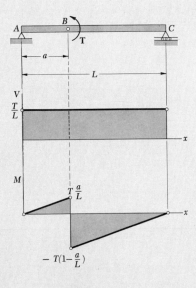

SAMPLE PROBLEM 7.7

The simple beam AC is loaded by a couple of moment T applied at point B. Draw the shear and bending-moment diagrams of the beam.

Solution. The entire beam is taken as a free body, and we obtain

$$\mathbf{R}_A = \frac{T}{L}\uparrow \qquad \mathbf{R}_C = \frac{T}{L}\downarrow$$

The shear at any section is constant and equal to T/L. Since a couple is applied at B, the bending-moment diagram is discontinuous at B; the bending moment decreases suddenly by an amount equal to T.

PROBLEMS

7.36. Using the methods of Sec. 7.5, solve Prob. 7.16.

7.37. Using the methods of Sec. 7.5, solve Prob. 7.17.

7.38. Using the methods of Sec. 7.5, solve Prob. 7.18.

7.39. Using the methods of Sec. 7.5, solve Prob. 7.19.

7.40. Using the methods of Sec. 7.5, solve Prob. 7.20.

7.41. Using the methods of Sec. 7.5, solve Prob. 7.25.

7.42. Using the methods of Sec. 7.5, solve Prob. 7.22.

7.43. Using the methods of Sec. 7.5, solve Prob. 7.23.

7.44. Using the methods of Sec. 7.5, solve Prob. 7.28.

7.45. Using the methods of Sec. 7.5, solve Prob. 7.29.

7.46 through 7.49. Draw the shear and bending-moment diagrams for the beam and loading shown.

7.50 through 7.53. Draw the shear and bending-moment diagrams for the beam and loading shown and determine the location and magnitude of the maximum bending moment.

7.54. Determine the equations of the shear and bending-moment curves for the beam and loading of Prob. 7.20. (Place the origin at point A.)

7.55. Determine the equations of the shear and bending-moment curves for the beam and loading of Prob. 7.17. (Place the origin at point A.)

7.56 and 7.57. Determine the equations of the shear and bending-moment curves for the given beam and loading. Also determine the magnitude and location of the maximum bending moment in the beam.

7.58. The rod AB is acted upon by a uniform downward load and by a uniformly varying upward load. Determine (a) the ratio w_1/w_0 required for equilibrium, (b) the equations of the shear and bending-moment curves, (c) the magnitude and location of the maximum bending moment in the rod.

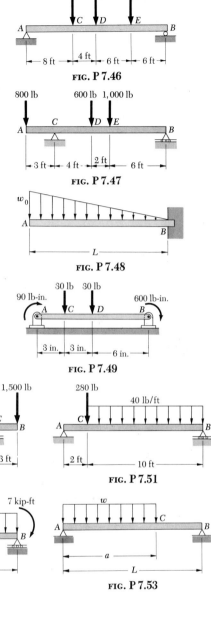

FIG. P 7.46

FIG. P 7.47

FIG. P 7.48

FIG. P 7.49

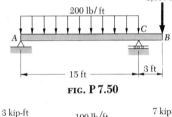

FIG. P 7.50

FIG. P 7.51

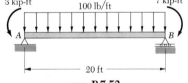

FIG. P 7.52

FIG. P 7.53

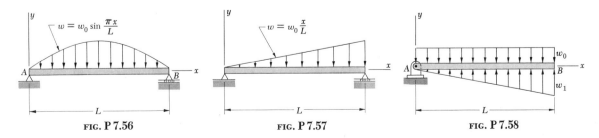

FIG. P 7.56   FIG. P 7.57   FIG. P 7.58

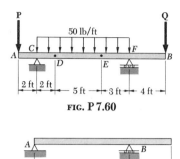

FIG. P 7.60

FIG. P 7.61

7.59. Solve Prob. 7.56 if the given loading is replaced by (a) the loading $w = w_0 \sin \dfrac{2\pi x}{L}$, (b) the loading $w = w_0 \sin \dfrac{n\pi x}{L}$.

*7.60. The beam AB is acted upon by the uniformly distributed load of 50 lb/ft and by two forces **P** and **Q**. It has been experimentally determined that the bending moment is $+200$ lb-ft at point D and $+75$ lb-ft at point E. Draw the shear and bending-moment diagrams for the beam.

*7.61. A uniform beam (w lb/ft) is supported as shown. Determine the distance a if the maximum absolute value of the bending moment is to be as small as possible. (See hint of Prob. 7.34.)

CABLES

*7.6. Cables with Concentrated Loads. Cables are used in many engineering applications, such as suspension bridges, transmission lines, aerial tramways, guy wires for high towers, etc. Cables may be divided into two categories, according to their loading: (1) cables supporting concentrated loads; (2) cables supporting distributed loads. In this section, we shall examine cables of the first category.

Consider a cable attached to two fixed points A and B and supporting n given vertical concentrated loads $\mathbf{P}_1, \mathbf{P}_2, \ldots, \mathbf{P}_n$ (Fig. 7.13a). We assume that the cable is *flexible,* i.e., that its resistance to bending is small and may be neglected. We further assume that the *weight of the cable is negligible* compared with the loads supported by the cable. Any portion of cable between successive loads may therefore be considered as a two-force member, and the internal forces at any point in the cable reduce to a *force of tension directed along the cable.*

We assume that each of the loads lies in a given vertical line, i.e., that the horizontal distance from support A to each of the loads is known; we also assume that the horizontal and vertical distances between the supports are known. We propose to determine the shape of the cable, i.e., the vertical distance from A to each of the points $C_1, C_2, \ldots, C_n$, and also the tension T in each portion of the cable.

We first draw the free-body diagram of the entire cable (Fig. 7.13b). Since the slope of the portions of cable attached at

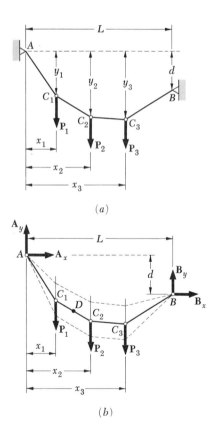

(a)

(b)

FIG. 7.13

A and B is not known, the reactions at A and B must be represented by two components each. Thus, four unknowns are involved, and the three equations of equilibrium are not sufficient to determine the reactions at A and B.† We must therefore obtain an additional equation by considering the equilibrium of a portion of the cable. This is possible if we know the coordinates x and y of a point D of the cable. Drawing the free-body diagram of the portion of cable AD (Fig. 7.14a) and writing $\Sigma M_D = 0$, we obtain an additional relation between the scalar components A_x and A_y and may determine the reactions at A and B. The problem would remain indeterminate, however, if we did not know the coordinates of D, unless some other relation between A_x and A_y (or between B_x and B_y) were given. The cable might hang in any of various possible ways, as indicated by the dashed lines in Fig. 7.13b.

Once A_x and A_y have been determined, the vertical distance from A to any point of the cable may be easily found. Considering point C_2, for example, we draw the free-body diagram of the portion of cable AC_2 (Fig. 7.14b). Writing $\Sigma M_{C_2} = 0$, we obtain an equation which may be solved for y_2. Writing $\Sigma F_x = 0$ and $\Sigma F_y = 0$, we obtain the components of the force **T** representing the tension in the portion of cable to the right of C_2. We observe that $T \cos \theta = A_x$; *the horizontal component of the tension force is the same at any point of the cable.* It follows that the tension T is maximum when $\cos \theta$ is minimum, i.e., in the portion of cable which has the largest angle of inclination θ. Clearly, this portion of cable must be adjacent to one of the two supports of the cable.

*7.7. Cables with Distributed Loads. Consider a cable attached to two fixed points A and B and carrying a *distributed load* (Fig. 7.15a). We saw in the preceding section that, for a cable supporting concentrated loads, the internal force at any point is a force of tension directed along the cable. In the case of a cable carrying a distributed load, the cable hangs in the shape of a curve, and the internal force at a point D is a force of tension **T** *directed along the tangent to the curve.* Given a certain distributed load, we propose in this section to determine the tension at any point of the cable. We shall also see in the following sections how the shape of the cable may be determined for two particular types of distributed loads.

† Clearly, the cable is not a rigid body; the equilibrium equations represent therefore *necessary but not sufficient conditions* (see Sec. 6.12).

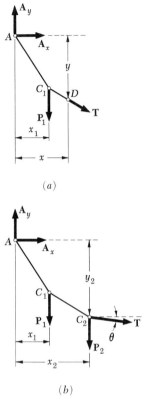

(a)

(b)

FIG. 7.14

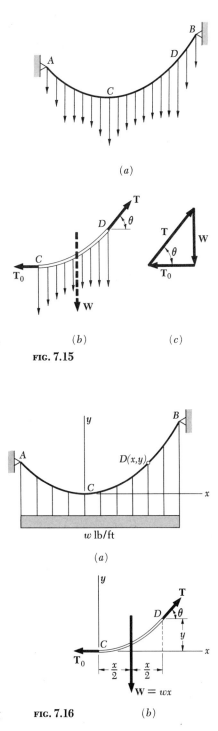

(a)

(b)   (c)

FIG. 7.15

(a)

w lb/ft

FIG. 7.16   (b)

Considering the most general case of distributed load, we draw the free-body diagram of the portion of cable extending from the lowest point C to a given point D of the cable (Fig. 7.15b). The forces acting on the free body are the tension force $\mathbf{T}_0$ at C, which is horizontal, the tension force $\mathbf{T}$ at D, directed along the tangent to the cable at D, and the resultant $\mathbf{W}$ of the distributed load supported by the portion of cable CD. Drawing the corresponding force triangle (Fig. 7.15c), we obtain the following relations:

$$T \cos \theta = T_0 \qquad T \sin \theta = W \qquad (7.5)$$

$$T = \sqrt{T_0^2 + W^2} \qquad \tan \theta = \frac{W}{T_0} \qquad (7.6)$$

From the relations (7.5), it appears that the horizontal component of the tension force $\mathbf{T}$ is the same at any point and that the vertical component of $\mathbf{T}$ is equal to the magnitude W of the load measured from the lowest point. Relations (7.6) show that the tension T is minimum at the lowest point and maximum at one of the two points of support.

*7.8. Parabolic Cable. Let us assume, now, that the cable AB carries a load *uniformly distributed along the horizontal* (Fig. 7.16a). Cables of suspension bridges may be assumed loaded in this way, since the weight of the cables is small compared with the weight of the roadway. Denoting by w the load per unit length (*measured horizontally*) and choosing coordinate axes with origin at the lowest point C of the cable, we find that the magnitude W of the total load carried by the portion of cable extending from C to the point D of coordinates x and y is $W = wx$. The relations (7.6) defining the magnitude and direction of the tension force at D become

$$T = \sqrt{T_0^2 + w^2x^2} \qquad \tan \theta = \frac{wx}{T_0} \qquad (7.7)$$

Moreover, the distance from D to the line of action of the resultant $\mathbf{W}$ is equal to half the horizontal distance from C to D (Fig. 7.16b). Summing moments about D, we write

$$+\!\!\curvearrowleft \ \Sigma M_D = 0: \qquad wx\frac{x}{2} - T_0 y = 0$$

$$y = \frac{wx^2}{2T_0} \qquad (7.8)$$

This is the equation of a *parabola* with a vertical axis and its vertex at the origin of coordinates. The curve formed by

cables loaded uniformly along the horizontal is thus a parabola.†
When the supports A and B of the cable have the same elevation, the distance L between the supports is called the *span* of the cable and the vertical distance h from the supports to the lowest point is called the *sag* of the cable (Fig. 7.17*a*).   If the span and sag of a cable are known, and if the load w per unit horizontal length is given, the minimum tension T_0 may be found by substituting $x = L/2$ and $y = h$ in formula (7.8). Formulas (7.7) and (7.8) will then define the tension at any point and the shape of the cable.

When the supports have different elevations, the position of the lowest point of the cable is not known and the coordinates x_A, y_A and x_B, y_B of the supports must be determined.   To this effect, we express that the coordinates of A and B satisfy Eq. (7.8) and that $x_B - x_A = L$, $y_B - y_A = d$, where L and d denote, respectively, the horizontal and vertical distances between the two supports (Fig. 7.17*b* and *c*).

The length of the cable from its lowest point C to its support B may be obtained from the formula

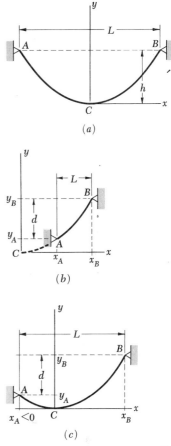

$$s_B = \int_0^{x_B} \sqrt{1 + \left(\frac{dy}{dx}\right)^2}\, dx \qquad (7.9)$$

Differentiating (7.8), we obtain the derivative $dy/dx = wx/T_0$; substituting into (7.9) and using the binomial theorem to expand the radical in an infinite series, we have

$$s_B = \int_0^{x_B} \sqrt{1 + \frac{w^2 x^2}{T_0^2}}\, dx$$

$$= \int_0^{x_B} \left(1 + \frac{w^2 x^2}{2T_0^2} - \frac{w^4 x^4}{8T_0^4} + \cdots\right) dx$$

$$= x_B \left(1 + \frac{w^2 x_B^2}{6T_0^2} - \frac{w^4 x_B^4}{40T_0^4} + \cdots\right)$$

and, since $wx_B^2/2T_0 = y_B$,

$$s_B = x_B \left[1 + \frac{2}{3}\left(\frac{y_B}{x_B}\right)^2 - \frac{2}{5}\left(\frac{y_B}{x_B}\right)^4 + \cdots\right] \qquad (7.10)$$

The series converges for values of the ratio y_B/x_B less than 0.5; in most cases, this ratio is much smaller, and only the first two terms of the series need be computed.

FIG. 7.17

----

† Cables hanging under their own weight are not loaded uniformly along the horizontal, and they do not form a parabola.   The error introduced by assuming a parabolic shape for cables hanging under their own weight, however, is small when the cable is sufficiently taut.   A complete discussion of cables hanging under their own weight is given in the next section.

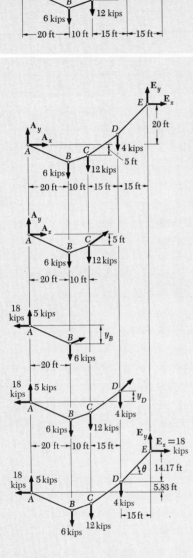

SAMPLE PROBLEM 7.8

The cable AE supports three vertical loads from the points indicated. If point C is 5 ft below the left support, determine (a) the elevations of points B and D, (b) the maximum slope and the maximum tension in the cable.

Solution. The reaction components $\mathbf{A}_x$ and $\mathbf{A}_y$ are determined as follows:

Free body: Entire cable

$$+\circlearrowleft \ \Sigma M_E = 0:$$

$$A_x(20 \text{ ft}) - A_y(60 \text{ ft}) + (6 \text{ kips})(40 \text{ ft})$$
$$+ (12 \text{ kips})(30 \text{ ft}) + (4 \text{ kips})(15 \text{ ft}) = 0$$

$$20A_x - 60A_y + 660 = 0$$

Free body: ABC

$$+\circlearrowleft \ \Sigma M_C = 0: \qquad -A_x(5 \text{ ft}) - A_y(30 \text{ ft}) + (6 \text{ kips})(10 \text{ ft}) = 0$$

$$-5A_x - 30A_y + 60 = 0$$

Solving the two equations simultaneously, we obtain

$$A_x = -18 \text{ kips} \qquad \mathbf{A}_x = 18 \text{ kips} \leftarrow$$
$$A_y = +5 \text{ kips} \qquad \mathbf{A}_y = 5 \text{ kips} \uparrow$$

a. **Elevation of Point** B. Considering the portion of cable AB *as a free body*, we write

$$+\circlearrowleft \ \Sigma M_B = 0: \qquad (18 \text{ kips})y_B - (5 \text{ kips})(20 \text{ ft}) = 0$$
$$y_B = 5.56 \text{ ft} \qquad \text{below } A \ \blacktriangleleft$$

Elevation of Point D. Using the portion of cable $ABCD$ *as a free body*, we write

$$+\circlearrowleft \ \Sigma M_D = 0:$$

$$-(18 \text{ kips})y_D - (5 \text{ kips})(45 \text{ ft}) + (6 \text{ kips})(25 \text{ ft}) + (12 \text{ kips})(15 \text{ ft}) = 0$$
$$y_D = 5.83 \text{ ft} \qquad \text{above } A \ \blacktriangleleft$$

b. **Maximum Slope and Maximum Tension.** We observe that the maximum slope occurs in portion DE. Since the horizontal component of the tension is constant and equal to 18 kips, we write

$$\tan \theta = \frac{14.17 \text{ ft}}{15 \text{ ft}} \qquad\qquad \theta = 43.4° \ \blacktriangleleft$$

$$T_{\max} = \frac{18 \text{ kips}}{\cos \theta} \qquad\qquad T_{\max} = 24.8 \text{ kips} \ \blacktriangleleft$$

SAMPLE PROBLEM 7.9

A light cable weighing 40 lb is attached to a support at A, passes over a small pulley at B, and supports a load P. Knowing that the sag of the cable is 1 ft, determine (a) the load P, (b) the slope of the cable at B, and (c) the total length of the cable from A to B. Since the ratio of the sag to the span is small, assume the cable to be parabolic. Also neglect the weight of the portion of cable from B to P.

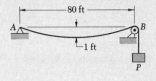

a. **Load P.** We denote by C the lowest point of the cable and draw the free-body diagram of the portion CB of cable. The weight **W** of the portion CB may be applied halfway between C and B since the load is assumed to be uniformly distributed along the horizontal. Summing moments about B, we write

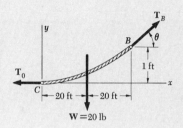

$$+ \textstyle\bigcirc\,\, \Sigma M_B = 0: \quad (20\ \text{lb})(20\ \text{ft}) - T_0(1\ \text{ft}) = 0 \quad T_0 = 400\ \text{lb}$$

From the force triangle we obtain

$$T_B = \sqrt{T_0^2 + W^2}$$
$$= \sqrt{(400\ \text{lb})^2 + (20\ \text{lb})^2} = 400.5\ \text{lb}$$

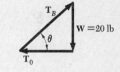

Since the tension on each side of the pulley is the same, we find

$$P = T_B = 400.5\ \text{lb} \quad \blacktriangleleft$$

b. **Slope of Cable at B.** We also obtain from the force triangle

$$\tan \theta = \frac{W}{T_0} = \frac{20\ \text{lb}}{400\ \text{lb}} = 0.05$$

$$\theta = 2.9° \quad \blacktriangleleft$$

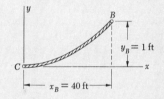

c. **Length of Cable.** Applying Eq. (7.10) between C and B, we write

$$s_B = x_B \left[1 + \frac{2}{3}\left(\frac{y_B}{x_B}\right)^2 + \cdots \right]$$

$$= 40\left[1 + (\tfrac{2}{3})(\tfrac{1}{40})^2 + \cdots \right] = 40.0167\ \text{ft}$$

The total length of the cable between A and B is twice this value,

$$\text{Length} = 2s_B = 80.033\ \text{ft} \quad \blacktriangleleft$$

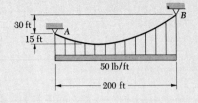

30 ft

15 ft

A

B

50 lb/ft

200 ft

SAMPLE PROBLEM 7.10

Cable *AB* supports a load distributed uniformly along the horizontal as shown. The lowest point of the cable is 15 ft below the support *A*. Determine the maximum and minimum values of the tension in the cable.

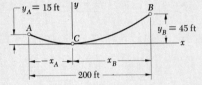

$y_A = 15$ ft

A

C

B

$y_B = 45$ ft

$-x_A$

x_B

200 ft

Solution. Since the load is distributed uniformly along the horizontal, the cable is parabolic; choosing the origin of coordinates at the lowest point *C*, the equation of the cable is given by Eq. (7.8),

$$y = \frac{wx^2}{2T_0} \qquad (1)$$

From the geometry of the sketch, we note that x_A is negative as drawn and write

$$y_A = 15 \text{ ft} \qquad y_B = 45 \text{ ft}$$

$$x_B - x_A = 200 \text{ ft} \qquad \text{or} \qquad x_A = x_B - 200 \text{ ft}$$

Substituting successively the coordinates of *A* and *B* into Eq. (1), we obtain

Point *A*: $\qquad y_A = \frac{wx_A^2}{2T_0} \qquad 15 = \frac{w(x_B - 200)^2}{2T_0} \qquad (2)$

Point *B*: $\qquad y_B = \frac{wx_B^2}{2T_0} \qquad 45 = \frac{wx_B^2}{2T_0} \qquad (3)$

Dividing (2) by (3) member by member and solving for x_B, we obtain

$$\frac{15}{45} = \frac{(x_B - 200)^2}{x_B^2}$$

$$x_B = 473 \text{ ft} \qquad \text{and} \qquad x_B = 126.8 \text{ ft}$$

The first root is discarded since it is larger than 200 ft.

Minimum Tension. The minimum tension occurs at *C* and equals T_0. Substituting the computed coordinates of point *B* into Eq. (1), we find

$$y = \frac{wx^2}{2T_0} \qquad 45 = \frac{(50)(126.8)^2}{2T_0} \qquad T_0 = 8{,}930 \text{ lb} \quad \blacktriangleleft$$

Maximum Tension. Since the slope is maximum at *B*, the maximum tension T_{max} occurs at *B*. Substituting the coordinates of *B* into Eq. (7.7), we find

$$T_{max} = \sqrt{T_0^2 + w^2x^2} = \sqrt{(8{,}930)^2 + (50)^2(126.8)^2}$$

$$T_{max} = 10{,}950 \text{ lb} \quad \blacktriangleleft$$

PROBLEMS

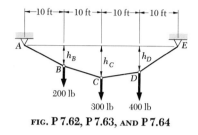

7.62. Three loads are suspended as shown from the cable. Knowing that $h_C = 6$ ft, determine (a) the components of the reaction at A, (b) the sag at points B and D.

7.63. Three loads are suspended as shown from the cable. Knowing that $h_C = 8$ ft, determine (a) the components of the reaction at E, (b) the maximum value of the tension in the cable.

FIG. P 7.62, P 7.63, AND P 7.64

7.64. Determine the sag at point C if the maximum tension in the cable is 1,300 lb.

7.65. If $a = 8$ ft and $b = 9$ ft, determine the components of the reaction at E for the cable and loading shown.

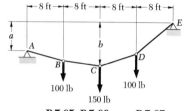

7.66. If $a = b = 5$ ft, determine the components of the reaction at E and the maximum tension in the cable.

FIG. P 7.65, P 7.66, AND P 7.67

7.67. Determine the distance a if the portion BC of the cable is horizontal and if the maximum tension in the cable is 650 lb.

7.68. The center span of the George Washington Bridge, as originally constructed, consisted of a uniform roadway suspended from four cables. The uniform load supported by each cable was $w = 9.75$ kips/ft along the horizontal. Knowing that the span L is 3,500 ft and that the sag h is 316 ft, determine the maximum and minimum tension in each cable.

7.69. Determine the length of each of the cables used in the center span of the George Washington Bridge. (See Prob. 7.68 for data.)

7.70. Two cables of the same gage are attached to a transmission tower at B. Since the tower is slender, the horizontal component of the resultant of the forces exerted by the cables at B is to be zero. Assuming the cables to be parabolic, determine the required sag h of cable AB.

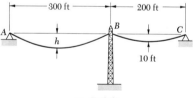

7.71. An electric wire, weighing 0.20 lb/ft, is strung between two insulators at the same elevation and 100 ft apart. If the maximum tension in the wire is to be 80 lb, determine the smallest value of the sag which may be used. (Assume the wire to be parabolic.)

FIG. P 7.70

7.72. Knowing that a 102-ft length of wire was used in spanning a horizontal distance of 100 ft, determine the approximate sag of the wire. Assume the wire to be parabolic. (*Hint.* Use only the first two terms of Eq. 7.10.)

7.73. A cable of length $L + \Delta$ is suspended between two points which are at the same elevation and a distance L apart.   (*a*) Assuming that Δ is small compared to L and that the cable is parabolic, determine the approximate sag in terms of L and Δ.   (*b*) If $L = 100$ ft and $\Delta = 4$ ft, determine the approximate sag.   (*Hint.*   Use only the first two terms of Eq. 7.10.)

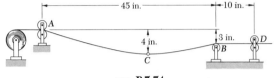

FIG. P 7.74

7.74. Before being fed into a printing press located to the right of D, a continuous sheet of paper weighing 0.20 lb/ft passes over rollers at A and B.   Assuming that the curve formed by the sheet is parabolic, determine the location of the lowest point C and the maximum tension in the sheet.

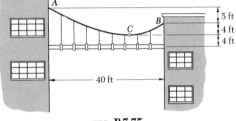

FIG. P 7.75

7.75. A steam pipe weighing 45 lb/ft, which passes between two buildings 40 ft apart, is supported by a system of cables as shown.   Assuming that the weight of the cable system is equivalent to a uniformly distributed loading of 5 lb/ft, determine the location of the lowest point C of the cable and the maximum cable tension.

°**7.76.** The total weight of cable AC is 60 lb.   Assuming that the weight of the cable is distributed uniformly along the horizontal, determine the sag h and the slope of the cable at A and C.

7.77. The loading of a cable varies linearly from zero at the lowest point to w_0 at each support.   Determine the equation of the curve assumed by each half of the cable and the tension at the center line.

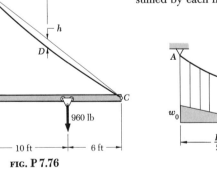

FIG. P 7.76

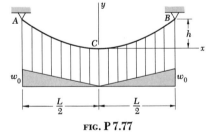

FIG. P 7.77

7.78. Solve Prob. 7.77 assuming that the distributed loading varies uniformly from zero at each end to a maximum value of w_0 at the center line.

°7.79. A cable *AB* of span *L* and a simple beam *A'B'* of the same span are subjected to identical vertical loadings as shown. Show that the magnitude of the bending moment at a point *C'* in the beam is equal to the product T_0h, where T_0 is the magnitude of the horizontal component of the tension force in the cable and *h* is the vertical distance between point *C* of the cable and the chord joining the points of support *A* and *B*.

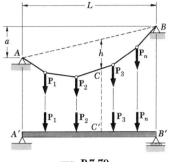

°7.80. Show that the curve assumed by a cable carrying a distributed load *w(x)* is defined by the differential equation $d^2y/dx^2 = w(x)/T_0$, where T_0 is the tension at the lowest point.

FIG. P 7.79

°7.81. Using the property indicated in Prob. 7.80, determine the curve assumed by a cable of span *L* and sag *h* carrying a distributed load $w = w_0 \cos(\pi x/L)$, where *x* is measured from mid-span. Also determine the maximum and minimum values of the tension.

°7.82. A large number of ropes are tied to a light wire which is suspended from two points *A* and *B* at the same level. Show that, if the lower ends of the ropes have been cut so that they lie in the same horizontal line, and if the ropes are kept uniformly spaced, the curve assumed by the wire *ACB* is

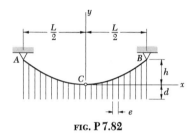

FIG. P 7.82

$$y + d = d \cosh(w_r/T_0 e)^{\frac{1}{2}} x$$

where w_r is the weight per unit length of the ropes, *d* is the length of the shortest rope, and *e* is the horizontal distance between adjacent ropes. (*Hint.* Use the property indicated in Prob. 7.80.)

°7.83. If the weight per unit length of the cable *AB* is $w_0/\cos^2\theta$, prove that the curve formed by the cable is a circular arc. (*Hint.* Use the property indicated in Prob. 7.80.)

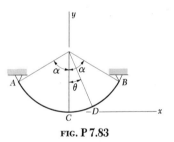

FIG. P 7.83

°7.9. Catenary. We shall consider now a cable *AB* carrying a load *uniformly distributed along the cable itself* (Fig. 7.18a). Cables hanging under their own weight are loaded in this way. Denoting by *w* the load per unit length (*measured along the cable*), we find that the magnitude *W* of the total load carried by a portion of cable of length *s* extending from the lowest point *C* to a point *D* is *W = ws*. Substituting this value for *W* in formula (7.6), we obtain the tension at *D*,

$$T = \sqrt{T_0^2 + w^2s^2}$$

In order to simplify the subsequent computations, we shall introduce the constant $c = T_0/w$. We thus write

$$T_0 = wc \qquad W = ws \qquad T = w\sqrt{c^2 + s^2} \qquad (7.11)$$

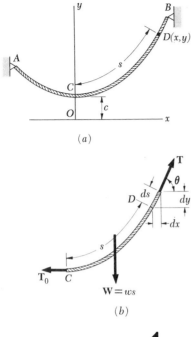

(a)

(b)

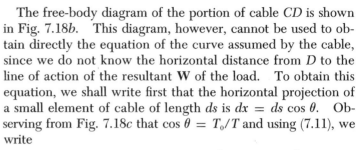

(c)

FIG. 7.18

The free-body diagram of the portion of cable CD is shown in Fig. 7.18b.   This diagram, however, cannot be used to obtain directly the equation of the curve assumed by the cable, since we do not know the horizontal distance from D to the line of action of the resultant $\mathbf{W}$ of the load.   To obtain this equation, we shall write first that the horizontal projection of a small element of cable of length ds is $dx = ds \cos \theta$.   Observing from Fig. 7.18c that $\cos \theta = T_0/T$ and using (7.11), we write

$$dx = ds \cos \theta = \frac{T_0}{T}\, ds = \frac{wc\, ds}{w\sqrt{c^2 + s^2}} = \frac{ds}{\sqrt{1 + s^2/c^2}}$$

Selecting the origin O of the coordinates at a distance c directly below C (Fig. 7.18a) and integrating from $C(0,c)$ to $D(x,y)$, we obtain†

$$x = \int_0^s \frac{ds}{\sqrt{1 + s^2/c^2}} = c\left[\sinh^{-1} \frac{s}{c} \right]_0^s = c \sinh^{-1} \frac{s}{c}$$

This equation, which relates the length s of the portion of cable CD and the horizontal distance x, may be written in the form

$$s = c \sinh \frac{x}{c} \tag{7.15}$$

The relation between the coordinates x and y may now be obtained by writing $dy = dx \tan \theta$.   Observing from Fig. 7.18c that $\tan \theta = W/T_0$ and using (7.11) and (7.15), we write

$$dy = dx \tan \theta = \frac{W}{T_0}\, dx = \frac{s}{c}\, dx = \sinh \frac{x}{c}\, dx$$

† This integral may be found in all standard integral tables.   The function

$$z = \sinh^{-1} u$$

(read "arc hyperbolic sine u") is the *inverse* of the function $u = \sinh z$ (read "hyperbolic sine z").   This function and the function $v = \cosh z$ (read "hyperbolic cosine z") are defined as follows:

$$u = \sinh z = \tfrac{1}{2}(e^z - e^{-z}) \qquad v = \cosh z = \tfrac{1}{2}(e^z + e^{-z})$$

Numerical values of these functions are found in *tables of hyperbolic functions*. The student is referred to any calculus text for a complete description of the properties of these functions.   In this section, we shall make use only of the following properties, which may be easily derived from the above definitions:

$$\frac{d \sinh z}{dz} = \cosh z \qquad \frac{d \cosh z}{dz} = \sinh z \tag{7.12}$$

$$\sinh 0 = 0 \qquad \cosh 0 = 1 \tag{7.13}$$

$$\cosh^2 z - \sinh^2 z = 1 \tag{7.14}$$

Integrating from $C(0,c)$ to $D(x,y)$ and using (7.12) and (7.13), we obtain

$$y - c = \int_0^x \sinh \frac{x}{c}\, dx = c \left[\cosh \frac{x}{c} \right]_0^x = c \left(\cosh \frac{x}{c} - 1 \right)$$

$$y = c \cosh \frac{x}{c} \qquad (7.16)$$

This is the equation of a *catenary* with vertical axis. The ordinate c of the lowest point C is called the *parameter* of the catenary. Squaring both sides of Eqs. (7.15) and (7.16), subtracting, and taking (7.14) into account, we obtain the following relation between y and s:

$$y^2 - s^2 = c^2 \qquad (7.17)$$

Solving (7.17) for s^2 and carrying into the last of the relations (7.11), we write these relations as follows:

$$T_0 = wc \qquad W = ws \qquad T = wy \qquad (7.18)$$

The last relation indicates that the tension at any point D of the cable is proportional to the vertical distance from D to the horizontal line representing the x axis.

When the supports A and B of the cable have the same elevation, the distance L between the supports is called the *span* of the cable and the vertical distance h from the supports to the lowest point C is called the *sag* of the cable. These definitions are the same that were given in the case of parabolic cables, but it should be noted that, because of our choice of coordinate axes, the sag h is now

$$h = y_A - c \qquad (7.19)$$

It should also be observed that certain catenary problems involve transcendental equations which must be solved by successive approximations (see Sample Prob. 7.11). When the cable is fairly taut, however, the load may be assumed uniformly distributed *along the horizontal* and the catenary may be replaced by a parabola. The solution of the problem is thus greatly simplified, while the error introduced is small.

When the supports A and B have different elevations, the position of the lowest point of the cable is not known. The problem may be solved then in a manner similar to that used for parabolic cables, by expressing that the cable must pass through the supports and that $x_B - x_A = L$, $y_B - y_A = d$, where L and d denote, respectively, the horizontal and vertical distances between the two supports.

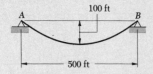

SAMPLE PROBLEM 7.11

A uniform cable weighing 3 lb/ft is suspended between two points A and B as shown. Determine (a) the maximum and minimum values of the tension in the cable, (b) the length of the cable.

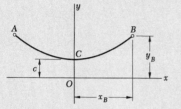

Solution. Equation of Cable. The origin of coordinates is placed at a distance c below the lowest point of the cable. The equation of the cable is given by Eq. (7.16),

$$y = c \cosh \frac{x}{c}$$

The coordinates of point B are

$$x_B = 250 \text{ ft} \qquad y_B = 100 + c$$

Substituting these coordinates into the equation of the cable, we obtain

$$100 + c = c \cosh \frac{250}{c}$$

$$\frac{100}{c} + 1 = \cosh \frac{250}{c}$$

The value of c is determined by assuming successive trial values, as shown in the following table:

c	$\dfrac{250}{c}$	$\dfrac{100}{c}$	$\dfrac{100}{c} + 1$	$\cosh \dfrac{250}{c}$
300	0.833	0.333	1.333	1.367
350	0.714	0.286	1.286	1.266
330	0.758	0.303	1.303	1.301
328	0.762	0.305	1.305	1.305

Taking $c = 328$, we have

$$y_B = 100 + c = 428 \text{ ft}$$

a. Maximum and Minimum Values of the Tension. Using Eqs. (7.18), we obtain

$$T_{\min} = T_0 = wc = (3 \text{ lb/ft})(328 \text{ ft}) \qquad T_{\min} = 984 \text{ lb} \quad \blacktriangleleft$$

$$T_{\max} = T_B = wy_B = (3 \text{ lb/ft})(428 \text{ ft}) \qquad T_{\max} = 1{,}284 \text{ lb} \quad \blacktriangleleft$$

b. Length of Cable. One-half the length of the cable is found by solving Eq. (7.17),

$$y_B^2 - s_{CB}^2 = c^2 \qquad s_{CB}^2 = y_B^2 - c^2 = (428)^2 - (328)^2 \qquad s_{CB} = 275 \text{ ft}$$

The total length of the cable is therefore

$$s_{AB} = 2s_{CB} = 2(275 \text{ ft}) \qquad s_{AB} = 550 \text{ ft} \quad \blacktriangleleft$$

PROBLEMS

7.84. An aerial tramway cable of length 600 ft and weighing 3.0 lb/ft is suspended between two points at the same elevation. Knowing that the sag is 150 ft, find the horizontal distance between supports and the maximum tension.

7.85. A 100-ft rope is strung between the roofs of two buildings, each of height 30 ft. The maximum tension is found to be 50 lb and the lowest point of the cable is observed to be 10 ft above the ground. Determine the horizontal distance between the buildings and the total weight of the rope.

7.86. A 200-ft steel surveying tape weighs 4 lb. If the tape is stretched between two points at the same elevation and pulled until the tension at each end is 16 lb, determine the horizontal distance between the ends of the tape. Neglect the elongation of the tape due to the tension.

7.87. A copper transmission wire weighs 0.50 lb/ft and is attached to two insulators at the same elevation and 300 ft apart. It has been established that the horizontal component of the tension in the wire must be 175 lb if the insulators are not to be bent. Determine (*a*) the length of cable which should be used, (*b*) the resulting sag, (*c*) the resulting maximum tension.

7.88. A tramway wire rope weighing 3.4 lb/ft is suspended across a canyon; it is attached to two supports at the same elevation and 600 ft apart. Knowing that the sag is 80 ft, determine the total length of the cable and the maximum tension.

7.89. A 400-lb counterweight is attached to a cable which passes over a small pulley at *A* and is attached to a support at *B*. If the sag is 10 ft, determine (*a*) the length of the cable from *A* to *B*, (*b*) the weight per unit length of the cable. Neglect the weight of the cable from *A* to *D*.

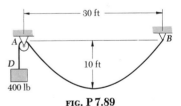

FIG. P 7.89

7.90. A chain of length 20 ft and total weight 40 lb is suspended between two points at the same elevation and 10 ft apart. Determine the sag and the maximum tension.

7.91. A 150-ft wire is suspended between two points at the same elevation and 100 ft apart. Knowing that the maximum tension is 30 lb, determine the sag and the total weight of the wire.

*7.92. Solve Prob. 7.74 assuming that the curve formed by the sheet of paper is a catenary.

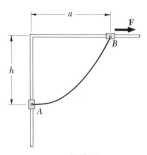

FIG. P 7.93

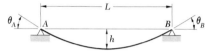

FIG. P 7.96, P 7.97, AND P 7.98

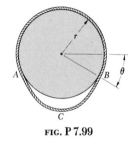

FIG. P 7.99

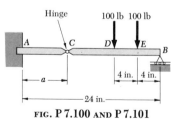

Hinge   100 lb 100 lb

FIG. P 7.100 AND P 7.101

°**7.93.** The 10-ft cable AB weighs 20 lb and is attached to collars at A and B which may slide freely on the rods shown. Neglecting the weight of the collars, determine (a) the magnitude of the horizontal force F so that $h = a$, (b) the corresponding value of h and a, (c) the maximum tension in the cable.

7.94. Denoting by θ the angle formed by a uniform cable and the horizontal, show that at any point $y = c/\cos\theta$.

°**7.95.** (a) Determine the maximum allowable horizontal span for a uniform cable of weight w per unit length if the tension in the cable is not to exceed the value T_m. (b) Using the result of part a, find the maximum span of a drawn-steel wire for which $w = 0.2$ lb/ft and $T_m = 6{,}000$ lb.

°**7.96.** A chain weighs 4 lb/ft and is supported as shown. Knowing that the span L is 24 ft, determine the *two* values of the sag h for which the maximum tension is 150 lb.

°**7.97.** Determine the sag-to-span ratio for which the maximum tension in the cable is equal to the total weight of the entire cable AB.

°**7.98.** A cable, of weight w per unit length, is suspended between two points at the same elevation and a distance L apart. Determine the sag-to-span ratio for which the maximum tension is as small as possible. What are the corresponding values of θ_B and T_m?

°**7.99.** A cable, of weight w per unit length, is looped over a cylinder and is in contact with the cylinder above points A and B. Knowing that $\theta = 30°$, determine (a) the length of the cable, (b) the tension in the cable at C. (*Hint.* Use the property indicated in Prob. 7.94.)

REVIEW PROBLEMS

7.100. Draw the shear and bending-moment diagrams for the beam and loading shown when $a = 4$ in.

7.101. Determine the distance a for which the maximum absolute value of the bending moment is as small as possible.

7.102. A $\frac{1}{2}$-in.-diameter wire rope weighing 0.40 lb/ft is suspended from two supports at the same elevation and 200 ft apart. If the sag is 50 ft, determine (a) the total length of the cable, (b) the maximum tension.

7.103. Concrete piles are designed primarily to resist axial loads, and their bending resistance is relatively small.   To lessen the possibility of breaking them, piles are often lifted at several points along their length. By using the arrangement shown, the concrete pile *AB* is lifted by four equal forces applied at points *C, D, E,* and *F.*   If the total weight of the pile is 16,000 lb, draw the shear and bending-moment diagrams of the pile.   Assume the weight of the pile to be uniformly distributed.

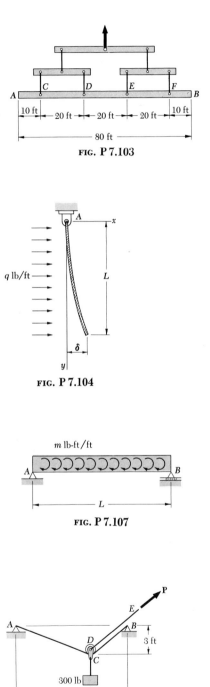

FIG. P 7.103

7.104. A heavy cable of length *L* weighs *w* lb/ft and is suspended from a support at *A.*   Wind blowing on the cable exerts a loading of *q* lb/ft distributed uniformly along the vertical.   Knowing that *q* is small compared to *w*, determine the equation of the curve formed by the cable.

7.105. The axis of the curved member shown is a parabola with vertex at *A.*   If a vertical load **P** of magnitude 600 lb is applied at *A*, determine the internal forces at *J*, when $h = 9$ in., $L = 30$ in., and $a = 20$ in.

FIG. P 7.104

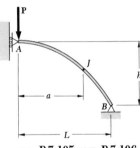

FIG. P 7.105 AND P 7.106

7.106. The axis of the curved member shown is a parabola with vertex at *A.*   Knowing that a vertical load **P** is applied at *A*, determine the magnitude and location of the maximum bending moment.

FIG. P 7.107

7.107. A beam *AB* is loaded by couples spaced uniformly along its length.   Assuming that the couples may be represented by a uniformly distributed couple loading of *m* lb-ft/ft, draw the shear and bending-moment diagrams for the beam when it is supported (*a*) as shown, (*b*) as a cantilever with a fixed support at *A* and no support at *B*.

7.108. A 300-pound load is attached to a small pulley which may roll on the cable *ACB*.   The pulley and load are held in the position shown by a second cable *DE* which is parallel to the portion *CB* of the main cable.   Determine (*a*) the reactions at *A* and *B*, (*b*) the tension in cable *ACB*, (*c*) the tension in cable *DE*.   Neglect the radius of the pulleys and the weight of the cables.

FIG. P 7.108

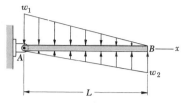

FIG. P 7.109

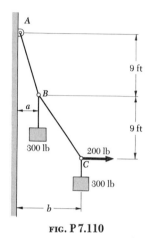

FIG. P 7.110

7.109. The rod AB is attached to a hinge at A and is free at B. Determine (*a*) the ratio of w_2 to w_1 for which the rod is in equilibrium, (*b*) the equations of the shear and bending-moment curves for the rod, (*c*) the magnitude and location of the maximum bending moment.

7.110. Cable ABC supports two 300-lb loads as shown. Determine the distances a and b when a 200-lb horizontal load is applied at C. Neglect the weight of the cable.

*7.111. Determine the magnitude and location of the maximum bending moment for the rod of Prob. 5.23. (Choose OB as a reference axis for θ.)

8. FRICTION

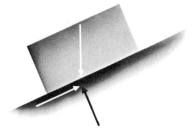

8.1. Introduction. In the preceding chapters, it was assumed that surfaces in contact were either *smooth* or *rough*. If they were smooth, it was assumed that the force each surface exerted on the other was normal to the surfaces and that the two surfaces could move freely with respect to each other. If they were rough, it was assumed that tangential forces could develop to prevent the motion of one surface with respect to the other.

This view was a simplified one. Actually, no perfectly smooth surface exists. When two surfaces are in contact, tangential forces, called *friction forces*, will always develop if one attempts to move one surface with respect to the other. On the other hand, these friction forces are limited in magnitude and will not prevent motion if sufficiently large forces are applied. The distinction between smooth and rough surfaces is thus a matter of degree. This will be seen more clearly in the present chapter, which is devoted to the study of friction and of its applications to common engineering situations.

There are two types of friction: *dry friction,* sometimes called *Coulomb friction,* and *fluid friction.* Fluid friction develops between layers of fluid moving at different velocities. Fluid friction is of great importance in problems involving the flow of fluids through pipes and orifices or dealing with bodies immersed in moving fluids. It is also basic in the analysis of the motion of *lubricated mechanisms.* Such problems are considered in texts on fluid mechanics. We shall limit our present study to dry friction, i.e., to problems involving rigid bodies which are in contact along *nonlubricated* surfaces.

8.2. The Laws of Dry Friction. Coefficients of Friction. The laws of dry friction are best understood by the following experiment. A block of weight W is placed on a horizontal plane surface (Fig. 8.1*a*). The forces acting on the block are

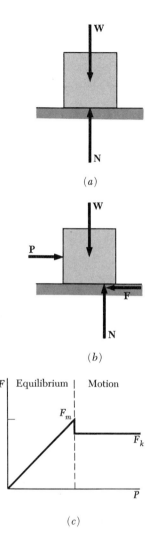

FIG. 8.1

its weight **W** and the reaction of the surface. Since the weight has no horizontal component, the reaction of the surface also has no horizontal component; the reaction is therefore *normal* to the surface and is represented by **N** in Fig. 8.1*a*. Suppose, now, that a horizontal force **P** is applied to the block (Fig. 8.1*b*). If **P** is small, the block will not move; some other horizontal force must therefore exist, which balances **P**. This other force is the *static-friction force* **F**, which is actually the resultant of a great number of forces acting over the entire surface of contact between the block and the plane. The nature of these forces is not known exactly, but it is generally assumed that these forces are due to the irregularities of the surfaces in contact and also, to a certain extent, to molecular attraction.

If the force **P** is increased, the friction force **F** also increases, continuing to oppose **P**, until its magnitude reaches a certain *maximum value* F_m (Fig. 8.1*c*). If **P** is further increased, the friction force cannot balance it any more and the block starts sliding. As soon as the block has been set in motion, the magnitude of **F** drops from F_m to a lower value F_k. This is because there is less interpenetration between the irregularities of the surfaces in contact when these surfaces move with respect to each other. From then on, the block keeps sliding with increasing velocity while the friction force, denoted by F_k and called the *kinetic-friction force*, remains approximately constant.

Experimental evidence shows that the maximum value F_m of the static-friction force is proportional to the normal component N of the reaction of the surface. We have

$$F_m = \mu_s N \tag{8.1}$$

where μ_s is a constant called the *coefficient of static friction*. Similarly, the magnitude F_k of the kinetic-friction force may be put in the form

$$F_k = \mu_k N \tag{8.2}$$

where μ_k is a constant called the *coefficient of kinetic friction*. The coefficients of friction μ_s and μ_k do not depend upon the area of the surfaces in contact. Both coefficients, however, depend strongly on the *nature* of the surfaces in contact. Since they also depend upon the exact condition of the surfaces, their value is seldom known with an accuracy greater than 5 per cent. Approximate values of coefficients of static friction are given in Table 8.1 for various dry surfaces. The corresponding values of the coefficient of kinetic friction would be about 25 per cent smaller.

Metal on metal	0.15–0.60
Metal on wood	0.20–0.60
Metal on stone	0.30–0.70
Metal on leather	0.30–0.60
Wood on wood	0.25–0.50
Wood on leather	0.25–0.50
Stone on stone	0.40–0.70
Earth on earth	0.20–1.00
Rubber on concrete	0.60–0.90

TABLE 8.1. *Approximate Values of Coefficient of Static Friction for Dry Surfaces*

From the description given above, it appears that four different situations may occur when a rigid body is in contact with a horizontal surface:

1. The forces applied to the body do not tend to move it along the surface of contact; there is no friction force (Fig. 8.2a).

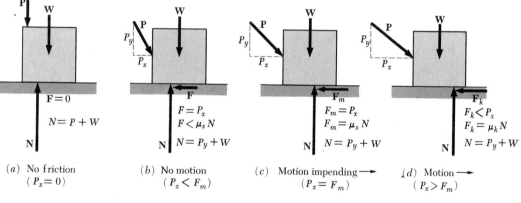

(a) No friction
($P_x = 0$)

(b) No motion
($P_x < F_m$)

(c) Motion impending →
($P_x = F_m$)

(d) Motion →
($P_x > F_m$)

FIG. 8.2

2. The applied forces tend to move the body along the surface of contact but are not large enough to set it in motion. The friction force **F** which has developed may be found by solving the equations of equilibrium for the body.   Since there is no evidence that the maximum value of the static-friction force has been reached, the equation $F_m = \mu_s N$ *cannot be used* to determine the friction force (Fig. 8.2b).

3. The applied forces are such that the body is just about to slide.   We say that *motion is impending*.   The friction force **F** has reached its maximum value F_m and, together with the normal force **N**, balances the applied forces.   Both the equa-

tions of equilibrium and the equation $F_m = \mu_s N$ *may be used.* We also note that the friction force has a sense opposite to the sense of impending motion (Fig. 8.2c).

4. The body is sliding under the action of the applied forces, and the equations of equilibrium do not apply any more. However, **F** is now equal to the kinetic-friction force $\mathbf{F}_k$ and the equation $F_k = \mu_k N$ may be used. The sense of $\mathbf{F}_k$ is opposite to the sense of motion (Fig. 8.2d).

8.3. Angles of Friction. It is sometimes found convenient to replace the normal force **N** and the friction force **F** by their resultant **R**. Let us consider again a block of weight **W** resting on a horizontal plane surface. If no horizontal force is applied to the block, the resultant **R** reduces to the normal force **N** (Fig. 8.3a). However, if the applied force **P** has a horizon-

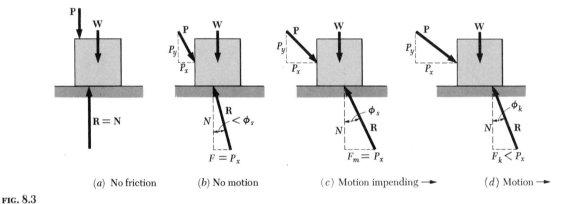

| (a) No friction | (b) No motion | (c) Motion impending → | (d) Motion → |

FIG. 8.3

tal component $\mathbf{P}_x$ which tends to move the block, the force **R** will have a horizontal component **F** and, thus, will form a certain angle with the vertical (Fig. 8.3b). If $\mathbf{P}_x$ is increased until motion becomes impending, the angle between **R** and the vertical grows and reaches a maximum value (Fig. 8.3c). This value is called the *angle of static friction* and is denoted by ϕ_s. From the force triangle shown in Fig. 8.3c, we note that

$$\tan \phi_s = \frac{F_m}{N} = \frac{\mu_s N}{N}$$

$$\tan \phi_s = \mu_s \tag{8.3}$$

If motion actually takes place, the magnitude of the friction force drops to F_k; similarly, the angle between **R** and **N** drops to a lower value ϕ_k, called the *angle of kinetic friction* (Fig. 8.3d). Using the force triangle of Fig. 8.3d, we write

$$\tan \phi_k = \frac{F_k}{N} = \frac{\mu_k N}{N}$$

$$\tan \phi_k = \mu_k \tag{8.4}$$

Another example will show how the angle of friction may be used to advantage in the analysis of certain types of problems. Consider a block resting on a board which may be given any desired inclination; the block is subjected to no other force than its weight **W** and the reaction **R** of the board. If the board is horizontal, the force **R** exerted by the board on the block is perpendicular to the board and balances the weight **W** (Fig. 8.4*a*). If the board is given a small angle of inclination θ, the force **R** will deviate from the perpendicular to the board by the angle θ and will keep balancing **W** (Fig. 8.4*b*); it will then have a normal component **N** of magnitude $N = W \cos \theta$ and a tangential component **F** of magnitude $F = W \sin \theta$.

If we keep increasing the angle of inclination, motion will soon become impending. At that time, the angle between **R** and the normal will have reached its maximum value ϕ_s (Fig. 8.4*c*). The value of the angle of inclination corresponding to impending motion is called the *angle of repose*. Clearly, the angle of repose is equal to the angle of static friction ϕ_s. If the angle of inclination θ is further increased, motion starts and the angle between **R** and the normal drops to the lower value ϕ_k (Fig. 8.4*d*). The reaction **R** is not vertical any more, and the forces acting on the block are unbalanced.

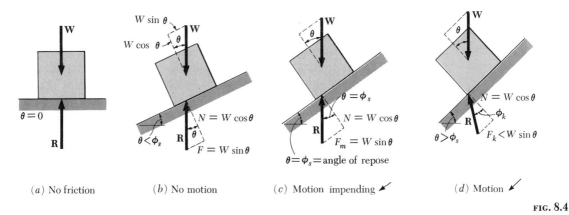

(*a*) No friction   (*b*) No motion   (*c*) Motion impending   (*d*) Motion

FIG. 8.4

8.4. Problems Involving Dry Friction.

Problems involving dry friction are found in many engineering applications. Some deal with simple situations such as the block sliding on a plane described in the preceding sections. Others involve more complicated situations as in Sample Prob. 8.3; many deal with the stability of rigid bodies in accelerated motion and will be studied in dynamics.   Also, a number of common machines and mechanisms may be analyzed by applying the laws of dry friction.   These include wedges, screws, journal and thrust bearings, and belt transmissions.   They will be studied in the following sections.

The *methods* which should be used to solve problems involving dry friction are the same that were used in the preceding chapters.   If a problem involves only a motion of translation, with no possible rotation, the body under consideration may usually be treated as a particle and the methods of Chap. 2 may be used.   If the problem involves a possible rotation, the body must be considered as a rigid body and the methods of Chap. 4 should be used.   If the structure considered is made of several parts, the principle of action and reaction must be used as was done in Chap. 6.

If the body considered is acted upon by more than three forces (including the reactions at the surfaces of contact), the reaction at each surface will be represented by its components N and F and the problem will be solved from the equations of equilibrium.   If only three forces act on the body under consideration, it may be found more convenient to represent each reaction by the single force R and to solve the problem by drawing a force triangle.

Most problems involving friction fall into one of the following *three groups:* In the *first group* of problems, all applied forces are given, and the coefficients of friction are known; we are to determine whether the body considered will remain at rest or slide.   The friction force F *required to maintain equilibrium* is unknown (its magnitude is *not* equal to $\mu_s N$) and should be determined, together with the normal force N, by drawing a free-body diagram and *solving the equations of equilibrium* (Fig. 8.5a).   The value found for the magnitude F of the friction force is then compared with the maximum value $F_m = \mu_s N$.   If F is smaller than or equal to F_m, the body remains at rest.   If the value found for F is larger than F_m, equilibrium cannot be maintained and motion takes place; the actual magnitude of the friction force is then $F_k = \mu_k N$.

In problems of the *second group*, all applied forces are given, and the motion is known to be impending; we are to determine the value of the coefficient of static friction.   Here again, we determine the friction force and the normal force by drawing a free-body diagram and solving the equations of

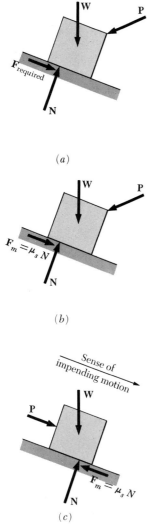

(a)

(b)

(c)

FIG. 8.5

equilibrium (Fig. 8.5*b*).   Since we know that the value found
for *F* is the maximum value F_m, the coefficient of friction may
be found by writing and solving the equation $F_m = \mu_s N$.

In problems of the *third group*, the coefficient of static friction is given, and it is known that motion is impending in a
given direction; we are to determine the magnitude or the direction of one of the applied forces.   The friction force should
be shown in the free-body diagram with a *sense opposite to that
of the impending motion* and with a magnitude $F_m = \mu_s N$ (Fig.
8.5*c*).   The equations of equilibrium may then be written, and
the desired force may be determined.

As noted above, it may be more convenient, when only three
forces are involved, to represent the reaction of the surface by
a single force **R** and to solve the problem by drawing a force
triangle.   Such a solution is used in Sample Prob. 8.2.

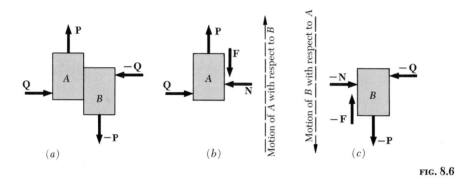

(*a*)   (*b*)   (*c*)

FIG. 8.6

When two bodies *A* and *B* are in contact (Fig. 8.6*a*), the
forces of friction exerted, respectively, by *A* on *B* and by *B* on
A are equal and opposite (Newton's third law).   It is important, in drawing the free-body diagram of one of the bodies,
to include the appropriate friction force with its correct sense.
The following rule should then be observed: *The sense of the
friction force acting on A is opposite to that of the motion (or
impending motion) of A as observed from B* (Fig. 8.6*b*).†   The
sense of the friction force acting on *B* is determined in a similar way (Fig. 8.6*c*).   Note that the motion of *A* as observed
from *B* is a *relative motion*.   Body *A* may be fixed; yet it will
have a relative motion with respect to *B* if *B* itself moves.   Also,
A may actually move down yet be observed from *B* to move up
if *B* moves down faster than *A*.

† It is therefore *the same as that of the motion of B as observed from A.*

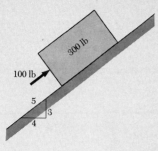

SAMPLE PROBLEM 8.1

A 100-lb force acts as shown on a 300-lb block placed on an inclined plane. The coefficients of friction between the block and the plane are $\mu_s = 0.25$ and $\mu_k = 0.20$. Determine whether the block is in equilibrium, and find the value of the friction force.

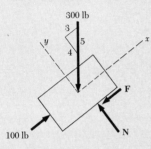

Force Required for Equilibrium. We first determine the value of the friction force *required to maintain equilibrium.* Assuming that **F** is directed down and to the left, we draw the free-body diagram of the block and write

$$+ \nearrow \Sigma F_x = 0: \qquad 100 \text{ lb} - \tfrac{3}{5}(300 \text{ lb}) - F = 0$$

$$F = -80 \text{ lb} \qquad \mathbf{F} = 80 \text{ lb} \nearrow$$

$$+ \nwarrow \Sigma F_y = 0: \qquad N - \tfrac{4}{5}(300 \text{ lb}) = 0$$

$$N = +240 \text{ lb} \qquad \mathbf{N} = 240 \text{ lb} \nwarrow$$

The force **F** required to maintain equilibrium is an 80-lb force directed up and to the right; the tendency of the block is thus to move down the plane.

Maximum Friction Force. The magnitude of the maximum friction force which may be developed is

$$F_{\max} = \mu_s N \qquad F_{\max} = 0.25(240 \text{ lb}) = 60 \text{ lb}$$

Since the value of the force required to maintain equilibrium (80 lb) is larger than the maximum value which may be obtained (60 lb), equilibrium will not be maintained and *the block will slide down the plane.*

Actual Value of Friction Force. The magnitude of the actual friction force is obtained as follows:

$$F_{\text{actual}} = F_k = \mu_k N$$
$$= 0.20(240 \text{ lb}) = 48 \text{ lb}$$

The sense of this force is opposite to the sense of motion; the force is thus directed up and to the right,

$$\mathbf{F}_{\text{actual}} = 48 \text{ lb} \nearrow \quad \blacktriangleleft$$

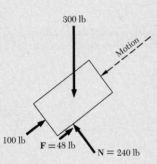

It should be noted that the forces acting on the block are not balanced; the resultant is

$$\tfrac{3}{5}(300 \text{ lb}) - 100 \text{ lb} - 48 \text{ lb} = 32 \text{ lb} \swarrow$$

SAMPLE PROBLEM 8.2

A wooden sled supporting a large stone is pulled up a track inclined at 15°. The combined weight of the sled and stone is 1,500 lb, and the coefficients of friction between the sled runners and the track are $\mu_s = 0.40$ and $\mu_k = 0.30$. Determine the force P required (a) to start the sled up the track, (b) to keep the sled moving up after it has been started, (c) to keep the sled from sliding down.

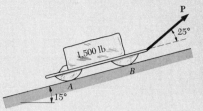

Solution. Since the normal component of the reaction of the track depends upon the unknown force P as well as upon the 1,500-lb weight, it would not be convenient to resolve the reactions R_A and R_B into components. Noting that R_A and R_B have the same direction (same angle of friction ϕ), we draw a force triangle including the 1,500-lb weight, the force P, and the sum $R = R_A + R_B$. The direction of R must be redetermined in each part of the problem. The law of sines is used to determine the magnitude of P in each part of the problem.

a. Force P to Start Sled Moving Up

$$\frac{P}{\sin 36.8°} = \frac{1,500 \text{ lb}}{\sin [180° - (50° + 36.8°)]}$$

$$P = 900 \text{ lb} \nearrow$$

$$\tan \phi_s = \mu_s = 0.40$$
$$\phi_s = 21.8°$$

$$15° + 21.8° = 36.8°$$

b. Force P to Keep Sled Moving

$$\frac{P}{\sin 31.7°} = \frac{1,500 \text{ lb}}{\sin [180° - (50° + 31.7°)]}$$

$$P = 796 \text{ lb} \nearrow$$

$$\tan \phi_k = \mu_k = 0.30$$
$$\phi_k = 16.7°$$

$$15° + 16.7° = 31.7°$$

c. Force P to Keep Sled from Sliding Down

$$\frac{P}{\sin 6.8°} = \frac{1,500 \text{ lb}}{\sin [180° - (130° + 6.8°)]}$$

$$P = 260 \text{ lb} \swarrow$$

Since the force P is directed downward, the sled will not slide down under its own weight.

$$21.8° - 15° = 6.8°$$

$$\phi_s = 21.8°$$

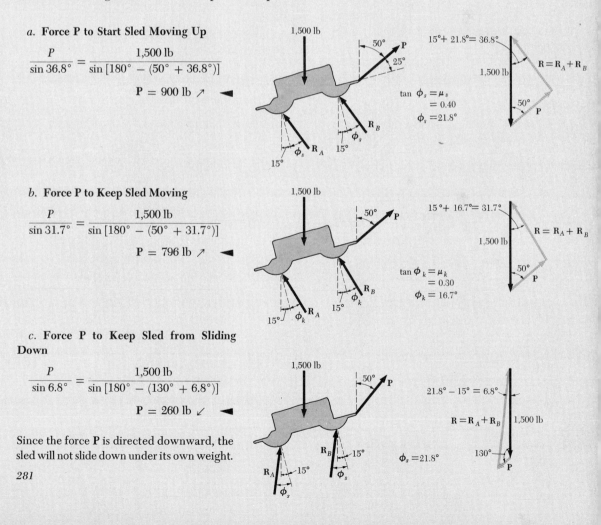

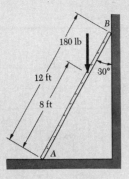

SAMPLE PROBLEM 8.3

A 12-ft ladder weighing 40 lb is placed against a vertical wall as shown. As a 180-lb man reaches a point 8 ft from the lower end A, the ladder is just about to slip. Knowing that the coefficient of static friction between the ladder and the wall is 0.20, determine the coefficient of friction μ_s between the ladder and the floor.

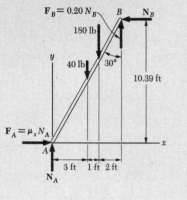

Solution. We draw the free-body diagram of the ladder. Since the ladder is about to slip, the forces of friction at A and B have reached their maximum values, equal to $\mu_s N_A$ and 0.20 N_B, respectively. The values of N_B, N_A, and μ_s are successively obtained from the equations of equilibrium,

$$+ \curvearrowright \Sigma M_A = 0:$$

$$(6 \text{ ft})0.20 N_B + (10.39 \text{ ft}) N_B - (3 \text{ ft})(40 \text{ lb}) - (4 \text{ ft})(180 \text{ lb}) = 0$$

$$N_B = 72.5 \text{ lb}$$

$$+ \uparrow \Sigma F_y = 0: \qquad N_A + 0.20 N_B - 40 \text{ lb} - 180 \text{ lb} = 0$$

$$N_A + 0.20(72.5 \text{ lb}) - 40 \text{ lb} - 180 \text{ lb} = 0$$

$$N_A = 205 \text{ lb}$$

$$\xrightarrow{+} \Sigma F_x = 0: \qquad \mu_s N_A - N_B = 0$$

$$\mu_s(205 \text{ lb}) - 72.5 \text{ lb} = 0$$

$$\mu_s = \frac{72.5 \text{ lb}}{205 \text{ lb}} \qquad\qquad \mu_s = 0.35 \quad \blacktriangleleft$$

PROBLEMS

8.1. A support block is acted upon by the two forces shown. Determine the magnitude of **P** required to start the block up the plane.

8.2. Determine the smallest magnitude of the force **P** which will prevent the support block from sliding down the plane.

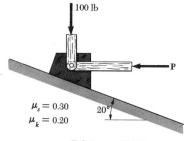

FIG. P 8.1 AND P 8.2

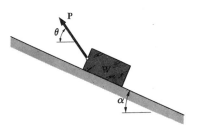

FIG. P 8.3 AND P 8.4

8.3. Denoting by ϕ_s the angle of static friction between the block and the plane, determine the magnitude and direction of the smallest force **P** which will cause the block to move up the plane.

8.4. A block of weight $W = 50$ lb rests on a rough plane as shown. Knowing that $\alpha = 20°$ and $\mu_s = 0.25$, determine the magnitude and direction of the smallest force **P** required (*a*) to start the block up the plane, (*b*) to prevent the block from moving down the plane.

8.5. Three packages A, B, and C, each of weight 10 lb, are placed on a conveyor belt which is at rest. Between the belt and both packages A and C the coefficients of friction are $\mu_s = 0.30$ and $\mu_k = 0.20$; between package B and the belt the coefficients are $\mu_s = 0.10$ and $\mu_k = 0.08$. The packages are placed on the belt so that they are in contact with each other and at rest. Determine which, if any, of the packages will move and the friction force acting on each package.

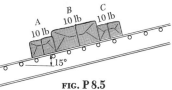

FIG. P 8.5

8.6. Solve Prob. 8.5 assuming that package B is placed to the right of both packages A and C.

8.7. A 200-lb block is used to secure one end of the cable shown. Determine the range of values of x for which the 200-lb block will not move.

8.8. Block A is positioned so that $x = 25$ in. Determine whether the block moves and find the value of the friction force.

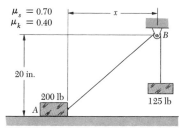
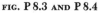

FIG. P 8.7 AND P 8.8

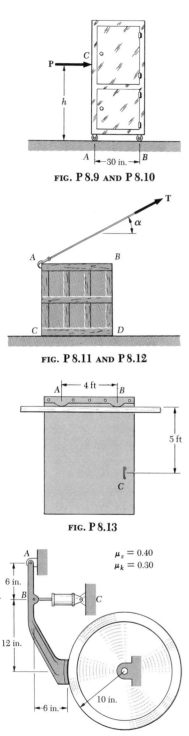

FIG. P 8.9 AND P 8.10

FIG. P 8.11 AND P 8.12

FIG. P 8.13

$\mu_s = 0.40$
$\mu_k = 0.30$

FIG. P 8.15 AND P 8.17

8.9. A 90-lb cabinet is mounted on casters which can be locked to prevent their rotation. The coefficient of friction between the floor and each caster is 0.30. Assuming that the casters at both A and B are locked, determine (a) the force $\mathbf{P}$ required to move the cabinet to the right, (b) the largest allowable value of h if the cabinet is not to tip over.

8.10. A 90-lb cabinet is mounted on casters which can be locked to prevent their rotation. The coefficient of friction is 0.30. If $h = 40$ in., determine the magnitude of the force $\mathbf{P}$ required to move the cabinet to the right (a) if all casters are locked, (b) if the casters at B are locked and the casters at A are free to rotate, (c) if casters A are locked and casters B are free to rotate.

8.11. A square packing crate, weighing 200 lb, is to be moved to the right along the floor without tipping. Knowing that the coefficient of friction between the crate and the floor is 0.40, determine (a) the largest allowable value of α, (b) the corresponding tension T.

8.12. A square packing crate, weighing 200 lb, is pulled by a cable as shown. The coefficient of friction between the crate and the floor is 0.30. If $\alpha = 30°$, determine (a) the tension T required to move the crate, (b) whether the crate will slide or tip.

8.13. A 180-lb sliding door is mounted on a horizontal rail as shown. The coefficients of static friction between the rail and the door at A and B are 0.20 and 0.30, respectively. Determine the horizontal force which must be applied to the handle C in order to move the door to the right.

8.14. Solve Prob. 8.13 assuming that the door is to be moved to the left.

8.15. A clockwise couple of magnitude 60 lb-ft is applied to the drum. Determine the smallest force which must be exerted by the hydraulic cylinder if the drum is not to rotate.

8.16. Solve Prob. 8.15 assuming that a counterclockwise couple of magnitude 60 lb-ft is applied to the drum.

8.17. The hydraulic cylinder exerts on point B a force of 500 lb directed to the right. Determine the moment of the friction force about the axle of the drum if the drum is rotating (a) clockwise, (b) counterclockwise.

8.18. A large number of thin steel plates are stacked on a factory floor as shown. The coefficients of friction between two adjacent plates and between the bottom plate and the floor are 0.35 and 0.25, respectively.

All the plates are to be moved to the right, without tipping or sliding with respect to each other, by applying a horizontal force **P**. Determine the largest allowable height h at which **P** may be applied.

8.19. A large number of thin steel plates of total weight 100 lb are stacked upon each other on a factory floor. In order to move *all* the plates to the right, it is observed that a force **P** of magnitude 27.5 lb is required and that this force cannot be applied at a height h greater than 3 in. Determine the coefficient of friction (*a*) between the floor and the bottom plate, (*b*) between two adjacent plates.

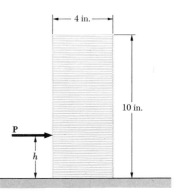

FIG. P 8.18 AND P 8.19

8.20. A 10-ft beam, weighing 1,200 lb, is to be moved to the left onto the platform. A horizontal force **P** is applied to the dolly, which is mounted on frictionless wheels. The coefficient of friction between all surfaces is 0.30. Knowing that the horizontal top surface of the dolly is slightly higher than the platform, determine the magnitude of **P** required to move the beam. (*Hint.* The beam is supported at A and D.)

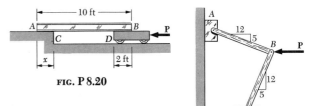

FIG. P 8.20

8.21. (*a*) Show that the beam of Prob. 8.20 cannot be moved if the horizontal top surface of the dolly is slightly *lower* than the platform. (*b*) How far can the beam be moved to the left if two 175-lb men stand on the beam at B?

8.22. Two links, of negligible weight, are connected by frictionless pins to each other and to two 10-lb blocks at A and C. The coefficient of friction is 0.30 at A and C. If neither block is to slip, determine the magnitude of the largest horizontal force **P** which can be applied at B.

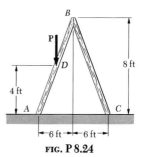

FIG. P 8.22

8.23. In Prob. 8.22 determine the magnitude of the smallest horizontal force **P** which must be applied at B if neither block is to slip.

8.24. Two identical uniform boards, each of weight 40 lb, are temporarily leaned against each other as shown. Knowing that the coefficient of friction between all surfaces is 0.40, determine (*a*) the largest magnitude of the force **P** for which equilibrium will be maintained, (*b*) the surface at which motion will impend.

FIG. P 8.24

8.25. Solve Prob. 8.24 assuming that the force **P** is applied at D and is directed horizontally to the right.

8.26. The movable bracket shown may be placed at any height on the 3-in.-diameter pipe. If the coefficient of static friction between the pipe and bracket is 0.25, determine the minimum distance x at which the load W can be supported. Neglect the weight of the bracket.

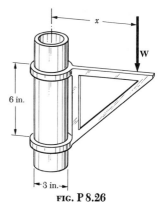

FIG. P 8.26

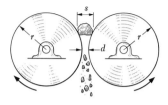

FIG. P 8.27

8.27. Two large cylinders, each of radius $r = 20$ in., rotate in opposite directions and form the main elements of a crusher for stone aggregate. The distance d is set equal to the maximum desired size of the crushed aggregate. If $d = 1$ in. and $\mu = 0.30$, determine the size s of the largest stones which will be pulled through the crusher by friction alone.

8.28. Two uniform rods, each of weight W, are held by frictionless pins A and B. It is observed that if the value of θ is greater than $10°$, the rods will not remain in equilibrium. Determine the coefficient of friction at C.

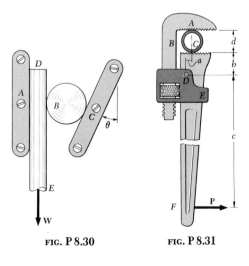

FIG. P 8.28

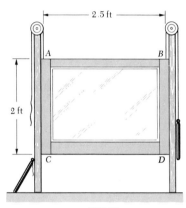

FIG. P 8.29

8.29. A window sash weighs 10 lb and is normally supported by two 5-lb sash weights. It is observed that the window remains open after one sash cord has broken. What is the smallest possible value of the coefficient of static friction? (Assume that the sash is slightly smaller than the frame and will bind only at points A and D.)

8.30. A rod DE and a small cylinder are placed between two guides as shown. The rod is not to slip downward, however large the force $\mathbf{W}$ may be; i.e., the arrangement is to be *self-locking*. Determine the minimum allowable coefficients of friction at A, B, and C.

8.31. A pipe of diameter d is gripped by the Stillson wrench shown. Portions AB and DE of the wrench are rigidly attached to each other and portion CF is connected by a pin at D. If the wrench is to grip the pipe and be self-locking, determine the required minimum coefficients of friction at A and at C, (a) in terms of the given letters, (b) if $a = \frac{1}{2}$ in., $b = 1$ in., $c = 10$ in., and $d = 1\frac{1}{4}$ in.

FIG. P 8.30

FIG. P 8.31

8.32. A block of weight W rests on an incline which forms an angle θ with the horizontal plane.   A horizontal force $\mathbf{P}$, parallel to the incline, is applied to the block.   Denoting by μ the coefficient of friction, determine (a) the magnitude of $\mathbf{P}$ required to move the block, (b) the direction in which the block moves.   (c) Obtain numerical values for parts a and b, when $\theta = 15°$, $\mu = 0.30$, and $W = 50$ lb.

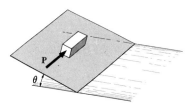

FIG. P 8.32

8.33. A uniform plank of weight $W = 60$ lb rests on two joists as shown.   The coefficient of friction between the joists and the plank is $\mu = 0.40$.   Determine the magnitude of the horizontal force $\mathbf{P}$ required to move the plank (a) when $a = 12$ ft, (b) when $a = 10$ ft.

8.34. Determine the smallest distance a for which the plank of Prob. 8.33 will slip at C.

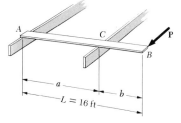

FIG. P 8.33

°8.35. A cylinder of weight W is placed in a V block as shown.   Denoting by ϕ the angle of friction between the cylinder and the block and assuming $\phi < \theta$, determine (a) the axial force $\mathbf{P}$ required to move the cylinder, (b) the couple $\mathbf{M}$, applied in the plane of the cross section of the cylinder, required to rotate the cylinder.

FIG. P 8.35

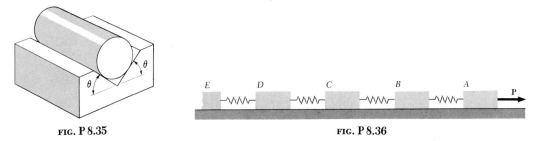

FIG. P 8.36

8.36. The mathematical model shown has been developed for the analysis of a certain structure.   It consists of a large number of 1-lb blocks connected in series by springs, each of constant $k = 0.20$ lb/in.   The coefficient of friction between the base and each block is 0.40.   At a time when the tension in each spring is zero, the magnitude of $\mathbf{P}$ is slowly increased from zero to a maximum of 0.50 lb; the magnitude of $\mathbf{P}$ is then slowly decreased until it becomes zero again.   For both the cases (1) when $P = 0.50$ lb and (2) when P is again zero, determine (a) the friction force acting on each block, (b) the tension in each spring, (c) the position of each block relative to its original position.

8.37. Solve Prob. 8.36 assuming that the magnitude of the force $\mathbf{P}$ increases to 1.00 lb and then decreases until it is again zero.

8.38. For the model of Prob. 8.36, construct a graph showing the magnitude of the force $\mathbf{P}$ versus the position of block A, (a) as P increases from zero to 1.00 lb, (b) as P decreases from 1.00 lb to zero.

8.39. Identical cylindrical cans, each of weight W, are raised to the top of an incline by a series of moving arms. Either one or two cans are moved by each arm. The coefficient of friction between all surfaces is $\mu = 0.20$. If $W = 2.00$ lb and $\theta = 12°$, determine the force parallel to the incline which the arm must exert on can A to move it. Does can A roll or slide?

°8.40. Solve Prob. 8.39 considering can C instead of can A.

°8.41. In Prob. 8.39 determine the range of values of θ for which can A will roll.

°8.42. In Prob. 8.39 determine the range of values of θ for which can C will roll.

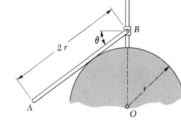

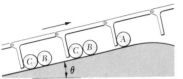

FIG. P 8.39

FIG. P 8.43 AND P 8.44

°8.43. A uniform slender rod is attached to a collar at B and rests on a *smooth* circular cylindrical surface of radius r. The angle of friction between the collar and the vertical guide is ϕ. Derive the equation which must be satisfied by the largest and smallest values of θ corresponding to equilibrium.

°8.44. A uniform slender rod is attached to a collar at B and rests on a circular cylindrical surface of radius r. The collar may slide without friction along a vertical guide. Denoting by ϕ the angle of friction between the rod and the surface, show that the largest and smallest values of θ corresponding to equilibrium must satisfy the equation

$$\tan \theta + \tan^2 \theta \tan (\theta \mp \phi) = 1$$

8.5. Wedges. Wedges are simple machines used to raise large stone blocks and other heavy loads. These loads may be raised by applying to the wedge a force usually considerably smaller than the weight of the load. Besides, because of the friction existing between the surfaces in contact, a wedge, if properly shaped, will remain in place after being forced under the load. Wedges may thus be used advantageously to make small adjustments in the position of heavy pieces of machinery.

Consider the 2,000-lb block *A* shown in Fig. 8.7*a*. This block rests against a vertical wall *B* and is to be raised a few inches by forcing a wedge *C* between block *A* and a second wedge *D*. We want to find the minimum value of the force **P** which must be applied to the wedge *C* to move the block.

The free-body diagrams of block *A* and of wedge *C* have been drawn in Fig. 8.7*b* and *c*. The forces acting on the block include its weight and the normal and friction forces at the surfaces of contact with wall *B* and wedge *C*. The magnitudes of the friction forces **F**$_1$ and **F**$_2$ are equal, respectively, to $\mu_s N_1$ and $\mu_s N_2$ since the motion of the block must be started. It is important to show the friction forces with their correct sense. Since the block will move upward, the force **F**$_1$ exerted by the wall on the block must be directed downward. On the other hand, since the wedge *C* moves to the right, the relative motion of *A* with respect to *C* is to the left and the force **F**$_2$ exerted by *C* on *A* must be directed to the right.

Considering now the free body *C* in Fig. 8.7*c*, we note that the forces acting on *C* include the applied force **P** and the normal and friction forces at the surfaces of contact with *A* and *D*. The weight of the wedge is small compared with the other forces involved and may be neglected. The forces acting on *C* are equal and opposite to the forces **N**$_2$ and **F**$_2$ acting on *A* and are denoted, respectively, by $-\mathbf{N}_2$ and $-\mathbf{F}_2$; the friction force $-\mathbf{F}_2$ must therefore be directed to the left. We check that the force **F**$_3$ is also directed to the left.

The total number of unknowns involved in the two free-body diagrams may be reduced to four if the friction forces are expressed in terms of the normal forces. Expressing that block *A* and wedge *C* are in equilibrium will provide four equations which may be solved to obtain the magnitude of **P**. It should be noted that, in the example considered here, it will be more convenient to replace each pair of normal and friction forces by their resultant. Each free body is then subjected to only three forces, and the problem may be solved by drawing the corresponding force triangles. The actual solution of the problem has been carried out in this way in Sample Prob. 8.4.

8.6. Square-threaded Screws. Square-threaded screws are frequently used in jacks, presses, and other mechanisms. Their analysis is similar to that of a block sliding along an inclined plane.

Consider the jack shown in Fig. 8.8. The screw carries a load **W** and is supported by the base of the jack. Contact be-

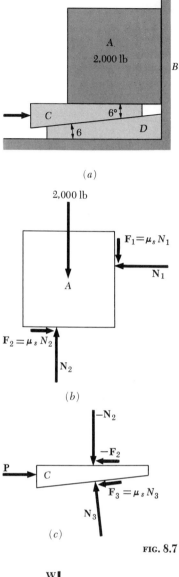

(*a*)

(*b*)

(*c*)

FIG. 8.7

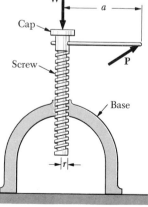

FIG. 8.8

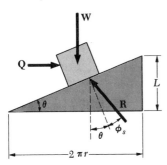

(*a*) Impending motion upward

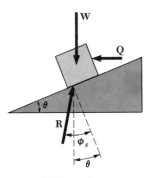

(*b*) Impending motion
downward with $\phi_s > \theta$

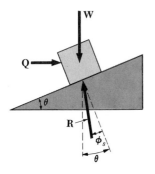

(*c*) Impending motion
downward with $\phi_s < \theta$

**FIG. 8.9. Block-and-incline analysis
of a screw**

tween screw and base takes place along a portion of their threads.   By applying a force **P** on the handle, the screw may be made to turn and to raise the load **W**.

The thread of the base has been unwrapped and shown as a straight line in Fig. 8.9*a*.   The correct slope was obtained by plotting horizontally the product $2\pi r$, where r is the mean radius of the thread, and vertically the *lead L* of the screw, i.e., the distance through which the screw advances in one turn.   The angle θ this line forms with the horizontal is the *lead angle*. Since the force of friction between two surfaces in contact does not depend upon the area of contact, the two threads may be assumed to be in contact over a much smaller area than they actually are and the screw may be represented by the block shown in Fig. 8.9*a*.   It should be noted, however, that, in this analysis of the jack, the friction between cap and screw is neglected.

The free-body diagram of the block should include the load **W**, the reaction **R** of the base thread, and a horizontal force **Q** having the same effect as the force **P** exerted on the handle. The force **Q** should have the same moment as **P** about the axis of the screw and its magnitude should thus be $Q = Pa/r$.   The force **Q**, and thus the force **P** required to raise the load **W**, may be obtained from the free-body diagram shown in Fig. 8.9*a*. The friction angle is taken equal to ϕ_s since the load will presumably be raised through a succession of short strokes.   In mechanisms providing for the continuous rotation of a screw, it may be desirable to distinguish between the force required to start motion (using ϕ_s) and that required to maintain motion (using ϕ_k).

If the friction angle ϕ_s is larger than the lead angle θ, the screw is said to be *self-locking;* it will remain in place under the load.   To lower the load, we must then apply the force shown in Fig. 8.9*b*.   If ϕ_s is smaller than θ, the screw will unwind under the load; it is then necessary to apply the force shown in Fig. 8.9*c* to maintain equilibrium.

The lead of a screw should not be confused with its *pitch*. The lead was defined as the distance through which the screw advances in one turn; the pitch is the distance measured between two consecutive threads.   While lead and pitch are equal in the case of *single-threaded* screws, they are different in the case of *multiple-threaded* screws, i.e., screws having several independent threads.   It is easily verified that, for double-threaded screws, the lead is twice as large as the pitch; for triple-threaded screws, it is three times as large as the pitch; etc.

SAMPLE PROBLEM 8.4

A 2,000-lb block is raised by forcing a wedge under it as shown. Determine the minimum value of the force **P** which must be applied to the wedge. The coefficient of static friction is 0.30 at all surfaces of contact.

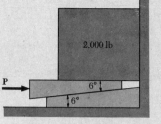

Solution. The free-body diagrams of the block and of the upper wedge are shown below; the corresponding force triangles are also shown. The sense in which friction takes place is obtained by considering the *relative motion* of the surfaces in contact (see Sec. 8.5). The force $\mathbf{R}_2$ exerted by the wedge on the block is obtained by applying the law of sines to the force triangle of the block. The force $\mathbf{R}_2$ exerted by the block on the wedge is equal and opposite; its value is used to draw the force triangle of the wedge, from which **P** is obtained.

Free Body: Block

$$\frac{R_2}{\sin 106.7°} = \frac{2{,}000 \text{ lb}}{\sin \left[180° - (106.7° + 16.7°)\right]}$$

$$R_2 = 2{,}300 \text{ lb}$$

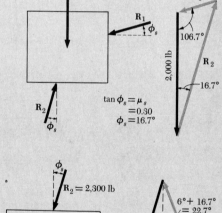

$$\tan \phi_s = \mu_s$$
$$= 0.30$$
$$\phi_s = 16.7°$$

Free Body: Wedge

$$\frac{P}{\sin (16.7° + 22.7°)} = \frac{2{,}300 \text{ lb}}{\sin (90° - 22.7°)}$$

$$P = 1{,}580 \text{ lb}$$
$$P = 1{,}580 \text{ lb} \rightarrow \quad \blacktriangleleft$$

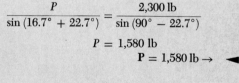

$$\phi_s = 16.7°$$

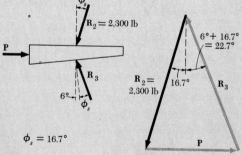

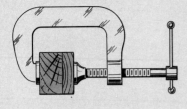

SAMPLE PROBLEM 8.5

A clamp is used to hold two pieces of wood together as shown. The clamp has a double square thread of mean diameter equal to 0.50 in. and with a pitch of 0.10 in. The coefficient of friction between threads is $\mu_s = 0.30$. If a maximum torque of 30 lb-ft is applied in tightening the clamp, determine (a) the force exerted on the pieces of wood, (b) the torque required to loosen the clamp.

a. **Force Exerted by Clamp.** Since the screw is double-threaded, the lead L is equal to twice the pitch, i.e., to $2(0.10 \text{ in.}) = 0.20 \text{ in.}$ The lead angle θ and the friction angle ϕ_s are obtained by writing

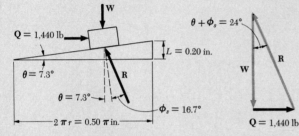

$$\tan \theta = \frac{L}{2\pi r} = \frac{0.20 \text{ in.}}{0.50\pi \text{ in.}} = 0.1273 \qquad \theta = 7.3°$$

$$\tan \phi_s = \mu_s = 0.30 \qquad\qquad \phi_s = 16.7°$$

The force **Q** which should be applied to the block representing the screw is obtained by expressing that its moment Qr about the axis of the screw is equal to the applied torque.

$$Q(0.25 \text{ in.}) = 30 \text{ lb-ft} \qquad Q = \frac{30 \text{ lb-ft}}{0.25 \text{ in.}} = \frac{360 \text{ lb-in.}}{0.25 \text{ in.}} = 1,440 \text{ lb}$$

The free-body diagram and the corresponding force triangle may now be drawn for the block; the magnitude of the force **W** exerted on the pieces of wood is obtained by solving the triangle.

$$W = \frac{Q}{\tan (\theta + \phi_s)} = \frac{1,440 \text{ lb}}{\tan 24°}$$

$$W = 3,230 \text{ lb} \quad \blacktriangleleft$$

b. **Torque Required to Loosen Clamp.** The force **Q** required to loosen the clamp and the corresponding torque are obtained from the free-body diagram and force triangle shown.

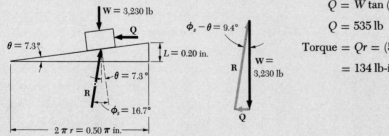

$$Q = W \tan (\phi_s - \theta) = (3,230 \text{ lb}) \tan 9.4°$$

$$Q = 535 \text{ lb}$$

$$\text{Torque} = Qr = (535 \text{ lb})(0.25 \text{ in.})$$

$$= 134 \text{ lb-in.}$$

$$\text{Torque} = 11.2 \text{ lb-ft} \quad \blacktriangleleft$$

PROBLEMS

8.45. The machine part *ABC* is supported by a frictionless hinge at *B* and by a wedge at *C*. Knowing that $\mu = 0.20$ at both surfaces of the wedge, determine (*a*) the force **P** required to move the wedge to the left, (*b*) the corresponding components of the reaction at *B*.

8.46. Solve Prob. 8.45 assuming that the wedge is to be moved to the right.

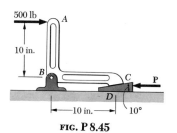

FIG. P 8.45

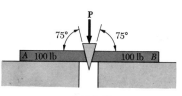

FIG. P 8.47

8.47. A wedge, of weight 4 lb, is to be driven between two plates *A* and *B*. The coefficient of static friction between all surfaces of contact is 0.35. Determine the magnitude of the force **P** required to start moving the wedge (*a*) if the plates are equally free to move, (*b*) if plate *B* is securely bolted to the surface.

8.48. The spring of the door latch has a constant of 1.5 lb/in. and in the position shown exerts a force of $\frac{1}{2}$ lb on the bolt. The coefficient of friction between the bolt and the guide plate is 0.40; all other surfaces are well lubricated and may be assumed to be frictionless. Determine the magnitude of the force **P** required to start closing the door.

8.49. In Prob. 8.48 determine the angle which the face of the bolt should form with the line *BC* if the force **P** required to close the door is to be the same for both the position shown and the position when *B* is almost at the guide plate.

8.50. Neglecting the weight of the wedge, determine the magnitude of the force **P** required to raise the 500-lb weight. The coefficient of friction is 0.30 at all surfaces.

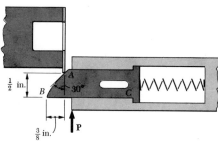

FIG. P 8.48

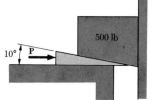

FIG. P 8.50

8.51. A 20° wedge is forced into a saw cut to prevent binding of the circular saw. The coefficient of friction between the wedge and the wood is 0.30. Knowing that a horizontal force **P** of magnitude 25 lb was required to insert the wedge, determine the magnitude of the forces exerted on the board by the wedge after it has been inserted.

8.52. A circular disk of radius $r = 2$ in. is eccentrically connected to a shaft A. A constant 10-lb force is applied to the horizontal follower BD. Knowing that $\mu = 0.20$, determine the magnitude M of the couple required to rotate the disk clockwise about A (a) if $\theta = 0°$, (b) if $\theta = 90°$.

8.53. Solve Prob. 8.52 for the case when (a) $\theta = 180°$, (b) $\theta = 270°$.

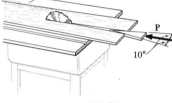

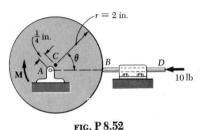

FIG. P 8.51

FIG. P 8.52

8.54. A 5° wedge is to be forced under a 1,400-lb machine base at A. Knowing that $\mu = 0.10$ at all surfaces, (a) determine the force **P** required to move the wedge, (b) indicate whether the machine will move.

8.55. Solve Prob. 8.54 assuming that the wedge is to be forced under the machine base at B instead of A.

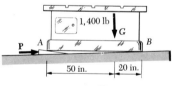

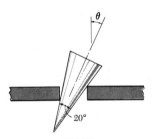

FIG. P 8.54

FIG. P 8.56

°8.56. A conical wedge is placed between two horizontal plates which are then slowly moved toward each other. Indicate what will happen to the wedge (a) if $\mu = 0.15$, (b) if $\mu = 0.25$.

8.57. Derive the following formulas relating the load W and the force **P** exerted on the handle of the jack discussed in Sec. 8.6: (a) $P = (Wr/a) \tan (\theta + \phi_s)$, to raise the load; (b) $P = (Wr/a) \tan (\phi_s - \theta)$, to lower the load if the screw is self-locking; (c) $P = (Wr/a) \tan (\theta - \phi_s)$, to hold the load if the screw is not self-locking.

8.58. High-strength bolts are now used in the construction of many buildings. For a 1-in.-nominal-diameter bolt the required minimum bolt tension is specified as 42,500 lb. It is further specified that a torque of 710 lb-ft be applied to the bolt and nut to obtain this tension. Determine the coefficient of friction for which these values are compatible. The mean diameter of the thread is 0.94 in. and the lead is 0.125 in. Neglect friction between the nut and washer, and assume the bolt to be square-threaded.

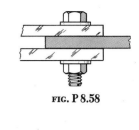

FIG. P 8.58

8.59. The square-threaded worm gear shown has a mean radius of $1\frac{1}{2}$ in. and a pitch of $\frac{3}{8}$ in. The large gear is subjected to a constant clockwise torque of 500 lb-ft. Knowing that the coefficient of friction between gear teeth is 0.10, determine the torque which must be applied to shaft AB in order to rotate the large gear counterclockwise. Neglect friction in the bearings at A, B, and C.

8.60. In Prob. 8.59 determine the torque which must be applied to shaft AB in order to rotate the large gear clockwise.

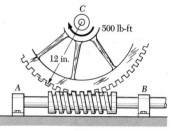

FIG. P 8.59

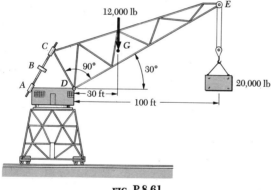

FIG. P 8.61

FIG. P 8.62

8.61. The main features of a screw-luffing crane are shown. Distances AD and CD are each 25 ft. The position of the boom CDE is controlled by the screw ABC which is single-threaded at each end (left-handed thread at A, right-handed thread at C). Each thread has a pitch of $1\frac{1}{4}$ in. and a mean diameter of 8 in. If $\mu = 0.08$, determine the moment of the couple which must be applied to the screw (*a*) to raise the boom, (*b*) to lower the boom.

8.62. The ends of two fixed rods A and B are each made in the form of a single-threaded screw of mean radius 0.25 in. and pitch 0.08 in. The coefficient of friction between the rods and the threaded sleeve is 0.15. Determine the moment of the couple which must be applied to the sleeve in order to draw the rods closer together. Rod A has a left-handed thread and rod B a right-handed thread.

8.63. In Prob. 8.62 a right-handed thread is used on *both* rods *A* and *B*. Determine the moment of the couple which must be applied to the sleeve in order to rotate it.

8.64. The vise shown consists of two members connected by two double-threaded screws of mean radius 0.20 in. and pitch 0.04 in. The lower member is threaded at *A* and *B* ($\mu_s = 0.25$), but the upper member is not threaded. It is desired to apply two equal and opposite forces of 100 lb on the blocks held between the jaws. (*a*) What screw should be adjusted first? (*b*) What is the maximum torque applied in tightening the second screw?

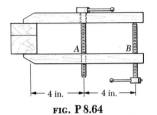

FIG. **P 8.64**

4 in.   4 in.

8.65. The vise of Prob. 8.64 has been tightened until the blocks are compressed by two equal and opposite 100-lb forces. The blocks are now to be removed from the vise. (*a*) What screw should be loosened? (*b*) What is the maximum torque applied in loosening the screw?

*8.7. Journal Bearings.   Axle Friction.   Journal bearings

are used to provide lateral support to rotating shafts and axles. Thrust bearings, which will be studied in the next section, are used to provide axial support to shafts and axles. If the journal bearing is fully lubricated, the frictional resistance depends upon the speed of rotation, the clearance between axle and bearing, and the viscosity of the lubricant. As indicated in Sec. 8.1, such problems are studied in fluid mechanics. The methods of this chapter, however, may be applied to the study of axle friction when the bearing is not lubricated or only partially lubricated. We may then assume that the axle and the bearing are in direct contact along a single straight line.

Consider two wheels, each of weight **W**, rigidly mounted on an axle supported symmetrically by two journal bearings (Fig. 8.10*a*). If the wheels rotate, we find that, to keep them rotating at constant speed, it is necessary to apply to each of them a couple **M**. A free-body diagram has been drawn in Fig. 8.10*c*, which represents one of the wheels and the corresponding half axle in projection on a plane perpendicular to the axle. The forces acting on the free body include the weight **W** of the wheel, the couple **M** required to maintain its motion, and a force **R** representing the reaction of the bearing. This force is vertical, equal, and opposite to **W** but does not pass through the center *O* of the axle; **R** is located to the right of *O* at a distance such that its moment about *O* balances the moment **M** of the couple. Contact between axle and bearing, there-

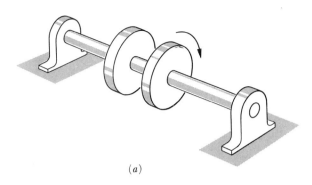

(a)

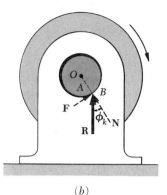

(b)

fore, does not take place at the lowest point A when the axle
rotates.   It takes place at point B (Fig. 8.10b) or, rather, along
a straight line intersecting the plane of the figure at B.   Physi-
cally, this is explained by the fact that, when the wheels are set
in motion, the axle "climbs" in the bearings until slippage occurs.   After sliding back slightly, the axle settles more or less
in the position shown.   This position is such that the angle
between the reaction $\mathbf{R}$ and the normal to the surface of the
bearing is equal to the angle of kinetic friction ϕ_k.   The distance from O to the line of action of $\mathbf{R}$ is thus $r \sin \phi_k$, where
r is the radius of the axle.   Writing that $\Sigma M_O = 0$ for the forces
acting on the free body considered, we obtain the magnitude
of the couple $\mathbf{M}$ required to overcome the frictional resistance
of one of the bearings:

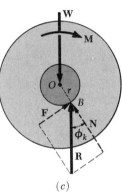

(c)

$$M = Rr \sin \phi_k \qquad (8.5)$$

Observing that, for small values of the angle of friction, $\sin \phi_k$
may be replaced by $\tan \phi_k$, that is, by μ_k, we write the approximate formula

$$M \approx Rr\mu_k \qquad (8.6)$$

In the solution of certain problems, it may be more convenient to let the line of action of $\mathbf{R}$ pass through O, as it does
when the axle does not rotate.   A couple $-\mathbf{M}$ of the same
magnitude as the couple $\mathbf{M}$ must then be added to the reaction
$\mathbf{R}$ (Fig. 8.10d).   This couple represents the frictional resistance
of the bearing.

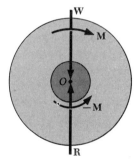

(d)

In case a graphical solution is preferred, the line of action
of $\mathbf{R}$ may be readily drawn (Fig. 8.10e) if we note that it must
be tangent to a circle centered at O and of radius

$$r_f = r \sin \phi_k \approx r\mu_k \qquad (8.7)$$

This circle is called the *circle of friction* of the axle and bearing and is independent of the loading conditions of the axle.

297

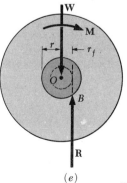

(e)

FIG. 8.10

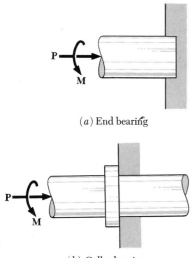

(*a*) End bearing

(*b*) Collar bearing

FIG. 8.11.   Thrust bearings

*8.8. Thrust Bearings.   Disk Friction.   Thrust bearings are used to provide axial support to rotating shafts and axles. They are of two types: (1) *end bearings* and (2) *collar bearings* (Fig. 8.11).   In the case of collar bearings, friction forces develop between the two ring-shaped areas which are in contact.   In the case of end bearings, friction takes place over full circular areas, or over ring-shaped areas when the end of the shaft is hollow.   Friction between circular areas, called *disk friction,* also occurs in other mechanisms, such as *disk clutches.*

To obtain a formula which is valid in the most general case of disk friction, we shall consider a rotating hollow shaft.   A couple **M** keeps the shaft rotating at constant speed while a force **P** maintains it in contact with a fixed bearing (Fig. 8.12). Contact between the shaft and the bearing takes place over a ring-shaped area of inner radius R_1 and outer radius R_2.   Assuming that the pressure between the two surfaces in contact is uniform, we find that the magnitude of the normal force ΔN exerted on an element of area ΔA is $\Delta N = P \Delta A / A$, where $A = \pi(R_2^2 - R_1^2)$, and that the magnitude of the friction force ΔF acting on ΔA is $\Delta F = \mu_k \Delta N$.   Denoting by r the distance from the axis of the shaft to the element of area ΔA, we express as follows the moment ΔM of ΔF about the axis of the shaft:

$$\Delta M = r \, \Delta F = \frac{r\mu_k P \, \Delta A}{\pi(R_2^2 - R_1^2)}$$

The equilibrium of the shaft requires that the moment **M** of the couple applied to the shaft be equal in magnitude to the sum of the moments of the friction forces ΔF.   Replacing ΔA by the infinitesimal element $dA = r \, d\theta \, dr$ used with polar coordinates, and integrating over the area of contact, we thus obtain the following expression for the magnitude of the couple

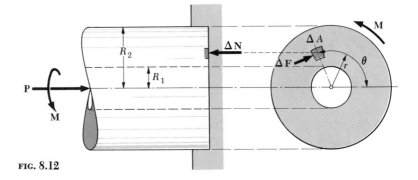

FIG. 8.12

M required to overcome the frictional resistance of the bearing:

$$M = \frac{\mu_k P}{\pi(R_2^2 - R_1^2)} \int_0^{2\pi} \int_{R_1}^{R_2} r^2 \, dr \, d\theta$$

$$= \frac{\mu_k P}{\pi(R_2^2 - R_1^2)} \int_0^{2\pi} \tfrac{1}{3}(R_2^3 - R_1^3) \, d\theta$$

$$M = \tfrac{2}{3}\mu_k P \frac{R_2^3 - R_1^3}{R_2^2 - R_1^2} \tag{8.8}$$

When contact takes place over a full circle of radius R, formula (8.8) reduces to

$$M = \tfrac{2}{3}\mu_k PR \tag{8.9}$$

The value of M is then the same as would be obtained if contact between shaft and bearing took place at a single point located at a distance $2R/3$ from the axis of the shaft.

The largest torque which may be transmitted by a disk clutch without causing slippage is given by a formula similar to (8.9), where μ_k has been replaced by the coefficient of static friction μ_s.

*8.9. Wheel Friction. Rolling Resistance. The wheel is one of the most important inventions of our civilization. Its use makes it possible to move heavy loads with relatively little effort. Because the point of the wheel in contact with the ground at any given instant has no relative motion with respect to the ground, the wheel eliminates the large friction forces which would arise if the load were in direct contact with the ground. In practice, however, the wheel is not perfect, and some resistance to its motion exists. This resistance has two distinct causes. It is due (1) to a combined effect of axle friction and friction at the rim and (2) to the fact that the wheel and the ground deform, with the result that contact between wheel and ground takes place, not at a single point, but over a certain area.

To understand better the first cause of resistance to the motion of a wheel, we shall consider a railroad car supported by eight wheels mounted on axles and bearings. The car is assumed to be moving to the right at constant speed along a straight horizontal track. The free-body diagram of one of the wheels is shown in Fig. 8.13a. The forces acting on the free body include the load **W** supported by the wheel and the normal reaction **N** of the track. Since **W** is drawn through the center O of the axle, the frictional resistance of the bearing

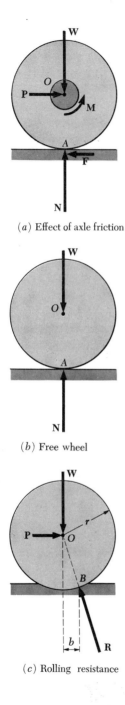

(a) Effect of axle friction

(b) Free wheel

(c) Rolling resistance

FIG. 8.13

should be represented by a counterclockwise couple **M** (see Sec. 8.7). To keep the free body in equilibrium, we must add two equal and opposite forces **P** and **F** forming a clockwise couple of moment −**M**. The force **F** is the friction force exerted by the track on the wheel, and **P** represents the force which should be applied to the wheel to keep it rolling at constant speed. Note that the forces **P** and **F** would not exist if there were no friction between wheel and track. The couple **M** representing the axle friction would then be zero; the wheel would slide on the track without turning in its bearing.

The couple **M** and the forces **P** and **F** also reduce to zero when there is no axle friction. For example, a wheel which is not held in bearings and rolls freely and at constant speed on horizontal ground (Fig. 8.13b) will be subjected to only two forces: its own weight **W** and the normal reaction **N** of the ground. No friction force will act on the wheel, regardless of the value of the coefficient of friction between wheel and ground. A wheel rolling freely on a horizontal ground should thus keep rolling indefinitely.

Experience, however, indicates that the wheel will slow down and eventually come to rest. This is due to the second type of resistance mentioned at the beginning of this section, known as the *rolling resistance*. Under the load **W**, both the wheel and the ground deform slightly, causing the contact between wheel and ground to take place over a certain area. Experimental evidence shows that the resultant of the forces exerted by the ground on the wheel over this area is a force **R** applied at a point B, which is not located directly under the center O of the wheel, but slightly in front of it (Fig. 8.13c). To balance the moment of **W** about B and to keep the wheel rolling at constant speed, it is necessary to apply a horizontal force **P** at the center of the wheel. Writing $\Sigma M_B = 0$, we obtain

$$Pr = Wb \qquad (8.10)$$

where r = radius of wheel
b = horizontal distance between O and B
The distance b is commonly called the *coefficient of rolling resistance*. It should be noted that b is not a dimensionless coefficient since it represents a length; b is usually expressed in inches. The value of b depends upon several parameters in a manner which has not yet been clearly established. Values of the coefficient of rolling resistance vary from about 0.01 in. for a steel wheel on a steel rail to 5.0 in. for the same wheel on soft ground.

SAMPLE PROBLEM 8.6

A pulley of diameter 4 in. can rotate about a fixed shaft of diameter 2 in. The coefficients of static and kinetic friction between the pulley and shaft are both assumed equal to 0.20. Determine (a) the smallest vertical force **P** required to raise a 500-lb load, (b) the smallest vertical force **P** required to hold the load, (c) the smallest horizontal force **P** required to raise the same load.

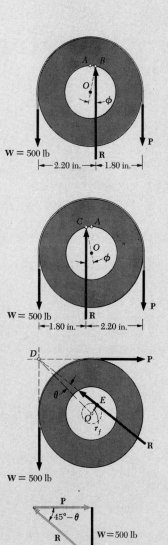

a. **Vertical Force P Required to Raise the Load.** When the forces in both parts of the rope are equal, contact between the pulley and shaft takes place at *A*. When **P** is increased, the pulley rolls around the shaft slightly and contact takes place at *B*. The free-body diagram of the pulley when motion is impending is drawn. The perpendicular distance from the center *O* of the pulley to the line of action of **R** is

$$r_f = r \sin \phi \approx r\mu \qquad r_f \approx (1 \text{ in.})0.20 = 0.20 \text{ in.}$$

Summing moments about *B*, we write

$$+\!\!\uparrow\ \Sigma M_B = 0: \quad (2.20 \text{ in.})(500 \text{ lb}) - (1.80 \text{ in.})P = 0$$

$$P = 611 \text{ lb} \qquad\qquad \mathbf{P = 611\ lb} \downarrow \quad \blacktriangleleft$$

b. **Vertical Force P to Hold the Load.** As the force **P** is decreased, the pulley rolls around the shaft and contact takes place at *C*. Considering the pulley as a free body and summing moments about *C*, we write

$$+\!\!\uparrow\ \Sigma M_C = 0: \quad (1.80 \text{ in.})(500 \text{ lb}) - (2.20 \text{ in.})P = 0$$

$$P = 409 \text{ lb} \qquad\qquad \mathbf{P = 409\ lb} \downarrow \quad \blacktriangleleft$$

c. **Horizontal Force P to Raise the Load.** Since the three forces **W**, **P**, and **R** are not parallel, they must be concurrent. The direction of **R** is thus determined from the fact that its line of action must pass through the point of intersection *D* of **W** and **P**, and must be tangent to the circle of friction. Recalling that the radius of the circle of friction is $r_f = 0.20$ in., we write

$$\sin \theta = \frac{OE}{OD} = \frac{0.20 \text{ in.}}{(2 \text{ in.})\sqrt{2}} = 0.0707 \qquad \theta = 4.1°$$

From the force triangle, we obtain

$$P = W \cot (45 - \theta) = (500 \text{ lb}) \cot 40.9°$$

$$P = 577 \text{ lb} \qquad\qquad \mathbf{P = 577\ lb} \rightarrow \quad \blacktriangleleft$$

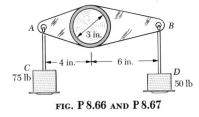

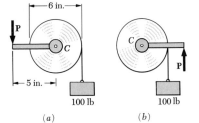

FIG. P 8.66 AND P 8.67

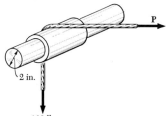

(a)   (b)

FIG. P 8.68

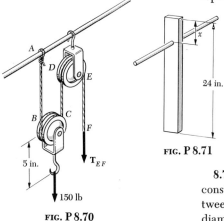

100 lb

FIG. P 8.69

FIG. P 8.70

FIG. P 8.71

PROBLEMS

8.66. A lever of weight 5 lb is loosely fitted onto a 3-in.-diameter shaft and is in equilibrium under the loads shown. It is observed that the lever will just start rotating if a 4-lb weight is added at D. Determine the coefficient of friction between the shaft and the lever.

8.67. Determine the size of the weight which must be added at C to cause the lever of Prob. 8.66 to rotate counterclockwise.

8.68. A windlass, of diameter 6 in., is used to raise a 100-lb load. It is supported by two axles and bearings of diameter 2 in., poorly lubricated ($\mu = 0.40$). Determine the magnitude of the force **P** required to raise the load for each of the two positions shown.

8.69. A bushing of outside diameter 3 in. fits loosely on a horizontal 2-in.-diameter shaft. A horizontal force **P** of magnitude 110 lb is required to raise the 100-lb load attached to the rope. Determine the coefficient of friction between the shaft and the bushing. Assume that the rope does not slip on the bushing.

8.70. A 150-lb load is to be raised by the block and tackle shown. Each of the 3-in.-diameter pulleys rotates on a $\frac{1}{2}$-in.-diameter axle. Knowing that $\mu = 0.20$, determine the tension in each portion of the rope as the load is being raised.

8.71. A uniform bar of length 24 in. hangs loosely on a horizontal shaft of diameter 1 in. The shaft is slowly rotated. If the distance x is 2 in., determine the angle at which the bar initially slips. The coefficient of friction is 0.10.

8.72. Determine the minimum value of x for which the bar of Prob. 8.71 will not slip when the shaft is slowly rotated through a full turn.

8.73. A scooter is to be designed to roll down a 2 per cent slope at constant speed. Assuming that the coefficient of kinetic friction between the 1-in. axles and the bearings is 0.10, determine the required diameter of the wheels. Neglect the rolling resistance between the wheels and the ground.

8.74. A certain railroad freight car has eight steel wheels of 32-in. diameter which are supported on 5-in.-diameter axles. Assuming $\mu = 0.015$, determine the horizontal force per ton of load required to move the car at constant velocity.

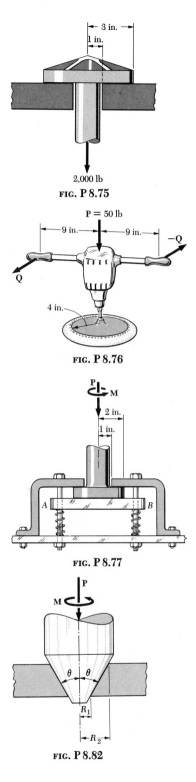

8.75. A couple of magnitude 60 lb-ft is required to start the vertical shaft rotating.   Determine the coefficient of static friction.

8.76. A vertical force of 50 lb is applied to a 10-lb electric polisher as it is operated on a horizontal surface.   Knowing that $\mu_k = 0.25$, determine the magnitude Q of the forces required to prevent rotation of the handles.   Assume the force between the disk and the surface to be uniformly distributed.

8.77. Four springs, each of constant 30 lb/in., are used to press plate AB against the head on the vertical rod.   In the position shown each spring has been compressed 2 in.   The plate AB may move vertically, but it is constrained against rotation by bolts which pass through holes cut in the plate.   Knowing that $\mu = 0.30$ and $P = 0$, determine the magnitude of the couple **M** required to rotate the rod.

8.78. In Prob. 8.77 determine the required magnitude of the force **P** if the rod is to just rotate when the magnitude of the couple **M** is 180 lb-in.   For what magnitude of the force **P** is the rod most easily rotated?

*8.79. Solve Prob. 8.76 assuming that between the disk and the surface the force per unit area varies uniformly from a maximum at the center to zero at the perimeter of the disk.

*8.80. As the surfaces of shaft and bearing wear out, the frictional resistance of a thrust bearing decreases.   It is generally assumed that the wear is directly proportional to the distance traveled by any given point of the shaft, and thus to the distance r from the point to the axis of the shaft.   Assuming, then, that the normal force per unit area is inversely proportional to r, show that the magnitude of the couple **M** required to overcome the frictional resistance of a worn-out end bearing (with contact over the full circular area) is equal to 75 per cent of the value given by formula (8.9) for a new bearing.

*8.81. Assuming that bearings wear out as indicated in Prob. 8.80, show that the magnitude of the couple **M** required to overcome the frictional resistance of a worn-out collar bearing is

$$M = \tfrac{1}{2}\mu_k P(R_1 + R_2)$$

where P = magnitude of the total axial force

R_1, R_2 = inner and outer radii of collar

*8.82. Assuming that the pressure between the surfaces of contact is uniform, show the magnitude of the couple required to overcome frictional resistance for the conical pivot shown is

$$M = \frac{2\,\mu_k P}{3\sin\theta}\ \frac{R_2^3 - R_1^3}{R_2^2 - R_1^2}$$

FIG. P 8.75

FIG. P 8.76

FIG. P 8.77

FIG. P 8.82

2,000 lb

$P = 50$ lb

9 in. 9 in.

Q $-Q$

4 in.

P

M

2 in.

1 in.

A B

P

M

θ θ

R_1

R_2

3 in.

1 in.

8.83. Determine the horizontal force required to move a 3,000-lb automobile along a horizontal road at constant velocity.   Neglect all forms of friction except rolling resistance, and assume the coefficient of rolling resistance to be 0.05 in.   The diameter of each tire is 24 in.

8.84. A circular disk of diameter 5 in. rolls at constant velocity down an incline which has a slope of $\frac{1}{8}$ in. per foot.   Determine the coefficient of rolling resistance.

8.85. Solve Prob. 8.73 including the effect of a coefficient of rolling resistance of 0.06 in.

8.86. Solve Prob. 8.74 including the effect of a coefficient of rolling resistance of 0.02 in.

8.10. Belt Friction.   Consider a flat belt passing over a fixed cylindrical drum (Fig. 8.14a).   We propose to determine the relation existing between the values T_1 and T_2 of the tension in the two parts of the belt when the belt is just about to slide toward the right.

Let us detach from the belt a small element PP' subtending an angle $\Delta\theta$.   Denoting by T the tension at P and by $T + \Delta T$ the tension at P', we draw the free-body diagram of the element of the belt (Fig. 8.14b).   Besides the two forces of tension, the forces acting on the free body are the normal component ΔN of the reaction of the drum and the friction force ΔF.   Since motion is assumed to be impending, we have $\Delta F = \mu_s\,\Delta N$.   It should be noted that if $\Delta\theta$ is made to approach zero, the magnitudes ΔN, ΔF, and the *difference* ΔT between the tension at P and the tension at P' will also approach zero; the value T of the tension at P, however, will remain unchanged.   This observation helps in understanding our choice of notations.

Choosing the coordinate axes shown in Fig. 8.14b, we write the equations of equilibrium for the element PP':

$$\Sigma F_x = 0: \quad (T + \Delta T)\cos\frac{\Delta\theta}{2} - T\cos\frac{\Delta\theta}{2} - \mu_s\,\Delta N = 0 \quad (8.11)$$

$$\Sigma F_y = 0: \quad \Delta N - (T + \Delta T)\sin\frac{\Delta\theta}{2} - T\sin\frac{\Delta\theta}{2} = 0 \quad (8.12)$$

Solving Eq. (8.12) for ΔN and substituting into (8.11), we obtain after reductions

$$\Delta T\cos\frac{\Delta\theta}{2} - \mu_s(2T + \Delta T)\sin\frac{\Delta\theta}{2} = 0$$

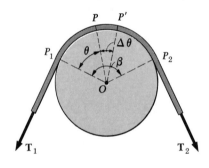

(a)

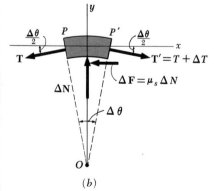

(b)

FIG. 8.14

We shall now divide both terms by $\Delta\theta$; as far as the first term is concerned, this will be simply done by dividing ΔT by $\Delta\theta$. The division of the second term is carried out by dividing the terms in the parentheses by 2 and the sine by $\Delta\theta/2$. We write

$$\frac{\Delta T}{\Delta\theta}\cos\frac{\Delta\theta}{2} - \mu_s\left(T + \frac{\Delta T}{2}\right)\frac{\sin(\Delta\theta/2)}{\Delta\theta/2} = 0$$

If we now let $\Delta\theta$ approach 0, the cosine approaches 1 and $\Delta T/2$ approaches zero as noted above. On the other hand, the quotient of $\sin(\Delta\theta/2)$ over $\Delta\theta/2$ approaches 1, according to a lemma derived in all calculus textbooks. Since the limit of $\Delta T/\Delta\theta$ is by definition equal to the derivative $dT/d\theta$, we write

$$\frac{dT}{d\theta} - \mu_s T = 0 \qquad \frac{dT}{T} = \mu_s\, d\theta$$

We shall now integrate both members of the last equation obtained from P_1 to P_2 (Fig. 8.14a). At P_1, we have $\theta = 0$ and $T = T_1$; at P_2, we have $\theta = \beta$ and $T = T_2$. Integrating between these limits, we write

$$\int_{T_1}^{T_2}\frac{dT}{T} = \int_0^\beta \mu_s\, d\theta$$

$$\ln T_2 - \ln T_1 = \mu_s\beta$$

$$\ln\frac{T_2}{T_1} = \mu_s\beta \qquad (8.13)$$

This relation may also be written in the form

$$\frac{T_2}{T_1} = e^{\mu_s\beta} \qquad (8.14)$$

The formulas we have derived apply equally well to problems involving flat belts passing over fixed cylindrical drums and to problems involving ropes wrapped around a post or capstan. They may also be used to solve problems involving band brakes. In such problems, it is the drum which is about to rotate, while the band remains fixed. The formulas may also be applied to problems involving belt drives. In these problems, both the pulley and the belt rotate; our concern is then to find whether the belt will slip, i.e., whether it will move *with respect* to the pulley.

Formulas (8.13) and (8.14) should be used only if the belt, rope, or brake is *about to slip*. Formula (8.14) will be used if

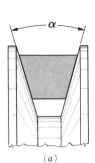

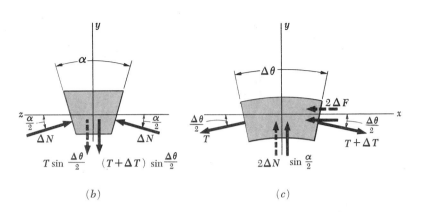

(a) (b) (c)

FIG. 8.15

T_1 or T_2 is desired; formula (8.13) will be preferred if either μ_s or the angle of contact β is desired.† We should note that T_2 is always larger than T_1; T_2 therefore represents the tension in that part of the belt or rope which *pulls*, while T_1 is the tension in the part which *resists*. We should also observe that the angle of contact β must be expressed in *radians*. The angle β may be larger than 2π; for example, if a rope is wrapped n times around a post, β is equal to $2\pi n$.

If the belt, rope, or brake is actually slipping, formulas similar to (8.13) and (8.14), but involving the coefficient of kinetic friction μ_k, should be used. If the belt, rope, or brake does not slip and is not about to slip, none of these formulas may be used.

The belts used in belt drives are often V-shaped. Such a belt, called a "V belt," is shown in Fig. 8.15a. It is seen that contact between belt and pulley takes place along the sides of the groove. The relation existing between the values T_1 and T_2 of the tension in the two parts of the belt when the belt is just about to slip may again be obtained by drawing the free-body diagram of an element of belt (Fig. 8.15b and c). Equations similar to (8.11) and (8.12) are derived, but the magnitude of the total friction force acting on the element is now $2\,\Delta F$, and the sum of the y components of the normal forces is $2\,\Delta N \sin{(\alpha/2)}$. Proceeding as above, we obtain

$$\frac{T_2}{T_1} = e^{\,\mu_s\beta/\sin{(\alpha/2)}} \tag{8.15}$$

† Since the determination of a power of e and that of a logarithm to the base e (ln) involves the use of the same scales on the slide rule, there is no need for distinguishing between formulas (8.13) and (8.14) in carrying out computations on the slide rule. In every case, the product $\mu_s\beta$ should be read on the D scale and the quotient T_2/T_1 on one of the LL scales.

SAMPLE PROBLEM 8.7

A hawser thrown from a ship to a pier is wrapped two full turns around a capstan. The tension in the hawser is 1,500 lb; by exerting a force of 30 lb on its free end, a longshoreman can just keep the hawser from slipping. (*a*) Determine the coefficient of friction between the hawser and the capstan. (*b*) Determine the tension in the hawser that could be resisted by the 30-lb force if the hawser were wrapped three full turns around the capstan.

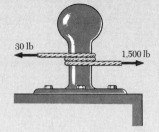

a. **Coefficient of Friction.** Since slipping of the hawser is impending, we use Eq. (8.13),

$$\ln \frac{T_2}{T_1} = \mu_s \beta$$

Since the hawser is wrapped two full turns around the capstan, we have

$$\beta = 2(2\pi \text{ radians}) = 12.6 \text{ radians}$$

$$T_1 = 30 \text{ lb} \qquad T_2 = 1{,}500 \text{ lb}$$

Therefore,

$$\mu_s \beta = \ln \frac{T_2}{T_1}$$

$$\mu_s(12.6 \text{ radians}) = \ln \frac{1{,}500 \text{ lb}}{30 \text{ lb}} = \ln 50 = 3.91$$

$$\mu_s = 0.31 \qquad \blacktriangleleft$$

b. **Hawser Wrapped Three Turns around Capstan.** Using the value of μ_s obtained in part *a*, we have now

$$\beta = 3(2\pi \text{ radians}) = 18.9 \text{ radians}$$

$$T_1 = 30 \text{ lb} \qquad \mu_s = 0.31$$

Substituting these values into Eq. (8.14), we obtain

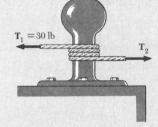

$$\frac{T_2}{T_1} = e^{\mu_s \beta}$$

$$\frac{T_2}{30 \text{ lb}} = e^{(0.31)(18.9)} = e^{5.86} = 350$$

$$T_2 = 10{,}500 \text{ lb} \qquad \blacktriangleleft$$

Note. See the footnote on page 306 for the use of the slide rule in problems dealing with belt friction.

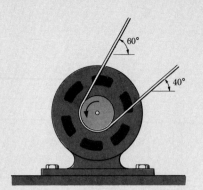

SAMPLE PROBLEM 8.8

A flat belt is used to transmit the 25-lb-ft torque developed by an electric motor. The belt is in contact with a drum of diameter 6 in., as shown. The coefficient of static friction between belt and drum is 0.30. Determine the minimum values of the tension in both parts of the belt which will assure no slippage.

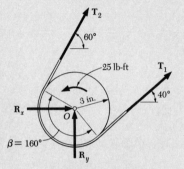

Solution. The free-body diagram of the drum is drawn. Summing moments about the center O of the drum, we write

$$+\curvearrowleft \ \Sigma M_O = 0: \qquad T_1(3 \text{ in.}) - T_2(3 \text{ in.}) + 25 \text{ lb-ft} = 0$$

$$(T_2 - T_1)(3 \text{ in.}) = 300 \text{ lb-in.}$$

$$T_2 - T_1 = 100 \text{ lb} \tag{1}$$

The angle of contact between belt and drum is

$$\beta = 160° = 160° \frac{2\pi \text{ radians}}{360°} = 2.79 \text{ radians}$$

Since the values of T_1 and T_2 corresponding to impending slippage are desired, we use Eq. (8.14).

$$\frac{T_2}{T_1} = e^{\mu_s \beta} \qquad \frac{T_2}{T_1} = e^{(0.30)(2.79)} = e^{0.837} = 2.31$$

$$T_2 = 2.31 T_1 \tag{2}$$

Substituting T_2 from Eq. (2) into Eq. (1), we obtain

$$2.31 T_1 - T_1 = 100 \text{ lb} \qquad\qquad T_1 = 76.4 \text{ lb} \ \blacktriangleleft$$

$$T_2 = T_1 + 100 \text{ lb} \qquad\qquad T_2 = 176.4 \text{ lb} \ \blacktriangleleft$$

PROBLEMS

8.87. A hawser is wrapped two full turns around a capstan head.   By exerting a force of 80 lb on the free end of the hawser, a seaman can resist a force of 5,000 lb on the other end of the hawser.   Determine (*a*) the coefficient of friction, (*b*) the number of times the hawser should be wrapped around the capstan if a 20,000-lb force is to be resisted by the same 80-lb force.

8.88. A rope weighing 0.5 lb/ft is wound $2\frac{1}{4}$ times around a horizontal bar.   What length x of rope should be left hanging if a load of 100 lb is to be supported?   The coefficient of static friction between the rope and the bar is 0.25.

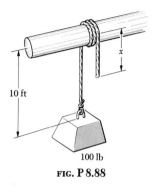

100 lb

FIG. P 8.88

8.89. Assume that the bushing of Prob. 8.69 has become frozen to the shaft and cannot rotate.   Determine the coefficient of friction between the bushing and the rope if a force **P** of magnitude 120 lb is required to raise the 100-lb load.

8.90. A rope *ABCD* is looped over two pipes as shown.   Knowing that $\mu = 0.30$, determine (*a*) the smallest weight W for which equilibrium is possible, (*b*) the angle θ for which the corresponding tension in portion *BC* of the rope is 50 lb.

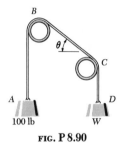

FIG. P 8.90

8.91. A flat belt is used to transmit a torque from pulley *A* to pulley *B*. The radius of each pulley is 3 in. and $\mu = 0.20$.   Determine the moment of the largest torque which can be transmitted if the maximum allowable tension is 800 lb.

8.92. Solve Prob. 8.91 assuming that the belt is looped around the pulleys in a single figure 8.

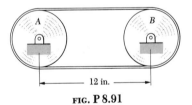

12 in.

FIG. P 8.91

8.93. A brake drum of radius $r = 5$ in. is rotating counterclockwise when a force **P** of magnitude 10 lb is applied at *A*.   Knowing that $\mu = 0.40$, determine the moment about O of the friction forces applied to the drum when $a = 8$ in. and $b = 10$ in.

8.94. Knowing that $r = 5$ in. and $a = 8$ in., determine the maximum value of μ for which the brake is not self-locking.   The brake drum revolves counterclockwise.

8.95. Knowing that $\mu = 0.40$, determine the minimum ratio of the distance a to the radius r for which the brake is not self-locking.   The brake drum revolves counterclockwise and $a > r$.

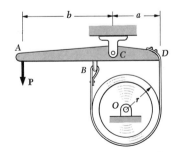

FIG. P 8.93, P 8.94, AND P 8.95

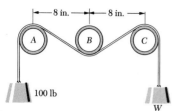

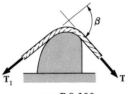

FIG. P 8.96 AND P 8.97

8.96. A cable is placed around three pipes, each of 4-in. outside diameter, located in the same horizontal plane.   Two of the pipes are fixed and do not rotate; the third pipe is rotated slowly.   Knowing that $\mu = 0.30$ for each pipe, determine the largest weight W which can be raised (*a*) if only pipe A is rotated, (*b*) if only pipe B is rotated, (*c*) if only pipe C is rotated.

8.97. A cable is placed around three pipes, each of 4-in. outside diameter, located in the same horizontal plane.   Pipes A and C are rotated slowly clockwise while pipe B is held fixed.   Knowing that $\mu = 0.30$ for each pipe, determine the largest weight W which can be raised.

8.98. A 50-ft rope passes over a small horizontal shaft; one end of the rope is attached to a bucket which weighs 5 lb.   The excess rope is coiled inside the bucket.   The coefficient of static friction between the rope and the shaft is 0.30, and the rope weighs 0.50 lb/ft.   (*a*) If the shaft is held fixed, show that the system is in equilibrium.   (*b*) If the shaft is slowly rotated, how far will the bucket rise before slipping?   Neglect the diameter of the shaft.

FIG. P 8.98

8.99. The shaft of Prob. 8.98 is slowly rotated.   Determine how far the bucket can be lowered before the rope slips on the shaft.

8.100. Prove that Eqs. (8.13) and (8.14) are valid for any shape of surface provided that the coefficient of friction is the same at all points of contact.

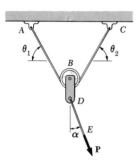

FIG. P 8.100

8.101. The axle of the pulley is frozen and cannot rotate with respect to the block.   Knowing that $\mu = 0.30$ between the cable ABC and the pulley and that $\theta_1 = \theta_2 = 60°$, determine the largest value of α for which the block is in equilibrium.   (Assume that the straight portions of cable meet at point D.)

*8.102. The axle of the pulley is frozen and cannot rotate with respect to the block.   The coefficient of friction between cable ABC and the pulley is 0.30.   For the case when $\alpha = 0°$ and $\theta_1 = 60°$, determine the largest value of θ_2 for which equilibrium exists.

8.103. Complete the derivation of Eq. (8.15), which relates the tension in both parts of a V belt.

FIG. P 8.101 AND P 8.102

8.104. Solve Prob. 8.91 assuming that the flat belt and pulley are replaced by a V belt and V pulley with $\alpha = 28°$.   (The angle α is as shown in Fig. 8.15*a*.)

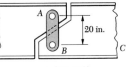

FIG. P 8.105

REVIEW PROBLEMS

8.105. In highway bridge construction the link arrangement shown is frequently used to allow for expansion due to changes in temperature. The coefficients of friction at each of the 2-in.-diameter pins A and B is 0.20. Knowing that the vertical component of the force in beam BC is 40,000 lb, determine (*a*) the horizontal component of the force in beam BC required to just move the link, (*b*) the angle that the corresponding total force in the link forms with the vertical.

8.106. The arrangement shown is used to measure the power output of a small turbine. The coefficient of kinetic friction is 0.15. When the flywheel is at rest, the reading of each spring is 15 lb. What will be the reading of each spring when the flywheel is rotating clockwise? Assume that the belt is of constant length.

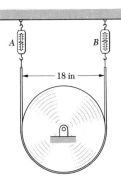

FIG. P 8.106

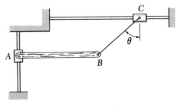

FIG. P 8.107

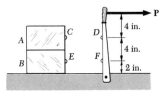

FIG. P 8.108

8.107. The uniform rod AB is connected to two collars, of negligible weight, by a pin at A and by the cord BC. The coefficient of friction between each collar and the rod upon which it may slide is denoted by μ. (*a*) Show that μ must be at least equal to 1.00 if the rod is to be maintained in a horizontal position. (*b*) If $\mu = 1.50$, determine the range of values of θ for which the rod will remain in a horizontal position.

8.108. The two 25-lb boxes A and B may be attached to the lever by means of either one or two horizontal links. The coefficient of friction between all surfaces is 0.30. Determine the magnitude of the force P required to move the lever (*a*) if a single link EF is used, (*b*) if a single link CD is used, (*c*) if two links EF and CD are used at the same time.

8.109. A band brake is used to control the speed of a flywheel as shown. What torque must be applied to the flywheel in order to keep it rotating at a constant speed, when $P = 10$ lb? Assume that the flywheel rotates clockwise.

8.110. Solve Prob. 8.109 assuming that the flywheel rotates counterclockwise.

8.111. A hot-metal ladle and its contents weigh 60 tons. Knowing that the coefficient of friction between the hooks and the pinion is 0.30, determine the tension in the cable AB required to start tipping the ladle.

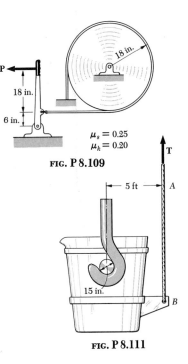

$\mu_s = 0.25$
$\mu_k = 0.20$

FIG. P 8.109

FIG. P 8.111

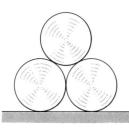

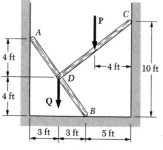

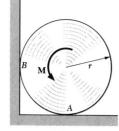

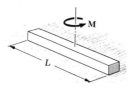

8.112. A rope is wrapped three complete turns around a post; the co-efficient of friction is 0.30.   (*a*) Determine the largest force which may be resisted at one end of the rope if a 10-lb force is applied at the other end.   (*b*) How many turns will be required if the force to be resisted is doubled, while the same 10-lb force is maintained at the other end?

8.113. Determine the smallest value of the coefficient of friction for which three identical cylindrical rods may be placed as shown.

8.114. A shaft of radius r and weight W is placed as shown; the coefficient of static friction between all surfaces is μ_s.   Determine the magnitude of the couple **M** required to start the shaft rotating in terms of r, W, and μ_s.

8.115. Two 10-ft beams are pin-connected at D and support two loads **P** and **Q** as shown.   Knowing that the coefficient of friction is zero at A, 0.25 at B, and 0.50 at C, determine the smallest value of P for which equilibrium is maintained when $Q = 240$ lb.   (*Hint*.   Note that C moves up when B moves to the right.)

8.116. A thin uniform bar of length L and weight W lies on a rough horizontal surface.   Denoting by μ the coefficient of friction, determine the magnitude of the couple **M** which must be applied to rotate the bar. Assume that the normal force between the surface and the bar is uniformly distributed.

9. DISTRIBUTED FORCES: MOMENTS OF INERTIA

MOMENTS OF INERTIA OF AREAS

9.1. Second Moment, or Moment of Inertia, of an Area. In Chap. 5, we analyzed various systems of forces distributed over an area. The two main types of forces considered were (1) weights of homogeneous plates of uniform thickness (Secs. 5.2 to 5.4) and (2) distributed loads on beams and hydrostatic forces (Secs. 5.6 and 5.7). In the case of homogeneous plates, the magnitude ΔW of the weight of an element of plate was proportional to the area ΔA of the element. In the case of distributed loads on beams, the magnitude ΔW of each elementary weight was represented by an element of area $\Delta A = \Delta W$ under the load curve; in the case of hydrostatic forces on submerged rectangular surfaces, a similar procedure was followed. Thus, in all cases considered in Chap. 5, the distributed forces were proportional to the elementary areas associated with them. The resultant of these forces, therefore, could be obtained by summing the corresponding areas, and the moment of the resultant about any given axis could be determined by computing the first moments of the areas about that axis.

In this chapter, we shall consider distributed forces $\Delta \mathbf{F}$ whose magnitudes depend not only upon the element of area ΔA on which they act but also upon the distance from ΔA to some given axis. More precisely, the magnitude of the force per unit area $\Delta F / \Delta A$ will vary linearly with the distance to the axis.

Consider, for example, a beam of uniform cross section, subjected to two equal and opposite couples applied at each end of the beam. Such a beam is said to be in *pure bending*, and it is shown in mechanics of materials that the internal forces in any section of the beam are distributed forces whose magnitudes $\Delta F = ky \, \Delta A$ vary linearly with the distance y from

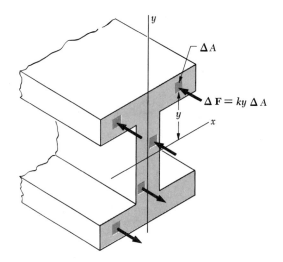

an axis passing through the centroid of the section.   This axis, represented by the x axis in Fig. 9.1, is known as the *neutral axis* of the section.   The forces on one side of the neutral axis are forces of compression, and on the other side forces of tension, while on the neutral axis itself the forces are zero.

The magnitude of the resultant **R** of the elementary forces $\Delta\mathbf{F}$ over the entire section is

$$R = \int ky\,dA = k\!\int y\,dA$$

The last integral obtained is recognized as the *first moment* of the section about the x axis; it is equal to $\bar{y}A$ and to zero, since the centroid of the section is located on the x axis.   The system of the forces $\Delta\mathbf{F}$ thus reduces to a couple.   The magnitude M of this couple (bending moment) must be equal to the sum of the moments $\Delta M_x = y\,\Delta F = ky^2\,\Delta A$ of the elementary forces.   Integrating over the entire section, we obtain

$$M = \int ky^2\,dA = k\!\int y^2\,dA$$

The last integral is known as the *second moment,* or *moment of inertia,*† of the beam section with respect to the x axis and is denoted by I_x.   It is obtained by multiplying each element of area dA by the *square of its distance* from the x axis and integrating over the beam section.   Since each product $y^2\,dA$ is positive, whether y is itself positive or negative (or zero if y is zero), the integral I_x will always be different from zero and positive.

---

† The term second moment is more proper than the term moment of inertia since, logically, the latter should be used only to denote integrals of mass (see Sec. 9.10).   In common engineering practice, however, moment of inertia is used in connection with areas as well as masses.

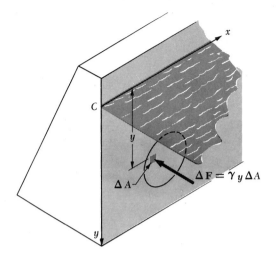

FIG. 9.2

Another example of second moment, or moment of inertia, of an area is provided by the following problem of hydrostatics: A vertical circular gate used to close the outlet of a large reservoir is submerged under water as shown in Fig. 9.2. What is the resultant of the forces exerted by the water on the gate, and what is the moment of the resultant about the line of intersection of the plane of the gate with the water surface (x axis)?

If the gate were rectangular, the resultant of the forces of pressure could be determined from the pressure curve, as was done in Sec. 5.7. Since the gate is circular, however, a more general method must be used. Denoting by y the depth of an element of area ΔA and by γ the specific weight of water, the pressure at the element is $p = \gamma y$, and the magnitude of the elementary force exerted on ΔA is $\Delta F = p \, \Delta A = \gamma y \, \Delta A$. The magnitude of the resultant of the elementary forces is thus

$$R = \int \gamma y \, dA = \gamma \int y \, dA$$

and may be obtained by computing the first moment of the area of the gate with respect to the x axis. The moment M_x of the resultant must be equal to the sum of the moments $\Delta M_x = y \, \Delta F = \gamma y^2 \, \Delta A$ of the elementary forces. Integrating over the area of the gate, we have

$$M_x = \int \gamma y^2 \, dA = \gamma \int y^2 \, dA$$

Here again, the integral obtained represents the second moment, or moment of inertia, I_x of the area with respect to the x axis.

9.2. Determination of the Moment of Inertia of an Area by Integration. We have defined in the preceding section the second moment, or moment of inertia, of an area A with re-

315

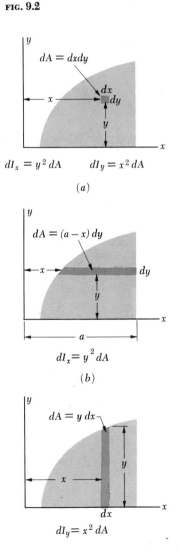

$dA = dx\,dy$

$dI_x = y^2\,dA \qquad dI_y = x^2\,dA$

(a)

$dA = (a - x)\,dy$

$dI_x = y^2\,dA$

(b)

$dA = y\,dx$

$dI_y = x^2\,dA$

(c)

FIG. 9.3

spect to the x axis.   Defining in a similar way the moment of inertia I_y of the area A with respect to the y axis, we write (Fig. 9.3*a*)

$$I_x = \int y^2 \, dA \qquad I_y = \int x^2 \, dA \qquad (9.1)$$

These integrals, known as the *rectangular moments of inertia* of the area A, may be more easily computed if we choose for dA a thin strip parallel to one of the axes of coordinates.   To compute I_x, the strip is chosen parallel to the x axis, so that all the points forming the strip are at the same distance y from the x axis (Fig. 9.3*b*); the moment of inertia dI_x of the strip is then obtained by multiplying the area dA of the strip by y^2. To compute I_y, the strip is·chosen parallel to the y axis, so that all the points forming the strip are at the same distance x from the y axis (Fig. 9.3*c*); the moment of inertia dI_y of the strip is $x^2 \, dA$.

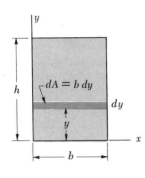

FIG. 9.4

Moment of Inertia of a Rectangular Area.   As an example, we shall determine the moment of inertia of a rectangle with respect to its base (Fig. 9.4).   Dividing the rectangle into strips parallel to the x axis, we obtain

$$dA = b \, dy \qquad dI_x = y^2 b \, dy \qquad I_x = \int_0^h by^2 \, dy = \tfrac{1}{3}bh^3 \quad (9.2)$$

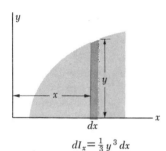

$$dI_x = \tfrac{1}{3} y^3 \, dx$$
$$dI_y = x^2 y \, dx$$

FIG. 9.5

Computing I_x and I_y from the Same Elementary Strips.   The formula just derived may be used to determine the moment of inertia dI_x with respect to the x axis of a rectangular strip parallel to the y axis such as the one shown in Fig. 9.3*c* and reproduced in Fig. 9.5.   Making $b = dx$ and $h = y$ in formula (9.2), we write

$$dI_x = \tfrac{1}{3}y^3 \, dx$$

On the other hand, we have

$$dI_y = x^2 \, dA = x^2 y \, dx$$

The same element may thus be used to compute the moments of inertia I_x and I_y of a given area (see Sample Prob. 9.3).

9.3. Polar Moment of Inertia.   An integral of great importance in problems concerning the torsion of cylindrical shafts and in problems dealing with the rotation of slabs is

$$J_O = \int r^2 \, dA \qquad (9.3)$$

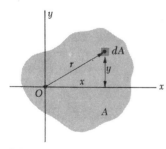

FIG. 9.6

where r is the distance from the element of area dA to the pole O (Fig. 9.6).   This integral is the *polar moment of inertia* of the area A with respect to O.

The polar moment of inertia of a given area may be computed from the rectangular moments of inertia I_x and I_y of the area if these integrals are already known. Indeed, noting that $r^2 = x^2 + y^2$, we write

$$J_o = \int r^2 \, dA = \int (x^2 + y^2) \, dA = \int y^2 \, dA + \int x^2 \, dA$$

that is,

$$J_o = I_x + I_y \qquad (9.4)$$

9.4. Radius of Gyration of an Area. Consider an area A which has a moment of inertia I_x with respect to the x axis (Fig. 9.7a). Let us imagine that we concentrate this area into a thin strip parallel to the x axis (Fig. 9.7b). If the area A, thus concentrated, is to have the same moment of inertia with respect to the x axis, the strip should be placed at a distance k_x from the x axis, defined by the relation

$$I_x = k_x^2 A$$

Solving for k_x, we write

$$k_x = \sqrt{\frac{I_x}{A}} \qquad (9.5)$$

The distance k_x is referred to as the *radius of gyration* of the area with respect to the x axis. We may define in a similar way the radii of gyration k_y and k_o; we write

$$I_y = k_y^2 A \qquad k_y = \sqrt{\frac{I_y}{A}} \qquad (9.6)$$

$$J_o = k_o^2 A \qquad k_o = \sqrt{\frac{J_o}{A}} \qquad (9.7)$$

Substituting for J_o, I_x, and I_y in terms of the radii of gyration in the relation (9.4), we observe that

$$k_o^2 = k_x^2 + k_y^2 \qquad (9.8)$$

Example. As an example, let us compute the radius of gyration k_x of the rectangle shown in Fig. 9.4. Using formulas (9.5) and (9.2), we write

$$k_x^2 = \frac{I_x}{A} = \frac{\frac{1}{3}bh^3}{bh} = \frac{h^2}{3} \qquad k_x = \frac{h}{\sqrt{3}}$$

The radius of gyration k_x of the rectangle is shown in Fig. 9.8. It should not be confused with the ordinate $\bar{y} = h/2$ of the centroid of the area. While k_x depends upon the *second moment*, or moment of inertia, of the area, the ordinate $\bar{y}$ is related to the *first moment* of the area.

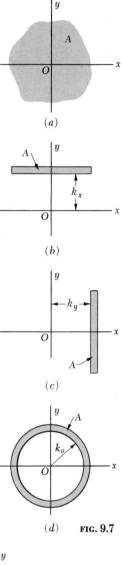

(a)

(b)

(c)

(d)   **FIG. 9.7**

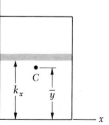

FIG. 9.8

SAMPLE PROBLEM 9.1

Determine the moment of inertia of a triangle with respect to its base.

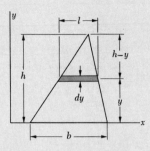

Solution. A triangle of base b and height h is drawn; the x axis is chosen to coincide with the base. A differential strip parallel to the x axis is chosen. Since all portions of the strip are at the same distance from the x axis, we write

$$dI_x = y^2 \, dA \qquad dA = l \, dy$$

From the similar triangles, we have

$$\frac{l}{b} = \frac{h-y}{h} \qquad l = b\frac{h-y}{h} \qquad dA = b\frac{h-y}{h} dy$$

Integrating dI_x from $y = 0$ to $y = h$, we obtain

$$I_x = \int y^2 \, dA = \int_0^h y^2 b \frac{h-y}{h} dy = \frac{b}{h} \int_0^h (hy^2 - y^3) \, dy$$

$$= \frac{b}{h}\left[h\frac{y^3}{3} - \frac{y^4}{4} \right]_0^h \qquad\qquad I_x = \frac{bh^3}{12} \quad \blacktriangleleft$$

SAMPLE PROBLEM 9.2

(*a*) Determine the centroidal polar moment of inertia of a circular area by direct integration. (*b*) Using the result of part *a*, determine the moment of inertia of a circular area with respect to a diameter.

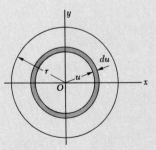

a. **Polar Moment of Inertia.** An annular differential element of area is chosen. Since all portions of this differential area are at the same distance from the origin, we write

$$dJ_0 = u^2 \, dA \qquad dA = 2\pi u \, du$$

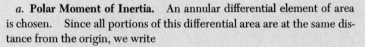

$$J_0 = \int dJ_0 = \int_0^r u^2(2\pi u \, du) = 2\pi \int_0^r u^3 \, du$$

$$J_0 = \frac{\pi}{2} r^4 \quad \blacktriangleleft$$

b. **Moment of Inertia.** Because of the symmetry of the circular area we have $I_x = I_y$. We then write

$$J_0 = I_x + I_y = 2I_x \qquad \frac{\pi}{2} r^4 = 2I_x \qquad I_x = \frac{\pi}{4} r^4 \qquad I_{\text{diameter}} = \frac{\pi}{4} r^4 \quad \blacktriangleleft$$

318

SAMPLE PROBLEM 9.3

(a) Determine the moment of inertia of the shaded area shown with respect to each of the coordinate axes. This area has also been considered in Sample Prob. 5.4. (b) Using the results of part a, determine the radius of gyration of the shaded area with respect to each of the coordinate axes.

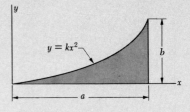

Solution. Referring to Sample Prob. 5.4, we obtain the following expressions for the equation of the curve and the total area:

$$y = \frac{b}{a^2} x^2 \qquad A = \tfrac{1}{3}ab$$

Moment of Inertia I_x. A vertical differential element of area is chosen. Since all portions of this element are *not* at the same distance from the x axis, we must treat the element as a thin rectangle. The moment of inertia of the element with respect to the x axis is

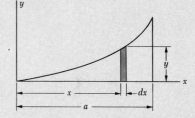

$$dI_x = \tfrac{1}{3}y^3\, dx = \frac{1}{3}\left(\frac{b}{a^2}x^2\right)^3 dx = \frac{1}{3}\frac{b^3}{a^6}x^6\, dx$$

$$I_x = \int dI_x = \int_0^a \frac{1}{3}\frac{b^3}{a^6}x^6\, dx = \left[\frac{1}{3}\frac{b^3}{a^6}\frac{x^7}{7}\right]_0^a$$

$$I_x = \frac{ab^3}{21} \quad \blacktriangleleft$$

Moment of Inertia I_y. The same vertical differential element of area is used. Since all portions of the element are at the same distance from the y axis, we write

$$dI_y = x^2\, dA = x^2(y\, dx) = x^2\left(\frac{b}{a^2}x^2\right) dx = \frac{b}{a^2}x^4\, dx$$

$$I_y = \int dI_y = \int_0^a \frac{b}{a^2}x^4\, dx = \left[\frac{b}{a^2}\frac{x^5}{5}\right]_0^a$$

$$I_y = \frac{a^3 b}{5} \quad \blacktriangleleft$$

Radii of Gyration k_x and k_y

$$k_x^2 = \frac{I_x}{A} = \frac{ab^3/21}{ab/3} = \frac{b^2}{7} \qquad\qquad k_x = \sqrt{\tfrac{1}{7}}\,b \quad \blacktriangleleft$$

$$k_y^2 = \frac{I_y}{A} = \frac{a^3 b/5}{ab/3} = \tfrac{3}{5}a^2 \qquad\qquad k_y = \sqrt{\tfrac{3}{5}}\,a \quad \blacktriangleleft$$

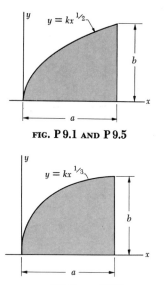

$y = kx^{1/2}$

b

a

FIG. P 9.1 AND P 9.5

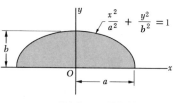

$y = kx^{1/3}$

b

a

FIG. P 9.2 AND P 9.6

PROBLEMS

9.1 through 9.4. Determine by direct integration the moment of inertia of the shaded area with respect to the y axis.

9.5 through 9.8. Determine by direct integration the moment of inertia of the shaded area with respect to the x axis.

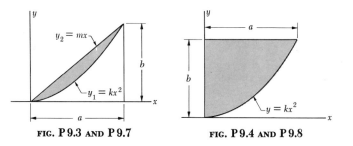

$y_2 = mx$

$y_1 = kx^2$

b

a

FIG. P 9.3 AND P 9.7

a

b

$y = kx^2$

FIG. P 9.4 AND P 9.8

9.9 Determine the moment of inertia and radius of gyration of the semielliptical area shown with respect to the x axis.

9.10. Determine the moment of inertia and radius of gyration of the semielliptical area shown with respect to the y axis.

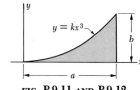

$\dfrac{x^2}{a^2} + \dfrac{y^2}{b^2} = 1$

b

O

a

FIG. P 9.9 AND P 9.10

$y = kx^3$

b

a

FIG. P 9.11 AND P 9.12

9.11. Determine the radius of gyration of the shaded area with respect to the x axis.

9.12. Determine the radius of gyration of the shaded area with respect to the y axis.

9.13. Determine the polar moment of inertia and the polar radius of gyration of an equilateral triangle of side a with respect to one of its vertices.

9.14. Determine the polar moment of inertia and the polar radius of gyration of a rectangle of base b and height h with respect to one of its corners.

9.15. Determine the polar moment of inertia and the polar radius of gyration of the semielliptical area of Prob. 9.9 with respect to O.

9.16. (*a*) Determine by direct integration the polar moment of inertia of the annular area shown. (*b*) Using the results of part *a*, determine the moment of inertia of the given area with respect to the *x* axis.

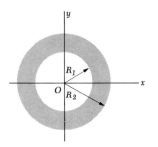
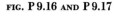

°**9.17.** (*a*) Show that the polar radius of gyration k_O of the annular area shown is approximately equal to the mean radius $R_m = (R_1 + R_2)/2$ for small values of the thickness $t = R_2 - R_1$. (*b*) Determine the percentage error introduced by using R_m in place of k_O for values of t/R_m respectively equal to 1, $\frac{1}{2}$, and $\frac{1}{10}$.

FIG. P 9.16 AND P 9.17

°**9.18.** Prove that the centroidal polar moment of inertia of a given area *A* cannot be smaller than $A^2/2\pi$. (*Hint.* Compare the moment of inertia of the given area with the moment of inertia of a circle of the same area and same centroid.)

°**9.19.** In the plane area shown, it is desired to have I_x directly proportional to the height *b*. Determine the equation of the curve bounding the area on the right.

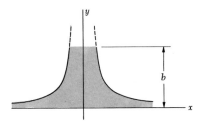

FIG. P 9.19

9.5. Parallel-axis Theorem. Consider the moment of inertia *I* of an area *A* with respect to an axis *AA'* (Fig. 9.9). Denoting by *y* the distance from an element of area *dA* to *AA'*, we write

$$I = \int y^2 \, dA$$

Let us now draw an axis *BB'* parallel to *AA'* through the centroid *C* of the area; this axis is called a *centroidal axis*. Denoting by *y'* the distance from the element *dA* to *BB'*, we write $y = y' + d$, where *d* is the distance between the axes *AA'* and *BB'*. Substituting for *y* in the integral representing *I*, we write

$$I = \int y^2 \, dA = \int (y' + d)^2 \, dA$$
$$= \int y'^2 \, dA + 2d\int y' \, dA + d^2\int dA$$

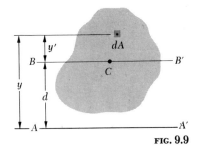

FIG. 9.9

The first integral represents the moment of inertia $\bar{I}$ of the area with respect to the centroidal axis *BB'*. The second integral represents the first moment of the area with respect to *BB'*; since the centroid *C* of the area is located on that axis, the second integral must be zero. Finally, we observe that the last integral is equal to the total area *A*. We write therefore

$$I = \bar{I} + Ad^2 \qquad (9.9)$$

This formula expresses that the moment of inertia *I* of an area with respect to any given axis *AA'* is equal to the moment of inertia $\bar{I}$ of the area with respect to a centroidal axis *BB'* parallel to AA' *plus* the product Ad^2 of the area A and of the square of the distance d between the two axes.   This theorem is known as the *parallel-axis theorem*.   Substituting k^2A for I and $\bar{k}^2A$ for $\bar{I}$, the theorem may also be expressed in the following way:

$$k^2 = \bar{k}^2 + d^2 \qquad (9.10)$$

A similar theorem may be used to relate the polar moment of inertia J_O of an area about a point O and the polar moment of inertia J_C of the same area about its centroid C.   Denoting by d the distance between O and C, we write

$$J_O = J_C + Ad^2 \qquad \text{or} \qquad k_O^2 = k_C^2 + d^2 \qquad (9.11)$$

Example 1.   As an application of the parallel-axis theorem, we shall determine the moment of inertia I_T of a circular area with respect to a line tangent to the circle (Fig. 9.10).   We found in Sample Prob. 9.2 that the moment of inertia of a circular area about a centroidal axis is $\bar{I} = \frac{1}{4}\pi r^4$.   We may write, therefore,

$$I_T = \bar{I} + Ad^2 = \frac{1}{4}\pi r^4 + \pi r^2 r^2 = \frac{5}{4}\pi r^4$$

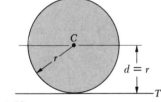

Example 2.   The parallel-axis theorem may also be used to determine the centroidal moment of inertia of an area when the moment of inertia of this area with respect to some parallel axis is known.   Consider, for instance, a triangular area (Fig. 9.11).   We found in Sample Prob. 9.1 that the moment of inertia of a triangle with respect to its base AA' is equal to $\frac{1}{12}bh^3$.   Using the parallel-axis theorem, we write

$$I_{AA'} = \bar{I}_{BB'} + Ad^2$$
$$\bar{I}_{BB'} = I_{AA'} - Ad^2 = \frac{1}{12}bh^3 - \frac{1}{2}bh(\frac{1}{3}h)^2 = \frac{1}{36}bh^3$$

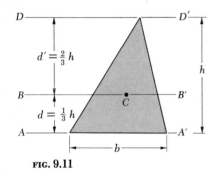

FIG. 9.10

FIG. 9.11

It should be observed that the product Ad^2 was *subtracted* from the given moment of inertia in order to obtain the centroidal moment of inertia of the triangle.   While this product is *added* in transferring *from* a centroidal axis to a parallel axis, it should be *subtracted* in transferring *to* a centroidal axis.   In other words, the moment of inertia of an area is always smaller with respect to a centroidal axis than with respect to any other parallel axis.

Returning to Fig. 9.11, we observe that the moment of inertia of the triangle with respect to a line DD' drawn through a vertex may be obtained by writing

$$I_{DD'} = \bar{I}_{BB'} + Ad'^2 = \frac{1}{36}bh^3 + \frac{1}{2}bh(\frac{2}{3}h)^2 = \frac{1}{4}bh^3$$

Note that $I_{DD'}$ *could not* have been obtained directly from $I_{AA'}$.   The parallel-axis theorem can be applied only if one of the two parallel axes passes through the centroid of the area.

9.6. Moments of Inertia of Composite Areas.   Consider a composite area A made of several component areas A_1, A_2,

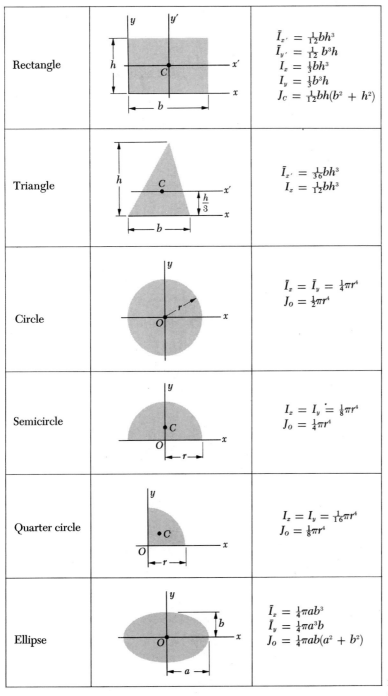

Rectangle	$\bar{I}_{x'} = \frac{1}{12}bh^3$ $\bar{I}_{y'} = \frac{1}{12}b^3h$ $I_x = \frac{1}{3}bh^3$ $I_y = \frac{1}{3}b^3h$ $J_C = \frac{1}{12}bh(b^2 + h^2)$
Triangle	$\bar{I}_{x'} = \frac{1}{36}bh^3$ $I_x = \frac{1}{12}bh^3$
Circle	$\bar{I}_x = \bar{I}_y = \frac{1}{4}\pi r^4$ $J_O = \frac{1}{2}\pi r^4$
Semicircle	$I_x = I_y = \frac{1}{8}\pi r^4$ $J_O = \frac{1}{4}\pi r^4$
Quarter circle	$I_x = I_y = \frac{1}{16}\pi r^4$ $J_O = \frac{1}{8}\pi r^4$
Ellipse	$\bar{I}_x = \frac{1}{4}\pi ab^3$ $\bar{I}_y = \frac{1}{4}\pi a^3b$ $J_O = \frac{1}{4}\pi ab(a^2 + b^2)$

FIG. 9.12. Moments of inertia of common geometric shapes

Shape		Nominal size, in.	Wt/ft, lb
Wide-flange section	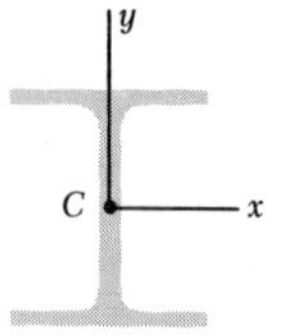	$16 \times 8\frac{1}{2}$† 14×8 8×8	64 43 31
American Standard beam	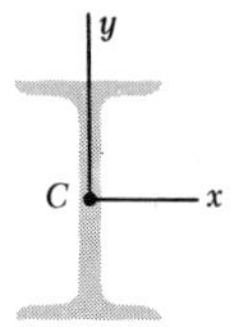	18×6 12×5 $6 \times 3\frac{3}{8}$	70 35 12.5
American Standard channel	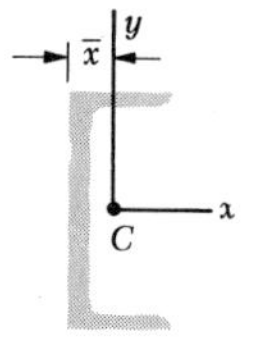	$10 \times 2\frac{5}{8}$ $8 \times 2\frac{1}{4}$ 6×2	25.0 11.5 8.2
Angles	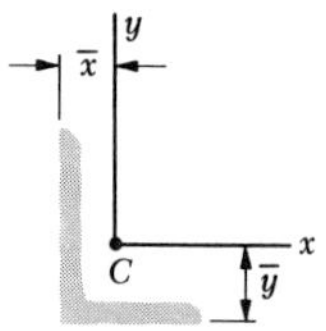	$6 \times 6 \times 1$‡ $4 \times 4 \times \frac{1}{2}$ $8 \times 6 \times 1$ $5 \times 3\frac{1}{2} \times \frac{1}{2}$	37.4 12.8 44.2 13.6

† Depth and width.   ‡ The last figure represents the thickness.

FIG. 9.13. **Properties of rolled-steel**

etc. Since the integral representing the moment of inertia of A may be subdivided into integrals computed over A_1, A_2, etc., the moment of inertia of A with respect to a given axis will be obtained by adding the moments of inertia of the areas A_1, A_2, etc., with respect to the same axis. The moment of inertia of an area made of several of the common shapes shown in Fig. 9.12 may thus be obtained from the formulas given in that figure. Before adding the moments of inertia of the component areas, however, the parallel-axis theorem should be used to transfer each moment of inertia to the desired axis. This is shown in Sample Probs. 9.4 and 9.5.

Area, in.^{2}	$\bar{I}_x$, in.^{4}	$\bar{k}_x$, in.	$\bar{y}$, in.	$\bar{I}_y$, in.^{4}	$\bar{k}_y$, in.	$\bar{x}$, in.
18.80	833.8	6.66	. . . .	68.4	1.91	
12.65	429.0	5.82	. . . .	45.1	1.89	
9.12	109.7	3.47	. . . .	37.0	2.01	
20.46	917.5	6.70	. . . .	24.5	1.09	
10.20	227.0	4.72	. . . .	10.0	0.99	
3.61	21.8	2.46	. . . .	1.8	0.72	
7.33	90.7	3.52	. . . .	3.4	0.68	0.62
3.36	32.3	3.10	. . . .	1.3	0.63	0.58
2.39	13.0	2.34	. . . .	0.7	0.54	0.52
11.00	35.5	1.80	1.86	35.5	1.80	1.86
3.75	5.6	1.22	1.18	5.6	1.22	1.18
13.00	80.8	2.49	2.65	38.8	1.73	1.65
4.00	10.0	1.58	1.66	4.1	1.01	0.91

structural shapes

The properties of the cross sections of various structural shapes are given in Fig. 9.13. As noted in Sec. 9.1, the moment of inertia of a beam section about its neutral axis is closely related to the value of the internal forces. The determination of moments of inertia is thus a prerequisite to the analysis and design of structural members.

It should be noted that the radius of gyration of a composite area is *not* equal to the sum of the radii of gyration of the component areas. In order to determine the radius of gyration of a composite area, it is necessary first to compute the moment of inertia of the area.

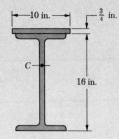

SAMPLE PROBLEM 9.4

The strength of a 16-in., 64-lb wide-flange beam is increased by attaching a 10- by $\frac{3}{4}$-in. plate to its upper flange as shown. Determine the moment of inertia and the radius of gyration of the composite section with respect to an axis through its centroid C and parallel to the plate.

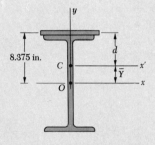

Solution. The origin of coordinates O is placed at the centroid of the wide-flange section, and the distance $\overline{Y}$ to the centroid of the composite section is computed by the methods of Chap 5. The area of the wide-flange section is found by referring to Fig. 9.13.

Section	Area	$\bar{y}$	$\bar{y}A$
Plate	7.5	8.375	62.8
Wide-flange section	18.8	0	0
	26.3	. . . .	62.8

$$\overline{Y}\Sigma A = \Sigma \bar{y}A \qquad \overline{Y}(26.3) = 62.8 \qquad \overline{Y} = 2.39 \text{ in.}$$

Moment of Inertia. The parallel-axis theorem is used to determine the moments of inertia of the wide-flange section and of the plate with respect to the x' axis. This axis is a centroidal axis for the composite section, but *not* for either of the elements considered separately. The value of $\bar{I}_x$ for the wide-flange section is obtained from Fig. 9.13.

For the wide-flange section

$$I_{x'} = \bar{I}_x + A\overline{Y}^2 = 833.8 + (18.8)(2.39)^2 = 941 \text{ in.}^4$$

For the plate

$$I_{x'} = \bar{I}_x + Ad^2 = (\tfrac{1}{12})(10)(\tfrac{3}{4})^3 + (7.5)(8.375 - 2.39)^2 = 269 \text{ in.}^4$$

For the composite area

$$I_{x'} = 941 + 269 = 1{,}210 \text{ in.}^4$$
$$I_{x'} = 1{,}210 \text{ in.}^4 \quad \blacktriangleleft$$

Radius of Gyration

$$k_{x'}^2 = \frac{I_{x'}}{A} = \frac{1{,}210 \text{ in.}^4}{26.3 \text{ in.}^2}$$
$$k_{x'} = 6.78 \text{ in.} \quad \blacktriangleleft$$

SAMPLE PROBLEM 9.5

Determine the moment of inertia of the shaded area with respect to the y axis.

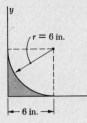

Solution. The given area may be obtained by subtracting a quarter circle from a square. The moments of inertia of the square and of the quarter circle are computed separately.

I_y *for Square.* Referring to Fig. 9.12, we obtain

$$I_y = \tfrac{1}{3} b^3 h = (\tfrac{1}{3})(6)^3(6) = 432 \text{ in.}^4$$

I_y *for the Quarter Circle.* Referring to Fig. 5.8, we locate the centroid C of the quarter circle with respect to side AA'.

$$a = \frac{4r}{3\pi} = \frac{(4)(6)}{3\pi} = 2.546 \text{ in.}$$

The distance b from the centroid C to the y axis is

$$b = 6 \text{ in.} - a = 6 \text{ in.} - 2.546 \text{ in.} = 3.454 \text{ in.}$$

Referring now to Fig. 9.12, we compute the moment of inertia of the quarter circle with respect to side AA'; we also compute the area of the quarter circle.

$$I_{AA'} = \tfrac{1}{16}\pi r^4 = \tfrac{1}{16}\pi(6)^4 = 254.5 \text{ in.}^4$$
$$A = \tfrac{1}{4}\pi r^2 = \tfrac{1}{4}\pi(6)^2 = 28.27 \text{ in.}^2$$

Using the parallel-axis theorem, we obtain the value of $\bar{I}_{y'}$,

$$I_{AA'} = \bar{I}_{y'} + Aa^2$$
$$\bar{I}_{y'} = I_{AA'} - Aa^2$$
$$= 254.5 - (28.27)(2.546)^2 = 71.2 \text{ in.}^4$$

Again using the parallel-axis theorem, we obtain the value of I_y,

$$I_y = \bar{I}_{y'} + Ab^2 = 71.2 + (28.27)(3.454)^2 = 408.5 \text{ in.}^4$$

I_y *for Given Area.* Subtracting the moment of inertia of the quarter circle from that of the square, we obtain

$$I_y = 432.0 \text{ in.}^4 - 408.5 \text{ in.}^4$$

$$I_y = 23.5 \text{ in.}^4 \quad \blacktriangleleft$$

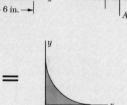

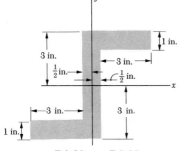

FIG. P 9.20 AND P 9.22

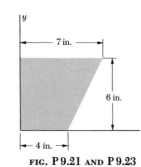

FIG. P 9.21 AND P 9.23

PROBLEMS

9.20 and 9.21. Determine the moment of inertia and the radius of gyration of the shaded area with respect to the x axis.

9.22 and 9.23. Determine the moment of inertia and the radius of gyration of the shaded area with respect to the y axis.

9.24. Knowing that the shaded area is equal to 30 in.^{2} and that its moment of inertia with respect to AA' is 1,200 in.^{4}, determine its moment of inertia with respect to BB', for $d_1 = 6$ in. and $d_2 = 2$ in.

9.25. Determine the shaded area and its moment of inertia with respect to a centroidal axis parallel to AA', knowing that its moments of inertia with respect to AA' and BB' are respectively 1,000 in.^{4} and 2,600 in.^{4}, and that $d_1 = 6$ in. and $d_2 = 4$ in.

9.26. The polar moments of inertia of the shaded area with respect to the corners A, B, and D of a 3-in. square are respectively $J_A = 1,300$ in.^{4}, $J_B = 1,660$ in.^{4}, and $J_D = 2,860$ in.^{4}. Determine the shaded area, its centroidal moment of inertia J_C, and the distance d from A to C.

9.27. The shaded area is equal to 50 in.^{2}. Determine its centroidal moments of inertia $\bar{I}_x$ and $\bar{I}_y$, knowing that $\bar{I}_x = 2\bar{I}_y$, and that the polar moment of inertia of the area about point A, at the distance $d = 6$ in. from C, is $J_A = 2,400$ in.^{4}.

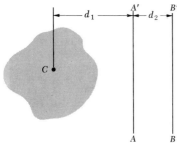

FIG. P 9.24 AND P 9.25

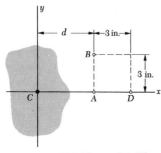

FIG. P 9.26 AND P 9.27

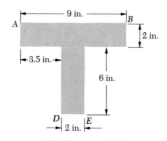

FIG. P 9.28 AND P 9.29

9.28. Determine the centroidal polar moment of inertia of the area shown.

9.29. Determine the moments of inertia $\bar{I}_x$ and $\bar{I}_y$ of the area shown with respect to centroidal axes respectively parallel and perpendicular to the side AB.

9.30. Determine the polar moment of inertia of the area shown with respect to (*a*) point *O*, (*b*) the centroid of the area.

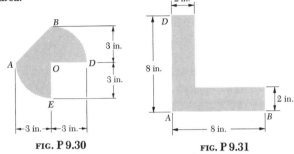

FIG. P 9.30

FIG. P 9.31

9.31. Determine the moments of inertia $\bar{I}_x$ and $\bar{I}_y$ of the area shown with respect to centroidal axes respectively parallel and perpendicular to the side *AB*.

9.32. A column is made of two 8-in., 11.5-lb American Standard channels welded to two 12- by $\frac{1}{4}$-in. steel plates. Determine the distance *d* for which the centroidal moments of inertia $\bar{I}_x$ and $\bar{I}_y$ of the column section are equal.

9.33. If the distance between the channels of the column of Prob. 9.32 is $d = 6$ in., determine the centroidal moments of inertia $\bar{I}_x$, $\bar{I}_y$, and J_C of the column section.

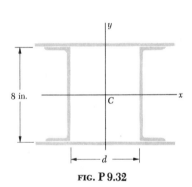

FIG. P 9.32

9.34. A steel plate, 8 by $\frac{1}{2}$ in., is welded to the flange of a 12-in., 35-lb American Standard beam as shown. Determine the moments of inertia and the radii of gyration of the combined section with respect to centroidal axes respectively parallel and perpendicular to the plate.

9.35. Three steel plates, 18 by 1 in., are riveted to four 6- by 6-in. angles, each 1 in. thick, to form the column whose cross section is shown. Determine the moments of inertia and the radii of gyration of the section with respect to centroidal axes respectively parallel and perpendicular to the flanges.

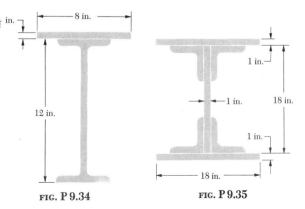

FIG. P 9.34

FIG. P 9.35

9.36 through 9.39. The panel shown forms the end of a trough which is filled with water to the line AA'. Referring to Sec. 9.1, determine the depth of the point of application of the resultant of the hydrostatic forces acting on the panel (center of pressure).

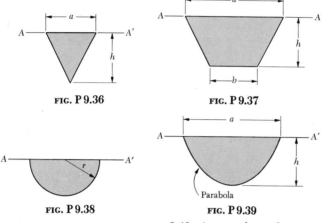

FIG. P 9.36

FIG. P 9.37

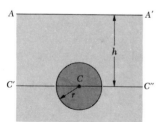

FIG. P 9.38

Parabola

FIG. P 9.39

9.40. A vertical circular gate of radius r is completely submerged in water. If the center of the gate is at a depth h, determine the depth of the center of pressure.

9.41. Assuming that the circular gate of Prob. 9.40 is hinged about its diameter $C'C''$, and denoting the specific weight of water by γ, determine (*a*) the reaction at each hinge, (*b*) the moment of the couple required to keep the gate closed.

°9.42. Show that the resultant of the hydrostatic forces acting on a submerged plane area A is a force $\mathbf{P}$ perpendicular to the area and of magnitude $P = \gamma A \bar{y} \sin \theta = \bar{p}A$ where γ is the specific weight of the liquid and $\bar{p}$ the pressure at the centroid C of the area. Show that $\mathbf{P}$ is applied at a point C_P, called the center of pressure, of coordinates $x_P = P_{xy}/A\bar{y}$ and $y_P = I_x/A\bar{y}$, where $P_{xy} = \int xy \, dA$ (see Sec. 9.7). Show also that the difference of ordinates $y_P - \bar{y}$ is equal to $\bar{k}_x^2/\bar{y}$ and thus depends upon the depth at which the area is submerged.

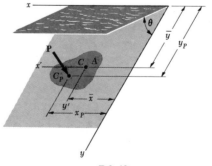

FIG. P 9.40

FIG. P 9.42

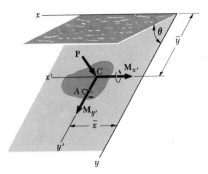

°9.43. Show that the system of hydrostatic forces acting on a sub-merged plane area A may be reduced to a force $\mathbf{P}$ at the centroid C of the area and two couples. The force $\mathbf{P}$ is perpendicular to the area and of magnitude $P = \gamma A\bar{y} \sin \theta$, where γ is the specific weight of the liquid, and the couples are represented by vectors directed as shown and of magnitude $M_{x'} = \gamma \bar{I}_{x'} \sin \theta$ and $M_{y'} = \gamma \bar{P}_{x'y'} \sin \theta$, where $\bar{P}_{x'y'} = \int x' y' \, dA$ (see Sec. 9.7). Note that the couples are independent of the depth at which the area is submerged.

FIG. P 9.43

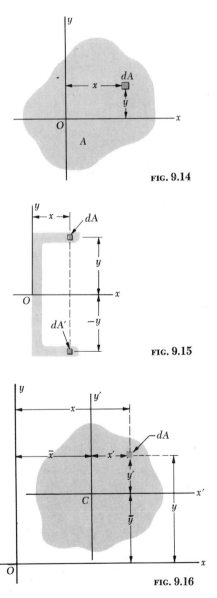

°9.7. Product of Inertia. The integral

$$P_{xy} = \int xy \, dA \qquad (9.12)$$

obtained by multiplying each element dA of an area A by its coordinates x and y and integrating over the area (Fig. 9.14) is known as the *product of inertia* of the area A with respect to the x and y axes. Unlike the moments of inertia I_x and I_y, the product of inertia P_{xy} may be either positive or negative.

When one or both of the x and y axes are axes of symmetry for the area A, the product of inertia P_{xy} is zero. Consider, for example, the channel section shown in Fig. 9.15. Since this section is symmetrical with respect to the x axis, we can associate to each element dA of coordinates x and y an element dA' of coordinates x and $-y$. Clearly, the contributions of any pair of elements chosen in this way cancel out, and the integral (9.12) reduces to zero.

A parallel-axis theorem similar to the one established in Sec. 9.5 for moments of inertia may be derived for products of inertia. Consider an area A and a system of rectangular coordinates x and y (Fig. 9.16). Through the centroid C of the area, of coordinates $\bar{x}$ and $\bar{y}$, we draw two *centroidal axes* x' and y' parallel, respectively, to the x and y axes. Denoting by x and y the coordinates of an element of area dA with respect to the original axes, and by x' and y' the coordinates of the same element with respect to the centroidal axes, we write $x = x' + \bar{x}$ and $y = y' + \bar{y}$. Substituting into (9.12), we obtain the following expression for the product of inertia P_{xy}:

$$P_{xy} = \int xy \, dA = \int (x' + \bar{x})(y' + \bar{y}) \, dA$$
$$= \int x'y' \, dA + \bar{y}\int x' \, dA + \bar{x}\int y' \, dA + \bar{x}\bar{y}\int dA$$

The first integral represents the product of inertia $P_{x'y'}$ of the area A with respect to the centroidal axes x' and y'. The next

FIG. 9.14

FIG. 9.15

FIG. 9.16

two integrals represent first moments of the area with respect to the centroidal axes; they reduce to zero, since the centroid C is located on these axes.   Finally, we observe that the last integral is equal to the total area A.   We write therefore

▶ $$P_{xy} = \overline{P}_{x'y'} + \overline{x}\overline{y}A \qquad (9.13)$$

°9.8. Principal Axes and Principal Moments of Inertia. Consider the area A and the coordinate axes x and y (Fig. 9.17). We assume that the moments and product of inertia

$$I_x = \int y^2\, dA \qquad I_y = \int x^2\, dA \qquad P_{xy} = \int xy\, dA \quad (9.14)$$

of the area A are known, and we propose to determine the moments and product of inertia I_u, I_v, and P_{uv} of A with respect to new axes u and v obtained by rotating the original axes about the origin through an angle θ.

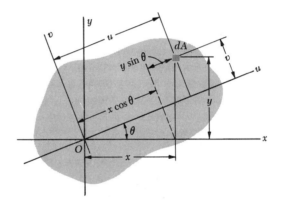

FIG. 9.17

We first note the following relations between the coordinates u, v and x, y of an element of area dA:

$$u = x \cos\theta + y \sin\theta \qquad v = y \cos\theta - x \sin\theta$$

Substituting for u and v into the expression for I_u, we write

$$\begin{aligned}
I_u &= \int v^2\, dA = \int (y \cos\theta - x \sin\theta)^2\, dA \\
&= \cos^2\theta \int y^2\, dA - 2 \sin\theta \cos\theta \int xy\, dA + \sin^2\theta \int x^2\, dA
\end{aligned}$$

Taking the relations (9.14) into account, we write

$$I_u = I_x \cos^2\theta - 2P_{xy} \sin\theta \cos\theta + I_y \sin^2\theta \quad (9.15)$$

Similarly, we obtain for I_v and P_{uv} the expressions

$$I_v = I_x \sin^2\theta + 2P_{xy} \sin\theta \cos\theta + I_y \cos^2\theta \qquad (9.16)$$
$$P_{uv} = I_x \sin\theta \cos\theta + P_{xy}(\cos^2\theta - \sin^2\theta) - I_y \sin\theta \cos\theta \quad (9.17)$$

We observe, by adding (9.15) and (9.16) member by member, that

$$I_u + I_v = I_x + I_y \tag{9.18}$$

This result could have been anticipated, since both members of (9.18) are equal to the polar moment of inertia J_O.

Using the trigonometric relations $\sin 2\theta = 2 \sin \theta \cos \theta$ and $\cos 2\theta = \cos^2 \theta - \sin^2 \theta$, we may write (9.15), (9.16), and (9.17) as follows:

$$I_u = \frac{I_x + I_y}{2} + \frac{I_x - I_y}{2} \cos 2\theta - P_{xy} \sin 2\theta \tag{9.19}$$

$$I_v = \frac{I_x + I_y}{2} - \frac{I_x - I_y}{2} \cos 2\theta + P_{xy} \sin 2\theta \tag{9.20}$$

$$P_{uv} = \frac{I_x - I_y}{2} \sin 2\theta + P_{xy} \cos 2\theta \tag{9.21}$$

Equations (9.19) and (9.21) are the parametric equations of a circle. This means that, if we choose a set of rectangular axes and plot a point M of abscissa I_u and ordinate P_{uv} for any given value of the parameter θ, all the points thus obtained will lie on a circle. To establish this property we shall eliminate θ from Eqs. (9.19) and (9.21); this is done by transposing $(I_x + I_y)/2$ in Eq. (9.19), squaring both members of Eqs. (9.19) and (9.21), and adding. We write

$$\left(I_u - \frac{I_x + I_y}{2}\right)^2 + P_{uv}^2 = \left(\frac{I_x - I_y}{2}\right)^2 + P_{xy}^2 \tag{9.22}$$

Setting

$$I_{av} = \frac{I_x + I_y}{2} \quad \text{and} \quad R = \sqrt{\left(\frac{I_x - I_y}{2}\right)^2 + P_{xy}^2} \tag{9.23}$$

we write the identity (9.22) in the form

$$(I_u - I_{av})^2 + P_{uv}^2 = R^2 \tag{9.24}$$

which is the equation of a circle of radius R centered at the point C of abscissa I_{av} and ordinate 0 (Fig. 9.18).

The two points A and B where the circle obtained intersects the axis of abscissas are of special interest: Point A corresponds to the maximum value of the moment of inertia I_u, while point B corresponds to its minimum value. Besides, both points correspond to a zero value of the product of inertia P_{uv}. Thus, the values θ_m of the parameter θ which correspond to the points

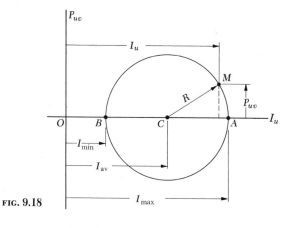

FIG. 9.18

A and *B* may be obtained by setting $P_{uv} = 0$ in Eq. (9.21). We obtain†

$$\tan 2\theta_m = -\frac{2P_{xy}}{I_x - I_y} \quad (9.25)$$

This equation defines two values $2\theta_m$ which are 180° apart and thus two values θ_m which are 90° apart. One of them corresponds to point *A* in Fig. 9.18 and to an axis through *O* in Fig. 9.17 with respect to which the moment of inertia of the given area is maximum; the other value corresponds to point *B* and an axis through *O* with respect to which the moment of inertia of the area is minimum. The two axes thus defined, which are perpendicular to each other, are called the *principal axes of the area about O*, and the corresponding values I_{max} and I_{min} of the moment of inertia are called the *principal moments of inertia of the area about O*. We check from Fig. 9.18 that

$$I_{max} = I_{av} + R \quad \text{and} \quad I_{min} = I_{av} - R \quad (9.26)$$

Substituting for I_{av} and R from formulas (9.23), we write

$$I_{max,\,min} = \frac{I_x + I_y}{2} \pm \sqrt{\left(\frac{I_x - I_y}{2}\right)^2 + P_{xy}^2} \quad (9.27)$$

Since the two values θ_m defined by Eq. (9.25) were obtained by setting $P_{uv} = 0$ in Eq. (9.21), it is clear that the product of inertia of the given area with respect to its principal axes is zero. Referring to Sec. 9.7, we note that, if an area possesses an axis of symmetry through a point *O*, this axis must be a principal axis of the area about *O*. On the other hand, a princi-

† This relation may also be obtained by differentiating I_u in Eq. (9.19) and setting $dI_u/d\theta = 0$.

pal axis does not need to be an axis of symmetry; whether or not an area possesses properties of symmetry, it will have two principal axes of inertia about any point O.

The properties established in this section hold for any point O located inside or outside the given area. If the point O is chosen to coincide with the centroid of the area, any axis through O is a centroidal axis; the two principal axes of the area about its centroid are referred to as the *principal centroidal axes of the area*.

*9.9. Mohr's Circle for Moments and Products of Inertia. The circle used in the preceding section to illustrate the relations existing between the moments and products of inertia of a given area with respect to axes passing through a fixed point O was first introduced by the German engineer Otto Mohr (1835–1918) and is known as *Mohr's circle*. We shall see that, if the moments and product of inertia of an area A are known with respect to two rectangular x and y axes through a point O, Mohr's circle may be used to determine graphically (a) the principal axes and principal moments of inertia of the area about O, or (b) the moments and product of inertia of the area with respect to any other pair of rectangular axes u and v through O.

Consider a given area A and two rectangular coordinate axes x and y (Fig. 9.19a). We shall assume that the moments of inertia I_x and I_y and the product of inertia P_{xy} are known, and we shall represent them on a diagram by plotting a point

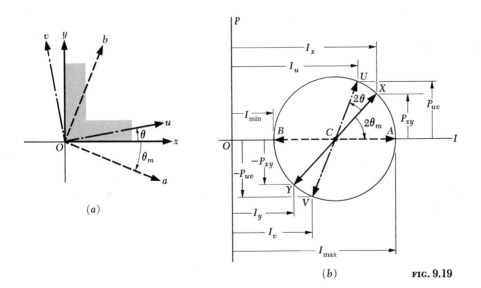

(a)   (b)   **FIG. 9.19**

X of coordinates I_x and P_{xy} and a point Y of coordinates I_y and $-P_{xy}$ (Fig. 9.19b).   Joining X and Y by a straight line, we define the point C of intersection of line XY with the I axis and draw the circle of center C and diameter XY.   Noting that the abscissa of C and the radius of the circle are respectively equal to the quantities I_{av} and R defined by the formulas (9.23), we conclude that the circle obtained is Mohr's circle for the given area about point O.   Thus the abscissas of the points A and B where the circle intersects the I axis represent respectively the principal moments of inertia I_{max} and I_{min} of the area.

We also note that, since tan $(XCA) = 2P_{xy}/(I_x - I_y)$, the angle XCA is equal in magnitude to one of the angles $2\theta_m$ which satisfy Eq. (9.25); thus the angle θ_m which defines in Fig. 9.19a the principal axis Oa corresponding to point A in Fig. 9.19b may be obtained by dividing in half the angle XCA measured on Mohr's circle.   We further observe that, if $I_x > I_y$ and $P_{xy} > 0$, as in the case considered here, the rotation which brings CX into CA is clockwise.   But, in that case, the angle θ_m obtained from Eq. (9.25) and defining the principal axis Oa in Fig. 9.19a is negative; thus the rotation bringing Ox into Oa is also clockwise.   We conclude that the senses of rotation in both parts of Fig. 9.19 are the same; if a clockwise rotation through $2\theta_m$ is required to bring CX into CA on Mohr's circle, a clockwise rotation through θ_m will bring Ox into the corresponding principal axis Oa in Fig. 9.19a.

Since Mohr's circle is uniquely defined, the same circle may be obtained by considering the moments and product of inertia of the area A with respect to rectangular axes u and v (Fig. 9.19a).   The point U of coordinates I_u and P_{uv}, and the point V of coordinates I_v and $-P_{uv}$, are therefore located on Mohr's circle, and the angle UCA in Fig. 9.19b must be equal to twice the angle uOa in Fig. 9.19a.   Since, as noted above, the angle XCA is twice the angle xOa, it follows that the angle XCU in Fig. 9.19b is twice the angle xOu in Fig. 9.19a.   Thus the diameter UV defining the moments and product of inertia I_u, I_v, and P_{uv} of the given area with respect to rectangular axes u and v forming an angle θ with the x and y axes may be obtained by rotating through an angle 2θ the diameter XY corresponding to the moments and product of inertia I_x, I_y, and P_{xy}.   We note that the rotation which brings the diameter XY into the diameter UV in Fig. 9.19b has the same sense as the rotation which brings the xy axes into the uv axes in Fig. 9.19a.

SAMPLE PROBLEM 9.6

Determine the product of inertia of the right triangle shown (a) with respect to the x and y axes and (b) with respect to centroidal axes parallel to the x and y axes.

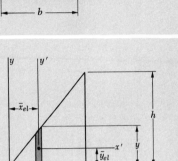

a. Product of Inertia P_{xy}. A vertical rectangular strip is chosen as the differential element of area. Using the parallel-axis theorem, we write

$$dP_{xy} = dP_{x'y'} + \bar{x}_{el}\bar{y}_{el}\, dA$$

Since the element is symmetrical with respect to the x' and y' axes, we note that $dP_{x'y'} = 0$. From the geometry of the triangle, we obtain

$$y = h\frac{x}{b} \qquad dA = y\, dx = h\frac{x}{b}\, dx$$

$$\bar{x}_{el} = x \qquad \bar{y}_{el} = \tfrac{1}{2}y = \tfrac{1}{2}h\frac{x}{b}$$

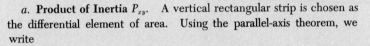

Integrating dP_{xy} from $x = 0$ to $x = b$, we obtain

$$P_{xy} = \int dP_{xy} = \int_0^b \bar{x}_{el}\bar{y}_{el}\, dA = \int_0^b x\left(\tfrac{1}{2}h\frac{x}{b}\right)h\frac{x}{b}\, dx$$

$$= \int_0^b \frac{h^2}{2b^2}x^3\, dx = \frac{h^2}{2b^2}\frac{b^4}{4}$$

$$P_{xy} = \tfrac{1}{8}b^2h^2 \qquad \blacktriangleleft$$

b. Product of Inertia $\bar{P}_{x'y''}$. The coordinates of the centroid of the triangle are

$$\bar{x} = \tfrac{2}{3}b \qquad \bar{y} = \tfrac{1}{3}h$$

Using the expression for P_{xy} obtained in part a, we apply the parallel-axis theorem and write

$$P_{xy} = \bar{P}_{x'y''} + \bar{x}\bar{y}A$$

$$\tfrac{1}{8}b^2h^2 = \bar{P}_{x'y''} + (\tfrac{2}{3}b)(\tfrac{1}{3}h)(\tfrac{1}{2}bh)$$

$$\bar{P}_{x'y''} = \tfrac{1}{8}b^2h^2 - \tfrac{1}{9}b^2h^2$$

$$\bar{P}_{x'y''} = \tfrac{1}{72}b^2h^2 \qquad \blacktriangleleft$$

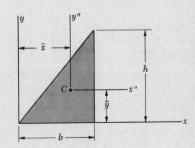

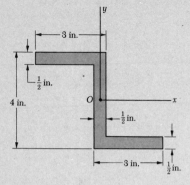

SAMPLE PROBLEM 9.7

For the section shown, the moments of inertia with respect to the x and y axes have been computed and are known to be

$$I_x = 10.91 \text{ in.}^4 \qquad I_y = 6.94 \text{ in.}^4$$

Determine (a) the principal axes of the section about O, (b) the values of the principal moments of inertia of the section about O.

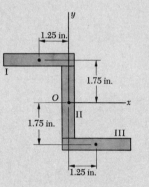

Solution. We first compute the product of inertia with respect to the x and y axes. The area is divided into three rectangles as shown. We note that the product of inertia $\bar{P}_{x'y'}$ with respect to centroidal axes parallel to the x and y axes is zero for each rectangle. Using the parallel-axis theorem $P_{xy} = \bar{P}_{x'y'} + \bar{x}\bar{y}A$, we thus find that for each rectangle P_{xy} reduces to $\bar{x}\bar{y}A$.

Rectangle	Area	$\bar{x}$	$\bar{y}$	$\bar{x}\bar{y}A$
I	1.5	-1.25	$+1.75$	-3.28
II	1.5	0	0	0
III	1.5	$+1.25$	-1.75	-3.28
				-6.56

$$P_{xy} = \Sigma \bar{x}\bar{y}A = -6.56 \text{ in.}^4$$

a. Principal Axes. Since the magnitudes of I_x, I_y, and P_{xy} are known, Eq. (9.25) is used to determine the values of θ_m,

$$\tan 2\theta_m = -\frac{2P_{xy}}{I_x - I_y} = -\frac{(2)(-6.56)}{10.91 - 6.94} = +3.31$$

$$2\theta_m = 73.2° \text{ and } 253.2°$$

$$\theta_m = 36.6° \qquad \text{and} \qquad \theta_m = 126.6° \quad \blacktriangleleft$$

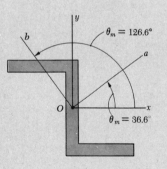

b. Principal Moments of Inertia. Using Eq. (9.27), we write

$$I_{\text{max, min}} = \frac{I_x + I_y}{2} \pm \sqrt{\left(\frac{I_x - I_y}{2}\right)^2 + P_{xy}^2}$$

$$= \frac{10.91 + 6.94}{2} \pm \sqrt{\left(\frac{10.91 - 6.94}{2}\right)^2 + (-6.56)^2}$$

$$I_{\text{max}} = 15.78 \text{ in.}^4 \qquad I_{\text{min}} = 2.07 \text{ in.}^4 \quad \blacktriangleleft$$

Noting that the area of the section is farther away from the a axis than from the b axis, we conclude that $I_a = I_{\text{max}} = 15.78 \text{ in.}^4$ and $I_b = I_{\text{min}} = 2.07 \text{ in.}^4$. This conclusion may be verified by substituting $\theta = 36.6°$ into Eqs. (9.19) and (9.20).

338

SAMPLE PROBLEM 9.8

For the section shown, the moments and product of inertia with respect to the x and y axes have been computed and are known to be

$$I_x = 10.91 \text{ in.}^4 \qquad I_y = 6.94 \text{ in.}^4 \qquad P_{xy} = -6.56 \text{ in.}^4$$

Using Mohr's circle, determine (a) the principal axes of the section about O, (b) the values of the principal moments of inertia of the section about O, (c) the moments and product of inertia of the section with respect to the u and v axes forming an angle of 60° with the x and y axes.

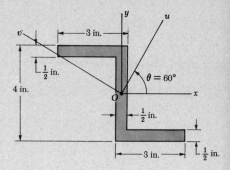

Solution. We first plot point X of coordinates $I_x = 10.91$, $P_{xy} = -6.56$, and point Y of coordinates $I_y = 6.94$, $-P_{xy} = +6.56$. Joining X and Y by a straight line, we define the center C of Mohr's circle. The abscissa of C, which represents I_{av}, and the radius R of the circle may be measured directly, or they may be determined analytically.

$$I_{av} = OC = \tfrac{1}{2}(I_x + I_y) = \tfrac{1}{2}(10.91 + 6.94) = 8.92 \text{ in.}^4$$
$$R = \sqrt{(CD)^2 + (DX)^2} = \sqrt{(1.98)^2 + (6.56)^2} = 6.85 \text{ in.}^4$$

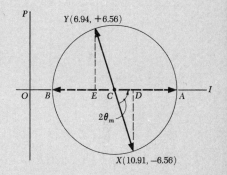

a. Principal Axes. The principal axes of the section correspond to points A and B on Mohr's circle and the angle through which we should rotate CX to bring it into CA defines $2\theta_m$. We have

$$\tan 2\theta_m = \frac{DX}{CD} = \frac{6.56}{1.98} = 3.31 \qquad 2\theta_m = 73.2° \rlap{$\,\curvearrowright$} \qquad \theta_m = 36.6° \rlap{$\,\curvearrowright$} \quad \blacktriangleleft$$

Thus the principal axis Oa corresponding to the maximum value of the moment of inertia is obtained by rotating the x axis through 36.6° counterclockwise; the principal axis corresponding to the minimum value of the moment of inertia may be obtained by rotating the y axis through the same angle.

b. Principal Moments of Inertia. The principal moments of inertia are represented by the abscissas of A and B. We have

$$I_{max} = OA = OC + CA = I_{av} + R = 8.92 + 6.85$$
$$I_{max} = 15.77 \text{ in.}^4 \quad \blacktriangleleft$$
$$I_{min} = OB = OC - BC = I_{av} - R = 8.92 - 6.85$$
$$I_{min} = 2.07 \text{ in.}^4 \quad \blacktriangleleft$$

c. Moments and Product of Inertia with Respect to uv Axes. The points U and V on Mohr's circle which correspond to the u and v axes are obtained by rotating CX and CY through an angle $2\theta = 2(60°) = 120°$ counterclockwise. The coordinates of U and V yield the desired moments and product of inertia. Noting that the angle that CU forms with the I axis is $\phi = 120° - 73.2° = 46.8°$, we write

$$I_u = OF = OC + CF = 8.92 + 6.85 \cos 46.8°$$
$$I_u = 13.61 \text{ in.}^4 \quad \blacktriangleleft$$
$$I_v = OG = OC - GC = 8.92 - 6.85 \cos 46.8°$$
$$I_v = 4.23 \text{ in.}^4 \quad \blacktriangleleft$$
$$P_{uv} = FU = 6.85 \sin 46.8°$$
$$P_{uv} = +4.99 \text{ in.}^4 \quad \blacktriangleleft$$

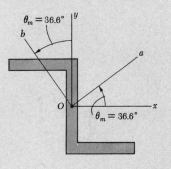

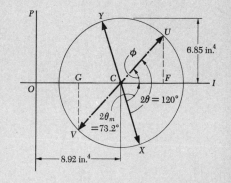

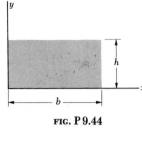

FIG. P 9.44

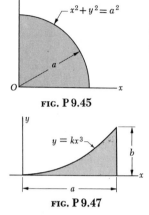

FIG. P 9.45

PROBLEMS

9.44 through 9.47. Determine by direct integration the product of inertia of the given area with respect to the x and y axes.

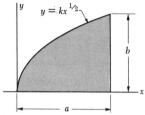

FIG. P 9.46

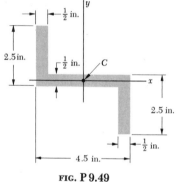

FIG. P 9.47

9.48 and 9.49. Using the parallel-axis theorem, determine the product of inertia of the area shown with respect to the centroidal x and y axes.

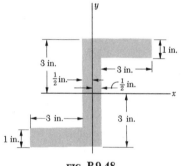

FIG. P 9.48

FIG. P 9.49

9.50 and 9.51. Using the parallel-axis theorem, determine the product of inertia of the angle cross section shown with respect to the centroidal x and y axes. Neglect the effect of fillets.

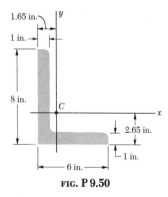

FIG. P 9.50

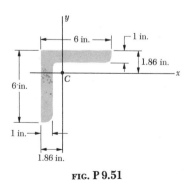

FIG. P 9.51

9.52. Determine the moments of inertia and the product of inertia of the rectangle shown with respect to the centroidal u and v axes.

9.53. Determine the moments of inertia and the product of inertia of the area of Prob. 9.48 with respect to new centroidal axes obtained by rotating the x and y axes through 30° counterclockwise.

9.54. Determine the moments of inertia and the product of inertia of the quarter circle of Prob. 9.45 with respect to new axes obtained by rotating the x and y axes about O (a) through 30° counterclockwise, (b) through 45° counterclockwise.

9.55. Determine the moments of inertia and the product of inertia of the angle cross section of Prob. 9.50 with respect to new centroidal axes obtained by rotating the x and y axes through 45° clockwise. (The moments of inertia $\bar{I}_x$ and $\bar{I}_y$ of the section are given in Fig. 9.13.)

9.56. Determine the orientation of the principal axes through the centroid and the corresponding values of the moments of inertia for the area of Prob. 9.48.

9.57. Determine the orientation of the principal axes through the centroid and the corresponding values of the moment of inertia for the angle cross section shown. Neglect the effect of fillets in computing $\bar{P}_{xy}$. (The moments of inertia $\bar{I}_x$ and $\bar{I}_y$ of the section are given in Fig. 9.13.)

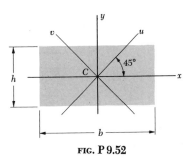

FIG. P 9.52

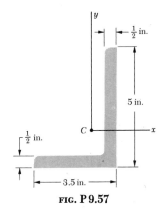

FIG. P 9.57

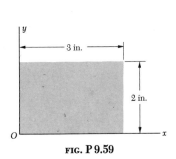

FIG. P 9.59

9.58. Determine the orientation of the principal axes through the centroid and the corresponding values of the moment of inertia for the angle cross section of Prob. 9.50. (The moments of inertia $\bar{I}_x$ and $\bar{I}_y$ of the section are given in Fig. 9.13.)

9.59. Determine the orientation of the principal axes through O and the corresponding values of the moment of inertia for the rectangle shown.

9.60. Using Mohr's circle, determine the moments of inertia and the product of inertia of the quarter circle of Prob. 9.45 with respect to new axes obtained by rotating the x and y axes about O (a) through 30° counterclockwise, (b) through 45° counterclockwise.

9.61. Using Mohr's circle, determine the moments of inertia and the product of inertia of the angle cross section of Prob. 9.50 with respect to new centroidal axes obtained by rotating the x and y axes through 45° clockwise. (The moments of inertia $\bar{I}_x$ and $\bar{I}_y$ of the section are given in Fig. 9.13.)

9.62. Solve Prob. 9.52, using Mohr's circle.

9.63. Using Mohr's circle, determine the moments of inertia and the product of inertia of the area of Prob. 9.48 with respect to new centroidal axes obtained by rotating the x and y axes through 30° counterclockwise.

9.64. Using Mohr's circle, determine the orientation of the principal axes through the centroid and the corresponding values of the moment of inertia for the angle cross section of Prob. 9.50. (The moments of inertia $\bar{I}_x$ and $\bar{I}_y$ of the section are given in Fig. 9.13.)

9.65. Solve Prob. 9.59, using Mohr's circle.

9.66. Using Mohr's circle, determine the orientation of the principal axes through the centroid and the corresponding values of the moment of inertia for the area of Prob. 9.48.

9.67. Solve Prob. 9.57, using Mohr's circle.

9.68. Using Mohr's circle, show that for any area the axes corresponding to the principal moments of inertia are 45° from the axes corresponding to the maximum product of inertia.

9.69. Using Mohr's circle, show that, for any regular polygon (such as a pentagon), (a) the moment of inertia with respect to every axis through the centroid is the same, (b) the product of inertia with respect to any pair of rectangular axes through the centroid is zero.

*9.70. The moments and product of inertia of a given area with respect to two rectangular axes x and y through O are respectively $I_x = 48$ in.^{4}, $I_y = 32$ in.^{4}, and $P_{xy} > 0$, while the minimum value of the moment of inertia of the area with respect to any axis through O is $I_{min} = 30$ in.^{4}. Using Mohr's circle, determine the orientation of the principal axes of the area through O and the value of I_{max}.

*9.71. Using Mohr's circle, determine the product of inertia P_{xy} of the area of Prob. 9.70 with respect to the x and y axes.

*9.72. Prove that the expression $I_u I_v - P_{uv}^2$, where I_u, I_v, and P_{uv} represent respectively the moments and product of inertia of a given area with respect to two rectangular axes u and v through a given point O, is independent of the orientation of the u and v axes. Considering the particular case when the u and v axes correspond to the maximum value of P_{uv}, show that the given expression represents the square of the tangent drawn from the origin of the coordinates to Mohr's circle.

*9.73. Using the invariance property established in the preceding problem, express the product of inertia P_{xy} of an area A with respect to two rectangular axes through O in terms of the moments of inertia I_x and I_y of A and of the principal moments of inertia $I_{\min}$ and $I_{\max}$ of A about O. Apply the formula obtained to calculate the product of inertia $\bar{P}_{xy}$ of the 8- by 6- by 1-in.-angle cross section shown in Fig. 9.13, knowing that its minimum moment of inertia is 21.3 in.[4]

MOMENTS OF INERTIA OF MASSES

9.10. Moment of Inertia of a Mass. Consider a small mass Δm mounted on a rod of negligible mass which may rotate freely about an axis AA' (Fig. 9.20a). If a couple is applied to the system, the rod and mass, assumed initially at rest, will start rotating about AA'. The details of this motion will be studied later in dynamics. At present, we wish only to indicate that the time required for the system to reach a given speed of rotation is proportional to the mass Δm and to the square of the distance r. The product $r^2 \, \Delta m$ provides, therefore, a measure of the *inertia* of the system, i.e., of the resistance the system offers when we try to set it in motion. For this reason, the product $r^2 \, \Delta m$ is called the *moment of inertia* of the mass Δm with respect to the axis AA'.

Consider now a body of mass m which is to be rotated about an axis AA' (Fig. 9.20b). Dividing the body into elements of mass Δm_1, Δm_2, etc., we find that the resistance offered by the body is measured by the sum $r_1^2 \, \Delta m_1 + r_2^2 \, \Delta m_2 + \cdots$. This sum defines therefore the moment of inertia of the body with respect to the axis AA'. Increasing the number of elements, we find that the moment of inertia is equal, at the limit, to the integral

$$I = \int r^2 \, dm \qquad (9.28)$$

The *radius of gyration* k of the body with respect to the axis AA' is defined by the relation

$$I = k^2 m \quad \text{or} \quad k = \sqrt{\frac{I}{m}} \qquad (9.29)$$

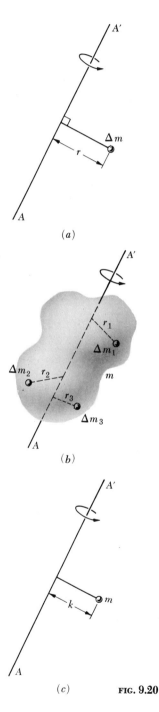

(a)

(b)

(c)　　　　**FIG. 9.20**

The radius of gyration k represents, therefore, the distance at which the entire mass of the body should be concentrated if its moment of inertia with respect to AA' is to remain unchanged (Fig. 9.20c).   Whether it is kept in its original shape (Fig. 9.20b) or whether it is concentrated as shown in Fig. 9.20c, the mass m wil! react in the same way to a rotation, or *gyration*, about AA'.

The radius of gyration of a mass is usually expressed in feet. Since the moment of inertia of a mass is the product of a mass (expressed in lb-sec²/ft) by a distance squared, it will generally be expressed in lb-ft-sec².

9.11. Parallel-axis Theorem.   Consider a body of mass m; the moment of inertia of the body with respect to an axis AA' is $I = \int r^2\,dm$, where r is the distance from the element of mass dm to AA' (Fig. 9.21).   Similarly, the moment of inertia of the body with respect to a centroidal † axis BB' parallel to the axis AA' and passing through the center of gravity G of the body is $\bar{I} = \int r'^2\,dm$, where r' is the distance from the element of mass to BB'.   Choosing two systems of axes as shown in Fig. 9.21, we write

$$r^2 = x^2 + z^2 \qquad r'^2 = x'^2 + z'^2$$

Observing that $x = x' + d$, where d is the distance between AA' and BB', and that $z = z'$, we write

$$r^2 = (x' + d)^2 + z'^2 = x'^2 + 2x'd + d^2 + z'^2$$
$$= r'^2 + 2x'd + d^2$$

Substituting for r^2 in the expression $I = \int r^2\,dm$, we write the moment of inertia of the body with respect to AA' as follows:

$$I = \int r^2\,dm = \int r'^2\,dm + 2d\int x'\,dm + d^2\int dm$$

The first integral represents the moment of inertia $\bar{I}$ about the centroidal axis BB'; the second integral represents the first moment of the body with respect to the $y'z'$ plane and, since this plane contains G, is equal to zero; the last integral is equal to the total mass m of the body.   We write, therefore,

$$I = \bar{I} + md^2 \tag{9.30}$$

Expressing the moments of inertia in terms of the corresponding radii of gyration, we may also write

$$k^2 = \bar{k}^2 + d^2 \tag{9.31}$$

†Note that the term centroidal is used to define an axis passing through the center of gravity G of the body, whether or not G coincides with the centroid of the volume of the body.

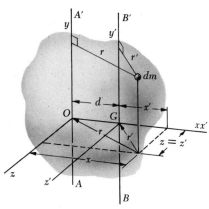

FIG. 9.21

where k and $\bar{k}$ represent the radii of gyration about AA' and BB', respectively.

9.12. Moments of Inertia of Thin Plates. Consider a thin plate of uniform thickness t, made of a homogeneous material of density ρ (density = mass per unit volume). The mass moment of inertia of the plate with respect to an axis AA' *contained in the plane* of the plate (Fig. 9.22a) is

$$I_{AA',\text{mass}} = \int r^2\, dm$$

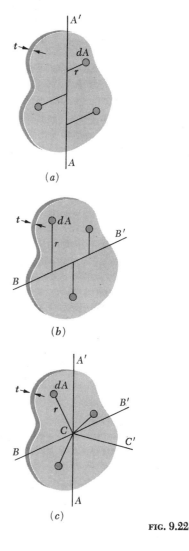

(a)

Since $dm = \rho t\, dA$, we write

$$I_{AA',\text{mass}} = \rho t \int r^2 dA$$

But r represents the distance of the element of area dA to the axis AA'; the integral is therefore equal to the moment of inertia of the area of the plate with respect to AA'. We have

$$I_{AA',\text{mass}} = \rho t I_{AA',\text{ area}} \qquad (9.32)$$

Similarly, we have with respect to an axis BB' perpendicular to AA' (Fig. 9.22b)

$$I_{BB',\text{ mass}} = \rho t I_{BB',\text{ area}} \qquad (9.33)$$

(b)

Considering now the axis CC' *perpendicular* to the plate through the point of intersection C of AA' and BB' (Fig. 9.22c), we write

$$I_{CC',\text{ mass}} = \rho t J_{C,\text{ area}} \qquad (9.34)$$

where J_C is the *polar* moment of inertia of the area of the plate with respect to point C.

Recalling the relation $J_C = I_{AA'} + I_{BB'}$ existing between polar and rectangular moments of inertia of an area, we write the following relation between the mass moments of inertia of a thin plate:

$$I_{CC'} = I_{AA'} + I_{BB'} \qquad (9.35)$$

Rectangular Plate. In the case of a rectangular plate of sides a and b (Fig. 9.23), we obtain the following mass moments of inertia with respect to axes through the center of gravity of the plate:

$$I_{AA',\text{mass}} = \rho t I_{AA',\text{area}} = \rho t(\tfrac{1}{12}a^3 b)$$

$$I_{BB',\text{mass}} = \rho t I_{BB',\text{area}} = \rho t(\tfrac{1}{12}ab^3)$$

Observing that the product ρabt is equal to the mass m of the plate, we write the mass moments of inertia of a thin rectangular plate as follows:

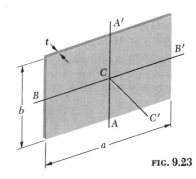

(c)

FIG. 9.22

FIG. 9.23

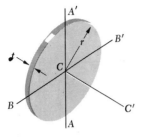

FIG. 9.24

$$I_{AA'} = \tfrac{1}{12}ma^2 \qquad I_{BB'} = \tfrac{1}{12}mb^2 \tag{9.36}$$
$$I_{CC'} = I_{AA'} + I_{BB'} = \tfrac{1}{12}m(a^2 + b^2) \tag{9.37}$$

Circular Plate. In the case of a circular plate, or disk, of radius r (Fig. 9.24), we write

$$I_{AA',\ \text{mass}} = \rho t I_{AA',\ \text{area}} = \rho t(\tfrac{1}{4}\pi r^4)$$

Observing that the product $\rho\pi r^2 t$ is equal to the mass m of the plate and that $I_{AA'} = I_{BB'}$, we write the mass moments of inertia of a circular plate as follows:

$$I_{AA'} = I_{BB'} = \tfrac{1}{4}mr^2 \tag{9.38}$$
$$I_{CC'} = I_{AA'} + I_{BB'} = \tfrac{1}{2}mr^2 \tag{9.39}$$

9.13. Determination of the Moment of Inertia of a Three-dimensional Body by Integration. The moment of inertia of a three-dimensional body is obtained by computing the integral $I = \int r^2\, dm$. If the body is made of a homogeneous material of density ρ, we have $dm = \rho\, dV$ and write $I = \rho \int r^2\, dV$. This integral depends only upon the shape of the body. In order to compute it, it will generally be necessary to perform a triple, or at least a double, integration.

However, if the body possesses two planes of symmetry, it is usually possible to determine its moment of inertia through a single integration by choosing as an element of mass dm the mass of a thin slab perpendicular to the planes of symmetry. In the case of bodies of revolution, for example, the element of mass should be a thin disk (Fig. 9.25). Using formula (9.39), the moment of inertia of the disk with respect to the axis of revolution may be readily expressed as indicated in Fig. 9.25. Its moment of inertia with respect to each of the other two axes of coordinates will be obtained by using formula (9.38) and the parallel-axis theorem. Integration of the expressions obtained will yield the desired moments of inertia of the body of revolution.

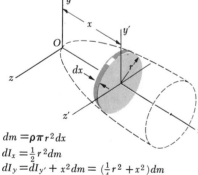

$dm = \rho\pi r^2\, dx$
$dI_x = \tfrac{1}{2}r^2\, dm$
$dI_y = dI_{y'} + x^2\, dm = (\tfrac{1}{4}r^2 + x^2)\, dm$
$dI_z = dI_{z'} + x^2\, dm = (\tfrac{1}{4}r^2 + x^2)\, dm$

FIG. 9.25. Determination of the moment of inertia of a body of revolution

9.14. Moments of Inertia of Composite Bodies. The moments of inertia of a few common shapes are shown in Fig. 9.26. The moment of inertia with respect to a given axis of a body made of several of these simple shapes may be obtained by computing the moments of inertia of its component parts about the desired axis and adding them together. We should note, as we already have noted in the case of areas, that the radius of gyration of a composite body *cannot* be obtained by adding the radii of gyration of its component parts.

Slender rod	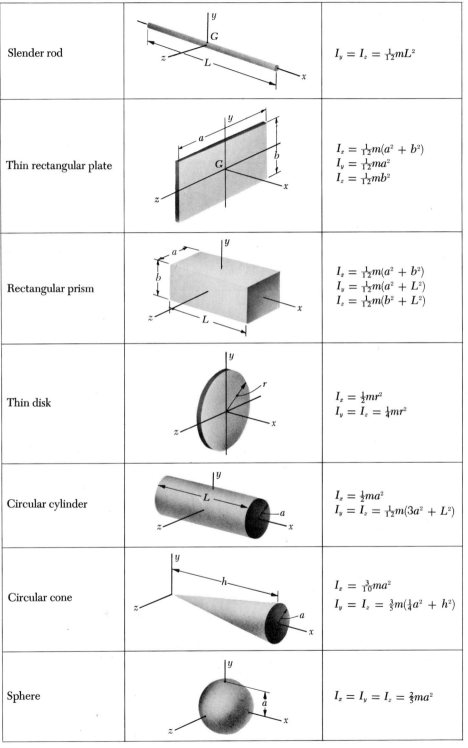	$I_y = I_z = \frac{1}{12}mL^2$
Thin rectangular plate		$I_x = \frac{1}{12}m(a^2 + b^2)$ $I_y = \frac{1}{12}ma^2$ $I_z = \frac{1}{12}mb^2$
Rectangular prism		$I_x = \frac{1}{12}m(a^2 + b^2)$ $I_y = \frac{1}{12}m(a^2 + L^2)$ $I_z = \frac{1}{12}m(b^2 + L^2)$
Thin disk		$I_x = \frac{1}{2}mr^2$ $I_y = I_z = \frac{1}{4}mr^2$
Circular cylinder		$I_x = \frac{1}{2}ma^2$ $I_y = I_z = \frac{1}{12}m(3a^2 + L^2)$
Circular cone		$I_x = \frac{3}{10}ma^2$ $I_y = I_z = \frac{3}{5}m(\frac{1}{4}a^2 + h^2)$
Sphere		$I_x = I_y = I_z = \frac{2}{5}ma^2$

FIG. 9.26. Mass moments of inertia of common geometric shapes

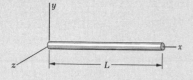

SAMPLE PROBLEM 9.9

Determine the mass moment of inertia of a slender rod of length L and mass m with respect to an axis perpendicular to the rod and passing through one end of the rod.

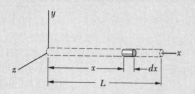

Solution. Choosing the differential element of mass shown, we write

$$dm = \frac{m}{L} dx$$

$$I_y = \int x^2\, dm = \int_0^L x^2 \frac{m}{L} dx = \left[\frac{m}{L} \frac{x^3}{3} \right]_0^L \qquad I_y = \frac{mL^2}{3} \quad \blacktriangleleft$$

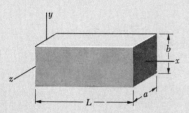

SAMPLE PROBLEM 9.10

Determine the mass moment of inertia of the homogeneous rectangular prism shown with respect to the z axis.

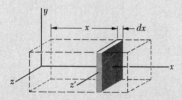

Solution. We choose as a differential element of mass the thin slab shown for which

$$dm = \rho ab\, dx$$

Referring to Sec. 9.12, we find that the moment of inertia of the element with respect to the z' axis is

$$dI_{z'} = \frac{b^2}{12} dm$$

Applying the parallel-axis theorem, we obtain the mass moment of inertia of the slab with respect to the z axis.

$$dI_z = dI_{z'} + x^2\, dm = \frac{b^2}{12} dm + x^2\, dm = \left(\frac{b^2}{12} + x^2 \right) \rho ab\, dx$$

Integrating from $x = 0$ to $x = L$, we obtain

$$I_z = \int dI_z = \int_0^L \left(\frac{b^2}{12} + x^2 \right) \rho ab\, dx = \rho abL \left(\frac{b^2}{12} + \frac{L^2}{3} \right)$$

Since the total mass of the prism is $m = \rho abL$, we may write

$$I_z = m \left(\frac{b^2}{12} + \frac{L^2}{3} \right) \qquad I_z = \tfrac{1}{12} m(b^2 + 4L^2) \quad \blacktriangleleft$$

We note that if the prism is slender, b is small compared to L and the expression for I_z reduces to $mL^2/3$ (see Sample Prob. 9.9).

SAMPLE PROBLEM 9.11

Determine the mass moment of inertia of a right circular cone with respect to (a) its longitudinal axis, (b) an axis through the apex of the cone and perpendicular to its longitudinal axis, (c) an axis through the centroid of the cone and perpendicular to its longitudinal axis.

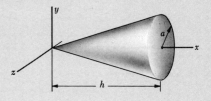

Solution. We choose the differential element of mass shown.

$$r = a\,\frac{x}{h} \qquad dm = \rho\pi r^2\,dx = \rho\pi\frac{a^2}{h^2}x^2\,dx$$

a. **Moment of Inertia I_x.** Using the expression derived in Sec. 9.12 for a thin disk, we compute the mass moment of inertia of the differential element with respect to the x axis.

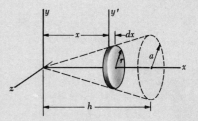

$$dI_x = \tfrac{1}{2}r^2\,dm = \frac{1}{2}\left(a\frac{x}{h}\right)^2\left(\rho\pi\frac{a^2}{h^2}x^2\,dx\right) = \tfrac{1}{2}\rho\pi\frac{a^4}{h^4}x^4\,dx$$

Integrating from $x = 0$ to $x = h$, we obtain

$$I_x = \int dI_x = \int_0^h \tfrac{1}{2}\rho\pi\frac{a^4}{h^4}x^4\,dx = \tfrac{1}{2}\rho\pi\frac{a^4}{h^4}\frac{h^5}{5} = \tfrac{1}{10}\rho\pi a^4 h$$

Since the total mass of the cone is $m = \tfrac{1}{3}\rho\pi a^2 h$, we may write

$$I_x = \tfrac{1}{10}\rho\pi a^4 h = \tfrac{3}{10}a^2(\tfrac{1}{3}\rho\pi a^2 h) = \tfrac{3}{10}ma^2 \qquad I_x = \tfrac{3}{10}ma^2 \quad \blacktriangleleft$$

b. **Moment of Inertia I_y.** The same differential element will be used. Applying the parallel-axis theorem and using the expression derived in Sec. 9.12 for a thin disk, we write

$$dI_y = dI_{y'} + x^2\,dm = \tfrac{1}{4}r^2\,dm + x^2\,dm = (\tfrac{1}{4}r^2 + x^2)\,dm$$

Substituting the expressions for r and dm, we obtain

$$dI_y = \left(\frac{1}{4}\frac{a^2}{h^2}x^2 + x^2\right)\left(\rho\pi\frac{a^2}{h^2}x^2\,dx\right) = \rho\pi\frac{a^2}{h^2}\left(\frac{a^2}{4h^2}+1\right)x^4\,dx$$

$$I_y = \int dI_y = \int_0^h \rho\pi\frac{a^2}{h^2}\left(\frac{a^2}{4h^2}+1\right)x^4\,dx = \rho\pi\frac{a^2}{h^2}\left(\frac{a^2}{4h^2}+1\right)\frac{h^5}{5}$$

Introducing the total mass of the cone m, we rewrite I_y as follows:

$$I_y = \tfrac{3}{5}(\tfrac{1}{4}a^2 + h^2)\tfrac{1}{3}\rho\pi a^2 h \qquad I_y = \tfrac{3}{5}m(\tfrac{1}{4}a^2 + h^2) \quad \blacktriangleleft$$

c. **Moment of Inertia $\bar{I}_{y''}$.** We apply the parallel-axis theorem and write

$$I_y = \bar{I}_{y'} + md^2$$

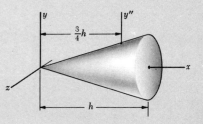

Solving for $\bar{I}_{y'}$ and recalling that $d = \tfrac{3}{4}h$, we have

$$\bar{I}_{y'} = I_y - md^2 = \tfrac{3}{5}m(\tfrac{1}{4}a^2 + h^2) - m(\tfrac{3}{4}h)^2$$

$$\bar{I}_{y''} = \tfrac{3}{20}m(a^2 + \tfrac{1}{4}h^2) \quad \blacktriangleleft$$

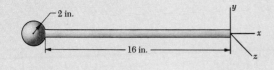

A portion of a governor consists of a 20-lb sphere welded to a 5-lb rod as shown. Determine the mass moment of inertia and the radius of gyration of the body with respect to the y axis.

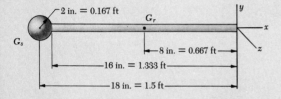

Moment of Inertia I_y. The mass moment of inertia of each component with respect to the y axis is computed in the following table. The expression for $\bar{I}_y$ of each component is obtained from Fig. 9.26, and the parallel-axis theorem is used to obtain the corresponding value of I_y. Note that all lengths should be expressed in feet.

	Weight	Mass, lb-sec²/ft	$\bar{I}_y + md^2$, lb-ft-sec²
Sphere	20 lb	$\dfrac{20}{32.2} = 0.621$	$\dfrac{2}{5}(0.621)(0.167)^2 + (0.621)(1.5)^2 = 1.404$
Rod...	5 lb	$\dfrac{5}{32.2} = 0.155$	$\dfrac{1}{12}(0.155)(1.333)^2 + (0.155)(0.667)^2 = 0.092$
		$m = 0.776$	$I_y = 1.496$

The moment of inertia of the composite body is

$$I_y = 1.496 \text{ lb-ft-sec}^2 \quad \blacktriangleleft$$

Radius of Gyration k_y

$$k_y^2 = \frac{I_y}{m} = \frac{1.496 \text{ lb-ft-sec}^2}{0.776 \text{ lb-sec}^2/\text{ft}} \qquad k_y = 1.388 \text{ ft} \quad \blacktriangleleft$$

PROBLEMS

9.74. Determine the mass moment of inertia of a thin elliptical plate of mass m with respect to (*a*) the axes AA' and BB' of the ellipse, (*b*) the axis CC' perpendicular to the plate.

FIG. P 9.74

9.75. A thin plate of mass m is cut in the shape of an isosceles triangle of base b and height h. Determine the mass moment of inertia of the plate with respect to (*a*) the centroidal axes AA' and BB' in the plane of the plate, (*b*) the centroidal axis CC' perpendicular to the plate.

9.76. Determine the mass moments of inertia of the plate of Prob. 9.75 with respect to the axes DD' and EE' parallel to the centroidal axes AA' and BB' respectively.

FIG. P 9.75

9.77. Determine the mass moment of inertia of a ring of mass m, cut from a thin uniform plate, with respect to (*a*) the diameter AA' of the ring, (*b*) the axis CC' perpendicular to the plane of the ring.

9.78. Determine by direct integration the mass moment of inertia and the radius of gyration of a sphere of radius a and uniform density ρ with respect to a diameter.

9.79. Determine by direct integration the mass moment of inertia and the radius of gyration with respect to the x axis of the paraboloid shown, assuming a uniform density ρ.

FIG. P 9.77

9.80 and 9.81. The area shown is revolved about the x axis to form a homogeneous solid of revolution of mass m. Express the mass moment of inertia of the solid with respect to the x axis in terms of m and a.

9.82. Determine by direct integration the mass moment of inertia and the radius of gyration of a circular cylinder of radius a, length L, and uniform density ρ, with respect to a diameter of its base.

9.83. Determine by direct integration the mass moment of inertia and the radius of gyration with respect to the y axis of the paraboloid shown, assuming a uniform density ρ.

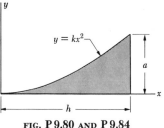

FIG. P 9.79 AND P 9.83

9.84 and 9.85. The area shown is revolved about the x axis to form a homogeneous solid of revolution of mass m. Express the mass moment of inertia of the solid with respect to the y axis in terms of m, a, and h.

$y = kx^2$

FIG. P 9.80 AND P 9.84

$y = kx^{1/3}$

FIG. P 9.81 AND P 9.85

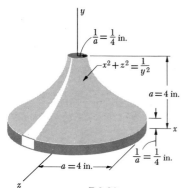

$$\frac{1}{a}=\frac{1}{4}\text{ in.}$$

$$x^2+z^2=\frac{1}{y^2}$$

$a=4$ in.

$$\frac{1}{a}=\frac{1}{4}\text{ in.}$$

$a=4$ in.

FIG. P 9.86

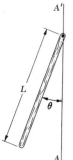

A'

L

θ

A

FIG. P 9.87

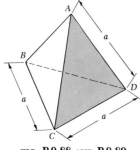

A

a

B

a

D

C

a

FIG. P 9.88 AND P 9.89

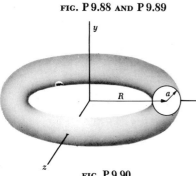

y

R

a

x

z

FIG. P 9.90

9.86. Determine by direct integration the mass moment of inertia and the radius of gyration of the body shown with respect to the y axis, assuming a uniform density ρ.

9.87. A slender rod of mass m and length L forms an angle θ with the vertical axis AA'. Determine the mass moment of inertia and the radius of gyration of the rod with respect to the axis AA'. Check the result obtained when $\theta = 90°$ with Sample Prob. 9.9.

°9.88. Determine by direct integration the mass moment of inertia of the regular tetrahedron shown with respect to an axis through A perpendicular to the base BCD. Express the result in terms of a and the mass m of the body.

°9.89. Determine by direct integration the mass moment of inertia of the regular tetrahedron shown with respect to an axis through A parallel to the base BCD. Express the result in terms of a and the mass m of the body and show that the result is independent of the orientation of the axis.

°9.90. Determine by direct integration the mass moment of inertia of the circular ring shown (*torus*) with respect to the y axis. Express the result in terms of R, a, and the mass m of the ring.

°9.91. Given an arbitrary solid and three rectangular axes x, y, and z, prove that the mass moment of inertia of the solid with respect to any one of the three axes cannot be larger than the sum of the moments of inertia of the solid with respect to the other two axes; i.e., prove that the inequality $I_x \leqslant I_y + I_z$ is satisfied, as well as two similar inequalities. Further prove that, if the solid is homogeneous and of revolution, and if x is the axis of revolution and y a transverse axis, then $I_y \geqslant \frac{1}{2}I_x$.

°9.92. Given a homogeneous solid of mass m and of arbitrary shape, and three rectangular axes x, y, and z of origin O, prove that the sum $I_x + I_y + I_z$ of the mass moments of inertia of the solid cannot be smaller than the similar sum computed for a sphere of the same mass and same material centered at O. Further prove, using the result of Prob. 9.91, that, if the solid is of revolution and if x is the axis of revolution, then its moment of inertia I_y about a transverse axis y must satisfy the inequality

$$I_y \geqslant \frac{3}{10}\,ma^2$$

where a is the radius of the sphere of the same mass and same material.

9.93. Determine the mass moment of inertia of a sphere of radius a and mass m with respect to a line tangent to the sphere.

9.94. A homogeneous hemisphere of radius a and mass m is oriented as shown. Determine the distance y for which the moment of inertia of the hemisphere with respect to the axis AA' is twice its moment of inertia with respect to the y axis.

9.95. In using the parallel-axis theorem, the error introduced by neglecting the centroidal moment of inertia is sometimes small. For a homogeneous sphere of radius a and mass m, (a) determine the mass moment of inertia with respect to an axis AA' at a distance R from the center of the sphere, (b) express as a function of a/R the relative error introduced by neglecting the centroidal moment of inertia, (c) determine the distance R in terms of a for which the relative error is 0.4 per cent.

9.96. Determine the mass moment of inertia of a thin spherical shell of radius a and mass m with respect to one of its diameters. (*Hint.* Consider the solid bounded by spherical surfaces of radius a and $a + \varepsilon$, respectively, and let ε approach zero after the moment of inertia has been expressed in terms of a, ε, and the mass of the solid.)

9.97. Determine the radius of gyration of the homogeneous solid shown with respect to the x axis.

9.98. Determine the radius of gyration of the homogeneous solid shown with respect to the y axis.

9.99. Determine the moment of inertia of the frustum of a right circular cone of mass m with respect to its axis of symmetry.

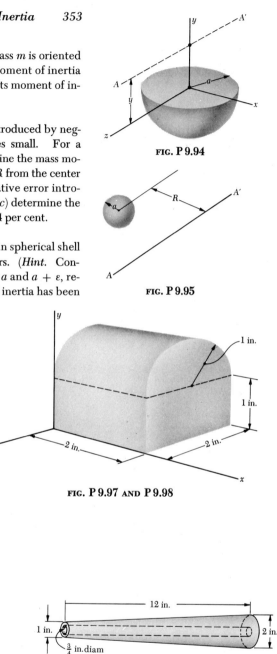

FIG. P 9.94

FIG. P 9.95

FIG. P 9.97 AND P 9.98

FIG. P 9.99

FIG. P 9.100

9.100. A $\frac{3}{4}$-in.-diameter hole is drilled through the entire length of a steel taper as shown. Determine the mass moment of inertia and the radius of gyration of the taper with respect to its axis of symmetry. (Specific weight of steel = 490 lb/ft³.)

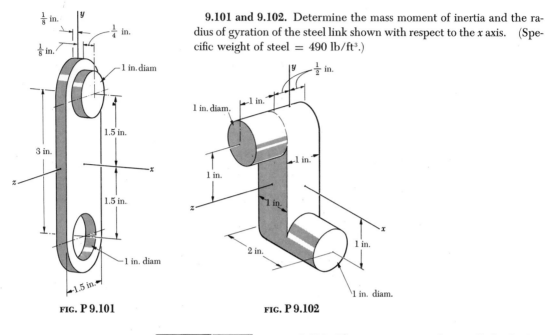

9.101 and 9.102. Determine the mass moment of inertia and the radius of gyration of the steel link shown with respect to the *x* axis. (Specific weight of steel = 490 lb/ft³.)

FIG. P 9.101

FIG. P 9.102

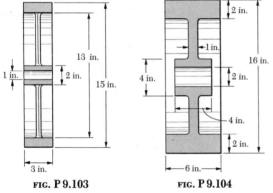

FIG. P 9.103

FIG. P 9.104

9.103. The cross section of a small flywheel is shown. The rim and hub are connected by eight spokes (two of which are shown in the cross section). Each spoke has a cross-sectional area of 0.1875 in.². Determine the mass moment of inertia and radius of gyration of the flywheel with respect to the axis of rotation. (Specific weight of steel = 490 lb/ft³.)

9.104. Determine the mass moment of inertia and radius of gyration of the steel flywheel shown with respect to the axis of rotation. The web of the flywheel consists of a solid plate 1 in. thick. (Specific weight of steel = 490 lb/ft³.)

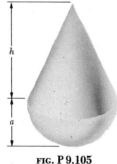

FIG. P 9.105

9.105. A hemisphere of radius *a* and a cone of height *h*, of the same density ρ, are attached as shown. (*a*) Determine the ratio *h*/*a* for which the moment of inertia of the composite body with respect to its axis of symmetry is equal to the moment of inertia of a sphere, of radius *a* and density ρ, with respect to one of its diameters. (*b*) Repeat the solution considering now the moment of inertia of the composite body with respect to a diameter of the base common to the cone and the hemisphere. (*Hint.* Solve the resulting cubic equation by trial and error.)

9.106. Geological evidence indicates that the earth consists of a central spherical *core* surrounded by two layers called respectively the *mantle* and the *crust*. The radii and density characterizing these three regions are as follows:

$$
\begin{aligned}
\text{core:} &\quad 0 < r < 2{,}140 \text{ miles, density} = 10.0 \\
\text{mantle:} &\quad 2{,}140 \text{ miles} < r < 3{,}940 \text{ miles, density} = 4.7 \\
\text{crust:} &\quad 3{,}940 \text{ miles} < r < 3{,}960 \text{ miles, density} = 3.0
\end{aligned}
$$

Knowing that the average density of the earth is 5.51, determine the ratio of the actual moment of inertia of the earth to the moment of inertia of a sphere of radius 3,960 miles having a uniform density of 5.51.

REVIEW PROBLEMS

9.107. (*a*) Determine $\bar{I}_x$ and $\bar{I}_y$ if $b = 6$ in. (*b*) Determine the dimension b for which $\bar{I}_x = 3\bar{I}_y$.

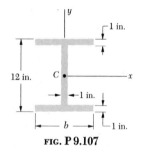

FIG. P 9.107

9.108. Determine the mass moment of inertia of the right circular cone of Sample Prob. 9.11 with respect to a diameter of its base.

9.109. Determine the radius of gyration of an equilateral triangle of side a with respect to one of its sides.

9.110. Determine the radius of gyration of the steel crankshaft shown with respect to the axis AA'.

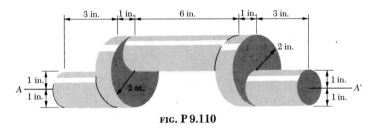
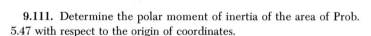

FIG. P 9.110

9.111. Determine the polar moment of inertia of the area of Prob. 5.47 with respect to the origin of coordinates.

9.112. Determine the centroidal moments of inertia $\bar{I}_x$ and $\bar{I}_y$ and the centroidal radii of gyration $\bar{k}_x$ and $\bar{k}_y$ for the structural shape shown. Neglect the effect of fillets.

9.113. Determine the orientation of the principal axes through the centroid C and the corresponding values of the moments of inertia for the structural shape shown. Neglect the effect of fillets and use the values of $\bar{I}_x$ and $\bar{I}_y$ obtained in Prob. 9.112.

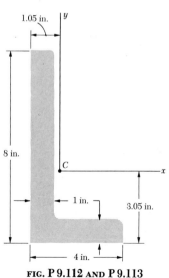

FIG. P 9.112 AND P 9.113

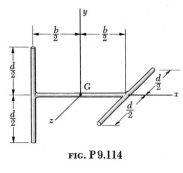

FIG. P 9.114

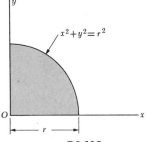

FIG. P 9.116

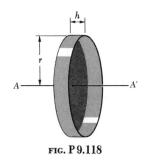

FIG. P 9.118

9.114. Three slender homogeneous rods, weighing w lb/ft, are welded together as shown. If $b = d = 1$ ft and $w = 3$ lb/ft, determine the mass moment of inertia and the radius of gyration of the assembly with respect to (*a*) the x axis, (*b*) the y axis, (*c*) the z axis.

9.115. For the assembly of Prob. 9.114 determine the value of the ratio d/b for which $I_x = I_y = I_z$.

9.116. Determine the product of inertia of the quarter-circular area shown with respect to (*a*) the x and y axes, (*b*) centroidal axes, respectively parallel to the x and y axes.

9.117. Determine the orientation of the principal axes through the origin and the corresponding values of the moments of inertia for the cross-sectional area of Prob. 5.35. (*Hint.* Make use of the result of Prob. 9.116*a*.)

9.118. The rotor of an electric clock motor consists of a disk of radius r and a rim of width h; both the disk and the rim are of uniform thickness t. Determine the ratio h/r for which the radius of gyration of the rotor with respect to the axis AA' is 0.80 r.

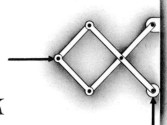

10. METHOD OF VIRTUAL WORK

10.1. Work of a Force. In the preceding chapters, problems involving the equilibrium of rigid bodies were solved by expressing that the external forces acting on the bodies were balanced. The equations of equilibrium $\Sigma F_x = 0$, $\Sigma F_y = 0$, $\Sigma M_A = 0$ were written and solved for the desired unknowns. We shall now consider a different method, which will prove more effective for solving certain types of equilibrium problems. This method is based on the concept of the *work of a force* and was first formally used by the Swiss mathematician Jean Bernoulli in the eighteenth century.

We shall first define the terms *displacement* and *work* as they are used in mechanics. Consider a particle which moves from a point A to a neighboring point A' (Fig. 10.1). If $\mathbf{r}$ denotes the position vector corresponding to point A, the small vector joining A and A' may be denoted by the differential $d\mathbf{r}$; the vector $d\mathbf{r}$ is called the *displacement* of the particle. Now let us assume that a force $\mathbf{F}$ is acting on the particle. The *work of the force $\mathbf{F}$ corresponding to the displacement $d\mathbf{r}$* is defined as the quantity

$$dU = \mathbf{F} \cdot d\mathbf{r} \qquad (10.1)$$

obtained by forming the scalar product of the force $\mathbf{F}$ and of the displacement $d\mathbf{r}$. Denoting respectively by F and ds the magnitudes of the force and of the displacement, and by α the angle formed by $\mathbf{F}$ and $d\mathbf{r}$, and recalling the definition of the scalar product of two vectors (Sec. 3.8), we write

$$dU = F \, ds \cos \alpha \qquad (10.1')$$

Being a *scalar quantity*, work has a magnitude and a sign, but no direction. We also note that work should be expressed in units such as ft-lb or in.-lb, obtained by multiplying units of length by units of force.

It follows from $(10.1')$ that the work dU is positive if the

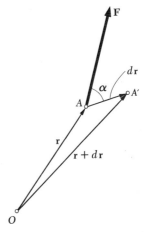

FIG. 10.1

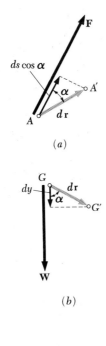

(a)

(b)

FIG. 10.2

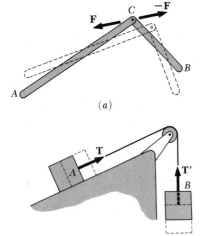

(a)

(b)

FIG. 10.3

angle α is acute, and negative if α is obtuse. Three particular cases are of special interest. If the force **F** has the same direction as $d\mathbf{r}$, the work dU reduces to $F\,ds$. If **F** has a direction opposite to that of $d\mathbf{r}$, the work is $dU = -F\,ds$. Finally, if **F** is perpendicular to $d\mathbf{r}$, the work dU is zero.

The work dU of a force **F** during a displacement $d\mathbf{r}$ may also be considered as the product of F and of the component $ds \cos \alpha$ of the displacement $d\mathbf{r}$ along **F** (Fig. 10.2a). This view is particularly useful in the computation of the work done by the weight **W** of a body (Fig. 10.2b). The work of **W** is equal to the product of W and of the vertical displacement dy of the center of gravity G of the body. If the displacement is downward, the work is positive; if it is upward, the work is negative.

A number of forces frequently encountered in statics *do no work*. They are forces applied to fixed points ($ds = 0$) or acting in a direction perpendicular to the displacement ($\cos \alpha = 0$). Among the forces which do no work are the following: the reaction at a smooth pin when the body supported rotates about the pin, the reaction at a smooth frictionless surface when the body in contact moves along the surface, the reaction at a roller moving along its track, the weight of a body when its center of gravity moves horizontally, the friction force acting on a wheel rolling without slipping (since at any instant the point of contact does not move). Examples of forces which *do work* are the weight of a body (except in the case considered above), the friction force acting on a body sliding on a rough surface, and most forces applied on a moving body.

In certain cases, the sum of the work done by several forces is zero. Consider, for example, two rigid bodies AC and BC connected at C by a *smooth pin* (Fig. 10.3a). Among the forces acting on AC is the force **F** exerted at C by BC. In general, the work of this force will not be zero, but it will be equal in magnitude and opposite in sign to the work of the force $-\mathbf{F}$ exerted at C by AC on BC, since these forces are equal and opposite and are applied to the same particle. Thus, when the total work done by all the forces acting on AB and BC is considered, the work of the two internal forces at C cancels out. A similar result is obtained if we consider a system consisting of two blocks connected by an *inextensible cord AB* (Fig. 10.3b). The work of the tension force **T** at A is equal in magnitude to the work of the tension force **T'** at B, since these forces have the same magnitude and the points A and B

move through the same distance; but in one case the work is positive, and in the other it is negative. Thus, the work of the internal forces again cancels out.

It may be shown that the total work of the internal forces holding together the particles of a rigid body is zero. Consider two particles A and B of a rigid body and the two equal and opposite forces $\mathbf{F}$ and $-\mathbf{F}$ they exert on each other (Fig. 10.4). While, in general, the displacements $d\mathbf{r}$ and $d\mathbf{r}'$ of the two particles are different, the components of these displacements along AB must be equal; otherwise, the particles would not remain at the same distance from each other, and the body would not be rigid. Therefore, the work of $\mathbf{F}$ is equal in magnitude and opposite in sign to the work of $-\mathbf{F}$, and their sum is zero.

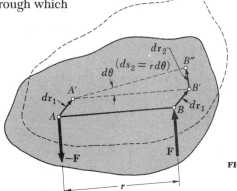

FIG. 10.4

In computing the work of the external forces acting on a rigid body, it is often convenient to determine the work of a couple without considering separately the work of each of the two forces forming the couple. Consider the two forces $\mathbf{F}$ and $-\mathbf{F}$ forming a couple of moment $\mathbf{M}$ and acting on a rigid body (Fig. 10.5). Any small displacement of the rigid body bringing A and B, respectively, into A' and B'' may be divided into two parts, one in which points A and B undergo equal displacements $d\mathbf{r}_1$, the other in which A' remains fixed while B' moves into B'' through a displacement $d\mathbf{r}_2$ of magnitude $ds_2 = r\,d\theta$. In the first part of the motion, the work of $\mathbf{F}$ is equal in magnitude and opposite in sign to the work of $-\mathbf{F}$, and their sum is zero. In the second part of the motion, only force $\mathbf{F}$ works, and its work is $dU = F\,ds_2 = Fr\,d\theta$. But the product Fr is equal to the magnitude M of the moment of the couple. Thus, the work of a couple of moment $\mathbf{M}$ acting on a rigid body is

$$dU = M\,d\theta \qquad (10.2)$$

where $d\theta$ is the small angle expressed in radians through which

FIG. 10.5

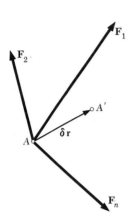

FIG. 10.6

the body rotates.   We again note that work should be expressed in units obtained by multiplying units of force by units of length.

*10.2. Principle of Virtual Work.   Consider a particle acted upon by several forces $\mathbf{F}_1$, $\mathbf{F}_2$, . . . $\mathbf{F}_n$ (Fig. 10.6).   We shall assume that the particle undergoes a small displacement from A to A'.   This displacement is possible, but it will not necessarily take place.   The forces may be balanced and the particle at rest, or the particle may move under the action of the given forces in a direction different from that of AA'.   The displacement considered is therefore an imaginary displacement; it is called a *virtual displacement* and is denoted by $\delta\mathbf{r}$. The symbol $\delta\mathbf{r}$ represents a differential of the first order; it is used to distinguish the virtual displacement from the displacement $d\mathbf{r}$ which would take place under actual motion.   As we shall see, virtual displacements may be used to determine whether the conditions of equilibrium of a particle are satisfied.

The work of each of the forces $\mathbf{F}_1$, $\mathbf{F}_2$, . . . , $\mathbf{F}_n$ during the virtual displacement $\delta\mathbf{r}$ is called *virtual work*.   The virtual work of all the forces acting on the particle of Fig. 10.6 is

$$\delta U = \mathbf{F}_1 \cdot \delta\mathbf{r} + \mathbf{F}_2 \cdot \delta\mathbf{r} + \cdots + \mathbf{F}_n \cdot \delta\mathbf{r}$$
$$= (\mathbf{F}_1 + \mathbf{F}_2 + \cdots + \mathbf{F}_n) \cdot \delta\mathbf{r}$$
$$= \mathbf{R} \cdot \delta\mathbf{r} \tag{10.3}$$

where $\mathbf{R}$ is the resultant of the given forces.   Thus, the total virtual work of the forces $\mathbf{F}_1$, $\mathbf{F}_2$, . . . , $\mathbf{F}_n$ is equal to the virtual work of their resultant $\mathbf{R}$.

The principle of virtual work for a particle states that, *if a particle is in equilibrium, the total virtual work of the forces acting on the particle is zero for any virtual displacement of the particle.*   This condition is necessary: if the particle is in equilibrium, the resultant $\mathbf{R}$ of the forces is zero, and it follows from (10.3) that the total virtual work δU is zero.   The condition is also sufficient: if the total virtual work δU is zero for any virtual displacement, the scalar product $\mathbf{R} \cdot \delta\mathbf{r}$ is zero for any $\delta\mathbf{r}$, and the resultant $\mathbf{R}$ must be zero.

In the case of a rigid body, the principle of virtual work states that, *if a rigid body is in equilibrium, the total virtual work of the external forces acting on the rigid body is zero for any virtual displacement of the body.*   The condition is necessary: if the body is in equilibrium, all the particles forming the body are in equilibrium and the total virtual work of the forces acting on all the particles must be zero; but we have seen in the preceding section that the total work of the internal forces is zero; the total work of the external forces must therefore also be zero.   The condition may also be proved to be sufficient.

The principle of virtual work may be extended to the case of a *system of connected rigid bodies.*   If the system remains connected during the virtual displacement, *only the work of the forces external to the system need be considered,* since the total work of the internal forces at the various connections is zero.

10.3. Applications of the Principle of Virtual Work.   The principle of virtual work is particularly effective when applied to the solution of problems involving machines or mechanisms consisting of several connected rigid bodies.   Consider for instance the toggle vise ACB of Fig. 10.7a, used to compress a wooden block.   We wish to determine the force exerted by the vise on the block when a given force P is applied at C, assuming that there is no friction.   Denoting by Q the reaction of the block on the vise, we draw the free-body diagram of the vise and consider the virtual displacement obtained by giving to the angle θ a positive increment $\delta\theta$ (Fig. 10.7b).   Choosing a system of

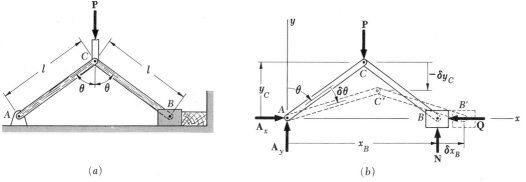

(a)

(b)

FIG. 10.7

coordinate axes with origin at A, we note that x_B increases while y_C decreases.   This is indicated in the figure by means of the positive increment δx_B and the negative increment $-\delta y_C$. The reactions A_x, A_y, and N will do no work during the virtual displacement considered, and we need only compute the work of P and Q.   Since Q and δx_B have opposite senses, the virtual work of Q is $\delta U_Q = -Q\,\delta x_B$.   Since P and the increment shown $(-\delta y_C)$ have the same sense, the virtual work of P is $\delta U_P = +P(-\delta y_C) = -P\,\delta y_C$.   The minus signs obtained could have been predicted by simply noting that the forces **Q** and **P** are directed opposite to the positive x and y axes, respectively.   Expressing the coordinates x_B and y_C in terms of the angle θ and differentiating, we obtain

$$x_B = 2l \sin \theta \qquad\qquad y_C = l \cos \theta$$
$$\delta x_B = 2l \cos \theta \; \delta\theta \qquad \delta y_C = -l \sin \theta \; \delta\theta \qquad (10.4)$$

The total virtual work of the forces **Q** and **P** is thus

$$\delta U = \delta U_Q + \delta U_P = -Q \; \delta x_B - P \; \delta y_C$$
$$= -2Ql \cos \theta \; \delta\theta + Pl \sin \theta \; \delta\theta$$

Making $\delta U = 0$, we obtain

$$2Ql \cos \theta \; \delta\theta = Pl \sin \theta \; \delta\theta \qquad (10.5)$$
$$Q = \tfrac{1}{2}P \tan \theta \qquad (10.6)$$

The superiority of the method of virtual work over the conventional equilibrium equations in the problem considered here is clear: by using the method of virtual work, we were able to eliminate all unknown reactions, while the equation $\Sigma M_A = 0$ would have eliminated only two of the unknown reactions.   We may take advantage of this characteristic of the method of virtual work to solve many problems involving machines and mechanisms.   *If the virtual displacement considered is consistent with the constraints imposed by the supports and connections, all reactions and internal forces are eliminated and only the work of the loads, applied forces, and friction forces need be considered.*

We shall observe that the method of virtual work may also be used to solve problems involving completely constrained structures, although the virtual displacements considered will never actually take place.   Consider, for example, the frame ACB shown in Fig. 10.8a.   If point A is kept fixed, while B is given a horizontal virtual displacement (Fig. 10.8b), we need consider only the work of **P** and **B**$_x$.   We may thus determine the reaction component **B**$_x$ in the same way as the force **Q** of the preceding example (Fig. 10.7b); we have

$$B_x = -\tfrac{1}{2}P \tan \theta$$

Keeping B fixed and giving to A a horizontal virtual displacement, we may similarly determine the reaction component $\mathbf{A}_x$. The components $\mathbf{A}_y$ and $\mathbf{B}_y$ may be determined by rotating the frame ACB as a rigid body about B and A, respectively.

The method of virtual work may also be used to determine

the configuration of a system in equilibrium under given forces. For example, the value of the angle θ for which the linkage of Fig. 10.7a is in equilibrium under two given forces **P** and **Q** may be obtained by solving Eq. (10.6) for tan θ.

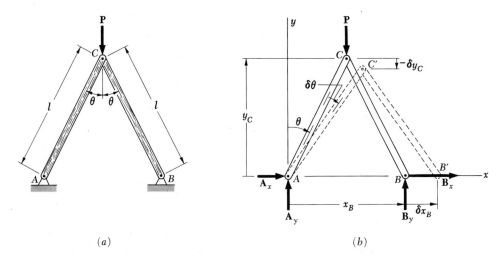

(a)   (b)   **FIG. 10.8**

*10.4. Real Machines. Mechanical Efficiency. In analyzing the toggle vise in the preceding section, we assumed that no friction forces were involved. Thus, the virtual work consisted only of the work of the applied force **P** and of the reaction **Q**. But the work of the reaction **Q** is equal in magnitude and opposite in sign to the work of the force exerted by the vise on the block. Equation (10.5), therefore, expresses that the *output work* $2Ql \cos \theta \, \delta\theta$ is equal to the *input work* $Pl \sin \theta \, \delta\theta$. A machine in which input and output work are equal is said to be an "ideal" machine. In a "real" machine, friction forces will always do some work, and the output work will be smaller than the input work.

Consider, for example, the toggle vise of Fig. 10.7a, and assume now that a friction force **F** develops between the sliding block B and the horizontal plane (Fig. 10.9). Using the conventional methods of statics and summing moments about A, we find $N = P/2$. Denoting by μ the coefficient of friction between block B and the horizontal plane, we have $F = \mu N = \mu P/2$. Recalling formulas (10.4), we find that the total virtual work of the forces **Q**, **P**, and **F** during the virtual displacement shown in Fig. 10.9 is

$$\delta U = -Q \, \delta x_B - P \, \delta y_C - F \, \delta x_B$$
$$= -2Ql \cos \theta \, \delta\theta + Pl \sin \theta \, \delta\theta - \mu Pl \cos \theta \, \delta\theta$$

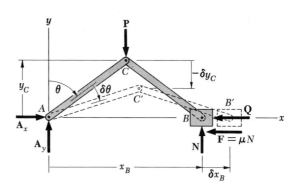

FIG. 10.9

Making $\delta U = 0$, we obtain

$$2Ql \cos \theta \; \delta\theta = Pl \sin \theta \; \delta\theta - \mu Pl \cos \theta \; \delta\theta \qquad (10.7)$$

which expresses that the output work is equal to the input work minus the work of the friction force.   Solving for Q, we have

$$Q = \tfrac{1}{2}P(\tan \theta - \mu) \qquad (10.8)$$

We note that $Q = 0$ when $\tan \theta = \mu$, that is, when θ is equal to the angle of friction ϕ, and that $Q < 0$ when $\theta < \phi$. The toggle vise may thus be used only for values θ larger than the angle of friction.

The *mechanical efficiency* of a machine is defined as the ratio

$$\eta = \frac{\text{output work}}{\text{input work}} \qquad (10.9)$$

Clearly, the mechanical efficiency of an ideal machine is $\eta = 1$, since input and output work are then equal, while the mechanical efficiency of a real machine will always be less than 1.

In the case of the toggle vise we have just analyzed, we write

$$\eta = \frac{\text{output work}}{\text{input work}} = \frac{2Ql \cos \theta \; \delta\theta}{Pl \sin \theta \; \delta\theta}$$

Substituting from (10.8) for Q, we obtain

$$\eta = \frac{P(\tan \theta - \mu)l \cos \theta \; \delta\theta}{Pl \sin \theta \; \delta\theta} = 1 - \mu \cot \theta \qquad (10.10)$$

We check that, in the absence of friction forces, we would have $\mu = 0$ and $\eta = 1$.   In the general case, when μ is different from zero, the efficiency η becomes zero for $\mu \cot \theta = 1$, that is, for $\tan \theta = \mu$, or $\theta = \tan^{-1} \mu = \phi$.   We check again that the toggle vise may be used only for values of θ larger than the angle of friction ϕ.

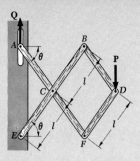

SAMPLE PROBLEM 10.1

Using the method of virtual work, determine the magnitude of the force **Q** required to maintain the equilibrium of the mechanism shown.

Solution. Choosing a coordinate system with origin at E, we write

$$y_A = 2l \sin \theta \qquad y_D = l \sin \theta$$

$$\delta y_A = 2l \cos \theta \, \delta\theta \qquad \delta y_D = l \cos \theta \, \delta\theta$$

Principle of Virtual Work. Since the reactions **A**, **E**$_x$, and **E**$_y$ will do no work during the virtual displacement, the total virtual work done by **P** and **Q** must be zero.

$$\delta U = 0: \qquad +Q \, \delta y_A - P \, \delta y_D = 0$$

$$+Q(2l \cos \theta \, \delta\theta) - P(l \cos \theta \, \delta\theta) = 0 \qquad Q = \tfrac{1}{2}P \blacktriangleleft$$

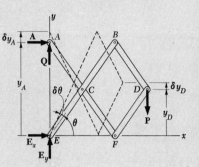

SAMPLE PROBLEM 10.2

Determine the expressions for θ and for the tension in the spring which correspond to the equilibrium position of the mechanism. The unstretched length of the spring is h, and the constant of the spring is k. Neglect the weight of the mechanism.

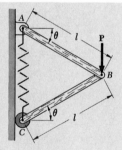

Solution. With the coordinate system shown

$$y_B = l \sin \theta \qquad y_C = 2l \sin \theta$$

$$\delta y_B = l \cos \theta \, \delta\theta \qquad \delta y_C = 2l \cos \theta \, \delta\theta$$

The elongation of the spring is

$$s = y_C - h = 2l \sin \theta - h$$

The magnitude of the force exerted at C by the spring is

$$F = ks = k(2l \sin \theta - h) \qquad (1)$$

Principle of Virtual Work

$$\delta U = 0: \qquad P \, \delta y_B - F \, \delta y_C = 0$$

$$P(l \cos \theta \, \delta\theta) - k(2l \sin \theta - h)(2l \cos \theta \, \delta\theta) = 0$$

$$\sin \theta = \frac{P + 2kh}{4kl} \blacktriangleleft$$

Substituting this expression into (1), we obtain

$$F = \tfrac{1}{2}P \blacktriangleleft$$

365

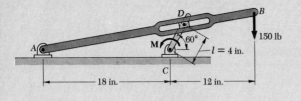

SAMPLE PROBLEM 10.3

Determine the couple **M** which must be applied to the crank CD to hold the mechanism in equilibrium. The block at D is pinned to the crank CD and is free to slide in a slot cut in member AB. This mechanism has been previously considered in Sample Prob. 6.8.

Solution. Referring to Sample Prob. 6.8, we obtain the following dimensions:

$$b = 2 \text{ in.} \qquad \alpha = 9.8°$$

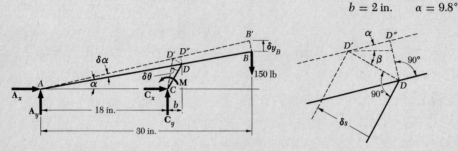

Virtual Displacement $\delta\theta$. After a virtual rotation $\delta\theta$ of the crank CD, the mechanism assumes the position indicated by the dashed lines. Member AB rotates through $\delta\alpha$ into AB', and the block D moves through δs into D'. Since the virtual rotation $\delta\theta$ represents a differential of the first order, DD' is perpendicular to CD.

$$\beta = 30° \qquad \delta s = l\,\delta\theta$$

The component of the displacement of the block perpendicular to member AB is

$$DD'' = \delta s \sin(\alpha + \beta) = (l\,\delta\theta)\sin(9.8° + 30°) = l\sin 39.8°\,\delta\theta \quad (1)$$

By similar triangles, we obtain

$$\frac{AB}{AD} = \frac{30 \text{ in.}}{18 \text{ in.} + b} \qquad \frac{AB}{AD} = \frac{30 \text{ in.}}{20 \text{ in.}} \quad (2)$$

Using the similar triangles ABB' and ADD'' together with (1) and (2), we find

$$\frac{BB'}{DD''} = \frac{AB}{AD} = \tfrac{30}{20} \qquad BB' = \tfrac{30}{20}DD'' = \tfrac{30}{20}l\sin 39.8°\,\delta\theta$$

Finally, since BB' is perpendicular to AB and $l = 4$ in., we obtain

$$\delta y_B = BB'\cos\alpha = [(\tfrac{30}{20})(4 \text{ in.})\sin 39.8°\,\delta\theta]\cos 9.8° = (3.78 \text{ in.})\,\delta\theta$$

Principle of Virtual Work

$$\delta U = 0: \qquad +M\,\delta\theta - (150 \text{ lb})\,\delta y_B = 0$$

$$+M\,\delta\theta - (150 \text{ lb})(3.78 \text{ in.})\,\delta\theta = 0$$

$$M = +567 \text{ lb-in.} \qquad\qquad \mathbf{M} = 567 \text{ lb-in.} \;\circlearrowright \;\blacktriangleleft$$

PROBLEMS

10.1. Determine the magnitude of the force **P** required to maintain the equilibrium of the linkage shown.

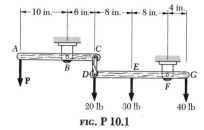

FIG. P 10.1

10.2. Using the principle of virtual work, determine the tension in the rope for each of the rope-and-pulley arrangements of Prob. 2.42.

10.3. Determine the weight *W* which balances the 10-lb load.

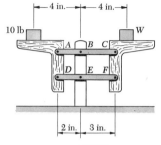

FIG. P 10.3

10.4. Determine the force **P** required to maintain the equilibrium of the linkage shown. All members are of the same length and the wheels at *A* and *B* roll freely on the horizontal rod.

10.5. Determine the vertical force **P** which must be applied at *A* to maintain the equilibrium of the linkage.

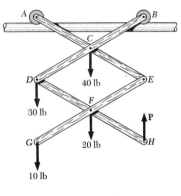

FIG. P 10.4

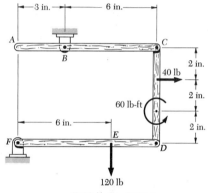

FIG. P 10.5 AND P 10.6

10.6. Determine the couple **M** which must be applied to member *AC* to maintain the equilibrium of the linkage.

10.7 and 10.8. The mechanism shown is acted upon by the force **P**; determine an expression for the magnitude of the force **Q** required to maintain equilibrium.

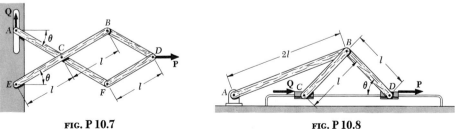

FIG. P 10.7   **FIG. P 10.8**

10.9. Three links, each of length l, are connected as shown. Knowing that the line of action of the force **Q** passes through point A, determine an expression for the magnitude of **Q** required to maintain equilibrium.

FIG. P 10.10

10.10. A slender rod of length l is attached to a collar at B and rests on a smooth circular cylinder of radius r. Knowing that the collar may slide freely along a vertical guide, determine an expression for the magnitude of the force **Q** required to maintain equilibrium.

10.11. Solve Prob. 10.10 assuming that the force **P** is removed and that a couple **M**, directed counterclockwise, is applied to rod AB.

10.12 and 10.13. Determine an expression for the magnitude of the couple **M** required to maintain equilibrium.

10.14. Solve Prob. 10.12 assuming that the force **P** is directed horizontally to the right.

10.15. If gripping forces of magnitude $Q = 450$ lb are desired, determine the magnitude P of the forces which must be applied to the pliers of Prob. 6.113. Also show that the required magnitude P is independent of the position of the object gripped by the jaws.

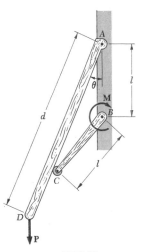

FIG. P 10.12

FIG. P 10.13

10.16. In Prob. 10.7 determine the magnitude of the force **Q** required for equilibrium, when $l = 15$ in., $\theta = 30°$, and $P = 200$ lb.

10.17. In Prob. 10.9 determine the magnitude of the force **Q** required for equilibrium, when $l = 20$ in., $\theta = 45°$, and $P = 400$ lb.

10.18. In Prob. 10.13 determine the magnitude of the force **P** required for equilibrium when $r = 4$ in., $l = 8$ in., $\theta = 60°$, and $M = 4,000$ lb-in. clockwise.

10.19. Determine the value of θ corresponding to the equilibrium position of the mechanism of Prob. 10.7, when $P = 50$ lb and $Q = 200$ lb.

°10.20. Determine the value of θ corresponding to the equilibrium position of the mechanism of Prob. 10.8, when $P = 100$ lb and $Q = 200$ lb.

10.21. Determine the value of θ corresponding to the equilibrium position of the mechanism of Prob. 10.9, when $P = 100$ lb and $Q = 150$ lb.

10.22. Determine the value of θ corresponding to the equilibrium position of the mechanism of Prob. 10.10, when $P = 250$ lb, $Q = 300$ lb, $r = 8$ in., and $l = 12$ in.

10.23. Two 15-in. bars AC and DE are connected by a pin at B and by a spring EC. When unstretched, the spring is 5 in. long; the constant of the spring is 15 lb/in. Determine the value of a corresponding to equilibrium.

10.24. Solve Prob. 10.23 assuming that the 20-lb force is applied at C and the 12-lb force is applied at D.

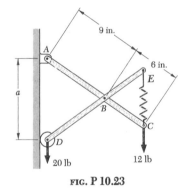

FIG. P 10.23

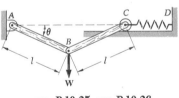

FIG. P 10.25 AND P 10.26

10.25. A vertical load **W** is applied to the linkage at B. The constant of the spring is k, and the spring is unstretched when AB and BC are horizontal. Neglecting the weight of the linkage, obtain an equation, in terms of θ, W, l, and k, which must be satisfied when the linkage is in equilibrium.

10.26. A load **W** of magnitude 100 lb is applied to the linkage.at B. Neglecting the weight of the linkage and knowing that $l = 10$ in., determine the value of θ corresponding to equilibrium. The constant of the spring is $k = 30$ lb/in., and the spring is unstretched when AB and BC are horizontal. (*Hint.* Obtain the approximate value of θ by solving by trial and error the equation obtained.)

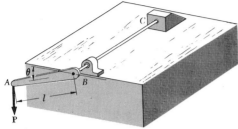

FIG. P 10.27

10.27. The lever AB is attached to the horizontal shaft BC which passes through a bearing and is welded to a fixed support at C. The torsional spring constant of the shaft BC is K; i.e., a couple of moment K is required to rotate end B through one radian. Knowing that the shaft is untwisted when AB is horizontal, determine the value of θ corresponding to the position of equilibrium, if $P = 20$ lb, $l = 10$ in., and $K = 100$ lb-in./radian.

10.28. Solve Prob. 10.27, if $P = 70$ lb, $l = 10$ in., and $K = 100$ lb-in./radian. Obtain an answer in each of the following quadrants: $0 < \theta < 90°$, $270° < \theta < 360°$, and $360° < \theta < 450°$. (It is assumed that K remains constant for the angles of twist considered.)

10.29. A block of weight W is pulled up a plane forming an angle α with the horizontal by a force **P** directed along the plane. If μ is the coefficient of friction between the block and the plane, derive an expression for the mechanical efficiency of the system. Show that the mechanical efficiency cannot exceed $\frac{1}{2}$ if the block is to remain in place when the force **P** is removed.

10.30. Derive an expression for the mechanical efficiency of the jack discussed in Sec. 8.6. Show that, if the jack is to be self-locking, the mechanical efficiency cannot exceed $\frac{1}{2}$.

10.31. In Prob. 10.7, assume that friction exists between the pin and the slot at A. Denoting by μ the coefficient of friction, determine the smallest and the largest magnitudes of the force **Q** for which equilibrium is maintained.

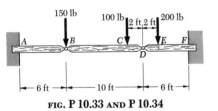

FIG. P 10.33 AND P 10.34

10.32. In Prob. 10.7, assume that the coefficient of friction between the pin and the slot at A is $\mu = 0.30$, and determine the smallest and the largest magnitudes of the force **Q** for which equilibrium is maintained when $\theta = 30°$ and $P = 200$ lb.

10.33. Using the method of virtual work, determine separately the force and the couple representing the reaction at A.

10.34. Using the method of virtual work, determine separately the force and the couple representing the reaction at F.

10.35. In Prob. 10.4 the force **P** is removed and the linkage is maintained in equilibrium by a cord which is attached to pins E and H. Determine the tension in the cord.

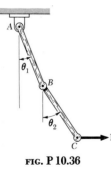

FIG. P 10.36

10.36. Two uniform rods, each of weight W and length l, are connected as shown. Using the method of virtual work, determine θ_1 and θ_2 corresponding to equilibrium.

10.37. Solve Prob. 10.36, assuming that the force **P** is replaced by a counterclockwise couple **M** applied on rod *BC*.

10.38. Determine the vertical movement of joint *G* if member *AB* is shortened 0.8 in. (*Hint.* Apply a vertical load at joint *G*, and, using the methods of Chap. 6, compute the force exerted by member *AB* on joints *A* and *B*. Then apply the method of virtual work for a virtual displacement making member *AB* shorter. This method should be used only for small changes in the length of members.)

10.39. Determine the vertical movement of joint *D* if the length of member *BF* is changed to 50 ft $1\frac{1}{2}$ in. (See hint of Prob. 10.38.)

10.40. Determine the horizontal movement of joint *D* if the length of member *BF* is changed to 50 ft $1\frac{1}{4}$ in. (See hint of Prob. 10.38.)

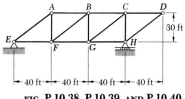

FIG. P 10.38, P 10.39, AND P 10.40

*10.5. Work of a Force during a Finite Displacement.
Consider a force **F** acting on a particle. The work of **F** corresponding to an infinitesimal displacement *d***r** of the particle was defined in Sec. 10.1 as

$$dU = \mathbf{F} \cdot d\mathbf{r} \tag{10.1}$$

The work of **F** corresponding to a finite displacement of the particle from A_1 to A_2 (Fig. 10.10*a*) is denoted by $U_{1\to2}$ and is obtained by integrating (10.1) along the curve described by the particle:

$$U_{1\to2} = \int_{A_1}^{A_2} \mathbf{F} \cdot d\mathbf{r} \tag{10.11}$$

Using the alternate expression

$$dU = F\, ds \cos \alpha \tag{10.1'}$$

given in Sec. 10.1 for the elementary work dU, we may also express the work $U_{1\to2}$ as

$$U_{1\to2} = \int_{s_1}^{s_2} (F \cos \alpha)\, ds \tag{10.11'}$$

where the variable of integration *s* measures the distance along the path traveled by the particle. The work $U_{1\to2}$ is represented by the area under the curve obtained by plotting $F \cos \alpha$ against *s* (Fig. 10.10*b*). In the case of a force **F** of constant magnitude acting in the direction of motion, formula (10.11) yields $U_{1\to2} = F(s_2 - s_1)$.

Recalling from Sec. 10.1 that the work of a couple of mo-

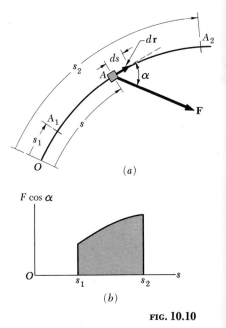

FIG. 10.10

ment **M** during an infinitesimal rotation $d\theta$ of a rigid body is

$$dU = M \, d\theta \qquad (10.2)$$

we express as follows the work of the couple during a finite rotation of the body:

$$U_{1\rightarrow 2} = \int_{\theta_1}^{\theta_2} M \, d\theta \qquad (10.12)$$

In the case of a constant couple, formula (10.12) yields

$$U_{1\rightarrow 2} = M(\theta_2 - \theta_1)$$

Work of a Weight. It was stated in Sec. 10.1 that the work of the weight **W** of a body during an infinitesimal displacement of the body is equal to the product of W and of the vertical displacement of the center of gravity of the body. With the y axis pointing upward, the work of **W** during a finite displacement of the body (Fig. 10.11) is obtained by writing

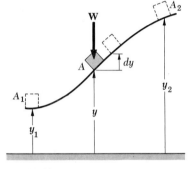

FIG. 10.11

$$dU = -W \, dy$$

$$U_{1\rightarrow 2} = -\int_{y_1}^{y_2} W \, dy = Wy_1 - Wy_2 \qquad (10.13)$$

or
$$U_{1\rightarrow 2} = -W(y_2 - y_1) = -W \, \Delta y \qquad (10.13')$$

where Δy is the vertical displacement from A_1 to A_2. The work of the weight **W** is thus equal to *the product of W and of the vertical displacement of the center of gravity of the body.* The work is *positive* when $\Delta y < 0$, that is, *when the body moves down.*

Work of the Force Exerted by a Spring. Consider a body A attached to a fixed point B by a spring; it is assumed that the spring is undeformed when the body is at A_0 (Fig. 10.12a). Experimental evidence shows that the magnitude of the force **F** exerted by the spring on a body A is proportional to the deflection x of the spring measured from the position A_0. We have

$$F = kx \qquad (10.14)$$

where k is the *spring constant,* expressed in lb/ft or lb/in. The work of the force **F** exerted by the spring during a finite displacement of the body from $A_1(x = x_1)$ to $A_2(x = x_2)$ is obtained by writing

$$dU = -F \, dx = -kx \, dx$$

$$U_{1\rightarrow 2} = -\int_{x_1}^{x_2} kx \, dx = \tfrac{1}{2}kx_1^2 - \tfrac{1}{2}kx_2^2 \qquad (10.15)$$

Care should be taken to express k and x in consistent units, that is, k in lb/ft and x in feet, or k in lb/in. and x in inches; in the first case, the work is obtained in ft-lb; in the second case, in in.-lb.   We note that the work of the force $\mathbf{F}$ exerted by the spring on the body is *positive* when $x_2 < x_1$, that is, *when the spring is returning to its undeformed position.*

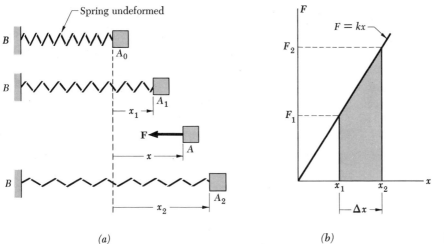

(a)   (b)   FIG. **10.12**

   Since Eq. (10.14) is the equation of a straight line of slope k passing through the origin, the work $U_{1\rightarrow2}$ of $\mathbf{F}$ during the displacement from A_1 to A_2 may be obtained by evaluating the area of the trapezoid shown in Fig. 10.12b.   This is done by computing the values F_1 and F_2 and multiplying the base Δx of the trapezoid by its mean height $\frac{1}{2}(F_1 + F_2)$.   Since the work of the force $\mathbf{F}$ exerted by the spring is positive for a negative value of Δx, we write

$$U_{1\rightarrow2} = -\tfrac{1}{2}(F_1 + F_2)\,\Delta x \qquad (10.16)$$

Formula (10.16) is usually more convenient to use than (10.15) and affords fewer chances of confusing the units involved.

*10.6.   Potential Energy.   Considering again the body of Fig. 10.11, we note from (10.13) that the work of the weight $\mathbf{W}$ during a finite displacement is obtained by subtracting the value of the function Wy corresponding to the second position of the body from its value corresponding to the first position.   The work of $\mathbf{W}$ is thus independent of the actual path followed; it depends only upon the initial and final values of the function Wy.   This function is called the *potential energy* of the body with respect to the *force of gravity* **W** and is denoted by V_g.   We write

$$U_{1 \to 2} = (V_g)_1 - (V_g)_2 \qquad \text{with } V_g = Wy \qquad (10.17)$$

We note that if $(V_g)_2 > (V_g)_1$, that is, *if the potential energy increases* during the displacement (as in the case considered here), *the work $U_{1 \to 2}$ is negative.*   If, on the other hand, the work of **W** is positive, the potential energy decreases.   Therefore, the potential energy V_g of the body provides a measure of *the work which may be done* by its weight **W**.   Since only the *change* in potential energy, and not the actual value of V_g, is involved in formula (10.17), an arbitrary constant may be added to the expression obtained for V_g.   In other words, the level from which the elevation y is measured may be chosen arbitrarily.   Note that potential energy is expressed in the same units as work, i.e., in ft-lb or in in.-lb.

Considering now the body of Fig. 10.12*a*, we note from formula (10.15) that the work of the elastic force **F** is obtained by subtracting the value of the function $\frac{1}{2}kx^2$ corresponding to the second position of the body from its value corresponding to the first position.   This function is denoted by V_e and is called the *potential energy* of the body with respect to the *elastic force* **F**.   We write

$$U_{1 \to 2} = (V_e)_1 - (V_e)_2 \qquad \text{with } V_e = \tfrac{1}{2}kx^2 \qquad (10.18)$$

and observe that, during the displacement considered, the work of the force **F** exerted by the spring on the body is negative and the potential energy V_e increases.   We should note that the expression obtained for V_e is valid only if the deflection of the spring is measured from its undeformed position.

The concept of potential energy may be used when forces other than gravity forces and elastic forces are involved.   It remains valid as long as the elementary work dU of the force considered is an *exact differential*.   It is then possible to find a function V, called potential energy, such that

$$dU = -dV \qquad (10.19)$$

Integrating (10.19) over a finite displacement, we obtain the general formula

$$U_{1 \to 2} = V_1 - V_2 \qquad (10.20)$$

which expresses that *the work of the force is independent of the path followed and is equal to minus the change in potential energy.*   A force which satisfies Eq. (10.20) is said to be a *conservative force.*†

† A detailed discussion of conservative forces is given in Sec. 13.6.

*10.7. **Potential Energy and Equilibrium.** The application of the principle of virtual work is considerably simplified when the potential energy of a system is known. In the case of a virtual displacement, formula (10.19) becomes $\delta U = -\delta V$. Besides, if the position of the system is defined by a single independent variable θ we may write $\delta V = (dV/d\theta)\delta\theta$. Since $\delta\theta$ must be different from zero, the condition $\delta U = 0$ for the equilibrium of the system becomes

$$\frac{dV}{d\theta} = 0 \qquad (10.21)$$

In terms of potential energy, the principle of virtual work states therefore that, *if a system is in equilibrium, the derivative of its total potential energy is zero.* If the position of the system depends upon several independent variables (the system is then said to possess *several degrees of freedom*), the partial derivatives of V with respect to each of the independent variables must be zero.

Consider, for example, a structure made of two members AC and CB and carrying a load **W** at C. The structure is supported by a pin at A and a roller at B, and a spring BD connects B to a fixed point D (Fig. 10.13a). The constant of the spring

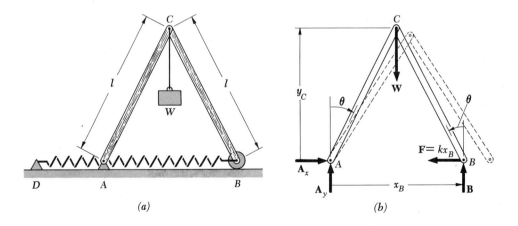

(a)   (b)   **FIG. 10.13**

is k, and it is assumed that the natural length of the spring is equal to AD, and thus that the spring is undeformed when B coincides with A. Neglecting the friction forces and the weight of the members, we find that the only forces which work during a displacement of the structure are the weight **W** and the force **F** exerted by the spring at point B. The total potential energy of the system will thus be obtained by adding the potential energy V_g corresponding to the gravity force **W** and the potential energy V_e corresponding to the elastic force **F**.

Choosing a coordinate system with origin at A and noting that the deflection of the spring, measured from its undeformed position, is $AB = x_B$, we write

$$V_e = \tfrac{1}{2}kx_B^2 \qquad V_g = Wy_C$$

Expressing the coordinates x_B and y_C in terms of the angle θ, we have

$$x_B = 2l \sin \theta \qquad\qquad y_C = l \cos \theta$$
$$V_e = \tfrac{1}{2}k(2l \sin \theta)^2 \qquad V_g = W(l \cos \theta)$$
$$V = V_e + V_g = 2kl^2 \sin^2 \theta + Wl \cos \theta \qquad (10.22)$$

The positions of equilibrium of the system are obtained by equating to zero the derivative of the potential energy V,

$$\frac{dV}{d\theta} = 4kl^2 \sin \theta \cos \theta - Wl \sin \theta = 0$$

$$\sin \theta = 0 \qquad 4kl \cos \theta - W = 0$$

There are therefore two positions of equilibrium, corresponding to the values $\theta = 0$ and $\theta = \cos^{-1}(W/4kl)$.†

10.8. Stability of Equilibrium. Consider the three uniform rods of length $2a$ and weight **W** shown in Fig. 10.14. While each rod is in equilibrium, there is an important difference between the three cases considered. Suppose that each rod is slightly disturbed from its position of equilibrium and then released: rod a will move back toward its original position, rod b will keep moving away from its original position, and rod c will remain in its new position. In case a, the equilibrium of the rod is said to be *stable;* in case b, the equilibrium is said to be *unstable;* and, in case c, to be *neutral.*

Recalling from Sec. 10.6 that the potential energy V_g with respect to gravity is equal to Wy, where y is the elevation of the point of application of **W** measured from an arbitrary level, we observe that the potential energy of rod a is minimum in the position of equilibrium considered, that the potential energy of rod b is maximum, and that the potential energy of rod c is constant. Equilibrium is thus *stable, unstable,* or *neutral* according to whether the potential energy is *minimum, maximum,* or *constant.*

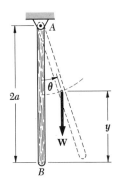

(*a*) Stable equilibrium

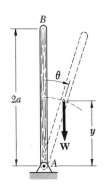

(*b*) Unstable equilibrium

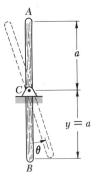

(*c*) Neutral equilibrium

FIG. 10.14

† The second position does not exist if $W > 4kl$ (see Prob. 10.51 for a further discussion of the equilibrium of this system).

That the result obtained is quite general may be seen as follows: We first observe that a force always tends to do positive work and thus to decrease the potential energy of the system on which it is applied. Therefore, when a system is disturbed from its position of equilibrium, the forces acting on the system will tend to bring it back to its original position if V is minimum (Fig. 10.15a) and to move it farther away if V is maximum (Fig. 10.15b). If V is constant (Fig. 10.15c), the forces will not tend to move the system either way.

Recalling from calculus that a function is minimum or maximum according to whether its second derivative is positive or negative, we may summarize as follows the conditions for the equilibrium of a system with one degree of freedom (i.e., a system the position of which is defined by a single independent variable θ):

$$\frac{dV}{d\theta} = 0 \qquad \frac{d^2V}{d\theta^2} > 0: \qquad \text{Stable equilibrium}$$

$$\frac{dV}{d\theta} = 0 \qquad \frac{d^2V}{d\theta^2} < 0: \qquad \text{Unstable equilibrium}$$

$$(10.23)$$

If both the first and the second derivatives of V are zero, it is necessary to examine derivatives of a higher order to determine whether the equilibrium is stable, unstable, or neutral. The equilibrium will be neutral if all derivatives are zero, since the potential energy V is then a constant. The equilibrium will be stable if the first derivative found to be different from zero is of even order, and if that derivative is positive. In all other cases the equilibrium will be unstable.

If the system considered possesses *several degrees of freedom*, the potential energy V depends upon several variables and it is thus necessary to apply the theory of functions of several variables to determine whether V is minimum. It may be verified that a system with two degrees of freedom will be stable, and the corresponding potential energy $V(\theta_1, \theta_2)$ will be minimum, if the following relations are satisfied simultaneously:

$$\frac{\partial V}{\partial \theta_1} = \frac{\partial V}{\partial \theta_2} = 0$$

$$\left(\frac{\partial^2 V}{\partial \theta_1\, \partial \theta_2} \right)^2 - \frac{\partial^2 V}{\partial \theta_1^2}\, \frac{\partial^2 V}{\partial \theta_2^2} < 0 \qquad (10.24)$$

$$\frac{\partial^2 V}{\partial \theta_1^2} > 0 \qquad \text{or} \qquad \frac{\partial^2 V}{\partial \theta_2^2} > 0$$

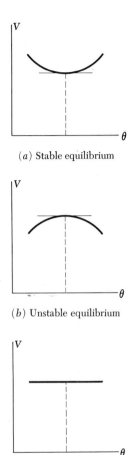

(a) Stable equilibrium

(b) Unstable equilibrium

(c) Neutral equilibrium

FIG. 10.15

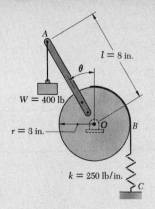

SAMPLE PROBLEM 10.4

A 400-lb weight is attached to the lever AO as shown. The constant of the spring BC is $k = 250$ lb/in., and the spring is unstretched when $\theta = 0$. Determine the position or positions of equilibrium, and state in each case whether the equilibrium is stable, unstable, or neutral.

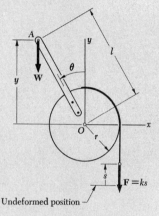

Potential Energy. Denoting by s the deflection of the spring from its undeformed position and placing the origin of coordinates at O, the potential energy of the system is

$$V_e = \tfrac{1}{2} ks^2 \qquad V_g = Wy$$

Measuring θ in radians, we have

$$s = r\theta \qquad\qquad y = l \cos \theta$$
$$V_e = \tfrac{1}{2} kr^2\theta^2 \qquad V_g = Wl \cos \theta$$
$$V = V_e + V_g = \tfrac{1}{2} kr^2\theta^2 + Wl \cos \theta$$

Positions of Equilibrium. Setting $dV/d\theta = 0$, we write

$$\frac{dV}{d\theta} = kr^2\theta - Wl \sin \theta = 0$$

$$\sin \theta = \frac{kr^2}{Wl} \theta$$

Substituting the given data, we obtain

$$\sin \theta = \frac{(250 \text{ lb/in.})(3 \text{ in.})^2}{(400 \text{ lb})(8 \text{ in.})} \theta \qquad \sin \theta = 0.703\theta$$

Solving by trial and error for θ, we find

$$\theta = 0 \qquad \text{and} \qquad \theta = 80.4° \quad \blacktriangleleft$$

Stability of Equilibrium. The second derivative of the potential energy V with respect to θ is

$$\frac{d^2V}{d\theta^2} = kr^2 - Wl \cos \theta = (250 \text{ lb/in.})(3 \text{ in.})^2 - (400 \text{ lb})(8 \text{ in.}) \cos \theta$$

$$= 2{,}250 - 3{,}200 \cos \theta$$

For $\theta = 0$: $\qquad \dfrac{d^2V}{d\theta^2} = 2{,}250 - 3{,}200 \cos 0° = -950 < 0$

The equilibrium is unstable for $\theta = 0°$. $\quad \blacktriangleleft$

For $\theta = 80.4°$: $\qquad \dfrac{d^2V}{d\theta^2} = 2{,}250 - 3{,}200 \cos 80.4° = +1{,}716 > 0$

The equilibrium is stable for $\theta = 80.4°$. $\quad \blacktriangleleft$

PROBLEMS

10.41. Show that the position of equilibrium is neutral in Probs. 10.1 and 10.3.

10.42. Show that the position of equilibrium is neutral in Prob. 10.4.

10.43. Two uniform rods, each of weight W, are attached to gears of equal radii as shown. Determine the positions of equilibrium of the system and state in each case whether the equilibrium is stable, unstable, or neutral.

10.44. A vertical force P of magnitude 10 lb is applied to rod CD at D. Knowing that the uniform rods AB and CD weigh 5 lb each, determine the positions of equilibrium of the system and state in each case whether the equilibrium is stable, unstable, or neutral.

FIG. P 10.43 AND P 10.44

10.45. Using the method of Sec. 10.7, solve Prob. 10.27. Determine whether the equilibrium is stable, unstable, or neutral. (*Hint.* The potential energy corresponding to the couple exerted by a torsion spring is $\frac{1}{2}K\theta^2$, where K is the torsional spring constant and θ is the angle of twist.)

10.46. In Prob. 10.28 determine whether each of the positions of equilibrium is stable, unstable, or neutral. (See hint of Prob. 10.45.)

10.47. Using the method of Sec. 10.7, solve Prob. 10.26. Determine whether the equilibrium is stable, unstable, or neutral.

10.48. (*a*) Obtain an equation defining the angle θ corresponding to the equilibrium position. (*b*) Determine the angle θ corresponding to the equilibrium position if $W = P$.

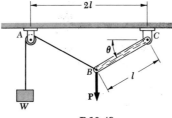

FIG. P 10.48

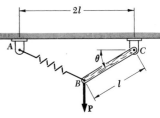

FIG. P 10.49

10.49. Knowing that the spring AB is of constant k and is unstretched when $\theta = 0$, (*a*) obtain an equation defining the angle θ corresponding to the equilibrium position, (*b*) determine the value of θ corresponding to the equilibrium position if $P = kl$.

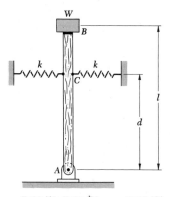

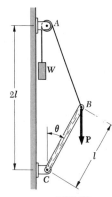

FIG. P 10.53, P 10.54, AND P 10.55

FIG. P 10.56

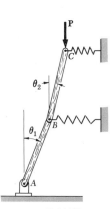

FIG. P 10.58

10.50. For the mechanism considered in Prob. 10.25, show that for any finite values of W and k there is only one equilibrium position. Further show that the equilibrium position is stable.

10.51. In Sec. 10.7, two positions of equilibrium were obtained for the system shown in Fig. 10.13, namely, $\theta = 0$ and $\theta = \cos^{-1}(W/4kl)$. Show that (a) if $W < 4kl$ the equilibrium is stable in the first position ($\theta = 0$) and unstable in the second, (b) if $W = 4kl$, the two positions coincide and the equilibrium is unstable, (c) if $W > 4kl$, the equilibrium is unstable in the first position ($\theta = 0$) and the second position does not exist. (*Note.* It is assumed that the system must deform as shown and that the system cannot rotate as a single rigid body about A when A and B coincide.)

10.52. For the mechanism of Sample Prob. 10.4, determine the largest vertical load W for which stable equilibrium exists when lever AO is vertical. Express the result in terms of l, r, and k.

10.53. The rod AB is attached to a hinge at A and to two springs each of constant k. If $l = 20$ in., $d = 15$ in., and $W = 750$ lb, determine the smallest value of k for which the equilibrium of rod AB is stable in the position shown. Each spring can act in either tension or compression.

10.54. If $W = 100$ lb, $l = 30$ in., and the constant of each spring is $k = 12$ lb/in., determine the smallest distance d for which the equilibrium of the rod AB is stable in the position shown. Each spring can act in either tension or compression.

10.55. If $d = 16$ in., $l = 24$ in., and the constant of each spring is $k = 50$ lb/in., determine the largest load W for which the equilibrium of the rod AB is stable in the position shown. Each spring can act in either tension or compression.

*10.56. Determine (a) the largest ratio P/W for which $\theta = 0$ is a stable position of equilibrium, (b) the smallest ratio P/W for which $\theta = 180°$ is a stable position of equilibrium, (c) the range of values of P/W for which both $\theta = 0$ and $\theta = 180°$ are stable positions of equilibrium.

*10.57. In Prob. 10.56 show that the value of θ defined by the equation $(5 - 4\cos\theta)^{1/2} = 2W/P$ corresponds to a position of equilibrium. Further show that this position of equilibrium is always unstable.

*10.58. Two bars AB and BC, each of length l and of negligible weight, are attached to springs each of constant k. The springs are undeformed and the system is in equilibrium when $\theta_1 = \theta_2 = 0$. Determine the largest value of the force $\mathbf{P}$ for which this equilibrium position is stable.

°**10.59.** Two rods, of negligible weight, are attached to drums of radius *r* which are connected by a belt and a spring of constant *k*. The spring is undeformed when $\theta_1 = \theta_2 = 0$. Determine the largest value of the force **P** for which the equilibrium position $\theta_1 = \theta_2 = 0$ is stable.

°**10.60.** Solve Prob. 10.59 knowing that $k = 20$ lb/in., $r = 3$ in., $l = 6$ in., and $W = 10$ lb.

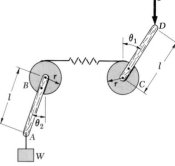

FIG. P 10.59

REVIEW PROBLEMS

10.61. Two bars *AB* and *BC* are attached to a single spring of constant *k* which is unstretched when the bars are vertical. Determine the largest value of the force **P** for which the equilibrium of the system is stable in the position shown.

10.62. Solve parts *b* and *c* of Prob. 6.118 by the method of virtual work.

10.63. Collar *B* may slide along rod *OC* and is attached by a pin to a block which may slide in the vertical slot. Derive an expression for the magnitude of the couple **M** required to maintain equilibrium.

10.64. Determine the value of θ corresponding to the equilibrium position of rod *OC* when $R = 10$ in., $P = 50$ lb, and $M = 2,000$ lb-in.

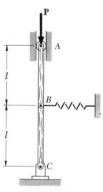

FIG. P 10.61

FIG. P 10.63 AND P 10.64

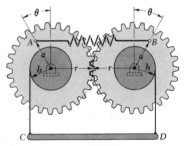

FIG. P 10.65

10.65. A spring *AB* of constant *k* is attached to two identical gears as shown. A uniform bar *CD* of weight *W* is supported by cords wrapped around drums of radius *b* which are attached to the gears. If the spring is undeformed when $\theta = 0$, obtain an equation defining the angle θ corresponding to the equilibrium position.

10.66. For the mechanism of Prob. 10.65 the following numerical values are given: $k = 50$ lb/in., $a = 4$ in., $b = 3$ in., $r = 6$ in., and $W = 200$ lb. Determine the values of θ corresponding to equilibrium positions and state in each case whether the equilibrium is stable, unstable, or neutral.

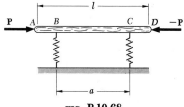

FIG. P 10.68

10.67. Solve Prob. 6.132 by the method of virtual work.

10.68. The horizontal bar AD is attached to two springs of constant k and is in equilibrium in the position shown. Knowing that the springs are equidistant from the center of the bar, determine the largest value of the magnitude P of the two equal and opposite *horizontal* forces **P** and $-\mathbf{P}$ for which the equilibrium position shown is stable.

10.69. Solve Prob. 10.68 assuming that the distance AB is twice as large as the distance CD.

10.70. Solve Prob. 6.77 by the method of virtual work.

10.71. Derive an expression for the magnitude P of the two equal and opposite forces **P** and $-\mathbf{P}$ required to maintain the equilibrium of the mechanism shown.

10.72. Determine the value of θ corresponding to the equilibrium position of the mechanism shown when $P = W$.

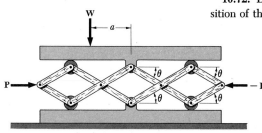

FIG. P 10.71 AND P 10.72

Appendix. GRAPHICAL METHODS IN STATICS

A.1. A Graphical Method for the Reduction of a System of Forces. A system of coplanar forces acting on a rigid body may be reduced graphically to one force or one couple by making use of the principle of transmissibility and the parallelogram law. Consider, for instance, the three forces $\mathbf{F}_1$, $\mathbf{F}_2$, and $\mathbf{F}_3$ (Fig. A.1a). The forces $\mathbf{F}_1$ and $\mathbf{F}_2$ may be moved along their lines of action until they act at the same point A (Fig. A.1b). They may then be added into their resultant $\mathbf{R}_{1,2}$ (Fig. A.1c). The forces $\mathbf{R}_{1,2}$ and $\mathbf{F}_3$ may in turn be moved along their lines of action until they act at the same point B (Fig. A.1d) and added into their resultant $\mathbf{R}_{1,2,3}$ (Fig. A.1e). If there were more than three forces, it would be possible to repeat this procedure until all the forces were added together.

This method is simple to understand and easy to remember; yet it is not always practical. Indeed, the construction may

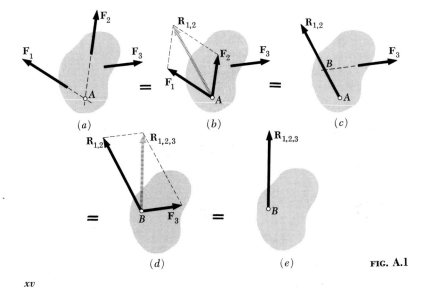

(a) (b) (c)

(d) (e) **FIG. A.1**

become quite cumbersome if many forces are involved. Besides, lines of action will perhaps intersect off the paper; and, obviously, the method fails completely if all the forces are parallel. We shall consider next another method for the graphical reduction of a system of forces, which is less direct but more effective.

A.2. Resultant of a System of Forces by the Method of the Force Polygon and String Polygon. Consider four forces $\mathbf{F}_1$, $\mathbf{F}_2$, $\mathbf{F}_3$, and $\mathbf{F}_4$ acting on a rigid body (Fig. A.2a). We draw the lines of action of the forces, extending them as far as possible on one side of the rigid body to divide the space outside the rigid body into four distinct regions. We write the letter a in one of these regions, and, moving clockwise around the body, we write successively b, c, d, and finally e in the region from which we started. The line of action of $\mathbf{F}_1$, which separates regions a and b, will be referred to as *line ab*. The lines of action of $\mathbf{F}_2$, $\mathbf{F}_3$, and $\mathbf{F}_4$ will be denoted similarly by *bc, cd,* and *de,* each time reading the letters clockwise around the body. This is *Bow's notation.*

We shall now draw the four given forces in tip-to-tail fashion in a separate diagram (Fig. A.2b). The tail of the first force is denoted by A and its tip, which is also the tail of the second force, by B; C, D, and E are defined in a similar way. We shall refer to each of these forces by the names of the points they join, naming first the letter corresponding to the tail and last the letter corresponding to the tip. Thus, the four given forces will be called $\overrightarrow{AB}$, $\overrightarrow{BC}$, $\overrightarrow{CD}$, and $\overrightarrow{DE}$, respectively.

Comparing the two figures we have drawn (Fig. A.2a and b), we note that a correspondence exists between *regions* in Fig. A.2a and *points* in Fig. A.2b. Each force *joins two points* in Fig. A.2b, while its line of action *separates two regions* of corresponding names in Fig. A.2a; thus, to the force $\overrightarrow{AB}$ joining points A and B corresponds the line of action ab separating regions a and b; to the force $\overrightarrow{BC}$ corresponds the line bc, to $\overrightarrow{CD}$ corresponds cd, and to $\overrightarrow{DE}$ corresponds de.

The magnitude, direction, and sense of the resultant are easily obtained by joining points A and E in Fig. A.2b. We shall see next how the line of action of the resultant $\overrightarrow{AE}$ may be determined by using the two figures simultaneously. We note that, according to the notation used, this line will be named ae.

We choose an arbitrary point O, called a *pole* (Fig. A.2d), and draw lines from O to each of the vertices of the force polygon. The lines OA, OB, OC, OD, and OE are called *rays*. We

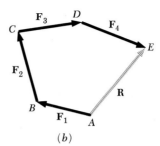

(a)

(b)

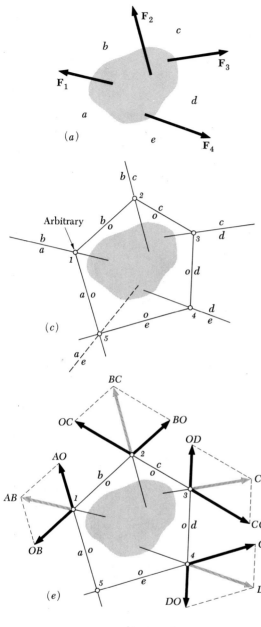

(c)

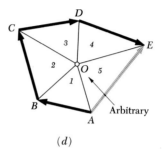

(d)

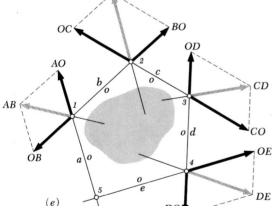

(e)

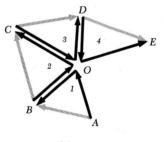

(f)

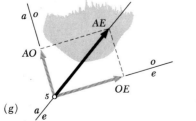

(g)

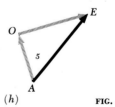

(h)

FIG. A.2

may now resolve each of the original forces $\overrightarrow{AB}$, $\overrightarrow{BC}$, $\overrightarrow{CD}$, and $\overrightarrow{DE}$ into components along the rays (Fig. A.2f).   We write

$$\overrightarrow{AB} = \overrightarrow{AO} + \overrightarrow{OB} \qquad \overrightarrow{BC} = \overrightarrow{BO} + \overrightarrow{OC}$$

$$\overrightarrow{CD} = \overrightarrow{CO} + \overrightarrow{OD} \qquad \overrightarrow{DE} = \overrightarrow{DO} + \overrightarrow{OE}$$

We note that the components $\overrightarrow{OB}$ and $\overrightarrow{BO}$ have the same magnitude and direction, but opposite sense.   Indeed, $\overrightarrow{OB}$ is a force with tail at O and tip at B, while $\overrightarrow{BO}$ has tail at B and tip at O. When all the components are added together, $\overrightarrow{OB}$ and $\overrightarrow{BO}$ cancel, and so do $\overrightarrow{OC}$ and $\overrightarrow{CO}$, and $\overrightarrow{OD}$ and $\overrightarrow{DO}$.   Only $\overrightarrow{AO}$ and $\overrightarrow{OE}$ remain and add up into the resultant $\overrightarrow{AE}$ (Fig. A.2h).   Algebraically, this is expressed as follows:

$$\overrightarrow{AE} = \overrightarrow{AB} + \overrightarrow{BC} + \overrightarrow{CD} + \overrightarrow{DE}$$

$$= \overrightarrow{AO} + \overrightarrow{OB} + \overrightarrow{BO} + \overrightarrow{OC} + \overrightarrow{CO} + \overrightarrow{OD} + \overrightarrow{DO} + \overrightarrow{OE}$$

$$= \overrightarrow{AO} + \overrightarrow{OE}$$

This construction is obviously not necessary to determine the magnitude and direction of $\overrightarrow{AE}$.   If, however, we repeat it, taking into account the lines of action of the forces as well as their magnitudes, this construction enables us to determine the line of action of the resultant.   We choose an arbitrary point (point *1*) on line *ab* (Fig. A.2c) and draw from point *1* a line parallel to ray *OA*.   This line, which separates region *a* from a central region *o*, is called the *string oa*.   From point *1*, we also draw *string ob* parallel to ray *OB*; this string will intersect line *bc* at point *2*.   From point *2*, we draw *string oc* parallel to ray *OC* and determine its point of intersection with *cd* (point *3*).   From point *3*, we draw *string od* parallel to *OD* and determine its point of intersection with *de* (point *4*). Finally, we draw *string oe* through point *4* in a direction parallel to *OE*, thus completing a polygon called the *string polygon*, or *funicular polygon* (from *funiculus*, Latin for "*string*"). The first string (*oa*) and the last string (*oe*) intersect at point *5*.

We now move force $\mathbf{F}_1$ (i.e., force $\overrightarrow{AB}$) along its line of action until it acts at point *1* and resolve it into its components $\overrightarrow{AO}$ and $\overrightarrow{OB}$ (Fig. A.2e), using the force triangle *1* of Fig. A.2f. We similarly attach force $\overrightarrow{BC}$ at point *2*, force $\overrightarrow{CD}$ at point *3*, and force $\overrightarrow{DE}$ at point *4* and resolve them into components, using the force triangles *2*, *3*, and *4*.   The components $\overrightarrow{OB}$ and $\overrightarrow{BO}$, being equal and opposite and having the same line of action *ob*, will cancel, and so will $\overrightarrow{OC}$ and $\overrightarrow{CO}$, and $\overrightarrow{OD}$ and $\overrightarrow{DO}$.   The system of forces reduces to $\overrightarrow{AO}$ and $\overrightarrow{OE}$.   These forces are moved along their respective lines of action (Fig. A.2g) until they act at point 5.   They may then be added into the resultant $\overrightarrow{AE}$, using the force triangle 5 of Fig. A.2*h*.   The line of action of the resultant is the line *ae* drawn through point 5 in a direction parallel to $\overrightarrow{AE}$.

Once the construction has been understood, it may be reduced to a few steps.   Since the magnitude and direction of the resultant are obtained from the force polygon, the string polygon will be used to determine only its line of action.   The necessary steps are the following:

1. Denote the various regions defined by the lines of action of the given forces, using lower-case letters and moving clockwise around the rigid body (Fig. A.2*a*).

2. Draw the force polygon, using capital letters corresponding to the lower-case letters used in step 1, and determine the magnitude, direction, and sense of the resultant (Fig. A.2*b*).

3. Choose an arbitrary pole *O* (either inside or outside the force polygon), and draw rays from *O* to each of the vertices of the force polygon (Fig. A.2*d*).

4. Starting from an arbitrary point on the line of action *ab*, draw the string polygon, each string parallel to the corresponding ray.   Through the point of intersection of the first and last strings (here *oa* and *oe*), draw a line parallel to the resultant; this is the line of action of the resultant (Fig. A.2*c*).

The shape of the string polygon depends upon the choice of the pole, and care should be taken to choose the pole so that no string will be parallel to the line of action it is supposed to intersect.   The size of the polygon generally depends upon the choice of its first vertex (unless all forces are parallel).   The line of action of the resultant does not, however, depend upon the choice of the pole or of the first vertex.

It may happen that *the resultant of the force polygon is zero*. In this case, the first and last vertices of the force polygon (here *A* and *E*) coincide.   The first and last rays (here *OA* and *OE*) also coincide, and the corresponding two strings (here *oa* and *oe*) have the same direction.   Two cases may be distinguished:

1. *The Two Strings Coincide.*   The forces they carry (here $\overrightarrow{AO}$ and $\overrightarrow{OE}$) may be canceled, and the given system of forces reduces to zero.   The rigid body is in equilibrium (see Sec. A.3).

2. *The Two Strings Are Parallel and Distinct.*   The given system reduces to the two forces they carry, i.e., to a couple. The moment of this resultant couple is equal to the product of the common ray *OA* and the perpendicular distance between the two parallel strings (see Sample Prob. A.2).

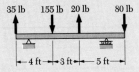

SAMPLE PROBLEM A.1

A 12-ft beam is subjected to the forces shown. Determine graphically the resultant of the given system of forces. (*Note.* This problem is the same as Sample Prob. 3.9. Again the reactions at the supports are not included in the given system of forces.)

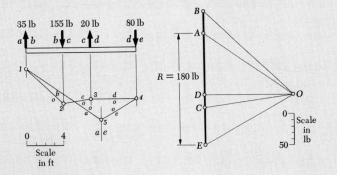

Solution. 1. Moving clockwise around the beam, we write the lower-case letters a, b, c, d, and e. Note that a and e are written in the same region.

2. Using the corresponding capital letters, we draw the force polygon $ABCDE$. Since all the forces are vertical, the polygon reduces to a vertical line. The resultant $\overline{AE}$ is directed downward, and its magnitude is 180 lb.

3. We choose an arbitrary pole O and draw rays OA, OB, OC, OD, and OE.

4. We choose an arbitrary point 1 on line ab and draw the following strings:

From point 1 on ab, we draw string oa parallel to OA.

From point 1 on ab, we draw string ob parallel to OB and obtain point 2 on bc.

From point 2 on bc, we draw string oc parallel to OC and obtain point 3 on cd.

From point 3 on cd, we draw string od parallel to OD and obtain point 4 on de.

From point 4 on de, we draw string oe parallel to OE.

5. The line of action ae of the resultant passes through the point of intersection (point 5) of strings oa and oe. Since the resultant is vertical (see step b), we draw the line of action of the resultant ae vertically through point 5.

SAMPLE PROBLEM A.2

In order to move a 173-lb crate, two men push on it while two other men pull on it by means of ropes. The force exerted by man A is 150 lb, and that exerted by man B is 50 lb; both forces are horizontal. Man C pulls with a force equal to 80 lb and man D with a force equal to 120 lb. Both cables form an angle of 30° with the vertical. Determine graphically the resultant of all forces acting on the crate.

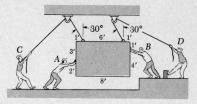

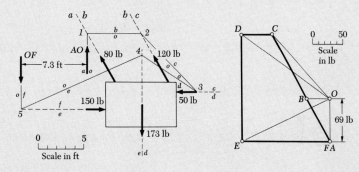

Solution. 1. We draw the free-body diagram of the crate and write the lower-case letters a, b, c, d, e, and f, moving clockwise around the crate.

2. Using the corresponding capital letters, we draw the force polygon $ABCDEF$ and note that F coincides with A. The polygon is closed, and the resultant $\overrightarrow{AF}$ is zero. The given forces must thus reduce either to a couple or to zero.

3. We choose pole O and draw the various rays; the rays OA and OF coincide.

4. Starting from an arbitrary point 1 on line ab, we draw the string polygon, obtaining successively the vertices 2, 3, 4, and 5. The strings oa and of are parallel but distinct, and the forces $\overrightarrow{AO}$ and $\overrightarrow{OF}$ that they carry have the same magnitude and opposite sense. The system of forces thus reduces to a counterclockwise couple. The moment of the couple is obtained by multiplying the common magnitude

$$AO = OF = 69 \text{ lb}$$

of the forces $\overrightarrow{AO}$ and $\overrightarrow{OF}$ by the perpendicular distance between strings oa and of (7.3 ft); the moment is found to be 504 lb-ft $\circlearrowright$.

PROBLEMS

A.1. Solve Prob. 3.77*a* graphically.

A.2. Solve Prob. 3.76 graphically.

A.3. Solve Prob. 3.59 graphically.

A.4. Solve Prob. 3.77*b* graphically.

A.5. Solve Sample Prob. 3.10*b* graphically.

A.6. Solve Prob. 3.82 graphically.

A.7. Solve Prob. 3.81 graphically.

A.8. Solve Prob. 3.84 graphically.

A.9. Solve Prob. 3.83*b* graphically.

A.10. Solve Prob. 3.77*c* graphically.

A.11 and A.12. Determine graphically the resultant of the force system shown.

A.13. Solve Prob. A.12 assuming that the 20-kip force acts downward.

°A.14. The 20-kip force in Prob. A.12 is removed and replaced by a vertical force **P** acting at the same point. Determine graphically the required magnitude and sense of **P** if the resultant of the four forces is to pass through a point 24 in. from the left end of the beam.

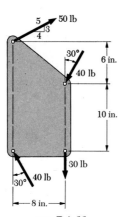

FIG. **P A.11**

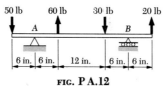

FIG. **P A.12**

A.3. Equilibrium of a Rigid Body by the Method of the Force Polygon and String Polygon. We saw in Sec. A.2 that, when a rigid body is in equilibrium, the force polygon is closed and the first and last strings of the string polygon coincide. Consider, for example, a rigid body in equilibrium under four forces. The corresponding string polygon and force polygon are shown in Fig. A.3. Note that, since the force polygon is closed, the same letter A is used to denote the tail of the first force and the tip of the last force. Similarly, the first and last regions that we meet while moving clockwise around the rigid body we denote by a single letter a and not by two different letters a and e as we did in Sec. A.2 when the rigid body was not in equilibrium.

Problems concerning the equilibrium of rigid bodies usually call for the determination of two unknown forces.† The force polygon, therefore, cannot be drawn completely at the outset of the solution; one of its vertices is unknown, and the object of the solution is to determine this vertex graphically. The exact procedure to follow varies from one problem to another, and the student is advised to turn now to the Sample Problems. A general outline of the method is described here for later reference.

1. The lines of action of all external forces are named according to Bow's notation, moving clockwise around the rigid body. If necessary, the lines of action of some of the forces are extended to the other side of the body, so that all known forces may be denoted by successive letters (see Sample Prob. A.3).

2. The force polygon is drawn, starting with the known forces. All the vertices of the force polygon may be plotted except one.

3. A pole O is chosen, and all the rays corresponding to known vertices are drawn.

4. Next, we draw the string polygon, choosing the first vertex on the line of action of one of the two unknown forces, and ending with the vertex located on the second unknown force. The last side of the string polygon is obtained by joining the first and last vertices. It should be noted that, if a force is unknown in magnitude and direction, the string polygon *must* be started at the point of application of that force (see Sample Prob. A.4).

5. We draw a ray from pole O in a direction parallel to the last side of the string polygon, thus defining the unknown vertex of the force polygon. The force polygon may now be completed and the unknown forces determined.

Note that, if a rigid body is in equilibrium under three nonparallel forces, the unknown forces may be determined more conveniently by observing that the lines of action of the three forces must be concurrent (Sec. 4.7).

---

†If three forces are unknown, their lines of action must be known. Two of the forces may then be replaced by a single force applied at the point of intersection of their lines of action.

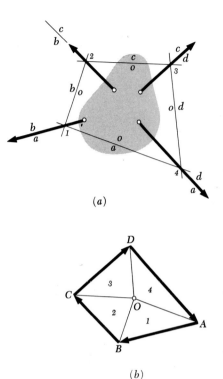

(a)

(b)

FIG. A.3

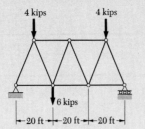

4 kips   4 kips

6 kips

|← 20 ft →|← 20 ft →|← 20 ft →|

SAMPLE PROBLEM A.3

Determine graphically the reactions at the points of support of the truss shown.

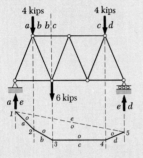

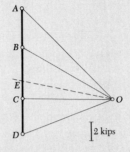

Solution. 1. The truss is drawn to scale, and the lines of action of the given loads and of the two unknown reactions are named according to Bow's notation, moving clockwise around the truss. The line of action of the 6-kip load has been extended to the other side of the truss, so that all known forces may be denoted by successive letters.

2. The force polygon is drawn, starting with load $\overrightarrow{AB}$ and proceeding with loads $\overrightarrow{BC}$ and $\overrightarrow{CD}$. The reaction $\overrightarrow{DE}$ at the roller is vertical, and so must be the reaction $\overrightarrow{EA}$ at the pin, since all applied loads are vertical. The location of point E, however, is not known, and the force polygon is incomplete.

3. A pole O is chosen, and the rays OA, OB, OC, and OD are drawn.

4. The string polygon is drawn. Point 1 is chosen on the line of action ea of one of the unknown reactions, and strings oa, ob, oc, and od are drawn in directions parallel, respectively, to the known rays OA, OB, OC, and OD. The vertices 2, 3, 4, and 5 are thus successively obtained. The last string oe may then be drawn by joining point 1 and point 5.

5. Ray OE is drawn from O in a direction parallel to string oe, thus defining point E. The force polygon is completed, and the reactions are measured on the force polygon. They are found to be

$$\overrightarrow{DE} = 6 \text{ kips} \uparrow \qquad \overrightarrow{EA} = 8 \text{ kips} \uparrow \quad ◄$$

SAMPLE PROBLEM A.4

A fixed crane weighs 2,000 lb and is used to lift a load of 5,000 lb. The center of gravity of the crane is located at G. Determine graphically the reactions at the points of support.

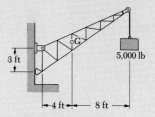

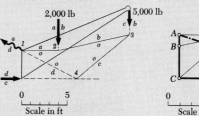

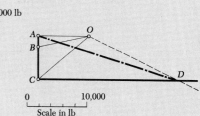

Scale in ft   Scale in lb

Solution. 1. A free-body diagram of the crane is drawn to scale. The lines of action of the given load, of the weight of the crane, and of the two unknown reactions are named according to Bow's notation, moving clockwise around the crane.

2. The force polygon is drawn, starting with the 2,000-lb weight $\overrightarrow{AB}$ and proceeding with the 5,000-lb load $\overrightarrow{BC}$. The reaction $\overrightarrow{CD}$ at the rocker is horizontal, but its magnitude is not known, and point D cannot be plotted. The reaction $\overrightarrow{DA}$ at the pin is unknown in magnitude and in direction and cannot be drawn. The force polygon is incomplete.

3. A pole O is chosen, and the rays OA, OB, and OC are drawn.

4. The string polygon is drawn. The line of action da of the reaction at the pin is not known, except for the fact that it passes through the pin. We must then choose the first vertex of the string polygon at the pin. If the string polygon were started at any other point, we would eventually have to find the point of intersection of a string with line da. This would be impossible since line da is not known. Having thus chosen point 1 at the pin, we draw strings oa, ob, and oc in directions parallel, respectively, to the known rays OA, OB, and OC. The vertices 2, 3, and 4 are obtained, respectively, on lines ab, bc, and cd. The last string od may then be drawn by joining point 1 and point 4.

5. We draw ray OD from O in a direction parallel to string od, and, since CD must be horizontal, we determine the vertex D of the force polygon. Side DA may now be drawn to complete the force polygon. The reactions $\overrightarrow{CD}$ and $\overrightarrow{DA}$ (magnitude and direction) are determined from the force polygon. We find

$$\overrightarrow{CD} = 22,700 \text{ lb} \rightarrow \qquad \overrightarrow{DA} = 23,700 \text{ lb} \searrow 17° \quad \blacktriangleleft$$

PROBLEMS

A.15. Solve Prob. 4.21 graphically.

A.16. Determine graphically the reactions for the truss and loading of Prob. 3.76.

A.17. Solve Sample Prob. 4.2 graphically.

A.18. Determine graphically the reactions for the beam and loading of Prob. A.12.

A.19. Solve Prob. 4.9 graphically.

A.20. Determine graphically the reactions for the truss and loading of Prob. 3.84.

A.21. Solve Prob. 4.23*a* and *b* graphically.

A.22. Solve Prob. 4.24*a* and *b* graphically.

*A.23. Solve Prob. 4.13 graphically.   (*Hint.*   Start the string polygon at the point of intersection of two of the unknown forces.)

*A.24. Solve Prob. 4.14*a* graphically (see hint of Prob. A.23).

*A.25. Solve Prob. 4.15 graphically (see hint of Prob. A.23).

*A.26. Solve Prob. 4.29 graphically.   (*Hint.*   Since the belt tensions are known to be equal, the line of action of their resultant may easily be determined.)

INDEX

xxvii

ANSWERS TO
EVEN-NUMBERED PROBLEMS

CHAPTER 2

2.2. 409 lb ⬈ 26.6°.

2.4. 4,000 lb ⬈ 9.2°.

2.6. 26.1 lb ⬊ 86.7°.

2.8. 67.4 lb ⬋ 35.2°.

2.10. 27.2°.

2.12. 604 lb.

2.14. 64.7 lb ←; 241 lb ↑.

2.16. $P = 69.3$ lb; 34.6 lb ⬋.

2.18. 150 lb →; 360 lb ↑.

2.20. 502 lb ⬉ 4.6°.

2.22. 111.8 lb ⬈ 8.8°.

2.26. (a) $\alpha = 48.2°$.   (b) Impossible.

2.28. 53.6 lb ⬊ 51.8°.

2.30. $T_{AC} = 175.9$ lb; $T_{BC} = 130.5$ lb.

2.32. $T_{AC} = 240$ lb; $T_{BC} = 320$ lb.

2.34. (a) 30°.   (b) $T_{AC} = 300$ lb; $T_{BC} = 520$ lb.

2.36. 6.09 lb ⬊ 7.5°.

2.38. $T_{AC} = T_{BC} = 174.5$ lb.

2.40. $P = 270$ lb; $Q = 642$ lb.

2.42. (a) 300 lb.   (b) 300 lb.   (c) 200 lb.
(d) 200 lb.   (e) 150 lb.

2.44. (a) 938 lb.   (b) 1,250 lb.

2.46. 1.252 in.

2.48. 201 lb ⬋ 39.7° or 414 lb ⬉ 39.7°.

2.50. (a) $+113.3$ lb; $+217$ lb; $+52.8$ lb.
(b) 63.1°; 30°; 77.8°.

2.52. (a) -260 lb; -410 lb; -121.2 lb.
(b) 121.3°; 145.1°; 104.0°.

2.54. 45.7°. $+279$ lb; $+69.5$ lb; $+278$ lb.

2.56. $+600$ lb; -300 lb; -200 lb.

2.58. 261 lb.   54.9°; 106.7°; 40.0°.

2.60. 31.0°; 115.4°; 106.6°.

2.62. $-1,200$ lb; $+600$ lb; -400 lb.

2.64. $T_{AB} = 13,000$ lb; $T_{AD} = 10,000$ lb.

2.66. 655 lb.

2.68. $T_{AD} = 168$ lb; $T_{BD} = 80$ lb; $T_{CD} = 90$ lb.

2.70. $T_{AD} = 31.2$ lb; $T_{BD} = 10.39$ lb; $T_{CD} = 22.9$ lb.

2.72. $T_{AD} = T_{BD} = T_{CD} = 25$ lb.

2.74. $P = 125$ lb. $T_{AC} = T_{BC} = 331$ lb.

2.76. $T_{AD} = 0; T_{CD} = T_{ED} = 43.8$ lb.

2.78. (a) 6 ft.   (b) A must be on or inside the circle
$x^2 + z^2 = 64$.

2.80. (a) 462 lb.   (b) 454 lb.

2.82. 800 lb.

2.84. (a) 48.2°; 109.5°; 131.8°.   (b) 48.2°; 109.5°;
48.2°.   (c) 153.4°; 116.6°; 90.0°.

2.86. $aa = 4,320$ lb ⬋; $cc = 4,320$ lb ⬈

2.88. (a) 120°.   (b) 100 lb.

2.90. $P = 115.5$ lb; $R = 200$ lb.

CHAPTER 3

3.2. -960 lb-in.; $\alpha = 15°$.

3.4. (a) -643 lb-in.; (b) 68.4 lb ←;
(c) 64.3 lb ⬈ 20°.

3.6. -510 lb-in.

3.8. $+3,300$ lb-in.

3.10. $M_B = (x_1 - x_2)F_y - (y_1 - y_2)F_x$.

3.12. $d = (xF_y - yF_x)/(F_x^2 + F_y^2)^{\frac{1}{2}}$.

3.14. (a) $\mathbf{M}_O = -58\mathbf{i} + 4\mathbf{j} + 32\mathbf{k}$.
(b) $\mathbf{M}_O = +6\mathbf{i} - 4\mathbf{k}$.   (c) $\mathbf{M}_O = -30\mathbf{i} + 12\mathbf{j}$.

3.16. $\mathbf{M}_O = (3,600 \text{ lb-ft})\mathbf{i} - (3,600 \text{ lb-ft})\mathbf{k}$.

3.18. $M_x = 600$ lb-ft, $M_y = 3,800$ lb-ft,
$M_z = -1,300$ lb-ft.

3.20. $\mathbf{M}_O = -(1,200 \text{ lb-in.})\mathbf{i} + (1,800 \text{ lb-in.})\mathbf{j}$
$- (1,200 \text{ lb-in. })\mathbf{k}$.

3.22. 3.53 in.

3.28. 56.4°.

3.30. 400 lb.

3.32. (a) 32.5°.   (b) 177.1 lb.

3.34. 4.00.

3.36. 1,146 lb.

3.40. (*a*) -328 lb-in.   (*b*) 288 lb-in.

3.42. (*a*) zero.   (*b*) 1,460 lb-in.   (*c*) 396 lb-in.

3.44. (*a*) 4,800 lb-ft.   (*b*) $-1,662$ lb-ft.

3.48. 5.91 in.

3.50. (*a*) 50 lb.   (*b*) 72 lb.   (*c*) 46.2 lb.

3.52. 1.50 in.

3.54. $M = 6,180$ lb-in.;

$\phi_x = 104.0°, \phi_y = 90.0°, \phi_z = 14.0°.$

3.56. $(0.555\,M)\mathbf{i} + (1.279\,M)\mathbf{j} + (0.894\,M)\mathbf{k}.$

3.58. (*a*) 65 lb $\angle$ 60°; 457 lb-in. $\,\rangle\,$.

     (*b*) 65 lb $\angle$ 60°; 288 lb-in. $\,\rangle\,$.

3.60. 22.0°.

3.62. $\mathbf{F}_A = Pb/(a + b)\downarrow; \mathbf{F}_B = Pa/(a + b)\downarrow.$

3.66. $\mathbf{F} = (3,000\text{ lb})\mathbf{i};$

$\mathbf{M} = -(4,050\text{ lb-in.})\mathbf{j} - (7,950\text{ lb-in.})\mathbf{k}.$

3.68. (*a*) $\mathbf{F} = (600\text{ lb})\mathbf{i} - (300\text{ lb})\mathbf{j} - (200\text{ lb})\mathbf{k},$

$\mathbf{M} = (3,600\text{ lb-ft})\mathbf{i} + (9,600\text{ lb-ft})\mathbf{j}$

$- (3,600\text{ lb-ft})\mathbf{k}.$

     (*b*) $\mathbf{F} = (600\text{ lb})\mathbf{i} - (300\text{ lb})\mathbf{j} - (200\text{ lb})\mathbf{k},$

$\mathbf{M} = -(1,200\text{ lb-ft})\mathbf{i} - (3,600\text{ lb-ft})\mathbf{k}.$

3.70. system at C.

3.72. $\mathbf{F} = (9\text{ lb})\mathbf{i} + (20\text{ lb})\mathbf{j} - (12\text{ lb})\mathbf{k},$

$\mathbf{M} = (150\text{ lb-in.})\mathbf{i} + (108\text{ lb-in.})\mathbf{j} - (20\text{ lb-in.})\mathbf{k}.$

3.74. *b* and *d*.

3.76. 9 kips $\downarrow$; 14.22 ft to right of A.

3.78. 130 lb $\angle$ 67.4°; 60 lb-in. $\,\rangle\,$.

3.80. $\mathbf{R} = 0; \mathbf{M} = 504$ lb-ft $\,\rangle\,$.

3.82. 88.9 lb $\angle$ 13.0°.   (*a*) 10.50 in. to left of B.

     (*b*) 2.42 in. below B.

3.84. 65.8 kips $\angle$ 61.7°; 22.7 ft to right of A.

3.86. (*a*) 46.2 lb $\angle$ 60°.   (*b*) 46.2 lb $\angle$ 60°.

3.88. (*a*) $\mathbf{F} = P \angle \theta; \mathbf{M}_E = Pa \cos \theta \sin 2\theta\,\rangle\,.$

     (*b*) 35.3°.

3.90. $\mathbf{R} = -(55\text{ lb})\mathbf{j} + (8.66\text{ lb})\mathbf{k};$

$\mathbf{M} = -(17.32\text{ lb-in})\mathbf{i} + (416\text{ lb-in.})\mathbf{j}$

$- (960\text{ lb-in.})\mathbf{k}.$

3.92. $\mathbf{P} = (40.0\text{ lb})\mathbf{j} + (17.32\text{ lb})\mathbf{k}.$

3.94. 80 kips; $x = 1.75$ ft, $z = -1.75$ ft.

3.96. 152 kips;

on edge AC at a point 10.53 ft from A.

3.98. (*a*) $\mathbf{F} = -(30\text{ lb})\mathbf{i} - (30\text{ lb})\mathbf{k},$

$\mathbf{M} = (40\text{ lb-ft})\mathbf{i} - (40\text{ lb-ft})\mathbf{k}.$

     (*b*) Horizontal, 1.333 ft below C, forming 45°

angle with the xy plane.

3.100. $R = \sqrt{3}\,P, M = -\sqrt{3}\,Pa$; at origin,

direction of axis, $\theta_x = \theta_y = \theta_z = 54.7°.$

3.102. (*a*) $\mathbf{R} = -(5\text{ lb})\mathbf{j};$

$\mathbf{M} = (40\text{ lb-in.})\mathbf{i} - (50\text{ lb-in.})\mathbf{j} - (35\text{ lb-in.})\mathbf{k}.$

     (*b*) $R = -5$ lb, $M = -50$ lb-in.; parallel to

the y axis at $x = 7$ in., $z = 8$ in.;

pitch $= 10$ in.

3.104. (*a*) $\mathbf{R} = \sqrt{2}\,P\,\mathbf{i}; \mathbf{M} = (Pa/\sqrt{2})(\mathbf{i} + \mathbf{j} - \mathbf{k}).$

     (*b*) $R = \sqrt{2}\,P, M = Pa/\sqrt{2};$

parallel to the x axis at $y = z = \frac{1}{2}a;$

pitch $= \frac{1}{2}a.$

3.106. $\mathbf{R} = -55\,\mathbf{j} + 8.66\,\mathbf{k},$

$\mathbf{M} = 30\sqrt{3}\,(20 - a)\mathbf{j} - 30(20 + a)\mathbf{k};$

$a = 10$ in.

3.108. $\mathbf{F}_B = -(20\text{ lb})\mathbf{i} + (30\text{ lb})\mathbf{j} + (60\text{ lb})\mathbf{k},$

$\mathbf{F}_{xz} = (80\text{ lb})\mathbf{i} - (40\text{ lb})\mathbf{k},$ at $x = 1.50$ in.,

$y = z = 0.$

3.112. $\mathbf{R} = 300$ lb, $\theta_x = \theta_z = 48.2°, \theta_y = 109.5°;$

$\mathbf{M} = 9,900$ lb-in., $\phi_x = 45°, \phi_y = 90°, \phi_z = 135°.$

3.114. $\mathbf{R} = 88.9$ lb $\angle$ 13.0°; (*a*) 1.086 in. below B;

     (*b*) 4.70 in. to right of B; (*c*) 2.61 in. above D.

3.116. (*a*) $\mathbf{R} = (150\text{ lb})\mathbf{i}; \mathbf{M} = (520\text{ lb-in.})\mathbf{i}$

$+ (300\text{ lb-in.})\mathbf{j} + (600\text{ lb-in.})\mathbf{k}.$

     (*b*) $R = 150$ lb, $M = 520$ lb-in.;

parallel to the x axis at $y = -4$ in.,

$z = +2$ in.; pitch $= 3.47$ in.

3.118. (*a*) $\mathbf{M}_O = -(900\text{ lb-in.})\mathbf{i} + (3,600\text{ lb-in.})\mathbf{j}$

$+ (2,800\text{ lb-in.})\mathbf{k}.$

     (*b*) 3,180 lb-in.

3.120. $\mathbf{Q} = (90\text{ lb})\mathbf{i} - (77.3\text{ lb})\mathbf{j}.$

3.122. 40 lb at B and 30 lb at F.

CHAPTER 4

4.2. $T = 250$ lb, $\mathbf{B}_x = 275$ lb $\rightarrow$, $\mathbf{B}_y = 217$ lb $\uparrow$.

4.4. (*a*) $T = \frac{1}{2}W(1 - r_1/r_2).$ (*b*) 200 lb.

4.6. (*a*) $T = (Pa/r) \sin \theta.$ (*b*) 115.9 lb.

4.8. 467 lb.

4.10. $\mathbf{A} = 2.89$ kips $\angle$ 60°, $\mathbf{B}_x = 2.56$ kips $\rightarrow$,

$\mathbf{B}_y = 7.50$ kips $\uparrow$.

4.12. $\mathbf{A} = 0.833$ kip $\uparrow$, $\mathbf{B}_x = 4.00$ kips $\leftarrow$,

$\mathbf{B}_y = 9.17$ kips $\uparrow$.

4.14. (*a*) $T = 800$ lb, $\mathbf{A} = 200$ lb $\rightarrow$, $\mathbf{D} = 200$ lb $\leftarrow$.

     (*b*) 12.5 in.

4.16. (*a*) $\mathbf{B} = 360$ lb $\nearrow$, $\mathbf{C} = 360$ lb $\swarrow$,

$\mathbf{D} = 200$ lb $\uparrow$.   (*b*) 2 and 3.

4.18. (*a*) $\mathbf{A} = 0, \mathbf{M}_A = M\,\rangle.$ (*b*) $\mathbf{B} = 0, \mathbf{M}_B = M\,\rangle.$

     (*c*) $\mathbf{A} = 2M/\sqrt{3}L\uparrow, \mathbf{B} = 2M/\sqrt{3}L\downarrow.$

     (*d*) $\mathbf{A} = M/L \angle 60°, \mathbf{B} = M/L \angle 60°.$

     (*e*) $\mathbf{A} = 2M/L \leftarrow, \mathbf{B} = 2M/L \rightarrow.$

(f) $\mathbf{A} = 2\sqrt{3}M/L \uparrow$, $\mathbf{B} = 2M/L \leftarrow$,
$\mathbf{D} = 4M/L \searrow$.

4.20. (a) $\mathbf{B} = 90$ lb $\uparrow$, $\mathbf{D} = 90$ lb $\downarrow$.
(b) $\mathbf{B} = 120$ lb $\leftarrow$, $\mathbf{D} = 120$ lb $\rightarrow$.
(c) $\mathbf{B} = 0$, $\mathbf{M}_B = 900$ lb-in. $\curvearrowright$.

4.22. 1,029 lb.

4.24. (a) $\mathbf{A} = 15.61$ lb $\angle$ $73.9°$, $\mathbf{B} = 4.33$ lb $\leftarrow$.
(b) $\mathbf{A} = \mathbf{B} = 7.5$ lb $\uparrow$.   (c) $\mathbf{A} = 18.75$ lb $\uparrow$,
$\mathbf{B} = 6.50$ lb $\leftarrow$, $\mathbf{C} = 7.50$ lb $\searrow$ $30°$.
(d) $\mathbf{A} = 15$ lb $\uparrow$, $\mathbf{M}_A = 90$ lb-in. $\curvearrowright$.

4.26. (a) $\mathbf{A}_x = 89.9$ lb $\leftarrow$, $\mathbf{A}_y = 20$ lb $\uparrow$,
$\mathbf{C} = 3.33$ lb $\rightarrow$.   (b) $\mathbf{A} = 47.5$ lb $\downarrow$,
$\mathbf{C}_x = 86.6$ lb $\leftarrow$, $\mathbf{C}_y = 67.5$ lb $\uparrow$.
(c) $\mathbf{C}_x = 86.6$ lb $\leftarrow$, $\mathbf{C}_y = 20$ lb $\uparrow$,
$\mathbf{M}_C = 569$ lb-in. $\curvearrowright$.

4.28. (a) $\mathbf{R}_A = 175$ lb $\uparrow$, $\mathbf{M}_A = 2,625$ lb-in. $\curvearrowright$.
(b) 1,313 lb.

4.30. $T = 62.6$ lb, $\mathbf{D} = 50.9$ lb $\searrow$ $63.3°$.

4.32. $82.8°$.

4.34. (a) $31.0°$.   (b) $34.7°$.   (c) Impossible.

4.36. $\sin\theta = (2M/WL)\cot\alpha$.

4.38. (a) $90°$.   (b) $90°$.   (c) $60°$.   (d) 20.3 in.

4.40. (1) Completely constrained; det.;
$\mathbf{A} = 12.02$ kips $\angle$ $56.3°$; $\mathbf{B} = 6.67$ kips $\leftarrow$.
(2) Improperly constrained; indet.; no equil.
(3) Completely constrained; det.;
$\mathbf{A} = \mathbf{C} = 5$ kips $\uparrow$.
(4) Completely constrained; indet.;
$\mathbf{A}_x = 6.67$ kips $\rightarrow$; $\mathbf{B}_x = 6.67$ kips $\leftarrow$;
($\mathbf{A}_y + \mathbf{B}_y = 10$ kips $\uparrow$).
(5) Improperly constrained; indet.; no equil.
(6) Partially constrained; det.; equil.;
$\mathbf{A} = \mathbf{C} = 5$ kips $\uparrow$.
(7) Completely constrained; det.;
$\mathbf{A} = 5$ kips $\uparrow$; $\mathbf{B} = 8.33$ kips $\searrow$ $36.9°$;
$\mathbf{C} = 6.67$ kips $\rightarrow$.
(8) Completely constrained; indet.;
$\mathbf{A}_{..} = 5$ kips $\uparrow$.

4.48. (a) $32.6°$.   (b) $\mathbf{C} = 210$ lb $\swarrow$; $\mathbf{D} = 234$ lb $\uparrow$.

4.50. $\mathbf{P} = Wa/b \leftarrow$,
$\mathbf{B} = W(1 + a^2/b^2)^{\frac{1}{2}} \angle \tan^{-1}(b/a)$.

4.52. (a) 1,252 lb.   (b) 406 lb.

4.54. $\alpha = 68.1°$, $\theta = 51.2°$.

4.56. $\sin^3\theta = 2a/L$.

4.58. (a) 5 lb $\uparrow$.   (b) 5.32 lb along leg.

4.60. (a) 1,800 lb.   (b) $\mathbf{A} = 0$.

4.62. $T_{AD} = T_{ED} = 262.5$ lb, $T_{CD} = 474$ lb.

4.64. $\mathbf{A} = -(1,025\text{ lb})\mathbf{i} + (3,250\text{ lb})\mathbf{j} - (1,680\text{ lb})\mathbf{k}$,
$T_{ECF} = 725$ lb, $T_{FBG} = 2,175$ lb.

4.66. (a) $36.9°$, (b) $53.1°$.

4.68. $W = 90$ lb; $x = 0.889$ ft, $z = 2.44$ ft.

4.70. $P = 24.2$ lb, $\mathbf{A} = (9.45\text{ lb})\mathbf{i} - (15.76\text{ lb})\mathbf{k}$,
$\mathbf{B} = (11.76\text{ lb})\mathbf{i} + (40\text{ lb})\mathbf{j} + (18.79\text{ lb})\mathbf{k}$.

4.72. $F_{CD} = 3$ lb, $\mathbf{A} = -(2.94\text{ lb})\mathbf{i} + (6.90\text{ lb})\mathbf{j}$,
$\mathbf{B} = (7.50\text{ lb})\mathbf{j}$.

4.74. $T = 70$ lb, $\mathbf{A} = (10\text{ lb})\mathbf{i} + (15\text{ lb})\mathbf{j} + (20\text{ lb})\mathbf{k}$.
$\mathbf{B} = (50\text{ lb})\mathbf{i} + (15\text{ lb})\mathbf{j}$.

4.76. $\mathbf{A}_y = (5.39\text{ lb})\mathbf{j}$, $\mathbf{B}_y = (16.2\text{ lb})\mathbf{j}$,
$\mathbf{C}_y = (38.4\text{ lb})\mathbf{j}$.

4.78. $\theta = M_0h/Wr^2$.

4.80. $M_0 = Wr\sin\theta/(h^2/r^2 - 4\sin^2\frac{1}{2}\theta)^{\frac{1}{2}}$.

4.82. $T_{CD} = 25$ lb, $\mathbf{A} = (20\text{ lb})\mathbf{i}$,
$\mathbf{B} = (12\text{ lb})\mathbf{j} + (9\text{ lb})\mathbf{k}$.

4.84. $\mathbf{D} = (75\text{ lb})\mathbf{i}$.

4.86. 180.3 lb.

4.88. $P = 21.0$ lb, $\theta_x = 65.2°$, $\theta_y = 69.6°$,
$\theta_z = 33.1°$.

4.90. $\mathbf{A}_x = 522$ lb $\leftarrow$, $\mathbf{A}_y = 777$ lb $\downarrow$; $T = 455$ lb.

4.92. $\mathbf{Q} = -(150\text{ lb})\mathbf{i}$, $\mathbf{B} = (180\text{ lb})\mathbf{i} + (52.0\text{ lb})\mathbf{j}$,
$\mathbf{C} = -(30\text{ lb})\mathbf{i} - (52.0\text{ lb})\mathbf{j}$.

4.94. (a) $T = M_0/[r(\cos\phi - c)]$,
where $c = 1/\sqrt{3 + 2\cos\phi}$.
(b) $T = 1.809\, M_0/r$,
$\mathbf{D} = \mathbf{E} = -(1.309\, M_0/r)\mathbf{j} + (0.809\, M_0/r)\mathbf{k}$.
(c) $-60° < \phi < 60°$.

4.96. Case 1: (a) $90°$, (b) 40 lb, $\mathbf{A} = 56.6$ lb $\angle$ $45°$,
(c) $0°$.
Case 2: (a) $26.6°$, (b) 17.89 lb,
$\mathbf{A} = 25.3$ lb $\angle$ $71.6°$, (c) $-63.4°$.
Case 3: (a) $45°$, (b) 14.14 lb,
$\mathbf{A} = 28.3$ lb $\angle$ $45°$, (c) $-45°$.

4.98. $\mathbf{B} = 2P/\sqrt{3}$ $\angle$ $60°$, $\mathbf{C} = 2P/\sqrt{3}$ $\searrow$ $60°$,
$\mathbf{D} = P\downarrow$.

4.100. $\mathbf{A} = (222\text{ lb})\mathbf{j}$,
$\mathbf{B} = -(800\text{ lb})\mathbf{i} + (222\text{ lb})\mathbf{j} - (600\text{ lb})\mathbf{k}$,
$\mathbf{C} = +(1,050\text{ lb})\mathbf{i} + (556\text{ lb})\mathbf{j} + (600\text{ lb})\mathbf{k}$.

CHAPTER 5

5.2. $\bar{x} = 5.94$ in.; $\bar{y} = 2.62$ in.

5.4. $\bar{x} = 0$; $\bar{y} = 0.459$ in.

5.6. $\bar{x} = 0$; $\bar{y} = 3.36$ in.

5.8. $\bar{x} = -0.774$ in.; $\bar{y} = 0$.

5.10. $\bar{x} = 4.80$ in.; $\bar{y} = 0$.

5.12. $\bar{x} = 8.00$ in.; $\bar{y} = 2.29$ in.

5.14. $\bar{x} = \dfrac{4r}{3} \dfrac{\sin^3 \alpha}{2\alpha - \sin 2\alpha}$.

5.16. $\bar{x} = 0; \bar{y} = 0.206$ in.

5.18. $\bar{x} = \dfrac{r \sin \alpha\,(1 + \cos \alpha)}{\alpha + \sin \alpha}; \bar{y} = 0$.

5.20. 0.494.

5.24. $\tan \theta = \dfrac{2W}{\pi\,(W + 2W_1)}$.

5.26. $\alpha = 43.9°; \theta_{\max} = 46.1°$.

5.28. $\bar{x} = 0.56$ in.; $\bar{y} = 0$.

5.30. $\bar{x} = 0.7666a; 2.22\%$.

5.32. $\bar{x} = \frac{2}{3}b; \bar{y} = \frac{1}{3}h$.

5.34. $\bar{x} = \frac{4}{7}a; \bar{y} = \frac{2}{5}b$.

5.42. $\bar{x} = \bar{y} = \frac{9}{20}$.

5.44. $\bar{x} = L/\pi; \bar{y} = \pi a/8$.

5.46. $\bar{x} = c; \bar{y} = \frac{1}{4}a$.

5.48. $\bar{x} = \bar{y} = (2a^2 - 1)/2a(1 + 2 \ln a)$.

5.50. (a) 792 in.³   (b) 1,263 in.³

5.52. $A = 4\pi^2 rR; V = 2\pi^2 r^2 R$.

5.54. 28.3 ft².

5.56. 8,200 ft³.

5.58. $V = 17.84$ in.³; $A = 58.0$ in.²

5.60. $\pi/4$.

5.62. 0.1737 in.³

5.64. 0.436.

5.66. $\mathbf{R} = 2,500$ lb $\downarrow$, 9.80 ft to right of A;
$\mathbf{A} = 969$ lb $\uparrow$, $\mathbf{B} = 1,531$ lb $\uparrow$.

5.68. $\mathbf{A} = 18.30$ kips $\uparrow$, $\mathbf{B} = 15.70$ kips $\uparrow$.

5.70. $\mathbf{A} = 2,740$ lb $\uparrow$, $\mathbf{B} = 3,660$ lb $\uparrow$.

5.72. (a) 0.500; $\mathbf{B} = \frac{1}{4}w_B L \uparrow$, $\mathbf{M}_B = 0$.
(b) 1.000; $\mathbf{B} = 0$, $\mathbf{M}_B = \frac{1}{6}w_B L^2$ ⤵.

5.74. (a) $\mathbf{R} = \frac{1}{2}(w_A + w_B)L \downarrow$,
$\bar{X} = (w_A + 2w_B)L/3(w_A + w_B)$.
(b) $\mathbf{A} = \frac{1}{6}L(2w_A + w_B) \uparrow$,
$\mathbf{B} = \frac{1}{6}L(w_A + 2w_B) \uparrow$.

5.76. (a) $\mathbf{R} = 1,966$ lb $\leftarrow$, 1.714 ft below A.
(b) $\mathbf{B} = 1,123$ lb $\rightarrow$.

5.78. 9 in.

5.80. $\mathbf{A} = 1,191$ lb $\rightarrow$, $\mathbf{B} = 1,200$ lb $\rightarrow$.

5.82. $\mathbf{R} = 19.90$ kips $\leftarrow$, 7.52 ft above B.

5.84. $\tan \theta = \dfrac{2}{3} \dfrac{\gamma b r^2}{W}$.

5.86. 3.94 ft.

5.88. 8.36 ft.

5.90. 0.792.

5.92. 6,350 lb ∠ 38.2°, through center of drum.

5.94. $7h/9$ above base of cylinder.

5.96. 4.31 in. from right end.

5.98. $\bar{x} = 0.0313$ in., $\bar{y} = 0.376$ in., $\bar{z} = 0$.

5.100. 1.457 in. above the base of the aluminum part.

5.102. $\bar{x} = 2$ in., $\bar{y} = 0.223$ in., $\bar{z} = 0.584$ in.

5.104. $\bar{x} = \bar{z} = 5.05$ in., $\bar{y} = 10.81$ in.

5.106. $\frac{1}{2}r$ above base.

5.110. $\bar{x} = 5h/8$.

5.112. $\bar{x} = 5h/6, \bar{y} = 20a/21\pi, \bar{z} = 0$.

5.114. $\bar{y} = 0.422$ in.

5.116. $0.785a$.

5.118. $\bar{y} = (\pi + 2)h/16$.

5.120. $\bar{x} = 0, \bar{y} = 5h/16, \bar{z} = -a/4$.

5.122. 17.66 in.³

5.124. $\mathbf{A} = 81.3$ lb $\uparrow$, $\mathbf{B} = 518.7$ lb $\uparrow$.

5.126. 1.645 ft.

5.128. 784 lb.

5.130. 1.412 ft.

5.132. $-10/9$.

CHAPTER 6

6.2 and 6.22. 1-2 = 2-4 = 240 lb T;
1-3 = 3-4 = 260 lb C; 2-3 = 100 lb C.

6.4 and 6.24. 1-2 = 3-4 = 8 kips T;
2-3 = 16 kips T; 2-6 = 3-7 = 4 kips C;
other members = 10 kips C.

6.6 and 6.26. 1-2 = 1-6 = 6-7 = 1 kip C;
1-4 = 4-7 = 2-4 = 4-6 = 1.414 kips T;
2-3 = 7-8 = 1 kip T;
2-5 = 5-8 = 3-5 = 5-7 = 1.414 kips C.

6.8 and 6.28. 1-2 = 2-3 = 200 lb T;
1-4 = 4-6 = 150 lb T; 3-5 = 5-6 = 250 lb C;
2-4 = 2-5 = 4-5 = 0.

6.10 and 6.30. 1-2 = 1,200 lb T; 1-4 = 1,300 lb C;
2-3 = 5-6 = 0; 2-4 = 2,400 lb C;
2-6 = 2,680 lb T; 3-6 = 1,500 lb C;
4-5 = 1,700 lb C; 4-6 = 1,697 lb C.

6.12 and 6.32. 1-2 = 2-4 = 30 kips T;
1-3 = 3-4 = 40 kips C; 2-3 = 36 kips T.

6.14. 2-3; 3-4; 9-10; 9-12; 11-12; 12-13; 13-14.

6.16. All simple trusses except 6.14 and 6.15.

6.18. $AB = AC = AD = P/\sqrt{6}$ *comp.*;
$BC = CD = DB = P/3\sqrt{6}$ *ten.*

6.20. (a) $A_x = +192$ lb, $A_y = 0$; $A_z = -144$ lb,
$B_x = -384$ lb, $B_y = +576$ lb, $C_y = -576$ lb.
(b) $AB = BC = 240$ lb C; $BE = 576$ lb C;
$CE = 624$ lb T; other members $= 0$.

6.34. 1-2 = 2-3 = 30 kips C; 1-4 = 2-6 = 4-9 = 0;
1-5 = 5-9 = 10 kips C; 1-6 = 31.6 kips T;
3-6 = 31.6 kips T; 3-7 = 7-10 = 70 kips T;

$3\text{-}8 = 84.8$ kips C; $4\text{-}5 = 5\text{-}6 = 20$ kips T;
$6\text{-}7 = 7\text{-}8 = 80$ kips T, $8\text{-}10 = 63.2$ kips C.

6.36. $1\text{-}2 = 3\text{-}4 = 874$ lb T; $1\text{-}5 = 614$ lb C;
$2\text{-}3 = 897$ lb T; $2\text{-}5 = 3\text{-}5 = 346$ lb C;
$4\text{-}5 = 980$ lb C; $4\text{-}6 = 1,225$ lb T.

6.38. $1\text{-}2 = 6\text{-}8 = 21.2$ kips C;
$1\text{-}3 = 3\text{-}5 = 5\text{-}7 = 7\text{-}8 = 15.0$ kips T;
$2\text{-}3 = 2\text{-}5 = 4\text{-}5 = 5\text{-}6 = 6\text{-}7 = 0$;
$2\text{-}4 = 4\text{-}6 = 15.8$ kips C.

6.40. $F_{DF} = 66.7$ kips C; $F_{DG} = 16.67$ kips C.

6.42. $F_{EF} = 12$ kips C; $F_{CE} = 9$ kips T.

6.44. 6 kips T.

6.46. $F_{DF} = 8.25$ kips T; $F_{DE} = 3$ kips C;
$F_{CE} = 8$ kips C.

6.48. $F_{BD} = 39$ kips T; $F_{BE} = 23.4$ kips C;
$F_{CE} = 18$ kips C.

6.50. $F_{BE} = 2.50$ kips C; $F_{DE} = 4.50$ kips T.

6.52. 6.67 kips C.

6.54. $F_{AB} = 0$; $F_{EJ} = \frac{2}{3}P$ *comp.*

6.56. $F_{AB} = Q$ *comp.*; $F_{EJ} = \frac{2}{3}Q$ *comp.*

6.58. $F_{CE} = 10$ kips C; $F_{DF} = 5$ kips T;
$F_{CF} = 7.07$ kips T.

6.60. $F_{CD} = 12$ kips C; $F_{CG} = 20$ kips T;
for this loading both F_{AD} and F_{BC} are zero.

6.62. (*a*) Completely constrained, indet.
(*b*) Partially constrained.
(*c*) and (*d*) Completely constrained, det.

6.64. (*a*) Partially constrained.
(*b*) Completely constrained, indet.
(*c*) and (*d*) Completely constrained, det.

6.66. $\mathbf{A}_x = 600$ lb $\leftarrow$; $\mathbf{A}_y = 800$ lb $\uparrow$; $\mathbf{C} = 900$ lb $\downarrow$;
$\mathbf{E}_x = 600$ lb $\rightarrow$; $\mathbf{E}_y = 900$ lb $\uparrow$.

6.68. $\mathbf{A}_x = 175$ lb $\leftarrow$; $\mathbf{A}_y = 200$ lb $\uparrow$; $\mathbf{B} = 220$ lb $\rightarrow$,
$\mathbf{D} = 375$ lb $\rightarrow$; $\mathbf{E}_x = 420$ lb $\leftarrow$, $\mathbf{E}_y = 200$ lb $\downarrow$.

6.70. $\mathbf{A} = 86.7$ lb $\searrow$ $63.5°$; $\mathbf{E} = 44.7$ lb $\swarrow$ $30°$;
$\mathbf{C} = 29.8$ lb $\swarrow$ $30°$; $\mathbf{D} = 74.5$ lb $\nwarrow$ $30°$.

6.72. (*a*) $\mathbf{A} = 13$ lb $\searrow$ $22.6°$; $\mathbf{B} = 13$ lb $\searrow$ $22.6°$.
(*b*) $\mathbf{A} = 13$ lb $\nwarrow$ $22.6°$; $\mathbf{B} = 13$ lb $\swarrow$ $22.6°$.
(*c*) $\mathbf{A} = 5$ lb $\downarrow$, $\mathbf{B} = 55$ lb $\downarrow$.

6.74. $\mathbf{E} = 132.0$ lb $\searrow$ $16.5°$; $\mathbf{F} = 169.3$ lb $\swarrow$ $41.6°$;
$\mathbf{C} = 339$ lb $\swarrow$ $41.6°$.

6.76. $\mathbf{A}_x = 750$ lb $\leftarrow$; $\mathbf{A}_y = 1,000$ lb $\uparrow$;
$\mathbf{E}_x = 750$ lb $\rightarrow$, $\mathbf{E}_y = 400$ lb $\downarrow$.

6.78. $\mathbf{A} = 200$ lb $\uparrow$, $\mathbf{E} = 200$ lb $\uparrow$, $\mathbf{M}_E = 0$.

6.80. $40.9°$.

6.82. $(0 < a < 30 \text{ ft})$: $A_x = 1,000(a/30)$;
$A_y = 1,000(1 - a/75)$.
$(30 \text{ ft} < a < 50 \text{ ft})$: $A_x = 1,000(50 - a)/20$;

$A_y = 1,000(50 - a)/33.3$.

6.84. *At each wheel:* (*a*) $\mathbf{A} = 1,188$ lb $\uparrow$;
$\mathbf{B} = 921$ lb $\uparrow$; $\mathbf{C} = 866$ lb $\uparrow$.
(*b*) $\mathbf{B} = 281$ lb $\uparrow$; $\mathbf{C} = 93.8$ lb $\downarrow$.

6.86. (*a*) $T = 491$ lb.
(*b*) *At each wheel:*
$\mathbf{A} = 1,277$ lb $\uparrow$; $\mathbf{B} = 689$ lb $\uparrow$; $\mathbf{C} = 1,009$ lb $\uparrow$.

6.88. $a \geqslant 7.20$ ft.

6.90. $F_{AF} = 3M_0/4a$ *ten.*;
$F_{BG} = F_{GD} = M_0/\sqrt{2}a$ *comp.*;
$F_{EH} = M_0/4a$ *ten.*

6.92. (*a*) Rigid; $\mathbf{A} = 2.24$ kips $\measuredangle$ $26.6°$;
$\mathbf{B} = 3.61$ kips $\searrow$ $56.3°$.   (*b*) Not rigid.

6.94. (*a*) Rigid; $\mathbf{A} = 4.00$ kips $\rightarrow$,
$\mathbf{B} = 5.66$ kips $\searrow$ $45°$.   (*b*) Not rigid.

6.96. $\mathbf{C}_x = 200$ lb $\leftarrow$, $\mathbf{C}_y = 150$ lb $\uparrow$, $\mathbf{D} = 300$ lb $\downarrow$,
$\mathbf{E}_x = 400$ lb $\rightarrow$, $\mathbf{E}_y = 300$ lb $\uparrow$,
$\mathbf{F}_x = 200$ lb $\leftarrow$, $\mathbf{F}_y = 150$ lb $\downarrow$.

6.98. $\mathbf{B} = 17.07$ lb $\leftarrow$; $\mathbf{E}_x = 36.3$ lb $\rightarrow$;
$\mathbf{E}_y = 32.0$ lb $\downarrow$; $\mathbf{H}_x = 19.20$ lb $\leftarrow$;
$\mathbf{H}_y = 32.0$ lb $\uparrow$.

6.100. $\mathbf{D} = 2M_0/3r$ $\measuredangle$ $30°$;
$\mathbf{E} = M_0(r + a)/3ra$ $\nwarrow$ $30°$;
$\mathbf{F} = M_0(r - a)/3ra$ $\measuredangle$ $30°$.

6.102. (*a*) 6 in.   (*b*) 7.07 in.

6.104. 15 lb; $\mathbf{B} = 40$ lb $\downarrow$.

6.106. $\mathbf{D} = 515$ lb $\nwarrow$ $29.1°$; $\mathbf{C} = 950$ lb $\rightarrow$.

6.108. (*a*) 175 lb-ft $\curvearrowright$.   (*b*) 75 lb-ft $\curvearrowright$.

6.110. (*a*) $\mathbf{M}_B = M_D \cos^2 \theta$ $\curvearrowright$.
(*b*) $\mathbf{B} = (M_D \cos \theta)/h$ $\measuredangle$ θ;
$\mathbf{D} = (M_D \cos \theta)/h$ $\nwarrow$ θ.

6.112. $14,625$ lb.

6.116. $T_1 = 350$ lb, $T_2 = 4,150$ lb.

6.118. (*a*) $\mathbf{B} = \mathbf{D} = 500$ lb $\uparrow$; $\mathbf{C} = 1,000$ lb $\downarrow$.
(*b*) 320 lb.   (*c*) 8 in.

6.120. $F_{AD} = 0$; $F_{BC} = 192.4$ lb T;
$F_{DG} = 1,052$ lb C.

6.122. (*a*) 240 lb-ft.   (*b*) $B = 0$; $M_B = -450$ lb-ft,
parallel to the x axis.

6.124. (*a*) $\mathbf{M}_S = 4M_A$ $\curvearrowright$.   (*b*) $\mathbf{M}_E = 3M_A$ $\curvearrowright$.

6.126. (*a*) $M_A = 577$ lb-in.   (*b*) $B = 0$;
$D_x = D_y = E_x = E_y = 0$; $D_z = -28.8$ lb;
$E_z = +28.8$ lb.

6.128. $15.6°$.

6.130. $\mathbf{G} = 480$ lb $\downarrow$; $\mathbf{D} = 200$ lb $\swarrow$, $\mathbf{F} = 400$ lb $\searrow$,
$\mathbf{H}_x = 120$ lb $\leftarrow$, $\mathbf{H}_y = 480$ lb $\uparrow$.

6.132. $1,600$ lb.

6.134. $F_{AB} = 2.47$ kips T; $F_{AC} = 9.00$ kips C;

$F_{GH} = 1.50$ kips C.

6.136. $\mathbf{C}_x = \mathbf{F}_x = 500$ lb $\rightarrow$, $\mathbf{C}_y = \mathbf{F}_y = 200$ lb $\uparrow$,
$\mathbf{D} = \mathbf{E} = 500$ lb $\leftarrow$.

6.138. *On the frame:* $\mathbf{F} = 1,611$ lb $\uparrow$, $\mathbf{A} = 500$ lb $\leftarrow$,
$\mathbf{D}_x = 500$ lb $\rightarrow$, $\mathbf{D}_y = 861$ lb $\downarrow$.

6.140. *1-2 = 2-7 = 6-11 = 3-8 = 6* kips C;
1-6 = 4.5 kips C; *1-7 = 7.5* kips T;
2-3 = 10 kips C; *2-8 = 5* kips T;
6-7 = 2 kips C; *6-12 = 2.5* kips T;
7-8 = 4 kips T; *7-12 = 1.50* kips C;
11-12 = 0.

CHAPTER 7

7.2. (On *JG*) $\mathbf{F} = 480$ lb $\swarrow$; $\mathbf{V} = 360$ lb $\nwarrow$;
$\mathbf{M} = 1,800$ lb-ft $\mathbf{\jmath}$.

7.4. (On *JA*) $\mathbf{F} = 38.7$ lb $\rightarrow$; $\mathbf{V} = 77.6$ lb $\downarrow$;
$\mathbf{M} = 310$ lb-in. $\mathbf{\jmath}$.

7.6. (On *JA*) $\mathbf{F} = \mathbf{V} = 0$; $\mathbf{M} = 1,000$ lb-ft $\mathbf{\jmath}$.

7.8. (On *CB*) (*a*) $\mathbf{F} = \mathbf{V} = 0$; $\mathbf{M} = \frac{1}{8}wL^2 \cos\theta$ $\mathbf{\jmath}$.
(*b*) $\mathbf{F} = \mathbf{V} = 0$; $\mathbf{M} = 450$ lb-ft $\mathbf{\jmath}$.

7.10. At *J* (On *JB*) $\mathbf{F} = 0$; $\mathbf{V} = 90$ lb $\uparrow$;
$\mathbf{M} = 900$ lb-in. $\mathbf{\jmath}$. At *K* (On *KD*) $\mathbf{F} = 0$;
$\mathbf{V} = 30$ lb $\downarrow$; $\mathbf{M} = 300$ lb-in. $\mathbf{\jmath}$.

7.12. (On *JC*) 54.5 lb-in. $\mathbf{\jmath}$.

7.14. (On *JC*) $\mathbf{F} = (\frac{1}{2}W - W\theta/\pi)\cos\theta$ $\searrow$;
$\mathbf{V} = (\frac{1}{2}W - W\theta/\pi)\sin\theta$ $\swarrow$;
$\mathbf{M} = \frac{1}{2}Wr(1 - \cos\theta)$
$- (Wr/\pi)(\sin\theta - \theta\cos\theta)$ $\mathbf{\jmath}$.

7.16. $M_B = +Pab/L$.

7.18. $M_B = +wa^2/2$.

7.20. $M_B = -wL^2/2$.

7.22. $M_A = -2,500$ lb-ft.

7.24. $M_C = +13.5$ kip-ft.

7.26. 5.00 ft.

7.28. $M_C = -1,200$ lb-ft.

7.30. $M_E = +960$ lb-in.

7.32. $M_D = -500$ lb-ft.

7.34. $a = 0.207L$.

7.46. $M_D = +132$ kip-ft.

7.48. $M_B = -w_0L^2/3$.

7.50. $M = +3,600$ lb-ft, 6 ft to the right of *A*;
$M = -4,500$ lb-ft at *C*.

7.52. $M = +200$ lb-ft, 8 ft to the right of *A*;
$M = -7,000$ lb-ft at *B*.

7.54. $V = -wx$; $M = -wx^2/2$.

7.56. $V = w_0(L/\pi)\cos(\pi x/L)$;
$M = w_0(L/\pi)^2\sin(\pi x/L)$;
$M_{max} = w_0(L/\pi)^2$, at $x = \frac{1}{2}L$.

7.58. (*a*) 1.500.
(*b*) $V = w_0L[\frac{1}{4} - (x/L) + \frac{3}{4}(x/L)^2]$,
$M = w_0L^2[\frac{1}{4}(x/L) - \frac{1}{2}(x/L)^2 + \frac{1}{4}(x/L)^3]$.
(*c*) $M_{max} = w_0L^2/27$, at $x = L/3$.

7.60. $V_D = +100$ lb, $M_C = -100$ lb-ft.

7.62. (*a*) $\mathbf{A}_x = 1,000$ lb $\leftarrow$, $\mathbf{A}_y = 400$ lb $\uparrow$.
(*b*) $h_B = 4$ ft, $h_D = 5$ ft.

7.64. 5 ft.

7.66. $\mathbf{E}_x = 800$ lb $\rightarrow$, $\mathbf{E}_y = 300$ lb $\uparrow$, $T_E = 854$ lb.

7.68. 50,200 kips, 47,200 kips.

7.70. 22.5 ft.

7.72. 8.66 ft.

7.74. 15 in. to the left of *B*, 1.940 in.

7.76. $h = 0.1429$ ft, $\theta_A = 38.2°$ ∇, $\theta_C = 35.5°$ ∇.

7.78. For $x \geqslant 0$: $y = 2h[3(x/L)^2 - 2(x/L)^3]$;
$T_0 = w_0L^2/12h$.

7.84. 495 ft, 1,125 lb.

7.86. 199.48 ft.

7.88. 628 ft, 2,230 lb.

7.90. 7.96 ft, 20.5 lb.

7.92. 15.02 in. to the left of *B*, 1.953 lb.

7.96. 2.05 ft, 33.4 ft.

7.98. $h/L = 0.338$, $\theta_B = 56.5°$,
$T_m = 0.754wL$.

7.100. $M_A = -240$ lb-in.; $M_D = +720$ lb-in.

7.102. (*a*) 230 ft. (*b*) 63.0 lb.

7.104. $y = (L/\delta)x$.

7.106. (On *JA*) $\mathbf{M}_{max} = \frac{1}{4}PL$ $\mathbf{\jmath}$, at $a = \frac{1}{2}L$.

7.108. (*a*) $\mathbf{A}_x = 267$ lb $\leftarrow$, $\mathbf{A}_y = 100$ lb $\uparrow$,
$\mathbf{B}_x = 228$ lb $\rightarrow$, $\mathbf{B}_y = 171$ lb $\uparrow$.
(*b*) $T_{ACB} = 285$ lb. (*c*) $T_{DE} = 48.5$ lb.

7.110. $a = 3$ ft, $b = 9$ ft.

CHAPTER 8

8.2. 5.77 lb.

8.4. (*a*) 28.0 lb $\searstyle$ 34.0°. (*b*) 5.23 lb $\searstyle$ 6.0°.

8.6. All packages move; $\mathbf{F}_A = 1.932$ lb $\nearrow$,
$\mathbf{F}_B = 0.773$ lb $\nearrow$, $\mathbf{F}_C = 1.932$ lb $\nearrow$.

8.8. Moves; 48.7 lb.

8.10. (*a*) 27.0 lb. (*b*) 22.5 lb. (*c*) 9.64 lb.

8.12. (*a*) 59.1 lb. (*b*) Slide.

8.14. 51.4 lb $\leftarrow$.

8.16. $\mathbf{B} = 612$ lb $\rightarrow$.

8.18. 2.86 in.

8.20. 135.0 lb.

8.22. 72.4 lb (motion impending at *C*).

8.24. (*a*) 11.43 lb. (*b*) Motion impending at *C*.

8.26. 12 in.

8.28. 0.353.

8.30. $\mu_B = \mu_C = \tan \frac{1}{2}\theta; \mu_A =$ any value.

8.32. (a) $P = W(\mu^2 \cos^2 \theta - \sin^2 \theta)^{\frac{1}{2}}$.

(b) $\tan \beta = (\mu^2 \cot^2 \theta - 1)^{\frac{1}{2}}$, where β is the angle between the direction of motion and the line of greatest slope of the plane.

(c) 6.52 lb, $\beta = 26.7°$.

8.34. $2L/3$.

8.36. All forces, tensions, and displacements are zero, except as follows:

Case 1: (a) $\mathbf{F}_A = 0.40$ lb $\leftarrow$, $\mathbf{F}_B = 0.10$ lb $\leftarrow$.

(b) $T_{AB} = 0.10$ lb.   (c) $\Delta_A = 0.50$ in. $\rightarrow$.

Case 2: (a) $\mathbf{F}_A = 0.10$ lb $\rightarrow$, $\mathbf{F}_B = 0.10$ lb $\leftarrow$.

(b) $T_{AB} = 0.10$ lb.   (c) $\Delta_A = 0.50$ in. $\rightarrow$.

8.38. Straight line segments connecting the following points: (0, 0), (0.40 lb, 0), (0.80 lb, 2 in.), (1.00 lb, 4 in.), (0.20 lb, 4 in.), (0, 3 in.).

8.40. 1.300 lb $\nearrow$, C rolls.

8.42. $0 < \theta < 14.0°$.

8.46. (a) 111.3 lb $\rightarrow$.   (b) $\mathbf{B}_x = 511$ lb $\leftarrow$, $\mathbf{B}_y = 500$ lb $\downarrow$.

8.48. 0.635 lb.

8.50. 473 lb.

8.52. (a) 4.50 lb-in. $\curvearrowright$.   (b) 6.60 lb-in. $\curvearrowright$.

8.54. (a) 115.6 lb $\rightarrow$.   (b) Machine will not move.

8.56. (a) Wedge is forced up and out from between plates.   (b) Wedge will become self-locked at $\theta = 4.0°$.

8.58. 0.378.

8.60. 3.71 lb-ft.

8.62. 10.08 lb-in.

8.64. (a) First adjust A.   (b) 6.37 lb-in.

8.66. 0.12.

8.68. (a) 72.8 lb.   (b) 62.8 lb.

8.70. $T_{AB} = 72.5$ lb, $T_{CD} = 77.5$ lb, $T_{EF} = 82.7$ lb.

8.72. 11.95 in.

8.74. 4.69 lb/ton.

8.76. 2.22 lb.

8.78. 60 lb, 240 lb.

8.84. 0.026 in.

8.86. 7.19 lb/ton.

8.88. 4.14 ft.

8.90. (a) 39.0 lb.   (b) 42.3°.

8.92. 113.5 lb-ft.

8.94. 0.441.

8.96. (a) 73.0 lb.   (b) 39.0 lb.   (c) 73.0 lb.

8.98. 3.17 ft.

8.102. 75.8°.

8.104. 185.1 lb-ft.

8.106. $T_A = 11.5$ lb, $T_B = 18.5$ lb.

8.108. (a) 3 lb.   (b) 4.5 lb.   (c) 6 lb.

8.110. 36.7 lb-ft.

8.112. (a) 2,860 lb.   (b) 3.37 turns.

8.114. $M = Wr\mu(1 + \mu)/(1 + \mu^2)$.

8.116. $M = \frac{1}{4}\mu WL$.

CHAPTER 9

9.2. $3a^3b/10$.

9.4. $2a^3b/15$.

9.6. $ab^3/6$.

9.8. $2ab^3/7$.

9.10. $\pi a^3b/8$, $a/2$.

9.12. $a\sqrt{2}/3$.

9.14. $(b^2 + h^2)bh/3$, $\sqrt{(b^2 + h^2)/3}$.

9.16. (a) $\frac{1}{2}\pi(R_2^4 - R_1^4)$.   (b) $\frac{1}{4}\pi(R_2^4 - R_1^4)$.

9.20. 56.0 in.⁴, 2.18 in.

9.22. 29.0 in.⁴, 1.555 in.

9.24. 2,040 in.⁴

9.26. $A = 40$ in.², $J_C = 300$ in.⁴, $d = 5$ in.

9.28. 283 in.⁴

9.30. (a) 77.1 in.⁴   (b) 74.9 in.⁴

9.32. 6.24 in.

9.34. 339 in.⁴, 4.89 in.; 31.3 in.⁴, 1.485 in.

9.36. $h/2$.

9.38. $3\pi r/16$.

9.40. $h + (r^2/4h)$.

9.44. $+b^2h^2/4$.

9.46. $+a^2b^2/6$.

9.48. $+30.0$ in.⁴

9.50. -32.3 in.⁴

9.52. $\bar{I}_u = \bar{I}_v = bh(b^2 + h^2)/24$, $\bar{P}_{uv} = -bh(b^2 - h^2)/24$.

9.54. (a) $(\pi - \sqrt{3})a^4/16$, $(\pi + \sqrt{3})a^4/16$, $+a^4/16$.

(b) $(\pi - 2)a^4/16$, $(\pi + 2)a^4/16$, 0.

9.56. $-32.9°$, 75.4 in.⁴, 9.6 in.⁴

9.58. $+28.5°$, 98.3 in.⁴, 21.3 in.⁴

9.60. (a) $0.0881a^4$, $0.305a^4$, $0.0625a^4$.

(b) $0.0713a^4$, $0.321a^4$, 0.

9.64. $+28.5°$, 98.3 in.⁴, 21.3 in.⁴.

9.66. $-32.9°$, 75.4 in.⁴, 9.6 in.⁴.

9.70. $-18.4°$, 50.0 in.⁴

9.74. (a) $I_{AA'} = ma^2/4$, $I_{BB'} = mb^2/4$.

(b) $I_{CC'} = m(a^2 + b^2)/4$.

9.76. $I_{DD'} = m(b^2/24 + d^2)$, $I_{EE'} = m(h^2/18 + d^2)$.

9.78. $8\pi\rho a^5/15$, $\sqrt{2/5}\, a$.

9.80. $5ma^2/18$.

9.82. $\pi\rho a^2 L(3a^2 + 4L^2)/12$, $\sqrt{(3a^2 + 4L^2)/12}$.

9.84. $5m(a^2/36 + h^2/7)$.

9.86. $(134.0)\rho$, 2.34 in.

9.88. $ma^2/20$.

9.90. $m(R^2 + \frac{3}{4}a^2)$.

9.94. $0.360a$ or $-1.110a$.

9.96. $2ma^2/3$.

9.98. 1.622 in.

9.100. 0.000424 lb-ft-sec², 0.644 in.

9.102. 0.000283 lb-ft-sec², 1.031 in.

9.104. 1.743 lb-ft-sec², 6.54 in.

9.106. 0.890.

9.108. $m(3a^2 + 2h^2)/20$.

9.110. 1.643 in.

9.112. 69.6 in.⁴, 11.64 in.⁴; 2.52 in., 1.029 in.

9.114. $I_x = 0.01553$ lb-ft-sec²,
$I_y = I_z = 0.0621$ lb-ft-sec²;
$k_x = 0.236$ ft, $k_y = k_z = 0.471$ ft.

9.116. $(a)\, P_{xy} = +r^4/8$.
$(b)\, \bar{P}_{x'y'} = r^4(1/8 - 4/9\pi) = -0.01647r^4$.

9.118. 0.1944.

CHAPTER 10

10.4. 50 lb ↑.

10.6. 480 lb-in. ↘.

10.8. $Q = P(AD)/(AC)$, where AC = distance from A to C, and AD = distance A to D.

10.10. $(Pl/r)\cos^2\theta$.

10.12. $\frac{1}{2}Pd\sin\theta$.

10.14. $\frac{1}{2}Pd\cos\theta$.

10.16. 173.2 lb.

10.18. 904 lb.

10.20. 52.2°.

10.22. 26.6°.

10.24. 11.8 in.

10.26. 30.7°.

10.28. 78.7°, 323.8°, 379.1°.

10.30. $\tan\theta/\tan(\theta + \phi_s)$.

10.32. 143.2 lb, 203.2 lb.

10.34. 280 lb ↑, 1,280 lb-ft ↘.

10.36. $\tan\theta_1 = 2P/3W$, $\tan\theta_2 = 2P/W$.

10.38. 0.356 in. ↓.

10.40. 0.625 in. →.

10.44. 78.7°, unstable; $-101.3°$, stable.

10.46. 78.7° and 379.1°, stable; 323.8°, unstable.

10.48. $(a)\, 2W/P = \cot\theta\,(5 - 4\cos\theta)^{\frac{1}{2}}$. $(b)\, 32.5°$.

10.52. kr^2/l.

10.54. 11.18 in.

10.56. $(a)\, 2$. $(b)\, \frac{2}{3}$. $(c)\, \frac{2}{3} < P/W < 2$.

10.58. $0.382kl$.

10.60. 7.50 lb.

10.64. 60°.

10.66. 11.0°, stable; 79.0°, unstable.

10.68. $ka^2/2l$.

10.70. $\mathbf{A} = 100$ lb ↑, $\mathbf{E} = 300$ lb ↑,
$\mathbf{M}_E = 2,000$ lb-ft ↘.

10.72. 18.4°.

APPENDIX ON GRAPHICAL METHODS

A.4. 150 lb ←, 50.7 in. above A.

A.10. Resultant is a couple; 4,000 lb-in. ↘.

A.12. $\mathbf{R} = 0$, $\mathbf{M} = 720$ lb-in. ↘.

A.14. 40 lb ↓.

A.16. $\mathbf{A} = 5$ kips ↑, $\mathbf{B} = 4$ kips ↑.

A.18. $\mathbf{A} = 30$ lb ↑, $\mathbf{B} = 30$ lb ↓.

A.20. $\mathbf{A} = 31.5$ kips ↗ 8.6°, $\mathbf{B} = 62.7$ kips ↑.

A.26. $T = 74.8$ lb, $\mathbf{C} = 168$ lb ↙ 39.8°.